Instructor's Curriculum Resource

to accompany

Kinn's **The Medical Assistant**

An Applied Learning Approach

The Latest *Evolution* in Learning.

Evolve provides online access to free learning resources and activities designed specifically for the textbook you are using in your class. The resources will provide you with information that enhances the material covered in the book and much more.

Visit the Web address listed below to start your learning evolution today

▶ **LOGIN:** *http://evolve.elsevier.com/Kinn/*

Evolve Instructor Resources include all content from Morton: Instructor's Curriculum Resource to accompany Kinn's The Medical Assistant: An Applied Learning Approach, *9th Edition.*

- **Content Updates**
  The latest content updates from the authors of the textbook and instructor materials to keep you current with recent developments in the teaching of medical assisting.

- **Complete Online Teaching Tool**
  Beginning and veteran instructors alike will be able to easily prepare their lectures, presentations, labs, and assessment with an extensive course lecture and lab guide, multiple course outlines for various length programs, individual chapter lesson plans, ready-made tests for each chapter, and slide set. Answer keys for all text and Student Study Guide questions are also included.

- **Kinn's Medical Assisting Online**
  The multidimensional enhancement to take you beyond the traditional classroom setting, these innovative new products offer complete courses that simulate the externship experience by creating a virtual medical practice where students have an opportunity to learn by doing. Instructors have the flexibility to tailor the program's content to support a traditional classroom learning experience, a true distance education course, or a combination of these two formats.

Think outside the book... *evolve*

Instructor's Curriculum Resource

to accompany

Kinn's **The Medical Assistant**

An Applied Learning Approach

NINTH EDITION

Tammy B. Morton, MS, RN, CS, CMA

Formerly Department Head, Medical Assisting Program
TriCounty Technical College
Pendleton, South Carolina

SAUNDERS

An Imprint of Elsevier

SAUNDERS

An Imprint of Elsevier
11830 Westline Industrial Drive
St. Louis, Missouri 63146

Instructor's Curriculum Resource to accompany
Kinn's The Medical Assistant: An Applied Learning Approach, 9th edition   1-4160-0197-2

International Standard Book Number: 1-4160-0197-2

Many thanks to Karen Sorrow, Kathy Duncan, Mary Helper, Adrianne Cochran, Christine Ambrose, and Jeanne Genz for helping make the project a success.

Acquisition Editor: Adrianne Cochran
Developmental Editor: Christine Ambrose
Publishing Services Manager: Gayle May
Designer: Mark Oberkrom

Printed in the United States of America

CE/MV-B

9 8 7 6 5 4 3 2 1

To my family,
friends, and former students
who have encouraged and supported me
throughout my teaching career

Contents

Introduction

Every healthcare instructor battles the same issues: limited time and massive volumes of material to cover. How do you develop a course that is interesting and accessible to the students while maintaining academic credibility? This Instructor's Curriculum Resource, a supplement to the text *Kinn's The Medical Assistant: An Applied Learning Approach, 9th Edition,* has been developed with these criteria in mind. The authors of *Kinn's The Medical Assistant* and its supplements, the Student Study Guide and Instructor's Curriculum Resource, have committed themselves to providing you with content that is both competency-based and accreditation-friendly. Designed to accommodate a wide variety of student learning types and instructor teaching styles, this package of supportive materials includes comprehensive curriculum materials in both print and electronic formats.

Accrediting agencies, including the Committee on Accreditation of Allied Health Programs (CAAHEP) and the Accrediting Bureau of Health Education Schools (ABHES), place demands on faculty and Medical Assistant Programs to maintain accreditation standards. While this resource gives instructors and department heads a blueprint for meeting such accreditation requirements, the concepts that are emphasized in the student activities and test questions offer invaluable preparation for students who are seeking certification. In fact, exercises in the clinical chapters incorporate coding and other administrative tasks to simulate actual workplace challenges.

This instructor teaching tool reinforces the "applied" theme of the textbook and Student Study Guide by emphasizing individual student learning styles and critical thinking skills. Beginning and veteran instructors alike will be able to easily prepare their lectures, presentations, labs, and assessment with an extensive course syllabus, multiple course outlines, individual chapter lesson plans, ready-made tests for each chapter, as well as an accurate and exhaustive Test Bank to accommodate a wide variety of examination styles. Answer keys for all text and Student Study Guide questions are also included. In addition, special tips for instructors with ESL (English-As-A-Second-Language) students have been provided, written by an ESL consultant. All of the printed materials from the Instructor's Curriculum Resource are also available in Word format on the free CD-ROM, making them fully customizable for use in any classroom.

The instructor CD-ROM includes a PowerPoint viewer and a set of over 1,500 PowerPoint slides. The slides include a summary of key chapter material, and can easily be customized to support your lectures and enhance your classroom presentation. All slides have been formatted to reflect the text design, and include nearly 300 images from the text. These slides can also be easily formatted within the PowerPoint program for student note taking, or as overhead transparencies. For your convenience, an outline of these slides is included in the print version of this resource.

Tammy B. Morton

Instructor's Curriculum Resource

to accompany

Kinn's **The Medical Assistant**
An Applied Learning Approach

Learning Styles Inventory

There are many different ways of examining learning styles but professionals agree that success of students has more to do with whether they can "make sense" of the information rather than whether or not they are "smart." Education that is based on attention to individual learning styles is sensitive to the different ways students learn and approach new material with a wide variety of methods so that all students have the opportunity to learn.

There are advantages and disadvantages to all four of the learning stages. When faced with a learning situation that does not match your learning preference, see how you can adapt your instructional strategies to individual learning styles. For example, if students are bored by lectures, look for opportunities to apply the information being presented into a real-world problem.

Investigating various learning styles tells you how you can combine different methods of perceiving and processing information. In his book *Becoming a Master Student,* David Ellis discusses these different methods of information perception, processing, and learning.*

Learners in ***Stage 1*** have a concrete/reflective style. These students want to know the purpose of the information and have a personal connection to the content. They like to consider a situation from many different points of view, observe others, and plan before taking action. Their strengths are in understanding people, brainstorming, and recognizing and creatively solving problems. If they fall into this stage you enjoy small group activities and learn well in study groups.

Stage 2 learners have an abstract/reflective style. These students are eager to learn just for the sheer pleasure of learning rather than because the material relates to their personal lives. They like to learn lots of facts and arrange new material in a logical and clear manner. Stage 2 learners plan studying and like to create ways of thinking about the material but don't always make the connection with the practical application of the material. If someone is a Stage 2 learner they prefer organized, logical presentations of material and, therefore, enjoy lectures and generally dislike group work. They also need time to process and think about the new material before applying it.

Learners in ***Stage 3*** have an abstract/active style. Learners with this combination of learning style want to experiment and test the knowledge they are learning. If a student is a Stage 3 learner they want to know how techniques or ideas work but you also want to practice what you are learning. Their strengths are in problem solving and making decisions but you may tend to lack focus and be hasty in your decision-making. They learn best with hands-on practice by doing experiments, projects, and lab activities. They also enjoy working alone or in small groups.

Stage 4 is made up of concrete/active learners. Students in this stage are concerned about how they can use what they learn to make a difference in their lives. If students fall into this stage, they like to relate new material to other areas of your life. they have leadership capabilities, can create on their feet, and are usually vocal in a group. They may have difficulty getting your work done

*Ellis D: *Becoming a Master Student,* ed 10. Boston, 2002, Houghton Mifflin.

completely and on time. Stage 4 learners enjoy teaching others and working in groups and learn best when they can apply the new information to real-world problems.

Have students complete the Learning Styles Questionnaire to help them determine their own strengths and weaknesses. Use the graph to analyze their responses. You may consider using the Instruction Sheet and questionnaire on a transparency or overhead projection system. The Learning Styles Questionnaire features style icons from the *Student Study Guide.*

Learning Styles Questionnaire Instructions

1. Have students answer the four categories of questions by placing one checkmark per row.
2. Tally the number of checkmarks in each column.

Column 1	Column 2	Column 3	Column 4
Watching	Doing	Thinking	Feeling

3. Compare the scores from Column one and Column two. Which is higher? _____

4. Compare columns three and four. Which is higher? _____

5. Use the answers to questions three and four along with the graph below to determine the student's learning style.

Reflective		Active	
Watching and Feeling	Watching and Thinking	Doing and Thinking	Doing and Feeling
Stage 1	Stage 2	Stage 3	Stage 4

Learning Styles Questionnaire

1. When I Learn:			
I take my time before acting	I like to see results	I like ideas and theories	I like to deal with my feelings
I like to watch and listen	I work hard	I rely on logic	I trust my hunches
I like to observe	I get involved	I like to evaluate things	I have strong feelings and reactions

2. I learn best when:			
I am careful	I am practical	I analyze ideas	I am receptive and open-minded

3. I learn by:			
Watching someone	Doing it myself	Thinking about it first	Relating it to something I already know
Relying on observations	Trying things	Relying on ideas	Relying on feelings

4. When I am learning:			
I am reserved	I am active	I am quiet	I am personally involved
I take my time	I am moving	I analyze ideas	I try to relate to the subject matter

Totals			

Nine-Month Curriculum

Month 1	**INTRODUCTION** Chapter 1: Becoming a Successful Student Chapter 2: The Healthcare Industry **UNIT ONE: INTRODUCTION TO MEDICAL ASSISTING** Chapter 3: The Medical Assisting Profession Chapter 4: Professional Behavior in the Workplace Chapter 5: Interpersonal Skills and Human Behavior Chapter 6: Medicine and Ethics Chapter 7: Medicine and Law
Month 2:	**UNIT TWO: ADMINISTRATIVE MEDICAL ASSISTING** Chapter 8: Computers in the Medical Office Chapter 9: Telephone Technique Chapter 10: Scheduling Appointments

	Chapter 11: Patient Reception and Processing
	Chapter 12: Written Communications and Mail Processing
	Chapter 13: Medical Records Management
Month 3	**UNIT THREE: FINANCIAL MANAGEMENT**
	Chapter 14: Professional Fees, Billing, and Collecting
	Chapter 15: Basics of Diagnostic Coding
	Chapter 16: Basics of Procedural Coding
	Chapter 17: The Health Insurance Claim Form
	Chapter 18: Third Party Reimbursement
	Chapter 19: Banking Services and Procedures
Month 4	**UNIT FOUR: MEDICAL PRACTICE AND HEALTH INFORMATION MANAGEMENT**
	Chapter 20: Medical Practice Management

	Chapter 21: Medical Practice Marketing and Customer Service
	Chapter 22: Health Information Management
	Chapter 23: Management of Practice Finances
Month 5	**UNIT FIVE: FUNDAMENTALS OF CLINICAL MEDICAL ASSISTING** Chapter 24: Infection Control Chapter 25: Patient Assessment Chapter 26: Patient Education Chapter 27: Nutrition and Health Promotion Chapter 28: Vital Signs Chapter 29: Assisting with the Primary Physical Examination **UNIT SIX: ASSISTING WITH MEDICATIONS** Chapter 30: Principles of Pharmacology Chapter 31: Pharmacology Math

	Chapter 32: Administering Medications
Month 6	**UNIT SEVEN: ASSISTING WITH MEDICAL SPECIALTIES** Chapter 33: Assisting with Medical Emergencies Chapter 34: Assisting in Ophthalmology and Otolaryngology Chapter 35: Assisting in Dermatology Chapter 36: Assisting in Gastroenterology Chapter 37: Assisting in Urology and Male Reproduction Chapter 38: Assisting in Obstetrics and Gynecology Chapter 39: Assisting in Pediatrics
Month 7	Chapter 40: Assisting in Orthopedic Medicine Chapter 41: Assisting in Neurology and Mental Health Chapter 42: Assisting in Endocrinology

	Chapter 43: Assisting in Pulmonary Medicine Chapter 44: Assisting in Cardiology Chapter 45: Assisting in Geriatrics
Month 8	**UNIT EIGHT: DIAGNOSTIC PROCEDURES** Chapter 46: Principles of Electrocardiography Chapter 47: Assisting with Diagnostic Imaging Chapter 48: Assisting in the Clinical Laboratory Chapter 49: Assisting in the Analysis of Urine Chapter 50: Assisting in Phlebotomy Chapter 51: Assisting in the Analysis of Blood Chapter 52: Assisting in Microbiology
Month 9	**UNIT NINE: ASSISTING WITH SURGERIES** Chapter 53: Surgical Supplies and Instruments

	Chapter 54: Surgical Asepsis and Assisting with Surgical Procedures
	UNIT TEN: CAREER DEVELOPMENT
	Chapter 55: Career Development and Life Skills

Twelve-Month Curriculum

Quarter 1 Admin I	**INTRODUCTION**
	Chapter 1: Becoming a Successful Student
	Chapter 2: The Healthcare Industry
	UNIT ONE: INTRODUCTION TO MEDICAL ASSISTING
	Chapter 3: The Medical Assisting Profession
	Chapter 4: Professional Behavior in the Workplace
	Chapter 5: Interpersonal Skills and Human Behavior
	Chapter 6: Medicine and Ethics
	Chapter 7: Medicine and Law
Quarter 2 Admin II	**UNIT TWO: ADMINISTRATIVE MEDICAL ASSISTING**
	Chapter 8: Computers in the Medical Office
	Chapter 9: Telephone Technique
	Chapter 10: Scheduling Appointments

	Chapter 11: Patient Reception and Processing
	Chapter 12: Written Communications and Mail Processing
	Chapter 13: Medical Records Management
Quarter 2 Finance I	**UNIT THREE: FINANCIAL MANAGEMENT**
	Chapter 14: Professional Fees, Billing, and Collecting
	Chapter 15: Basics of Diagnostic Coding
	Chapter 16: Basics of Procedural Coding
	Chapter 17: The Health Insurance Claim Form
	Chapter 18: Third Party Reimbursement
	Chapter 19: Banking Services and Procedures
Quarter 3 Management I	**UNIT FOUR: MEDICAL PRACTICE AND HEALTH INFORMATION MANAGEMENT**
	Chapter 20: Medical Practice Management

	Chapter 21: Medical Practice Marketing and Customer Service
	Chapter 22: Health Information Management
	Chapter 23: Management of Practice Finances
Quarter 1 Clinical I	**UNIT FIVE: FUNDAMENTALS OF CLINICAL MEDICAL ASSISTING** Chapter 24: Infection Control Chapter 25: Patient Assessment Chapter 26: Patient Education Chapter 27: Nutrition and Health Promotion Chapter 28: Vital Signs Chapter 29: Assisting with the Primary Physical Examination
Quarter 3 Pharmacology I	**UNIT SIX: ASSISTING WITH MEDICATIONS** Chapter 30: Principles of Pharmacology Chapter 31: Pharmacology Math

	Chapter 32: Administering Medications
Quarter 2 Clinical II	**UNIT SEVEN: ASSISTING WITH MEDICAL SPECIALTIES**
	Chapter 33: Assisting with Medical Emergencies
	Chapter 34: Assisting Ophthalmology and Otolaryngology
	Chapter 35: Assisting in Dermatology
	Chapter 36: Assisting in Gastroenterology
	Chapter 37: Assisting in Urology and Male Reproduction
	Chapter 38: Assisting in Obstetrics and Gynecology
	Chapter 39: Assisting in Pediatrics
Quarter 3 Clinical III	Chapter 40: Assisting in Orthopedic Medicine
	Chapter 41: Assisting in Neurology and Mental Health
	Chapter 42: Assisting in Endocrinology

	Chapter 43: Assisting in Pulmonary Medicine
	Chapter 44: Assisting in Cardiology
	Chapter 45: Assisting in Geriatrics
Quarter 4 Diagnostic Procedures I	**UNIT EIGHT: DIAGNOSTIC PROCEDURES** Chapter 46: Principles of Electrocardiography Chapter 47: Assisting with Diagnostic Imaging Chapter 48: Assisting in the Clinical Laboratory Chapter 49: Assisting in the Analysis of Urine Chapter 50: Assisting in Phlebotomy Chapter 51: Assisting in the Analysis of Blood Chapter 52: Assisting in Microbiology
Quarter 4 Clinical IV	**UNIT NINE: ASSISTING WITH SURGERIES** Chapter 53: Surgical Supplies and Instruments

Chapter 54: Surgical Asepsis and Assisting with Surgical Procedures

UNIT TEN: CAREER DEVELOPMENT

Chapter 55: Career Development and Life Skills

Three-Semester Curriculum

Semester 1 Admin I	**INTRODUCTION**
	Chapter 1: Becoming a Successful Student
	Chapter 2: The Healthcare Industry
	UNIT ONE: INTRODUCTION TO MEDICAL ASSISTING
	Chapter 3: The Medical Assisting Profession
	Chapter 4: Professional Behavior in the Workplace
	Chapter 5: Interpersonal Skills and Human Relations
	Chapter 6: Medicine and Ethics
	Chapter 7: Medicine and Law
Semester 2 Admin II	**UNIT TWO: ADMINISTRATIVE MEDICAL ASSISTING**
	Chapter 8: Computers in the Medical Office
	Chapter 9: Telephone Technique
	Chapter 10: Scheduling Appointments

	Chapter 11: Patient Reception and Processing
	Chapter 12: Written Communications and Mail Processing
	Chapter 13: Medical Records Management
Semester 2 Finance and Management	**UNIT THREE: FINANCIAL MANAGEMENT** Chapter 14: Professional Fees, Billing, and Collecting Chapter 15: Basics of Diagnostic Coding Chapter 16: Basics of Procedural Coding Chapter 17: The Health Insurance Claim Form Chapter 18: Third Party Reimbursement Chapter 19: Banking Services and Procedures **UNIT FOUR: MEDICAL PRACTICE AND HEALTH INFORMATION MANAGEMENT** Chapter 20: Medical Practice Management

	Chapter 21: Medical Practice Marketing and Customer Service Chapter 22: Health Information Management Chapter 23: Management of Practice Finances
Semester 1 Clinical I	**UNIT FIVE: FUNDAMENTALS OF CLINICAL MEDICAL ASSISTING** Chapter 24: Infection Control Chapter 25: Patient Assessment Chapter 26: Patient Education Chapter 27: Nutrition and Health Promotion Chapter 28: Vital Signs Chapter 29: Assisting with the Primary Physical Examination **UNIT SIX: ASSISTING WITH MEDICATIONS** Chapter 30: Principles of Pharmacology Chapter 31: Pharmacology Math

	Chapter 32: Administering Medications
Semester 2 Clinical II *Many programs offer separate Medical terminology courses along with CPR and First Aid Certification.	**UNIT SEVEN: ASSISTING WITH MEDICAL SPECIALTIES** Chapter 33: Assisting with Medical Emergencies Chapter 34: Assisting in Ophthalmology and Otolaryngology Chapter 35: Assisting in Dermatology Chapter 36: Assisting in Gastroenterology Chapter 37: Assisting in Urology and Male Reproduction Chapter 38: Assisting in Obstetrics and Gynecology Chapter 39: Assisting in Pediatrics Chapter 40: Assisting in Orthopedic Medicine Chapter 41: Assisting in Neurology and Mental Health Chapter 42: Assisting in Endocrinology

	Chapter 43: Assisting in Pulmonary Medicine
	Chapter 44: Assisting in Cardiology
	Chapter 45: Assisting in Geriatrics
Semester 3 Clinical III and Externship	**UNIT EIGHT: DIAGNOSTIC PROCEDURES** Chapter 46: Principles of Electrocardiography Chapter 47: Assisting with Diagnostic Imaging Chapter 48: Assisting in the Clinical Laboratory Chapter 49: Assisting in the Analysis of Urine Chapter 50: Assisting in Phlebotomy Chapter 51: Assisting in the Analysis of Blood Chapter 52: Assisting in Microbiology **UNIT NINE: ASSISTING WITH SURGERIES** Chapter 53: Surgical Supplies and Instruments

	Chapter 54: Surgical Asepsis and Assisting with Surgical Procedures
	UNIT TEN: CAREER DEVELOPMENT Chapter 55: Career Development and Life Skills

24-Month Curriculum

| Semester 1 Admin I | **INTRODUCTION**

Chapter 1: Becoming a Successful Student

Chapter 2: The Healthcare Industry

UNIT ONE: INTRODUCTION TO MEDICAL ASSISTING

Chapter 3: The Medical Assisting Profession

Chapter 4: Professional Behavior in the Workplace

Chapter 5: Interpersonal Skills and Human Relations

Chapter 6: Medicine and Ethics

Chapter 7: Medicine and Law |
| Semester 2 Admin II | **UNIT TWO: ADMINISTRATIVE MEDICAL ASSISTING**

Chapter 8: Computers in the Medical Practice

Chapter 9: Telephone Technique

Chapter 10: Scheduling Appointments |

	Chapter 11: Patient Reception and Processing
	Chapter 12: Written Communications and Mail Processing
	Chapter 13: Medical Records Management
Semester 3 Finance and Management	**UNIT THREE: FINANCIAL MANAGEMENT**
	Chapter 14: Professional Fees, Billing, and Collecting
	Chapter 15: Basics of Diagnostic Coding
	Chapter 16: Basics of Procedural Coding
	Chapter 17: The Health Insurance Claim Form
	Chapter 18: Third Party Reimbursement
	Chapter 19: Banking Services and Procedures
	UNIT FOUR: MEDICAL PRACTICE AND HEALTH INFORMATION MANAGEMENT
	Chapter 20: Medical Practice Management

	Chapter 21: Medical Practice Marketing and Customer Service
	Chapter 22: Health Information Management
	Chapter 23: Management of Practice Finances
Semester 2 Clinical I	**UNIT FIVE: FUNDAMENTALS OF CLINICAL MEDICAL ASSISTING**
	Chapter 24: Infection Control
	Chapter 25: Patient Assessment
	Chapter 26: Patient Education
	Chapter 27: Nutrition and Health Promotion
	Chapter 28: Vital Signs
	Chapter 29: Assisting with the Primary Physical Examination
	UNIT SIX: ASSISTING WITH MEDICATIONS
	Chapter 30: Principles of Pharmacology
	Chapter 31: Pharmacology Math

	Chapter 32: Administering Medications
Semester 3 Clinical II *Many programs offer separate Medical terminology courses along with CPR and First Aid Certification.	**UNIT SEVEN: ASSISTING WITH MEDICAL SPECIALTIES** Chapter 33: Assisting with Medical Emergencies Chapter 34: Assisting in Ophthalmology and Otolaryngology Chapter 35: Assisting in Dermatology Chapter 36: Assisting in Gastroenterology Chapter 37: Assisting in Urology and Male Reproduction Chapter 38: Assisting in Obstetrics and Gynecology Chapter 39: Assisting in Pediatrics Chapter 40: Assisting in Orthopedic Medicine Chapter 41: Assisting in Neurology and Mental Health Chapter 42: Assisting in Endocrinology

	Chapter 43: Assisting in Pulmonary Medicine
	Chapter 44: Assisting in Cardiology
	Chapter 45: Assisting in Geriatrics
Semester 4 Clinical III and Externship	**UNIT EIGHT: DIAGNOSTIC PROCEDURES** Chapter 46: Principles of Electrocardiography Chapter 47: Assisting with Diagnostic Imaging Chapter 48: Assisting with the Clinical Laboratory Chapter 49: Assisting in the Analysis of Urine Chapter 50: Assisting in Phlebotomy Chapter 51: Assisting in the Analysis of Blood Chapter 52: Assisting in Microbiology **UNIT NINE: ASSISTING WITH SURGERIES** Chapter 53: Surgical Supplies and Instruments

	Chapter 54: Surgical Asepsis and Assisting with Surgical Procedures
	UNIT TEN: CAREER DEVELOPMENT
	Chapter 55: Career Development and Life Skills

Blank Lesson Plan Template

Lesson Plan	Action verbs for writing objectives:
Date: _____	*Knowledge:* define, match, repeat, select
Topic: _____ Time: _____	*Comprehension:* express, explain, restate, discuss, demonstrate, describe
Lesson No: _____	
Opening: _____	*Application:* organize, solve, transfer, classify, choose, illustrate, practice
_____	
PreTest:	*Analysis:* distinguish, compare, list, subdivide, contrast, debate
	Synthesis: design, plan, solve
Content Objectives (At least 1 per $\frac{1}{2}$ hour) Time: _____	*Evaluation:* judge, assess, compare, critique, rate
• _____	
• _____	
• _____	
• _____	
• _____	
Post objectives on overhead, in syllabus, or on flip chart for each class.	
Read aloud.	
Content Outline: (Choose activities from Chapter Activities and Lesson Plans, pp. 00-00)	
Time: _____	
• _____	
• _____	
• _____	
• _____	
• _____	
• _____	
• _____	

Assignment:	
PostTest: Choose from objectives; give oral and written directions	
Learning Equipment Needed List: Transparencies, forms, activity supplies, clinical supplies *Additional items:* _____	

Instructor Notes: _____
 	
    • _____
 	
    • _____
 	
    • _____	

Chapter Activities

INTRODUCTION

Chapter 1: Becoming a Successful Student

1. Have students complete the Learning Styles Questionnaire.
2. Have students keep a time management journal.

Chapter 2: The Healthcare Industry

1. Assign poster projects or papers about the major contributors to modern medicine.
2. Search *Caduceus* and *staff of Aesculapius* on the internet.
3. Find web sites for WHO, AMA and NIH.

UNIT ONE: INTRODUCTION TO MEDICAL ASSISTING

Chapter 3: The Medical Assisting Profession

1. Have students look up *physicians* in the Yellow pages and discuss the specialties in your area.
2. Have students write a paper about certification requirements for medical assistants.

Chapter 4: Professional Behavior in the Workplace

1. Have student write a dress code policy for a fictitious practice and share with the class.
2. Have a discussion about behaviors that students feel are unprofessional.

Chapter 5: Interpersonal Skills and Human Behavior

1. Have students prepare short skits on non-verbal communication.
2. Use role play to help students understand defense mechanisms.

Chapter 6: Medicine and Ethics

1. Allow students to choice a controversial topic and prepare a poster to share with the class.
2. Host a pro and con style debate about human cloning or another medical ethical issue.

Chapter 7: Medicine and Law

1. Have groups of students prepare a mock malpractice trial on video tape and play it in class.
2. Ask the Risk Manager from the local hospital to be a guest speaker.
3. Examine and discuss a blank contract from a car dealership or finance company. Place the contract on an overhead and allow students to find the elements of the contract.

UNIT TWO: ADMINISTRATIVE MEDICAL ASSISTING

Chapter 8: Computers in the Medical Office

1. Have students bring in an ad for computers. Consulting the ad for actual specifications, instruct them to examine the components of a computer.
2. Tour an IS or IT department of your school, local business, or hospital.

Chapter 9: Telephone Technique

1. Use toy phones and role play the "do's and don'ts" of answering the telephone.
2. Have students write some scenarios of the types of calls they might expect to receive in the medical office.

Chapter 10: Scheduling Appointments

1. Have students visit a doctor or chiropractors office and ask them about their method of scheduling.

Chapter 11: Patient Reception and Processing

1. Practice filing out patient information forms in class.
2. Ask students to design a waiting room for a specialty office.

Chapter 12: Written Communications and Mail Processing

1. Practice folding blank pieces of paper into different types of envelopes.
2. Have students address an envelope to a fellow classmate. These can be used later for birthdays and holidays.
3. Visit a post office.
4. Put various letter styles on an overhead and ask the class to identify them.

Chapter 13: Medical Records Management

1. Have each student make a list of 10 celebrity names. Place these on index cards, shuffle, and ask students to put them in proper indexing order. Use a timer and give a small prize to the winner.

UNIT THREE: FINANCIAL MANAGEMENT

Chapter 14: Professional Fees, Billing, and Collecting

1. Prepare collection letters in class.
2. Design a fee schedule using E&M codes.

Chapter 15: Basics of Diagnostic Coding

1. Search the internet for *ICD-9 coding*.
2. Practicing coding diagnosis.

Chapter 16: Basics of Procedural Coding

1. Search the internet for *CPT coding*.
2. Practicing coding E&M and procedure codes.

Chapter 17: The Health Insurance Claim Form

1. Complete a blank HCFA 1500 form.

Chapter 18: Third-Party Reimbursement

1. Look up *Medicare, Campus, TriCare,* and *Medicaid* on the internet.
2. Have students practice getting a surgery pre-certified. Have one student pretend to be the medical assistant and the other pretend to be an insurance company representative.

Chapter 19: Banking Services and Procedures

1. Tour a local bank.
2. Practice reconciling a bank statement.

UNIT FOUR: MEDICAL PRACTICE AND HEALTH INFORMATION MANAGEMENT

Chapter 20: Medical Practice Management

1. Set up mock interviews with students.
2. Have students prepare an agenda and a travel itinerary.
3. Ask students to identify community resources and services. Have them present this information to the class.

Chapter 21: Medical Practice Marketing and Customer Service

1. Build a simple medical office website in MS Word. Use the instructions in the Help file.

Chapter 22: Health Information Management

1. Search for information about HIPPA on the internet.

Chapter 23: Management of Practice Finances

1. Set up a petty cash fund with play money and have students bring receipts to class.
2. Inventory the school's lab.
3. Practice filing out W-4 forms.
4. Set up a peg board.

UNIT FIVE: FUNDAMENTALS OF CLINICAL MEDICAL ASSISTING

Chapter 24: Infection Control

1. Invite the Infection Control Coordinator from a local hospital to speak to the class.
2. Visit the OSHA website.

Chapter 25: Patient Assessment

1. Have the class practice asking closed and open-ended questions.
2. Play a game to see which students can identify subjective and objective data.

Chapter 26: Patient Education

1. Allow students to choice a topic for and plan a teaching project. Have them do demonstrations, posters or make teaching brochures.

Chapter 27: Nutrition and Health Promotion

1. Ask students to bring an empty food package and discuss the nutritional content of each.
2. Search *bulimia* and *anorexia nervosa* on the internet.
3. Have students do a 24-hour diet recall.

Chapter 28: Vital Signs

1. Host a free blood pressure screening at your school.
2. Have students take vital signs on each class member.

Chapter 29: Assisting with the Primary Physical Examination

1. Quiz the students on body systems.
2. Have students demonstrate positioning.

UNIT SIX: ASSISTING WITH MEDICATIONS

Chapter 30: Principles of Pharmacology

1. Have students start a collection of drug cards.
2. Have students practice using a PDR.

Chapter 31: Pharmacology Math

1. Ask the area doctor's offices to save empty drug sample packages. Set up a lab where students have to determine correct amounts.

Chapter 32: Administering Medications

1. Practice pouring colored rubbing alcohol into medicine cups.
2. Have student identify different syringes.
3. Make index cards with the names of intramuscular site and have students pin them on each others clothing near the correct area.

UNIT SEVEN: ASSISTING WITH MEDICAL SPECIALTIES

Chapter 33: Assisting with Medical Emergencies

1. Ask the class to collect appropriate items for a first aid kit and then donate it to the local scouts, seniors group, or a local church.
2. Have each student make a poster about each emergency that is discussed in the chapter.
3. Practice CPR and basic first aid in the lab.

Chapter 34: Assisting in Ophthalmology and Otolaryngology

1. Ask students examine each other's acuity using a Snelling chart.
2. Practice Rinne and Weber tests with tuning forks.

Chapter 35: Assisting in Dermatology

1. Search the web for various dermatological conditions.
2. Have students prepare a poster about selected skin diseases.

Chapter 36: Assisting in Gastroenterology

1. Visit an endoscopy or GI lab.
2. Search for *colonoscopy* on the internet.

Chapter 37: Assisting in Urology and Male Reproduction

1. Have students complete a research project on BHP, prostate and testicular cancer.

Chapter 38: Assisting in Obstetrics and Gynecology

1. Arrange for students to visit a childbirth education class.

Chapter 39: Assisting in Pediatrics

1. Using baby dolls, have students practice measuring head circumference.
2. Arrange for students to spend an afternoon at a daycare center.

Chapter 40: Assisting in Orthopedic Medicine

1. Have student teach each other how to walk with crutches.
2. Use pictures to have students identify various fractures.

Chapter 41: Assisting in Neurology and Mental Health

1. Look up *MS, MG,* and *ALS* on the internet.
2. Ask students to research addition and depression and identify community resources.

Chapter 42: Assisting in Endocrinology

1. Ask students to plan a 3-day meal plan using an 1800 calorie ADA diet.
2. Have students make a list of resources for people with various endocrine disorders.
3. Ask a podiatrist to come speak on foot care.

Chapter 43: Assisting in Pulmonary Medicine

1. Obtain materials from the American Lung Association. Have students pick

Chapter 44: Assisting in Cardiology

1. Visit a cardiac catheter lab or cardiac rehabilitation center.

Chapter 45: Assisting in Geriatrics

1. Have students wear thick gloves and sunglasses coated with petroleum jelly to class one day, so that they can see the frustrations of living with arthritis and limited vision.
2. Have students prepare patient teaching brochures on some of the common illnesses of aging.

UNIT EIGHT: DIAGNOSTIC PROCEDURES

Chapter 46: Principles of Electrocardiography

1. Have students make EKG leads out of yarn and clothespins. Have them label each lead and place them on their partners clothing.

Chapter 47: Assisting with Diagnostic Imaging

1. Ask students to draw a position or body plane out of a hat and demonstrate the position for the class.

Chapter 48: Assisting in the Clinical Laboratory

1. Have the class prepare an MSDS for the school lab using common chemicals and searching MSDS on the internet.

Chapter 49: Assisting in the Analysis of Urine

1. Have student draw various urine casts.

Chapter 50: Assisting in Phlebotomy

1. Search the Internet for *phlebotomy* or *venipuncture.*
2. Have students make a poster that explains when to use various colored collection tubes.

Chapter 51: Assisting in the Analysis of Blood

1. Ask student to draw various blood cells and describe their functions.
2. Visit an allergist's office.

Chapter 52: Assisting in Microbiology

1. Practice collecting throat cultures.
2. Practice streaking culture plates.

UNIT NINE: ASSISTING WITH SURGERIES

Chapter 53: Surgical Supplies and Instruments

1. Prepare instruments for sterilization.
2. Set up a lab and have students identify instruments by site or photo.

Chapter 54: Surgical Asepsis and Assisting with Surgical Procedures

1. Don sterile gloves.
2. Set up and add to sterile fields.

UNIT TEN: CAREER DEVELOPMENT

Chapter 55: Career Development and Life Skills

1. Have students prepare resumes and cover letters.

Chapter Summaries

CHAPTER 1

Becoming a Successful Student

Key Points

- To become a successful medical assistant, you must first become a successful student. This chapter helps you discover the way you learn best and provides multiple strategies to assist you in your journey toward success.

- Consider your history as a student. What do you think helped you be successful? What do you think needs improvement?

- Over time you have developed a method for **perceiving** and **processing** information. This pattern of behavior is called your **learning style.**

- To learn new material, two things must happen. First is your perception of the information. This is the method you have developed over time that helps you examine the material and recognize it as real.

- The next step is to process the information. Processing the information is how you internalize it and make it your own. Investigating various learning styles tells you how you can combine different methods of perceiving and processing information.

Perceiving

- Some people are **concrete** perceivers who learn information through direct experience by doing, acting, sensing, or feeling.

- Other learners are **abstract** perceivers who take in information through analysis, observation, and **reflection.**

Processing

- Two different methods exist for processing material. **Active** processors prefer to jump in and start doing things immediately. They make sense of the new material by immediately using it.

- **Reflective** processors, however, have to think about the information before they can internalize it. They prefer to observe and consider what is going on.

Stage 1

Stage 1 learners have a concrete/reflective style. These students want to know the purpose of the information and have a personal connection to the content. They like to consider a situation from many different points of view, observe others, and plan before taking action.

Stage 2

Stage 2 learners have an abstract/reflective style. These students are eager to learn just for the sheer pleasure of learning rather than because the material relates to their personal lives. They like to learn lots of facts and arrange new material in a logical and clear manner. Stage 2 learners plan studying and like to create ways of thinking about the material but do not always make the connection with the practical application of the material.

Stage 3

Learners in *Stage 3* have an abstract/active style. Learners with this combination of learning style want to experiment and test the knowledge they are learning.

Stage 4

Stage 4 is made up of concrete/active learners. Students in this stage are concerned about how they can use what they learn to make a difference in their lives.

All four of the learning stages have pluses and minuses. In a learning situation that does not match your learning preference, see how you can adapt your individual learning to make the best of the information.

Time Management

The following time-management skills are designed to help you effectively deal with the demands on your time.

1. *Determine your purpose.* What do you want to accomplish this semester, in this course, or unit of study? What do you want to achieve as a student? What is one thing you can do to help achieve your goals?

2. *Identify your main concern.* Besides school, what other demands do you have on your time? Based on the learning goals you have established, what do you need to do to accomplish your goals?

3. *Be organized.* What materials, books, research, and supplies do you need to have an effective study time? What preparation is needed to make the most of your time?

4. *Stop procrastinating.* Avoiding working on your goals may be the reason you do not achieve them.

5. *Remember you.* It is very easy to become overwhelmed with responsibilities both in school and at home. Part of successful time management includes setting aside time to do things you enjoy.

Problem Solving and Conflict Management

- The first step in reaching an equitable solution to a problem or conflict situation is to identify the central issue.

- Once you understand the situation and how you feel about it, then you must decide if it is worth the effort to solve it.

- After you have gathered the details about the problem or conflict, and you have decided to act, determine possible solutions. One way to do this is to ask for advice or brainstorm ideas with individuals you respect.

- After brainstorming for possible solutions, get feedback regarding the workability of the suggested solutions. Another way of approaching the problem is to list the pros and cons of possible solutions.

- Before deciding which solution to try, critically analyze the consequences of each proposed solution.

- Finally you are ready to implement the chosen solution.

- It is best if you attempt to solve the conflict in a private place at a prescheduled time.

Study Skills

Study skills include memory techniques, active learning, brain tricks, reading methods, and note-taking strategies.

- The first of these involves organizing information into recognizable groups so the brain can find it more easily. You can organize information by learning the big picture before trying the details.

- A useful study skill for some learners is to be physically active while learning. Some students learn best if they walk or talk out loud while studying.

- Another method for encouraging your brain to remember material is to review the material soon after class. This minireview will help the new information become part of your long-term memory system.

- As you read, highlight important words or thoughts, and stop periodically to summarize the material.

- The first step in effective note taking is to come to class prepared.

- The more familiar you are with the material, the easier it will be to determine the important parts of the instructor's lecture.

- Pay attention to the instructor and look for clues about what he or she thinks is important.

- Organize the information as much as possible while you are writing in either an outline or paragraph format. Use only one side of the paper for easier reading, and leave blank spaces where needed to fill in details later.

- Use key words to help you remember the material, and create pictures or diagrams to help visualize it.

Test-Taking Strategies

- The first step to taking charge of your success is to go into a test adequately prepared.

- Before you start the test, make sure you read directions carefully, and if possible, begin with the easiest or shortest questions to build your confidence.

- With multiple-choice questions, try to identify key words or clues in each question. Read the question carefully and answer it in your head before you review the provided answers.

- True/false questions give you a 50:50 chance of being correct. Remember that if any part of the question is not true, the statement is false.

CHAPTER 2

The Healthcare Industry

Key Points

The History of Medicine

- Aesculapius, the son of Apollo, was revered as the god of medicine. The early Greeks worshiped the healing powers of Aesculapius and built temples in his honor.

- A common medical icon is the staff of Aesculapius, which depicts a serpent encircling a staff, and signifies the art of healing. The staff of Aesculapius has been adopted by the American Medical Association as the symbol of medicine.

- The mythologic staff belonging to Apollo, the caduceus, which is a staff encircled by two serpents, is the medical insignia of the United States Army Medical Corps and is often misused as a symbol of the medical profession.

Medicine in Ancient Times

- In the well-developed societies of the Egyptians, Babylonians, and Assyrians, the men who acted as physicians used the little knowledge they had to try to treat illness and injury.

- Moses presented rules of health to the Hebrew people around 1205 B.C. He was thus the first advocate of preventive medicine and is considered the first public health officer.

- Hippocrates, known as the Father of Medicine, is the most famous of the ancient Greek physicians. He was born in 450 B.C. on the island of Cos in Greece. He is best remembered for the Hippocratic Oath that his pupils repeated, an oath administered to many physicians for more than 2000 years.

- Galen was a Greek physician who migrated to Rome in 162 A.D.; he was known as the Prince of Physicians. He is considered the Father of Experimental Physiology and the first experimental neurologist.

- In early times, medical knowledge developed slowly, and distribution of knowledge was poor. Before the invention of the printing press, there was very little exchange of scientific knowledge and ideas.

- Another development important to science occurred in the seventeenth century, when European academies or societies were established, consisting of small groups of men who met to discuss subjects of mutual interest.

- One of the earliest of the academies was the Royal Society of London, formed in 1662.

- The passage of the Medical Act of 1858 in Great Britain was considered one of the most important events in British medicine.

- In the United States, medical education was greatly influenced by the Johns Hopkins University Medical School in Baltimore.

- Its clinical work was superior because the school was a partner with Johns Hopkins Hospital, which had been created expressly for teaching and research by members of the medical faculty.

- Andreas Vesalius (1514-1564) was a Belgian anatomist known as the Father of Modern Anatomy.

- This work marked a turning point by breaking with traditional beliefs in Galen's theories.

- In 1628, William Harvey (1578-1657) announced his discovery that the heart acts as a muscular pump, forcing and propelling the blood throughout the body.

- Anton van Leeuwenhoek (1632-1723) learned how to use a simple biconvex lens to magnify the minute world of organisms and structures that had never been seen before.

- In 1661, Marcello Malpighi described the pulmonary and capillary network connecting the smallest arteries with the smallest veins.

- The famous English scientist, John Hunter (1728-1793), is known as the Founder of Scientific Surgery.

- Edward Jenner (1749-1823) was a student of John Hunter and a country physician from Dorsetshire, England. He is considered one of the immortals of preventive medicine for his origination of the smallpox vaccine.

- Ignaz Philipp Semmelweis (1818-1865) directed that in his wards, the students were to wash and disinfect their hands before examining women and delivering children.

- Pasteur (1822-1895), a Frenchman, did brilliant work as a chemist, but his studies in bacteriology made him one of the most famous men in medical history.

- Joseph Lister (1827-1912) revolutionized surgery through the application of Pasteur's discoveries. He understood the similarity between the infections in postsurgical wounds and the processes of putrefaction.

- Robert Koch (1843-1910) is a familiar name to all bacteriologists, because of his famous Koch's Postulates. These are criteria that must be met before an organism can be accepted as the causative agent in a given disease.

- Crawford Williamson Long (1815-1878) was the first to use ether as an anesthetic agent.

- Roentgen discovered the x-ray in 1895 while experimenting with electrical currents passed through sealed glass tubes.

- Marie and Pierre Curie discovered radium in 1898, and they were awarded the 1902 Nobel Prize in Physics for their work on radioactivity.

Women in Medicine

- Florence Nightingale (1820-1910) is known as the founder of nursing and fondly called "the lady with the lamp."

- Clara Barton (1821-1912) organized a Red Cross Committee in Washington, forming the American Red Cross.

- Elizabeth Blackwell (1821-1910) was the first woman in the United States to receive the Doctor of Medicine degree from a medical school.

- Margaret Sanger (1883-1966) was born in Corning, New York, and trained as a nurse at the White Plains Hospital. She became the American leader of the birth control movement.

- Dr. Elisabeth Kubler-Ross, a Swiss-born psychiatrist, was shocked at the treatment of terminally ill patients at her hospital in New York. She wrote the best-selling *On Death and Dying,* which helped professionals and laypersons to understand the stages of grief.

Modern Heroes

- Jonas Edward Salk and Albert Sabin almost eradicated polio, once the killer and crippler of thousands in the United States. The vaccine, developed in 1952, was later distributed nationally.

- Christiaan Barnard, a South African surgeon, performed the first human heart transplant in 1967.

World Health Organization

- The World Health Organization, founded in 1948, is a specialized agency of the United Nations. The organization promotes cooperation between nations in their effort to control and eliminate diseases worldwide.

Department of Health and Human Services

- DHHS is made up of more than 300 programs that include medical and social science research, immunization services, financial assistance for low-income families, child-support enforcement services, improvement of infant and maternal health, child and elder abuse prevention services, and various programs for elderly Americans.

USAMRIID

- The primary focus of the United States Army Medical Research Institute of Infectious Diseases is protecting military service members, but the Institute conducts key research programs in national defense and infectious diseases that benefit everyone.

- USAMRIID is the only laboratory facility operated by the Department of Defense that is equipped to study Biosafety Level IV viruses and pathogens.

Centers for Disease Control and Prevention

- The headquarters of the Center for Disease Control and Prevention are located in Atlanta, Georgia. The CDC is the leading U.S. federal agency concerned with the health and safety of people throughout the world. It is a clearinghouse for information and statistics associated with healthcare.

National Institutes of Health

- The mission of the NIH is to uncover new knowledge that will lead to better health for everyone. As a part of public health service, it seeks to improve the health of the American people, supports and conducts biomedical research into the causes and prevention of diseases, and uses a modern communications system to furnish biomedical information to healthcare professionals.

Types of Healthcare Facilities

- Hospitals
- Ambulatory care
- Diagnostic laboratories
- POLs, or privately owned laboratories
- Home health agencies

Medical Practices

- Sole proprietorship
- Partnerships
- Group practice
- Corporations

Healthcare Professionals

- Doctors of Medicine
- Doctors of Osteopathy
- Doctors of Chiropractic
- Dentists
- Optometrists
- Doctor of Podiatric Medicine
- Other doctorates

Licensed or Certified Professionals

- Physician assistants
- Nurse practitioners
- Nurse anesthetists
- Registered nurses
- Licensed practical/vocational nurses

- Medical technologists
- Medical laboratory technicians
- Physical therapists
- Respiratory therapists
- Occupational therapists
- Diagnostic medical and cardiac sonographers
- Radiology technicians
- Paramedics and emergency medical technicians
- Registered dieticians

CHAPTER 3

The Medical Assisting Profession

Key Points

- According to the United States Department of Labor's Occupational Outlook Handbook, medical assisting is expected to be one of the ten fastest-growing occupations through the year 2008.

The History of Medical Assisting

- The first medical assistant was probably a neighbor of a physician who was called on to help when an extra pair of hands was needed. As the practice of medicine became more organized and more complicated, some physicians hired registered nurses to help in their office practices.

- Gradually, record keeping, data reporting, and an increasing number of business details became important to physicians, and they realized a need for an assistant with both administrative and clinical training.

- Community and junior colleges began offering training programs that focused on both administrative and clinical skills in the late 1940s. Medical assistant organizations at the local and state levels began developing around 1950, and soon after, certifying examinations were available.

The Scope of Practice of a Medical Assistant

- The duties that medical assistants perform vary not only from office to office, but even within the same clinic.

- They perform routine duties within the offices of many types of health professionals, including physicians, chiropractors, podiatrists, and others.

- Medical assistants work under the direct supervision of a physician in the office and perform tasks delegated by the doctor or supervisor.

- The two major categories of duties that medical assistants perform are administrative and clinical.

Classroom Training

- Formal training is essential for today's medical assistant. Many community colleges, junior colleges, and private career institutions offer courses in medical assisting.

- After satisfactory completion of the program, the student receives a certificate or diploma. Students who attend community and junior colleges to study medical assisting may complete additional educational requirements to obtain an associate degree.
- Courses at the community college level usually take 1 to 2 years to complete, and offer enrollment 2 or 3 times per year. Private career institutions offer training that usually takes 7 to 10 months to complete, and offer enrollment as often as monthly.

Externships/Internships

- Most medical assisting training programs require an externship or internship before the student graduates.
- This type of on-the-job training allows the student to use the skills learned in the classroom setting with actual patients and staff members.

Continuing Education

- Continuing education classes are available to enhance the knowledge of the professional medical assistant.
- Continuing education units (**CEUs**) may be required to maintain the medical assistant's certification.

Professional Appearance

- The essentials of a professional appearance are good health, good grooming, and suitable dress.
- Good health requires getting adequate sleep, eating balanced meals, and exercising enough to keep fit.
- Good grooming is little more than attention to the details of personal appearance.
- Uniforms or scrubs should be laundered daily, because medical assistants are exposed to ill patients throughout the workday.
- Shoes should be appropriate for a uniform and be spotless and comfortable. White shoes must be kept white by daily cleansing.

Professional Organizations

- American Association of Medical Assistants and Certified Medical Assistants
- American Medical Technologists and Registered Medical Assistants
- American Association of Medical Assistants
- Certified Medical Assistants
- The AAMA was formally organized in 1956 as a federation of several state associations that had been functioning independently. Today the AAMA has 43 state societies and more than 350 local chapters.

- The organization, whose national headquarters are located in Chicago, Illinois, has been a driving force behind establishing a national certification program for medical assistants.

- It also has been instrumental in the accreditation of medical assisting training programs in community colleges and private career institutes and in setting the minimal standards for entry-level medical assistants.

- Since 1963, the AAMA has administered the Certified Medical Assistant (CMA) examination. Those that pass the examination are awarded the CMA credential. Examinations are given in January and June of each year at more than 280 centers throughout the United States.

- Certification is available to graduates of medical assisting programs accredited by the CAAHEP or by ABHES. Recertification is required every 5 years and can be accomplished through CEUs or reexamination.

American Medical Technologists

Registered Medical Assistants

- In the early 1970s, the American Medical Technologists (AMT), a national certifying body for laboratory professionals, began offering a certifying examination for medical assistants. This led to the formation of the Registered Medical Assistant (RMA) program within the AMT organization in 1976.

- The RMA examination can be scheduled nearly every day of the year other than Sundays and holidays at Prometric Testing Centers, with more than 300 locations throughout the United States.

- Applicants for the RMA examination must be graduates of a medical assisting course accredited by ABHES or by CAAHEP.

CMA versus RMA

- Both of the certifying examinations are national credentials. The CMA credential is offered by the AAMA, and the RMA credential is offered by the AMTs.

- Because medical assistants are not required to be licensed, both of these examinations are voluntary.

- Most employers today require at least one certification.

CHAPTER 4

Professional Behavior in the Workplace

Key Points

- Some of the characteristics of professionals include loyalty, dependability, courtesy, initiative, flexibility, credibility, confidentiality, and a good attitude.

- Confidentiality is vitally important in the medical profession.

- Patients depend on medical personnel to keep their health information confidential and private.

- Breach of patient confidentiality is one reason for which an employee can be immediately terminated, and can result in litigation between the patient and the physician employer.

- Professionalism is the characteristic of being or conforming to the technical or ethical standards of a profession.

- It is exhibiting courtesy, being conscientious, and conducting oneself in a business-like manner at the workplace.

- Professionalism is vitally important in the medical profession.

- Because most patients are not at their best when visiting the physician's office, the attitude of the staff plays an important role in patients' attitudes while in the office.

- Medical assistants need patience when working with those who are ill.

- A smile or a reassuring pat on the back will go a long way and be encouraging.

- Office politics can be negative or positive. A person who uses others to promote through the company or takes credit for a team effort may be using office politics in a negative way.

- However, the person who strategically plans advancement by outstanding performance, dependability, and teamwork uses office politics positively.

- Knowing when to speak and when to listen will help the medical assistant to play the game of politics well in the medical facility.

- Teamwork makes any job easier to complete.

- By helping those who may be overwhelmed with duties, the medical assistant may find willing co-workers to offer help when the situation is reversed.

- If two assistants both have duties they dislike, they might trade the duties and both be satisfied.

- Insubordination can be grounds for immediate dismissal. Insubordination is being disobedient to any authority figure, usually the supervisor.

- When given a task to complete, the medical assistant should carry out the order unless it is unlawful or unethical.

- Assigning priorities to tasks can help the medical assistant to accomplish more tasks.

- Ranking tasks can be used for work, home, and extracurricular activities alike. Tasks can be thought of as those that must, should, or could be done today.

- In each of these categories, number the tasks in the order they should be completed.

- Write goals down and review them often to check progress.

- Taking small steps toward goals will help assure that they are eventually reached. Set goals in each area of life, and break the tasks down into manageable parts.

- Goals should not be unreasonable or unattainable, but should provide the opportunity for small successes along the way to reaching the ultimate goal.

- If the medical assistant feels that the duty should have been performed by someone else or there was some reason it should not have been performed, consult the supervisor.

- Discuss the issue and attempt to reach an agreement about the appropriateness of performing the task in the future.

CHAPTER 5

Interpersonal Skills and Human Behavior

Key Points

First Impressions

- Patients are the reason for the existence of the facility, and they should be offered the best customer service available.

- When the patient approaches, even though you are wearing a name badge, introduce yourself and smile. Show your smile both facially and in your voice and eyes, and genuinely welcome the patient to the office.

- Once an impression is formed in the patient's mind, it is very difficult to change, so make positive the first impressions of your office.

Verbal Communication

- Oral communication depends on words and sounds.
- The voice lifts at the end of a question.
- It drops at the end of a statement.
- The medical assistant should speak clearly and enunciate words properly.
- Always speak at a clearly audible level; at times, it will be necessary to increase or decrease the volume of speech.
- Eye contact is critical.

Nonverbal Communication

- Nonverbal communications are messages conveyed without the use of words.
- They are transmitted by body language, gestures, and mannerisms that may or may not be in agreement with the words a person speaks.
- Appearance is an integral part of nonverbal communication.
- How can appearance influence communication?

Space

- Public space is usually accepted as a distance of 12 to 25 feet, and social space is usually considered to be 4 to 12 feet.

- Personal space ranges from 1.5 to 4 feet, and intimate contact includes physical touching to about a foot and a half.

Touch

- Touch is a powerful communicator.

- In the medical profession, as in any other, touch can be comforting or can promote a sexual harassment suit.

- The medical assistant should not, however, be afraid to touch the patient appropriately, such as a pat on the back or a squeeze of the hand.

- What is battery?

Posture

- Posture can signal depression, excitement, anger, or even an appeal for help.

- When the physician sits at the front of the chair and leans forward, he or she is giving the message of caring and interest.

Positioning

- Sitting behind a desk promotes an air of authority.

- Standing or sitting across a room may convey a negative message of denying involvement or reluctance to talk.

The Communication Process

- The sender is the person who sends a message through a variety of different **channels.**
- Channels can be spoken words, written messages, and body language.
- The sender **encodes** the message, which simply means choosing a specific way of expression by using words and other channels.
- The receiver **decodes** the message according to his or her understanding of what is being communicated.
- **Feedback** can be verbal expressions or body language, such as a simple nod of understanding.

Listening

- People need to know that they are being heard.
- When listening to someone who is attempting to communicate, the first rule is to look at the speaker and pay attention.

Questioning

- An open question requires more than a "yes" or "no" answer.
- It forces the patient to provide more detail and expand on thoughts.

Defense Mechanisms

- Verbal aggression
- Sarcasm
- Rationalization
- Compensation
- Regression
- Repression
- Apathy
- Displacement
- Denial
- Physical avoidance
- Projection

Conflict

- Conflict is defined as the struggle resulting from incompatible or opposing needs, drives, wishes, or external or internal demands.
- Conflict is not always negative.
- Assertion is stating or declaring positively, often forcefully or aggressively.
- Too much aggression can make a person seem pushy, so it should be controlled and used at appropriate times.

Barriers to Communication

- Physical impairment
- Language
- Prejudice

- Stereotyping
- Perception

Multicultural Issues

- What multicultural issues might exist in your community?

Maslow's Hierarchy of Needs

- The needs we have as humans, at the most basic level, are those that involve our physical well-being. These include food, rest, sleep, water, air, and sex.
- The second level includes issues related to our safety. We need to feel safe and secure in our homes and our environments, as well as in the places where we work.
- The third level involves our social needs for love, a sense of belonging, and interaction with others.
- The fourth level relates to our self-esteem.
- The last level is the self-actualization stage, in which we maximize our potential.

A Good Night's Sleep

- The two main phases of sleep are non–rapid-eye-movement (NREM) and rapid-eye-movement (REM) sleep.
- During NREM sleep, the eyes are fairly still, and the body relaxes and slows down.
- After the body moves through the four stages of NREM, it enters REM sleep.
- During REM sleep, the brain is highly active, and the eyes move rapidly.
- Dreaming occurs during REM sleep.

Healthful Nutrition

- A balanced diet is essential to ensure that our organs and systems function at optimal levels.
- Exercise regularly and take walks to provide cardiovascular benefits to the body.
- Do not skip meals in an effort to lose weight, and choose foods from the four basic food groups.
- Avoid unhealthful snacks and sodas, and drink at least 8 to 10 glasses of water every day.

Healthy Self-Esteem

- Self-esteem is a confidence and satisfaction in oneself. To have a good self-esteem, an individual must be self-aware, and that means taking a look at your strengths, your weaknesses, and what you have to offer as a person.

CHAPTER 6

Medicine and Ethics

Key Points

- A system of ethics deals with judgments of right and wrong or actions on issues that have implications of a moral right and wrong.

- Etiquette deals with courtesy, customs, and manners.

- Ethics should not be confused with etiquette.

- Rights are claims that are made by a person or group on society, a group, or an individual.

- Ethical distress is a problem for which there is an obvious solution, but some type of barrier hinders the action that should be taken.

- An ethical dilemma is a situation in which two or more solutions exist, but in choosing one, something of value is lost in not choosing the other.

- A dilemma of justice involves allocation of benefits and how they are to be fairly distributed.

- Two or more authority figures, each with an idea of how to handle a certain situation, are the center of the locus-of-authority ethical problem.

- Making an ethical decision is easier when approached logically with a five-step process.

- The steps include
  - Gathering relevant information
  - Identifying the type of ethical problem
  - Determining the ethics approach to use
  - Exploring the practical alternatives
  - Completing the action

- First, gather relevant information. Then identify the type of problem. After determining the ethical approach to use, explore alternatives. Then all that is left is to complete the action and make the decision.

- The American Medical Association (AMA) Code of Ethics has four components:
  - Principles of medical ethics
  - Fundamental elements of the patient/physician relationship
  - Current opinions of Council on Ethical and Judicial Affairs (CEJA) with annotations
  - Reports of CEJA

- Although healthcare professionals do not have to abide by the opinions of the CEJA, the opinions are highly regarded, and many professionals practice in accordance with these opinions.

Ethical Duty

- A **duty** is an obligation that a person has or is perceived to have.

- **Nonmaleficence** refers to refraining from harming the self or another person.

- **Beneficence** refers to bringing about good.

- **Fidelity** is the concept of keeping promises.

- **Veracity** refers to the duty to tell the truth.

- **Justice,** in relation to medical ethics, deals with the fair distribution of benefits and burdens among individuals or groups in society having legitimate claims on those benefits.

Ethical Problems

- Ethical **distress** is the problem faced when a certain course of action is indicated, but some type of hindrance or barrier prevents that action. The professional knows the right thing to do, but for whatever reason, cannot do it.

- The ethical **dilemma** is a situation in which the medical professional is faced with two or more acceptable and correct choices, but doing one precludes doing another. A choice must be made, and there may be a loss of something of value if a second choice is eliminated. This could be viewed as the proverbial "rock and a hard place," whereby a choice must be made that has a greater effect than may be seen on the surface.

- The third type of ethical problem is the dilemma of **justice.** This problem focuses on the fair distribution of benefits to those who are entitled to them. Choices must be made as to who receives these benefits and in what portion. A few examples of a dilemma of justice would include organ donations and distribution of scarce or expensive medications.

- In **locus-of-authority issues,** two or more authority figures have their own ideas about how a situation should be handled, but only one of those authorities will prevail. If one physician believes that a patient should have surgery, and another does not, how does the patient decide?

The Medical Assistant

- An ethical medical assistant will not wish to participate in known substandard or unlawful practices, especially those that might be harmful to patients.

- The medical assistant has an ethical obligation to keep abreast of current developments that affect the practice of medicine and care of the patients.

- Membership in a professional organization provides access to continuing education for maintaining knowledge and skills pertaining to the performance of medical assisting.

Confidentiality

- Confidentiality is of major importance in the medical profession.

- It is unethical to reveal patient confidences to anyone, and this includes family, spouse, best friends, and other medical assistants.

- This is such a serious issue that breach of patient confidentiality is sufficient reason for immediate termination of an employee.

Human Immunodeficiency Virus (HIV)

- Some individuals might hesitate to be tested because of concern that their name will be reported to various agencies.
- Unique identifiers maintain the confidentiality of patients who are tested for HIV.
- With the unique identifiers, patients have much more confidence that the chances of discrimination due to HIV status are lessened.

Genetic Testing

- Many ethical concerns surround the advent of genetic testing.
- Many patients are concerned as to how the information gained will be used and who will have access to the information.
- Questions arise regarding this ownership of the information.
- Discrimination could be possible with the knowledge of a person's genetic blueprint.

CHAPTER 7

Medicine and Law

Key Points

- **Law** is a custom or practice of a community, a rule of conduct or action prescribed or formally recognized as binding or enforceable by a controlling authority.

- Law is the system by which society gives order to our lives.

- Legal issues are interwoven throughout many aspects of the physician's office, and the wording of statutes and regulations is often long and complicated.

- Medical assistants, as well as all staff members and physicians, must be ever conscious of the fact that in today's **litigious** society, steps must be taken to protect themselves from lawsuits.

- **Jurisprudence,** the science and philosophy of law, comes from the Latin words *juris,* which means "law, right, equity, or justice," and *prudentia,* which means "skill or good judgment."

- The United States Constitution is the supreme law of the land, which takes **precedence** over federal statutes, court opinions, and state constitutions.

- A law enacted at the federal level, which must be passed by Congress, is called an **act.**

- **Statutes** are laws that have been enacted by state legislative bodies.

- Local governments create and enact **ordinances.**

- Much of our law is based on previous **judicial** and jury decisions, which are called **precedents.** Often judges and juries follow precedents when making a decision on a case before them.

- The two basic categories of **jurisprudence** are **criminal** law and **civil** law.

Criminal Law

- Criminal law governs violations of the law that are punishable as offenses against the state or government. Such offenses involve the welfare and safety of the public as a whole rather than of one individual.
  - Misdemeanors
  - Felonies
  - Treason

- A minor crime, as opposed to a felony, is called a **misdemeanor.** These crimes are punishable by fine or imprisonment in a city or county jail rather than in a penitentiary.

- Misdemeanors are punishable by imprisonment for 1 year or less.

- A **felony** is a major crime, such as murder, rape, or burglary, and is punishable by a greater sentence than that given for a misdemeanor. Federal law and most state statutes classify felonies as crimes punishable by imprisonment for more than 1 year.

- **Treason** is the most serious crime and is the offense of attempting to overthrow the government. High treason constitutes a serious threat to the stability or continuity of the government, such as attempts to kill the president.

Civil Law

Civil law is concerned with acts that are not criminal, but involve relationships of individuals with other individuals, organizations, or government agencies.

- *Tort law*
- *Contract law*
- *Administrative law*

Tort

Tort law provides a remedy for a person or group who has suffered harm from the wrongful acts of others.

- Medical professional liability, or medical malpractice, falls into the category of tort law.

The Four D's of Tort
Four elements must be established in every tort action:

- Duty
- Dereliction of duty
- Direct cause
- Damages

Duty

- First, the plaintiff must establish that the defendant was under a legal duty to act in a particular fashion.

Dereliction of duty

- Second, the plaintiff must demonstrate that the defendant breached this duty by failing to conform his or her behavior accordingly.

Direct cause

- Third, the plaintiff must prove that the breach of the legal duty proximately caused some injury or damage.

Damages

- Fourth, the plaintiff must prove damages, the injury or loss suffered.

Contract Law

- A contract is an agreement creating an obligation.

- A contract does not have to be formalized in writing to be binding on the parties involved.

- Oral contracts also are valid in many states in most situations.

Four Elements of a Contract

- First, there must be **manifestation of assent** or a "meeting of the minds." This element is proven by an "offer" and the "acceptance" of that offer. The parties to the contract must understand and agree on the intent of the contract.

- Second, the contract must involve **legal subject matter.** An obligation that requires an illegal action, like a gambling contract, is not an enforceable contract.

- Third, both parties must have the **legal capacity** to enter into a contract. This means that the parties must be adults of sound mind or emancipated minors.

- Last, some type of **consideration** must be exchanged. A consideration is something of value; for example, money exchanged for the physician's time.

Administrative Law

Administrative law involves regulations set forth by governmental agencies.
  - The Internal Revenue Service (IRS) has thousands of regulations and codes.
  - The laws that allow the IRS to collect taxes and pursue restitution are **administrative laws.**
  - Other agencies that are involved with administrative law include the Social Security Administration, Occupational Safety and Health Administration (OSHA), Immigration & Naturalization Service, and the Centers for Medicare & Medicaid Services (formerly HCFA).

- The physician invites an offer by establishing availability.

- The patient accepts the invitation and makes an offer by arriving for or requesting treatment.

- The physician accepts the offer by accepting the patient and undertaking treatment.

- The physician may explicitly accept the patient's offer or implicitly accept the offer by exercising independent medical judgment on behalf of the patient.

- The patient's responsibility in this agreement includes the liability for payment for services and a willingness to follow the advice of the physician.

Professional Negligence

- Professional negligence in medicine falls into one of three general classifications:
  - **Malfeasance** *The performance of an act that is wholly wrongful and unlawful*
  - **Misfeasance** *The improper performance of a lawful act*
  - **Nonfeasance** *The failure to perform an act that should have been performed*

- In medicine, negligence is defined as the performance of an act that a reasonable and **prudent** physician *would not* do or the failure to do an act that a reasonable and prudent physician *would* do.

- The standard of prudent care and conduct is not defined by law, but is left to the determination of a judge or jury, usually with the help of **expert witnesses.**

- **Contributory negligence** exists when the patient contributes to his or her own condition and can lessen the damages that can be collected or even prevent them from being collected altogether.

Types of Damages

- Nominal damages
- Punitive damages
- Compensatory damages
- General damages
- Special damages

Standard of Care

The courts hold that a physician must:

- Use reasonable care, attention, and diligence in the performance of professional services.
- Follow his or her best judgment in treating patients.
- Possess and exercise the best skill and care that are commonly possessed and exercised by other reputable physicians in the same type practice in the same or a similar locality.

Implied Consent

- A physician must have consent to treat a patient even though this consent is usually implied by virtue of the patient's appearance at the office for treatment.
- This **implied consent** is sufficient for common or simple procedures that are generally understood to involve little risk.

Informed Consent

- **Informed consent** involves a deeper understanding of the patient's condition and a full explanation of the plan for treatment. Informed consent is not satisfied merely by having the patient sign a form.
- A discussion must occur during which the physician provides the patient or the patient's legal representative with enough information to decide whether to undergo the treatment or seek an alternative.
- After such discussion, the patient either consents or refuses to consent to the proposed therapy and signs a consent form.

Minors

Consent is not required for minors when:
  - Consent may be assumed, such as in a life-threatening situation;
  - A certain treatment is required by law, such as a vaccination or radiograph for school entry or safety;
  - A court order has been issued, as in a situation in which parents withhold consent for a necessary treatment for religious reasons.

Emancipated Minors

- Emancipation is defined by statute and varies from state to state. An emancipated minor is a person younger than the age of majority (usually 18 to 21 years) who meets one or more of these conditions:
    - is married;
    - is in the armed forces;
    - is living separate and apart from parents or a legal guardian;
    - is self-supporting.

Statutes of Limitations

- A statute of limitations specifies a period after which a lawsuit cannot be filed. The statute of limitations varies from state to state, and differs for various types of litigation.

Depositions

- A deposition is testimony taken from a party or witness to the litigation and is not limited to the parties named in the lawsuit.

- A witness who is not a party to the lawsuit may be summoned by **subpoena** for the deposition. The deposition is usually taken in an attorney's office in the presence of a court reporter and is taken under oath. The person giving the deposition is called the deponent.

- The transcribed deposition, once finished, is sent to the deponent for review, and the deponent is at liberty to request any necessary changes or corrections in the document.

Legal Disclosures

- Certain infectious diseases must be reported.

- Births and deaths must be reported. In some states, detailed information about stillbirths is required.

- Physicians also must report cases that may have been a result of violence, such as gunshot wounds, knife injuries, or poisonings.

- Any death from accidental, suggestive, or unexplained causes also must be reported.

- In some states, occupational diseases and injuries must be reported within specific time limits.

Discuss these laws...

- Patient Self-Determination Act

- Patient Bill of Rights

- Controlled Substances Act of 1970

- Uniform Anatomical Gift Act

- Health Insurance Portability and Accountability Act of 1996

- Occupational Safety and Health Act and the Bloodborne Pathogens Standard of 1992

- Clinical Laboratory Improvement Act (CLIA)

Licensure

- Examination
- Reciprocity
- Endorsement

Registration and Reregistration

- After a license is granted, periodic reregistration is necessary annually or biennially.
- A physician can be concurrently registered in more than one state.
- The issuing body notifies the physician when re-registration is due.
- Continuing education units (CEUs) are granted to physicians for attending approved seminars, lectures, scientific meetings, and formal courses in accredited colleges and universities.
- A total of 50 hours a year is the average requirement for a license renewal.
- The medical assistant may be expected to help the physician arrange for completing the required units for license renewal.

Revocation or Suspension

- Conviction of a crime
- Unprofessional conduct
- Personal or professional incapacity

CHAPTER 8

Computers in the Medical Office

Key Points

- For many years, the computer has been used in medical facilities, including the physician's office.

- The development of software, the decrease in cost of computer hardware, and the time saving that the computer brings to the office make it well worth the investment.

- Computers are now standard equipment in healthcare facilities. It is essential that the medical assistant have a good understanding of the way computers work and their capabilities.

- Some of the ways that computers assist workers in medical offices are by
  - performing repetitive tasks
  - reducing errors
  - speeding production
  - recalling information on command
  - saving time
  - reducing paperwork
  - allowing more creative and productive use of the worker's time

Input

Input includes any information that enters the computer. It can take a variety of forms, from commands that are entered from the keyboard to data from another computer or device, like a scanner.
  - The device that feeds data into a computer is called an input device, such as a mouse, scanner, or keyboard.

Processing

Processing is the act of manipulating the data currently in the computer to carry out a certain task.

Output

Output is anything that exits the computer. Output can appear in many forms, such as binary numbers, characters, pictures, printed pages, or the simple image on the monitor.

- Output devices include monitors, speakers, and printers.

Storage

- The act of retaining data or applications is called storage.

- Data can be stored on disks, on CDs, or on separate drives, such as a zip drive.

Hardware

The physical pieces that can be touched and seen are called **hardware.**

- Most personal computers have a microprocessor, monitor, keyboard, mouse, and printer.

- The microprocessor is the central unit of the computer that contains the logic circuitry, which carries out the instructions of a computer's programs.

- Microprocessors, sometimes called "central processing units," are differentiated by three basic elements: *bandwidth, clock speed,* and *instruction set.*

Inside the Computer

- Motherboard

- Disk drives

- CD ROM

- Expansion boards

- Software

- Modems

- Speakers and microphones

Peripheral Devices

- Scanner

- Digital cameras

- Zip drives

- Software

- **Systems software** serves as the operating system of the computer and allows it to run and carry out the functions that the computer performs.

- For instance, Windows XP, Linux, and the now somewhat antiquated DOS are all types of operating systems software.

- **Applications software** includes the programs in the computer that carry out the work for the actual users of the computer.

- Examples of applications software include Microsoft Office, MediSoft, and Medical Manager.

- Applications programs are designed to perform specific tasks such as word processing, billing, accounting, appointment setting, insurance form preparation, payroll, and database management.

File Formats

- *JPEG*

JPEG stands for joint *photographic experts group* and is often used for photographs.

- *GIF*

GIF stands for *graphics interchange format,* which supports color and is often used for scanned images and illustrations rather than photographs.

- *DOC*

A file that includes the extension *.doc* is usually a file created by a word processor or word processing software, and stands for *document.*

- *TXT*

A text file usually has the extension *.txt* after its name. Characters in a text file are represented by their **ASCII codes.**

- *RTF*

RTF stands for *rich text format.* This type of file combines ASCII codes with special commands that distinguish variations, such as a certain **font.**

- *BMP*

Bit-mapped graphics are indicated by the extension *.bmp.* These are compiled by a graphics image set in rows or columns of dots.

Computer Networking

- *LAN*

A LAN is a local-area network, or a computer network spanning a relatively small area. Most LANs are contained in a single building or group or buildings, but LANs can be connected to other LANs even at a distance.

- *MAN*

MAN stands for metropolitan-area network. A MAN spans an area that does not exceed a metropolitan area or city and connects several LANs.

- *WAN*

A WAN is a wide-area network, which spans a relatively large geographic area. Typically a WAN consists of two or more LANs or MANs. These networks can be connected through public networks, such as a telephone system, or through leased lines or satellites. The largest WAN is the Internet.

- *HAN*

An HAN is a home-area network, which connects computers inside a user's home.

- *CAN*

A CAN is a campus-area network, often used on college campuses and sometimes on military bases.

Servers

- File servers are used for file storage, and database servers are used to process database queries.

- Some servers are considered to be dedicated servers, meaning they perform tasks only as servers, although a server also may operate as a normal computer.

The Internet

- The Internet is a global network that connects millions of computers.

- Each computer connected to the Internet is called a host and is independent of all the others.

- Internet Service Providers (ISPs) are companies that provide access to the Internet.

Domains

- .com

for commercial businesses

- .org

for organizations, usually nonprofit

- .edu

for educational institutions

- .gov

for governmental agencies

- .net

for network organizations

Browsers

- The most commonly used browsers are Netscape Navigator and Microsoft Internet Explorer.

- These browsers are able to display graphics as well as text and can present **multimedia** information, the quality of which is dependent on the computer system in use and the Internet connection speed.

Computer Security

- Encryption is the translation of data into a code not readily understood by most users.

- Firewalls are often used to prevent individuals from accessing private networks.

- Passwords

Viruses

- Viruses are programs or pieces of code loaded onto a computer, usually without the owner's knowledge, which can act just like a physical virus.

- Antivirus software is an important part of any computer system.

Computers and Ergonomics

- Repetitive strain injury (RSI)
- Eyestrain

CHAPTER 9

Telephone Technique

Key Points

- Calls to the physician's office come from a wide variety of sources. New or established patients may call to set appointments.

- Insurance companies may seek information about a claim. Hospitals, nursing facilities, or other healthcare units may need to report the progress of a patient. Laboratory results may be arriving for a patient who is very ill.

- Routine sales calls and telemarketing calls come to the office, in addition to personal calls to the physician and staff members.

Voice

- A pleasing telephone voice is friendly and uplifting.

- The speaker should pronounce words clearly and distinctly.

- Vary the pitch of the voice and avoid monotone speaking.

- Always be courteous, use tact, and talk directly into the handset so that the caller can clearly hear what is being said.

Handset

- The telephone handset should be held around the middle of the shaft, and the mouthpiece situated approximately 1 inch from the lips in front of the teeth.

- Do not hold the mouthpiece beneath the chin, because the voice may not be heard clearly.

- Do not lean the head downward to hold the phone between the ear and the shoulder, to avoid sore muscles and neck problems.

Customer Service

- It is vital to be courteous to patients and other callers to the medical facility.

- Customer service is important, because many patients have choices among their healthcare providers as to which physician provides their care, and the attitude of staff members may play a large part in their decisions.

- With good customer care, patients will continue to see the provider, and they will refer other patients to the physician; this is one of the best ways to help a practice grow.

The Physician

- The physician's time is valuable and is centered around his or her patients.
- It would be physically impossible for the physician to take all of the calls from those who wished to talk each day.
- The medical assistant must screen the physician's call and make decisions about who should be put through to the doctor.
- Offer to take a message; attempt to find out the caller's needs and how they can be resolved.
- The patient should not feel that the physician is totally inaccessible, but the patient in the office must have his or her full attention.
- Seven distinct items are needed for a phone message, including the name of the person to whom the call should be directed and the name of the person calling.
- The caller's telephone number and the reason for the call must be noted.
- The medical assistant should describe the action to be taken.
- Always note the date and time of the call, as well as the initials of the person taking the call, so that if there is any question, that person can be identified and asked.

Angry Callers

- Never return anger when a caller is angry.
- Remain calm and speak in tones that are perhaps slightly quieter than those of the caller to prompt the caller to lower his or her voice.
- Offer to help the angry person, and ask questions to gain control of the conversation, moving it toward solution.

Complaints

- Callers who have a complaint should be handled as are angry callers. Remain calm, and offer to help.
- Take a serious interest in what the caller has to say.
- Emphasize that his or her concerns are important to the staff and the physician.
- Find the source of the problem and determine exactly what the caller wants or expects for its resolution.
- Always follow up complaints and be sure that they were resolved as much to the caller's satisfaction as possible.

Emergencies

- When an emergency call comes to the medical office:
  - First, obtain a phone number where the caller can be reached in case there is a sudden disconnection.
  - Ask about the chief symptoms and when they started. Find out if the patient has had similar symptoms in the past and what happened in that situation.
  - Determine if the patient is alone, has transportation, or needs an ambulance dispatched to the location. In severe emergencies, do not hang up the phone until the ambulance or police arrive.

- The introductory pages of the telephone book contain several sections of useful information, such as area codes, emergency service information, long-distance calling information, time zones, government listings, and community service numbers.

- It may be helpful to tear these pages out and place them in clear sheet protectors in a binder for easy reference.

CHAPTER 10

Scheduling Appointments

Key Points

- When scheduling appointments, the medical assistant must consider the patients' needs, the physician's preferences, and the available facilities.

- Make every attempt to schedule the patient at his or her most convenient time to help avoid no-shows. The physician's preferences are of high priority.

- However, most physicians are flexible and will make adjustments according to the needs of the office.

- The availability of facilities within the office are perhaps the most inflexible.

- If a certain room or piece of equipment is being used by one patient, it usually cannot be used by another.

The Appointment Book

- When choosing an appointment book, all of the needs of the office should be considered.

- If there are multiple physicians, arrange the book so that each doctor is readily identified.

- Books that open flat on the surface of the desk are much easier to handle, but if there is not enough space to open the book entirely, another style might be better.

- The book should provide enough space to write all of the patient information needed in the various time slots, such as the name, phone number, and reason for the visit.

- Computerized scheduling programs are in demand today because of the ease in operation and in making changes to the schedule.

- The computer can find the first available time much more quickly than a person scanning through an appointment book.

- Most programs can prepare reports and even notify patients automatically by email of the impending appointment.

- Web-based self-scheduling programs allow patients to see the physician's available appointments and book their own dates and times.

- Self-scheduling would vastly reduce calls to the office, because many everyday calls are requests to schedule appointments.

- Patients could make an appointment at midnight, if they desired.

Types of Schedules

- Open office hours allow patients to come to the physician's office when it is convenient and wait in turn to see the doctor.

- Scheduling specific appointments is the most popular method of seeing patients.

- Flexible office hours allow patients to see the doctor during the evening and often on weekends.

- Many of today's medical offices have some flexible scheduling because most families now have two working parents.

- Wave scheduling brings two to three patients to the office at the same time, and they are seen in the order of their arrival.

- This type of scheduling can be modified in many ways to suit the needs of the facility.

- Other scheduling methods include double booking and grouping of like procedures.

- When the office is running 15 minutes behind schedule, the medical assistant should briefly explain the delay to the waiting patients and then offer to reschedule their appointments.

- Keep the patients informed of wait times until the schedule resumes.

- Giving the patient a choice in appointment times is a part of good customer service.

- Offer the patient a choice of 2 days, morning or afternoon, and two times.

- This method helps to ensure a show for the appointment and better meets the needs of the patient.

- Because the appointment schedule might be called into a court of law, it is vital that the handwriting in the book be completely legible.

- Even if the book is 5 years old, the person charged with testifying in court should be able to read all entries clearly.

- Scribbled, messy handwriting implies incompetence, and the courtroom is not the place for this impression.

- Patients that arrive late might be told to arrive 15 minutes before the time written in the book.

- Some offices book these patients as the last appointment of the day: if they do not arrive promptly, they do not see the physician.

- Talking with the patient and gaining an understanding of why the patient arrives late usually will vastly improve the situation.

- The office can work with the patient to choose the best times that will result in a show appointment.

- Some patients accidentally forget the appointment with the physician, and some are habitually careless about remembering their scheduled time.

- Small emergencies often come up, and in today's busy business world, some patients just cannot get away from their own offices or other obligations to visit the doctor.

- In some cases, the patient does not keep an appointment to avoid dealing with the health issues.

CHAPTER 11

Patient Reception and Processing

Key Points

- The office mission statement is the philosophy of why the office exists. Physicians often develop the mission statement themselves; it outlines their vision and reasons for entering medical practice.

- Some doctors allow the office staff to assist in the statement development. All employees should become familiar with the mission statement and promote its ideas to all patients and visitors.

- Patient amenities include such things as a VCR, television, computer, telephone, and a desk where patients can sit and balance a checkbook or review work while away from the office.

- These features turn the time spent in the physician's office into productive minutes instead of wasteful ones.

- Some offices prepare for patient arrivals the evening before, and some, in the morning.

- Patient charts must be pulled and reviewed, checking for completed laboratory tests, posting of results, and assuring that there are ample progress notes for this visit.

- Rooms should be checked and inventoried to make certain that there are enough supplies on hand, and that they present a clean, neat appearance.

- People like hearing their own names, and a better relationship is built between the staff and patients when the names are used often. Patients feel that the office staff cares enough about them to acknowledge them, and the practice adds a personal touch.

- The medical assistant should escort the patient to the examination rooms and other areas of the office. Always tell the patient when to disrobe and exactly what should be removed. Offer to assist with disrobing, if the patient needs extra help.

- Take care that the patients' purse or wallet is in a secure place. Be sure that doors do not open and expose the disrobed patient. Instruct them as to when they may leave, or whether they should wait after seeing the physician.

- Ask often if the patient has any questions.

- Some medical offices place patient charts in a door file to alerts the physician that the patient is ready to be seen.

- The chart may be placed horizontally or vertically, one placement meaning that the patient is ready for the doctor, and the other meaning that the doctor is finished with the patient.

- Other offices place the charts in door files in a certain order. For example, if Exam Rooms 1, 2, and 3 are available, patients are seen in that order by the physician.

- Talkative patients are sometimes lonely and enjoy the social interaction of their visits to the physician's office.

- Be as courteous as possible with talkative patients, expressing to them when necessary that another patient is waiting, or the physician needs assistance.

- When this is said with a smile, most patients understand.

- Closing duties can be easily remembered by making an association of each duty with a certain letter, and then making a word from those letters.

- Lists posted close to the door will help, or developing a checklist of closing duties will help the medical assistant recall what to do before leaving for the day.

- The personal touch will help the patient feel at home and comfortable in the office.

- An attractive reception area with various patient amenities will provide a warm atmosphere.

- Using the patient's name often and a gentle touch will impart a sense of caring as well.

CHAPTER **12**

Written Communications and Mail Processing

Key Points

- The medical assistant is responsible for making certain that equipment is in good working order.

- Warranties should always be mailed when new equipment is purchased, and the correct maintenance procedures should be followed to keep machines working at an optimal levels.

- Supplies should be ordered before they run out, and prices should be compared to find the best quality for the best price available.

- The four basic sizes of letterhead stationery follow:
  - Standard or letter-size stationery, which is most commonly used for business purposes, is $8\frac{1}{2} \times 11$ inches.
  - Monarch or executive stationery is $8\frac{1}{2} \times 10\frac{1}{2}$ inches and is used for informal business correspondence.
  - Baronial stationery is $5\frac{1}{2} \times 8\frac{1}{2}$ inches.
  - Legal stationery is $8\frac{1}{2} \times 14$ inches.

- The medical assistant should be familiar with the various parts of speech and their correct use in a sentence.

- Nouns name something, such as a person, place, or thing; pronouns are substitutes for nouns.

- Verbs are action words, and express movement, a condition, or a state of being.

- Adjectives usually describe nouns, whereas adverbs usually describe verbs or adjectives.

- Prepositions are connecting words, as are conjunctions.

- Interjections show strong feelings, often followed by an exclamation point.

- A personal tool collection will help the medical assistant with the written communications in the medical office.

- An up-to-date dictionary, a medical dictionary, a composition handbook, an English-language reference manual, and a thesaurus will be valuable additions to the tool library.

- Before answering any type of correspondence, read the piece carefully.

- A highlighter may be used to mark questions that must be answered, or notes may be written on the correspondence in pencil.

- A draft of the reply should be written first and then rewritten in its final form.

- Subsequent letters will be much easier to draft if the medical assistant develops a portfolio containing sample letters and other types of communications.

- Once a letter is written, it can be saved on the computer or on a disk, or printed and placed in a binder for easy viewing.

- If printed in a binder, it is wise to note the file name as it is saved on the computer, so that the document can be easily found again.

- This is an excellent way to save time in the busy medical office.

- Block is an efficient but less attractive letter style, wherein all lines begin flush with the left margin of the paper.

- Modified block is similar, but some lines begin at the center of the page instead of the left margin.

- Modified block with indented paragraphs is identical to block style, with the exception of the indention of the paragraphs.

- Simplified letter style contains lines that begin flush at the left margin, but other items are omitted, such as the salutation and complimentary closing.

- The four standard parts of a business letter include the heading, the opening, the body, and the closing.

- The heading includes the letterhead and date line; the opening includes the inside address and any attention or salutation line.

- The body is the message of the document, and the closing is the signature, complimentary closing, reference initials, and special notations.

- To save money, consult the post office when mailing, checking for better rates and using zip codes. Consult a local post office when mailing in bulk to obtain the best rates.

CHAPTER 13

Medical Records Management

Key Points

- Several types of equipment and supplies are necessary to manage patient records.

- A variety of shelving units and filing containers are available.

- Open shelving allows the maximized use of color-coded charts, which make finding misfiles quick and easy.

- Many file folder styles are available, and there are several types of forms to use within the patient charts.

- The preference of the physician and staff members who use these tools is important, as well as concerns such as cost and availability.

- The medical assistant should be conservative when ordering supplies and purchasing equipment, ordering only the number needed to save on costs.

Five basic steps are involved in filing documents:

- The papers are conditioned, which is the preparatory stage for filing.

- Releasing the documents means that they are ready to be filed because they have been reviewed or read, and some type of mark is placed on the document to indicate this.

- Indexing involves the decision as to where the document should be filed, and coding is placing some type of mark on the paper relative to that decision.

- Sorting is placing the files in filing sequence.

- The last step is the actual filing and storing of the document.

- Alphabetic filing is a simple and traditional filing system, whereby documents are filed in alphabetic order.

- Numeric filing systems use a number code to give order to the files. An alphanumeric system is a combination of the two.

- Color coding is an excellent way to keep patient charts in order and swiftly to locate misfiled charts.

- The medical assistant can tell at a glance when a chart is out of place.

- Color coding also makes retrieval of files and refiling quick and easy.

- Medical records must be accurate so that the right care can be given to the patient. The record also helps to provide continuity of care between providers, so that there is no lapse in treatment of the patient.

- The record serves as indication and proof in court that certain treatments and procedures were performed on the patient, so it can be excellent legal support if it is well maintained and accurate.

- Medical records also aid researchers with statistical information.

- The physician owns the physical medical record, whereas the patient owns the information contained within.

- The problem-oriented medical record categorizes each problem that a patient has and elaborates on the findings and treatment plan for all concerns. Detailed progress notes are kept for every problem.

- This method separates each of the patient's concerns and addresses them separately, whereas a traditional record may address all problems and concerns at one time.

- The problem-oriented medical record helps to assure that all individual problems are addressed.

- Very simply, subjective information is provided by the patient, whereas objective information is provided by the physician or provider.

- Subjective information includes items such as the patient address, social security number, insurance information, and the patient's explanation of the his or her condition.

- Objective information is obtained through the questions the physician asks and the observations made during the examination.

- Correct procedures must be followed when making corrections to a patient chart. Draw a single line through the incorrect information, and then initial and date it.

- Some offices require a notation of "Corr." or "correction" on the chart as well. The medical assistant should never try to alter the medical record or cover up an error in charting.

CHAPTER 14

Professional Fees, Billing, and Collecting

Key Points

- Medical services are valuable to the patient who receives them.

- The physician sets fees based on three commodities.

- The physician offers the patient his or her *time* and makes the most accurate *judgments* about the patient's medical condition possible.

- The *services* provided to the patient also figure into the fees that are set for various procedures.

- Many third-party payors use the usual, customary, and reasonable method of determining fees for procedures.

- The usual fee is what the physician normally charges for a given service.

- The customary fee is the range of fees charged by physicians who have similar experience in the same geographic area.

- Services or procedures that are exceptionally complicated and require extra time deserve a reasonable fee that may be higher than the usual fee.

- Providing estimates for medical care helps patients to plan their finances when an illness or injury occurs.

- Estimates help avoid the possibility of later misquoting the fee.

- The office staff should keep a copy of the estimate in the patient's chart to help avoid misunderstandings and confusion over charges.

Professional Courtesy

- Some physicians choose to extend professional courtesy to other physicians, medical professionals, and medical staff employees.

- This means that the physician either discounts or eliminates the charges for all or part of the services provided.

- The decision to offer professional courtesy is made by the physician.

Payment

- Payment for medical services is accomplished in several ways.

- Most physicians prefer that payment be received at the time of service.

- When the extension of credit is offered, internal billing is necessary.

- Some offices contract with external billing services.

- Patients may have some type of insurance or managed-care policy that pays at least a portion of the bill. When patients fail to meet their obligations, outside collection services may be used.

- The first statement should always be itemized. This provides the patient and the guarantor with a record of each procedure and each charge. Insurance companies require itemized bills to reimburse for the charges.

- Rarely patients do not meet their obligations by paying bills.

- Some do not have the money to pay for medical services, and if they do not have health insurance, it could be even more difficult to obtain medical care.

- The financial problems that the patient faces may be temporary or may be a long-standing situation.

- Only a few patients are actually unwilling to pay, so the medical assistant should work with the patient to develop a payment plan that the patient can meet.

Skips

- Immediate action should be taken when the office classifies a patient as a "skip." Search the patient chart for all possible telephone numbers, and call those that the patient has given.

- Do not reveal that the patient owes money. If it is necessary to leave a message, do not indicate that the call is from a physician's office.

- The employer may be called unless the patient has not given permission to call the place of business.

- Never communicate with a third party more than once unless invited to call back.

- A certified letter may be sent, and when address corrections are requested, the new address is often obtainable.

- Unless the "skip" is found quickly, the account is generally turned over to a collection agency.

- For collection calls to patients or guarantors, be sure to call within accepted calling hours, which are 8 a.m. to 9 p.m.

- Be sure to identify the person speaking, and always be respectful and courteous.

- State the purpose for the call, and keep the conversation business-like and professional.

- Keep a positive attitude, and convey to the patient that the call is to help devise a way that the obligations to the physician can be met.

- Never threaten the patient, and make every effort to get a commitment as to when payment can be expected. Most important, follow up on collection calls to assure that patients sent in the payment as promised.

CHAPTER 15

Basics of Diagnostic Coding

Key Points

Why Use ICD Codes?

- In addition to the logistic layout of a standard system used in billing, some pertinent reasoning behind the use of International Classification of Diseases–9th edition–Clinical Modification (ICD-9-CM) codes include the following:

- Store and retrieve data

- Maximize reimbursement by accurate coding

- Shorten claims-processing time

- Measure compliance with clinical guidelines

Volume I

- Volume I contains five appendices and 17 chapters. This is referred to as the Tabular List.

- This volume classifies diseases and injuries according to etiology and organ system, dividing them into groups:
  - Anatomic system type of condition
  - Related groups of codes
  - Three-digit codes (category codes)
  - Fourth-digit codes (subcategory codes)
  - Fifth-digit codes (subclassification codes)

- Each of the 17 chapters in Volume I is subdivided as follows:
  - **Section:** Group of three-digit code numbers describing a general disease category.
  - **Category:** A three-digit code representing a specific disease within the section.
  - **Subcategory:** A further breakdown of the category, assigning a fourth digit.
  - **Subclassification:** Five-digit code giving the highest level of definition to the disease state.

Volume II

- Volume II contains an alphabetic index of disease and injury. This volume contains more information than contained in the Tabular List and is divided into three sections:
  - Index of diseases
  - Poison and external causes of adverse effects of drugs and other chemical substances
  - Alphabetic index of external cause of injury and poisoning

Symbols

☐   The "lozenge" symbol precedes a disease code when indicating that the content of a four-digit category has been moved or modified.

§   This "section mark" symbol is only used in the Tabular List of Diseases and precedes a code denoting a footnote on the page.

●   The "bullet" symbol indicates a new entry.

▲   The "triangle" indicates a revision in the tabular list and a code change in the alphabetic index.

►◄   These symbols mark both the beginning and ending of new or revised text.

♀   Female diagnosis only.

♂   Male diagnosis only.

√4th Code requires a fourth digit.

√5th Code requires a fifth digit.

Abbreviations

● NEC Not elsewhere classifiable. The category number for the term including NEC is to be used only when the coder lacks the information necessary to code the term to a more specific category.

● NOS Not otherwise specified. This abbreviation is the equivalent of "unspecified."

Punctuation

[ ]   Brackets are used to enclose synonyms, alternative wordings, or explanatory phrases.

( )   Parentheses are used to enclose supplementary words that may be present or absent in the statement of a disease or procedure without affecting the code number to which it is assigned.

:   Colons are used in the Tabular List after an incomplete term that needs one or more of the modifiers that follow to make it assignable to a given category.

{ }   Braces enclose a series of terms, each of which is modified by the statement appearing to the right of the brace.

BOLD – used for all codes and titles in the Tabular List.

ITALICIZED – used for exclusion notes and to identify a diagnosis that cannot be used as primary.

The following steps are always necessary to assign the appropriate ICD-9-CM code:

● Identify the key terms in the diagnostic statement, determining the main reason for the encounter. Keep in mind that the definitive diagnosis should be coded first. Some important points to remember:

● Check documentation regarding preexisting condition. Be sure this condition is currently being treated and is not part of the past medical history.

● *Never code conditions described as "rule out," "suspected," "probable," or "questionable."* (You don't want to give patients a disease they don't have!)

● If a patient requests that a different diagnosis be used that is not the correct or appropriate diagnosis for the visit, stating that their insurance company will not reimburse, you have a legal and ethical responsibility to code the diagnosis correctly.

● If no definitive diagnosis is made, code the symptoms.

CHAPTER 16

Basics of Procedural Coding

Key Points

Current Procedural Terminology (CPT)

Why use CPT?

- Medicare and most commercial insurance companies use CPT to identify and classify claims for payment.

- Although it is standard in a physician practice, CPT is not recognized in some facilities or under special guidelines in an insurance company.

- Physician practices use CPT to
  – Submit claims
  – Track utilization
  – Measure physician productivity

Format of CPT

- Three levels of CPT:
  – Level I (one) are national codes developed by the American Medical Association (AMA) and contained in current CPT Manual. They are five-digit codes and two-digit modifiers.
  – Level II (two), known as Healthcare Financing Administration Common Procedure Coding System (HCPCS), are national codes developed by the Council of Medical Specialties (CMS) to describe medical services and supplies not covered in CPT. They consist of alpha characters (between A and V) and four digits. Modifiers are either alphanumeric or two letters (between AA and VP).
  – Level III (three) are local codes. Unlike Levels I and II, these codes are not common to all carriers. They are assigned by local Medicare carriers to describe new procedures that are not yet in Levels I and II. These codes start with a letter (W to Z) followed by four digits. Please note: when the HIPAA standards for electronic transactions are implemented, Level III (three) codes will no longer be recognized for reimbursement reporting.

Symbols

Symbols appear in the listings to serve as instructional notes. Understanding their meaning and using their guidance is crucial to accurate coding.

- ● New procedure
- ▲ Code revision

+   CPT add-on codes
Ø   Exempt from the use of modifier 51
▶◀ Revised guidelines, cross-references and explanations
→   With a circle around it refers to *CPT Assistant*
*   Surgical procedure only

Classifications of Sections

Section is a general grouping of codes like Surgery, Medicine, Laboratory, or Radiology. It is the largest grouping in CPT.

- **Subsection** better defines the section

- **Subheading** further defines the subsection.

- **Category** defines the specific procedures.

Steps in CPT Coding

- Know your CPT code book: there are changes each year, so even if you have been coding for years, you must read the *introduction, guidelines, and notes.*

- Review all services and procedures performed on the day of the encounter; include all medications administered and trays and equipment used.

- Find the procedures and/or services in the index in the back of the CPT book. This will direct you to a code (not a page number!). The code you are looking for may be listed as a procedure, body system, service, or abbreviation (this will usually refer to the full spelling).

- Read the description in the code and any related descriptions that follow a semicolon; this will lead you to the most accurate code. If the service is an Evaluation and Management code, identify
  - A new or established patient
  - Whether this is a consultation
  - Where the service performed
  - The level of service
  - Check to see if there is a reason to use a modifier
  - **Assign the five-digit CPT code**

Modifiers

- When used, modifiers explain circumstances that alter a service that has been provided.

- Multiple modifiers: Sometimes more than one modifier is needed. When this happens, the first modifier used is –99 or 09999.

Understanding Evaluation and Management (E&M)

- **Type of service:** Services covered in the E&M section are physician visits in all locations for "well" and "sick" visits, patient transport, case-management services, preventive medicine services, and prolonged services.

- **Place of service:** For payment purposes, the place of service must match the type of service. Some examples of places of service include
  - Office (11)
  - Patient's home (12)
  - Inpatient hospital (21)
  - Outpatient hospital (22)

- **Patient status:** Many of the CPT codes are classified by whether a patient is a new or an established patient.
  - A new patient is new to the practice or has not been seen by the specialty in group practice for a period of more than 3 years.
  - An established patient is one that has a continuing relationship with the practice and is unlikely to depart from baseline health.

Levels of E&M Services

- **Problem focused:** A problem-focused history concentrates on the chief complaint; it looks at the symptoms, severity, and duration of the problem. It usually does not include a review of systems (ROS) or family and social history.

- **Expanded problem focused:** The physician does the same as above but includes an ROS that relate to the chief complaint. Usually a past, family, and social history is not included.

- **Detailed:** The physician will document a more extensive history, ROS, and will document pertinent past, family, and social histories.

- **Comprehensive:** The physician will document responses to **all** of the components listed earlier. This type of history is usually done on an initial visit with patients who have a significant history of illness.

Medical Decision Making

- **Straightforward:** One diagnosis/management option, one test ordered or reviewed, and full recovery expected.

- **Low complexity:** Limited (two) diagnoses/management options, limited (two) tests ordered or reviewed, and low risk of complications.

- **Moderate complexity:** Multiple (three) diagnoses/management options, moderate (three) data ordered or reviewed, and moderate risk of complications and/or death if patient is not treated.

- **High complexity:** Extensive (four or more) diagnoses/management options, extensive (four or more) data ordered or reviewed, and the risk to the patient for complications if the problem untreated is great.

Examination

- *Body areas:* Head, including face and neck; chest, including breasts and axillae; abdomen; genitourinary; back, including spine; and extremities.

- **Organ systems:** Constitutional; eyes, ears, nose, throat, and mouth; cardiovascular; respiratory; gastrointestinal (GI); genitourinary (GU); musculoskeletal; skin; neurologic; psychiatric; and hematologic/lymphatic.

- **Problem focused:** Limited to the single body area or single system mentioned in the chief complaint.

- **Expanded problem focused:** In addition to the limited body area or system, related body areas/organ systems are examined.

- **Detailed:** An extended examination is made of related body areas/organ systems.

- **Comprehensive:** A "complete" multisystem examination is performed.

CHAPTER 17

The Health Insurance Claim Form

Key Points

- For a better understanding of the medical insurance claims process, the medical assistant should familiarize himself or herself with the language and terms used in this area of administrative work.

- Insurance claims can be submitted in two forms: paper and electronic. There are advantages and disadvantages for both; however, electronic claims normally have fewer errors and historically are paid faster.

- Clean claims are those that can be processed and paid quickly; dirty claims contain errors and/or omissions that often result in rejection, greatly slowing the reimbursement process.

- The insurance claim cycle begins when the patient first makes an appointment. The medical assistant should follow an established list of guidelines for Healthcare Financing Administration (HCFA)-1500 form completion, including obtaining a signed authorization to release information.

- There are 33 blocks in the HCFA-1500 claim form, and except for a few blocks that ask for standard information, completion requirements vary from payor to payor.

- The medical assistant should familiarize himself or herself with each major payor's unique requirements to maximize reimbursement.

- Optical character recognition (OCR) scanning is the electronic transfer of information from claim forms to data banks that simplifies and speeds the claims process.

- Specific guidelines should be followed when completing claims to facilitate OCR scanning. The medical assistant should know and follow these guidelines precisely.

- Claim rejection and delay cost the medical facility time and money. Establish and adhere to proven methods of preventing claim rejections.

- It is important to track claims once they are submitted.

- An insurance claim register, or log, can be created and used as one method of tracking claims.

- A routine should be established for claims follow-up.

CHAPTER 18

Third-Party Reimbursement

Key Points

Coordination of Benefits (COB)

- The **policyholder's** own plan is primary for that individual. An exception occurs if the policyholder is laid off or retired and is not a Medicare recipient. In this case, the policyholder's plan pays second.

- The primary coverage for dependents of the policyholder is determined by the birthday rule.

- The insurance plan of the policyholder whose birthday comes first in the calendar year (month and day, not year) provides primary coverage for each dependent.

- If neither situation applies, the plan that has been in existence longer is the primary payor.

- The primary plan for dependents of legally separated or divorced parents is more complicated.

- The birthday rule is in effect if the parent who has custody of the dependent has not remarried. If the custodial parent has remarried, that parent's plan is primary for that dependent.

- If one parent has been decreed by the court to be the responsible party, that parent's policy is primary. This is not always the parent with legal custody of the child.

- If one of the plans originated in a state not having the COB law, the plan that did originate in a state having a COB law will determine the order of benefits.

- The medical assistant should have an understanding of the purpose of health insurance. This will help in the workplace not only by facilitating his or her knowledge of the subject, but also in educating patients. The trend for insurance policies to encourage "preventive medicine" can be appreciated.

- Insurance policies fall into many different categories and are available in many different forms.

- The ability to differentiate among the various types of insurance policies gives medical assistants a solid background in what is available on the market, what is included in each policy category, and the function of each.

- It also is important for the medical assistant to understand and appreciate that many people in this country still cannot afford and do not receive quality healthcare.

- Insurance packages are often tailored to the needs of each individual or group, and the ways to combine benefits are limitless.

- Health insurance policies normally contain a combination of the different benefits discussed in the narrative of this chapter (e.g., surgical, basic medical, and major medical).

- Benefits are determined and paid in one of several ways: indemnity schedules; service benefit plans; determination of the usual, customary, and reasonable (UCR) fee; and relative value studies.

- The medical assistant should become familiar with each of these methods and understand the ramifications of all.

- Healthcare has changed tremendously in recent years, and the cost of quality healthcare has skyrocketed.

- Efforts have been made in both the public and private sector to introduce various healthcare reform methods to contain these costs.

- Healthcare reform has had little success on a national level; however, individual states are now beginning to pass laws that have resulted in some improvement.

- The medical assistant should become well informed on the issues of healthcare reform and keep current by reading pertinent magazines and periodicals and paying close attention to news broadcasts.

- Managed care is a broad term used to describe a variety of health plans developed to provide healthcare services at lower costs.

- There is much confusion as to what all managed care entails.

- To understand managed care fully, it is necessary to know its history and how it evolved.

- When the medical assistant is employed in a medical facility, he or she will no doubt be working with one or more managed care plans.

- Therefore it is important to know the various types [e.g., health maintenance organization (HMO), IPS, preferred provider option (PPO)] and to understand how each functions. Managed care has had both positive and negative effects on modern medicine. The bottom line is to be well informed.

- The maze of managed care options can create confusion in even the best informed people.

- There are three HMO plans alone.

- PPOs are another popular managed care option in which physicians sign a contract with a PPO organization and agree to allow PPO members a discount for healthcare services. It may be difficult for the medical assistant to become an expert on every type of managed care; however, he or she should research those that are the most common in his or her area of practice and concentrate on them.

- Other major third-party payors the medical assistant should become familiar with are Blue Cross/Blue Shield, Medicaid, Medicare, CHAMPVA/TRICARE, and Workers' Compensation.

- Medicare is the largest third-party insurer in the country, making quality healthcare affordable for the elderly and selected other groups.

- Medicaid is another government-sponsored health care plan for individuals who qualify for these benefits.

- Workers' Compensation covers employees who are injured or who become ill as a result of accidents or adverse conditions in the workplace.

- Disability programs reimburse individuals for monetary losses incurred as a result of an inability to work for reasons other than those covered under Workers' Compensation.

- Many problems can be prevented for both the patient and the medical office if the medical assistant develops and follows a procedure for verifying insurance benefits before services are rendered.

- This procedure includes gathering as much information as possible about the demographics of the patient and his or her insurance coverage.

- A pragmatic and tactful discussion with all new patients explaining the established policy that the medical office adheres to regarding the insurance claims process and the collection of fees not covered by their policy will pay off in the end.

- It is important for the medical assistant, and patients alike, to realize that fees for medical procedures and services differ from office to office, based on the type of practice and the needs of the facility.

- Until the advent of managed care, most physicians operated on a *fee-for-service* basis in which the provider would render his or her services and charge accordingly.

- In recent years, government and managed care organizations have greatly influenced what healthcare providers can charge.

- Many third-party payors base reimbursements on what is referred to as the *allowable charge*.

- Other fee schedule types include the Relative Value Scale (RVS) and the Resource-Based Relative Value Scale (RBRVS).

CHAPTER **19**

Banking Services and Procedures

Key Points

- The Internet has changed conventional banking as we know it, and it offers expansive opportunities. As with everything, however, e-banking has both advantages and disadvantages, and it should be thoroughly researched before opening an online account.

- For an instrument (e.g., check) to be "negotiable," it must meet certain criteria:
  - Be written and signed by a **maker,**
  - Contain a promise or order to pay a sum of money,
  - Be payable on demand or at a fixed future date, and
  - Be payable to order or bearer.

- The many advantages of using checks include the following:
  - They are safe and convenient,
  - Expenditures can be quickly calculated, and
  - They provide a permanent record for tax purposes.

- The three most common types of bank accounts are checking accounts, savings accounts, and money market savings accounts. Each is slightly different, and each has its special uses.

- Normally, when a mistake is made on a check, it should be marked VOID and a new check written. Some banks will accept minor errors if the maker initials the error. Erasures are not allowed, nor is whiteout.

- The four kinds of endorsements are as follows:
  - blank endorsement, in which the payee simply signs his or her name on the back of the check
  - restrictive endorsement, which specifies which bank and what specific account the funds are to be deposited in
  - special endorsement, which names a specific person as payee on the back of the check
  - qualified endorsement, which disclaims future liability. This type of endorsement is used when the person who accepts the check has no personal claim in the transaction.

- When a deposited check is returned, the maker should be contacted immediately, informed of the situation, and asked to remedy the situation by either immediately depositing funds in his or her account to cover the check, or paying the bill with alternative means—cash or money order.

- The procedure for reconciling a bank statement is simple and straightforward; however, until it is done a few times, it can be confusing.

CHAPTER 20

Medical Practice Management

Key Points

- Management is an important aspect of running a professional medical office.

- The physician counts on the office manager to run the business aspects of the office so that he or she can focus on good patient care.

- A high degree of trust is placed on the office manager.

- A good office manager is fair and flexible.

- Good communications skills and attention to details are necessary.

- The manager should care about the employees and have a sense of fairness.

- The ability to remain calm in a crisis is important, as is the use of good judgment and ability to organize tasks.

- Charismatic leaders inspire allegiance and dedication, while encouraging individuals to overcome great obstacles.

- The transactional leader is structured and organized, hardworking, and a planner.

- The transformational leader is excellent during times of transition, and is effective at building relationships.

- Power can be both positive and negative.

- Power should not be manipulative or coercive.

- Expert power is based on a high degree of knowledge about a certain subject.

- Using rewards is one form of implementing power, and legitimate power is that of position or status.

- Referent power is granted from subordinates to those who lead by example.

- Employees are motivated by various factors, including money, praise, insecurity, honor, prestige, needs, love, fear, satisfaction, and many others.

- The effective manager attempts to discover what motivates employees to do a good job.

- Intrinsic motivation comes from within the employee, whereas extrinsic motivation has an outside source.

- Asking for help, first and foremost, can prevent burnout.

- Managers often take on too many duties and do not delegate as much as they should.

- Exercise and rest help prevent burnout, as does understanding one's own personal limitations.

- Focused goals are important and help keep the manager working on the most critical tasks.

- Resumes and applications should be reviewed for accuracy and completeness.

- Gaps in employment dates should be fully explained, and office managers should verify any references given.

- Documents should be legible, and the information contained should be consistent without oversights.

- The phone voice of an applicant is important because most employees have occasion to answer the phone at work.

- The employee's voice should be clear and easily understandable.

- Good grammar skills must be used to reflect a professional image.

- After interviewing a prospective candidate, the office manager should verify the facts on the resume and application, and check several references.

- A comparison should be made between the candidates and the top two or three chosen for a possible second interview.

- It is wise to involve other staff members when choosing new employees for the office.

- Mentors assist new employees by offering information regarding policies and procedures.

- The mentor can be a helpful advocate that the new employee can approach with questions about any aspect of the medical office.

- Staff meetings may be held to relay information, solve a problem, or brainstorm ideas.

- Some meetings are designed as work sessions, whereas others may be scheduled to discuss new policies or changes in procedures.

Medical Practice Marketing and Customer Service

Key Points

- When preparing to implement marketing strategies, the medical assistant should first evaluate what is currently being done in marketing.

- Then decide on the objectives of the marketing plan are and how they will be measured.

- Last, develop a specific plan and timeline for implementing each phase.

- A target market is a very specific group of people or individuals that the medical facility wishes to serve.

- Where the individuals live, the lifestyle they are accustomed to, and the personalities of the individuals all are ways to classify them into a specific target market.

- When identifying a target market, ask "Who are our patients?" "What do our patients want?" and "Why do they want it?"

- These questions will help the medical facility to design a marketing plan to meet the needs of these individuals.

- Suggestions from patients and employees should always be welcomed in the medical office.

- These people often see the facility from a different point of view, and their suggestions can enhance the atmosphere and services offered.

- A marketing plan must always address the "four p's": product, placement, price, and promotion.

- The product in a medical office includes the services and any actual retail items that might be sold.

- Placement relates to the location of the office and its convenience to the patients, and the placement of retail items in the facility.

- Price represents the charges for goods and services.

- Promotion entails the ways in which the services are promoted to the general public and the target market.

- To develop a marketing plan, the facility should first assess the efforts that have been made and their results.

- Then the plan is developed, which should include very specific steps for each aspect of the endeavor.

- After the plan is executed, the staff must evaluate its effectiveness and then determine whether the goals were met.

- The evaluation is important in planning future marketing strategies.

- Involvement in the community is an excellent way to give to the medical profession and to remain in the public eye. These efforts can result in new patients for the facility. The public sees medical professionals as caring and compassionate, so volunteer activities reinforce this attitude and help to meet patient expectations.

- Advertising is defined as a medium that creates or changes attitudes, beliefs, and perceptions though purchased broadcast time, printed material, or other forms of communication.

- Public relations is similar, but relies more on news broadcasts or reports, magazine or newspaper articles, and radio reports to reach the audience.

- The new medical practice can be promoted by placing an announcement in the newspaper about its opening. Some physicians hold an open house, inviting the public to visit the office. A website is an excellent promotional tool that should be listed on business cards and stationery. Community service and volunteer activities that mention the practice also will help to spread the word about the available services.

- Identifying with the patient is an effective customer-service tool.

- The medical assistant should express his or her understanding about the patient's concerns.

- Then tell the patient that the situation can be resolved and how it will be resolved.

- Four magic words in customer service are, "Let me help you."

Customers

- External customers are those that visit the facility, such as patients. However, staff members and employees are internal customers, who wish to derive a sense of satisfaction in working for the medical office.

- The internal customers are just as important as the external customers.

CHAPTER 22

Health Information Management

Key Points

- Both physicians and employees of medical facilities use health information in many ways. The information helps to assure continuity of care from provider to provider. It assists manufacturers in determining side effects of drugs. It provides statistical information regarding primary and secondary diagnoses. Health information also helps the medical facility plan for future needs and capital equipment.

- There are nine characteristics of high-quality health data. Validity refers to the accuracy of the information; reliability means that the information can be counted on to be accurate, and medical decisions can be made based on the information. Completeness simply means that the information is available in its entirety, and recognizability refers to the data being understood by the users.

- Timely information allows the provider to make decisions based on the latest data about a patient or a treatment. Relevance refers to the usefulness of the health information, and accessibility means that the information is easily available to the provider. Security encompasses the effort to keep unauthorized people from accessing health information. Legality refers to the correctness of the information and its authentication by the healthcare provider.

- Four concerns surround quality assurance, including the overuse, underuse, misuse, and variations in use of healthcare services. Overused services are excessive and cause cost increases, as in using the emergency room for nonemergencies. Underuse means that patients do not take advantage of many services they should be using, especially if they are at-risk patients.

- Misuse of services often reflects errors, such as laboratory errors or misdiagnoses. Variations in services simply means that in various parts of the country, individuals use services in different ways, which can influence the quality of care overall in the United States.

HIPPA

- The Health Insurance Portability and Accountability Act is a milestone in support of patient privacy issues. The most widely publicized sections deal with the right to patient privacy. The act will give a degree of control to patients and allow them information about who accesses their records. They also must give specific authorization for the use and dissemination of the information contained in the medical record.

- The National Center for Health Statistics (NCHS) is a part of the Centers for Disease Control. Health statistics are important, because they allow providers to treat their patients more effectively.

- For instance, if a certain area has a high number of outbreaks of a particular disease, the physician may be better prepared to cope with patients with the symptoms of that disease, treating them faster and promoting a full recovery.

- Health statistics provide information about these types of issues. The NCHS helps to compile information such as the number of human immunodeficiency virus (HIV) infections, teen pregnancies, and other vital health data that are useful to medical professionals.

- Some of the statistics kept by the NCHS include alcohol and drug use information, births, deaths, communicable diseases, infant health and mortality, and life expectancy.

- Total quality management is management and control activities based on the leadership of top management and supported by the involvement of all employees and departments in an effort to provide quality assurance.

- The Joint Commission on Accreditation of Healthcare Organizations (JCAHO) is a nonprofit organization that offers accreditation services to facilities that wish to excel in healthcare services. Accreditation is voluntary; however, more than 17,000 healthcare facilities in the United States are accredited by the JCAHO.

- Without strong healthcare standards, quality cannot exist. The focus of quality assurance has shifted in recent years from just meeting the minimal standards to providing optimal quality.

- People expect high-quality healthcare when they request treatment. Today's organizations that seek accreditation or focus their efforts on quality will exceed standards, and not just meet them.

CHAPTER 23

Management of Practice Finances

Key Points

- The financial records of any business should at all times show how much was earned in a given period; how much was collected; how much is owed; and the distribution of expenses incurred.

- *Accounts payable* refers to the amounts of money owed by a business and not yet paid, whereas *accounts receivable* refers to amounts owed to the business that are not yet paid.

- The three most common bookkeeping systems in use today include the single-entry system, double-entry system, and pegboard system.

- The *single-entry method* is the oldest accounting method, and uses a general journal, a cash payment journal, and an accounts receivable ledger. Payroll records and petty cash records also may be included.

- The *double-entry system* requires an entry on each side of the accounting equation, and the sides must always balance. It is more difficult to use than the single-entry system.

- The *pegboard system* may be expensive to implement at first, but allows the user to perform several accounting functions at once. It is often called the write-it-once system.

- A trial balance will reflect discrepancies between the journal and the ledger. It does not reveal errors in the individual accounts, but will show errors in the overall balances of accounts.

- The Internal Revenue Service requires that several employment records be kept for at least 4 years.

- These records include the Social Security number of the employee; the number of withholding allowances claimed; the amount of gross salary; and all deductions for Social Security and Medicare taxes; federal, state, and city or other subdivision withholding taxes; state disability insurance; and state unemployment tax.

- Several deductions are taken from the employee's wages as required by law.

- These deductions are based on the total earnings of the employee; the number of withholding allowances claimed; the marital status of the employee; and the length of the pay period involved.

- Five common reports are used for accounting in the small business office. These reports are the statement of income and expense, the cash-flow statement, the trial balance, the accounts receivable trial balance, and the balance sheet.

- The Employee's Withholding Allowance Certificate, or form W-4, specifies the number of withholding allowances the employee claims. The more allowances claimed, the less money taken from the employee's paycheck.

- The Federal Insurance Contributions Act requires that a certain amount of money be deducted from an employee's wages and designated for Medicare and social security programs.

- The current percentages are 1.45% for the Medicare contribution and 6.2% for social security. Both the employer and employee contribute these amounts.

- The physician's office must set a budget each fiscal year to prepare for all of the expenses that will be involved in running the office.

- Without a well-planned budget, the physician cannot control expenses. The expenditures from the past year should be evaluated when planning the new budget, paying particular attention to the expense categories that exceeded expected amounts.

CHAPTER 24

Infection Control

Key Points

- Pathogenic microorganisms are disease-causing microbes that fall into the categories of viruses, bacteria, protozoa, fungi, or rickettsia.

- The *chain of infection* is the method of infectious disease spread.

- It consists of the infectious agent and the reservoir host, continues with the means or portal of exit from the host, the mode of transmission, the means or portal of entry into a new host, and the presence of a susceptible host.

- To stop the spread of infection, at least one of these links must be broken.

The Inflammatory Response

- The inflammatory response is the body's reaction to the introduction of a foreign substance or antigen.

- It involves the release of inflammation mediators that, through three separate actions, result in an increase of white blood cells (WBCs) at the site of the injury.

- First, blood vessels at the site dilate, causing an increase in the local blood flow that results in redness or inflammation and heat.

- Blood vessel walls become more permeable, which helps in releasing WBCs to the site.

- The WBCs begin to form a fibrous capsule around the injury site to protect surrounding cells from the damage or the source of infection.

- Blood plasma also filters out of the more permeable vessel walls resulting in edema that puts pressure on the nerves and causes pain.

- Finally, *chemotaxis,* the release of chemical agents, attracts WBCs to the site.

- The increased number of WBCs at the site result in phagocytosis, or the engulfing and destruction of microorganisms and damaged cells.

- Destroyed pathogens, cells, and WBCs collect in the area and form a thick, white substance called pus.

- The body's immune system operates on two different levels. Humoral immunity creates specific antibodies to combat antigens, and cell-mediated immunity attacks the source of the infection at the cellular level.

- Acute diseases have a rapid onset and short duration;
  Chronic diseases last over a long period, perhaps a lifetime;
  Latent diseases cycle through relapse and remission phases.

- Bacterial infections can be treated with antibiotics, but viral infections, because they involve viral takeover of cellular DNA or RNA material, cannot be treated with antibiotics.

- The Occupational Safety and Health Administration (OSHA) has designated certain body fluids including cerebrospinal fluid (CSF), synovial, pleural, pericardial, peritoneal, mucous, and amniotic fluids as potentially infectious for blood-borne pathogens. Blood, vaginal and seminal secretions, saliva, and human tissue also are in this category.

- Protective equipment must be used if there is any chance that you will be involved in any of the following activities:
  – Touching a patient's blood and body fluids, mucous membranes, or skin that is not intact
  – Handling items and surfaces contaminated with blood and body fluids
  – Performing venipuncture, finger punctures, injections, and other vascular-access procedures
  – Assisting with any surgical procedure. If a glove is torn or an injury occurs, remove and replace the glove with a new glove as soon as safety permits. Remove the instrument involved in the incident from the sterile field.
  – Handling, processing, and disposing of all specimens of blood and body fluids
  – Cleaning and decontaminating spills of blood or other body fluids

- The Exposure Control Plan must be available for employee review and contain specifics on controls for blood-borne pathogens including personal protective equipment (PPE), training, hepatitis B immunization, record keeping, and the labeling and disposal of all biohazard waste.

- Postexposure follow-up involves immediate cleansing of the site, examination of the source individual and worker's blood, administration of prophylactic medications, health counseling, and confidential treatment of all medical records.

- The OSHA Compliance Guidelines stipulate the management and implementation of barrier protection devices, environment protection, housekeeping controls, and administration of the hepatitis B immunization.

- Medical asepsis involves the removal or destruction of pathogens. and surgical asepsis is the destruction of all microorganisms.

- Medical aseptic techniques are used to create an environment that is as free of pathogens as possible, whereas surgical asepsis, or sterile technique, is used when the patient's skin or mucous membranes are disrupted.

- Sanitization is the cleaning of contaminated articles or surfaces to reduce the numbers of micro-organisms; disinfection is the process of killing pathogenic organisms; and sterilization results in the destruction of all microorganisms.

- The medical assistant must take every opportunity to teach patients about infection control and the potential danger of blood and body fluids.

- This includes demonstrating aseptic techniques, the proper management of infectious materials at home, and the importance of frequent and consistent hand washing.

- The medical assistant is responsible for applying infection-control procedures in all situations at all times to prevent cross-contamination and the development of nosocomial infections in patients.

CHAPTER 25

Patient Assessment

Key Points

- Holistic care includes assessing the patient's health status with physical, cognitive, psychosocial, and behavioral data.
- The medical history consists of the patient's database, medical history, family and social histories, and the review of systems.

Preparing the Appropriate Environment

- *Ensure privacy*
- *Refuse interruptions*
- *Prepare comfortable surroundings*
- *Take notes judiciously*

Open-Ended Questions

- What brings you to the doctor?
- How have you been getting along?
- You mentioned having dizzy spells. Tell me more about that.

Closed Questions

- Do you have a headache?
- What is your birth date?
- Have you ever broken a bone?

Health History of a Child

- The environment should be safe and attractive.
- Do not keep children and their caregivers waiting any longer than necessary, because they become anxious and/or distracted quickly.

- Do not offer a choice unless the child can truly make one. If part of the treatment requires that the child receive an injection, asking the child if he or she would like the shot now will receive an automatic "No." However, giving a choice of stickers after the injection is appropriate.

- Praising the child during the examination helps decrease anxiety and increase self-esteem. When possible, direct questions toward the child so he or she feels part of the process.

- Involving the child in the examination by permitting her to manipulate the equipment may help relieve anxiety. If possible, use your imagination, and make a game of the assessment or the procedure.

- A typical defense mechanism seen in sick or anxious children is regression. The child may refuse to leave the mother's lap or may want to hold a favorite toy during the procedure as a comfort measure. Look for signs of anxiety such as thumb sucking or rocking during the assessment.

- Developing a professional helping relationship with patients is the responsibility of all healthcare workers.

- The helping relationship involves consistent application of respectful patient care that recognizes the impact of patient anxieties on interactions and responses to treatment.

- The Linear Communication Model illustrates communication as an interactive process between the sender and receiver of the message, with feedback a crucial part of the process.

- Active-listening techniques, which include restatement, reflection, and clarification, help the medical assistant go beyond hearing the message to actually listening to and appropriately responding to the patient's main point.

- Approximately 90% of patient interactions occur through nonverbal language. The key to successful patient interaction is congruence between verbal and nonverbal messages.

Nonverbal Communication

Rules That Will Help You Learn to Listen

- Listen to the main points in the discussion.

- Attend to both verbal and nonverbal messages.

- Be patient and nonjudgmental.

- Do not interrupt.

- Never intimidate your patient.

- Use active-listening techniques: restatement, reflection, and clarification

- Certain communication styles can be misleading or restrict the patient's response.

- The medical assistant must be alert to using such techniques as providing reassurance, giving advice, using medical terminology, asking leading questions, and talking too much.

- These behaviors interfere with gathering complete data during the interview and are an obstacle to developing rapport with your patient.

- Patients use defense mechanisms to protect themselves in emotionally challenging situations.

- The medical assistant must consistently apply nonjudgmental therapeutic communication skills to maintain professional relationships.

- Therapeutic communication techniques vary according to the age and developmental level of the patient.

- The medical assistant should be aware of how to interact most effectively with various age groups, including young children, adolescents, adults, and their families.

- Age-specific application of interview styles assures clear communication between the health professional and the patient.

- The patient interview is divided into the introduction, the body, and the summary or closing.

- Throughout the interview, the medical assistant should use professional interview techniques such as empathetic patient care, sensitivity to patient diversity, active-listening skills, appropriate nonverbal communication, attention to the interview environment, avoidance of communication barriers, and use of open and closed questions and/or statements.

- The ability to document accurately and completely is a necessary skill for all medical assistants.

- Documentation should describe the patient's chief complaint, with all pertinent signs and symptoms, and demonstrate the correct use of medical terminology and appropriate abbreviations.

- Any error in the medical record must be corrected according to legally approved methods.

- The three main forms of medical record systems include the problem-oriented medical record (POMR) method, which uses subjective, objective, assessment, plan, and evaluation (SOAPE) charting to define the patient's health problems.

- The most frequently used form of medical record keeping is the SOMR, which organizes patient data into specific sections, and, finally, the computerized medical record (CMR), which organizes computer records for patient data.

- The perfect time to initiate patient education is during the initial patient interview. The medical assistant should take advantage of every "teaching moment" to get to know the patient and to promote patient wellness.

- Risk-management practices focus on reducing the chances of professional liability claims.

- Accurate and complete documentation on the patient's chart is crucial for successful risk management.

- In addition, maintaining strict confidentiality of patient information and factual, nonjudgmental, legible recording of patient data are essential to professional patient care.

CHAPTER 26

Patient Education

Key Points

- The holistic model suggests patient education should consider all aspects of patient life including physical, psychological, emotional, social, economic, and spiritual needs.

- The guidelines for patient education include providing knowledge and skills that promote recovery and health, including family in education interventions; encouraging patient ownership of the education process; promoting safe use of medications and treatments; encouraging healthy behaviors; and providing information on how to access community resources.

- Patient factors that affect learning include the patient's perception of disease versus the actual state of disease; the need for information; age and developmental level; mental and emotional state; the influence of multicultural and diversity factors; individual learning style; and the impact of physical disabilities on the education process.

- Education approaches for patients with language barriers include addressing the patient formally and courteously; using nonverbal language to promote understanding; integrating pictures or models that illustrate the material; observing the patient for understanding or confusion; using simple lay language; demonstrating procedures; implementing teaching in small manageable steps; providing written instructions; and using an interpreter when available.

- Potential barriers to patient education include patient learning style; physical limitations; age and developmental level; emotional or mental state that interferes with learning; use of defense mechanisms; cultural or ethnic factors; language; the patient experiencing pain; patient motivation to learn; and limited time for teaching.

- Effective teaching materials and methods include the use of printed materials, videos, and approved Internet sites to gather information; referral to community resources and experts; demonstration/return demonstration of medical skills; patient journals of events; and involvement of family members in the education process.

- The parts of the teaching plan assessing learning needs; determining teaching priorities; using appropriate teaching materials and methods; gathering feedback repeatedly to assure patient understanding; eliminating learning barriers; summarizing the material at the end of each education session; planning for the next meeting; evaluating the effectiveness of the session; and completely and accurately documenting the details of the teaching intervention.

- The role of the medical assistant in patient education is to reinforce physician instructions and information by encouraging patients to take an active role in their health; using "teaching moments" effectively; keeping information relevant to the patient; establishing and maintaining patient rapport; communicating clearly; being aware of learning factors; and being flexible with the teaching plan.

- Appropriate patient education reflects the patient Bill of Rights emphasis on patient confidentiality as well as informed consent. Risk-management practices related to patient education include accurate and complete documentation of patient education sessions and sensitivity to the diverse needs of the patient.

CHAPTER 27

Nutrition and Health Promotion

Key Points

- Nutrients consist of carbohydrates, fats, proteins, vitamins, minerals, and water. Their primary functions are to provide the body with energy, protection, and insulation; to build and repair tissues; and to regulate metabolic processes.

- Dietary fiber plays an important role in maintaining regularity and helping to prevent cancer and heart disease.

- **Carbohydrates (CHO)** are chemical organic compounds composed of carbon, hydrogen, and oxygen and are derived primarily from plant products. They are divided into three groups based on the complexity of their molecules: simple sugars, complex carbohydrates (starch), and dietary fiber. The primary function of carbohydrates is to provide the body with a ready source of energy.

- **Protein** builds and repairs tissue as well as assisting with metabolic functions.

- Dietary **fat** provides essential fatty acids and is needed for the absorption of fat-soluble vitamins. Adipose tissue helps protect the organs of the body, insulates, and serves as a concentrated form of stored energy.

- Fat, a storage form of fuel, is used to back up carbohydrates as an available energy source. Fat is a much more concentrated form of fuel; it produces 9 kcal/g of energy when metabolized. Dietary fats, or *lipids,* provide essential fatty acids and are needed for the absorption of fat-soluble vitamins.

- The main building blocks of fat are *fatty* acids, which can be either saturated or unsaturated. The chemical structure of a *saturated* fatty acid contains all the hydrogen possible and therefore is denser, heavier, and solid at room temperature.

- Examples of saturated fats are dairy products, eggs, lard, meat, and **hydrogenated** fats such as margarine. Some fats, such as those in soft-type margarines, are partially hydrogenated. These fats are usually soft at room temperatures. Most saturated fats come from animal sources.

- *Unsaturated* fatty acids can take on more hydrogen under the proper conditions and therefore are less heavy and less dense. If fatty acids have one unfilled hydrogen bond, the fat is called *monoun-saturated.* Olives and olive oil, peanuts and peanut oil, canola oil, pecans, and avocados contain monounsaturated fats.

- *Polyunsaturated* fats, such as safflower, corn, cottonseed, and soy oils have two or more unfilled hydrogen bonds. Unsaturated fats are found in plants and are usually liquid at room temperature.

- Cholesterol is a nonessential nutrient that plays a vital role in metabolic activities. It is synthesized only in animal tissue and so is not found in plant foods. The primary food sources of cholesterol are egg yolks and organ meats, although all animal sources of food contain cholesterol. As a nonessential nutrient, it also is manufactured within the body, particularly in the liver.

- The good fats, or high-density lipoproteins (HDLs), carry free cholesterol from body tissues to the liver for metabolism and excretion.

- The bad fats, or low-density lipoproteins (LDLs), and very low-density lipoprotein (VLDLs), carry fat and cholesterol to the cells. LDLs and VLDLs form atherosclerotic plaques on arterial walls that frequently result in heart disease, hypertension, and strokes. However, serum LDL levels can often be successfully changed through diet.

Antioxidants

- Our bodies have developed mechanisms to protect us against toxins created by oxidation through utilization of antioxidant vitamins C and E and β-carotene, but the amounts are not always sufficient. When enough antioxidants are circulating in the blood, cholesterol is prevented from oxidizing.

Water

- Water is all too often overlooked when nutritional status is evaluated. The body is approximately 80% water and can survive longer without food than it can without water. Water is part of almost every vital body process.

Functions of Water

- Plays a key role in the maintenance of body temperature
- Acts as a solvent and the medium for most biochemical reactions
- Acts as the vehicle for transport of substances such as nutrients, hormones, antibodies, and metabolic waste
- Acts as a lubricant for joints and mucous membranes

Functions of Protein

- Builds and repairs body tissue
- Aids in the body's defense mechanisms against disease
- Regulates body secretions and fluids
- Provides energy

Vitamins and Minerals

Vitamins are essential for metabolic functions and are classified as soluble in either fat or water. They regulate the synthesis of body tissues as well as aid in the metabolism of nutrients. Vitamins also play a vital role in disease prevention.

- Minerals help maintain electrolytes and acid-base balance as well as regulate muscular action and nervous activities throughout the body.

- The Food Guide Pyramid was developed by the government as a visual representation of dietary guidelines. The pyramid is divided into six sections and depicts how the proportions of each basic food group contribute to a balanced diet.

- The physician's assessment of the patient's nutritional status includes an evaluation of the patient's current health and lifestyle habits, as well as body fat measurements. Body fat can be measured as a waste-to-hip ratio, using calipers to measure fat-folds, or calculating the body mass index (BMI).

- Therapeutic nutrition uses diet to help treat or prevent disease. Diets can be modified in many ways, including changing consistency and taste, monitoring caloric levels, altering amounts and types of specific nutrients, and managing the fiber content of foods. Two examples of diet therapies are the diabetic diet and the heart-healthy diet, both of which can have significant impact on patient wellness.

- The government requires all food manufacturers to follow certain guidelines for labeling packages. Labels provide facts on the nutritional value of foods. The food label can be a valuable tool in patient compliance with specialized diets.

Eating Disorders

- Anorexia nervosa is characterized by self-induced starvation. These individuals are typically adolescents when first diagnosed and are perfectionists who are extremely sensitive to failure and any criticism. They use not eating as a way of controlling their feelings, and they fear becoming grossly overweight if they allow themselves to eat.

- Bulimia is more common than anorexia and is characterized by cycles of bingeing and purging. This behavior pattern usually begins in adolescence when an individual who is slightly overweight diets but fails to achieve the expected results. Psychologically the person believes that self-worth is related to being thin. Usually the pattern begins with some form of stress that upsets the individual, who then turns to food for consolation.

- Health promotion considers all aspects of patient care including the concepts of general wellness, adequate nutrition, environmental health and safety, health education needs, and disease prevention. The components of health promotion include exercise, stress management, regular physical examinations, and health screening.

- The medical assistant plays a key role in nutrition and health promotion, serving as a patient advocate and liaison between the patient and community resources. It is important for the medical assistant to understand various implications of nutrition and specific diets so he or she is capable of answering patient questions and thereby promoting compliance with treatment.

Health Problems Related to Poor Nutrition

- Anemia: low iron or folate intake
- Cancer: high-fat, low-fiber diet (cancer of the colon, breast, cervix)
- Constipation: low fiber, inadequate fluids; high-fat diet; sedentary lifestyle
- Diabetes: high-calorie, high-fat diet; obesity
- Hypercholesterolemia: high-fat, low-fiber diet
- Hypertension: high-calorie, high-fat diet; obesity
- Osteoporosis: low calcium intake; inadequate vitamin D, or lack of sun exposure

CHAPTER 28

Vital Signs

Key Points

- The measurement of vital signs is an important aspect of almost every visit of a patient to the medical office. These signs are the human body's indicators of internal **homeostasis** and represent the general state of health of the patient.

- Accuracy is essential. A change in one or more of the patient's vital signs may indicate a change in general health. Variations may indicate the presence or disappearance of a disease process and, therefore, a change in the treatment plan.

- The *vital signs* are the patient's temperature, pulse, respiration, and blood pressure. These four signs are abbreviated *TPR* and *BP* and may be referred to as *cardinal signs*.

- Anthropometric measurements are not considered vital signs but are usually obtained at the same time as the vital signs.

- These measurements include height, weight, and other body measurements, such as fat composition and head and chest circumference.

- The vital signs are influenced by many factors, both physical and emotional.

- Most patients, for one reason or another, are apprehensive during an office visit. These emotions may alter the vital signs, and it is necessary for the medical assistant to help the patient relax before taking any readings.

Normal Ranges for Vital Signs

Temperature

- *Body temperature* is defined as the balance between the heat lost and the heat produced by the body. It is measured in degrees.

- An increase in body temperature is thought to be the body's defensive reaction, because heat is believed to inhibit the growth of some bacteria and viruses.

Fever

- *Continuous* fever rises and falls only slightly during a 24-hour period. It remains above the patient's average normal range and is called continuous because that is exactly what the pattern shows.

- *Intermittent* fever comes and goes, or it spikes and then returns into average range.

- *Remittent* fever has great fluctuation but never returns to the average range. It is a constant fever with fluctuating levels and thus is remittent.

- Temperatures that are considered **febrile:**
  - Rectal or *aural* (ear) temperatures greater than 100.4° F (38° C)
  - Oral temperatures greater than 99.5° F (37.5° C)
  - Axillary temperatures greater than 98.6° F (37° C)
  - *Fever of unknown origin* (FUO) is a fever greater than 100.9° F (38.3° C) for 3 weeks in adults and 1 week in children without a known diagnosis

Temperature Readings

- A clinical thermometer is used to measure body temperature and is calibrated in either the Fahrenheit or the Celsius scale. The Fahrenheit (F) scale has been used most frequently in the United States to measure body temperature, but hospitals and many ambulatory care settings often use the Celsius scale.

- The formulas for conversion from one system to the other are as follows:

- $C = (F - 32) \times 5/9$

- $F = \dfrac{9 \times C}{5} + 32$

- Rectal temperatures, when taken accurately, are approximately 1° F or 0.6° C higher than oral readings.

- Axillary temperatures are approximately 1° F or 0.6° C lower than accurate oral readings.

Types of Thermometers

- Digital

- Tympanic

- Disposable

- Axillary

- Rectal

Pulse

- Pulse reflects the palpable beat of the arteries as they expand with the beat of the heart.

- To measure the pulse, use an artery that is close to the body surface that can be pushed against a bone.

Pulse Sites

- The most common sites used to feel this rhythmic throbbing are at the following arteries: temporal, carotid, apical, brachial, radial, femoral, popliteal, and dorsalis pedis

Characteristics of Pulse

- When you are taking a pulse, there are four important characteristics to note: (1) rate, (2) rhythm, (3) volume of the pulse, and (4) condition of the arterial wall.

- Record the number of beats in 1 minute. Assess the pulse, including rate, rhythm, volume, and elasticity.

Three-Point Scale for Measuring Pulse Volume

- 3+ = full, bounding

- 2+ = normal pulse

- 1+ = weak, thready

Respiration

- One complete inspiration and expiration is called a *respiration*.

- To determine the respiratory rate of a patient, note three important characteristics: rate, rhythm, and depth.

Counting Respirations

- The respiratory rate is easily controlled, and patients self-consciously alter their breathing rates when they are being watched.

- Therefore count the respirations while appearing to count the pulse. Keep your eyes alternately on the patient's chest and your watch while you are counting the pulse rate, and then, without removing your fingers from the pulse site, determine the respiration rate.

- Count the respirations for 30 seconds, and multiply the number by 2.

- Note any variation or irregularity in the rate. Record the respiration count on the medical record.

Blood Pressure

- Blood pressure is a reflection of the pressure of the blood against the walls of the arteries.

- Blood pressure is read in millimeters of mercury, abbreviated mm Hg. However, the abbreviations do not have to be included when documenting the reading on the patient's medical record.

- Blood pressure is recorded as a fraction, with the systolic reading as the numerator (top) and the diastolic reading as the denominator (bottom) (for example, 130/80).

Factors Affecting Blood Pressure

- Volume is the amount of blood in the arteries.

- Peripheral resistance of blood vessels refers to the relation of the *lumen* or diameter of the vessel to the amount of blood flowing through it.

- Vessel elasticity refers to a vessel's capability to expand and contract to supply the body with a steady flow of blood.

- The condition of the heart muscle, or myocardium, is of primary importance to the volume of blood flowing through the body.

Hypertension

- 50 million Americans have hypertension that requires treatment.

- Prevalence increases with age, and it occurs more frequently in African Americans.

- Risk factors for developing hypertension include cigarette smoking, diabetes mellitus, hyperlipidemia, male gender, postmenopausal women, obesity, stress, and family history.

- Treatments include medications and lifestyle changes, such as weight loss, limiting alcohol intake, stopping smoking, aerobic exercise, and a diet that is low in fat and sodium and high in fiber.

- Patient should be scheduled for regular follow-up visits every 3 to 6 months depending on the severity of the hypertension.

- **Hypotension** is abnormally low blood pressure and may be caused by shock, both emotional and traumatic; hemorrhage; central nervous system disorders; and chronic wasting diseases. Persistent readings of 90/60 mm Hg or less are usually considered hypotensive.

- The sphygmomanometer must be used with a stethoscope. The objective of the procedure is to use the inflatable cuff to obliterate (cause to disappear) circulation through an artery. The stethoscope is placed over the artery just below the cuff, and then the cuff is slowly deflated to allow the blood to flow again.

- As blood flow resumes, cardiac-cycle sounds are heard through the stethoscope, and gauge readings are taken when the first (systolic) and the last (diastolic) sounds are heard.

Anthropometric Measurement

- Height

- Weight

- BMI

Conversion Formulas

- To convert kilograms to pounds: 1 kg = 2.2 pounds
  Multiply the number of kilograms by 2.2.

  Example: If a patient weighs 68 kg, $68 \times 2.2 = 149.6$ pounds

- To convert pounds to kilograms: 1 pound = 0.45 kg
  Multiply the number of pounds by 0.45 **or** divide the number of pounds by 2.2 kg

  Example: If a patient weighs 120 pounds, $120 \times 0.45 = 54$ kg, **or** $120 \div 2.2 = 54.5$ kg

- Patient education regarding vital signs includes confirming the ability of the patient to monitor vital signs at home as needed, providing assistance in working home-based equipment, and confirming understanding of the need to comply with physician recommendations.

- Legal and ethical implications for the medical assistance include following physician guidelines with patient disclosure, accurate monitoring and recording of vital signs, and consistently being alert to inaccurate readings or potential carelessness.

The Role of the Medical Assistant in Obtaining Vital Signs

- Monitoring vital signs is a key responsibility of the medical assistant.

- It is crucial that medical assistants correctly measure and describe all facets of each vital sign.

- Accurately and clearly documenting this information also is crucial.

- Take advantage of all opportunities to answer questions and help the patient understand the significance of healthy vital signs.

- Maintain patient privacy throughout all procedures.

- Include family or caregivers in patient care as indicated.

- Use community resources to promote holistic patient care.

- Be sensitive to cultural and ethnic factors that may affect patient compliance with physician recommendations, such as diet, exercise, weight control, and the use of medication.

CHAPTER 29

Assisting with the Primary Physical Examination

Key Points

- An *organ* is composed of two or more types of tissue bound together to form a more complex structure with a common purpose or function. An organ may have one or many functions and may be considered a unit in one or several systems.

- A body *system* is composed of several organs and their associated structures. These structures work together to perform a specific function within the body. There are 11 systems in the human body; each system has specific units, and each performs specific functions. Put these 11 systems together, and we have a human being.

Vocabulary

- **bruit** Abnormal sound or murmur heard on auscultation of an organ, vessel, or gland

- **emphysema** Pathologic accumulation of air in the tissues or organs; in the lungs, the bronchioles become plugged with mucus and lose elasticity

- **manipulation** Moving or exercising a body part by an externally applied force

- **murmur** Abnormal sound heard when auscultating the heart that may or may not be pathologic

- **nodule** Small lump, lesion, or swelling felt when palpating the skin

- **sclera** White part of the eye that forms the orb

- **transillumination** Inspection of a cavity or organ by passing light through its walls

- **trauma** Physical injury or wound caused by an external force or violence

- **uremia** Toxic renal condition characterized by an excess of urea, creatinine, and other nitrogenous end products in the blood

Instruments

- The instruments typically used during the physical examination enable the physician to see, feel, and listen to parts of the body.

- All equipment must be in good working order, properly disinfected, and readily available for the physician's use during the examination.

- *Nasal speculum:* Stainless-steel instrument used to inspect the lining of the nose, nasal membranes, and internal septum. Squeezing the handles of the nasal speculum causes the tips spread apart to dilate the nostrils, allowing the physician to visualize the internal aspects.

- *Ophthalmoscope:* Instrument used to inspect the inner structures of the eye. It has a stainless-steel handle containing batteries, onto which a head is attached. The head is equipped with a light, magnifying lenses, and an opening through which the eye is viewed.

- *Otoscope:* Instrument used to examine the external auditory canal and tympanic membrane. The stainless steel handle contains batteries, onto which a head is fastened. The head contains a light focused through a magnifying lens and disposable ear speculum.

- Examination rooms are usually equipped with wall-mounted electrical units for the ophthalmoscope, otoscope, disposable speculums, and sphygmomanometer.

- *Tongue depressor:* Flat, wooden blade used to hold down the tongue when examining the throat.

- *Reflex hammer:* Sometimes referred to as a percussion hammer. This stainless steel instrument has a hard rubber head used to test neurologic reflexes of the knee and elbow by striking the tendons.

- *Tuning fork:* Used to check a patient's auditory acuity and to test bone vibration. This stainless steel instrument consists of a handle and two prongs that produce a humming sound when the physician strikes the prongs against his or her hand.

- *Stethoscope:* Listening device used for auscultating certain areas of the body, particularly the heart and lungs. This instrument comes in many shapes and sizes. All have two earpieces connected to flexible rubber or vinyl tubing. At the distal end of the tubing is a diaphragm or bell (many have both) that when placed securely on the patient's skin enables the physician to hear internal body sounds.

- *Gloves:* Disposable latex gloves protect the physician and the patient from microorganisms. Under Standard Precautions, gloves are to be worn whenever there is a possibility of contact with all body fluids, broken skin or wounds, or contaminated items.

- *Tape measure:* Flexible ribbon ruler usually printed in inches and feet on one side and in centimeters and meters on the opposite side Measurement is used to assess infant length and head circumference, wound size, etc.

Methods of Examination

- *Inspection* uses observation to detect significant physical features or objective data. This method of examination focuses on the patient's general appearance (the general state of health, including posture, mannerisms, grooming) and more detailed observations, including body contour, gait, symmetry, visible injuries and deformities, tremors, rashes, and color changes.

- *Palpation* uses the sense of touch. A part of the body is felt with the hand to determine its condition or that of an underlying organ. Palpation may include touching the skin or the more firm feeling of the abdomen for underlying masses. This technique involves a wide range of perceptions: temperature, vibrations, consistency, form, size, rigidity, elasticity, moisture, texture, position, and contour.

- *Percussion* involves tapping or striking the body, usually with the fingers or a small hammer, to elicit sounds or vibratory sensations. Percussion aids in the determination of the position, size, and density of an underlying organ or cavity. The effect of percussion is both heard and felt by the examiner. It is helpful in determining the amount of air or solid matter in an underlying organ or cavity.

- *Auscultation* uses a stethoscope to listen to sounds arising from the body. Auscultation is a difficult method of examination because the physician must distinguish between a normal and an abnormal sound. It is particularly useful in evaluating sounds originating in the lungs, heart, and abdomen such as **murmurs, bruits,** and bowel sounds.

- *Mensuration* is the process of measuring. Measurements are recorded of the patient's height and weight, the length and diameter of an extremity, the extent of flexion or extension of an extremity, the uterus during pregnancy, the size and depth of a wound, or the pressure of a grip.

- *Manipulation* is the forceful, passive movement of a joint to determine the range of extension or flexion of a part of the body.

- *Supine (horizontal recumbent)* describes the patient lying flat with face upward. This position is used for the examination of the frontal portion of the body, including the heart, breasts, and abdominal organs.

- *Dorsal recumbent* position places the patient lying face upward, with the weight distributed primarily to the surface of the back. This is accomplished by flexing the knees so that the feet are flat on the table. This position relieves muscle tension in the abdomen.

- *Lithotomy* position describes the patient on the back, with the knees sharply flexed, the arms placed at the sides or folded over the chest, and the buttocks to the edge of the table. The feet are supported in table stirrups.

- *Fowler's* position describes the patient sitting on the examination table with the head elevated 90 degrees or simply sitting at the edge of the table. This position is useful for examinations and treatments of the head, neck, and chest or for patients who find it difficult to breathe lying down.

- *Semi-Fowler's* position is a modification of Fowler's position. Instead of the head being at a full 90-degree angle, the head is lowered to a 45-degree angle.

- *Prone* describes the patient lying face down on the table, on the ventral surface of the body. This is the opposite of the supine position and is another one of the recumbent positions.

- *Sims'* position is sometimes called the lateral position. The patient is placed on the left side; the left arm and shoulder are drawn back behind the body so that the body's weight is predominantly on the chest. The right arm is flexed upward for support. The left leg is slightly flexed, and the buttocks are pulled to the edge of the table.

- *Knee-chest* position describes the patient resting on the knees and the chest, with the head turned to one side. The arms can be placed under the head for support and comfort or bent and at the sides of the table near the head. The thighs are perpendicular to the table and are slightly separated. The buttocks extend up into the air, and the back should be straight.

- *Trendelenburg* position describes the patient supine on a table that has been raised at the lower end to about 45 degrees. This places the patient's head lower than the legs.

CHAPTER 30

Principles of Pharmacology

Key Points

- Drugs are generally classified according to their actions on the body or according to the body system they affect. Drugs may have multiple actions and therefore multiple classifications.

Drug Types

Adrenergic

- *Action:* Constricts blood vessels, narrows the lumen of a vessel
- *Examples:* Epinephrine: phenylephrine (Neo-Synephrine)
- *Primary use:* Stop superficial bleeding, increase and sustain blood pressure, and relieve nasal congestion

Analgesic

- *Action:* Lessens the sensory function of the brain
- *Examples:* Nonnarcotic: aspirin; acetaminophen (Tylenol); ibuprofen (Advil, Motrin); narcotic: meperidine (Demerol); hydrocodone (Vicodin); propoxyphene (Darvon)
- *Primary use:* Pain relief

Anesthetic

- *Action:* Produces insensibility to pain or the sensation of pain
- *Examples:* Bupivacaine (Marcaine); lidocaine (Xylocaine)
- *Primary use:* Local or general anesthesia

Antianxiety

- *Action:* Produces insensibility to pain or the sensation of pain
- *Examples:* Bupivacaine (Marcaine); lidocaine (Xylocaine)
- *Primary use:* Local or general anesthesia

Antibiotic

- *Action:* Kills or inhibits the growth of microorganisms
- *Examples:* Cefaclor (Ceclor); tetracycline (Acromycin); amoxicillin (Augmentin)
- *Primary use:* treatment of bacterial invasions and infections

Anticholinergic

- *Action:* Parasympathetic blocking agent, reduces spasm in smooth muscle
- *Examples:* Scopolamine; atropine sulfate
- *Primary use:* Dry secretions

Anticoagulant

- *Action:* Delays or blocks the clotting of blood
- *Examples:* Heparin; warfarin sodium (Coumadin)
- *Primary use:* Treatment for blood clots

Antidepressant

- *Action:* Treats depression
- *Examples:* Fluoxetine (Prozac); imipramine pamoate (Tofranil); amitriptyline (Elavil)
- *Primary use:* Mood elevator

Antiemetic

- *Action:* Acts on hypothalamus center in the brain
- *Examples:* Prochlorperazine (Compazine); trimethobenzamide (Tigan); metoclopramide (Reglan)
- *Primary use:* Prevent and relieve nausea and vomiting

Antiepileptic (Anticonvulsant)

- *Action:* Reduces excessive stimulation of the brain
- *Examples:* Phenytoin (Dilantin); phenobarbital; carbamazepine (Tegretol)
- *Primary use:* Epilepsy and other convulsive disorders

Antifungal

- *Action:* Slows or retards the multiplication of fungi
- *Examples:* Miconazole (Monistat); nystatin (Mycostatin); amphotericin B
- *Primary use:* Treat systemic or local fungal infections

Antihistamine

- *Action:* Counteracts the effects of histamine by blocking action in tissues; may be used to inhibit gastric secretions

- *Examples:* Brompheniramine maleate (Dimetane); chlorpheniramine (Chlor-Trimeton); diphenhydramine (Benadryl); promethazine (Phenergan); cimetidine (Tagamet); ranitidine (Zantac)

- *Primary use:* Relief of allergies; prevention of gastric ulcers

Antihypertensive

- *Action:* Blocks nerve impulses that cause arteries to constrict; or slows heart rate, decreasing its contractility; or restricts the hormone aldosterone in the blood

- *Examples:* Atenolol (Tenormin); doxazosin mesylate (Cardura); metoprolol (Lopressor); methyldopa (Aldomet)

- *Primary use:* Reduce and control blood pressure

Antiinflammatory

- *Action:* Reduces inflammation or acts as antirheumatic

- *Examples:* Nonsteroidal anti-inflammatory drugs (NSAIDs): ibuprofen (Advil, Motrin); naproxen (Naprosyn). Steroidal: dexamethasone (Decadron); prednisone (Cortisone)

- *Primary use:* Treatment of arthritic and other inflammatory disorders

Antineoplastic

- *Action:* Inhibits the development of and destroys cancerous cells

- *Examples:* Interferon alfa-2a (Roferon-A); hydroxyurea (Hydrea); cyclophosphamide (Cytoxan); fluorouracil (Adrucil)

- *Primary use:* Cancer chemotherapy

Antispasmodic

- *Action:* Relieves or prevents spasms from musculoskeletal injury or inflammation

- *Examples:* Methocarbamol (Robaxin); carisoprodol (Soma)

- *Primary use:* Sport injuries

Antitussive (Cough Suppressant)

- *Action:* Inhibits the cough center

- *Examples:* Narcotic: codeine sulfate; nonnarcotic: dextromethorphan (Romilar, Robitussin DM)

- *Primary use:* Temporarily suppresses a nonproductive cough; reduces the thickness of secretions

Bronchodilator

- *Action:* Relaxes the smooth muscle of the bronchi

- *Examples:* Aminophylline (Aminophyllin); theophylline (Theo-Dur); epinephrine (Adrenalin, Sus-Phrine); albuterol (Ventolin, Proventil); isoproterenol (Isuprel)

- *Primary use:* Treats asthma, bronchospasm; promotes bronchodilation

Cathartic (Laxative)

- *Action:* Increases peristaltic activity of the large intestine

- *Examples:* Magnesium hydroxide (milk of magnesia); bisacodyl (Dulcolax); casanthranol (Peri-Colace); psyllium hydrophilic muciloid (Metamucil)

- *Primary use:* Increases and hasten bowel evacuation (defecation)

Contraceptive

- *Action:* Inhibits conception

- *Examples:* Medroxyprogesterone acetate (Depo-Provera); norgestrel (Ovrett); ethinyl estradiol and ethynodiol diacetate (Demulen 1/35)

- *Primary use:* Family planning

Decongestant

- *Action:* Relieves local congestion in the tissues

- *Examples:* Ephedrine or phenylephrine (Neo-Synephrine); pseudoephedrine (Sudafed); oxymetazoline (Afrin)

- *Primary use:* Relief of nasal and sinus congestion due to common cold, hay fever, or upper respiratory tract disorders

Diuretic

- *Action:* Inhibits the reabsorption of sodium and chloride in the kidneys

- *Examples:* Hydrochlorothiazide (Dyazide, Esidrix, HydroDiuril); furosemide (Lasix); triamterene (Dyrenium)

- *Primary use:* Increases urinary output, decreases blood pressure

Expectorant

- *Action:* Increases secretions of mucus from the bronchial tubes

- *Examples:* Diphenhydramine (Benylin); guaifenesin guaiacolate (Fenesin, Robitussin)

- *Primary use:* Reduces upper respiratory tract congestion

Hemostatic

- *Action:* Controls bleeding, a blood coagulant
- *Examples:* Phytonadione, vitamin K (Konakion); absorbable hemostatics, such as absorbable gelatin sponge (Gelfoam) and absorbable knitted fabric (Surgicel), are applied directly to a wound.
- *Primary use:* Control of acute or chronic blood-clotting disorder; formation of absorbable, artificial clot

Hypnotic (Sedative)

- *Action:* Induces sleep and lessens the activity of the brain
- *Examples:* Secobarbital (Seconal); flurazepam (Dalmane); tamazepam (Restoril)
- *Primary use:* Treats insomnia; lower doses sedate

Hormone Replacement

- *Action:* Replaces or compensates for hormone deficiency
- *Examples:* Insulin (Humulin); levothyroxine sodium (Synthroid); estrogen (Premarin)
- *Primary use:* Maintenance of adequate hormone levels

Miotic

- *Action:* Causes the pupil of the eye to contract
- *Examples:* Carbachol (Isopto Carbachol); isoflurophate (Floropryl); pilocarpine (Isopto Carpine)
- *Primary use:* Counteract pupil dilation

Mydriatic (Anticholinergic)

- *Action:* Dilates the pupil of the eye
- *Examples:* Atropine sulfate (Isopto-Atropine)
- *Primary use:* Ophthalmologic examinations

Narcotic

- *Action:* Depress the central nervous system and cause insensibility or stupor.
- *Examples:* Natural narcotics: opium group (codeine phosphate, morphine sulfate); synthetic narcotics: meperidine (Demerol), methadone (Dolophine), and propoxyphene HCl (Darvon).
- *Primary use:* Pain relief

Sympathetic Blocking Agent

- *Action:* Blocks certain functions of the adrenergic nervous system

- *Examples:* Propranolol (Inderal); metaprolol (Lopressor); phentolamine (Regitine); prazosin (Minipress)

- *Primary use:* Treating cardiovascular conditions

Six Parts of a Prescription

- *Superscription:* Patient's name and address, the date, and the symbol Rx (for the Latin recipe, meaning "take").

- *Inscription:* Main part of the prescription; name of the drug, dosage form, and strength.

- *Subscription:* Directions for the pharmacist; size of each dose, amount to be dispensed, and the form of the drug, such as tablets or capsules.

- *Signature:* Directions for the patient; usually preceded by the symbol Sig: (for the Latin *signa,* meaning "mark"). This is where the physician indicates what instructions are to be put on the label to tell the patient how, when, and in what quantities to use the medication.

- *Refill information:* May be regulated by federal law if the drug is a controlled substance; must write number of times refill allowed on the script.

- *Physician signature:* Must include manual signature of physician and Drug Enforcement Administration (DEA) number when indicated.

Pharmacokinetic Terms

- *Absorption:* How a drug is absorbed into the body's circulating fluids, which depends on the route by which it is administered.

- *Distribution:* How a drug is transported from the site of administration to the various points in the body.

- *Metabolism:* How the drug is inactivated, including the time it takes for a drug to be detoxified and broken down into by-products.

- *Excretion:* The route by which a drug is excreted, or eliminated, from the body and the amount of time such a process requires.

- Several federal agencies combine forces to regulate drugs in the United States. The Food and Drug Administration (FDA) regulates the development and sale of all prescription drugs and over-the-counter drugs (OTCs); the DEA enforces laws designed to control drug abuse and educates the public on drug-abuse prevention; the Federal Trade Commission (FTC) regulates OTC advertisement.

- DEA regulations for the management of controlled substances include specific record-keeping guidelines; physician registration; and the inventory, storage, and disposal of controlled substances.

- Prescriptions written for controlled substances must comply with both state and federal regulations. The prescription must include details on the patient; information on the physician including the DEA number; the amount of drug written out; and manual signature by the physician.

- Orders for Schedule II drugs cannot be phoned in, except in an absolute emergency, and cannot be refilled; Schedule III, IV, and V drugs may be prescribed by phone and refilled up to 5 times in a 6-month period. In some states, Schedule V drugs can be dispensed by the pharmacist without a physician prescription.

- A single drug may have as many as three names: chemical, generic, and trade. The chemical name is the drug's formula; the generic or official name is assigned to the drug and may reflect the chemical name; the trade or brand name is the name given the compound by the developing pharmaceutical company and is protected by copyright for 17 years.

- Using drug reference materials is crucial to the safe administration of medications. Most drug reference books supply the action, indication, contraindications, precautions, adverse reactions, dosage, administration guidelines, and method of packaging. The most frequent drug reference guide is the Physician's Desk Reference (PDR), but package inserts also can be used.

- The clinical uses of drugs include therapeutic or curative; palliative drugs to relieve symptoms; prophylactic medications that prevent the occurrence of a condition; diagnostic drugs to help determine disease cause; and replacement drugs that provide substances that normally occur in the body.

- OTC drugs may interfere or interact with prescription drugs. Some safety measures for the use of OTCs include carefully reading directions, taking only the recommended dose, discarding when expired, informing the physician of OTC use, and being aware of OTC contraindications in certain conditions.

- Pharmacokinetics includes absorption, which is dependent on the routs of administration (oral, parenteral, mucous membrane, or topical); distribution through the bloodstream; metabolism in the liver; and excretion, primarily through the kidneys.

- Multiple factors affect drug action including weight, age, gender, diurnal rhythms, pathological factors, immune responses, psychological factors, tolerance, accumulation, idiosyncrasy, and drug-to-drug interactions.

- The legal responsibilities of medication management include compliance with DEA regulations regarding controlled substances as well as maintaining complete and accurate documentation on all medications administered and prescribed for each patient.

CHAPTER 31

Pharmacology Math

Key Points

- It is the responsibility of the medical assistant to be absolutely certain that the medication prepared and administered to the patient is exactly what is ordered by the physician.

- Although many times drugs are delivered by the pharmacy in unit-dose packs, the dosage ordered may differ from the dose on hand.

- In this case, the medical assistant must be prepared to calculate the correct dose accurately before dispensing and administering the medication.

- There is never a margin of error in drug calculations because even a minor mistake may result in serious complications for the patient; therefore the medical assistant must take meticulous care in calculating all drug dosages.

- If the dosage ordered by the physician is different the dosage on hand, the medical assistant must complete three basic steps for accurate calculation of the prescribed dose:

- Based on the type of system printed on the label, determine if the physician order is in the same mathematical system of measurement. If the systems vary (the order is in teaspoons, but the label states the medication is prepared in milliliters), then accurately convert the order so it matches the system used on the label.

- Perform the calculation in equation form, using the appropriate formula.

- Check your answer for accuracy, and ask someone you trust to confirm your calculations.

- All three of these steps must be completed before the medication is dispensed and administered.

- Confirm your calculations with the physician if you have any doubt of their accuracy.

- The first step in safely calculating the drug dosage is accurate reading of the label of the drug on hand to determine if the physician order and the packaged drug are in the same system of measurement.

- To do this, it is important to understand some of the basic terms used on drug labels:
  Drug label terms must be understood to implement pharmacology math formulas.
  - *Strength:* The potency of the drug stated as a percentage of drug in the solution (2% epinephrine), as a solid weight (grams, milligrams, pounds, grains), or as a millequivalent or unit.
  - *Dosage:* The size or amount of the drug available in the drug package. This could be in milliliters, teaspoons, or the number of tablets. For example, the label may read "Imitrex, 6 mg/ 0.5 ml" which means that 6 mg of the drug is in each 0.5 ml.
  - *Solute:* The pure drug that is dissolved in a liquid to form a solution.
  - *Solvent or diluent:* The liquid, which is usually sterile water that dissolves the solute.

Systems of Measurement

- There are three different systems of measurement: the metric system, the apothecary system, and the household system.

Metric System

- The *metric system* of weights and measures is now used throughout the world as the primary system for weight (mass), capacity (volume), and length (area).
- Units in the metric system are converted by moving the decimal point in multiples of 10.
- When going from larger to smaller units of measurement, as in converting grams to milligrams, the answer will be a larger number, so move the decimal point to the *right*. Therefore, 0.35 g = 350 mg.
- If converting a smaller unit of measurement to a larger one, the answer will be a smaller number, so move the decimal point to the *left*. For example, 150 ml = 0.15 L.
- The following equivalents can be used to make conversions within the metric system:

  1 kg = 1000 g   1 kl = 1000 L

  1 g = 1000 mg   1 L = 1000 ml

Apothecary System

- With the *apothecary system,* the basic unit of weight for a solid medication is the grain (gr), and the basic unit of volume for a liquid medication is the minim.
- As in the metric system, these two units are related: the grain is based on the weight of a single grain of wheat, and the minim is the volume of water that weighs 1 grain.

Household Measurements

- The household system is used in most American households. This system of measurement is important for the patient at home who has no knowledge of the metric or apothecary systems; however, is not completely accurate, so it should never be used in the medical setting.

Pediatrics

Fried's Law

- This calculation is for children younger than 1 year and is based on the age of the child in months compared with a child aged $12\frac{1}{2}$ years.

- $$\text{Pediatric Dose} = \frac{\text{Child's Age in Months}}{150 \text{ months}} \times \text{Adult Dose}$$

Young's Rule

- Young's rule is for children older than 1 year.
- Pediatric dose $= \dfrac{\text{Child's age in years}}{\text{Child's age in years} + 12} \times$ Adult dose

Clark's Rule

- This rule is based on the weight of the child.
- This system is much more accurate, because children of any age can vary greatly in size and body weight.
- Pediatric Dose $= \dfrac{\text{Child's Weight in Pounds}}{150 \text{ pounds}} \times$ Adult Dose

West's Nomogram

- West's nomogram calculates the body surface area of infants and young children.
- Reconstituting powdered injectables requires the medical assistant to add a particular amount of solvent (as recommended on the drug label) to a vial of powdered or crystal medication.
- Once the solute and solvent are combined and mixed in the vial, a solution of medication is formed, and the strength is based on equivalents printed on the drug label.
- Once the medication is mixed, it is important for the medical assistant to read the label carefully to determine how much of the drug must be withdrawn to equal the physician's order.
- This process frequently requires the use of the standard conversion formula to determine the accurate dose for administration.
- The medical assistant who prepares, dispenses, and administers medications is ethically and legally responsible for his or her own actions.
- It is important for medical assistants to be aware of state laws that monitor medication administration by allied health workers.

CHAPTER 32

Administering Medications

Key Points

- Safety precautions in the management of medication administration should be consistently applied.

- Safe drug administration includes understanding the physician order, looking up the drug if it is unknown, and using the three label checks and the seven rights every time a drug order is completed.

- Patient-assessment factors that affect medication administration include the continual evaluation of the patient's physical condition as well as such holistic factors as the impact of the patient's history, an accurate list of drug allergies, the patient's ability to understand the drug regimen and to afford the treatment, as well as special patient factors based on age, weight, and condition.

- Precautions in medication administration must be used with pregnant and lactating women because drugs can pass through the placenta into the developing fetus as well as into the breast milk.

- Pediatric administration is usually based on the weight of the child, and special precautions must be used because of alterations in the absorption, distribution, metabolism, and excretion of drugs in the child's body.

- Children also require a special approach for drug administration to be successful.

- Geriatric patients are more sensitive to the effects of medications because of altered metabolic rates, loss of subcutaneous fat, and accompanying chronic diseases.

- Aging patients are more likely to be taking more than one medication, so drug interactions are a potential problem.

- A holistic approach to medication management in aging patients includes a nutritional assessment, investigation of the cost of drug therapy, and adapted patient-education methods.

- Drugs are packaged in a variety of forms with administration guidelines. Oral medications include both solid and liquid preparations; mucous membrane medications are absorbed either rectally, vaginally, orally, nasally, or through the skin topically. Each form of medication has specific guidelines for administration, but all require the consistent use of the three label checks and the seven rights.

Solid Oral Dosage Forms

- The basic forms are tablets, capsules, and lozenges (troches).

- Tablets are compressed powders or granules that, when wet, break apart in the stomach or in the mouth, if they are not swallowed quickly.

- Tablets may be *sugar* coated to taste better, or **enteric coated,** such as Ecotrin (aspirin), to protect the stomach mucosa.

- Buffered tablets also are designed to prevent stomach irritation by combining the drug with a buffering agent, which decreases the amount of acidity in the compound. Buffered or enteric-coated tablets should never be crushed or dissolved.

- Only those tablets that are **scored** can be cut in half. This is accomplished with a pill cutter.

- Some tablets are coated with a volatile liquid that is meant to dissolve in the mouth, such as an antacid tablet. Caplets are oblong capsules.

- Capsules are gelatin coated and dissolve in the stomach, or they may be coated with substances that protect them from the acid action of the stomach.

- Timed- or sustained-release (SR) capsules or spansules are designed to dissolve at different rates, over time, to reduce the number of times a patient has to take a medication. These drugs should never be crushed or dissolved because it negates their timed-released action.

Liquid Oral Dosage Forms

- Many types of liquid forms are available. They differ mainly in the type of substance used to dissolve the drug: water, oil, or alcohol.
    - *Solutions:* Drug substances contained in a homogeneous mixture with a liquid.
    - *Syrups:* Solutions of sugar and water, usually containing flavoring and medicinal substances. Cough syrups are the most common.
    - *Aromatic waters:* Aqueous solutions containing volatile oils such as oil of spearmint, peppermint, or clove.
    - *Liquors:* Solutions that contain a nonvolatile material, such as alcohol, as the solute.
    - *Suspensions:* Insoluble drug substances contained in a liquid.
    - *Emulsions:* Mixtures of oil and water that improve the taste of otherwise distasteful products such as cod liver oil.
    - *Gels and magmas:* Minerals suspended in water. Minerals settle; therefore products containing minerals must be shaken before use. Milk of magnesia is an example.

- Parenteral medications are manufactured in either ampules or single- or multi-dose vials. The ordered route of administration, drug characteristics, and individual patient factors determine the correct gauge and length of needle needed for administration.

- The appropriate syringe is determined by the type of medication ordered and the amount of drug to be administered. Specialty syringe units, such as the Nova Pen and the EpiPen are designed for the quick administration of certain medications in public or in an emergency.

- Occupational Safety and Health Administration (OSHA) guidelines include using syringe units with retractable needle covers; wearing disposable nonsterile gloves and other appropriate protective gear when administering any medication that involves coming into contact with blood or body fluids; never recapping a contaminated needle and immediately discarding it into a sharps container; disposing of contaminated nonsharp materials in biohazard containers; disinfecting contaminated work areas; and washing hands before and after procedures.

- Parenteral routes of administration include intradermal (ID), subcutaneous (SC), and a variety of intramuscular (IM) sites. The type of medication, the physician's order, and the unique characteristics of individual patients determine the route and site of administration.

- Patient education is absolutely crucial to the correct administration of medication by patients at home. The patient should understand the purpose of the drug; the time, frequency, and amount of the dose; any special storage requirements; and the typical side effects.

- The more the patient knows and understands about how to take the medication and why it is prescribed, the greater the chances that the drug treatment will be successful.

- The medical assistant must be extremely knowledgeable when preparing and administering medications in the physician's office.

- If there are any questions about the order, ask for clarification before proceeding.

- Legal responsibilities include the prevention of error by carefully following safe practice procedures in pouring and administering drugs.

- The medial assistant must comply with individual state laws governing medications and their administration.

- Precise charting of the administration of medications as well as the management of prescriptions cannot be overemphasized.

CHAPTER 33

Assisting with Medical Emergencies

Key Points

- The medical assistant should be familiar with the healthcare facility's policy and procedures for the management of emergencies and maintain certification in cardiopulmonary resuscitation (CPR). Perform only the procedures for which you are trained; always notify the physician or activate emergency medical services (EMS) if the physician is unavailable.

- The medical assistant must make sure the facility is accident proof to prevent patient injuries on site; participate in planning for emergency situations; and post emergency telephone numbers for reference during an emergency.

- It is necessary to have a central location, either a crash cart or emergency bag, for all emergency supplies, equipment, and medications. Emergency supplies must be consistently inventoried and maintained.

- Managing emergencies requires a clam, efficient approach to the situation.

- Assess the nature of the emergency and determine whether EMS should be activated or if the patient requires an immediate or urgent appointment.

- Gather as many details as possible about the situation, and refer to the physician when in doubt.

Telephone Triage

- Telephone triage is one of the most important tasks of the medical assistant. Emergency action principles should be used to determine the level of patient emergency.

- These include determining whether the situation is life threatening and obtaining contact information about the patient as well as all pertinent information regarding the injury and patient signs and symptoms.

- This information must be shared with the doctor, and all details documented on the patient chart.

Syncope

- Was the patient injured?

- Does the patient have a history of heart disease, seizures, or diabetes?

Home Care Advice

- Does not necessarily indicate a serious disease. If injured from a fall, the patient may need to be treated.

- Patient should get up very slowly to prevent recurrence, take it easy, and drink plenty of fluids.

- If patient is to be seen, someone should accompany him or her to the clinician's practice.

Animal Bites

- What kind of animal (pet or wild)?

- How severe is the injury?

- Where are the bites?

- When did the bite occur?

Home Care Advice

- Health department or police should be notified.

- Every effort must be made to locate the animal and monitor its health.

- If the skin is not broken, then wash well and observe for signs of infection.

Insect Bites and Stings

- Does the patient have a history of anaphylactic reaction to insect stings?

- Does the patient have difficulty breathing, a widespread rash, or trouble swallowing?

Home Care Advice

- If there is a history of anaphylaxis and the patient has an EpiPen system, it should be administered immediately and EMS notified.

- Activate EMS if the patient has systemic symptoms.

- Use an antihistamine (diphenhydramine; Benadryl) to relieve local pruritis.

Asthma

- Does the patient show signs of cyanosis?

- Has the patient used the prescribed inhalers?

Home Care Advice

- The asthmatic patient who is unable to speak in sentences, has poor color, and is struggling to breathe even after inhaler use must be seen immediately or EMS activated.

Burns

- Where are the burns located, and what caused them?
- Are there signs of shock (i.e., moist clammy skin, altered consciousness, rapid breathing and pulse)?
- Are there signs of infection (foul odor, cloudy drainage) in a burn older than 2 days?

Home Care Advice

- Activate EMS for burns on the face, hands, feet, and perineum or those caused by electricity, a chemical, or associated with inhalation.
- Activate EMS if there are signs of shock.
- Patient must receive a tetanus shot if it has been longer than 10 years since the last one.
- Schedule an urgent appointment if signs of infection are reported.

Wounds

- Is the bleeding steady or pulsating?
- How and when did the injury occur?
- Does the patient have any bleeding disorders or take anticoagulant drugs?
- Is the wound open and deep?

Home Care Advice

- Pulsating bleeding usually indicates arterial damage; activate EMS.
- If bleeding is from a powerful force, other injuries may exist.
- If the patient takes anticoagulants or has diabetes or anemia, schedule an urgent appointment.
- Gaping, deep wounds require sutures.

Head Injury

- Did the patient faint or have a seizure?
- Is the patient confused, vomiting, or is there clear drainage from nose or ears?

Home Care Advice

- If the answer is "yes" to any of these symptoms, activate EMS.
- Always follow Standard Precautions when caring for a patient with a medical emergency.
- Documentation of emergency treatment should include information about the patient: vital signs; allergies, current medications and pertinent health history; chief complaint; sequence of events including any changes in the patient's condition since the incident; and physician orders and procedures performed.
- Life-threatening emergencies require immediate assessment, referral to the physician, and if the physician is not present, activation of EMS. While waiting for assistance, determine the presence of breathing and circulation.

- Administer rescue breaths or CPR if indicated. Depending on the patient's signs and symptoms, monitor the patient for signs of a heart attack; administer the Heimlich maneuver if there is an obstructed airway; evaluate for signs of a cerebrovascular accident (CVA); and assess for shock.

- Common ambulatory care emergencies require an assessment either by phone or on site of the patient's current condition and need for physician evaluation.

- Each of these situations requires the medical assistant calmly to gather pertinent information from the patient and follow through with the facility's policy and physician orders on management of the emergency.

- Patients should know how to contact emergency personnel, and families with young children should have poison control numbers posted.

- Educating patients on how to care for minor emergencies at home is an important part of telephone triage in the ambulatory care setting.

- Encouraging patients to participate in community safety workshops and becoming CPR certified may avoid emergencies as well as save lives.

Good Samaritan Laws

- They may vary from state to state but are designed to protect any individual, whether a healthcare professional or lay person, from liability if he or she provides assistance at the site of an emergency.

- The law does not require a medically trained person to act, but if emergency care is given in a reasonable and responsible manner, the healthcare worker is protected from being sued for negligence.

- This protection, however, does not extend into the workplace.

CHAPTER 34

Assisting in Ophthalmology and Otolaryngology

Key Points

- The ophthalmologist is a medical physician specializing in the diagnosis and treatment of the eye, whereas the optometrist examines the eyes and treats visual defects, and an optician fills prescriptions for corrective lenses.

- The anatomy of the eye begins with the outer covering, the conjunctiva, and the three layers of tissue: the sclera, choroid, and retina. The inner layer is where light rays are converted into nervous energy for interpretation by the brain.

- Vision begins with the passage of light through the cornea where it is refracted and then passes through the aqueous humor and pupil into the lens.

- The ciliary muscle adjusts the curvature of the lens to refract the light rays again so they pass into the retina, triggering the photoreceptor cells of the rods and cones.

- Light energy is then converted into an electrical impulse, which is sent through the optic nerve to the brain, where interpretation occurs.

- Refractive errors include hyperopia, myopia, presbyopia, and astigmatism.

- All result from a problem with bending light so it can be accurately focused on the retina.

- They are usually caused by defects in the shape of the eyeball and can be corrected with glasses, contact lenses, or surgery.

- Eye disorders can range with problems with eye movement as strabismus and nystagmus to infections of the eye, including hordeolums, chalazions, keratitis, conjunctivitis, and blepharitis.

- Disorders of the eyeball include corneal abrasions, cataracts, glaucoma, and macular degeneration.

- Diagnostic procedures for the eye begin with a visual examination of the eye with an ophthalmoscope. Next the eyelids are examined for abnormalities, and the pupils are tested for PERRLA (pupils equal, round, and reactive to light and accommodation).

- More-advanced techniques include the use of a slit-lamp to view the fine details of the eye and the exophthalmometer to measure the pressure in the central renal artery.

- Distance visual acuity is typically assessed with a Snellen chart; near visual acuity is tested with a near-vision acuity chart; and a patient can be tested for a color-vision defect with the Ishihara test.

- Eye irrigations relieve inflammation, remove drainage, dilute chemicals, or wash away foreign bodies. Sterile technique and equipment must be used to avoid contamination.

- Medication may be instilled into the eye to treat an infection, to soothe an eye irritation, to anesthetize the eye, or to dilate the pupils before examination or treatment.

The Ear

- The external ear consists of the auricle or pinna and the external auditory canal, which transmits sound waves to the tympanic membrane.

- The middle ear is an air-filled cavity that contains the ossicles. The sound vibration passes through the tympanic membrane, causing the ossicles to vibrate. This bone-conducted vibration passes through the oval window into the inner ear.

- The organ of Corti in the cochlea of the inner ear converts the sound waves into nervous energy that is sent to the brain for interpretation. The semicircular canals in the inner ear help maintain equilibrium.

- A conductive hearing loss is caused by a problem that originates in the external or middle ear that prevents the sound vibrations from passing through the external auditory canal, limits the vibrations of the tympanic membrane, or interferes with the passage of bone-conducted sound in the middle ear.

- A sensorineural hearing loss results from damage to the organ of Corti or the auditory nerve and prevents the sound vibration from becoming nervous stimuli that can be interpreted by the brain as sound.

- Two common types of otitis are seen in patients.

- The first affects the external ear canal and is called otitis externa, or swimmer's ear.

- Otitis media is an inflammation of the normally air-filled middle ear, resulting in a collection of fluid behind the tympanic membrane.

- Otitis media can be either serous or suppurative. Impacted cerumen that has pushed tightly up against the eardrum is a frequent cause of conductive hearing loss, because the sound vibrations cannot pass through the cerumen to initiate movement of the tympanic membrane.

- Ménière's disease is a chronic, progressive condition that affects the labyrinth and causes recurring attacks of vertigo, tinnitus, a sensation of pressure in the affected ear, and advancing hearing loss.

- The ear examination begins with an otoscopic examination and can include various tuning fork tests and more advanced audiometric testing.

- An ear irrigation is performed to remove excessive or impacted cerumen; to remove a foreign body; or to treat the inflamed ear with an antiseptic solution.

- Medication that is to be instilled into the ear generally is given to soften impacted cerumen, to relieve pain, or is an antibiotic drop needed to fight an infectious pathogen.

- Examination of the nose and throat begins with examination of the nasal cavity and then visual examination of the throat and the nasopharynx. Throat cultures may be done to determine the presence of a streptococcal infection.

- Patients with vision or hearing impairments face serious challenges and require individualized attention to meet their health education needs.

- Teaching adaptations may be required to meet the special needs of these patients.

- Those with vision losses may need large-print forms and handouts, increased levels of lighting, or oral rather than written instructions.

- Individuals with hearing deficits may benefit from printed instructions, demonstrations on how to manage treatments, or even sign-language interpretation.

- Family members should be included in the patient's treatment plan, and referrals to appropriate community or professional resources may be very beneficial.

CHAPTER 35

Assisting in Dermatology

Key Points

- The skin carries out several essential functions: it acts as a barrier to protect vital internal organs against infection and injury, it helps dissipate heat and regulate body temperature, and it synthesizes vitamin D when exposed to ultraviolet light. In addition, the various sensory receptors in the skin enable it to respond to such sensations as heat, cold, pain, and pressure.

- The skin is made up of three layers. The epidermis, which is the thin uppermost layer; the dermis, which is the thicker layer beneath, often referred to as the true skin, and makes up about 90% of the skin mass; and the subcutaneous layer, which is composed primarily of fatty or *adipose* tissue.

- The diagnoses of skin lesions are based on the color, level of elevation, and texture of the lesion; the presence of pruritus, excoriation, pain, or drainage; and whether the lesion is a primary or secondary growth.

- Integumentary system infections include bacterial infections such as impetigo, acne vulgaris, furuncles, carbuncles, and cellulites; fungal infections including a variety of tinea growths; viral infections that cause warts, herpes simplex, and herpes zoster outbreaks; and scabies or pediculosis infestations.

- Inflammatory and vascular integumentary system disorders include a variety of seborrheic dermatitis inflammations; contact dermatitis; eczema; psoriasis; and two autoimmune disorders, systemic lupus erythematosus and scleroderma.

Thermal Injuries

- The most frequent thermal injuries are burns, which are classified as superficial (first degree), partial thickness (second degree), or full thickness (third degree), depending on the depth of the wound.

- The most important concern in the treatment of burns is the prevention of infection.

- Cold injuries are usually less severe than burns, but prolonged exposure can result in infection, gangrene, amputation, and in severe situations, death.

- Frostbite can either be superficial or deep.

Cancer

- Benign masses are encapsulated, and although they may grow in size, they remain within a confining shell, whereas malignant tumors invade and take over surrounding tissues.

- Local invasion of surrounding tissue occurs when malignant cells break through the basement membrane that separates epithelial cells from connective tissue. Here the cancerous cells can invade blood and lymph vessels, which can then carry the malignant cells to organs throughout the body.

- Grading and staging describe the extent of malignant involvement so the physician can plan appropriate treatment.

- Grading is the histologic, or cellular, classification of the tumor. The more poorly differentiated the cells from the tumor, the less they look like normal cells, and the poorer the prognosis.

- Staging involves using physical examination and diagnostic tests (such as bone or liver scans) to determine the degree of tumor spread.

- The size and depth of the primary tumor, the level of lymph node involvement, and the presence of metastatic spread determine whether the patient has a carcinoma *in situ,* a tumor that is localized to the organ of origin, a direct spread beyond the primary organ, lymph node metastasis, or a confirmed secondary tumor growth at a distant metastasis.

- The warning signs of cancer include any change in bowel or bladder habits; a sore that does not heal; unusual bleeding or discharge; a thickening or a lump in the breast or elsewhere; indigestion or difficulty in swallowing; an obvious change in a wart or mole; or a nagging cough or hoarseness.

- Any of these warning signs should be reported to the physician immediately. Early detection and self-examination are crucial to cancer survival.

- The three cancerous lesions of the skin are basal cell, squamous cell, and malignant melanoma. Basal cell carcinoma is very slow growing and is the most frequently seen form of skin cancer.

- Squamous cell carcinoma grows rapidly and is more serious because it has a tendency to metastasize. The many forms of melanoma are all pigmented lesions (usually brown, tan, blue, red, black, or white) that are asymmetric with irregular borders and are usually larger than 6 mm.

- Treatment depends on the type of lesion, the level of invasion, and location. The physician may surgically remove the tumor or destroy it with cryosurgery, electrodesiccation, or the application of chemotherapeutic agents.

- The **ABCD** rule for early detection of a malignant melanoma includes examination of the site for any of the following: **a**symmetry, irregular **b**order, change in **c**olor, and an increase in the **d**iameter. If a mole displays any of these characteristics, a dermatologist should check it immediately.

- Dermatologic procedures include allergy skin testing that can be done with scratch, intradermal, or patch tests; drawing blood for a radioallergosorbent (RAST) test; treating allergies with immunotherapy; performing a wound culture; and assisting with appearance-modification procedures including chemical peels, dermabrasion, and laser resurfacing.

CHAPTER 36

Assisting in Gastroenterology

Key Points

- The gastrointestinal (GI) system is responsible for the preparation, digestion, absorption, and excretion of nutrients and waste materials.

- The GI system begins at the mouth and ends at the anal canal.

- The digestive process starts in the mouth with mastication and enzyme action. The bolus of food is swallowed and passed from the esophagus into the stomach, where digestion continues with the addition of hydrochloric acid and further enzyme action, and ends in the duodenum with pancreatic juices and emulsification of fat by bile, which is excreted by the liver and stored in the gallbladder.

- Absorption of nutrients takes place in the ileum and jejunum, with absorption of fluids in the large intestine. Ultimately, waste materials are excreted through the anus.

- The abdominal cavity can be divided into four sections or quadrants, the right and left upper quadrants and right and left lower quadrants.

- Another, more specific method of dividing the abdominal cavity is into nine regions: the right hypochondrias, epigastric, and left hypochondriac; the right lumbar, umbilical, and left lumbar; and the right inguinal, hypogastric, and left inguinal.

- The purpose of these anatomic markers is to be able to identify clearly the location of the GI problem.

- Patients with GI disorders may complain of nausea with pallor, diaphoresis, and tachycardia; vomiting because of pain, stress, GI upset, or an inner ear or intracranial pressure disturbance; diarrhea due to an infection, allergy, or malabsorption problem; constipation because of a low-fiber diet or inadequate fluids, side effect of medication, or a bowel obstruction or tumor; and abdominal pain that varies in intensity and quality.

- It is important for the medical assistant to identify the location of the patient's discomfort by using either abdominal quadrants or regions and to note the onset, duration, and frequency of all symptoms.

Gastrointestinal Cancer

- GI tumors can include those in the
  - mouth that appear as either a white mass or an ulcer
  - esophagus, causing dysphagia
  - stomach, which causes anorexia and weight loss but is difficult to diagnose in the early stages

- liver, which is usually secondary to metastasis from another cancerous site with hepatomegaly and portal hypertension
- pancreas, which is usually advanced when diagnosed
- colorectum, with changes in bowel function and anemia

- Esophageal and gastric disorders include hiatal hernias, in which part of the stomach pushes through the hiatal sphincter of the diaphragm causing gastroesophageal reflux disorder (GERD); peptic ulcers, which are associated with *Helicobacter pylori* infections that are treated with a combination of antibiotics and proton-pump inhibitors; and pyloric stenosis, which is seen most frequently in first-born male infants, causing projectile vomiting, and must be corrected by surgery. These disorders are usually diagnosed symptomatically and with the use of a barium swallow or upper GI series of radiographs. Medical treatment includes the use of cisapride (Propulsid), esomeprazole (Nexium), famotidine (Pepcid), cimetadine (Tagamet), or ranitidine (Zantac). Surgery may be indicated for repair of a hiatal hernia or gastric ulcers if perforation occurs.

- Intestinal disorders include a variety of food poisonings, all of which cause mild to severe gastroenteritis; antiemetics and antidiarrheal medications are used to control symptoms.

- Dumping syndrome may occur as a postsurgical complication to weight-loss surgery and results in widespread GI complaints.

- Inflammatory bowel disease *(IBS)* is a recurrent functional bowel disorder causing alternating bouts of diarrhea, flatulence, and constipation and is treated pharmaceutically with bulk-forming agents, antidiarrheals, antispasmodics, and anticholinergics.

- Acute appendicitis is diagnosed by a positive McBurney sign and is treated surgically.

- Regional enteritis or Crohn's disease causes localized areas of ulceration in the intestinal tract and is treated medically to decrease inflammation, manage symptoms, and maintain nutritional status.

- Ulcerative colitis causes inflammatory ulcers from the anus and moving proximally through the colon; it is treated like Crohn's disease, but surgical removal of the colon is curative.

- Malabsorption disorder: Celiac disease is due to a genetic defect in the ability to metabolize gluten.

- Diverticular disease, due to small herniations of the muscular lining of the colon, is managed with dietary changes and surgery with advanced diverticulitis.

- The abdominal musculature can become weakened; hernias are surgically repaired.

- Hemorrhoids, varicose veins of the anus, are treated with stool softeners, high-fiber diets, or surgical repair.

- Disorders of the liver include hepatitis either from viral infection or chemical reaction, including alcohol abuse and a complication of drug metabolism; mild inflammation temporarily impairs function, but severe inflammation may lead to necrosis and serious complications including jaundice, cirrhosis, and portal hypertension.

- The gallbladder stores bile that is excreted by the liver to aid in fat metabolism and may develop cholelithiasis or cholecystitis and have to be surgically removed to relieve patient symptoms.

- Hepatitis can be caused by exposure to chemicals or drug side effects. Viral hepatitis is an infection of the liver that causes an acute inflammatory process of hepatocytes. Several forms of this virus are A, B, C, D, E, and G. Hepatic cells are capable of regeneration, so dependent on the degree of liver involvement, the patient may recover completely or develop widespread necrosis, cirrhosis, and liver failure.

- The medical assistant's role in the GI examination includes providing patient support and education, gathering and recording specific details about the patient's complaints, instilling rectal medications as ordered, and assisting the physician with the examination and diagnostic procedures performed in the ambulatory care setting.

- Diagnostic procedures for the GI system include laboratory studies such as liver panels; urinary tests for bilirubin and amylase; and stool tests for occult blood, intestinal parasites, and fat excretion. Radiologic and endoscopic tests include barium swallow, upper GI series, barium enema, oral cholecystogram, sigmoidoscopy, and colonoscopy.

- The role of the medical assistant in the proctologic examination includes patient support and preparation; positioning and draping the patient for the procedure; monitoring vital signs before and during the procedure; and assisting the physician with the procedure.

CHAPTER 37

Assisting in Urology and Male Reproduction

Key Points

- The urinary system is made up of two kidneys located bilaterally in the retroperitoneum, two ureters, the urinary bladder, and the urethra. The main function of the urinary system is to remove waste products from the body.

- The urinary system also helps to maintain homeostasis by regulating water, electrolytes, and acid-base levels; activating vitamin D, which encourages calcium ion absorption; secreting the hormone erythropoietin, which helps control the rate of red blood cell formation; and maintaining blood pressure by the secretion of the enzyme rennin.

- Three processes are involved in urine formation: filtration, reabsorption, and excretion. The outer layer of the kidney, the *cortex,* contains the functional unit of the kidney, the nephron unit, where waste materials are filtered and substances reabsorbed.

- By the time the waste material reaches the calyx, it is in the form of urine, which is emptied out of the kidneys through bilateral ureters to the urinary bladder. When the bladder is full, sphincters open, and urine flows into the urethra.

- The urinary tract is made up of a continuous mucosal lining, which gives organisms that enter the urethra a direct pathway through the system.

- A wide range of symptoms occur in patients with disorders of the renal system, with the most common involving changes in the frequency of urination. Dysuria (difficult or painful urination), urgency, retention, and incontinence are all common symptoms.

- Abnormal functions of any part of the urinary tract can often be determined with urinalysis, blood urea nitrogen (BUN) levels, and with analysis of creatinine clearance.

- Diagnostic procedures for the urologic system include the kidney-ureter-bladder radiograph (KUB), which is a flat plate of the abdomen that shows the size, shape, location, and malformations of the kidneys and bladder; and renal scanning, which is a nuclear scan to determine size, shape, and function of the kidney or to diagnose obstruction or hypertension; cystography or voiding cystography, a radiograph with contrast dye to study the bladder; an intravenous pyelogram, radiographs after a dye is injected to show passage through the urinary system and diagnose tumors, calculi, or obstructions; and renal arteriogram, in which dye is injected into the renal artery to visualize blood flow through the kidneys.

- Renal computed tomography (CT) provides transverse views of the kidneys to detect tumors, abscesses, or hydronephrosis; renal ultrasound can detect functional defects in the kidneys or polycystic disease.

- Cystoscopy provides an endoscopic view of the urethra and bladder; and the retrograde pyelogram visualizes the bladder, ureters, and kidneys after injection of a dye.

- Most urinary tract infections (UTIs) are ascending, starting with pathogens in the perineal area and infecting the continuous mucosa up through the urethra, bladder, ureters, to the kidneys. Infection and inflammation of the urethra is called *urethritis,* and that of the bladder is *cystitis.* Resident flora of the colon, among them, *Escherichia coli,* are the usual causative agents.

- *Pyelonephritis,* an inflammation of the renal pelvis and kidney, is the most common type of renal disease. It is caused by bacteria that ascend from the lower urinary tract in conditions such as urinary retention or obstruction that promote urinary stasis and the growth of bacteria.

- Acute glomerulonephritis, the degenerative inflammation of the glomeruli, usually develops in children and adolescents about 2 weeks after a streptococcal infection such as strep throat or scarlet fever.

- Chronic glomerulonephritis causes progressive, irreversible renal damage that may result in renal failure and is caused by an antigen-antibody reaction within the glomerular capsule that ultimately destroys the nephron unit.

- Renal calculi are created when salts in the urine collect in the kidney or when fluid intake is low, creating a highly concentrated filtrate. They are a common problem and tend to recur if the cause of formation is not treated.

- Small stones usually do not cause any difficulty until they grow large enough to lodge in the ureters or renal pelvis. This blockage also can result in hydronephrosis, which is a backup of urine causing dilation of the calyses and increased pressure on the nephron units.

- Polycystic kidney disease is an autonomic dominant genetic disorder that is slowly progressive and irreversible, causing the formation of multiple grape-like cysts in the kidney. As the cysts enlarge, they compress the surrounding tissue, causing necrosis, uremia, and renal failure.

- Bladder cancer is characterized by one or more tumors, which can reappear. The tumor is invasive and can metastasize through the blood or surrounding pelvic lymph nodes.

- Adenocarcinoma of the kidney is a primary tumor that is initially asymptomatic, so it frequently has metastasized before being diagnosed. Wilms' tumor is cancer of the kidney in children due to an inherited genetic defect.

- Acute renal failure has a sudden, severe onset caused by exposure to toxic chemicals, severe or prolonged circulatory or cardiogenic shock that might occur from serious burns or heart disease, or an acute bilateral kidney infection or inflammation.

- Chronic renal failure is a slowly progressive process that is caused by the gradual destruction of the ability of the kidneys to filter waste materials. Dialysis, or cleansing of the blood, is used to treat acute renal failure until the problem is reversed or for those patients with end-stage renal disease until a transplant can be performed.

- There are two forms of dialysis, hemodialysis and peritoneal.

- Hemodialysis uses a machine known as an artificial kidney to filter out waste products in the blood and return the cleansed blood to the body.

- Peritoneal dialysis uses dialyzing fluid in the patient's abdomen to absorb waste products, which are drained from the abdominal cavity by gravity into a container. It can be done by the patient at home.

- Pediatric urologic disorders include enuresis, which is the inability to control urination and may be caused by physical or psychological disorders; urine reflux disorder, which is the backward flow of urine into the ureters when voiding, which is usually caused by an infection.

- Cryptorchidism, the failure of one or both testes to descend into the scrotum, can be corrected with an orchidopexy surgical procedure.

- The development of a hydrocele, a buildup of fluid in the scrotum, may be a congenital disorder or acquired because of injury.

Male Reproductive System

- The male reproductive system is made up of a pair of testes contained in the scrotum. The testes consist of lobules that contain the seminiferous tubules, where spermatozoa are produced. The sperm cells are tadpole-like structures less than 0.1 mm long, which are carried to the epididymis for maturation.

- The epididymis is a long coiled tube that rests on the top and lateral sides of each testis. Peristaltic waves in the epididymis help the sperm move into the vas deferens, where the sperm are stored until ejaculation.

- The prostate gland surrounds the urethra at the base of the bladder. It secretes a thin fluid with an alkaline pH that neutralizes the acidic sperm-containing fluid and vaginal secretions to provide an optimal pH for fertilization.

- The organ of male copulation is the penis, which has a slightly enlarged end, called the glans penis.

- Hormone production is an important aspect of the male reproductive system. As a group, the male sex hormones are called androgens. The most influential product of hormone production is testosterone, which stimulates the testes to enlarge, increases body hair growth, thickens skin and bone, increases muscle growth, and matures sperm cells.

- Inflammation of the prostate usually develops in the presence of infection. The common symptoms are dysuria, tenderness of the prostate region, and secretion of pus from the tip of the penis.

- The swelling of the prostate gland, benign prostatic hypertrophy, partially blocks the flow of urine, creating a medium for bacterial infection that can lead to cystitis. The diagnosis is made from patient complaints and a digital rectal examination, during which the physician can palpate the enlarged gland. Treatment includes the use of α-adrenergic blockers or surgical removal of the prostrate gland through a transurethral resection.

- Cancer of the prostate is common in men older than 50 years and ranks as the second highest cause of male cancer deaths after lung cancer. The patient may experience urinary obstruction, increased bouts of urinary infection, and frequent nocturia. Diagnosis is made with a digital rectal examination that identifies a firm or irregular area in the prostate and the prostate-specific antigen (PSA) blood test.

- Male genital pathology includes epididymitis, usually due to a urinary tract infection, prostatitis, or a sexually transmitted disease (STD). Patients have severe low abdominal and testicular pain, as well as swelling and tenderness of the scrotum.

- The inflammation of the glans penis and of the mucous membrane beneath it is known as balanitis. It occurs most often in uncircumcised patients with narrow foreskins that do not retract easily and in diabetics.

- Antibiotics are used for infections, cleansing for buildup of smegma; avoidance of chemicals that cause reactions can help avoid the problem.

- Testicular tumors usually occur in young men and are generally malignant. The patient complains of a hard, painless, mass affecting one testicle.

- Treatment of the tumors is usually a combination of orchidectomy, radiation therapy, and sometimes chemotherapy.

- Impotence is the inability to achieve and maintain an erection sufficient for intercourse. It has many causes, both psychologic and physiologic. This condition can be treated medically with sildenafil (Viagra).

- Male infertility may be caused by cryptorchidism, stricture, and varicoceles, low sperm count and motility, obstruction of the vas deferens, and hormonal imbalances. Examination of sperm samples is helpful in making a diagnosis of infertility.

- There is no cure for viral STDs such as human immunodeficiency virus (HIV) or herpes, and bacterial causes of infection are becoming increasingly resistant to antibiotic therapy. STDs are frequently asymptomatic and can cause serious health problems, even death.

- Bacterial STDs include gonorrhea and chlamydia infections, which tend to coexist. Symptoms are associated with acute urethritis and epididymitis.

- Chlamydia is resistant to penicillin; thus a regimen of antibiotics other than penicillin should be used if the patient has been diagnosed with both conditions.

- Syphilis begins with a chancre on the male genitalia within a few days to a few weeks after exposure. It is diagnosed with the VDRL or RPR.

CHAPTER **38**

Assisting in Obstetrics and Gynecology

Key Points

- The female reproductive system is made up of the external genitalia, including the vulva, labia majora, and labia minora.

- The internal organs include the vagina, with rugae formation in the walls so it can expand when the baby is born; the bottom of the uterus, the cervix, which must dilate and efface for the vaginal birth of a child; the uterus, the internal lining of which is the endometrium, and the middle lining is the myometriun; the fallopian tubes that extend from the fundus of the uterus and carry the fertilized egg back to the uterus; and the ovaries, which produce an egg or ovum.

- The average menstrual cycle lasts 28 days, starting with the follicular phase, when hormones mature a graafian follicle, so that an ovum can be released while the endometrial wall is thickening.

- The ovum passes into the fallopian tube, which moves it toward the uterus. The luteal phase then begins; extensive growth of the endometrium continues, but if conception does not occur, the menstrual cycle begins with the breakdown of the endometrium and menstrual flow.

- Barrier contraceptive methods include the use of a condom, a diaphragm, or a cervical cap. Both the diaphragm and cap use spermicidal agents as well. All barrier methods are relatively inexpensive and reversible but must be used each time there is intercourse. Hormonal contraceptives include Depo-Provera injections every 12 weeks, Norplant implants that provide contraception for 5 years, or oral contraceptives that must be taken daily as prescribed.

- Menstrual disorders include amenorrhea or the absence of menstruation for a minimum of 6 months, whereas with oligomenorrhea, the woman has not had a period for from 35 days to 6 months. Abnormal menstrual bleeding includes menorrhagia, which is excessive menstrual blood loss, such as a menses lasting longer than 7 days. Metrorraghia is spotting or bleeding between menstrual cycles.

- Endometriosis is characterized by the presence of functional endometrial tissue outside the uterus. The ectopic endometrial tissue responds to routine hormone changes so that it proliferates, degenerates, and bleeds as does the endometrium of the uterus throughout the menstrual cycle. This causes inflammation at the site of the implantation that recurs with each cycle, ultimately leading to adhesions and obstructions of the affected tissue. The primary symptom of endometriosis is dysmenorrhea and frequently dyspareunia.

- Gynecologic infections include a yeast infection called candidiasis; cervicitis, which is an inflammation of the cervix form a pathogen; pelvic inflammatory disease (PID), which is any acute or chronic infection of the reproductive system ascending from the vagina (vaginitis), cervix (cervicitis), uterus (endometritis), fallopian tubes (salpingitis), and ovaries (oophoritis).

165

- Benign tumors of the reproductive system include uterine fibroids, composed mainly of smooth muscle and some fibrous connective tissue of unknown cause. Ovarian cysts are sacs of fluid or semisolid material that form on or near the ovaries. They can occur in the follicle or the corpus luteum at any time between puberty and menopause.

- Polycystic ovary disease is a hormonal problem that causes cysts to develop over enlarged ovaries. Women with this disorder have hormonal abnormalities that cause anovulation and multiple symptoms.

- Fibrocystic breast disease is the presence of multiple palpable nodules in the breasts, usually associated with pain and tenderness that fluctuate with the menstrual cycle. Over time the cysts enlarge, and the connective tissue of the breast is replaced with dense and firm fibrous tissue.

- Malignant tumors include cervical, endometrial, and ovarian cancers that vary in their diagnostic features and symptoms. Breast cancer can be of multiple origins including ductal, lobular, or invasive carcinoma that has invaded surrounded tissue and metastasized. Treatment of all forms of reproductive cancer is dependent of the staging and grading of the tumors.

- Positional disorders of the pelvic region include a cystocele, which is a protrusion of the bladder into the anterior wall of the vagina. The bladder becomes angled, and urinary retention is common, with frequent cystitis.

- A rectocele is a protrusion of the rectum into the posterior wall of the vagina. In a uterine prolapse, the cervix has dropped into the vaginal area. This may progress to both the uterus and the cervix protruding from the vaginal opening. If severe, all three of these structural abnormalities can be corrected with surgery.

- Pregnancy occurs when the ovum and sperm meet in the fallopian tube and a zygote is formed. The zygote implants in the uterine wall, and the placenta begins to form, which provides hormonal support for the pregnancy.

- The fetus is surrounded by an amniotic sac and floats in amniotic fluid. The fetus's oxygen and nutrient needs are met by maternal blood that passes through the placenta to the umbilical cord, and waste material passes out along the same path. The embryonic period ends at 12 weeks, and by then all tissues and organs have developed.

- During the remainder of the pregnancy, the organs mature and begin to function, and the fetus grows.

- Pregnancy is divided into trimesters: the first, second, and third. The first trimester is a crucial time for fetal organ development; the second brings quickening and many physiologic changes in the mother; and during the third, organ systems mature until the birth of the infant.

- Labor consists of three stages; dilation and effacement of the cervix; birth; and expulsion of the placenta.

- The complications of pregnancy begin with fertility problems and the potential loss of the pregnancy from different types of abortions (miscarriages).

- Placental abnormalities pose a threat to the well-being of the fetus as well.

- These include placenta previa, in which the placenta covers the cervical os; and abruptio placentae, in which the placenta breaks away from the uterine wall.

- Both cause maternal hemorrhage, threaten the fetal oxygen supply, and require cesarean birth to protect the fetus and mother.

- Maternal disorders include the pregnancy-induced glucose metabolic disorder, gestational diabetes, which requires dietary changes and possible insulin therapy during the pregnancy; and hypertension, which may progress to toxemia, a life-threatening increase in blood pressure with edema, uremia, and possible seizure activity.

- Menopause is the permanent ending of menstruation because ovarian function stops. Perimenopause begins when hormone-related changes start to appear and lasts until the final menses. Some women experience few or no symptoms, whereas others have hot flashes, concentration problems, mood swings, irritability, migraines, vaginal dryness, urinary incontinence, dry skin, and sleep disorders.

- The physician may prescribe low-dose oral contraceptives or hormone-replacement therapy; soy products or supplements; vitamins E and B$_6$; avoidance of caffeine and spicy foods; a low-fat diet high in calcium; as well as regular weight-bearing exercise.

- The medical assistant's role in the gynecologic and reproductive examinations includes preparing the patient for the examination; equipping the room; making sure supplies are available and properly prepared; assisting with the examination; positioning and draping the patient as needed; assisting with the Pap smear or any other procedure; and providing support and understanding for the patient.

Diagnostic tests for the female reproductive system include

- Ultrasonography during pregnancy to determine the number of fetuses, age and gender of the fetus, fetal abnormalities, and position of the placenta;

- Chorionic villi sampling or amniocentesis to perform genetic testing for anomalies or inherited disorders;

- α-Fetoprotein (AFP) blood tests to diagnose neural tube defects;

- Mammography, which provides an x-ray image of the breast tissue to identify abnormal masses that would otherwise go undetected in a breast-palpation examination; and

- Colposcopy procedures that visualize abnormal cervical tissue for evaluation or biopsy; cryosurgery to treat cervical ulcers or cervicitis; and a variety of tests done during pregnancy.

CHAPTER 39

Assisting in Pediatrics

Key Points

- The terms *growth* and *development* are often used together and refer to the combination of changes a child goes through as he or she matures. Growth refers to measurable changes such as height and weight, whereas development considers qualitative maturation in motor, mental, and language skills.

- By age 6 months, the child's birth weight has doubled; at 1 year, it has tripled, and length has increased by 50%. By age 2 years, the child has reached approximately 50% of adult height. This same growth rate continues through the school-age period, 6 to 12 years, which leads to a growth spurt that indicates impending puberty. In adolescence, ages 12 to 18 years, the adolescent gains almost half of his or her adult weight, and the skeleton and organs double in size.

- Child development occurs rapidly during the first year of life, and by age 3 years, the child is showing increased autonomy. During the preschool stage, the child becomes increasingly independent, and by school-age, the child has perfected fine motor skills and has expanded reading and writing skills. The adolescent, or transition, stage is when the individual attempts to establish an adult identity. This is usually done through trial and error by experimenting with adult roles and behavior patterns.

- Pediatric gastrointestinal disorders include infant colic; diarrhea, caused by a variety of different microorganisms, including bacteria, viruses, and parasites, and treated medically when it continues for more than 2 days; failure to thrive, caused by a physiologic factor (such as malabsorption disease or cleft palate) or a nonorganic cause associated with the parent-child relationship; and obesity, with treatment for children who are more than 40% over their ideal weight.

- Disorders of the respiratory system include the common cold, which may lead to secondary bacterial infections including strep throat or otitis media due to accumulation of either serous or suppurative fluid in the middle ear.

- Croup, a viral disorder that affects primarily the larynx with edema and spasm to the vocal cords, results in a high-pitched, raspy cough.

- Bronchiolitis, a viral infection of the small bronchi and bronchioles, has an acute onset of wheezing and dyspnea because of necrosis, inflammation, edema, increased secretions, and bronchospasm in the respiratory pathway; asthma causes bronchospasms that decrease the amount of air that can pass through the airways and inflammation of the bronchioles, causing edema and secretion of mucus.

- Influenza, an acute, highly contagious viral infection of the respiratory tract, is transmitted by direct contact with moist secretions, causing high fevers and pulmonary complications.

- Pediatric infectious diseases include conjunctivitis, caused by bacterial or viral infection that produces a white or yellowish pus and is highly contagious.

- Tonsillitis, typically caused by *Streptococcus A,* causes painful, enlarged, and inflamed tonsils with fever and malaise.

- Fifth disease, also called *erythema infectiosum,* is a mild infection caused by parvovirus B19, causing a mild fever, general malaise, and flushed cheeks.

- Chickenpox is caused by a member of the herpesvirus group, begins with a slight fever and skin lesions that last for about 2 weeks and usually leaves the child with lifetime immunity.

- Meningitis, inflammation of the membranes that cover the brain and spinal cord, is caused by bacteria or viruses; bacterial meningitis is the more dangerous.

- Hepatitis B virus infection can lead to serious and chronic infection of the liver and can be transmitted across the placenta or during the birth process if the mother is infected.

- Reye's syndrome, linked with the use of aspirin during a viral illness, is characterized by fatty invasion of the inner organs, especially the liver, and swelling of the brain.

- Pediatric inherited disorders include cystic fibrosis, an autosomal recessive genetic disorder that causes exocrine glands to produce abnormally thick secretions and affects primarily the lungs and pancreas, causing buildup of mucus in the lungs and blockage of the pancreatic ducts, resulting in malabsorption problems and an emphysema-like lung condition.

- Duchenne's muscular dystrophy is an X-linked genetic disease that causes progressive muscle degeneration and subsequent replacement of muscle fibers with fat and fibrous connective tissue, ultimately causing either cardiac or respiratory failure.

- It is recommended that all children be vaccinated against diphtheria, tetanus, pertussis, hepatitis B, the *Haemophilus influenzae b* virus that can cause some forms of meningitis, polio, measles, mumps, rubella, pneumonia, and chickenpox.

- Well-child visits are typically scheduled from ages 2 weeks through 15 years to focus on maintaining the health of the child with basic system examinations, immunizations, and upgrading of the child's medical history record. Sick-child visits occur whenever needed and usually on short notice.

- The medical assistant is responsible for assisting the pediatrician with examinations; upgrading patient histories; performing ordered screening tests such as vision, hearing, urinalysis, and hemoglobin checks; administering immunizations; measuring and weighing children as needed; and providing patient and caregiver support.

- The medical assistant should be involved in parent education regarding injury prevention in children. Unintentional injuries are the leading cause of death and disability for children in the United States. Injuries cause more childhood deaths than all diseases combined. The primary causes of childhood injuries include motor vehicle accidents, drowning, burns, falls, poisoning, aspiration with airway obstruction, and firearms.

CHAPTER 40

Assisting in Orthopedic Medicine

Key Points

- The main structures of the musculoskeletal system include the skeletal muscles, which provide movement; tendons, which connect muscles to bones; bones, which provide support, protection, and mineral storage; and ligaments, which connect bone to bone.

- Tendons are the tough bands that connect muscles to bones, whereas ligaments provide support by connecting bone to bone and preventing a joint from moving beyond its normal range of motion (ROM). Ligament injury occurs when a joint if forced beyond its normal ROM. Bursae prevent friction between different tissues in the musculoskeletal system.

- Musculoskeletal system disorders account for more missed days at work and more doctors' office visits than nearly any other medical problems. Musculoskeletal disorders frequently result from trauma and also may be caused by bacteria, fungi, or viruses or may have an autoimmune origin.

- Common diagnostic procedures routinely performed in the orthopedic office include inspection, palpation and percussion, and radiographic studies. It is necessary to rule out bone fractures in many traumatic injuries, and this can only be done by obtaining radiographs of the injured area. Other diagnostic tools include computed tomography (CT), magnetic resonance imaging (MRI), and diagnostic ultrasound.

- The most common ambulatory assistive devices are crutches, canes, walkers, and wheelchairs. The most important aspects of using these assistive devices in an orthopedic practice are to fit them properly to the patient and to give the patient adequate instruction on how to use them.

- Cold should always be used immediately after an injury to help decrease pain and inflammation, inhibit additional swelling, and help to relieve pain.

- Heat should be used on injuries after 48 hours to promote circulation and healing, decrease swelling, and cause soft-tissue relaxation in the treated area.

- Physical therapy is critical in the treatment of musculoskeletal conditions because the goals include restoring normal ROM, muscle strength, and function of the injured part as quickly as possible. Other physical therapy treatment goals include decreasing pain and preserving muscle mass.

- In active ROM assessment or exercise, the patient provides and controls the movement of the specific body area. In passive ROM assessment or exercise, the therapist provides and controls the movement of a specific body area.

CHAPTER 41

Assisting in Neurology and Mental Health

Key Points

- The two main parts of the human nervous system are the central nervous system (CNS), which includes the brain and spinal cord, and the peripheral nervous system (PNS), which includes all of the nerves outside of the CNS.

- The main function of the nervous system is to control the body and thus maintain homeostasis. It does this by receiving messages in the CNS from the PNS and then sending a response to the appropriate location in the body, again via the PNS.

- The CNS is well protected, first by bone, and then by a series of membranous coverings (meninges) called the dura mater, arachnoid, and the pia mater.

- The brain is made up of the cerebrum (all expressions of artistic and verbal processes and thought), cerebellum (controls balance, equilibrium, posture, and muscle coordination), and the brainstem (vision, hearing, respirations, heart rate, blood pressure, and waking and sleeping).

- Symptoms of possible serious neurologic conditions include headache, nausea and vomiting, change in vision, or change in level of consciousness.

- The most common brain disorders resulting from trauma include concussion and contusion. More severe injuries may result in intracranial bleeding.

- The most common work-related neurologic condition is a repetitive stress disorder called carpal tunnel syndrome.

- Frequently used diagnostic tests in neurology include electroencephalogram (EEG), lumbar puncture, radiograph, computed tomography (CT) scan, and magnetic resonance imaging (MRI).

- Depression is among the most commonly encountered mental health disorders and has a variety of symptoms that could easily be overlooked or attributed to some other condition.

- When assisting in neurology, the medical assistant must be particularly careful to recognize signs and symptoms that can frequently be quite subtle, but can be extremely significant in helping with accurate assessment and diagnosis of the patient.

CHAPTER 42

Assisting in Endocrinology

Key Points

- The endocrine system is a network of ductless glands and other structures that secrete hormones directly into the bloodstream. These hormones directly affect the function of specific target tissues and organs.

- Hormones are chemical transmitters produced by the body and transported to target tissue or organs by the bloodstream.

- Diabetes insipidus and diabetes mellitus are different diseases. Diabetes insipidus is a metabolic condition characterized by excessive secretion of urine. Diabetes mellitus is a disorder that results from a deficiency or complete lack of the hormone insulin.

- Gigantism and acromegaly are both diseases of the pituitary gland involving growth hormone (GH). When this condition affects children whose epiphyseal disks have not closed, gigantism is the result. In adults, the disorder causes excessive growth of the facial bones and extremities. This condition is called acromegaly.

- Iodine supplements are used to reduce the size of the thyroid enlargement called a goiter.

- Type 1 or immune-mediated diabetes mellitus usually develops before age 30 years and is sometimes called juvenile diabetes. Type 2 diabetes develops gradually and is called maturity or adult-onset diabetes. Both conditions result from deficiencies of insulin; however, type 1 diabetics do not produce any insulin, and type 2 diabetics usually produce insulin in insufficient amounts.

- A daily food plan for a diabetic patient will help the individual to be aware of the possible complications of the disease and the need for developing an informed food plan.

- Some primary complications of diabetes mellitus include hypoglycemia, ketoacidosis, and diabetic coma. Secondary complications can appear many years after diagnosis. Diabetic coronary artery disease, strokes, retinopathy, nephropathy, neuropathy, and atherosclerosis are a few secondary complications.

- Basic foot care is important for diabetic patients. It is important for a patient to recognize potential problems with circulation and to report any injuries to the feet.

- A fasting blood glucose test uses a blood sample taken usually the first thing in the morning after the individual has been without food or drink (fasting) for a period of 12 hours. The fasting sample is a more accurate assessment of the blood glucose level than is a random blood glucose sample because of the fasting state.

- A glucose tolerance test (GTT) is a blood test to measure the body's ability to metabolize a concentrated oral glucose load. The GTT starts with a fasting blood glucose and measures the glucose levels from 1 to 5 hours.

- Glycosylated hemoglobin test accurately measures the glucose control of a diabetic for the preceding 5 to 6 weeks. The blood test may be performed without a fasting specimen.

- A type 1 diabetic can be treated with controlled doses of insulin; a mild case of type 2 diabetes can be controlled with exercise and diet. More severe cases of type 2 diabetes need medication to control sensitivity to insulin or to add insulin to the body.

- Various types of blood testing are available to provide management options. In the clinical setting, a diabetic can have a fasting level or a hemoglobin A_{1C} to measure the fasting or the level of the glucose of the RBCs of the past weeks. Many hand-held glucose monitors are available to fit the individual needs of the diabetic's lifestyle.

CHAPTER 44

Assisting in Cardiology

Key Points

- The heart is a muscular organ that pumps blood through all the arteries of the body, thus circulating a continuous supply of oxygen and nutrients to the cells and picking up the metabolic waste products from them.

- It has three layers of tissue surrounded by a double-membrane sac called the pericardium; the epicardium or the first layer of the heart; the middle muscular layer or the myocardium; and the inner layer, the endocardium, which forms the heart valves.

- The blood flow through the heart begins in the right atrium, which receives deoxygenated blood from the inferior and superior vena cavae. The right atrium contracts, and blood passes through the tricuspid valve into the right ventricle. The right ventricle contracts, and the blood passes from the right ventricle to the lungs via the pulmonary artery. Oxygenation occurs in the lungs, and the blood returns to the left atrium through the pulmonary veins. The left atrium contracts, and blood passes through the mitral (bicuspid) valve into the left ventricle. The left ventricle contracts, and oxygen-rich blood is sent out to the body through the aorta (the largest artery in the body).

- Multiple risk factors for cardiac disease include genetic predisposition and familial history; hypertension; diabetes; and elevated blood cholesterol levels. Lifestyle factors, including high-fat, high-caloric diets; obesity; smoking; lack of exercise; hypertension; and stress also contribute to premature death of cardiovascular disease.

- In coronary artery disease, the arteries supplying the myocardium become narrowed by atherosclerotic plaques. The process causes narrowing of the lumen of the arteries and inhibition of the normal flow of blood, thus depriving the heart of an adequate nutritious blood supply. The cardinal symptom of myocardial ischemia is angina pectoris, followed by pressure or fullness in the chest, syncope, edema, unexplained coughing spells, and fatigue.

- Women may exhibit a different clinical picture from that traditionally expected in men. Ischemia over a prolonged period leads to necrosis of a portion of the myocardium, resulting in a myocardial infarction (MI).

- Symptoms of an MI are very similar to those of angina, but MI is identified by pain lasting longer than 30 minutes that is unrelieved by rest or nitroglycerin tablets. An MI is diagnosed by electrocardiogram changes and elevated cardiac enzymes 6 to 12 hours after the episode.

- Medical treatment includes the use of thrombolytic medications to dissolve the coronary artery blockage, aspirin and β-blockers, angiotensin-converting enzyme (ACE) inhibitors, anticoagulants, and anticholesterol agents. When occlusion has taken place in one of the two coronary arteries that supply blood to the myocardium, either percutaneous transluminal coronary angioplasty or open-heart surgery may be indicated.

- The two types of hypertension are primary and secondary. Secondary hypertension occurs because of a disease process in another body system, and primary hypertension is idiopathic and is diagnosed if the patient's blood pressure is consistently greater than 140/90.

- Chronic elevated blood pressure can result in left ventricular hypertrophy, angina, MI, or heart failure. Hypertension also is a major cause of stroke and nephropathy.

- Some of the risk factors for developing hypertension include a family history of hypertension or stroke, hypercholesterolemia, smoking, high sodium intake, diabetes, excessive alcohol intake, aging, prolonged stress, and race.

- Congestive heart failure occurs when the myocardium is unable to pump an adequate amount of blood to meet the needs of the body. It typically develops over time because of weakness in the left ventricle from chronic hypertension or MI of the ventricular wall; valvular heart disease; or pulmonary complications.

- Typically, heart failure initially occurs on one side of the heart followed by the other side.

- Left heart failure is usually due to essential hypertension or left ventricle disease, whereas right heart failure can develop from lung disease.

- Left heart failure causes a backup of blood in the lungs, resulting in pulmonary edema. Signs and symptoms include dyspnea, orthopnea, nonproductive cough, rales, and tachycardia.

- Right-sided heart failure causes a backup of blood in the right atrium, which prevents complete emptying of the vena cava, resulting in systemic edema, especially in the legs and feet.

- Both types of heart failure cause fatigue, weakness, exercise intolerance, dyspnea, and sensitivity to cold temperatures.

- Rheumatic heart disease develops because of an unusual immune reaction that occurs approximately 2 weeks after an untreated β-hemolytic streptococcal infection.

- The inflammation in the heart can involve all layers of heart tissue.

- Endocarditis is the most common heart complication.

- Vegetations form along the outer edges of the valve cusps, causing scarring and stenosis.

- Disorders of the valves of the heart may be caused by a congenital defect or an infection such as endocarditis or rheumatic heart disease. Two specific problems can occur with valve disease.

- The valve can be stenosed, which restricts the forward flow of blood, or it can be incompetent, so blood can leak backward.

- The most common valve defect is mitral valve prolapse (MVP), an incompetence in the mitral valve, because of a congenital defect or vegetation and scarring from endocarditis.

- Blood vessels are divided into two systems that begin and end with the heart. Vessels are classified according to their structure and function as arteries, which carry oxygenated blood away from the heart; capillaries, the microscopic vessels that are responsible for the exchange of oxygen and carbon dioxide in the tissue; and veins, the vessels that carry deoxygenated blood back to the heart.

SHOCK

- Shock is the general collapse of the circulatory system including decreased cardiac output, hypotension, and hypoxemia. Initial signs are extreme thirstiness, restlessness, and irritability. The body attempts to compensate for the circulatory collapse with vasoconstriction of peripheral blood vessels, so blood may be pooled in the vital organs. This vasconstriction causes a generalized feeling of cool, clammy skin; pallor; tachycardia; and decreased urinary output.

- Symptoms progress to a rapid, weak, and thready pulse; tachypnea; and altered levels of consciousness. If the process is not reversed, the central nervous system becomes depressed, and acute renal failure may occur.

- Varicose veins are dilated, tortuous, superficial veins that develop because the valves do not completely close, allowing blood to flow backward, thus causing the vein to distend from the increased pressure.

- Deep vein thrombosis is a thrombus with inflammatory changes that has attached to the deep venous system of the lower legs and caused a partial or complete obstruction of the vessel. If a thrombus becomes dislodged and begins to circulate through the general circulation, it is then called an embolus.

- Arteriosclerosis is a general term for the thickening and loss of elasticity of arterial walls associated with the aging process. Arteriosclerosis can occur in arteries throughout the body and cause systemic ischemia and necrosis over time.

- Atherosclerosis is a form of arteriosclerosis in which there is the formation of an atheroma, a buildup of cholesterol, cellular debris, and platelets along the inside vessel wall.

- An aneurysm is a ballooning or dilation of the wall of a vessel caused by weakening of the vessel wall.

- Cardiovascular diagnostic procedures include Doppler studies of the patency of blood vessels; angiography to visualize arterial pathways; echocardiography to assess the structure and movement of the parts of the heart, especially the valves; and cardiac catheterization to visualize the heart chambers, valves, and coronary arteries.

CHAPTER 45

Assisting in Geriatrics

Key Points

- In the 2000 census, 12.4% (or approximately one in eight) of the U.S. population was older than 65 years. The "oldest old" (people older than 85) are the most rapidly growing age group. It is projected that people older than 65 will represent 16% of the population in 2020 and increase to 20% by 2030.

- The aging population will affect all aspects of society. To provide better services to the aging consumer, it is necessary to understand the aging process, which includes the physical and sensory changes encountered by older people. This knowledge enables the healthcare professional to recognize the special needs of the aged and to develop effective management and communication skills for better service to the older client.

- Table 45-1 summarizes the changes in anatomy and physiology associated with aging. These changes occur across all body systems. Normal age-related changes can be expected and compensated for, but these become more serious in the presence of poor health habits and chronic disease.

- General changes include a(n):
  - increase in arteriosclerosis;
  - increase in time needed to learn new material;
  - sharp decline in estrogen for women and increased risk of osteoporosis;
  - increase in malabsorption problems and constipation;
  - decrease in muscle mass,
  - tendency to gain weight, and deterioration of joint cartilage;
  - decreased elasticity of lung tissue;
  - presbycusis and presbyopia; and
  - the prostate enlarges, and bladder muscles weaken.

- All of these age-related changes can be managed through regular aerobic exercise and strength training; weight control; a diet rich in fruits, vegetables, whole grains, and low in fat; avoidance of sun damage to skin; pelvic muscle exercises; and annual physical examinations with health screening.

- The major health issues for aging people are related to an increase in atherosclerosis and potential cardiovascular disease:
  - hypertension;
  - type 2 diabetes mellitus;
  - tendency toward hyperthermia and hypothermia;
  - seborrheic keratosis;
  - arthritis; osteoporosis; increased risk of injury from falls;
  - dementia due to metabolic, cardiovascular, or Alzheimer's disease;
  - pneumonia, aspiration, and reactivation of tuberculosis;

– cataracts, glaucoma, and macular degeneration; depression; malnutrition; increased urinary tract infections,
– incontinence, and prostate enlargement;
– menopausal changes in the vaginal mucosa;
– sleep disorders such as apnea and periodic leg movement disorder (PLMD); and
– the impact of medications on general health.

- A commonly used screening tool for dementia is the Folstein Mini Mental Status Exam, a 5-minute screening test designed to evaluate basic mental function in the patient's ability to recall facts, write, and calculate numbers. It provides the physician with a quick way to determine whether more in-depth testing is needed.

- To screen for depression, the physician may use the Geriatric Depression Scale short form, which questions the patient about daily activities, interests, and feelings.

- Nutritional status can be assessed through a comprehensive patient interview that considers all potential barriers to adequate nutrition.

- The medical assistant can contribute to determining the nutritional status of older patients by considering oral health, gastrointestinal (GI) complaints, sensorimotor changes, diet influences, and social and mental influences when conducting patient interviews.

- Complaints of sleeping difficulties increase with age. The amount of time spent sleeping may be slightly longer than that for a younger person, but the quality of sleep decreases. Older people are often light sleepers and experience periods of wakefulness in bed. The amount of time spent in the deepest stages of sleep decreases with age. Other factors that might influence sleep patterns are medications, caffeine, alcohol, depression, and environmental or physical changes. Common sleep problems in older adults include PLMD, in which the person experiences periodic jerking of the legs during sleep, and sleep apnea.

- Aging persons prefer to remain in their home environment as long as possible. Adult day care centers can provide supervision for older adults who may be taken care of by family members in the evening but need care during the day. They also serve as respite for a caregiver.

- Assisted-living facilities can be retirement homes or board-and-care homes. These facilities are appropriate for older adults who need assistance with some activities of daily living, such as bathing, dressing, and walking. Skilled nursing facilities provide 24-hour medical care and supervision. In addition to medical care, residents receive care including physical, personal, occupational, and speech therapy.

- The medical assistant's role in caring for the older patient is to develop effective communication skills that are reflective of age-related sensorimotor changes. To reinforce independence, aging patients require more time, so should be scheduled for longer appointments.

- Adequate lighting in the waiting room with forms in large print; an examination room that is equipped with furniture, magazines, and treatment folders especially designed for the elderly patient; and inviting a professional in the management of the elderly patient for in-service training improves the quality of elder care.

- Ask the patient directly what is wrong rather than discussing the patient with family members. Give the patient your full attention rather than continuing with multiple tasks while he or she is speaking. Older people may take a little longer to process information, but they are capable of understanding. Do not hurry through explanations or questions, but take time to review a form or give instructions. Use referrals and community resources for patient and family support.

- Effective communication with aging patients includes addressing the patient with an appropriate title; introducing yourself and the purpose of a procedure before touching the patient; establishing eye contact and getting the patient's attention before beginning to speak; using expanded speech, gestures, demonstrations, or written instructions in block print; repeating the message as needed for understanding; observing the patient's nonverbal behaviors as cues to indicate if he or she understands; allowing time to process information; avoiding distractions; and involving family members as needed.

- Legal and ethical issues for aging patients include obtaining adequate informed consent; using of advance directives; and staying alert for signs of possible elder abuse.

CHAPTER 46

Principles of Electrocardiography

Key Points

- The heart beats in response to an electrical signal that originates in the sinoatrial (SA) node in the right atrium, spreads over the atria, and causes atrial contraction.

- This impulse continues to the atrioventricular (AV) node, through the bundle of His, and then through the right and left bundle branches, eventually causing ventricular contraction.

- The horizontal lines on the electrocardiogram (ECG) paper permit the determination of the intensity of the electrical activity or the relative strength of the heartbeat.

- The stronger the beat, the greater the vertical deflection on the paper. The vertical lines represent time.

- The large squares each represent 0.2 seconds. Five of them equal 1 second.

- Taking an ECG requires knowledge of where to place the electrodes accurately and how to connect the leads to obtain the most accurate recording possible.

- The medical assistant also must be able to recognize and correct the most common types of artifacts on the ECG recording.

- Patient preparation for an ECG or a stress test includes explaining why and how the procedure is to be done.

- When the patients understands the test, their fears are allayed, and they are much less anxious during the testing procedure.

- The P wave results from the contraction or depolarization of the atria.

- The QRS complex results from the contraction or depolarization of the ventricles.

- The T wave occurs when the ventricles relax or repolarize, getting ready for the next contraction.

- The 12-lead ECG consists of three limb leads (I, II, and III), three augmented leads (aVR, aVL, and aVF), and six precordial or chest leads (V_1, V_2, V_3, V_4, V_5, and V_6).

- These leads record the electrical activity from different directions, giving the physician a picture of the functioning of different areas of the heart.

CHAPTER 47

Assisting in Diagnostic Imaging

Key Points

- Radiography and fluoroscopy are both x-ray imaging procedures with a wide variety of applications. Often both techniques are used for a single study.

- Radiography produces still images, usually on photographic film, whereas fluoroscopy enables the radiologist to view the x-ray image directly and to observe motion.

- Magnetic resonance imaging uses a strong magnetic field and radio-wave pulses to produce images of all parts of the body, including bone, soft tissue, and blood vessels.

- Nuclear medicine studies demonstrate the functions of organs and tissues by mapping the radiation given off within the body when radioactive tracers have been ingested or injected into the patient.

- Sonography is a very safe imaging method that demonstrates soft tissues by using high-frequency sound waves.

- Preparation for chest radiography involves undressing to the waist and donning a gown; for an upper gastrointestinal (GI) series, the patient must fast and avoid water, chewing gum, and smoking for at least 8 hours before the examination; preparation for a lower GI series is an extensive bowel cleansing that may involve a low-residue or clear-liquid diet, forced fluids, cathartics, a suppository, and a low-volume enema.

- Preparation for intravenous urethrography (IVU) requires some bowel preparation, such as a cathartic on the previous evening, and nothing by mouth (NPO) orders for a period before the examination.

- When a computed tomography (CT) examination of the abdomen with an oral contrast medium is scheduled, the patient may be instructed to fast, and must arrive at the imaging center from 1 to 2 hours in advance to drink the oral contrast medium.

- The principal components of the x-ray machine are the tube in its barrel-shaped housing. The collimator is mounted on the tube housing.

- The tube housing with its attachments is mounted on the tube support, which may be suspended from the ceiling or attached to a tube stand that runs in a track on the floor.

- The radiographic table and an upright cassette holder provide support for the patient and the film and incorporate a grid device. The control console in the control booth is where the operator selects the exposure settings and makes the exposure.

- The three body planes are the sagittal plane that divides the body into right and left parts, the coronal plane that divides the body into anterior and posterior parts, and the transverse plane that divides the body into superior and inferior parts.

- For a frontal projection (anteroposterior [AP] or posteroanterior [PA]), the coronal plane is parallel to the film, and the sagittal plane is perpendicular to it. For a lateral projection, the sagittal plane is parallel to the film, and the coronal plane is perpendicular to it. Neither the sagittal plane nor the coronal plane is parallel to the film on an oblique projection.

- For a PA projection, the patient is facing the film, with the coronal plane parallel to the film. Lateral projections require the coronal plane to be perpendicular to the film.

- For an oblique projection, neither the coronal nor the sagittal plane is parallel to the film. For an axial or semiaxial projection, the x-ray beam is angled toward the patient's head or feet, along the long axis of the body.

- The image-receptor system for radiography usually consists of a cassette with two intensifying screens that give off light when stimulated by x-ray energy, and double-emulsion film that lies between the intensifying screens.

- The film is exposed on both sides, principally by the light emitted from the screens. This system greatly reduces the amount of radiation and exposure time involved in making exposures compared with direct exposure of film by x-rays.

- Cassettes are unloaded and reloaded in the darkroom under safelight illumination only.

- Precautions include ensuring that the door is locked, that your hands are clean and dry, and that the film is not creased, bent, or scraped in the process of loading and unloading.

- Take care that the cassette is reloaded with only one fresh film and latched securely.

- Keep the loading bench clean to prevent dirt from getting into the cassette.

- Film identification is essential for knowing the identity of the patient represented in the image and the date and location of the examination. Serious errors in diagnosis and treatment might occur if films are not correctly identified.

- The identification information is typed on a card that is inserted into a photographic printer in the darkroom. The printer stamps the information on the film after it is removed from the cassette and before it is processed.

- The health risks associated with radiography are extremely small and consist of a slightly increased likelihood of developing cataracts, cancer, or leukemia.

- There also is a potential for minimal decrease in life span and for a negative outcome when exposure occurs to the abdominal area during pregnancy.

- Exposure to the reproductive organs may cause genetic changes that can be passed on to future generations.

- The principal safety precaution for x-ray equipment operators and staff is to stay completely behind the lead barrier of the control booth during exposures. Occupationally exposed persons must not hold patients or cassettes during exposures.

- Any staff required to be in the x-ray room during an exposure should be shielded by a lead apron, should stay as far from radiation sources as possible, and should minimize the time they are in the room.

- The risks associated with x-ray exposure during pregnancy are very small, unless the exposure is in excess of 5 rad to the abdominal area. These risks include the possibility of spontaneous abortion, birth defects, growth retardation, and cancer or leukemia in childhood.

- Inadvertent exposure during pregnancy is avoided by posting warning signs in the x-ray department and by asking women of childbearing age whether there is any possibility that they may be pregnant.

- Diagnostic images are the property of the facility in which they are made. They are a part of the legal medical record and must be retained and accessible for a period specified by state law, usually 5 to 7 years.

- Images may be loaned or transferred to other healthcare providers to assist in the patient's care, in which case, the patient signs a release, the images are sent directly to the borrowing provider if possible, and a record is kept of the loan.

- Only licensed practitioners of the healing arts are permitted to order x-ray examinations or to interpret x-ray images.

CHAPTER 48

Assisting in the Clinical Laboratory

Key Points

- The clinical laboratory is responsible for analysis of blood and body fluids, providing the physician with test results that become part of the essential data needed to diagnose and manage a patient's condition.

- Most physicians' offices that perform laboratory testing will do so in the areas of urinalysis, hematology, chemistry, and microbiology. Routine urinalysis, complete blood counts, pregnancy testing, and throat cultures are some of the tests that might be performed in an office laboratory.

- United States government agencies that regulate the laboratory include the U.S. Department of Labor, the U.S. Department of Health and Human Services, and the Environmental Protection Agency (EPA). Professional agencies that provide guidelines include the national Committee for Clinical Laboratory Standards and the College of American Pathologists.

- Although all of the agencies provide recommendations for procedures in the clinical laboratory, not all have the power of enforcing them. The U.S. Dept of Labor and the EPA can impose stiff fines for failing to follow regulations, but the standard precautions set forth by the Centers for Disease Control are recommended but not enforceable.

- Risks can be minimized in all areas of the laboratory by using common sense and by having a formal safety training program and an up-to-date safety manual.

- The laboratory requisition must have all information needed to identify the patient, the ordering physician, the test ordered, and the specific details regarding the collection (such as time and source) of the specimen.

- Chain of Custody is a method used to ensure that a specimen provided by a patient who may be involved in a legal matter is handled in a fashion that will not compromise the test results.

- All individuals who handle or test the specimen must be identified in writing and provide a signature.

- Quality assurance involves procedures undertaken to ensure that each patient is provided excellent care. Quality control—ensuring that laboratory testing is accurate and reliable—is part of a quality-assurance program.

- Greenwich time uses the designation of a.m. and p.m., whereas military time uses the 24-hour clock, so that 3:15 p.m. is equivalent to 1515.

- Although the Celsius (Centigrade) thermometer is used in the clinical laboratory, in everyday life, we use the Fahrenheit system. The incubator is usually set at 37° C (98° F), the autoclave sterilizes at 121° C (254° F), and refrigerator temperature is 2° to 8° C (35 to 46° F).

- Liquid volume is measured in liters, distance is measured in meters, and mass is measured in grams. Prefixes commonly used in the clinical laboratory include milli (0.001), centi (0.01), micro (0.000001), deci (0.1), and kilo (1000).

- Pipettes must be chosen according to the job they are to perform. A pipetting device such as a bulb or pump should be attached, and particular attention must be given to the emptying of the pipette. The mouth should never be used in pipetting.

- Dilutions are prepared by mixing volumes of sample such as blood, body fluids, or reagents, and volumes of diluent such as water, saline, or buffer. The term *dilution* refers to parts in total volume and is an expression of concentration.

- The parts of the microscope can be divided into the illumination system (light source, condenser, and iris diaphragm lever), the frame (base, adjustment knobs, arm, stage, stage control), and the magnification system (objective lenses on the revolving nosepiece, oculars).

- Centrifuges are available for different types of centrifugation needs. The proper tube must be used, and it must be protected from breakage. Centrifuge loads must be carefully balanced. Specimens must be capped to prevent aerosols. Under no circumstances should centrifuges be opened while they are in operation.

- Autoclaves provide sterilization by exposing materials to steam under pressure. The steam must reach a temperature of 121° C. Specialized tape or spore strips must be used to ensure that the proper temperature has been reached.

CHAPTER 49

Assisting in the Analysis of Urine

Key Points

- Routine urinalysis is performed primarily as a screening test to detect metabolic and physiologic disorders.

- Urine is formed through a filtration mechanism in the kidney via the nephrons. It is stored in the bladder and voided through the urethra.

- Some urine collections must be timed around meals or fasts. Routine urinalysis requires no special preparation, whereas a clean catch midstream requires cleansing of the external genitalia. Only urine that will be cultured must be collected in a sterile container

- The physical examination of the urine involves determination of color, turbidity, and specific gravity. Odor and foam color may be noted.

- The chemical examination of urine involves determination of levels of glucose, pH, protein, ketones, blood, bilirubin, urobilinogen, nitrite, specific gravity, and leukocyte esterase.

- Formed elements in the urine sediment include casts, cells, and crystals. Artifacts may be present, but they are not reported.

- Timed urine specimens are collected to determine the amount of a particular analyte in the urine during a given time frame.

- Proper patient instruction is necessary for an acceptable clean-catch midstream urine sample. Both men and women are given instructions for cleaning the external genitalia to avoid contaminating the urine.

- A complete urinalysis involves the physical assessment, chemical assessment, and microscopic assessment. The three must correlate with each other.

- Most testing of urine requires reagent strips or tablets. It is essential that these supplies be stored in dark, cool, moisture-free areas.

- The Clinitest detects reducing sugars, including glucose, in the urine. It is superior to the reagent strip test because it detects sugars other than glucose.

- The sulfosalicylic acid test is a precipitation test that evaluates the amount of protein in the urine.

- Pregnancy testing done in the physician's office laboratory is based on the same principle as the tests available over the counter. Pregnancy tests detect human chorionic gonadotropin, a hormone produced by the placenta.

CHAPTER 50

Assisting in Phlebotomy

Key Points

- Venipuncture requires the following equipment: a double-pointed needle, evacuated collection tubes, and an adapter or a syringe fitted with a needle, a tourniquet, an alcohol prep pad, gauze or cotton, a sterile bandage, latex gloves, and biohazard disposal container.

- The tourniquet is used to prevent venous flow out of the site, causing the veins to bulge. This makes veins easier to locate and puncture.

- The venipuncture needle has a shaft with one end cut at an angle (bevel). The other end attaches to the syringe or to an adapter and is called the hub.

- The opening in the tip is called the lumen and is measured in gauge numbers. Needles should be disposed of in a sharps container, and the medical assistant should avoid recapping a needle.

- Syringes are more commonly used for blood collection from the elderly, whose veins tend to be more fragile; from children, whose veins tend to be small; and from the obese, whose veins tend to be deep. Using a syringe allows a more controlled draw.

- A winged infusion set (butterfly) is used on blood draws from the hand and from children. The needle has a small lumen and is more easily inserted into small veins.

- Whole blood will coagulate unless mixed with an anticoagulant. Many are available, and the anticoagulant must be matched with the test to avoid interfering with results.

- When clotted blood is centrifuged, the cells and liquid separate; the liquid portion is referred to as serum. When anticoagulated blood is centrifuged, the liquid that remains is referred to as plasma.

- Evacuated tubes should be collected in a specific order to prevent carryover of tube additives.

- The routine venipuncture begins with greeting and identifying the patient. The medical assistant then assembles the equipment, locates the vein, draws the blood, removes and properly disposes of the needle, tends to the puncture site, labels the tubes, and delivers them to the laboratory. The medical assistant observes standard precautions during the procedure.

- Tourniquets are snugly tied around the upper arm (or wrist for a hand draw) in a fashion that permits easy release. Leaving the tourniquet on for a prolonged period results in hemoconcentration.

- Needles are inserted into the vein at a 15- to 30-degree angle. This angle may have to be increased for obese patients. Do not probe excessively if you are unsuccessful. This may lead to a hematoma or nerve damage. Before the needle is removed, release the tourniquet. Immediately after removal, apply pressure to the puncture site with gauze.

- The median cephalic vein is the vein of choice for phlebotomy, but blood can be drawn from the cephalic vein and the median basilic vein. Avoid the basilic vein if possible.

- Capillary puncture is preferred to venipuncture for certain tests such as hematocrit or hemoglobin analysis, and it also is routinely performed on children younger than 2 years.

- The middle two fingers (the lateral sides of each) are generally used for capillary puncture; in infants, the heel is the site of choice. The center of the heel must be avoided.

- Dermal puncture devices are made of sharp sterile metal. Some are designed to make a cut of a specified depth, and some have internal safety devices that retract the blade after use.

- Capillary blood can be collected in microtainer devices, capillary pipettes, or on filter paper test cards.

- Capillary puncture is performed much like venipuncture. No tourniquet is used, however. The first drop of blood is routinely wiped away after the puncture because it is contaminated with tissue fluid.

CHAPTER 51

Assisting in the Analysis of Blood

Key Points

- The hematology section of the laboratory deals with the *counting* of red blood cells, white blood cells, and platelets; *differentiating* white blood cells on a stained smear; *measuring* the percentage of red blood cells in blood (hematocrit); and *determining* the oxygen-carrying capacity of the blood (hemoglobin).

- The *complete blood cell count (CBC)* is the most frequent laboratory procedure ordered on blood. It gives a fairly complete look at the components of blood and can provide a wealth of information concerning a patient's condition.

- *Whole blood* is composed of formed elements suspended in a clear yellow liquid portion called plasma. Plasma makes up about 55% of the blood by volume.

- The remaining 45% consists of the formed cellular elements, which are the erythrocytes (red blood cells), leukocytes (white blood cells), and thrombocytes (platelets). These cellular elements all have special functions.

- Thrombocytes are not true cells but rather are cytoplasmic fragments of a large cell in the bone marrow, the megakaryocyte. They are the smallest formed elements of the blood. The typical shape is discoid, but when they are activated, they become globular and form finger-like cytoplasmic extensions called *pseudopodia*.

- Plasma is a highly complex liquid is involved in the structure and function of the blood cells.

- Plasma also is the carrier for the formed elements and other substances such as proteins, carbohydrates, fats, hormones, enzymes, mineral salts, gases, and waste products.

- Plasma is composed of about 90% water, 9% protein, and 1% various other chemical substances. When the plasma proteins and other components are used up during the clotting process, the remaining liquid is called *serum*.

- The hematocrit (Hct) is a measurement of the percentage of packed red blood cells in a volume of blood. The test is based on the principle of separating the cellular elements from the plasma and is aided by centrifugation.

- The hemoglobin (Hgb) determination is a rough measure of the oxygen-carrying capacity of the blood. Determining hemoglobin concentration can be performed as part of the CBC or as an individual test.

- The white blood cell count gives an approximation of the total number of leukocytes in circulating blood. The count is performed to aid the physician in determining if an infection is present or to aid in the diagnosis of leukemia. It also may be used to follow the course of a disease and to determine whether the patient is responding to treatment.

- The normal white blood cell count varies with age. It is higher in newborns and decreases throughout life. The average adult range is between 4500 and 12,000 cells/mm^3. Many factors affect the white blood cell count. An increase in white blood cell numbers is called *leukocytosis*.

- A blood smear allows viewing the cellular components of the blood in as natural a state as possible. The morphology of the leukocytes, erythrocytes, and platelets can be studied. Their size, shape, and maturity can be evaluated. Examining a blood smear is part of a CBC.

- The erythrocyte sedimentation rate (ESR) is a laboratory test that measures the rate at which erythrocytes gradually separate from plasma and settle to the bottom of a specially calibrated tube in an hour. The test is not specific for a particular disease but is used as a general indication of inflammation. Increases are found in such conditions as acute and chronic infections, rheumatoid arthritis, tuberculosis, hepatitis, cancer, multiple myeloma, rheumatic fever, and lupus erythematosus.

- Coagulation testing is usually performed in the hematology laboratory. The medical assistant may be asked to perform a test to determine prothrombin time by using a hand-held, Clinical Laboratories Improvement Act (CLIA)-waived instrument that uses whole blood or citrated plasma. The "protime" (or prothrombin time) is a method of measuring how well the blood clots.

- Serologic testing provides information about past or present infections by antigen–antibody reactions. Most serologic testing done in the physician's office is done with individual testing kits. When performing a serologic test, the first step is to review the package insert provided by the manufacturer.

- CLIA-waived tests that can be performed by a medical assistant include bladder tumor associated antigen (BTA), *Helicobacter pylori* antibodies, and infectious mononucleosis antibodies. The BTA test is a rapid, single-step immunoassay. The disposable test device contains two monoclonal antibodies that detect the presence of an antigen shed by the bladder cells. To use the BTA test, five drops of urine are placed into the sample well of the test device, and positive or negative results are provided in 5 minutes.

- There are two major blood antigen systems: the ABO (or Landsteiner) system and the Rh system. In the ABO system, there are four major blood groups: A, B, O, and AB. A person is either Rh positive or Rh negative.

CHEMISTRY

- Increasingly, clinical chemistry testing is performed in the physician's office laboratory. Several clinical chemistry tests are CLIA-waived and can be performed by the medical assistant.

- Glucose is used as a fuel by many of the cells within the body; under normal circumstances, it is the only substance used by the brain. Maintenance of blood glucose levels within the normal range is vitally important to the homeostasis of the acid–base balance of the human body. Understanding the importance of glucose helps in understanding why glucose is the most frequently tested analyte.

- Cholesterol is a fat-like substance (lipid) present in cell membranes. It also is needed to form bile acids and steroid hormones. Cholesterol travels in the blood in distinct particles containing both lipid and proteins. These particles are called lipoproteins. The cholesterol level in the blood is determined partly by inheritance and partly by acquired factors such as diet, calorie balance, and level of physical activity.

- During the last two decades, diabetes researchers have developed several new laboratory tests that help in the evaluation of blood glucose level. These tests are named glycohemoglobin, fructosamine, and glycosylated protein tests. These are not substitutes for monitoring blood glucose levels. Instead, they give different information about the diabetic's health and add a new dimension to the evaluation of diabetes.

- Automated blood chemistry analyzers are often used to perform blood chemistry testing. It is not uncommon for several analytes to be detected at once. The physician may order a chemistry panel, such as a renal or liver panel, to determine the levels of several related analytes.

TOXICOLOGY

- Toxicology is the study of poisonous substances and their effects on the body. The toxicology laboratory performs testing on body fluids and tissues to monitor therapeutic drugs such as digoxin (a cardiac medication) and theophylline (an asthma medication), or to detect poisonings by herbicides, metals, animal toxins, and poisonous gasses (such as carbon monoxide).

- Laboratory testing for illegal drugs or alcohol also is done. Most commonly it is done as an employment, insurance, or governmental requirement. Although serum (blood) testing is more accurate for current impairment and/or time of ingestion, urine is the specimen of choice for most routine screening.

- For routine screening, a random specimen is usually collected. Often safeguards ensure that the specimen is fresh and truly from the patient. In some cases, a strict chain of custody is required. The substance being tested for or its metabolite often remains in the urine much longer than the impairment or intoxication. This is one reason that urine screening is favored over serum or blood screening.

CHAPTER 52

Assisting in Microbiology

Key Points

- Specimens for the microbiology laboratory must be collected in sterile containers. Transport systems are available if the specimen cannot be plated immediately. These systems often contain a transport medium that keeps the organisms alive but does not let them multiply.

- All microbes require nutrients to stay alive. Aerobes require oxygen; anaerobes die in the presence of oxygen. Most pathogens prefer an incubation temperature of 37° C.

- Viruses differ from bacteria in that they are not cells. Viruses are composed of a core of nucleic acid surrounded by a protein coat. They do not metabolize, and they cannot replicate on their own.

- Bacteria are prokaryotic, whereas fungi, protozoa, and parasites are eukaryotic. Many different species cause disease.

- Identification of bacteria begins with the observation of their morphology. Cocci are spherical organisms, bacilli are rod-shaped, and spirilla are spiral-shaped.

- Staphylococci are cocci in clusters; streptococci and streptobacilli are the organisms arranged in chains; and diplococci and diplobacilli refer to the organisms arranged in pairs.

- The most important stain in microbiology is the Gram stain. The four steps of applying the test involve the addition of the primary stain, crystal violet; the mordant, iodine; the decolorizer, alcohol; and the counterstain, safranin. Gram-positive bacteria stain purple, and gram-negative bacteria stain pink or red.

- Growth medium consists of nutrients selected for certain species. A medium can be liquid, or it can be made solid by the addition of agar. Solid media can be prepared as petri plates or as tube media.

- Media can be all-purpose and support the growth of many species. They can be selective, permitting only a certain type of microbe to grow.

- Media also can be differential, allowing differentiation of species based on color changes caused by different biochemical reactions. Enriched media support the growth of fastidious bacteria.

- A number of rapid methods have been developed for use in the laboratory. Generally, these tests identify some component of the infectious agent and do not require culture.

- Antimicrobial susceptibility testing uses disks impregnated with antimicrobial agents dropped onto the surface of an agar plate inoculated with a pathogen.

- The pathogen will display susceptibility, resistance, or an intermediate reaction to the antimicrobial agent. These determinations are made by measuring the zone of inhibition around each disk and comparing with a chart provided by the manufacturer.

- The medical assistant must be aware that patient confidentiality is of utmost importance but certain infections, such as sexually transmitted diseases and tuberculosis, must be reported to the Centers for Disease Control and Prevention and to the local board of health.

CHAPTER **53**

Surgical Supplies and Instruments

Key Points

- The solutions used in minor surgery include sterile water for mixing with medications or rinsing instruments; sterile saline for injection or wound irrigations; antiseptic skin cleansers such as povidone-iodine (Betadine) or chlorohexidine (Hibiclens) for site preparations; local anesthetics including ethyl chloride or fluori-methane topical applications, as well as lidocaine, chloroprocaine (Nescaine), or bupivacaine (Sensorcaine) injectables.

- These local anesthetics may be packaged with or without epinephrine. The physician also may use topical silver nitrate to control local bleeding.

- Surgical instruments are classified according to their use as cutting, grasping, retracting, probing, or dilating tools.

- The components of the instrument include the type of handle, the closing mechanism, and the jaws. Instrument tips may be either straight or curved.

- Surgical instruments are expensive and must be cared for properly to maintain function and maximize life. Instruments must be examined when purchased for proper working order and possible faults with mechanisms. Stainless steel instruments should be kept separate from other metal types.

- Each instrument must be cleaned according to manufacturer guidelines, unlocked, and disinfected immediately after use. Some instruments must be washed by hand with a mild, low-sudsing neutral pH solution and soft brush. Most instruments can be cleaned with an ultrasonic washer, which is an especially good method for sharp instruments to avoid possible injury.

- The instruments used in minor surgical procedures are dependent on the type of procedure and physician preference.

- Many disposable prewrapped surgical packs are available, but if packs are wrapped and autoclaved in the ambulatory care setting, it is important to be familiar with what is needed for a particular procedure as well as what the operating physician prefers to use.

- Suture material is available as absorbable for internal sutures or nonabsorbable for skin closures. Catgut or vicryl are the two most popular absorbable materials, whereas nonabsorbable sutures can be made of silk, nylon, or staples.

- Suture material range in size from smaller gauges for finer tissues below 0 (zero) and thicker gauges above 0 and come in various lengths.

- Surgical needles are either straight or curved. The sharper the curve, the deeper the surgeon can pass the needle. Most needles are manufactured with the suture material attached. A wide range of suture material is packaged attached to a variety of needle types. The medical assistant must ask the physician for his or her preference.

Surgical Asepsis and Assisting with Surgical Procedures

Key Points

- Proper surgical aseptic technique can prevent unnecessary postoperative infections in surgical patients.

- A "break" in technique at any step along the way can have dire consequences for the patient. Everyone on the surgical team is responsible for preventing and correcting breaks in technique.

- Air currents carry bacteria, so body motions over a sterile field and talking should be kept to a minimum.

- Sterile team members should always face each other.

- Always keep the sterile field in your view. Never turn your back on a sterile field or wander away from it.

- Nonsterile persons should never reach over a sterile field.

- EVERYTHING STERILE IS WHITE, and EVERYTHING THAT IS NOT STERILE IS BLACK.

- THERE IS NO GRAY! Sterile surfaces must NEVER come into contact with nonsterile surfaces.

- Indicator can be used to prove that a package was indeed in the steam autoclave during a sterilization run. Other indicators can prove that the contents of the package were exposed to a sufficient temperature for a sufficient length of time to achieve sterilization.

- Muslin wrappers must be inspected before each use for holes and must be discarded if any are found.

- All hinged instruments are wrapped in the open position to allow full steam penetration of the joint.

- Place a gauze sponge around the tips of sharp instruments to prevent them from piercing the wrapping material.

- If a number of instruments are to be placed on a stainless steel tray for wrapping, place a double-folded towel on the tray first and then the instruments. This helps to protect them.

- When using sterilizing bags, insert the jaws of the instruments first to ensure that the grasping end of the instrument can be reached easily when the bag is opened.

- Indicate on the wrapper what is in the package, or label it with a code. This code should correspond to a list of instruments that is stored with the pack after sterilization.

- Label with the contents, the date sterilized, and your initials. Use a permanent marker, and never a ballpoint pen.

- The legal and ethical concerns with regard to infection control affect everyone on the surgical team. It is necessary for all individuals involved in the surgical care of a patient to be aware of all legal and ethical practices that apply to excellent patient care.

- The most important legal concern for all involved is the informed consent, without which surgery cannot be legally performed on the patient without risking the possibility of a charge of battery. The consent also clearly limits what procedure can be done.

- Education of the surgical team takes many forms including using information sheets or pamphlets to be given to the patient before surgery, having conversations with the patient about the procedure, and giving them postoperative information sheets to prevent and minimize complications.

- The informed patient is more relaxed, cooperative, and much more pleasant to deal with when contrasted with the uninformed, frightened patient who did not receive adequate explanations from the surgical office staff.

- When planning office surgery, follow certain procedures the time of the appointment. This should include the following:
  - Have the necessary consent forms ready to sign.
  - Give the patient all the necessary preoperative instructions, such as medications to be used and special skin-cleansing instructions.
  - Tell the patient to bring a relative or friend to drive him or her home after the surgery.
  - Tell the patient to leave jewelry and other valuables at home.
  - Call the patient the day before the scheduled surgery to confirm any special instructions.

CHAPTER 55

Career Development and Life Skills

Key Points

- Because approximately 85% of individuals do not have any formal training in job-search skills, taking time to learn the best methods will place the medical assistant at an advantage.

- Training decreases the time spent looking for work and increases the benefits and salary offered when the applicant uses good negotiating skills. The medical assistant also will be more comfortable during interviews and throughout the job-search process.

- Employers have three basic expectations of their medical assistant employees. They desire an employee with a good appearance, who looks as if he or she fits in the medical profession.

- The medical assistant also should be dependable and have the skills to do the job for which he or she was hired.

- Three types of skill strengths may be used by employees. Job skills are those used to actually perform a job, like venipunctures or scheduling appointments.

- Self-management skills are usually a part of the medical assistant's personality, such as honesty and dependability.

- Transferable skills are those that can be taken from one job to another or used on any job. Examples include the ability to communicate effectively or lead and manage individuals.

- Networking and contacting employers directly are the two best methods of job searching. Networking involves developing a network of individuals that can assist in finding employment. This group may include co-workers, other students, relatives, or friends who provide leads to potential employers.

- Contacting employers directly includes taking resumes to specific offices or setting appointments to gain knowledge about the facility, and then later using that knowledge during the job search. These two methods are more effective than most traditional means of finding a job

- Avoid errors on a resume. Be sure that everything is spelled correctly, but do not rely on the computer spell-check alone. Proofread the document, and have someone else proofread it to catch errors that may be overlooked.

- Salary expectations should never be stated on the resume, and a photograph should not be included. Do not include personal information such as height and weight.

- Demographic information on other employers should be taken to interviews and kept handy when filling out job applications.

- The medical assistant should never have to ask for a phone book to look up the address of a former employer. This demonstrates a lack of preparation and planning on the part of the potential employee.

Test Bank

CHAPTER **1**

Becoming a Successful Student

MATCHING

Directions: Match each term with the correct definition.

a. Learning style
b. Reflection
c. Professional behaviors
d. Processing

e. Empathy
f. Perceiving
g. Critical thinking

_____ 1. The constant practice of considering all aspects of a situation in deciding what to believe or what to do.

_____ 2. Those actions that identify the medical assistant as a member of a healthcare profession, including dependability, respectful patient care, initiative, positive attitude, and teamwork.

_____ 3. How an individual looks at information and sees it as real.

_____ 4. The way an individual perceives and processes information to learn new material.

_____ 5. How individuals internalize new information and make it their own.

_____ 6. The process of considering new information and internalizing it to create new ways of examining information.

_____ 7. Sensitivity to the individual needs and reactions of patients.

COMPLETION

Directions: Fill in the blank with the best answer.

8. Medical assistants play a vital role in the healthcare team and are expected to display such

_____ as dependability, respectful patient care, empathy, initiative, positive attitude, and teamwork.

9. Learning styles are determined by your individual method of _____ or examining new material and the way that you process it or make it your own.

10. _____ can evaluate conflicting information and make a decision to act based on their knowledge and willingness to be open-minded to all possibilities.

11. Learning _____ are the ways that you like to learn and that have proven successful in the past.

12. People are either _____ or abstract perceivers and either _____ or reflective processors.

13. Problem solving and _____ management techniques are key to your success.

14. The first step to reaching a solution to a problem or conflict is to identify the _____ .

15. Methods for determining possible solutions to a conflict are to brainstorm or to make a _____ list.

16. Once you have decided on a solution to the problem, it is essential to _____ the outcomes of your solution and decide whether it solved the problem or whether another approach should be tried.

17. Creating a _____ _____ can be an effective way to represent the main idea of the topic and its important details with a figure or picture.

Word List
Active
Concrete
Conflict
Critical thinkers
Evaluate
Mind map
Perceiving
Preferences
Problem or central issue
Professional behaviors
Pros and cons

SHORT ANSWER

18. Summarize three time management strategies that can help you put time on your side.

19. Identify and explain four study skills that can help you become a successful student.

20. Describe three strategies that can help you become successful at taking tests.

CHAPTER **2**

The Healthcare Industry

MULTIPLE CHOICE

Directions: Circle the letter of the choice that best completes the statement or answers the question.

1. Which of the following statements describes the major contribution of the Greeks and Romans to modern medicine?
   a. the development of the concept of the modern hospital
   b. the formal study of human emotions, such as love and lust
   c. their study and written documentation of many body functions
   d. the mythology on which many medical terms are based

2. How did the studies of the ancient Greek physicians influence the progress of medicine during the period of history known as the "Dark Ages?"
   a. encouraged the founding of research centers and scientific experiments
   b. discouraged further study because these physicians were considered to be the final authority
   c. had no real effect because the early Christians ignored their writings
   d. encouraged the founding of hospitals and the humane treatment of patients

3. Which of the following organizations became the most famous medical school in the world in the 1800s?
   a. Royal Society of London
   b. General Medical Council of Britain
   c. Carnegie Foundation
   d. Johns Hopkins University

4. What was Abraham Flexner's contribution to medical education in North America?
   a. the founding of a statutory body that set standards for physicians
   b. the establishment of admission standards for medical students
   c. the transformation of the curriculum and methods for teaching medicine
   d. the preparation and publication of a report that rated the quality of medical schools

5. Which scientist first described the manner in which the heart functions as a pump that continually circulates the blood?
   a. Edward Jenner
   b. William Harvey
   c. John Hunter
   d. Andreas Vesalius

6. What was John Hunter's major contribution to modern medicine?
   a. development of vaccination as a means of protection against disease
   b. discovery of the nature of tissues with use of the microscope
   c. development of surgical techniques on the basis of pathological evidence
   d. grinding of lenses through which bacteria and protozoa could be observed

7. Smallpox, among other diseases, used to be *pandemic*. This means that it:
   a. was caught by many of the people who lived in a given country
   b. was nearly always fatal for anyone who caught it
   c. was common on farms where people worked closely with animals
   d. was caused by unsanitary conditions and contaminated water

8. What contribution made by Ignaz Philipp Semmelweis drastically reduced deaths that commonly took place in hospitals?
   a. promotion of the use of vaccinations in Hungary
   b. insistence on the disinfection of physicians' hands before assistance with childbirth
   c. encouragement of better educational methods for hospital personnel
   d. discovery that heat killed disease-causing microorganisms in contaminated water

9. Which assumption did Joseph Lister argue against when he made his contribution to medicine?
   a. surgical techniques must be based on an accurate knowledge of human anatomy
   b. sterilization is best achieved with the use of heat
   c. putrefaction is a natural part of the healing process
   d. surgical infection is God given and inevitable

10. The term *chemotherapy* refers to which of the following medical procedures?
    a. treatment of diseases with x-ray examinations
    b. diagnosis of diseases that are caused by chemical agents entering the body
    c. treatment of diseases with injection of chemicals into the body to destroy microorganisms
    d. alleviation of pain with the use of anesthetic agents

11. Which two scientists developed a vaccine that brought polio under control?
    a. Helen Tausig and Alfred Blalock
    b. Albert Sabin and Jonas Salk
    c. Alexander Fleming and Howard Florey
    d. Walter Reed and Sir Frederick Grant Banting

12. Which procedure was first performed by Dr. Christiaan Barnard?
    a. operation to save babies born with malformed hearts
    b. heart transplant from one human to another
    c. catheterization for diagnosis of heart disease
    d. injection of penicillin for the cure of infectious diseases

13. Which of the following statements about the professional corporation form of business organization is NOT true?
    a. the professional employees are liable for their own acts
    b. corporations are not restricted by legal requirements as are smaller sole proprietorships and partnerships
    c. tax advantages exist that are related to fringe benefits for the corporation and its employees
    d. reorganization of the corporation after a change in shareholders is not necessary

14. Which statement best describes the main difference between the DO and the MD?
    a. the training for the DO includes more courses and a longer residency
    b. only the MD can prescribe drugs for the prevention and treatment of disease
    c. the DO places more emphasis on the relationship of musculoskeletal structure to the function of organs and tissues within the body
    d. the license for the MD has more requirements and is more difficult to obtain

15. Which healthcare professional is trained to practice medicine under the supervision of a physician?
    a. medical technologist
    b. paramedic
    c. medical assistant
    d. physician assistant

16. Which allied health professional works with a physician who specializes in the care of the eye?
    a. surgical technologist
    b. ophthalmic medical technician
    c. cytotechnologist
    d. audiologist

17. Medical assistants who are interested in learning more about disorders of the skin should apply for employment with a:
    a. dermatologist
    b. allergist
    c. psychiatrist
    d. cosmetic surgeon

18. The medical specialty that deals with the causes of diseases that affect the body is called:
    a. internal medicine
    b. preventive medicine
    c. immunology
    d. pathology

19. The allied health specialist who performs ultrasound diagnostic procedures under the supervision of a physician is called a:
    a. cytotechnologist
    b. diagnostic medical sonographer
    c. electrodiagnostic technologist
    d. perfusionist

20. A medical doctor who specializes in the treatment of disorders of the eye is called an:
    a. otolaryngologist
    b. optometrist
    c. obstetrician
    d. ophthalmologist

21. Which legislation most affects the quality of laboratory reports and results?
    a. OSHA
    b. CLIA
    c. CDC
    d. WHO

22. What type of registered nurse has advanced training to diagnose and treat common illnesses?
    a. anesthetist
    b. practitioner
    c. dietician
    d. practical

23. The agency that most commonly inspects facilities for safety violations is:
    a. CDC
    b. OSHA
    c. CLIA
    d. DHHS

24. A method of prioritizing patients so that the most urgent cases receive care first is called:
    a. case management
    b. accreditation
    c. triage
    d. quality control

25. The caduceus is a staff that historically belonged to:
    a. Apollo
    b. Zeus
    c. Poseidon
    d. Aesculapius

26. The Father of Medicine contributed which of the following advances to medicine?
    a. dissection techniques
    b. more than 500 treatises on medicine
    c. Hippocratic Oath
    d. robotics

27. The organization that is committed to research and delivery of needed drugs and medical supplies to various areas of the world is the:
    a. CDC
    b. WHO
    c. OSHA
    d. DHHS

28. The organization that is a clearinghouse for information and statistics associated with healthcare is:
    a. CDC
    b. USAMRIID
    c. WHO
    d. DHHS

29. The highest level of biosafety that is studied at USAMRIID is:
    a. level II
    b. evel III
    c. level IV
    d. level V

30. Which of the following patients is NOT receiving ambulatory care?
   a. a patient in a freestanding emergency center
   b. a patient in a day surgery center
   c. a hospital inpatient
   d. a patient in a physician's office

31. Which of the following is NOT true about a group practice?
   a. contains three or more physicians in full-time practice
   b. does not share income and expenses
   c. may or may not practice one specific specialty
   d. may or may not form a corporation

32. Which of the following individuals is considered to be one of the most brilliant minds working on the AIDS crisis today?
   a. C. Everett Koop
   b. David Ho
   c. Eve Slater
   d. Antonia Novello

33. Which of the following individuals was the fifth most cited scientist during the period between 1981 and 1994?
   a. Antonia Novello
   b. Marcia Angell
   c. Eve Slater
   d. Anthony Fauci

34. Which of the following physicians are trained to find pressure points and weight distribution problems?
   a. podiatrists
   b. chiropractors
   c. osteopaths
   d. dentists

35. A person who manages systems consistent with the medical, administrative, ethical, and legal requirements of the healthcare delivery system is called:
   a. an orthotist
   b. a medical assistant
   c. a perfusionist
   d. a health information administrator

TRUE OR FALSE

Directions: Circle the best answer.

36.   T   F   An occupational therapist works to help patients regain functions and improve quality of life.

37.   T   F   Chiropractors only treat bone and joint disorders.

38.   T   F   Physician assistants are allowed to write prescriptions in most states.

39.   T   F   Paramedics are usually supervised by MTs.

40. T   F   A standard is an item or indicator that is used as a measure of quality or compliance.

41. T   F   Holistic refers to the individual parts of the body rather than all of its systems.

42. T   F   The first cervical vertebrae is called the axis, on which the head rests.

43. T   F   Doctors of Osteopathy usually practice allopathic medicine.

44. T   F   The Pasteur Institute began as a clinic for rabies treatment.

45. T   F   Clara Barton was also known as the Lady with the Lamp.

COMPLETION

Directions: Fill in the blank with the best answer.

46. A(An) _____ treats life-threatening illnesses and supervises ambulance services.

47. _____ therapists are trained to use oxygen therapy and measure lung capacity.

48. The credentials DDS and DMD are used by _____.

49. Systematic expositions or arguments in writing that include a methodical discussion of the fact and principles involved to reach a conclusion are called _____.

50. _____ are important points or groups of statistical values that indicate the quality of care provided in a healthcare institution.

51. A person who is able to walk and is not bedridden is considered to be _____.

52. The first Hispanic to be named Surgeon General was _____.

53. The principal US agency for providing essential human services is _____.

54. A person who is totally lacking in something of need is said to be _____.

55. The person named Honorary Chairperson for Planned Parenthood when it was formed in 1941 was _____.

56. A(An) _____ is trained in diagnosis and treatment of patients who have conditions related to genetically linked diseases.

57. Things that contribute to comfort, enjoyment, or convenience are called _____.

58. The act of extending medical or professional privileges to an individual is called _____.

59. Any contact between a physician and patient that ends in treatment or evaluation is called a(an)

_____.

60. _____ means existing in, belonging to, or determined by factors present in an individual since birth.

Word List

Encounter
Respiratory
Amenities
Treatises
Paramedic
Innate
Credentialing
Dentists
DHHS
Indicators
Geneticist
Ambulatory
Indigent
Margaret Sanger
Antonia Novello

CHAPTER 3

The Medical Assisting Profession

MULTIPLE CHOICE

Directions: Circle the letter of the choice that best completes the statement or answers the question.

1. How have the advancement of medical technology and the increased use of computers influenced the medical assisting profession?
   a. replaced many medical assistants with more specialized medical employees
   b. limited the responsibilities of medical assistants to clinical tasks
   c. increased the amount of training necessary to become a proficient medical assistant
   d. provided more work opportunities for medical assistants in hospital settings

2. A recent graduate of a comprehensive medical assisting training program could apply for all of the following positions EXCEPT:
   a. medical receptionist
   b. physical therapist assistant
   c. billing and collection specialist
   d. transcriptionist

3. Which of the following skills would NOT be an appropriate expectation of the competent medical assistant?
   a. performing insurance coding and billing
   b. giving instructions to patients about self-care after treatments
   c. using the computer to perform a variety of office functions
   d. diagnosing common patient symptoms

4. Which quality in a medical assistant is most likely to promote positive relations in the medical office?
   a. businesslike behavior
   b. consistent high grades during medical assisting training
   c. attractiveness
   d. sincere interest in patient welfare

5. You are beginning your externship in a large office that has three medical assistants. What is the best way to learn about your job responsibilities?
   a. ask for a job description and clear directions for daily activities
   b. spend a lot of time getting to know the patients
   c. wait politely until someone has time to explain your duties
   d. perform only those tasks that you are directed to do

6. Which statement best describes the relationship of administrative and clinical medical assisting responsibilities?
   a. administrative duties require the least interpersonal contact
   b. both are of equal importance in maintaining a high-quality medical practice
   c. clinical duties offer more variety in the type of work performed
   d. clinical tasks are more difficult to learn than are administrative tasks

7. Which is the most important consideration in choosing a uniform?
   a. it should be becoming and flattering to your body type
   b. it should not be wrinkled by the end of the workday
   c. it should give a professional neat appearance
   d. it should be fashionable

8. Which professional organization also certifies laboratory professionals?
   a. AAMA
   b. American Association of Medical Transcriptionists
   c. Professional Secretaries International
   d. AMT

9. Because they are key public relations representatives for the physicians for whom they work, it is critical that medical assistants NEVER:
   a. perform all duties as quickly and as efficiently as possible
   b. impress patients with their competence
   c. show sincere concern for each patient
   d. tell patients who are ill that they have an excellent chance for recovery

10. What would be the best way for new medical assistant graduates to become good team players in the medical office?
    a. show consideration and appreciation for the experienced staff
    b. share what they learned in school about the latest techniques in healthcare
    c. be careful to only perform those tasks designated in the job description and no other duties
    d. try to develop close friendships with everyone on the staff after working hours

11. Which is NOT a good reason for becoming an active member of a medical assisting professional organization?
    a. improved chances for promotion at work
    b. ensuring fair pay by asking others about their salaries
    c. networking opportunities
    d. professional growth through continuing education

12. The best way to earn a favorable evaluation on your externship would be to:
    a. show integrity and practice high ethical standards
    b. be friendly with your supervisor and other senior staff members and keep co-workers at a distance
    c. impress the physician with your knowledge about medicine
    d. show your willingness by performing tasks that have not been assigned to you even if regular duties are not yet completed

13. Which statement is true regarding the status of students during the externship, as compared with that of regular employees?
    a. students should not waste their supervisor's time asking a lot of questions
    b. students can expect the physician to treat their medical problems
    c. attendance expectations are generally less strict for students
    d. students are expected to perform under the same professional standards as regular employees

14. The first national organization formed for medical assistants was:
    a. CAAHEP
    b. ABHES
    c. AMT
    d. AAMA

15. Which credential is NOT offered by the AMT?
    a. COLT
    b. RMA
    c. CMA
    d. RPT

16. Mandatory means:
    a. embracing a variety of subjects
    b. involving entry into the living body
    c. training in more than one area
    d. containing or constituting a command

17. Extra advantages or benefits from working in a specific job are called:
    a. prerequisites
    b. perks
    c. commissions
    d. extras

18. Why is *bargain help* often the most expensive?
    a. the physician must pay additional taxes for bargain help
    b. bargain help makes the most efficient medical assistants
    c. extra time must be spent in training or correcting mistakes
    d. more benefits are given to bargain help

19. Which of these versatile careers could be entered as a result of medical assistant training?
    a. billing specialist
    b. medical receptionist
    c. coder
    d. all of the above

20. Which of the following are important to remember during an externship?
    a. do not worry about reconciling petty cash
    b. ask the physician to treat your daughter's ear infection
    c. never handle drugs or money without permission
    d. feel free to correct co-workers when they perform a procedure incorrectly

21. What is the biggest difference between the RMA certification and the CMA certification?
    a. the CMA examination is more difficult
    b. the RMA examination is more difficult
    c. the RMA examination is less expensive
    d. one is a professional organization; the other is not

22. Which of the following is NOT a part of the medical assistant's creed?
    a. I am loyal to myself
    b. I endeavor to be more effective
    c. I am true to the ethics of my profession
    d. I aspire to greater service

23. The medical assistant should consider which of these factors when seeking employment?
    a. pay rate
    b. benefits
    c. perks
    d. all of the above

24. The first medical reference listed on a medical assistant graduate's resume is often the:
    a. first paying job
    b. volunteer work done during school
    c. first actual job
    d. externship

25. Continuing educational units are important because they:
    a. are always required
    b. keep the medical assistant up to date with new techniques and information
    c. provide a day off while attending seminars
    d. none of the above

TRUE OR FALSE

Directions: Circle the best answer.

26.   T   F   Both men and women can be equally successful as medical assistants.

27.   T   F   Medical assistants may perform electrocardiography and prepare patients for x-ray examinations.

28.   T   F   Individuals working in the medical assisting field have a mandatory retirement age.

29.   T   F   Most medical assisting positions are in hospitals.

30.   T   F   The medical assisting student should treat the externship experience as a probationary period on an actual job.

31.   T   F   Medical assistants always wear white uniforms.

32.   T   F   Long nails and colored polish are always acceptable in the medical profession.

33.   T   F   Cross training means that one individual is trained to do a variety of duties.

34.   T   F   Something that is incapable of being perceived is said to be intangible.

35.   T   F   Profit sharing is never a part of the benefit package for medical assistants.

COMPLETION

Directions: Fill in the blank with the best answer.

36. Medical assistant organizations at the local and state level began developing around the decade of the _____.

37. Medical assistants are trained on how to collect a blood specimen with _____.

38. Medical assisting attracts _____ students who may be older than the average postsecondary student by a decade or more.

39. Medical assisting today is one of the most respected _____ _____ fields in the healthcare industry.

40. A type of on-the-job training that allows medical assistants to put their skills to use before graduation is called a(an) _____.

41. The awarding of a certificate from a third party on the basis of knowledge demonstrated is called _____.

42. A person with a wide range of abilities or skills is said to be _____.

43. Approximately _____ % of medical assistants work in physician offices.

44. Participation in a recognized professional organization shows that medical assistants take their career _____.

45. A(An) _____ _____ should be worn on the right shoulder of the uniform when working.

46. The AMT offers an examination called the _____ that medical assistants who have clinical duties may wish to take after 6 months of employment.

47. The abbreviation for the AAMA's bimonthly journal is _____.

48. The Department of Labor publication that forecasts occupational trends is called the _____ _____ _____.

49. The amount of medical knowledge gained is said to double every _____ years.

50. Medical assistants should always read the _____ _____ so that they will know what is expected by the employer or externship office.

Word List

CMA Today
Job description
Versatile
1950s
Allied health
Certification
Phlebotomy
Seriously
Occupational Outlook Handbook
Nontraditional
Internship/externship
5
COLT
60
Name tag

CHAPTER **4**

Professional Behavior in the Workplace

MULTIPLE CHOICE

Directions: Circle the letter of the choice that best completes the statement or answers the question.

1. Disobedience to authority is called:
   a. morale
   b. tenacity
   c. insubordination
   d. initiative

2. The mental and emotional condition, enthusiasm, loyalty, or confidence of an individual or group with regard to the function or tasks at hand is called:
   a. morale
   b. tenacity
   c. insubordination
   d. initiative

3. To intentionally put off doing something that should be done is to:
   a. initiate
   b. wait
   c. dominate
   d. procrastinate

4. To talk or widely disseminate opinion with no discernible source, or a statement that is not known to be true, is called:
   a. rumor
   b. libel
   c. discrimination
   d. slander

5. Deciding which tasks are most important is called:
   a. modification
   b. teaching
   c. prioritizing
   d. procrastinating

6. Faithfulness or allegiance to a cause, ideal, custom, institution, or product is called:
   a. flexibility
   b. courtesy
   c. dependability
   d. loyalty

7. A task that is noted as a B priority:
   a. must be done today
   b. should be done today
   c. could be done today
   d. is not a real priority

8. A task that is noted as an E priority is probably a(an):
   a. important task
   b. task that should be done early in the day
   c. errand
   d. extra task for that day

9. When medical assistants look for the opportunity to help and assist others, they are said to be:
   a. taking initiative
   b. flexible
   c. courteous
   d. dependable

10. When medical assistants are able to adapt to various situations, they are considered to be:
    a. dependable
    b. flexible
    c. courteous
    d. loyal

11. Probably the most important asset a medical assistant can offer the employer is:
    a. confidentiality
    b. teamwork
    c. a good attitude
    d. credibility

12. A connotation is:
    a. the mental and emotional condition
    b. something suggested by a word or thing
    c. behavior toward others
    d. exchange of skills

13. Office politics:
    a. are always negative
    b. are always a source of tension
    c. can be positive
    d. are underhanded schemes

14. If medical assistants have a conflict with a co-worker, they should first:
   a. go to the physician
   b. go to the person with whom they have an issue
   c. go to the office manager
   d. resign

15. Confidentiality is important because:
   a. laws protect the patient against breach of confidentiality
   b. the patient has a right to privacy
   c. the patients trust the medical professionals to keep their medical information confidential
   d. all of the above

16. Which is one of the most common physical places where confidentiality is breached?
   a. elevators
   b. examination rooms
   c. the physician's office
   d. the reception room

17. Corresponding in size, amount, extent, or degree and equal in measure is the definition for:
   a. commensurate
   b. characteristics
   c. persona
   d. reproach

18. Which of the following statements about professionalism is NOT true?
   a. it must be practiced at all times in the workplace
   b. it can lead to wage increases and promotions
   c. unacceptable behavior is detrimental to the medical assistant's career
   d. student medical assistants are naturally professional on the externship even if they are not professional at school

19. Note taking can help the medical assistant to:
   a. avoid forgetting orders from the physician
   b. remember dosages for medication
   c. complete duties assigned in a staff meeting
   d. all of the above

20. Which of the following statements is NOT true regarding goal setting?
   a. goals should be reasonable
   b. determination and persistence help the medical assistant to reach goals
   c. celebrating should be delayed until the last goal is reached
   d. goals should be measurable and specific

TRUE OR FALSE

Directions: Circle the best answer.

21.   T   F   When patients have a problem, they should be referred to the person who knows the most about that particular situation.

22.   T   F   Legible neat handwriting can make a huge difference in a lawsuit.

23.   T   F   In some cases, it is acceptable for the medical assistant to share personal difficulties with patients.

24.   T   F   Often the success of a business is directly related to effective communication.

25.   T   F   Personal baggage does not ever interfere with the medical assistant's ability to perform job duties.

26.   T   F   It is not the medical assistant's fault if a poor attitude is displayed after a reprimand by the supervisor.

27.   T   F   Checking personal email several times a day in the medical office is acceptable.

28.   T   F   Credibility is the perceived competence or character of a person.

29.   T   F   The personality that people project in public is their persona.

30.   T   F   Medical assistants should never trade or rotate their duties, even with the permission of the office manager.

COMPLETION

Directions: Fill in the blank with the best answer.

31. When supervisors give a medical assistant a task to do, they count on the medical assistant's _____ so that the task is carried out accurately and in a timely manner.

32. _____ is defined as exhibiting a courteous, conscientious, and generally businesslike manner in the workplace.

33. _____ is the ability to adapt to a wide variety of situations.

34. _____ is the belief that a person can be trusted.

35. _____ is an individual's social façade or front that reflects the role in life that the individual is playing.

36. One of the surest symptoms of a fear of failure is _____.

37. The medical assistant should use some _____ when discussing private personal affairs with the supervisor.

38. Great exaggerations and manipulations of the truth can affect employee _____.

39. When educating the patient, the medical assistant should have a professional _____ of concern and helpfulness.

40. Patients expect professional behavior and base much of their trust and confidence in those who exhibit this type of _____ in the medical office.

Word List
Dependability
Professionalism
Credibility
Demeanor
Morale
Procrastination
Flexibility
Discretion
Persona
Attitude

CHAPTER **5**

Interpersonal Skills and Human Behavior

MULTIPLE CHOICE

Directions: Circle the letter of the choice that best completes the statement or answers the question.

1. Which is NOT likely to be one of the factors that influence the first impression we make on others?
   a. what we say
   b. what we do
   c. what we know
   d. how we look

2. Which of the following is NOT the role of the medical assistant in communicating with patients?
   a. advising
   b. listening
   c. observing
   d. responding

3. Which of the following is NOT one of the stages of grief?
   a. bargaining
   b. depression
   c. dealing
   d. acceptance

4. What is the first step to avoid prejudice when dealing with people?
   a. avoid judging people by their appearance or lifestyle
   b. do not react negatively to others
   c. treat all people with equal respect
   d. honestly examine and evaluate your own personal prejudices

5. The principal reason for requesting feedback when communicating with patients is to determine whether they:
   a. have a vision problem
   b. are cooperative
   c. understand what you are saying
   d. are mentally alert

6. Which aspect of our communication is most likely to convey our true feelings and beliefs?
   a. nonverbal communication
   b. verbal communication
   c. the way we verbalize a phrase or word
   d. spoken words only

7. What is meant by the "litigious nature of today's society?"
   a. crowding has caused people to need more personal space
   b. patients are more likely to bring lawsuits than in the past
   c. a growing diversity of cultures is represented in the United States
   d. fewer people have access to needed medical care

8. The principal message that you will give an American patient if you avoid eye contact while communicating is that you:
   a. are angry
   b. are in a hurry
   c. do not understand what the patient is saying
   d. are not telling the truth

9. Which statement is FALSE regarding the interpretation of gestures and body language that you may encounter among the patients in a medical setting?
   a. they are less significant than verbal communication
   b. they vary widely in meaning
   c. your knowledge of them will influence patient relations
   d. they may require special accommodations

10. The defense mechanism in which unwanted desires or impulses are excluded from the consciousness and left to operate in the unconscious is called:
    a. rationalization
    b. repression
    c. regression
    d. displacement

11. Something that is difficult to understand or perceive is:
    a. internal noise
    b. perception
    c. subtle
    d. volatile

12. Verbal expressions or body language, such as a nod of understanding, are called:
    a. internal noise
    b. external noise
    c. channels
    d. feedback

13. Even when two people are speaking at the same time, various channels of communication are used, such as:
    a. words
    b. body language
    c. facial expressions
    d. all of the above

14. A lack of feeling, emotion, interest, or concern is a defense mechanism called:
    a. apathy
    b. sympathy
    c. projection
    d. denial

15. The psychological defense mechanism in which confrontation with a personal problem or with reality is avoided by denying the existence of the problem or reality is called:
    a. physical avoidance
    b. denial
    c. regression
    d. compensation

16. Sounds or factors outside the brain that interfere with the communication process are called:
    a. internal noise
    b. feedback
    c. external noise
    d. channels

17. That which advances beyond the usual or proper limits is called:
    a. paraphrasing
    b. malediction
    c. litigious
    d. encroachment

18. When patients cry, the medical assistant should never:
    a. ask what is wrong
    b. let the patients leave without reasonable assurance they are safe
    c. tell the physician
    d. call the police

19. If a patient hesitates when speaking, they might:
    a. be lying
    b. have more to say
    c. feel fear
    d. all of the above

20. When patients verbally attack someone without addressing the original complaint, they are using which defense mechanism?
    a. regression
    b. projection
    c. verbal aggression
    d. sarcasm

21. Personal space ranges from:
    a. 1.5 to 4 ft
    b. up to 1.5 ft
    c. 12 to 25 ft
    d. 4 to 12 ft

22. Which of the following patients is probably in shock?
    a. the patient who explodes over every little situation
    b. the patient who bargains with God to live a longer life
    c. the patient who remains calm and speaks clearly during conflict
    d. the patient who cannot think or move

23. The needs we have as humans, at the most basic level, include:
    a. esteem and recognition
    b. love
    c. safety
    d. food and shelter

24. The stage in Maslow's hierarchy of needs in which we maximize our potential is:
    a. self-actualization
    b. esteem and recognition
    c. love and belonging
    d. safety and security

25. Pleasers are people who are most likely looking for:
    a. achievement
    b. acceptance
    c. approval
    d. actualization

26. Dreaming occurs during what stage of sleep?
    a. NREM
    b. REM
    c. RAM
    d. ROM

27. We are able to control two things in life: our attitude and our:
    a. income
    b. nonverbal communication
    c. tardiness
    d. actions

28. Procrastination is often a symptom of the fear of:
    a. failure
    b. promotion
    c. comfort zones
    d. self-improvement

29. A person who approaches sensitive subjects in an attempt to get even or hurt another person is labeled a:
    a. withholder
    b. joker
    c. beltliner
    d. trapper

30. A person who refuses to face up to a conflict either by giving in or by pretending nothing is wrong is labeled as a(an):
    a. kitchen sink fighter
    b. gunnysacker
    c. avoider
    d. pseudo accommodator

31. A person who will not allow relationships to change from the way they once were is labeled as a:
    a. Benedict Arnold
    b. subject changer
    c. mind reader
    d. contract tyrannizer

32. A person who attacks other parts of a partner's life, instead of expressing the feelings about the object of dissatisfaction, is labeled as a:
    a. distracter
    b. blamer
    c. guiltmaker
    d. trivial tyrannizer

33. A standard mental picture that is held in common by members of a group and that represents an oversimplified opinion, prejudiced attitude, or uncritical judgment is called a:
    a. language
    b. perception
    c. stereotype
    d. multicultural issue

34. If the patient asks the medical assistant what the medical assistant would do in a similar medical situation, the medical assistant should:
    a. advise the patient as to the best course of action
    b. suggest that the patient seek counseling
    c. refuse to discuss the issue at all
    d. refer the patient to the physician for advice

35. At which time or in which instance is it appropriate to touch the patient?
    a. when the patient has just discovered he or she is HIV positive
    b. when the patient is crying
    c. when the patient has lost a close family member
    d. all of the above

TRUE OR FALSE

Directions: Circle the best answer.

36.   T   F   The perception of the receiver in communication is not important.

37.   T   F   Paraphrasing is listening to what the sender is communicating, analyzing the words, and then restating them to confirm that the receiver has understood the message as the sender intended it.

38. T F   Physical avoidance is a defense mechanism through which a person avoids a place or person because of the painful memories that are invoked.

39. T F   The struggle that results from incompatible or opposing needs, drives, wishes, or external or internal demands is called malediction.

40. T F   It is acceptable to tell a patient "I know how you feel."

41. T F   Culture shock is the state of being in unfamiliar surroundings and being away from the things that were present every day.

42. T F   Choosing which relationships to enter greatly increases the chances that they will be healthy relationships.

43. T F   To feel well and accomplish goals in life, one must develop positive attitudes and positive responses to the pressures of everyday life.

44. T F   Patients are usually right at home in their comfort zones on the first visit to the physician's office.

45. T F   Avoiders love the opportunity for a good fight.

COMPLETION

Directions: Fill in the blank with the best answer.

46. The _____ formed in the early moments of meeting someone remain in our thoughts long after the first words are spoken.

47. To utter articulate sounds or be distinct in speech is to _____.

48. _____ noise includes the person's own thoughts, prejudices, and opinions.

49. Nonconsensual touching may be considered _____.

50. Any biological factor that would preclude the communicator from sending or receiving accurate messages, such as not feeling well or being overly tired, is called _____ noise.

51. Active listening is the skill of_____ and clarifying what the speaker has said.

52. Most people use _____ _____ during times in which they feel pressured or attacked in some way.

53. _____ is a lack of feeling, emotion, interest, or concern.

54. It is always helpful to have a _____ staff member to communicate with patients who speak another language.

55. When people almost bring what is bothering them to the surface, but never quite express it, they are considered a _____ _____.

56. The first stage of grief is _____.

57. The third stage of grief is _____.

58. The second stage of grief is _____.

59. The last stage of grief is _____.

60. The fourth stage of grief is _____.

Word List
Acceptance
Anger
Apathy
Bargaining
Battery
Bilingual
Crisis tickler
Defense mechanisms
Denial
Depression
Enunciate
Internal
Opinions
Paraphrasing
Physiological

CHAPTER 6

Medicine and Ethics

MULTIPLE CHOICE

Directions: Circle the letter of the choice that best completes the statement or answers the question.

1. Which word or phrase best describes those actions that strive to achieve the highest good for humanity as a whole?
   a. ethics
   b. etiquette
   c. precepts
   d. social contracts

2. Which of the following statements is true regarding the revisions made to the AMA Code of Ethics in 1980?
   a. the number of sections was increased to include the growing number of ethical concerns
   b. the preamble was eliminated to allow more space for expansion of the sections
   c. the standards were modified to reflect a legal rather than a moral approach to medicine
   d. changes to the language were made to achieve a balance between contemporary legal standards and our society's professional standards

3. Which statement best describes the practice known as *fee splitting*?
   a. the unethical practice of basing the physician's fee on the success of the treatment
   b. the unethical practice in which physicians are paid for referring patients
   c. the lowering of the physician's fee as a way to help poor patients
   d. an appropriate method of allowing two physicians to work together in treating a patient

4. Which statement best describes the practice of physicians waiving co-payments required by insurance companies?
   a. may violate insurer policies if done routinely
   b. is a humane way to provide medical care to needy patients
   c. is promoted by insurance companies to encourage preventive care
   d. encourages patients to take advantage of the medical payment system

5. If a patient calls the office to ask for information about a medical condition and the physician is not available, what is the best way for the medical assistant to handle the situation?
   a. give out only those details believed to be in the best interest of the patient
   b. check the patient's medical record to ensure accurate information
   c. take the patient's name and telephone number and ask the physician to call when available
   d. ask the patient to call back later when the physician will be able to take the call

6. What is the greatest ethical problem created with the use of computers and patient databases in the modern medical office?
   a. important patient information can be lost because of lack of knowledge in the use of the computer
   b. unauthorized persons may gain access to confidential medical records
   c. many patients believe that computers represent an impersonal way of conducting business
   d. it has increased the cost of providing medical care

7. *Ghost surgery* is a term describing an unethical situation in which:
   a. the patient has not signed a consent form for surgery
   b. a physician other than the one approved by the patient performs the surgery
   c. a family member has made the decision for a patient to undergo surgery
   d. the surgery performed is not medically necessary

8. An obligation that people have or perceive themselves to have is called a(an):
   a. duty
   b. reparation
   c. right
   d. opinion

9. The person who normally decides what is ethical on a daily basis in the medical office is:
   a. the physician
   b. the individual faced with an ethical choice
   c. the office manager
   d. the patient

10. With regard to medical ethics, which term deals with the fair distribution of benefits and burdens among individuals or groups in society having legitimate claims on those benefits?
    a. reparation
    b. veracity
    c. justice
    d. beneficence

11. Which type of ethical problem is characterized by two or more courses of action with the result that, regardless of which course of action is taken, something of value will be lost?
    a. ethical dilemma
    b. ethical distress
    c. locus of authority
    d. distributive justice

12. With regard to ethical distress, what stands in the way of the correct ethical choice?
    a. morals
    b. ethics
    c. concern
    d. barriers

13. The first in the five-step process of ethical decision making is:
    a. determining the ethics approach to use
    b. gathering relevant information
    c. exploring the practical alternatives
    d. identifying the type of ethical problem

14. What is the strongest argument for the use of unique identifiers for patients with HIV?
    a. to make processing insurance claims easier
    b. to ensure that patients receive proper care
    c. to keep the identity of patients who are HIV positive confidential
    d. to keep a list of the names of those who are HIV positive on record

15. Which of the following statements is NOT true regarding the human genome?
    a. experts need to educate Congress, federal agencies, and governments about the use of genetic information
    b. the genome project formally began in 1890
    c. the mapping of the human genome has raised questions about confidentiality and privacy issues
    d. major healthcare agencies, such as the CDC, DHHS, NIH, and FDA, are involved in the genome project

16. What is the opinion of CEJA with regard to abortion?
    a. agrees fully
    b. agrees with stipulations
    c. disagrees
    d. has no opinion

17. What is the opinion of CEJA with regard to physician-assisted suicide?
    a. agrees fully
    b. agrees with stipulations
    c. disagrees
    d. has no opinion

18. What is the opinion of CEJA with regard to surrogate motherhood?
    a. agrees fully
    b. agrees with stipulations
    c. disagrees
    d. has no opinion

19. Which area of ethical question involves the development of new drugs and procedures?
    a. organ donation
    b. human cloning
    c. quality of life
    d. clinical trials

20. Another name for somatic cell nuclear transfer is:
    a. human cloning
    b. organ donation
    c. genetic counseling
    d. artificial insemination

21. With regard to capital punishment, CEJA agrees that a physician can ethically:
    a. give the lethal injection
    b. certify the death
    c. give the lethal injection and certify the death
    d. completely abstain from participation in capital punishment

22. In allocation of health resources, the criteria should be which of the following?
    a. likelihood of benefit
    b. duration of benefit
    c. urgency of need
    d. all of the above

23. Which of the following does CEJA not only agree is ethical but also encourages participation in?
    a. capital punishment
    b. abortion
    c. organ donation
    d. human cloning

24. How many active members of the AMA serve as CEJA members?
    a. five
    b. seven
    c. nine
    d. 11

25. The document that expresses the wishes of patients in case of terminal illness or an accident after which patients cannot express their wishes is called a:
    a. power of attorney
    b. DNR order
    c. will
    d. living will

26. The tendency of something or someone to act in a certain manner under given circumstances is called:
    a. idealism
    b. introspection
    c. disposition
    d. veracity

27. Refraining from the act of harming or committing evil is called:
    a. nonmaleficence
    b. beneficence
    c. duty
    d. fidelity

28. The prime objective of the medical profession is to:
    a. heal patients
    b. render service to humanity
    c. make money
    d. all of the above

29. If the medical assistant believes that the employer is participating in unethical behavior, the first course of action should be:
    a. to be absolutely sure of the facts and circumstances
    b. to quit immediately
    c. to turn the employer in to the local medical society and police
    d. to do nothing

30. Which of the following are practicing physicians required to do with regard to the opinions of CEJA?
    a. operate their practice in accordance with all of the CEJA opinions
    b. consider a different career if they cannot abide by the CEJA opinions
    c. consider the opinions but operate their practice in accordance with their own belief system
    d. follow the opinions without any deviation

31. One who pleads the cause of another or defends a cause or proposal is a(an):
    a. attorney
    b. defender
    c. counselor
    d. advocate

32. The earliest written code of ethics was:
    a. Oath of Hippocrates
    b. AMA Code of Ethics
    c. Code of Hammurabi
    d. Percival's Code of Medical Ethics

33. Idealism means:
    a. a devotion to, or conformity with, the truth
    b. faithfulness to something to which one is bound by pledge or duty
    c. the practice of forming ideas or living under the influence of ideas
    d. consequences produced by a cause or following from a set of conditions

34. When a person has wronged another person, that person has the duty to:
    a. become a surrogate
    b. express fidelity
    c. express an opinion
    d. make reparations

35. The type of ethical problem in which two or more agents think they each know what is best for the patient but only one agent can prevail is called:
    a. distributive justice
    b. locus of authority
    c. ethical dilemma
    d. ethical distress

TRUE OR FALSE
Directions: Circle the best answer.

36.   T   F   *Roe vs. Wade* was heard by the Supreme Court in 1970.

37.   T   F   An inward reflective examination of one's own feelings and thoughts is called introspection.

38.   T   F   CEJA is in favor of all abortions at any time.

39.   T   F   Norma McCorvey was the real Jane Roe in *Roe vs. Wade*.

40.   T   F   Logically, the control of gametes should be left to the man and woman who produced them.

41.   T   F   The physician involved in caring for the patient should be an advocate for the family as opposed to the patient being treated.

42.   T   F   If a person appears in the medical office with an official press badge, the medical assistant must make information available.

43.   T   F   Ghost surgery is now ethically acceptable.

44.   T   F   Physicians who know that they have an infectious disease should not engage in any activity that creates an identified risk of transmission to the patient.

45.   T   F   Requesting payment at the time services are rendered is unethical.

COMPLETION

Directions: Fill in the blank with the best answer.

46. A physician may be subject to civil or criminal _____ for violation of government laws.

47. _____ waiver of insurance co-payments may violate the policies of some insurers.

48. Administering a lethal drug to a patient to promote death is called _____.

49. A physician committed to saving life and relieving suffering may sometimes find those two goals _____.

50. The realm embracing property rights that belong to the community at large is called _____ _____.

51. A formal expression of judgment or advice by an expert is called a(an) _____.

52. Something that is _____ is oriented or directed toward social needs and problems.

53. _____ are defined as claims that a person or group makes on society.

54. The provision of care to medical colleagues or their families and staff is called _____ _____.

55. A devotion to, or conformity with, the truth is _____.

56. Although attorneys often accept clients on a(an) _____ fee basis, it is unethical for a physician to do so.

Word List
Contingent
Routine

Incompatible
Opinion
Rights
Veracity
Liability
Euthanasia
Public domain
Sociological
Professional courtesy

ETHICAL PROBLEMS DIAGRAMS

57. Draw the diagram representing ethical dilemma.

58. Draw the diagram representing ethical distress.

59. Draw the diagram representing locus of authority.

60. Draw the diagram representing distributive justice.

CHAPTER **7**

Medicine and Law

MULTIPLE CHOICE

Directions: Circle the letter of the choice that best completes the statement or answers the question.

1. What is the most serious action by a licensing board that can be taken against a physician who is found to be practicing under the influence of narcotic drugs?
   a. expulsion from the local medical society
   b. suspension of medical license
   c. accusation of unethical conduct
   d. revoking of medical license

2. Most states require by law that physicians report all of the following events EXCEPT:
   a. confirmed cases of AIDS
   b. abortions
   c. births
   d. deaths

3. Which statement best describes the difference between criminal and civil law?
   a. criminal law governs crimes against society as a whole; civil law governs crimes against individuals
   b. criminal law governs serious and violent crimes; civil law governs less serious crimes
   c. criminal law regulates professional behavior that might harm clients; civil law regulates behavior in nonprofessional situations
   d. criminal law regulates individual actions; civil law regulates group actions

4. Emancipated minors are persons under legal age who:
   a. have petitioned the court for emancipation
   b. are in college
   c. work full-time
   d. live independently of their parents

5. If a physician decides to end the professional relationship with a patient, what must the physician do to help avoid being sued for abandonment?
   a. call the patient personally and explain that the physician is withdrawing from the case
   b. send the patient's records to a physician believed to be competent to handle the case
   c. thoroughly document in writing the reasons and methods for withdrawing from the case
   d. return any money collected for the most recent treatment given

6. Which of the following is NOT one of the "four D's" of negligence included in a report by the AMA Committee of Medicolegal Problems?
   a. damages
   b. deceit
   c. derelict
   d. duty

7. Experience has shown which of the following to be the major influence on whether a patient sues a physician for malpractice?
   a. the trust developed between the physician and patient
   b. the reputation of the physician in the community
   c. the professional expertise of the physician
   d. the patient's medical insurance company

8. The formal action of a legislative body or a decision or determination of a sovereign state, a legislative council, or a court of justice is called:
   a. ordinance
   b. act
   c. law
   d. code

9. A minor crime, as opposed to a felony, punishable by fine or imprisonment in a city or county jail rather than a penitentiary is called a:
   a. felony
   b. misdemeanor
   c. larceny
   d. statute

10. An officer of the US courts who serves as a messenger to the judge is called a:
    a. marshal
    b. deputy
    c. bailiff
    d. reporter

11. Which of the following is NOT a type of criminal law?
    a. treason
    b. misdemeanor
    c. tort
    d. felony

12. Which of the following is NOT a type of civil law?
    a. administrative
    b. regulatory
    c. tort
    d. contract

13. A document issued by a court requiring a person to be in court at a specific time and place to testify as a witness is called a:
   a. deposition
   b. interrogatory
   c. subpoena duces tecum
   d. subpoena

14. United States District Courts handle which kind of cases?
   a. civil
   b. criminal
   c. both
   d. neither

15. Which of the following is the highest level of state courts?
   a. municipal
   b. district
   c. county
   d. state supreme court

16. Evidence brought before a court by document or display is called:
   a. discovery
   b. documentary evidence
   c. testimony
   d. slander

17. Civil cases must be proven by:
   a. reasonable doubt
   b. discovery
   c. preponderance of the evidence
   d. any means necessary

18. The improper performance of a lawful act is:
   a. misfeasance
   b. malfeasance
   c. nonfeasance
   d. feasance

19. Which type of civil law usually relates to medical malpractice?
   a. administrative law
   b. contract law
   c. prudent law
   d. tort law

20. The failure to perform a duty, with respect to the four D's of negligence, is called:
   a. damages
   b. direct cause
   c. derelict
   d. defense

21. Damages that are designed to compensate for any actual damages caused by a negligent person are called:
    a. punitive
    b. compensatory
    c. nominal
    d. general

22. Which of the following is NOT necessary information when providing a patient with informed consent?
    a. alternative procedures or treatments
    b. cost
    c. patient diagnosis
    d. risks and benefits of having or not having the treatment

23. Which of the following requires that all healthcare facilities develop and maintain written procedures to ensure that all adult patients receive information about living wills and advance directives?
    a. Controlled Substances Act of 1970
    b. Patient's Bill of Rights
    c. Patient Self-Determination Act
    d. Uniform Anatomical Gift Act

24. Questions to the parties involved in a lawsuit that must be answered within a certain time frame and are considered to be answered under oath are a part of a(an):
    a. deposition
    b. interrogatory
    c. subpoena
    d. discovery

25. Which of the following statements is true about arbitration?
    a. it is cheaper than taking a case through the court system
    b. it is not as legally binding as a regular court decision
    c. an attorney still must be present to represent each side during arbitration
    d. it is not as confidential as a case brought through the court system

26. Which of the following regulates safety in the workplace?
    a. OSHA
    b. CLIA
    c. DHHS
    d. CMS

27. Which of the following is a goal of HIPAA?
    a. raise administrative costs of healthcare and privacy issues
    b. make unique identifiers mandatory
    c. make regulating privacy more time consuming
    d. prevent fraud and abuse

28. To specify as a condition or requirement of an agreement or offer is to:
    a. testify
    b. discover
    c. stipulate
    d. assent

29. An authoritative decree or direction is called an:
    a. asset
    b. appeal
    c. arbitration
    d. ordinance

30. A rule of conduct or action prescribed or formally recognized as binding or enforceable by a controlling authority is called a:
    a. verdict
    b. precedent
    c. law
    d. fine

31. Some states have a subcategory for misdemeanors called:
    a. infractions
    b. felonies
    c. stipulations
    d. precedents

32. A thing that is marked by wisdom or judiciousness is said to be:
    a. intelligent
    b. sharp
    c. prudent
    d. decedent

33. If an attorney lodges an objection to a question, what should the witness do?
    a. go ahead with the answer unless the attorney is from the opposing side
    b. wait for the judge to rule on the objection before speaking at all
    c. refuse to answer the question
    d. look at the attorney to get a clue as to how to proceed

34. Why might a witness be accused of perjury?
    a. for lying under oath in court
    b. for not appearing in court
    c. for making inappropriate comments in court
    d. for dressing in an unacceptable manner in court

35. Which of the following is NOT true regarding a legal contract?
    a. one party to the contract makes an offer
    b. one party to the contract accepts an offer
    c. the subject matter must be legal
    d. the subject matter can be either legal or illegal, as long as there was an agreement

36. In which of the following ways might a person obtain a license to practice medicine in the United States?
    a. reciprocity
    b. jurisdiction
    c. statute
    d. precedence

37. When people are found to be responsible for an act or circumstances, they are said to be:
    a. libel
    b. liable
    c. litigious
    d. perjured

38. A person who provides testimony to a court in a certain field or subject to verify facts is called a(an):
    a. emancipated minor
    b. judge
    c. witness
    d. expert witness

39. A case decided before the current case, which may be referenced by either side to show how a previous court acted, is called a(an):
    a. ordinance
    b. decedent
    c. due process
    d. precedent

40. A legal representative for a minor is called a(an):
    a. attorney
    b. guardian ad litem
    c. bailiff
    d. arbitrator

TRUE OR FALSE

Directions: Circle the correct answer.

41.   T   F   The legal term for a deceased person is decedent.

42.   T   F   If something is relevant in a court case, it has significant and demonstrable bearing on the matter at hand.

43.   T   F   The pretense of curing disease is called prudent.

44.   T   F   Reasonable doubt arises from evidence or lack of evidence.

45.   T   F   Discovery is the post-trial disclosure of pertinent facts or documents.

46.   T   F   The burden of proof in a criminal case rests with the defendant.

47.   T   F   To prove a case in civil court, the scales of justice must tip heavily one way or another.

48. T F General damages are designed to punish the party who committed the wrongdoing.

49. T F Good Samaritan statutes allow people to collect damages when a person helps in an emergency and there is a detrimental result.

50. T F The statute of limitations is the same in all states for all types of cases.

COMPLETION

Directions: Fill in the blank with the best answer.

51. Schedule _____ drugs have no medical use in the United States.

52. Schedule _____ drugs have a high abuse potential, with severe risk of mental and physical dependence.

53. Schedule _____ drugs, such as Valium and Darvocet, have less of an abuse potential.

54. Schedule _____ drugs include those with abuse potential, such as hydrocodone and acetaminophen with codeine.

55. MSDS stands for _____ _____ _____ _____.

56. Because no law can cover every situation that might arise when judging workplace safety, OSHA can use the _____ _____ clause to cite a facility for an unsafe situation.

57. One third of the workplace injuries that occur in healthcare settings happen with needles during the _____ process.

58. The form that identifies the Log of Work-Related Injuries and Illnesses is OSHA Form

    _____.

59. The summary of work-related injuries must be posted in a common area for viewing by all employees between February 1 and _____ of each year.

60. With the National Fire Protection Rating system, a chemical with a moderate hazard would be given the numeral _____.

Word List
General duty
2
300
Disposal
Material safety data sheet
I
II
III
IV
April 30

Introduction to Medical Assisting Certification Review

MULTIPLE CHOICE

1. How have the advancement of medical technology and the increased use of computers influenced the medical assisting profession?
   a. replaced many medical assistants with more specialized medical employees
   b. limited the responsibilities of medical assistants to clinical tasks
   c. increased the amount of training required to become a proficient medical assistant
   d. provided many more work opportunities for medical assistants in hospital settings

2. A recent graduate of a comprehensive medical assisting training program could apply for all of the following positions EXCEPT:
   a. medical receptionist
   b. physical therapist assistant
   c. billing and collection specialist
   d. transcriptionist

3. Which quality in a medical assistant is most likely to promote positive patient relations in the medical office?
   a. behaves in a professional and businesslike manner
   b. maintained high grades in medical assisting training
   c. is attractive and well-groomed
   d. has a sincere interest in patient welfare

4. You are beginning your externship in a large office that has three medical assistants. What is the best way to learn about your job responsibilities?
   a. ask for a job description and clear directions
   b. watch what the experienced medical assistants do
   c. wait politely until someone has time to explain your duties
   d. perform only those tasks which you are directed to do

5. Which group has MOST influenced the growth of training opportunities for medical assistants?
   a. American Association of Medical Assistants
   b. American Medical Association
   c. community colleges
   d. private vocational colleges

6. Which of the following types of training is considered to be the MOST effective for someone who wants to start a career as a medical assistant?
   a. self-teaching using at-home study materials
   b. formal programs offered at community colleges and private vocational schools
   c. on-the-job training under the supervision of a physician
   d. chapter meetings of the American Association of Medical Assistants

7. In choosing a uniform, which is the MOST important consideration?
   a. it is becoming and flattering to your body type
   b. it will not be wrinkled by the end of the workday
   c. it gives a professional, clinical appearance
   d. it should be white

8. The skills needed by most competent medical assistants include all EXCEPT which of the following?
   a. excellent communication skills
   b. high level of computer ability
   c. ability to perform basic math computations
   d. knowledge of infection control

9. Which is the best reason for becoming an active member of a medical assisting professional organization?
   a. improved chances for promotion at work
   b. professional growth through continuing education
   c. networking opportunities
   d. opportunity to demonstrate your dedication

10. Which of the following is the MOST important benefit that you gain from your medical assisting externship experience?
    a. earning a small salary to help repay school expenses
    b. acquiring practical experience and applying your classroom skills
    c. demonstrating your knowledge and skills to a potential employer
    d. meeting healthcare professionals who can help you find employment

11. The best way to earn a favorable evaluation on your externship would be to:
    a. demonstrate integrity and practice high ethical standards
    b. be very friendly with your supervisor and other senior staff members
    c. impress the physician with your knowledge and skills
    d. demonstrate your willingness by performing tasks that have not been assigned to you

12. Which statement is TRUE regarding the status of students during the externship, as compared to those of regular employees?
    a. They should not waste their supervisor's time asking a lot of questions.
    b. They cannot be sued for medical malpractice.
    c. Attendance expectations are generally less strict for them.
    d. They are expected to perform under the same professional standards.

13. What is the principal difference between the personal inventory and the resume?
    a. the resume never includes information about extracurricular activities
    b. the resume contains actual dates of past employment
    c. the personal inventory does not require regular updating
    d. the personal inventory contains more complete and detailed information

14. Which of the following should NOT be included in the heading of your resume?
    a. your telephone number
    b. your address
    c. your full name
    d. your birth date

15. What would be the best attitude to display when applying for your first position as a medical assistant?
    a. willing to take any position offered
    b. very eager to get the position
    c. prepared and self-confident
    d. modest and aware of your inexperience

16. Under what circumstances would it be appropriate to include extracurricular activities on your resume?
    a. they are related to the job requirements of the medical assistant
    b. they demonstrate your ability to organize your time
    c. you have won awards for achievement in those areas
    d. all of the above

17. Which statement is TRUE regarding the medical symbol known as the "caduceus"?
    a. It was adopted by the American Medical Association as the symbol of medicine.
    b. It represents the United States Army Medical Corps.
    c. It consists of one snake wrapped around a staff.
    d. It represents the Greek god of medicine who took the form of a serpent.

18. Who was an early advocate of preventive medicine and could be considered history's first public health officer?
    a. Moses
    b. Aesculapius
    c. Hippocrates
    d. Hygeia

19. Which of the following organizations provided the world's best medical training at the end of the 1800s?
    a. Royal Society of London
    b. General Medical Council of Britain
    c. Carnegie Foundation
    d. Johns Hopkins University

20. Which scientist first described the manner in which the heart functions as a pump that continually circulates the blood?
    a. Edward Jenner
    b. William Harvey
    c. John Hunter
    d. Andreas Vesalius

21. Which of the following statements about the professional corporation form of business organization is NOT true?
    a. The professional employees are liable only for their own acts.
    b. They are less restricted by legal requirements than smaller sole proprietorships and partnerships.
    c. There are tax advantages related to fringe benefits for the corporation and the employees.
    d. It is not necessary to reorganize the corporation after the death of a major shareholder.

22. Which statement best describes the main difference between the Doctor of Osteopathy (DO) and the Doctor of Medicine (MD)?
    a. The training for the DO includes more courses and a longer residency.
    b. Only the MD can prescribe drugs for the prevention and treatment of disease.
    c. The DO places more emphasis on the relationship of musculoskeletal structure to the function of organs.
    d. The license for the MD has more requirements and is more difficult to obtain.

23. Which approach to providing healthcare has most influenced the practice of medicine in the United States in the past 10 years?
    a. insurance coverage through managed care
    b. organization of physicians into medical group practices
    c. government payments for medical care
    d. increase in physician control of managing patient treatment

24. Which allied health professional works with a physician who specializes in the care of the eye?
    a. surgical technologist
    b. ophthalmic medical technician
    c. cytotechnologist
    d. audiologist

25. Which statement describes the dominant feature of holistic medicine?
    a. Most physical diseases can be traced to psychological causes.
    b. Mainly natural methods, such as the use of herbs, are considered for treatments.
    c. All body systems are interrelated and must be considered when diagnosing ailments.
    d. Physicians have a major responsibility in determining the state of their own health.

26. The most appropriate treatment for a patient with a recently healed broken leg who needs to resume his normal activities would be:
    a. acceleration
    b. manipulation
    c. rehabilitation
    d. physical medicine

27. The principal purpose of managed care is to provide patients with:
    a. access to needed specialists
    b. proper care at the least possible cost
    c. a supervising physician who understands their health needs
    d. adequate preventive healthcare

28. Who sets the cost of medical services in "fee-for-service arrangements"?
   a. local medical societies
   b. federal government
   c. insurance companies
   d. physicians

29. Which of the following was created as a response to the federal government's concern about over utilization of medical services that was formally addressed in Public Law 93-222?
   a. health maintenance organizations
   b. fee-for-service plans
   c. managed care groups
   d. Medicare

30. The principal characteristic that differentiates a corporation from sole proprietorships and partnerships in the medical field is that it:
   a. is more strictly regulated by the American Medical Association
   b. offers better protection against malpractice lawsuits
   c. is an artificial entity, legally separate from its shareholders
   d. provides higher salaries for employees

31. The medical specialty that deals with the causes and effects of diseases is called:
   a. internal medicine
   b. preventive medicine
   c. immunology
   d. pathology

32. The allied health specialist who performs ultrasound diagnostic procedures under the supervision of a physician is called a:
   a. cytotechnologist
   b. diagnostic medical sonographer
   c. electrodiagnostic technologist
   d. perfusionist

33. With whom can the medical assistant share information about an elderly patient's condition if the patient has not signed a release form?
   a. a close family member who cares for the patient
   b. the patient's medical insurance company
   c. a local medical school that is conducting research on the patient's illness
   d. none of the above

34. Which statement best describes the practice known as "fee splitting"?
   a. It is the unethical practice of basing the physician's fee on the success of the treatment.
   b. It is the unethical practice in which physicians are paid for referring patients.
   c. It refers to the lowering of the physician's fee as a way to help poor patients.
   d. It is an appropriate method of allowing two physicians to work together in treating a patient.

35. Which statement best describes the practice of physicians waiving copayments required by insurance companies?
   a. It may be illegal if done on a regular basis.
   b. It is a humane way to provide medical care for needy patients.
   c. It is promoted by insurance companies to encourage preventive care.
   d. It encourages patients to take advantage of the medical payment system.

36. When it is appropriate for the medical office to request that a patient pay for treatment at the time it is given?
    a. never
    b. only if the patient has a history of paying late
    c. only for patients who have no medical insurance
    d. always

37. If a patient calls the office to ask for information about his medical condition and the physician is not available, what is the best way for the medical assistant to handle the situation?
    a. give out only those details which she believes to be in the best interest of the patient
    b. check the patient's medical record to ensure that she gives out accurate information
    c. take the patient's name and telephone number and ask the physician to call when he is available
    d. ask the patient to call back later when she believes the physician will be able to take the call

38. What is the greatest ethical problem created by the use of computers and patient databases in the modern medical office?
    a. important patient information can be lost due to lack of knowledge of the use of the computer
    b. unauthorized persons may gain access to confidential medical records
    c. many patients believe that computers represent an impersonal way of conducting business
    d. it has increased the cost of providing medical care

39. Which action should the medical assistant take if she believes that a prescription for a medication has an error?
    a. report it immediately to the physician
    b. refer to the Physician's Desk Reference and make the needed correction
    c. assume that the physician wrote the correct order
    d. advise the patient to double-check the prescription with the pharmacy

40. How does a "living will" help avoid problems for the children of a very ill, incompetent parent?
    a. it allows the physician to perform euthanasia in order to help the patient
    b. it gives the physician the responsibility for deciding what is best for the patient
    c. it prevents the patient's children from fighting over their inheritance
    d. it advises the patient's children of the parent's wishes regarding the provision of life support

41. When physicians are proven to have practiced immorally, what is the most serious penalty that can be imposed on them by the medical society?
    a. public announcement of their behavior
    b. expulsion from the society
    c. refusal by other physicians to refer patients
    d. a financial penalty based on the seriousness of the offense

42. The principal purpose of administrative law is to:
    a. promote the practice of ethical business and professional standards
    b. provide the means for government agencies to set and enforce regulations
    c. set the requirements for contracts to be valid and enforceable
    d. govern minor offenses such as misdemeanors and infractions

43. If a physician decides to end his professional relationship with a patient, what must he do in order to help avoid being sued for abandonment?
    a. call the patient personally and explain that he is withdrawing from his case
    b. send the patient's records to a physician whom he believes competent to handle the case
    c. thoroughly document in writing his reasons and methods for withdrawing from the case
    d. return any money collected for the most recent treatment given

44. Which of the following is NOT one of the "four Ds" of negligence included in a report by the AMA Committee on Medicolegal Problems?
    a. damages
    b. deceit
    c. derelict
    d. duty

45. Experience has shown which of the following to be the major influence on whether a patient sues his physician for malpractice?
    a. the personal relationship developed between the physician and patient
    b. the reputation of the physician in the community
    c. the professional expertise of the physician
    d. the patient's medical insurance company

46. When obtaining informed consent from a patient for medical treatment, all of the following factors must be discussed except:
    a. the risk involved
    b. the exact fee that the physician will charge
    c. the expected benefits
    d. other possible treatments

47. The Good Samaritan Acts were created in order to:
    a. require action on the part of anyone who witnesses an emergency
    b. create training methods and protocols for emergency healthcare procedures
    c. provide protection for volunteers against lawsuits charging improper care
    d. prohibit healthcare professionals from charging fees for rendering emergency care

CHAPTER **8**

Computers in the Medical Office

MULTIPLE CHOICE

Directions: Circle the letter of the choice that best completes the statement or answers the question.

1. Which of the following is an output device?
   a. printer
   b. scanner
   c. light pen
   d. keyboard

2. When a floppy disk is formatted, it:
   a. becomes usable in a computer
   b. organizes the disk into tracks and sectors
   c. both a and b
   d. none of the above

3. Storage devices include all of the following EXCEPT:
   a. hard disk drive
   b. modem
   c. CD-ROM drive
   d. Zip drive

4. All of the following are advantages to using laser printers EXCEPT:
   a. cost
   b. speed
   c. quality of printing
   d. efficiency

5. Microcomputers perform which of the following functions?
   a. input
   b. storage
   c. processing
   d. all of the above

6. Which of the following is internal memory that CANNOT be overwritten and is not erased when the computer is turned off?
   a. RAM
   b. ROM
   c. CPU
   d. hard disk

7. An application program is software that is designed to:
   a. perform a variety of tasks, such as word processing, database functions, and patient billing
   b. provide the computer with a set of basic instructions for executing other programs
   c. interpret the program instructions
   d. all of the above

8. Which of the following is an advantage of a computerized office database?
   a. all information about providers, patients, insurance carriers, diagnosis and procedure codes, charges, and payments is together and readily accessible
   b. it can be used by more than one person at the same time if networked
   c. it has the ability to link related pieces of information to process insurance claims
   d. all of the above

9. A mouse is a(an):
   a. output device
   b. input device
   c. storage device
   d. processor

10. A dialog box in Windows is:
    a. a box used to turn on and off options
    b. a window that appears requesting more information from the user
    c. a standard value used by the software
    d. a location on screen in which files are stored

11. A series of computers that are linked together allowing them to share information is a(an):
    a. database
    b. clearinghouse
    c. network
    d. Internet

12. Which kind of printer would be most beneficial for printing multipart insurance claim forms?
    a. laser
    b. inkjet
    c. dot matrix
    d. bubble jet

13. A communication tool that is used to send and receive messages and computer-generated documents is called:
    a. cellular phone
    b. voice mail
    c. pager
    d. electronic mail

14. Which of the following is used to make sure that all office computer programs and data are secure in case of a mishap, fire, or natural disaster?
    a. RAM
    b. microprocessor
    c. write-protection
    d. backup functions

15. Which of the following is NOT a part of the hardware of a computer system?
    a. hard copy
    b. monitor
    c. disk drive
    d. printer

16. Clock speed is expressed as:
    a. baud
    b. bytes
    c. megabytes
    d. megahertz

17. Which of the following is NOT a type of printer?
    a. monochrome
    b. dot matrix
    c. laser
    d. ink jet

18. Which of the following is a photographic file?
    a. doc
    b. txt
    c. rtf
    d. jpeg

19. Which of the following is the largest?
    a. wan
    b. lan
    c. can
    d. han

20. Which of the following domains is used by universities?
    a. .com
    b. .gov
    c. .org
    d. .edu

21. The work of sorting and manipulating information is performed in the computer by the:
    a. application software
    b. CPU
    c. CD-ROM
    d. ROM

22. The most commonly used input device that allows the computer operator to select commands by interfacing with the monitor screen is called the:
    a. cursor
    b. scanner
    c. control key
    d. mouse

23. The smallest piece of information on a computer is the:
    a. bit
    b. byte
    c. megabyte
    d. gigabyte

24. Which printer would be the best selection if you plan to prepare multicolored newsletters with computer-generated graphics and illustrations?
    a. dot matrix
    b. ink jet
    c. color laser
    d. letter quality

25. Which printer uses replaceable cartridges that must be factored in the of planning the long-range cost of the machine?
    a. dot matrix
    b. ink jet
    c. plain
    d. letter quality

26. The most common use for diskettes today is for:
    a. storing information
    b. giving instructions to the computer while it is being used
    c. substituting for the Zip drive
    d. formatting the computer

27. Which of the following is an example of computer software?
    a. email
    b. internal memory
    c. floppy diskette
    d. Word 2002

28. If you want to transfer paper files to a computerized system without inputting all the data from the keyboard, you could use a:
    a. modem
    b. disk operating system
    c. scanner
    d. magnetic disk drive

29. For which task might a database management software program be used in the medical office?
    a. preparing letters and reports
    b. tracking accounts payable
    c. preparing invoices for insurance billing
    d. organizing and storing patient information

30. What special type of hardware would you need to file your insurance claims electronically?
   a. network system
   b. modem
   c. scanner
   d. magnetic tape drive

31. The aspect of computer science that deals with computers taking on the attributes of humans is called:
   a. virtual reality
   b. artificial intelligence
   c. cyberspace
   d. telecommunications

32. The language that is used to create documents for use on the Internet is:
   a. HTTP
   b. DSL
   c. URL
   d. HTML

33. A special high-speed storage that might be a part of the computer's main memory or can be a separate storage device is called the:
   a. Zip drive
   b. device driver
   c. cache
   d. cursor

34. The presentation of graphics, animation, video, and sound on a computer in an integrated way or all at once is called:
   a. pasting
   b. query
   c. multimedia
   d. java

35. Which of the following is NOT one of the items that will differentiate microprocessors?
   a. instruction set
   b. bandwidth
   c. clock speed
   d. memory

36. Which of the following is a peripheral device?
   a. monitor
   b. keyboard
   c. scanner
   d. CPU

37. Which of the following is NOT a peripheral device?
   a. digital camera
   b. Zip drive
   c. keyboard
   d. light pen

38. The main circuit board for the computer to which other devices are attached is called the:
    a. CPU
    b. motherboard
    c. expansion board
    d. modem

39. Software applications that allow the computer to surf the Internet are called:
    a. browsers
    b. cache
    c. cookies
    d. flash

40. Encrypted data are called:
    a. flash
    b. cipher text
    c. crackers
    d. firewalls

TRUE OR FALSE

Directions: Circle the best answer.

41.	T	F	Search engines are programs in which a topic, word, or group of words can be entered and the engine searches the Internet for matches.
42.	T	F	A HAN would be used in an educational facility.
43.	T	F	Zip drives can hold between 100 and 250 megabytes of data.
44.	T	F	A server manages shared network resources.
45.	T	F	The hard drive is used to burn a new CD from information on a computer.
46.	T	F	DVD stands for digital video disk.
47.	T	F	A gigabyte is about 5 million bytes of data.
48.	T	F	Advertisements found on a webpage that can be animated to attract the user's attention are called banners.
49.	T	F	Cyberspace is the physical space of the online world of computer networks in which communication takes place.
50.	T	F	Magnetically creating tracks on a disk where information will be stored is called backup.

COMPLETION

Directions: Fill in the blank with the best answer.

51. The code representing English characters as numbers in which each is given a number from 0 to 127 is called _____ code.

52. A device used to connect any number of LANs that communicate with other routers and determine the best route between any two hosts is called a(n) _____.

53. A(An) _____ specifies the global address of documents or information on the Internet.

54. A picture, often on the desktop of a computer, that represents a program or an object is called a(an) _____, and by clicking on it, the user is taken into the program.

55. The pointer or flat bar appearing on the monitor that shows where the next character will appear is called the _____.

56. The magnetic creation of tracks on a disk where information will be stored, usually done by the manufacturer of the disk, is called _____.

57. _____ is the interface that allows computers to record and manipulate sound.

58. A suite of communications protocols used to connect users or hosts to the Internet is called _____.

59. The word used to describe selling and buying goods over the Internet is called _____.

60. Devices that load a program or data stored on a disk into the computer are called _____.

Word List
Ecommerce
Formatting
Icon
ASCII
MIDI
Disk drives
Router
URL
TCP/IP
Cursor

CHAPTER 9

Telephone Techniques

MULTIPLE CHOICE

Directions: Circle the letter of the choice that best completes the statement or answers the question.

1. A telephone call that is operator assisted and includes several physicians at separate offices is a(an):
   a. conference call
   b. message-unit call
   c. international call
   d. referenced call

2. The technical terminology or characteristic idiom of a particular group is called:
   a. salutation
   b. monotone
   c. jargon
   d. enunciation

3. Which of the following can be used to keep a record of incoming telephone calls so that no message is overlooked?
   a. conference call
   b. pager
   c. telephone log
   d. voice mail

4. A system that selects the order of patients to receive urgent medical treatment is often referred to as:
   a. triage
   b. selection
   c. streamlining
   d. matrixing

5. Which of the following best describes the primary goal of "screening" telephone calls?
   a. preventing calls from reaching the physician
   b. handling them at the lowest level possible
   c. selecting which calls should be forwarded to which staff members through an understanding of the purpose of the call
   d. determining whether the calls are emergencies

6. Which one of the following greetings is recommended as appropriate for handling incoming calls in an extremely busy medical office?
   a. "Good morning. This is Dr. Bewell's office. Ms. Blakely speaking."
   b. "Dr. Bewell's office. Ms. Blakely speaking."
   c. "Thank you for calling Dr. Bewell's office. This is Ms. Blakely."
   d. "Dr. Bewell's office."

7. If you are in the habit of preplanning phone calls, you always:
   a. practice out loud ahead of time what you are going to say in the call
   b. think of what to say when dialing the call
   c. have any needed files or reference materials in front of you
   d. make a master list in the morning of calls that need to be made during the day

8. If your office is in New York and you need to contact a supplier in Seattle, which New York time would be the earliest that you should call to place an order, assuming that the supplier opens at 8:00 a.m.?
   a. 8:00 a.m.
   b. 9:00 a.m.
   c. 10:00 a.m.
   d. 11:00 a.m.

9. Which of the following types of communication tools can be used to record verbal messages?
   a. voice mail
   b. fax
   c. email
   d. call waiting

10. Which of the following types of communication tools can be used for two-way communication?
    a. voice mail
    b. fax
    c. beeper
    d. cell phone

11. Which of the following types of calls should be limited in the professional setting?
    a. local
    b. long distance
    c. toll free
    d. personal

12. Inflection is:
    a. the choice of words
    b. the highness or lowness of sound
    c. the quality of being clear
    d. a change in pitch

13. Diction is:
    a. the choice of words with regard to clearness
    b. the highness or lowness of sound
    c. the quality of being clear
    d. a change in pitch

14. Pitch is:
    a. the choice of words
    b. the highness or lowness of sound
    c. the quality of being clear
    d. a change in pitch

15. Enunciation is:
    a. the choice of words
    b. the highness or lowness of sound
    c. articulation of clear sounds
    d. a change in pitch

16. The mouthpiece of the telephone handset should be held:
    a. below the chin
    b. three fingers from the lips
    c. 1 inch from the chin
    d. 1 inch from the lips

17. The medical assistant should be extremely careful when using a speakerphone because:
    a. the service is expensive
    b. it is distracting
    c. it can be traced
    d. confidentiality can be violated

18. Why is it unsatisfactory to answer the office phone by only saying "Hello?"
    a. the caller may think they have the wrong number
    b. it saves time
    c. it makes the caller feel rushed
    d. it is okay if you are in a hurry

19. Which of the following is NOT required when taking a telephone message?
    a. the caller's name and phone number
    b. time and date
    c. the name of the person to whom the call is directed
    d. the caller's account number

20. If your office is in California and it is noon, what time is it on the East Coast?
    a. 8:00 a.m.
    b. 9:00 a.m.
    c. 3:00 p.m.
    d. 4:00 p.m.

21. If your office is on the West Coast, what time is the latest time to call the East Coast?
    a. 11:00 a.m.
    b. 1:00 p.m.
    c. 2:00 p.m.
    d. 4:00 p.m.

22. Which of the following is NOT important when taking incoming calls at the physician's office?
    a. answering the phone promptly
    b. getting off the phone in less than 2 minutes
    c. identifying the caller
    d. minimizing wait time

23. Which of the following are common sources of incoming calls to the physician's office?
    a. other physicians
    b. new patients
    c. laboratories
    d. all of the above

24. A pleasing telephone voice is developed by using:
    a. customer service
    b. monotone
    c. clarity
    d. professional jargon

25. The medical assistant may help an angry caller to calm down by:
    a. speaking in a lower tone of voice
    b. getting angry in return
    c. passing the situation off to the office manager immediately
    d. calling the physician into the situation

26. When a patient calls with a complaint:
    a. use an approach similar to that of angry callers
    b. find the source of the problem
    c. present options of solutions to the patient
    d. all of the above

27. Federal, state, county, and city government pages are often organized in telephone directories as the:
    a. yellow pages
    b. white pages
    c. blue pages
    d. orange pages

28. What information should the medical assistant get from patients when they request a prescription?
    a. patient's last diagnosis
    b. patient's last laboratory results
    c. treatments that the patient has tried
    d. patient's medical history

29. Which of the following is NOT true about calling a pharmacy with a prescription?
    a. verify that the pharmacy staff member took the prescription down accurately
    b. note the time and date the prescription was called in to the pharmacy in the chart
    c. transcribe the information correctly when writing it down
    d. call the prescription in before verifying it with the physician

30. Which of the following is NOT true about ending a call?
    a. close the conversation with some form of "goodbye"
    b. hang up before the caller
    c. do not encourage inappropriate chatting
    d. thank the person for calling

TRUE OR FALSE

Directions: Circle the best answer.

31.   T   F   Phone and message records can be used in court.

32.   T   F   Direct calls are more expensive than operator-assisted calls.

33.   T   F   Always ask permission before placing a call on hold.

34.   T   F   Most physicians do not expect the medical assistant to screen calls.

35.   T   F   It is important that the medical assistant stay in control of incoming calls.

36.   T   F   A patient must give oral permission before a member of the physician's staff can give information to third-party callers.

37.   T   F   Wyoming falls into the Central time zone.

38.   T   F   New York falls into the Eastern time zone.

39.   T   F   Placing and receiving personal calls should be avoided during business hours.

40.   T   F   All sales calls are an interruption to the physician's day.

COMPLETION

Directions: Fill in the blank with the best answer.

41. A(An) _____ used in a phone greeting would include "good morning" or "good afternoon."

42. Callers who refuse to _____ themselves should not be put through to the physician.

43. Performing many tasks at the same time is called _____.

44. Having a keen sense of what to do or say to maintain good relations with others is called _____.

45. A minimum of _____ items of information are needed to correctly take a phone message.

46. The office should have a clear set of _____ to the office written so that when they are requested, they are easily given.

47. Patients often call the office to find out if the physician is a(an) _____ for their insurance program.

48. Some managed care organizations require a physician _____ before a patient may see a specialist.

49. To foster growth is to _____.

50. Many _____ calls require the good judgment of the medical assistant answering the phone.

51. Answering services usually provide a(an) _____ to answer the phone rather than a recording device.

52. One alternative to using directory assistance is using the _____ to find phone numbers.

53. The continental United States is divided into _____ standard time zones.

54. Call _____ allows the user to send calls to another designated number, such as a cell phone.

55. Legible and complete phone messages are vitally important because they can be brought into _____ and offered as evidence.

Word List
Emergency
Identify
Four
Seven
Salutation
Provider
Operator
Court
Referral
Tact
Cultivate
Forwarding
Multitasking
Directions
Internet

CHAPTER **10**

Scheduling Appointments

MULTIPLE CHOICE

Directions: Circle the letter of the choice that best completes the statement or answers the question.

1. A tickler file is an effective organizational tool to help the medical assistant:
   a. mail appointment reminders
   b. remember patient names
   c. learn to schedule efficiently
   d. manage office hours effectively

2. Which of the following features is NOT a basic requirement of the office appointment book?
   a. appropriate size
   b. color coding of days
   c. easy to write in
   d. space for notations

3. What information would you need to properly matrix the appointment book?
   a. days and hours the physician performs hospital rounds
   b. employee vacation days
   c. patient preferences regarding appointment times
   d. appointment times for friends of the physician

4. The way to organize appointment scheduling so that it best supports the success of the practice is to:
   a. schedule as many patients as possible throughout the entire day
   b. allow frequent rest breaks
   c. include a lot of time for the physician's administrative activities
   d. consider the preferences of the physician

5. The principal advantage of using the wave method when designing the scheduling process is that it:
   a. allows flexibility to accommodate the unpredictable
   b. gives priority to established patients
   c. provides more breaks for the staff
   d. enables the physician to see more patients each day

6. Which is the best approach to efficiently handle the scheduling of patients who are due for an appointment?
   a. send out a reminder that asks the patient to call for an appointment
   b. call the patient at work
   c. schedule a date and time and notify the patient
   d. it is the patient's responsibility to remember

7. An effective way to deal with patients who are always late for appointments is to:
   a. refuse to schedule them after this happens several times
   b. have them wait until it is convenient for the physician
   c. advise them that they disrupt the office schedule
   d. give them the last appointment of the day

8. What is the most important action to take when changing a patient's appointment time?
   a. finding out and noting why the time must be changed
   b. reminding them of any past due balances
   c. emphasizing the importance of keeping the new appointment
   d. erasing the patient's name from the original slot

9. Why is it necessary to include a note in the patient's chart when the patient does not show up for a scheduled appointment?
   a. to bill for the time
   b. to keep count of the number of no-shows for a possible drop in the future
   c. to provide you with a reminder to call and reschedule
   d. in case of future legal consequences regarding the patient's care

10. When informing patients that you must postpone their appointments because of the absence of the physician, it is good practice to:
    a. give them the name of one or more alternative physicians
    b. explain exactly why the physician cannot see them
    c. offer them priority over patients already scheduled in the future
    d. be extremely apologetic about the inconvenience

11. If you work for a physician who is frequently called away from the office, it is a good practice to:
    a. warn patients about this possibility when they make appointments
    b. design a reception area that offers extra patient services during long waits
    c. note alternative appointment times for each patient for rescheduling purposes
    d. create a scheduling system that best accommodates these delays

12. Which is the least satisfactory method of scheduling for the patient?
    a. wave
    b. double-booking
    c. modified wave
    d. categorization or grouping

13. A matrix in the schedule:
    a. avoids overcrowding
    b. keeps from booking during meetings and hospital rounds
    c. is only used in large offices
    d. is done at the end of the day

14. Which of the following is NOT an advantage to computerized appointment scheduling?
    a. the computer cannot select times on the basis of patient needs
    b. the computer can keep track of future appointments
    c. more than one person can access the system at a time
    d. ample appointment setting software is available

15. The appointment setting method by which patients log on to the Internet and view a facility's schedule to set their own appointment is called:
    a. flexible office hours
    b. self-scheduling
    c. grouping procedures
    d. advance booking

16. If a patient has been waiting more than _____ minutes past their appointment time, the medical assistant should offer to reschedule the appointment.
    a. 5
    b. 15
    c. 20
    d. 30

17. The information in the appointment book must be legible because:
    a. it could be entered into court proceedings as evidence
    b. it provides a clear indication as to what patient is coming at what time
    c. it allows all persons using the appointment book to clearly read it
    d. all of the above

18. Which of the following is true concerning scheduling new patients?
    a. financial arrangements should be explained when the appointment is made if the patient is expected to pay at the time of service
    b. only offer the patient the times reserved for new patient appointments without flexibility
    c. assume that the patient will look up directions on the Internet
    d. wait to obtain information about the chief symptom until the patient arrives for the appointment

19. The first prerequisite for scheduling an outpatient admission or procedure is:
    a. a signed consent form
    b. the telephone number of the diagnostic or inpatient facility
    c. the patient's demographic information
    d. an oral or written order for the procedure from the physician

20. When scheduling an inpatient admission, be sure that the patient understands which of the following?
    a. date and time to report for the admission
    b. what preadmission testing is necessary
    c. name, address, and phone number of the facility
    d. all of the above

21. The open office hours method of scheduling is also known as:
    a. tidal wave scheduling
    b. self-scheduling
    c. wave scheduling
    d. flexible office scheduling

22. Which types of outpatient procedures might be scheduled by the physician's office?
    a. MRIs
    b. CT scans
    c. blood work
    d. all of the above

23. The medical assistant must remember that the physician has other types of appointments that need special notation in the appointment book, such as:
    a. new patients
    b. physicals
    c. surgeries
    d. established patients

24. A person who fails to keep an appointment without giving advance notice is called a:
    a. disruption
    b. no-show
    c. cancellation
    d. reschedule

25. When an obstetrician devotes two afternoons per week to seeing pregnant patients, the physician is using an appointment scheduling method called:
    a. wave scheduling
    b. advance booking
    c. grouping procedures
    d. modified wave scheduling

26. When a requested appointment time is not available, the medical assistant should:
    a. explain why the time is not available and offer a substitute date and time
    b. insist that the patient accept the next available appointment
    c. immediately put the patient on a waiting list for that time slot
    d. suggest the patient see an alternate physician in the practice

27. When patients need a series of appointments, it is best to:
    a. schedule them individually
    b. let the patients call when they are ready to come in
    c. try to set the appointments for the same day of the week at the same time
    d. any method of scheduling will be effective

28. Patients may fail appointments because:
    a. they have been pressed for a payment but do not have the funds to pay
    b. they are in denial and are having difficulty facing the illness
    c. the office consistently runs behind schedule
    d. all of the above

29. What should the medical assistant remember when dealing with the appointments on the appointment book if the physician is ill?
    a. apologetically explain the nature of the physician's illness
    b. do not disclose the nature of the physician's illness
    c. do not lose the patient by referring to another physician
    d. tell the patients that the physician is out of town

30. When the physician is scheduled at outside facilities, the medical assistant must be sure to allow time for:
    a. emergencies
    b. travel
    c. returning phone calls
    d. the physician's late arrival

TRUE OR FALSE

Directions: Circle the correct answer.

31.   T   F   Open office hours do not work well for most practices.

32.   T   F   Wave scheduling may involve several patients arriving at the same time.

33.   T   F   Appointments for established patients usually take longer.

34.   T   F   A physician may discontinue care if the patient habitually fails to show up for appointments.

35.   T   F   When rescheduling an appointment, the first appointment date and time must be removed.

36.   T   F   Physicians rarely use medical bags for outside visits, so they do not need to be a concern for the medical assistant.

37.   T   F   If a late patient is scheduled as the last patient of the day and does not show up before the office closes, the medical assistant is obligated to wait until the patient arrives.

38.   T   F   Outpatient testing is no longer common for physicians.

39.   T   F   A documented physician's order is needed by most outside facilities before a patient is admitted.

40.   T   F   Everyone benefits from a full schedule of kept appointments.

COMPLETION

Directions: Fill in the blank with the best answer.

41. To throw a thing into disorder is called a(an) _____.

42. Patients who are returning to the office and have previously seen the physician are called

_____ _____.

43. Approaching a situation with haste or caution is using _____.

44. If a thing is considered _____, it is an indispensable part of a whole.

45. Two-way communication is also called _____.

46. If a symptom is coming and going at intervals and not continuous, it is said to be _____.

47. Responding to requests for immediate care and treatment after evaluating the urgency of the need and prioritizing the treatment is called _____.

48. A person who fails to keep an appointment without giving advance notice is called a(an)

    _____.

49. _____ means relating to a combination of social and economic factors.

50. A space of time in between events is called a(an) _____.

51. Competency as a result of training or practice is called _____.

52. Something in which a thing originates, develops, or is contained is called a(an) _____.

53. A thing that is necessary to an end or to carry out a function is called a(an)

    _____.

54. Patients must feel confident that the physician spent enough _____ to address their concerns.

55. Periodically, _____ calls will necessitate rescheduling appointments.

Word List
Integral
Triage
Time
No-show
Disruption
Expediency
Emergency
Socioeconomic
Intermittent
Established patients
Proficiency
Interaction
Prerequisite
Interval
Matrix

CHAPTER **11**

Patient Reception and Processing

MULTIPLE CHOICE

Directions: Circle the letter of the choice that best completes the statement or answers the question.

1. What is the most important reason for ensuring that sufficient quantities of all supplies exist each day in the medical office?
   a. maintain office reputation for efficiency
   b. prevent inconvenience for staff
   c. avoid interruption of patient flow
   d. prevent need for restocking patient examination rooms

2. Which statement is true regarding the handling of charts for patients who have appointments on a given day?
   a. pull all files before the first patient arrives and arrange in the order that patients are scheduled
   b. pull all files the night before and organize them alphabetically
   c. pull the file for each patient as the patient arrives and give to the physician
   d. check files for accuracy and completeness while the patient is with the physician

3. Which patients should be personally escorted to examination and treatment areas and given detailed instructions about what to do?
   a. new
   b. established
   c. consultations
   d. all of the above

4. What is the best way to decide whether patients need special assistance in disrobing or otherwise?
   a. ask all patients if you can be of assistance
   b. wait for patients to request help
   c. use special consideration with patients who display a disability
   d. offer help to patients who appear ill or upset

5. The medical assistant should follow all of these practices regarding patient arrivals EXCEPT:
   a. personally escort the patient from reception to the appropriate room
   b. tell the patient the specific items of clothing to remove
   c. explain exactly how to put on the gown
   d. have the patient wait in the examination room instead of the waiting room

6. The use of phonetic writing in the medical office can help you to:
   a. better understand medical abbreviations
   b. pronounce patient names correctly
   c. learn the meaning of medical terms
   d. take notes quickly and accurately

7. Patients often base their perceptions of an entire medical facility on:
   a. all of their experiences with medical professionals
   b. their previous healthcare experiences
   c. fears about their health
   d. what they see when entering the facility for the first time

8. The office mission statement:
   a. may reflect the reason that the physician went into practice
   b. may reflect the reason for the existence of the facility
   c. may be prominently displayed at the facility
   d. all of the above

9. Which of the following would be considered a patient amenity?
   a. writing table in the reception area
   b. examination gowns in the examination rooms
   c. rest rooms
   d. on-site laboratory

10. Which of the following is NOT true regarding chart placement in the medical facility?
    a. the chart should be placed in the door holder when the patient is ready for the physician
    b. offices should develop convenient signals regarding chart placement that everyone understands
    c. charts can be left in the patient examination room while the patient is waiting for the physician
    d. charts may be placed in either horizontal or upright positions in the door holder, depending on the physician's preference

11. The patient's name should be used:
    a. on greeting the patient at arrival
    b. when the patient leaves the office
    c. during the examination
    d. all of the above

12. Which of the following should be removed from the patient reception area as quickly as possible?
    a. talkative patients
    b. angry patients
    c. children
    d. patient relatives

13. Which of the following should most often be added to the patient chart on each visit?
    a. medical history form
    b. progress notes form
    c. patient information sheet
    d. insurance information sheet

14. Which of the following do patients NOT expect to find in the reception area?
    a. good ventilation
    b. television
    c. pleasant room temperature
    d. good lighting

15. The statistical characteristics of human populations are called:
    a. numbers
    b. perceptions
    c. demographics
    d. phonetics

16. If a chart if marked in some way as a reminder that specific actions need to be taken, it is said to be:
    a. mnemonic
    b. depleted
    c. sequential
    d. flagged

17. Which of the following is NOT an appropriate way to deal with a talkative patient?
    a. alert the physician that the patient tends to be talkative
    b. allow the patient to ask only three questions while seeing the physician
    c. schedule the patient as the last of the day
    d. intercom the physician while the physician is seeing the talkative patient, mentioning that the next patient is ready to be seen

18. It is helpful to devise an easy way to remember office closing duties, such as using a:
    a. mnemonic device
    b. lengthy checklist
    c. tickler file
    d. phonetic device

19. Which of the following is NOT true regarding patient examination rooms?
    a. patients enjoy a magazine rack so they can read while waiting for the physician
    b. the examination table should face the entrance to the room, so the patient is clearly visible when the physician enters
    c. the examination room should be tidied immediately after use and the next patient escorted in
    d. the examination room should not be used to clear out the reception area

20. Which information item is NOT included on a Patient Information Sheet that new patients are required to complete?
    a. social security number
    b. name and address of nearest relative
    c. name of spouse, if applicable
    d. summary of medical history

TRUE OR FALSE

Directions: Circle the best answer.

21.   T   F   Physician journals may be displayed as reading material in the reception area.

22.   T   F   Advance preparation for patient arrival helps the day progress smoothly and in a more relaxed way.

23.   T   F   The medical assistant must take care not to offer medical advice to the patient.

24.   T   F   If the patient brings a relative to the physician appointment, the patient implies consent to discussion of the patient's care with the relative.

25.   T   F   The appearance of the reception room influences the patient's perception of the entire office.

26.   T   F   Any toys placed in the waiting area should be washable.

27.   T   F   Patient charts pulled for the day should be placed in alphabetic order.

28.   T   F   Writing a phonetic spelling of a patient's name will help in pronouncing it correctly.

29.   T   F   A crowded reception room means that the physician is popular and competent.

30.   T   F   The medical assistant should only offer to assist patients who are obviously handicapped.

COMPLETION

Directions: Fill in the blank with the best answer.

31. Uncertainty in new surroundings can often create _____.

32. All patients should leave the medical facility feeling that they were treated with _____.

33. It is possible to violate patient _____ when using a sign-in register.

34. When the office staff commits to making the patient feel welcome, success of the practice is _____.

35. Patients expect to see the physician at the exact _____ time.

36. The patient should be given a(an) _____ of times and dates when making a return appointment.

37. The medical assistant should review the forms the patient fills out to be sure that they are _____.

38. Furniture in a pediatric physician's office should be _____.

39. If something is marked by accord in sentiment or action, it is said to be _____.

40. Something conducive to comfort, convenience, or enjoyment is called a(an) _____.

Word List

Confidentiality
Choice
Harmonious
Anxiety
Complete
Amenity
Respect
Appointment
Durable
Inevitable

CHAPTER **12**

Written Communications and Mail Processing

MULTIPLE CHOICE

Directions: Circle the letter of the choice that best completes the statement or answers the question.

1. Annotating incoming letters for physicians can help them by:
   a. preventing them from wasting time with "junk" mail sorting
   b. drawing their attention to the most important parts of the letters
   c. researching the information needed to answer the letter
   d. offering suggested responses

2. Which of the following would NOT be an appropriate responsibility of the medical assistant regarding office copiers and printers?
   a. understanding basic equipment maintenance
   b. studying the manuals that accompany the machines
   c. learning how to use all equipment properly
   d. memorizing the service contracts

3. Which size letterhead is appropriate for most business correspondence?
   a. $5\frac{1}{2} \times 8\frac{1}{2}$ in
   b. $7\frac{1}{4} \times 10\frac{1}{2}$ in
   c. $8\frac{1}{2} \times 11$ in
   d. 17×22 in

4. General and medical dictionaries and spelling guides are:
   a. not necessary if you have a word processing spell checker
   b. necessary only if you have trouble with spelling
   c. essential tools for every medical office
   d. books to learn from while you are in school

5. What is the most serious negative result of misspelling medical terms on patient records and in correspondence?
   a. appearance of professional incompetence on the part of the medical assistant
   b. embarrassment for the medical assistant
   c. a negative impression of the physician
   d. failure to meet requirements of insurance auditors

6. The best style to use when composing business letters in the medical office is:
    a. the one with which you are most comfortable
    b. the one that is preferred by your physician
    c. the one that is most formal
    d. the one that is highly technical and organized

7. The principal function of a well-organized portfolio of business letters is to help the medical assistant:
    a. write correctly
    b. save time
    c. use one consistent style
    d. spell accurately

8. Which letter style combines efficiency with an attractive page layout?
    a. modified-block
    b. block
    c. simplified
    d. none of the above

9. Which letter style would be most appropriate to use when writing a fast business letter to someone?
    a. modified-block
    b. block
    c. simplified
    d. modified-block with indented paragraphs

10. Which of the following dates is written correctly for inclusion in the heading of a letter?
    a. 5/1/04
    b. May 1st, 2004
    c. May 1, 2004
    d. May 1, '04

11. Which of the following is the correct way to write the first line of an inside address in a letter to John Kidwell, a pediatrician?
    a. John Kidwell, Pediatrician
    b. Dr. John Kidwell, MD
    c. Doctor John Kidwell
    d. John Kidwell, MD

12. What is the purpose of noting "c: Alice Adams, MD" at the bottom of a letter?
    a. it requests that the receiver make a copy of the letter for Dr. Adams
    b. it instructs the medical assistant to send the same letter to Dr. Adams
    c. it advises the receiver that a duplicate letter has been sent to Dr. Adams
    d. it tells the receiver that Dr. Adams has more information about the subject of the letter

13. The number of characters allowed for a state code is:
    a. five
    b. two
    c. 13
    d. one

14. Arrange these names in alphabetic order. Select the sequence of the numbers when the names are in alphabetic order.
    (1) Morton, Dianne
    (2) Marsh, Danielle
    (3) McDouglass, Dillard
    (4) MacDouglas, David

    a. (1), (2), (3), (4)
    b. (3), (2), (4), (1)
    c. (2), (3), (1), (4)
    d. (4), (2), (3), (1)

15. Arrange these names in alphabetic order. Select the sequence of the numbers when the names are in alphabetic order.
    (1) Woods-Jones, Stefanie
    (2) Ross, Kim
    (3) Mitchell, Pat
    (4) Jones, Sandra

    a. (1), (2), (3), (4)
    b. (3), (2), (4), (1)
    c. (2), (3), (1), (4)
    d. (4), (3), (2), (1)

16. Which type of special postal service would you use for a heavy expensive piece of medical equipment being returned to the manufacturer for a refund?
    a. registered
    b. first class
    c. certified
    d. special delivery

17. Which statement is TRUE regarding the procedures that the medical assistant should perform when handling incoming mail?
    a. do not open any mail addressed to the physician
    b. check carefully for any enclosures mentioned in letters
    c. initial each item
    d. organize all correspondence in alphabetic order

18. A marking in paper resulting from differences in thickness usually produced by the pressure of a projecting design in the mold is called a:
    a. girth
    b. portfolio
    c. watermark
    d. bond

19. Which of the following words is spelled incorrectly?
    a. homeostasis
    b. pallietive
    c. pleura
    d. sagittal

20. Which of the following words is spelled incorrectly?
    a. pamphlet
    b. questionnairre
    c. height
    d. committee

21. Which of the following words is spelled incorrectly?
    a. leukemia
    b. flexure
    c. hemorhage
    d. parenteral

22. Which of the following words is spelled incorrectly?
    a. wheal
    b. prosthesis
    c. rhyhmical
    d. vacuum

23. Which of the following words is spelled incorrectly?
    a. perseverence
    b. pruritus
    c. infarction
    d. cirrhosis

24. Words that replace nouns so that they do not have to constantly be repeated are called:
    a. verbs
    b. prepositions
    c. pronouns
    d. interjections

25. Which of the following is NOT a basic sentence structure pattern?
    a. subject-complement
    b. subject-object
    c. subject-clause
    d. subject-predicate

26. A measure around a body or item is called:
    a. girth
    b. bond
    c. ream
    d. flush

27. A group of words containing a subject and predicate is called a:
    a. flush
    b. clause
    c. portfolio
    d. grammar

28. Types of incoming mail would NOT include:
   a. bills for office purchases
   b. laboratory reports
   c. the physician's monthly statements
   d. payments for services

29. Which of the following is the usual business envelope size?
   a. no. 5
   b. no. 10
   c. no. $6^3/_4$
   d. no. $5^3/_4$

30. How many characters are allowed for a city name on an envelope?
   a. ten
   b. 13
   c. 16
   d. 18

31. If proof of mailing is needed, what might the medical assistant ask the post office for?
   a. special handling
   b. insured mail
   c. certificate of mailing
   d. certificate of delivery

32. Setting even with the edge of a typed page or column, or having no indentation, is called:
   a. flush
   b. annotated
   c. archaic
   d. superfluous

33. The substance number represents:
   a. the number of reams of paper in a case
   b. the quantity of paper being 20 lbs
   c. the number based on the weight of a ream of paper
   d. the measurement around a body or item

34. Which of the following letters should the physician sign personally?
   a. orders for office supplies
   b. collection letters to delinquent accounts
   c. letters of solicitation
   d. referral and consultation reports

35. The medical facility can save mailing costs by:
   a. using correct zip codes
   b. presorting
   c. using correct postage
   d. all of the above

TRUE OR FALSE

Directions: Circle the correct answer.

36.   T   F   A watermark is an indication of the quality of the paper.

37.   T   F   Typewriters are almost archaic now, with the use of computers in the medical office.

38.   T   F   Legal-sized paper is $5\frac{1}{2} \times 8\frac{1}{2}$.

39.   T   F   Simplified letter style means that the lines are flush with the right margin.

40.   T   F   Nouns express a person, place, thing, idea, or concept.

41.   T   F   An adjective describes a verb.

42.   T   F   A declarative sentence asks a question.

43.   T   F   Mail is classified according to type, weight, and destination.

44.   T   F   The United Parcel Service, Federal Express, and the US Postal Service are all private delivery services.

45.   T   F   Notations such as "special delivery" should be typed on the envelope in the upper left corner under the return address.

COMPLETION

Directions: Fill in the blank with the best answer.

46. Business envelopes are usually number _____.

47. The bottom margin of a letter should be _____ inch.

48. The best way to send a letter of great importance is via _____ mail.

49. To place in a specific division of a system of classification is to _____.

50. Generally, a business letter is _____ spaced.

51. Reference initials identify the _____ of a letter.

52. _____ means to furnish with notes, which are usually critical or explanatory.

53. All of the documents that leave the physician's office should project a professional _____.

54. Good _____ is essential to writing effective professional business letters.

55. Connecting words that show a relationship between nouns, pronouns, or other words in a sentence are called _____.

Word List

1
Single
Image
Prepositions
10
Certified
Annotating
Typist
Categorize
Grammar

CHAPTER 13

Medical Records Management

MULTIPLE CHOICE

Directions: Circle the letter of the choice that best completes the statement or answers the question.

1. Which of the following is NOT a method of organizing a medical record?
   a. source-oriented
   b. problem-oriented
   c. progressively
   d. chronologically

2. Information that is gained by questioning the patient or that is taken from a form is called:
   a. confidential information
   b. subjective information
   c. objective information
   d. necessary information

3. Which of the following are NOT needed when describing a patient's chief symptom?
   a. remedies the patient has tried to relieve symptoms
   b. duration of pain
   c. time when symptoms were first noticed
   d. number of family members who are healthy

4. A filing system in which an intermediary source of reference, such as a file card, must be consulted to locate specific files is called a(an):
   a. shelf filing system
   b. indirect filing system
   c. direct filing system
   d. shingling system

5. Releasing a record, with regard to filing it, means:
   a. removing pins and paper clips
   b. deciding where to file a particular item
   c. placing a mark indicating that the item is ready for filing
   d. arranging papers in filing sequence

6. How would you properly index the name "Jill Freeman, MD" for filing if you had another patient with the same name but without the title?
   a. Dr. Jill Freeman
   b. Freeman, Dr. Jill
   c. Freeman, Jill
   d. Freeman, Jill MD

7. How would you properly index the name "Amanda M. Stiles-Duncan" for filing?
   a. Stilesduncan, Amanda M.
   b. Stiles Duncan, Amanda M.
   c. Duncanstiles, Amanda M.
   d. Duncan, Amanda M. Stiles

8. Who is the legal owner of a patient's record?
   a. the patient
   b. the physician or agency where services were provided
   c. the patient's insurance company
   d. both the patient and the physician

9. Continuity of care means:
   a. an aggregate of activities designed to ensure adequate quality, especially in manufactured products or in the service industries
   b. a formal examination of an organization's or individual's accounts
   c. that which continues smoothly from one provider to another, so that the patient receives the most benefit
   d. granted or endowed with a particular authority

10. A legal instrument authorizing one to act as the agent of the grantor is called a:
    a. power of attorney
    b. will
    c. medical record release
    d. requisite

11. Which of the following are common types of filing equipment found in a medical office?
    a. rotary circular files
    b. lateral files
    c. automated files
    d. all of the above

12. Which of the following is NOT an advantage to color coding filing systems?
    a. patient charts can be found quickly
    b. it is easy to tell when a file is misplaced
    c. patient charts can be refiled quickly
    d. all of the above are advantages of color coding

13. Which statement is NOT true regarding the reasons for keeping accurate medical records?
    a. the medical record provides critical information for other caregivers
    b. effects of various treatments can be tracked and statistics gleaned from them
    c. the patient's family may wish to examine the records and correct errors
    d. accurate records are vital for financial reimbursements

14. Which of the following is NOT objective information?
   a. progress notes
   b. family history
   c. diagnosis
   d. physical examination and findings

15. What is the most important reason to tell the physician of an error in charting that is discovered later?
   a. the error could affect the health and well-being of the patient
   b. to protect your job
   c. to be sure that you are not accused of making the error
   d. to keep the patient from discovering the error

16. Which statement is INCORRECT about correcting charting errors?
   a. insert the correction above or immediately after the error
   b. draw two clear lines through the error
   c. in the margin, initial and date the error correction
   d. do not hide charting errors

17. Which of the following steps for records release is out of order?
   a. explain to the patient that the release form is necessary
   b. have the patient sign the form in the space indicated
   c. review the record release form with the patient and ask if it is understood
   d. make a copy of the form for the patient chart

18. The medical record should be released only with a:
   a. verbal order from the physician
   b. written order from the physician
   c. written release from the patient
   d. verbal order from the office manager

19. Medical facilities should keep records on minors for how long?
   a. indefinitely
   b. until the minor is deceased
   c. for 10 years
   d. until the minor reaches the age of majority, plus 3 years

20. Which of the following is NOT an advantage of a numeric filing system?
   a. allows periodic expansion without shifting folders
   b. provides additional confidentiality to the chart
   c. filing activity is greatest at the beginning of the system
   d. saves time in record retrieval and refiling

21. An informed consent form must address which of the following?
   a. risks and benefits of the procedure
   b. reasonable alternatives to the procedure
   c. risks and benefits of not performing the procedure
   d. all of the above

22. The three stages of machine transcription do NOT include:
    a. keyboarding the dictated text to a printed document
    b. reviewing the dictated text with the patient
    c. dictating into a dictation unit
    d. listening to what has been dictated

23. When preparing a file for a new patient, the medical assistant should:
    a. be sure the patient's name is spelled correctly
    b. review the forms the patient filled out for completeness
    c. copy the insurance card or ensure that insurance information is included
    d. all of the above

24. An item used to provide space for the temporary filing of materials is called a(an):
    a. OUTguide
    b. OUTfolder
    c. shingle
    d. caption

25. The most efficient type of medical record is the:
    a. computer-based medical record
    b. paper-based medical record
    c. both are equally efficient
    d. neither are efficient

26. The method of filing whereby one report is laid on top of the older report, resembling a roof, is called:
    a. alphanumeric filing
    b. gleaning
    c. shingling
    d. pressboard filing

27. Files for patients who have died, moved away, or otherwise terminated their relationship with the physician are called:
    a. inactive files
    b. closed files
    c. active files
    d. dead files

28. HIPAA recommends that physicians keep the records on patients who have died for at least:
    a. 1 year
    b. 2 years
    c. 3 years
    d. 4 years

29. The medical assistant should consider which of the following when selecting filing equipment?
    a. fire protection
    b. cost of space and equipment
    c. confidentiality requirements
    d. all of the above

30. A strong highly glazed composition paper or heavy card stock is called:
   a. augment
   b. pressboard
   c. microfilm
   d. shingle

TRUE OR FALSE

Directions: Circle the best answer.

31.　T　F　The patient owns the medical record.

32.　T　F　An aggregate of activities designed to ensure adequate quality is called quality control.

33.　T　F　Subjective information is that which the physician observes during the physical examination of the patient.

34.　T　F　A standard nationwide rule exists to follow in establishing a records retention schedule.

35.　T　F　Conditioning papers involves including a mark that indicates the papers are ready for filing.

36.　T　F　The three basic filing methods are alphabetic, numeric, and alphanumeric.

37.　T　F　Numeric filing is a direct filing system.

38.　T　F　A provisional diagnosis is one that is not a final diagnosis and that is usually made before test results are obtained.

39.　T　F　When adding documents to the patient chart, the most recent information should be placed on top.

40.　T　F　Keeping a copy of a patient consent form in the chart is not necessary.

COMPLETION

Directions: Fill in the blank with the best answer.

41. _____ information is provided by the patient.

42. To make greater, more numerous, larger, or more intense is to _____.

43. When a patient is transferred from one facility to another, the _____ of care assures that there are no lapses in treatment and that smooth transitions occur.

44. Computer-based medical records are sometimes called _____ health records.

45. The concise account of the patient's symptoms in the patient's own words is the _____ _____.

46. _____ of an entry in a medical record is never acceptable.

47. To be granted or endowed with a particular authority or right is to be _____.

48. _____ information is observed by the physician.

49. Deciding where to file a particular chart based on the name of the patient is called

_____.

50. A _____ file is a follow-up system used to help the medical assistant remember when a certain task needs to be done.

Word List
Indexing
Obliteration
Continuity
Objective
Vested
Chief complaint
Tickler
Augment
Electronic
Subjective

CHAPTER **14**

Professional Fees, Billing, and Collecting

MULTIPLE CHOICE

Directions: Circle the letter of the choice that best completes the statement or answers the question.

1. The medical assistant may help with all of the following tasks related to the physician's fees for services rendered EXCEPT:
   a. determining the amounts charged for procedures
   b. informing patients about the fees
   c. collecting payments from patients
   d. making arrangements for long-term payments

2. Which factor is NOT usually considered by physicians when determining how much to charge for a procedure?
   a. time required
   b. amount of knowledge and decision making involved
   c. type of procedure
   d. ability of patient to pay

3. When working under a managed care plan, physicians agree to:
   a. base fees on national trends
   b. charge fees that are based on local community averages
   c. accept fees that are predetermined by the plan
   d. set fees within certain ranges provided by the plan

4. Why might a physician receive only $185.00 for a procedure for which the insurance company was billed $255.00?
   a. the fee profile increased since being set by the company
   b. the insurance company's fee schedule allows only $185.00
   c. $225.00 is above the maximum range charged by the other physicians in the area
   d. all of the above

5. When filling a basic insurance claim, if the physician believes that the insurance company will only pay $185.00 of the $255.00 fee, how should the service be billed?
   a. bill the insurance company $255.00 and advise the patient that the bill will be for $70.00 after the insurance pays the claim
   b. bill the insurance company $185.00 and bill the patient $70.00
   c. bill the insurance company $185.00 and write off the $70.00
   d. bill the insurance company $295.00 and bill the patient $70.00

6. What information is gathered to determine an individual physician's fee profile?
   a. economic status of the patients
   b. the actual charges over a given time period
   c. type of specialty practiced
   d. average fees of other physicians in the area

7. Which of the following best describes the concept of *professional courtesy*?
   a. referral system in which physicians send patients to colleagues for consultation and treatment
   b. charging reduced or no fee for services rendered to other medical professionals
   c. practice of not undercharging for services and thus lowering the insurance company fee schedules
   d. reducing fees charged for treatment of friends and family members

8. It is not recommended that physicians charge for any of the following situations EXCEPT:
   a. late payments
   b. no-show appointments
   c. emergency walk-ins
   d. telephone consultations

9. If a patient tells you that a close friend will pay the medical bills if the patient is unable to do so, you must:
   a. orally verify this arrangement with the friend
   b. request that the patient give the friend power of attorney
   c. secure a written agreement from the friend
   d. meet with the friend in person

10. Which factor determines whether patients must sign a truth in lending disclosure as required by Regulation Z?
    a. their bill is divided into two payments
    b. the physician includes a finance charge
    c. the person has a poor credit history
    d. payments will be made over a period longer than 6 months

11. Which of the following information must NOT be given out when responding to a request for credit information on a patient?
    a. the highest amount the account has ever reached
    b. current balance on the patient's account
    c. your opinion about the patient's ability to pay
    d. how long the patient has had an account

12. Which is the best way to work with patients regarding financial matters?
    a. always apologize for having to ask them for payment
    b. discuss billing policies only if the patient asks about them
    c. be firm about enforcing office payment policies
    d. explain the office financial policies when they make an appointment

13. Identify the statement about medical office credit policies that is NOT a recommended practice.
    a. include billing, insurance, and collection procedures
    b. write fairly detailed guidelines to follow when making credit decisions
    c. develop general policies so that each account can be considered individually
    d. fully disclose these policies to patients

14. Which of the following is NOT true about the use of independent billing services?
    a. it reduces calls to the office regarding billing matters
    b. it allows office staff more time to work with patients
    c. it depersonalizes billing disputes
    d. it drastically reduces the cost of billing and monitoring accounts

15. Which of the following would be the LEAST helpful for encouraging patients to make prompt payments?
    a. clearly itemized statements
    b. including self-addressed envelopes with statements
    c. sending collection letters to all patients with a balance due
    d. firmly stating policies regarding collection procedures

16. When preparing the first statements sent to patients to bill for medical services, the charges should be itemized:
    a. if they were not explained to the patient before the patient received the services
    b. on all first statements sent out
    c. for bills that will also be submitted to an insurance carrier
    d. if many of your patients call with billing questions

17. The purpose of a charge slip is to:
    a. provide an itemized billing statement on which the physician notes charges
    b. explain charges to patients in advance of treatment
    c. provide estimates of future treatments
    d. allow patients to apply for credit

18. Under which circumstances would a cycle billing system be most advantageous for the medical office?
    a. most companies in the area pay employees at the end of each month
    b. the patient load is moderate and most of the patients pay at the time of their visits
    c. the physician wishes to stabilize cash flow
    d. all billing is handled by an outside service

19. Who should be billed for the treatment of an emancipated minor?
    a. the minor
    b. the parent who came to the office with the minor
    c. the parent who is financially responsible for the minor
    d. the guardian

20. The smallest percentage of people who do not pay their medical bills:
    a. are disorganized and irresponsible
    b. are dissatisfied with the physician's services
    c. spend more than they earn
    d. never intend to pay

21. Legal and appropriate procedures that you can use when attempting to locate patients with outstanding balances who move and leave no forwarding address include all of the following EXCEPT:
    a. informing the patient's employers that money is owed to the physician
    b. calling the emergency contact listed on the patient information sheet
    c. calling references that are listed on patient registration cards
    d. asking neighbors for information about patients' new locations

22. When a patient files for bankruptcy, the appropriate procedure is to:
    a. attempt to collect from the patient's insurance company
    b. bill the patient as usual
    c. contact the patient directly and demand payment in full
    d. file a creditor's claim with the court or write off the bill

23. All of the following statements describe advantages of using small claims court to collect delinquent accounts EXCEPT:
    a. it is faster than regular court action
    b. it is necessary to hire a lawyer to represent the physician
    c. the claim takes less time to prepare and present than a lawsuit
    d. it is relatively inexpensive to use small claims court

24. Which of the following is TRUE about giving patient estimates for treatment?
    a. it may help simplify collection by preventing misunderstandings
    b. it may help to avoid forgetting that a fee was quoted
    c. it may help eliminate the possibility of later misquoting the fee
    d. all of the above

25. An organization under contract to the government and some private plans to act as financial representatives is a:
    a. fiscal agent
    b. fiscal augment
    c. third-party payor
    d. guarantor

26. The column in the pegboard system used to enter charges is the:
    a. credit column
    b. debit column
    c. adjustment column
    d. balance column

27. Which of the following examples would you enter in the credit column?
    a. payments received for medical services rendered
    b. additional charges placed on the patient's account
    c. fees for returned checks
    d. none of the above

28. All of the following might be found in the adjustment column EXCEPT:
    a. professional discounts
    b. write-offs
    c. new charges
    d. disallowances

29. When using the telephone to collect accounts, the medical assistant should:
    a. call at whatever time the patient can be reached
    b. try to get a definite commitment on a date that payment will be made
    c. insist on payment within 2 weeks
    d. apologize for calling and requesting payment

30. Which of the following times are NOT acceptable for collection calls?
    a. 9:00 a.m.
    b. 11:30 a.m.
    c. 8:00 a.m.
    d. 9:30 p.m.

31. Which of the following billing types has statements sent at given times of the month, such as a fourth of the accounts receivable the first week and so on through the month?
    a. monthly billing
    b. cycle billing
    c. third-party billing
    d. twice-a-month billing

32. Transferring or carrying from a book of original entry to a ledger is called:
    a. posting
    b. paying
    c. receiving
    d. billing

33. All of the following are considered special bookkeeping entries EXCEPT:
    a. refunds
    b. credit balances
    c. payments
    d. adjustments

34. Payment for medical services is accomplished in which of the following ways?
    a. internal insurance or other third-party billing
    b. payment at the time of service
    c. outside billing and collection assistance
    d. all of the above

35. Most medical offices accept which of the following forms of payment?
    a. debit cards
    b. credit cards
    c. checks
    d. all of the above

TRUE OR FALSE

Directions: Circle the best answer.

36.   T   F   Most physicians prefer that patients pay at the time of service.

37.   T   F   Credit information is not as confidential as patient medical information.

38.   T   F   A credit balance occurs when a patient has overpaid.

39.   T   F   A physician's fee profile is used in determining the amount of third-party liability for services under the contracted program.

40.   T   F   Patients appreciate discussion of fees in advance of procedures.

41.   T   F   The guarantor is not always the patient.

42.   T   F   It is not the responsibility of the physician's office staff to discuss additional fees that the patient might incur.

43.   T   F   Repeated telephone collection calls are acceptable if the patient owes a balance.

44.   T   F   The physician is the only person who should sign collection letters.

45.   T   F   If a patient can pay a medical bill without incurring hardship, and still refuses to pay, litigation to collect is acceptable.

46.   T   F   When a patient is classified as a "skip," the office should wait 1 month before initiating collection efforts.

COMPLETION

Directions: Fill in the blank with the best answer.

47. The balance owed a creditor on an account is known as _____.

48. The slips used for billing that are attached to charts while the patient is in the office are called _____ forms.

49. An exchange or transfer of goods, services, or funds is called a(an) _____.

50. The _____ fee is a range of the usual fees charged for the same service by physicians with similar training and experience practicing in the same geographical area.

51. _____ slips may help to simplify the collection process because there is no misunderstanding as to the agreed fee for a procedure.

52. _____ paper does not require carbon to make a copy.

53. Refunds after all payments are made on an account usually result in a patient balance of _____.

54. The Truth in Lending Act is enforced by the Federal _____ Commission.

55. Patients who are unable to afford medical bills are sometimes said to be medically _____.

56. A statement of transactions during a fiscal period and the resulting balance is called a(an) _____.

57. Amounts paid on patient accounts are called _____.

58. A compilation of preestablished fee allowances for given services or procedures is called a fee _____.

59. Funds paid out are called _____.

60. The person who makes or gives a guarantee of payment for a bill is called a(an) _____.

Word List
Disbursements
Zero
Guarantor
Account
Customary
Trade
Indigent
Estimate
Encounter
Receipts
Transaction
NCR
Schedule
Payables

CHAPTER **15**

Basics of Diagnostic Coding

MULTIPLE CHOICE

Directions: Circle the letter of the choice that best completes the statement or answers the question.

1. An ICD-9 code identifies the:
   a. procedure
   b. supplies
   c. condition
   d. attending physician

2. A V-code describes:
   a. an illness
   b. an emergency
   c. a poisoning
   d. a condition other than an illness

3. An E-code can be used to identify:
   a. a disease
   b. a diagnosis
   c. an accident
   d. a physical examination

4. To code an annual checkup, the medical assistant would need to use a(an):
   a. E-code
   b. V-code
   c. modifier
   d. diagnosis code

5. Which of the following could be a code for the diagnosis of hypertension?
   a. E905.2
   b. V50.3
   c. 401.9
   d. 99213

6. Which of the following could be an ICD-9 code for a snakebite?
   a. E905.2
   b. V50.3
   c. 401.9
   d. 99213

7. When a coder lacks the information necessary to code a term to a more specific category, which of the following abbreviations is used?
   a. NEC
   b. NOS
   c. ICD
   d. CPT

8. The purpose of the ICD-9-CM is to:
   a. shorten claims processing time
   b. facilitate measurement of compliance with clinical guidelines
   c. maximize reimbursement with accurate coding
   d. all of the above

9. A preexisting condition that will cause an increase in the length of stay of an inpatient by at least 1 day is called a(an):
   a. comortality
   b. comorbidity
   c. complication
   d. etiology

10. If something is required by an authority or by law, it is said to be:
    a. prerequisite
    b. requisite
    c. mandated
    d. ancillary

11. The definition of disease or procedure is signified by the following notation:
    a. PDX
    b. SDX
    c. MSP
    d. DEF

12. Which of the following is a definitive diagnosis?
    a. dehydration
    b. nausea
    c. vomiting
    d. none of the above

DIAGNOSIS CODING

Directions: Properly code the following diagnoses.

13. Acute serous otitis media _____

14. Acute myocardial infarction of anterior wall, initial episode _____

15. Morbid obesity _____

16. Carbon monoxide poisoning _____

17. Complication of transplanted organ, heart _____

18. Tubal pregnancy _____

19. Cardiomegaly _____

20. Cataract associated with diabetes _____

21. Primary genital syphilis _____

22. Color blindness _____

23. Acute eustachian salpingitis _____

24. Chronic hypotension _____

25. Croup _____

26. Chronic tonsillitis and adenoiditis _____

27. Grave's disease _____

28. Diabetic coma with ketoacidosis _____

29. Transitory tachypnea of newborn _____

30. Accidental hypothermia _____

31. Exposure to venereal disease _____

32. Screening mammogram for patient at high risk _____

33. Contact dermatitis from solvent _____

34. Dysmenorrhea _____

35. Ventricular fibrillation _____

36. Botulism _____

37. Retinal hemorrhage _____

38. Fetal alcohol syndrome _____

39. Down syndrome _____

40. Pushing from a tall building _____

41. Diverticulitis of colon _____

42. HIV infection _____

43. Rupture of appendix _____

44. Fibrocystic breast disease _____

45. Acute juvenile rheumatoid arthritis _____

COMPLETION

Directions: Fill in the blanks with the best answer.

46. A direction given to the coder to look elsewhere if the main term or subterm for that entry is not sufficient for coding the information is _____.

47. _____ is the cause of the disorder.

48. Instructions or guides in classification assignments are called _____.

49. A condition that an insured person had before the issuance of an insurance policy is said to be

    _____.

50. The condition determined to be chiefly responsible for the patient's admission to the hospital is

    the _____ diagnosis.

51. Converting verbal or written descriptions into numeric and alphanumeric designations is called

    _____.

52. A three-digit code representing a specific disease within the section is called the

    _____.

53. The five-digit code giving the highest level of specificity to the disease state is the

    _____.

54. The abbreviation that is the equivalent of "unspecified" is _____.

55. Another word for encounter form is _____.

Word List
Subclassification
NOS
Principal
Superbill
Coding
Notes
Preexisting
Etiology
Category
"see also"

CHAPTER **16**

Basics of Procedure Coding

MULTIPLE CHOICE

Directions: Circle the letter of the choice that best completes the statement or answers the question.

1. Which codes have two-digit modifiers?
   a. ICD-9-CM
   b. CPT
   c. HCPCS
   d. E-codes

2. Which of the following is a CPT code?
   a. E905.2
   b. V50.3
   c. 401.9
   d. 99213

3. Which of the following could be an Evaluation and Management code for an office visit?
   a. E905.2
   b. V50.3
   c. 401.9
   d. 99213

4. Evaluation and Management codes are found in which book?
   a. CPT
   b. HCPCS
   c. ICD-9-CM
   d. textbooks

5. Procedures that are grouped together and paid as one are called:
   a. downcodes
   b. upcodes
   c. bundled codes
   d. unbundled codes

6. HCPCS are considered to be:
   a. level I codes
   b. level II codes
   c. level III codes
   d. level IV codes

7. The relative incidence of a disease is called:
   a. mortality
   b. component
   c. morbidity
   d. comorbidity

8. A general grouping of codes, such as surgery or medicine, is the largest group in the CPT and is called the:
   a. section
   b. subsection
   c. subheading
   d. category

9. Which place of service code usually designates the physician's office?
   a. 31
   b. 25
   c. 22
   d. 11

10. The office visit level that usually focuses on the chief symptom without a review of systems or family history is called:
    a. problem focused
    b. expanded problem focused
    c. detailed
    d. comprehensive

11. Which of the following play a role in the complexity of the decision-making process used in the treatment of a patient?
    a. number of diagnoses or management options
    b. amount and complexity of data reviewed
    c. risk of complications and morbidity or mortality
    d. all of the above

12. The helpful comments provided at the beginning of each section in the CPT are called:
    a. explanations
    b. guidelines
    c. regulations
    d. rules

PROCEDURE CODING

Directions: Properly code the following procedures.

13. Follow-up inpatient consultation, established patient, problem-focused _____

14. Office consultation, new patient, comprehensive _____

15. Hospital observation, care, discharge _____

16. New patient office visit, comprehensive history, moderate complexity decision-making _____

17. New patient office visit, problem-focused history, straightforward decision-making _____

18. Established patient office visit, expanded, problem-focused history, low-complexity decision-making _____

19. Emergency department visit, comprehensive history, high-complexity decision-making _____

20. Normal initial newborn care _____

21. Family psychotherapy without patient present _____

22. Dipstick urinalysis _____

23. Blood alcohol level _____

24. Cholesterol level _____

25. Blood glucose _____

26. Oral polio vaccine _____

27. Electrocardiogram, routine 12-lead _____

28. Spinal chiropractic manipulative treatment, 1-2 regions _____

29. Handling of specimen for transfer from office to laboratory _____

30. Automated CBC with manual differential WBC _____

31. Paternity test _____

32. ABO blood typing _____

33. Diagnostic amniocentesis _____

34. Bilateral oophorectomy _____

35. Reduction mammoplasty _____

36. MRI of temporomandibular joint _____

37. Routine venipuncture _____

38. Direct nasal mucous membrane allergy test _____

39. Initial prosthetic training, 15 minutes _____

40. Simple pulmonary stress test _____

41. Serum albumin _____

42. Confirmation of cocaine, qualitative _____

43. Blood uric acid _____

44. Critical care provided to patient for 50 minutes _____

45. Removal of the spleen, total _____

COMPLETION

Directions: Fill in the blank with the best answer.

46. It is important to have the _____ edition of the CPT manual.

47. The total income produced by a given source is called _____.

48. CPT was first published in 1966 by the _____.

49. The process of reviewing procedures and services for medical necessity is called _____.

50. _____ explain circumstances that alter a service that has been provided.

51. _____ is a deliberate increase in a CPT code to receive higher reimbursements and should never be done.

52. The CPT is a method of measuring physician _____.

53. A constituent part, or a part of a larger group, is called a(an) _____.

54. Evaluation and management codes are often used for physician office _____.

55. Almost all evaluation and management services contain a degree of _____.

Word List
Upcoding
Component
Visits
Counseling
Utilization
Revenue
Modifiers
Productivity
AMA
Latest

CHAPTER **17**

The Health Insurance Claim Form

MULTIPLE CHOICE

Directions: Circle the letter of the choice that best completes the statement or answers the question.

1. The number used by the IRS that identifies a business or individual functioning as a business entity for income tax reporting is the:
   a. social security number
   b. employer identification number
   c. insurance claim number
   d. routing number

2. Which of the following is NOT an advantage of paper claims over electronic claims?
   a. start-up cost is minimal
   b. documentation explaining unusual circumstances can be easily attached
   c. there is a greater chance for rejection
   d. they are accepted by most third-party payors

3. Which block on the insurance claim form tells whether or not the claim is related to a work injury or auto accident?
   a. 6
   b. 9
   c. 10
   d. 15

4. What is the most common place of service code used for claims filed from a physician's office?
   a. 11
   b. 21
   c. 26
   d. 35

5. Which act is responsible for implementation of various acts that protect an individual's health insurance and privacy standards?
   a. OSHA
   b. CLIA
   c. HIPAA
   d. CMS

6. A claim that is incorrect in some manner or does not present a logical picture of the patient's situation is called a:
   a. dingy claim
   b. clean claim
   c. dirty claim
   d. invalid claim

7. A claim that is missing some type of information is called a(an):
   a. incomplete claim
   b. dingy claim
   c. invalid claim
   d. rejected claim

8. Which of the following guidelines should NOT be followed when completing insurance claims?
   a. obtain a signed authorization form for release of information
   b. record the name of the subscriber because it may be different from that of the patient
   c. make certain that any necessary attachments are included with the completed form
   d. all of the above should be followed

9. The insured's name should be placed in which block of the insurance claim form?
   a. 1
   b. 4
   c. 8
   d. 12

10. If a physician chooses to accept assignment, which block would indicate so on the claim form?
    a. 21
    b. 24
    c. 26
    d. 27

11. An organization that processes claims and performs other business-related functions for a health plan is called a:
    a. clearinghouse
    b. beneficiary
    c. third-party administrator
    d. third-party payor

12. Hard copies of claims that are completed and sent via surface mail are called:
    a. electronic claims
    b. paper claims
    c. dirty claims
    d. clean claims

13. An organization that offers a healthcare provider the service of receiving claims transmissions, checking and preparing the claims for processing, and submitting claims to the applicable insurance payor is called a:
    a. clearinghouse
    b. beneficiary
    c. third-party administrator
    d. third-party payor

14. The person who pays the premium to the insurance company is the:
    a. policyholder
    b. carrier
    c. provider
    d. beneficiary

15. Which of the following is NOT an advantage of paper claims?
    a. start-up cost is minimal
    b. accepted by most third-party payors
    c. greater chance for rejection
    d. forms are readily available

16. Which of the following is NOT an advantage of electronic claims?
    a. cost savings in postage
    b. initial start-up is expensive
    c. reduced claim rejection
    d. generation of claim status reports

17. The current form used to process most insurance claims is the:
    a. CMS-1450
    b. CMS-1500
    c. CMS-1491
    d. CMS-1490S

18. If the patient wishes the payment to go directly to the physician, the patient is approving the:
    a. assignment of benefits
    b. release of information
    c. PIN number
    d. employer identification number

19. Which of the following would be helpful to the medical assistant in completing claims?
    a. keeping insurance forms in a central location
    b. completing the forms as soon as possible after service is rendered
    c. completing the forms by category
    d. all of the above

20. An organization that contracts with the government to handle and mediate insurance claims from medical facilities is a:
    a. provider
    b. third-party payor
    c. fiscal intermediary
    d. third-party administrator

21. The record that can be used to track information and verify that it was processed correctly is called a(an):
    a. electronic claim
    b. audit trail
    c. carrier-direct system
    d. electronic data interchange

22. If a patient has a second health insurance plan, the information about that plan should be noted in which block of the CMS-1500?
    a. 13
    b. 6
    c. 24
    d. 11

23. The date of service for the procedure to be billed is noted in which section of block 24?
    a. a
    b. b
    c. d
    d. g

24. The ID number of a referring physician is noted in block:
    a. 4
    b. 17
    c. 27
    d. 32

25. The name and address of the facility where services were rendered is in block:
    a. 25
    b. 10
    c. 32
    d. 18

TRUE OR FALSE

Directions: Circle the correct answer.

26.   T   F   Claim processing issues are at the heart of most provider-payor conflicts.

27.   T   F   The company, individual, or group that provides medical services to a patient is the provider.

28.   T   F   Paper claims usually contain no errors and are paid quickly.

29.   T   F   The patient is not always the beneficiary of an insurance reimbursement.

30.   T   F   Only a few insurance carriers use optical character recognition scanners to transfer the information on claim forms to computers.

31.   T   F   The CMS-1500 claim form is completed in the same manner for every insurance carrier.

32.   T   F   The MM DD YYYY format should be used for all dates on the claim form.

33.   T   F   Some of the blocks on the insurance claim form do not have to be completed.

34.   T   F   Physicians must always accept assignment on insurance claims.

35.   T   F   Claim rejection and delay cost the physician money.

COMPLETION

Directions: Fill in the blank with the best answer.

36. The act developed in 1996 designed to protect individuals' health insurance and privacy standards is called _____.

37. The document that means a service cannot be claimed to Medicare, and if the notice is not signed in advance of the service taking place, the charges cannot be collected from the patient, is called a(an) _____.

38. Block 22 of the CMS-1500 is the space reserved for the Medicaid _____ code.

39. When the charge is expressed in whole dollars, use two _____ in the cents column.

40. A claim that is missing some type of information is considered either a rejected claim or a(an) _____ claim.

41. A signature used for electronic claims that consists of lines of text or a text box and is attached through a software program is called a(an) _____ signature.

42. A tickler file is also called a(an) _____ file.

43. The medical assistant should _____ the front and the back of the insurance card and place it in the medical record.

44. There should not be any _____ data on electronic claims except for signatures.

45. Diagnosis codes are placed first in block _____.

46. Procedure codes are placed in block _____.

47. If the procedure that is being billed was an emergency procedure, that is marked in block 24 _____.

48. Dates of services are placed in block 24 _____.

49. If Medicare is the primary payor, the word _____ should appear in block 11.

50. If the physician is PAR, accept assignment should be checked _____.

51. If claims are submitted electronically, about _____ weeks should pass before expecting reimbursement.

52. It is helpful to create a _____ list of codes for the office.

53. The diagnosis must be coded accurately and must correspond with the _____.

54. _____ precede procedure code modifiers.

55. The biggest _____ in getting set up for electronic claims is waiting for state and federal approvals.

Word List
Suspense
a
Treatment
Digital
21
Handwritten
None
Photocopy
i
Master
Advance Beneficiary Notice
Dashes
Obstacle
Incomplete
3
Yes
Resubmission
24
Zeros
HIPAA

CHAPTER 18

Third-Party Reimbursement

MULTIPLE CHOICE

Directions: Circle the letter of the choice that best completes the statement or answers the question.

1. The purpose of health insurance is to:
   a. pay all medical bills
   b. provide income during times of illness
   c. help individuals and families offset the costs of medical care
   d. be able to choose one's own physician

2. The deductible is:
   a. a specific amount of money paid out-of-pocket before the insurance carrier begins paying
   b. a type of co-insurance collected at the time of service
   c. a term used in managed care for an approved referral
   d. limitations on an insurance contract for which benefits are not payable

3. Insurance benefits are determined by:
   a. indemnity schedules
   b. service benefit plans
   c. relative value studies
   d. all of the above

4. Which of the following is NOT one of the parts of the RBRVS?
   a. physician time
   b. physician work
   c. charge-based professional liability expenses
   d. charge-based overhead

5. Which classification of reimbursement provides protection against especially large medical bills resulting from catastrophic or prolonged illnesses?
   a. basic medical
   b. major medical
   c. surgical
   d. hospitalization

6. A tax-deferred bank or savings account combined with a low-premium/high-deductible insurance policy is called a:
   a. managed care plan
   b. medical savings account
   c. disability income insurance
   d. co-insurance

7. If a parent has been decreed by a court to provide insurance for the children from a divorced family:
   a. the birthday rule does not apply
   b. the birthday rule only applies in specific circumstances
   c. the birthday rule states that this parent's insurance is primary
   d. the birthday rule does not deal with children in divorced families

8. Which of the following is NOT a type of managed care?
   a. HMO
   b. Medicaid
   c. PPO
   d. IPA

9. The traditional fee-for-service option for military dependants is called:
   a. TRICARE Prime
   b. TRICARE Extra
   c. TRICARE Standard
   d. CHAMPVA

10. Utilization review committees:
    a. decide whether or not a patient is covered by medical insurance
    b. decide which patients should have medical procedures performed first
    c. ensure that medical services rendered are medically necessary
    d. provide counseling to patients regarding their insurance coverage

11. The type of referral used for emergency cases that is often immediately approved is called a:
    a. regular referral
    b. STAT referral
    c. urgent referral
    d. normal referral

12. The term meaning that a patient is not required to have a referral to see a specialist is:
    a. plan referral
    b. self referral
    c. automatic referral
    d. referral

13. Which of the following items of information are NOT needed to assign a DRG?
    a. patient's age
    b. patient's gender
    c. patient's principal diagnosis
    d. patient's occupation

14. The diagnosis that is determined to be the major cause of a hospital admission is called a:
    a. pertinent diagnosis
    b. primary diagnosis
    c. principal diagnosis
    d. partial diagnosis

15. When tracking insurance claims, the medical assistant should:
    a. keep a log of insurance claims filed
    b. transmit electronically whenever possible
    c. have all the necessary manuals and code books readily available
    d. all of the above

16. Which of the individuals is probably NOT eligible for Medicare?
    a. a 67-year-old woman
    b. a blind 66-year-old man
    c. a 34-year-old amputee
    d. a 57-year-old business owner

17. Medicare Part A does NOT cover:
    a. inpatient hospital
    b. home healthcare
    c. physician office visits
    d. hospice services

18. Medicare Part B does NOT cover:
    a. outpatient hospital care
    b. physician's office visits
    c. durable medical equipment
    d. inpatient hospital

19. The Health Maintenance Act of 1973 defined the characteristics of an HMO to include all of the following EXCEPT:
    a. voluntary group of enrollees
    b. agreed set of basic and supplemental health maintenance and treatment services
    c. organized system for providing healthcare
    d. mandatory coverage

20. The type of HMO model in which the facility is owned by the HMO is the:
    a. staff model
    b. prepaid group practice model
    c. independent practice association
    d. exclusive provider organization

21. The oldest and largest system of independent health insurers is:
    a. CHAMPUS
    b. Blue Cross/Blue Shield
    c. TRICARE
    d. Medicare

22. Which of the following individuals would probably not qualify for Medicaid?
    a. a person receiving food stamps
    b. a person receiving Aid to Families with Dependent Children
    c. a person employed full-time with medical benefits
    d. a person receiving Supplementary Security Income

23. After the deductible has been met, Medicare pays what percent of covered charges?
    a. 65%
    b. 70%
    c. 80%
    d. 85%

24. An insurance policy designed specifically for the use of one person and that person's dependents is called a(an):
    a. coordination of benefits
    b. individual policy
    c. managed care plan
    d. service benefit plan

25. A policy provision frequently found in medical insurance whereby the policyholder and the insurance company share the cost of covered losses in a specified ratio is called the:
    a. co-insurance
    b. co-payment
    c. deductible
    d. premium

TRUE OR FALSE

Directions: Circle the correct answer.

26.   T   F   Small companies may have to increase premiums and co-payments as health insurance costs rise.

27.   T   F   Many states have developed a patient bill of rights to protect from service denials and other HMO limitations.

28.   T   F   Dental insurance usually does not cover routine cleanings but will cover most procedures at 100%.

29.   T   F   The RBRVS is one of the outcomes of the Medicare Physician Payment Reform that was enacted in 1989.

30.   T   F   Forms of present-day managed healthcare plans began as far back as the Great Depression.

31.   T   F   QMB stands for quality medical benefits.

32.   T   F   Disability income insurance provides periodic payments to individuals to replace their income when sickness or injury results in being unable to work.

33.   T   F   The most critical area of a referral is the comments section.

34.   T   F   The medical assistant must use tact and good communication skills when talking with patients about insurance issues.

35.   T   F   The *Federal Register* is the official monthly publication for rules, proposed rules, and notices of federal agencies and organizations.

COMPLETION

Directions: Fill in the blank with the best answer.

36. An organization that provides a wide range of comprehensive healthcare services for a specified group at a fixed periodic payment rate is called a(an) _____.

37. A(An) _____ _____ plan is not restricted to a fee schedule.

38. A traditional health insurance plan that pays for all or a share of the cost of covered services regardless of which physician, hospital, or other licensed healthcare provider is used is called a(an) _____ plan.

39. A term used in managed care for an approved referral is _____.

40. The mechanism used in group health insurance to designate the order in which multiple carriers are to pay benefits to prevent duplicate payments is _____ of benefits.

41. The _____ the deductible, the lower the premium cost.

42. Hospital insurance policies often set a(an) _____ amount payable per day.

43. _____ care is an umbrella term for all healthcare plans that provide healthcare in return for preset scheduled payments.

44. The *Federal Register* was created because of a need for a(an) _____ location to keep track of rules and regulations.

45. The _____ diagnosis is the most critical factor in the assignment of DRGs.

46. One of the responsibilities of the medical assistant with regard to health insurance is to keep the patient _____.

47. A form of co-insurance that is paid at the time of service is a(an) _____.

48. An insurance plan funded by an organization having a large enough employee base that they can afford to fund their own insurance program is called a(an) _____ plan.

49. A payment method used by many managed care organizations wherein a fixed amount of money is reimbursed to the provider for patients enrolled during a specific time period, no matter what services were rendered, is called a(an) _____ plan.

50. The person who is responsible for paying the bill is the _____.

Word List

Indemnity
Self-insured
Managed
Guarantor
Principal
Centralized
Capitation
Maximum
Informed
Higher
Authorization
Coordination
Co-pay
Service benefit
HMO

CHAPTER 19

Banking Services and Procedures

MULTIPLE CHOICE

Directions: Circle the letter of the choice that best completes the statement or answers the question.

1. Which of the following is NOT an example of a negotiable instrument?
   a. cashier's check
   b. money order
   c. credit card
   d. personal check

2. What is the most common reason why the ending balances in checkbooks and bank statements usually do not match?
   a. transactions are made between the preparation and receipt of the statement
   b. it is common to make errors when recording checks and deposits in the checkbook
   c. banks often make mistakes in the preparation of statements
   d. patients have written insufficient fund checks that do not appear on the statement

3. Which type of bank account would be best for maintaining funds that are used for paying seasonal expenses, such as insurance premiums?
   a. regular savings
   b. money market savings
   c. interest-bearing checking that requires a high minimum balance
   d. regular checking

4. If you are not using a pegboard check-writing system, what is the first thing you must do when writing a check?
   a. enter the payee's name on the check
   b. date the check correctly
   c. fill in the check stub
   d. write the exact amount to be paid on the check

5. What is represented by the number in the "balance forward" box on the check stub?
   a. the amount of the check to be written
   b. the amount you have in the account before writing the check
   c. the amount you have remaining in the account after writing the check
   d. the total deposits made since the last check was written

6. If you make a mistake when writing a check, the best practice is to:
   a. write "void" on it and file with canceled checks
   b. destroy it immediately
   c. cross out the error and write in the correction
   d. erase the error and write in the correction

7. In which situation should you request the bank to issue a stop-payment order on a check that you wrote in payment for a medical supply order?
   a. the check was accidentally written for more than was owed
   b. the payment did not reach the payee within a reasonable amount of time
   c. the vendor to whom you wrote the check refuses to deliver the order
   d. all of the above

8. Why is it usually poor policy to accept third-party checks from patients?
   a. this type of check is illegal
   b. third-party checks are not negotiable
   c. the check will likely bounce
   d. you cannot verify the reliability of the maker

9. If a bank cashes a check that is later returned for insufficient funds, who is charged to recover the amount lost?
   a. the check's maker
   b. the person who received the money
   c. the person to whom the check was written
   d. the person who last endorsed the check

10. When should you deposit checks received from patients and other sources?
    a. at the same time you pay the bills
    b. as soon as possible after you receive them
    c. when you reconcile the bank statement each month
    d. at the end of every week

11. Which of the following is NOT one of the four types of endorsements?
    a. blank
    b. quality
    c. restrictive
    d. special

12. What is the first thing the medical assistant should do when a check is returned unpaid by the bank?
    a. contact the person who wrote the check
    b. file it with the district attorney's office
    c. send a letter refusing to see the person as a patient until the matter is resolved
    d. write off the account

13. Which type of bonding covers all employees in a facility?
    a. position-schedule bonding
    b. personal bonding
    c. blanket-position bonding
    d. general bonding

14. A check drawn on the bank's own account signed by an authorized bank official is called a:
    a. bank draft
    b. voucher check
    c. cashier's check
    d. certified check

15. Any individual, corporation, or legal party who signs a check or any type of negotiable instrument is considered the:
    a. maker
    b. payor
    c. drawer
    d. payee

16. Online banking is often called:
    a. m-banking
    b. e-banking
    c. quick banking
    d. none of the above

17. Which of the following would make an instrument nonnegotiable?
    a. written and signed by a maker
    b. containing a promise or order to pay a sum of money
    c. payable on demand or at a fixed future date
    d. payable to the order of payor

18. What are some of the advantages of Internet banking?
    a. no waiting in lines
    b. banking can be done from home
    c. account information is available 24 hours a day
    d. all of the above

19. A capital sum of money due as a debt or used as a fund for which interest is either charged or paid is called:
    a. disbursement
    b. reconciliation
    c. principal
    d. holder

20. The country is divided into how many Federal Reserve districts?
    a. 8
    b. 10
    c. 12
    d. 14

21. An insured account requiring a minimum balance that draws interest at a higher percentage than a regular savings account is called a(an):
    a. money market savings account
    b. individual retirement account
    c. checking account
    d. business savings account

22. The part of the ABA number following the dash on top in the fraction designates:
    a. cities in which Federal Reserve Banks are located
    b. number issued to each bank for identification purposes
    c. the Federal Reserve District in which the bank is located
    d. the amount of money in the bank account

23. A plan in which payments are transferred, usually electronically, by a paying agency directly to the account of a recipient is called:
    a. disbursement
    b. direct deposit
    c. customer-oriented banking
    d. endorsement banking

24. Something legally transferable to another party is considered:
    a. principal
    b. negotiable
    c. convenient
    d. legally binding

25. The person authorized to act as the agent when executing a power of attorney is called an:
    a. attorney at law
    b. attorney of power
    c. attorney ad litem
    d. attorney in fact

TRUE OR FALSE

Directions: Circle the best answer.

26.   T   F   Cashier's checks are sometimes known as officer's or treasurer's checks.

27.   T   F   One disadvantage of e-banking is learning the software.

28.   T   F   The person who writes a check is called a drawee.

29.   T   F   If a mistake is made on a check, draw one line through the error and make the correction.

30.   T   F   A stop payment order can protect the payor from loss as a result of stolen, lost, or incorrectly drawn checks.

31.   T   F   A limited check does not have a time restriction as to when it can be cashed.

32.   T   F   Money orders are best when a person is traveling.

33.   T   F   To maximize money, bills should be paid immediately when they arrive.

34.   T   F   Bank statements should be checked immediately on receipt and scanned carefully for errors.

35.   T   F   Blank endorsements make checks payable to the bearer.

36.   T   F   The three most common types of bank accounts are checking accounts, savings accounts, and money market savings accounts.

COMPLETION

Directions: Fill in the blanks with the best answer.

37. When an account is opened at a bank, the depositor is required to complete a(an) _____ card.

38. The medical assistant should be _____ rather than reactive when it comes to problem patients.

39. The name of the last endorser of the check shows who last _____ the money.

40. Often fees charged by banks to business accounts depend on the services _____.

41. _____ bonds reimburse the physician for any monetary loss caused by employees.

42. A signature on the back of a check whereby the rights of the check are transferred to another party is called a(an) _____.

43. A series of laws adopted by most states that regulate the fields of sales of goods and other entities is the _____.

44. Networks of banks that exchange checks with each other are called _____.

45. A(An) _____ check has a detachable form that is used to itemize or specify the purpose for which the check is drawn.

46. _____ is a charge or payment in exchange for the use of money.

47. The _____ _____ status is what distinguishes an IRA from an ordinary savings account.

48. A(An) _____ endorsement is used in preparing checks for deposit to the physician's checking account.

49. The _____ discloses any errors that may exist in the checkbook or, on rare occasions, the bank statement.

50. A person presenting a check for payment might be called the _____.

Word List
Proactive
Reconciliation
Tax-favored
Interest
UCC
Endorsement
Holder

Voucher
Restrictive
Rendered
Fidelity
Clearinghouses
Received
Signature

CHAPTER **20**

Medical Practice Management

MULTIPLE CHOICE

Directions: Circle the letter of the choice that best completes the statement or answers the question.

1. Which of the following documents lists the order in which business is to be conducted during a meeting?
   a. agenda
   b. bylaws
   c. itinerary
   d. minutes

2. When arranging travel to a professional conference, the medical assistant prepares which of the following?
   a. calendar of meeting dates
   b. agenda
   c. itinerary
   d. goals and objectives

3. An office with more than _____ employee(s) should have one person designated as a supervisor or office manager.
   a. one
   b. two
   c. three
   d. four

4. Leaders that are structured and organized and who ensure that their subordinates understand their duties are called:
   a. charismatic
   b. transformational
   c. transactional
   d. democratic

5. Which of the following are qualities of an effective leader or office manager?
   a. sense of fairness
   b. good communications skills
   c. good judgment
   d. all of the above

6. Something that spurs an individual to action or rewards an individual for performing a task is known as:
   a. morale
   b. incentive
   c. appraisal
   d. circumvention

7. Which of the following is a more intrinsic motivation?
   a. praise
   b. title
   c. promotion
   d. bonus

8. The type of power that is evident when a person is knowledgeable about a subject is called:
   a. coercive power
   b. expert power
   c. legitimate power
   d. referent power

9. Being disobedient to authority is termed:
   a. cohesive
   b. impenetrable
   c. meticulous
   d. insubordination

10. The exhaustion of physical or emotional strength or motivation, usually as a result of prolonged stress or frustration, is called:
    a. disparaging
    b. micromanaging
    c. burnout
    d. blatant

11. Which of the following is NOT true about change?
    a. change should be enjoyed
    b. change rarely happens
    c. individuals should be ready to change quickly
    d. change should be anticipated

12. Teams are more effective if they are:
    a. motivated
    b. cohesive
    c. happy
    d. all of the above

13. Burnout may be made worse by:
    a. understanding personal limitations
    b. taking on additional duties
    c. exercise
    d. considering options, including changing jobs

14. Some managers assign a person to assist new employees during the initial probationary period. This person is called a:
    a. mentor
    b. supervisor
    c. co-worker
    d. subordinate

15. The power of influence:
    a. is always positive
    b. is always negative
    c. can be either positive or negative
    d. is neither positive or negative

16. Which of the following is true about healthy employee-employer relationships?
    a. all of them make successful friendships
    b. it may be difficult to reprimand employees who are also friends
    c. a friendly relationship never interferes with the work relationship
    d. it is never wise to develop any kind of friendship with employees

17. New employees should experience orientation in which of the following areas?
    a. office policies
    b. nature of the practice
    c. physical environment
    d. all of the above

18. A long-term medical assistant should be terminated immediately, without notice, for which of the following events?
    a. being late more than three times
    b. displaying a poor attitude
    c. embezzlement
    d. calling in sick more than twice

19. An office manager will be more effective if:
    a. all employees are treated in exactly the same manner
    b. the office manager looks at all sides of a dispute
    c. only selected individuals are included in office meetings
    d. the office manager reports all problems involving employees to the physician

20. When closing a practice:
    a. a public announcement should be placed in the paper several months in advance
    b. all patients should be told to come and pick up their medical records
    c. wait until 1 month before closing to make the announcement
    d. offer the patient database to other physicians

21. A well-written patient information folder may reduce calls to the physician's office by up to:
    a. 10%
    b. 15%
    c. 30%
    d. 50%

22. Which subjects CANNOT be discussed in a job interview?
    a. religion
    b. work history
    c. previous terminations of employment
    d. none of the above can be discussed in the interview

23. Essential skills that must be developed by teams to experience success include:
    a. mutual accountability
    b. common purpose
    c. complementary skills
    d. all of the above

24. The office manager can easily determine all but which of the following by looking at an applicant's application or resume?
    a. work experience
    b. personality
    c. educational background
    d. skills

25. What can be evaluated by looking at the job application?
    a. handwriting
    b. ability to follow instructions
    c. ability to provide complete information
    d. all of the above

26. The process of inciting a person to some action or behavior is called:
    a. reprimand
    b. motivation
    c. circumvention
    d. appraisal

27. Which of the following is NOT necessary information on an itinerary?
    a. date and time of departure
    b. date and time of return
    c. mode of transportation
    d. contact name at hotels

28. Which of the following is an unlawful preemployment inquiry?
    a. are you over 18 years of age?
    b. do you have a mental impairment that could interfere with this job?
    c. have you been convicted of a crime?
    d. how many children do you have?

29. Which of the following questions is legally allowed during an initial interview for employment as a medical assistant?
    a. when did you graduate from medical assisting school?
    b. are you married?
    c. do you plan to have children?
    d. what church do you attend?

30. Which of the following often explains the reason for the existence of the practice?
    a. physician biography
    b. financial policy
    c. philosophy of the practice
    d. record retention policy

31. A patient has been diagnosed as having colitis and wants more information on the subject. Which of the following is the most appropriate initial setup for the medical assistant to take?
    a. give the patient an educational pamphlet
    b. lend the patient a medical assisting text
    c. lend the patient one of the physician's books
    d. refer the patient to the public library

32. The practice is experiencing an increased number of telephone calls from established patients with questions about office insurance policies. Which of the following is the most effective method to solve this problem?
    a. ask the physician to summarize office policies on a patient's first visit
    b. designate one of the staff to handle all information calls
    c. develop and distribute a practice information booklet with insurance information
    d. place an office procedure manual in the office lobby

33. Patient instruction sheets include:
    a. preparation for x-ray examinations and tests
    b. how to collect a urine specimen
    c. taking medications
    d. all of the above

34. Which is NOT a type of leader?
    a. charismatic
    b. transitional
    c. transformational
    d. laissez-faire

35. Which is NOT a type of manager?
    a. democratic
    b. aristocratic
    c. autocratic
    d. laissez-faire

TRUE OR FALSE

Directions: Circle the best answer.

36. T F Management problems can often be avoided by careful definition of the areas of responsibility for each staff member.
37. T F Micromanagement is managing with extreme or excessive care in the treatment of details.
38. T F A chain of command is unwise in a physician's office.
39. T F It is not important to consider employee morale when making management decisions.

40.   T   F   Intrinsic motivation is more difficult to discover as compared with extrinsic motivation but is longer lasting.

41.   T   F   A person who is currently employed should never be approached to accept a new position.

42.   T   F   If a manager does not make a habit of writing formal reprimands to employees not performing as expected, there may not be sufficient evidence to terminate employment.

43.   T   F   Interviews should be conducted when no one else is in the office.

44.   T   F   Continuous staff development and training are crucial parts of managing a successful medical practice.

45.   T   F   The best time to terminate an employee is usually at the beginning of the day.

COMPLETION

Directions: Fill in the blank with the best answer.

46. No supervisor enjoys giving a(an) _____ that is less than positive.

47. The office manager should evaluate the applicant's _____ when setting the interview time on the phone because this is an important attribute for medical assistants.

48. All _____ should be carefully checked before hiring a new employee.

49. The office manager should allow a minimum of _____ hours for a prospective employee to make a decision on a job offer.

50. A performance evaluation or _____ includes a judgment of both the quality and quantity of work, personal appearance, attitudes, and team spirit.

51. _____ of duties provides an opportunity for employees to grow and learn new skills and allows managers to concentrate on the most critical aspects of their own jobs.

52. Many employees can be _____ to become productive staff members with a little patience on the part of the manager.

53. _____ power is manipulative, and the leader using this type of power usually makes threats or uses fear to accomplish goals.

54. Before advertising for a new employee, be sure that the job _____ is reviewed so that a fair interview and evaluation can be conducted.

55. The types of staff meetings include informational, problem solving, _____, or work sessions.

56. A list or outline of things to be considered or done is called a(an) _____.

57. When employees do not leave their employment over a long period of time, the office is said to have good employee _____.

58. Successful managers know that their employees should be encouraged to perform at _____ levels.

59. New employees should be required to read the entire office _____ manual.

60. To avoid charges of abandonment, physicians who are closing their practice should notify all active patients at least _____ months in advance.

Word List
Description
Voice
24
Optimal
Brainstorming
Delegation
References
Evaluation
Retention
Policy/procedure
Coercive
3
Agenda
Redirected
Appraisal

CHAPTER **21**

Medical Practice Marketing and Customer Service

MULTIPLE CHOICE

Directions: Circle the letter of the choice that best completes the statement or answers the question.

1. Which of the following is NOT one of the three steps followed in preparing to implement marketing strategies?
   a. decide what objectives are most important
   b. develop a specific plan
   c. discuss other physician's specific marketing plans
   d. evaluate what is currently being done to increase patient flow

2. Something that is capable of being appraised at an actual or approximate value is said to be:
   a. tangible
   b. viable
   c. believable
   d. archaic

3. What is the first step in developing a plan?
   a. research
   b. planning the concept
   c. assessment
   d. evaluation

4. What is the final step in developing a plan?
   a. research
   b. planning the concept
   c. assessment
   d. evaluation

5. The four P's do NOT include:
   a. product
   b. practicality
   c. placement
   d. price

6. Placement might refer to:
   a. location of the office
   b. setup inside the office
   c. location of retail objects in the office
   d. all of the above

7. The employees of the office should be involved in promoting the practice because:
   a. the physician has services to offer the community
   b. a full schedule is more financially rewarding for the physician
   c. the employees should see the practice as a business
   d. all of the above

8. Which of the following resources might be free to the medical practice?
   a. advice columns in newspapers
   b. involvement in the local community
   c. participation in health fairs
   d. all of the above

9. When an effort is made to create or change an attitude, belief, or perception through purchased broadcast time or print space, the company is usually:
   a. advertising
   b. conducting public relations
   c. performing public service
   d. none of the above

10. A good advertising agency is:
    a. the cheapest
    b. the most expensive
    c. budget conscious
    d. willing to accept payments

11. The first step in building a website is to:
    a. upload the pages to a web server
    b. design the pages
    c. define the objectives of the website
    d. locate an appropriate web server

12. A music file used for a website might be identified by the word or extension:
    a. jpeg
    b. midi
    c. gif
    d. url

13. A word or graphic on a page that takes the viewer to another page or another website is called a:
    a. hyperlink
    b. hypertext
    c. uniform resource locator
    d. cookie

14. What is generally used to keep others from altering the information on a website?
a. link lock
b. sophisticated software
c. password
d. copyright

15. Some websites count the number of times they are accessed with a:
a. URL
b. cookie
c. hyperlink
d. counter

16. Who would most likely be an internal customer in the medical practice?
a. the patient
b. the patient's family
c. the employees
d. the physician

17. Patients expect the staff to treat them with:
a. concern
b. care
c. confidentiality
d. all of the above

18. Which action shows the best customer service?
a. offering coffee to all patients
b. greeting all patients by name
c. waving as patients enter the office
d. using a sign-in sheet

19. Without _____, many businesses fail.
a. insurance benefits
b. growth
c. marketing efforts
d. none of the above

20. The process of using marketing and education strategies to reach and involve diverse audiences through key messages and programs is called:
a. advertising
b. targeting
c. outreach
d. marketing

TRUE OR FALSE

Directions: Circle the correct answer.

21.   T   F   The medical facility should determine the characteristics of a typical member of the target market before developing a marketing plan.

22.   T   F   Physicians should not consider college students as a viable market.

23.   T   F   The four P's of marketing include promotion.

24.   T   F   Keeping the office open later one night per week is a marketing strategy.

25.   T   F   It is preferable that an advertising agency have experience in the medical field.

26.   T   F   A monthly e-newsletter is a great marketing idea.

27.   T   F   Providing all employees with business cards is not a good strategy for a new practice.

28.   T   F   The most important part of a website is the graphics.

29.   T   F   Most public relations strategies are expensive.

30.   T   F   A URL is a web address.

COMPLETION

Directions: Fill in the blank with the best answer.

31. Something toward which effort is directed is a(an) _____.

32. The process or technique of promoting, selling, and distributing a product or a service is _____.

33. A specific group of individuals to whom a marketing plan is focused is the _____ market.

34. Color choices, _____, and fonts will enhance the look of a professional website.

35. Be careful not to _____ photographs and graphics on a website.

36. Poorly chosen phrases that suggest poor attitudes give the patient or visitor a(an) _____ view of the facility.

37. Once files have been uploaded to a website, the site should be _____ to ensure that it looks the way the it is supposed to look.

38. Patients first expect to be treated with the _____ rule.

39. Providing good customer service is a(an) _____ that each employee must make in the medical facility.

40. _____ boxes are a great way to get patient and employee input.

Word List
Overdo
Tested
Objective
Target
Suggestion
Marketing
Golden
Animation
Negative
Commitment

CHAPTER **22**

Health Information Management

MULTIPLE CHOICE

Directions: Circle the letter of the choice that best completes the statement or answers the question.

1. Healthcare information is used to:
   a. determine how many patients enter a facility with the same diagnosis
   b. decide what equipment is needed to meet the needs of the patient population
   c. help the facility plan for the needs of next week and next year
   d. all of the above

2. Which of the following are NOT characteristics of quality health data?
   a. reliability
   b. completeness
   c. security
   d. authenticated

3. Quality assurance is concerned with:
   a. under use of medical services
   b. overuse of medical services
   c. misuse of medical services
   d. all of the above

4. An example of under use of medical services includes:
   a. indigent patients using a hospital for delivery of their babies
   b. more than the average number of tonsillectomies in one fiscal year
   c. mammograms for at-risk patients
   d. antibiotic prescriptions

5. A nosocomial infection is usually acquired in a:
   a. physician's office
   b. hospital
   c. school
   d. home

6. The NCHS keeps statistics on:
   a. suicide
   b. sexually transmitted diseases
   c. teenage pregnancy
   d. all of the above

7. Which of the following would most likely be a sentinel event?
   a. a total power failure in a hospital
   b. a baby born before the due date
   c. a death after emergency surgery
   d. all of the above

8. The characteristic of quality data that ensures multiple users can obtain the data at one time is:
   a. completeness
   b. recognizability
   c. accessibility
   d. validity

9. HIPAA became effective in:
   a. April 2003
   b. April 2002
   c. August 2002
   d. August 2003

10. The nonprofit organization that assists healthcare facilities by providing accreditation services is:
    a. OSHA
    b. ABHES
    c. JCAHO
    d. JCHAO

11. Which of the following are functions of NCHS?
    a. monitoring trends in health status and healthcare delivery
    b. identification of health problems
    c. support of biomedical and health services research
    d. all of the above

12. Most healthcare facilities are now interested in:
    a. meeting minimum accreditation standards
    b. meeting most accreditation standards
    c. exceeding standards and providing optimal healthcare to patients
    d. providing good care to patients

13. Which of the following is one of Deming's Fourteen Points for Management?
    a. avoid new philosophies
    b. institute training on the job
    c. increase dependence on inspection to achieve quality
    d. award business on the basis of the price tag

14. Which of the following is NOT one of Deming's Fourteen Points for Management?
    a. remove barriers that rob people of their right to pride in workmanship
    b. create consistency of purpose toward improvement of product and service
    c. make sure managers work to accomplish the transformation to quality service
    d. break down barriers between departments

15. Health information professionals perform which of the following tasks on data?
    a. collect
    b. integrate
    c. analyze
    d. all of the above

16. The organization that supports health information personnel is:
    a. AAMA
    b. AHIMA
    c. AMT
    d. ABHES

17. HIPAA places great restrictions on patient information used:
    a. by the physician alone while pondering the patient's diagnosis
    b. by the person completing the health insurance claim as an employee in the office
    c. for marketing purposes or solicitation of sales
    d. none of the above

18. The quality data characteristic that suggests that information in the database about a patient can be trusted is:
    a. reliability
    b. recognizability
    c. completeness
    d. relevance

19. Which of the following statements is accurate?
    a. under use of healthcare services is not a concern
    b. misuse of healthcare services is not common
    c. variations in use of healthcare services are common
    d. overuse of healthcare services is not a concern

20. A pharmacy is not allowed to:
    a. offer patient information to another entity that in turn uses that information to solicit sales of related products to a patient
    b. offer patients a discount program that requires a special card to participate
    c. offer discounted drugs to patients
    d. offer suggestions regarding over-the-counter drugs

TRUE OR FALSE

Directions: Circle the best answer.

21.   T   F   Transposing is changing the relative place or normal order of something or altering its sequence.

22.   T   F   Health information management is a relatively new profession.

23. T F The validity of health data is synonymous with accuracy.

24. T F Third-party payors use healthcare information to find ways to intentionally deny claims.

25. T F HIPAA was developed in part to ensure the confidentiality of medical records.

26. T F Health information management is not a large part of today's healthcare facility.

27. T F HIPAA compliance is not the medical assistant's responsibility.

28. T F Questions that patients have about HIPAA should be directed to the Department of Health and Human Services, not answered in the physician's office.

29. T F The healthcare facility should encourage the use of slogans, exhortations, and targets that ask for zero defects.

30. T F All employees must make a commitment for total quality management to be effective.

COMPLETION

Directions: Fill in the blank with the best answer.

31. Activities designed to increase the quality of a product or service through process or system changes that increase efficiency or effectiveness are called _____ _____.

32. Encoded is another word for _____.

33. _____, with regard to medical records, is a verification that a record is correct with a signature, initials, or computer keystroke by the maker.

34. _____ are established by authority, custom, or general consent as a model or example.

35. Something that contains error or assumption is said to be _____.

36. A(An) _____ makes a particular treatment or procedure inadvisable.

37. An unexpected occurrence involving death or serious physical or psychological injury, or the risk thereof, is called a(an) _____ _____.

38. To manage to get around, especially through ingenuity or stratagem, is called _____.

39. If a thing contains incongruous elements or is markedly distinct in quality or character, it is said to contain _____.

40. An infection originating in a hospital is said to be _____.

Word List
Contraindication
Disparities
Quality assurance
Standards
Nosocomial
Encrypted
Sentinel event
Circumvent
Authenticated
Erroneous

CHAPTER **23**

Management of Practice Finances

MULTIPLE CHOICE

Directions: Circle the letter of the choice that best completes the statement or answers the question.

1. Complete and correct financial records are necessary for:
   a. prompt billing and collection procedures
   b. professional financial planning
   c. accurate reporting of income
   d. all of the above

2. A system of recording, classifying, and summarizing financial transactions is called:
   a. bookkeeping
   b. accounting
   c. accruing
   d. depreciation

3. The chronological record of the medical practice is the:
   a. daily journal
   b. ledger journal
   c. disbursement journal
   d. monthly journal

4. Cardinal rules for bookkeeping include:
   a. good penmanship
   b. legible records
   c. straight columns of figures
   d. all of the above

5. Minor unpredictable expenses should be paid from the:
   a. regular checking account
   b. savings account
   c. petty cash
   d. whatever is most available

6. The financial records of any business should always show:
   a. how much has been collected
   b. how much is owed
   c. how much was earned in a given period
   d. all of the above

7. The disbursement journal should show:
   a. every amount paid out
   b. interest accrued
   c. total payables
   d. all of the above

8. Which of the following words or phrases CANNOT be used interchangeably?
   a. capital
   b. interest
   c. proprietorship
   d. net worth

9. A trial balance should be done:
   a. once per week
   b. twice per week
   c. once per month
   d. twice per month

10. Which statement best describes the relationship between bookkeeping and accounting?
    a. accounting is a summary of the activities of bookkeeping
    b. bookkeeping takes care of all the reporting activities of accounting
    c. accounting plans the bookkeeping process
    d. bookkeeping involves the recording activities of accounting

11. The *cash basis* system of accounting used by most physicians means that one:
    a. uses credit as little as possible
    b. records charges as income at the time received
    c. maintains a simple bookkeeping system
    d. records expenses at the time they are incurred

12. The purpose of the disbursement journal is to keep a record of the amount:
    a. in the checking account
    b. owed by the physician
    c. paid out for various expenses
    d. owed to the physician

13. Which accounting system has the least chance of errors because of the small amount of posting necessary?
    a. double-entry
    b. pegboard
    c. single-entry
    d. there is little difference between the three

14. Which accounting system requires the least initial expense and training to set up and use?
    a. double-entry
    b. pegboard
    c. single-entry
    d. there is little difference between the three

15. If you summarized the physician's financial situation in the basic accounting equation, which of the following would be included in the liability component?
    a. the value of the office equipment owned
    b. amounts owed by insurance companies
    c. amount of cash in the checking account
    d. amount owed to a medical supply company

16. At the end of the day, you discover a numeric error on an encounter form. All of the following actions should be taken EXCEPT:
    a. erase the error cleanly before writing in new numbers
    b. reinsert the ledger card before making the correction
    c. make a new receipt for the patient
    d. ensure that the proper amount was billed to the insurance company

17. The purpose of the accounts receivable ratio is to give information about:
    a. the percentage of patients who receive bills rather than paying at time of service
    b. the total amount that patients owe the physician at any given time
    c. the percentage of accounts that are past due
    d. how fast patient accounts are being paid

18. Assets = liabilities + :
    a. capital
    b. interest
    c. proprietorship
    d. income

19. Disbursements in a medical office might include:
    a. rent
    b. utilities
    c. dues
    d. all of the above

20. Which of the following is NOT a common summary report?
    a. trial balance
    b. invoice
    c. statement of income and expense
    d. balance sheet

21. For every disbursement from the petty cash fund, what should be completed?
    a. balance sheet
    b. invoice
    c. packing slip
    d. voucher

22. To determine that the books for the practice are in balance, the medical assistant can perform a(an):
    a. trial balance
    b. balance sheet
    c. cash flow statement
    d. end-of-day summary

23. W-2 forms should be given to all employees before what date each year?
    a. January 1
    b. December 31
    c. January 31
    d. December 1

24. The Transmittal of Income and Tax Statement must be transmitted annually with Form:
    a. W-2
    b. W-3
    c. W-4
    d. W-5

25. All of the following are determinants of withholding amounts EXCEPT:
    a. number of withholding allowances claimed
    b. length of the pay period involved
    c. total earnings of the employee
    d. insurance deductions

26. Which of the following records must be available for review by the IRS?
    a. social security numbers for employees
    b. number of withholding allowances claimed
    c. amount of gross salary
    d. all of the above

27. Which form is used to apply for a social security card?
    a. SS-5
    b. SS-4
    c. SS-3
    d. SS-2

28. When the end-of-month accounts receivable figures agree with the figure arrived at by adding all the account card balances, the accounts are said to be:
    a. false
    b. in balance
    c. out of balance
    d. matching

29. Which of the following is NOT a drawback to the single-entry accounting system?
    a. errors are not easily detected
    b. there are no built-in controls
    c. it satisfies governmental reporting regulations
    d. periodic analyses are inadequate for financial planning

30. The properties owned by a business are called:
    a. assets
    b. liabilities
    c. equities
    d. accounts

TRUE OR FALSE

Directions: Circle the correct answer.

31. T F Petty cash funds are usually kept in a locked cash drawer or box.

32. T F Computer posting software is a timesaver in the medical office.

33. T F Single-entry bookkeeping is expensive to use.

34. T F A pegboard system, either manual or computerized, is common in the medical office.

35. T F There is no way to find errors made in posting without doing the entire day sheet over.

36. T F A packing slip describes the contents of a package.

37. T F A profit and loss statement is also known as a statement of income and expense.

38. T F Most employers must file a quarterly federal tax return.

39. T F FUTA deals with office credit policies.

40. T F The Employee's Withholding Allowance Certificate is Form W-4.

41. T F Annual FUTA returns must be filed before January 1 following the close of the calendar year.

42. T F Most states have federal unemployment compensation laws.

43. T F Expenses in the medical office should be monitored on a monthly basis to remain within the budget.

44. T F An accurately completed purchase order helps to eliminate mistakes in the order and in shipment.

45. T F Some medical offices require the person who has been charged with handling financial duties to be bonded.

COMPLETION

Directions: Fill in the blank with the best answer.

46. The summary of unpaid accounts is called the accounts receivable _____.

47. The method of accounting in which income is recorded when earned and expenses are recorded when incurred is called the _____ basis of accounting.

48. A summary of accounts paid out is called the _____ journal.

49. The money value of a property or of an interest in a property in excess of claims or liens against it is called _____.

50. An accounting period of 12 months is a(an) _____ year.

51. A request for payment is called a(an) _____.

52. Something that is owed is called a(an) _____.

53. Accounts _____ are debts incurred and not yet paid.

54. The daily journal day sheet is a(an) _____ record of the practice, similar to a financial diary.

55. To estimate the budget for a new year, expenses from the _____ year should be evaluated.

56. Records must be _____ and completed on a daily basis.

57. Each employer must have a federal tax _____ number.

58. The petty cash fund is a(an) _____ fund.

59. Figure _____ should be kept straight, and figures should be well-formed.

60. Receipts are usually deposited in a(an) _____ account.

Word List
Accrual
Identification
Payable
Checking
Columns
Previous
Liability
Chronological
Statement
Equities
Fiscal
Disbursements
Accurate
Revolving
Control

CHAPTER **24**

Infection Control

MULTIPLE CHOICE

Directions: Circle the letter of the choice that best completes the statement or answers the question.

1. What action do viruses take when they enter the body's cells?
   a. multiply and form colonies
   b. produce poisonous secretions
   c. incorporate into the cell's reproductive material
   d. create resistant spores

2. Which of the following scenarios is the only time recapping a needle is considered an appropriate procedure?
   a. a biohazard sharps container is not close by
   b. the procedures performed do not involve venipuncture
   c. you know the patient is free of infectious disease
   d. after withdrawing medication from a vial

3. Which of the following is NOT a major area that must be covered in the medical facility's exposure control plan required by OSHA?
   a. list of potentially dangerous tasks performed by facility employees
   b. specific steps for providing effective patient treatment
   c. procedures for treating employees that come into contact with infectious materials
   d. safety procedures to reduce employee exposure to blood-borne pathogens

4. What are the two most important factors in performing an effective hand wash?
   a. friction and running warm water
   b. antibacterial soap and hot water
   c. length of time spent and type of soap
   d. position of hands and temperature of water

5. The process used to wash and remove blood and tissue from medical instruments is called:
   a. asepsis
   b. disinfection
   c. sanitization
   d. sterilization

6. The most important step in achieving asepsis is:
   a. washing hands
   b. removing jewelry
   c. rinsing with alcohol
   d. using surgical soap
   e. wearing gloves

7. The method that completely destroys microorganisms is:
   a. disinfection
   b. sterilization
   c. sanitization
   d. boiling
   e. fumigation

8. While a blood specimen is being prepared for laboratory analysis, the container tips over and blood spills on the laboratory table. Which of the following is the most appropriate management of the spill?
   a. cover the spill with paper towels, pour 10% bleach solution on the towels, wait 15 minutes, wipe up the spill while wearing gloves, and discard the paper towels in an infectious waste container
   b. spray the spill with a strong detergent and allow the table to dry
   c. wipe up the spill with paper towels, spray disinfectant on the table every 15 minutes for 30 minutes, and discard the paper towels in the wastebasket
   d. wipe up the spill with soapy cloth towels, rinse the table thoroughly with water, and discard the towels in the contaminated laundry bin
   e. wipe up the spill with a sponge and water, rinse the sponge thoroughly, and allow the table to dry

9. According to OSHA regulations, under which of the following circumstances is recapping needles allowed?
   a. when an antiseptic cleaner is used
   b. when the needles are reusable
   c. when the patient is disease-free
   d. when wearing gloves
   e. when recapping an unused needle

10. For which of the following is a medical assistant required to wear a mask while taking the patient's medical history?
    a. hepatitis C
    b. rheumatic fever
    c. AIDS
    d. active tuberculosis
    e. food poisoning

11. Which of the following is the recommended method for disposal of needles in a puncture-proof container?
    a. cutting the needle
    b. bending the needle
    c. keeping the needle intact
    d. recapping the needle
    e. removing the needle from the syringe

12. The CDC does NOT recommend standard precautions for which of the following body fluids if the fluid does not contain visible blood?
    a. amniotic
    b. cerebrospinal
    c. pleural
    d. synovial
    e. urine

13. Which of the following procedures is appropriate for preparing blood and other potentially infectious materials for transport?
    a. decontaminating the hazardous waste container
    b. freezing the materials before transport
    c. relabeling containers provided for waste
    d. placing the materials in a leak-proof container during collection
    e. washing the container with household detergent

14. Gloves, gowns, and goggles are examples of:
    a. asepsis
    b. personal protective equipment
    c. engineering controls
    d. sterilization

15. Blunt needles, needleless systems, and resheathing syringes are examples of:
    a. asepsis
    b. personal protective equipment
    c. engineering controls
    d. sterilization

16. On the basis of your understanding of the chain of infection, what would be the most effective method for controlling the spread of conjunctivitis in a daycare center?
    a. conjunctivitis is not contagious
    b. close the daycare center until all children are symptom-free
    c. wash hands thoroughly each time a symptomatic child is contacted
    d. immediately send the child home to prevent the spread of the disease

17. A bacterial spore:
    a. requires sanitization to be destroyed
    b. is the active form of an infectious microorganism
    c. can be destroyed with most disinfectants
    d. is a resistant bacterial reproductive cell that can become active and cause disease

18. Inflammation mediators that are released at the site of cellular damage perform which of the following functions:
    a. increase blood flow to the site
    b. increase the permeability of blood vessel walls
    c. cause more RBCs to be attracted to the site of injury
    d. a and b are true
    e. all are true

19. Cell-mediated immunity:
    a. causes destruction of pathogens at the site of infection
    b. results in the production of antibodies
    c. is stimulated by the presence of an antigen
    d. creates immunity to disease

20. Relapse and remission are seen frequently in what types of infections?
    a. chronic infections
    b. latent infections
    c. infections with rapid onset
    d. infections that cause fevers

21. Viral infections:
    a. are treated effectively with antibiotics
    b. include malaria and gonorrhea
    c. are treated with a focus on palliative care
    d. may form spores

22. Anita Simons, CMA was assisting with pediatric immunizations when she received an accidental needlestick. What is the *first* thing Anita should do?
    a. report the incident to a supervisor
    b. screen the child for HIV and HBV
    c. complete an incident report form
    d. thoroughly wash the needlestick site

23. What should NOT be done when sanitizing instruments?
    a. wear latex gloves when cleaning sharp instruments
    b. use a separate work area to avoid cross contamination
    c. prevent coagulation of blood on instruments
    d. separate sharp and blunt instruments

24. For disinfection to be effective, what must the medical assistant do?
    a. perform disinfection before sanitization
    b. ensure sanitized instruments are still moist before disinfection begins
    c. if the patient is HIV positive, use twice the amount of recommended disinfectant solution
    d. soak instruments in a closed container

TRUE OR FALSE

Directions: Circle the best answer.

25.   T   F   Relapse is the disappearance of the clinical symptoms of disease.

26.   T   F   A germicide is an agent that destroys pathogenic microorganisms.

27.   T   F   An antiseptic is an agent that can be used on the skin to inhibit the growth of microorganisms.

28.   T   F   Hepatitis A is transmitted through blood and body fluids.

29.   T   F   The same virus causes both chicken pox and shingles.

30.   T   F   HBV is transmitted via contaminated food or water.

31.   T   F   Meningococcal meningitis is transmitted through respiratory tract secretions.

32.   T   F   Giardiasis is a roundworm that is transmitted via contaminated water.

33.   T   F   Lyme disease is caused by a rickettsia and can be treated with antibiotics.

34.   T   F   Employees must provide their own alternative to latex gloves if they show signs of latex anaphylaxis.

35.   T   F   Employers must provide employees with hepatitis B immunization at a reduced fee within 10 days of the start of employment.

36.   T   F   Hands do not have to be washed if the healthcare worker conscientiously uses gloves during all possible times of exposure.

COMPLETION

Directions: Fill in the blank with the best answer.

37. A(An) _____ disorder is one in which the body reacts against its own tissues.

38. _____ is a skin eruption that results in hives.

39. The _____ route of administration is the injection or introduction of substances into the body other than through the digestive tract.

40. A(An) _____ is a foreign substance that results in the production of a specific antibody.

41. _____ is a yeast-like fungus that typically affects the vaginal and oral mucosa.

42. A(An) _____ agent is a medication that relieves patient symptoms but does not cure a disease.

43. A(An) _____ _____ is an infection that is acquired in a healthcare setting and is often caused by a lack of standard precautions with the facility.

44. A(An) _____ is an insect or tick that transmits the causative organisms of a disease.

45. The _____ _____ virus causes chicken pox.

46. _____ is caused by the itch mite and is spread through direct contact.

47. Fungal infections are also called _____ infections.

48. _____ infections persist for a long period of time.

49. A(An) _____ is a contaminated object, such as an improperly sterilized instrument, that causes the transmission of a disease.

50. _____ _____ are surface bacteria that are introduced by contaminated objects or by exposure to microorganisms that can be destroyed if managed properly.

Word List

Antigen

Autoimmune

Candidiasis

Chronic

Fomite

Mycotic

Nosocomial infection

Palliative

Parenteral

Scabies

Transient bacteria

Urticaria

Varicella zoster

Vector

CHAPTER **25**

Patient Assessment

MULTIPLE CHOICE

Directions: Circle the letter of the choice that best completes the statement or answers the question.

1. Which of the following actions is NOT usually appropriate for showing your interest in patients?
   a. hugging them reassuringly when you greet them
   b. leaning toward them when you are listening to them
   c. moving in a confident manner as you work with them
   d. using a friendly tone of voice when speaking to them

2. The section of the medical history that helps uncover existing or potential health problems is called the:
   a. database
   b. past history
   c. social history
   d. systems review

3. What does it mean when medical assistants display empathy when dealing with patients?
   a. they feel sorry for patients who have serious health problems
   b. they are able to hear what the patient says without judging the content
   c. they can detach themselves emotionally from the problems of their patients
   d. they truly like and care about each of their patients

4. Which of the following factors is likely to have the most influence on the accuracy and completeness of the information secured from the patient during the interview for the medical history?
   a. the comfort of the chairs in the meeting area
   b. the medical assistant's ability to take complete and detailed notes
   c. the privacy of the area in which the interview takes place
   d. the efficiency of the medical assistant in conducting the interview

5. While you are taking the medical history of a new patient, the patient mentions having occasional headaches that are quite painful. What is the best way for you to proceed with the interview?
   a. express concern and note this information in writing
   b. ask him a direct question about the pain
   c. reassure him that it is probably nothing serious
   d. ask him an open-ended question about the headaches

6. What is the best way to collect specific information about a patient when conducting the medical history interview?
   a. summarize the facts revealed by the patient when answering questions
   b. ask direct questions that can be answered briefly
   c. restate what the patient says to check the accuracy of what you hear
   d. encourage the patient to explain the answers fully

7. During the physical examination, the patient reports a continual ache in the right elbow. This information is called a/an:
   a. functional problem
   b. objective finding
   c. sign
   d. symptom

8. Which medical record system has a standard format that makes it easy to read and audit?
   a. chronological
   b. problem-oriented
   c. progress note
   d. source-oriented

9. Which statement best describes what it means to have good rapport with patients?
   a. you use language that they understand
   b. they respect you as a professional
   c. you have smooth pleasant relationships with them
   d. you are friendly and reassuring

10. Why would you take a patient's vital signs at both the beginning and the end of the office visit for a physical examination?
    a. to evaluate the effectiveness of treatment given during the visit
    b. because the patient was anxious on first arrival at the office
    c. to reassure the patient that the patient is receiving adequate care
    d. to ensure the accuracy of the procedures by double-checking the results

11. Which of the following information includes insurance information?
    a. family history
    b. past history
    c. social history
    d. database
    e. ROS

12. Which of the following information includes demographic information?
    a. family history
    b. past history
    c. social history
    d. database
    e. ROS

13. Which of the following information includes the physical examination?
    a. family history
    b. past history
    c. social history
    d. database
    e. ROS

14. Which of the following information includes childhood diseases?
    a. family history
    b. past history
    c. social history
    d. database
    e. ROS

15. Which of the following information includes diet, smoking history, and alcohol consumption?
    a. family history
    b. past history
    c. social history
    d. database
    e. ROS

16. Which of the following involves repeating or paraphrasing the patient's comments?
    a. restatement
    b. clarification
    c. reflection

17. Which of the following involves asking a question or summarizing a patient's thoughts?
    a. restatement
    b. clarification
    c. reflection

18. Which of the following involves stating an observation or recognition of a patient's feelings?
    a. restatement
    b. clarification
    c. reflection

19. Which of the following is a closed-ended question?
    a. "Tell me about your headache."
    b. "Does your head hurt?"
    c. "How are you feeling?"

20. Which of the following is an open-ended question?
    a. "How old are you?"
    b. "Do you smoke?"
    c. "What brings you to the physician today?"

TRUE OR FALSE

Directions: Circle the best answer.

21.   T   F   It is acceptable to conduct a patient interview in a quiet corner of the waiting room.

22.   T   F   Value systems are learned beliefs and behaviors that can impact therapeutic relationships.

23.   T   F   Research on the significance of body language indicates that 50% of the message received by patients is interpreted from the caregiver's nonverbal language.

24.   T   F   When conducting a patient interview, the medical assistant should sit behind a desk with arms crossed and wait for the patient to establish eye contact.

25.   T   F   The most effective distance between a patient and the medical assistant conducting an interview is approximately 2 to 3 feet.

26.   T   F   The best method for ensuring that the patient understands a patient education intervention is to have the patient repeat back to you the details learned.

27.   T   F   Providing patients with automatic reassurance when they express a concern is part of a therapeutic relationship.

28.   T   F   Children should always be given a choice about whether they want to take their medicine or not.

29.   T   F   Issues of privacy are important to adolescent patients.

30.   T   F   An example of an objective sign of disease is the patient's reported level of pain.

31.   T   F   Gathering details regarding patient use of over-the-counter medications is not necessary when conducting a patient interview.

32.   T   F   It is acceptable to skip lines when documenting to give the physician room to enter a note after the patient is seen.

33.   T   F   Documenting that the patient reports a headache of 3 days is part of the objective data in the POMR record.

COMPLETION

Directions: Fill in the blank with the best answer.

34. _____ care recognizes that patient health is affected by multiple factors, not just physical ones.

35. The physician's initial impression of the patient's presenting problem is called the _____ diagnosis.

36. When a verbal message matches the sender's nonverbal body language, the message is considered _____.

37. The medical assistant must consistently request _____ from the patient to determine the patient's understanding of the message.

38. During the _____ phase of the interview, medical assistants should introduce themselves and identify the purpose of the interview.

39. The _____ of the interview should summarize the information learned while communicating with the patient and outline patient expectations of care.

40. _____ are subjective reports given by patients about how they feel with a particular health problem.

41. A(An) _____ disease is one that can be proved via laboratory or other diagnostic studies.

42. Documentation of patient symptoms must always include the _____, _____, and frequency of signs and symptoms.

43. _____ data include the patient's blood pressure, TPR, and weight.

Word List
Closing
Congruent
Duration
Feedback
Holistic
Initiation
Objective
Onset
Organic or physical
Symptoms
Working

CHAPTER **26**

Patient Education

COMPLETION

Directions: Fill in the blank with the best answer.

1. Patient factors that have an impact on learning include the patient's _____ of disease versus the actual state of disease.

2. The holistic model suggests patient education should consider all aspects of patient life, including the _____ psychological, emotional, social, economic, and spiritual needs.

3. Essential factors in _____ management for the ambulatory care setting include conducting adequate patient education and follow-up.

4. Providing adequate, correct, understandable information to patients is integral to the _____ consent mandate within the Patient's Bill of Rights.

5. It is important that the medical assistant be aware of the various _____ available in the community for patient education and referral.

6. Both videotapes and Internet sites allow patient learning to be self-directed and _____.

7. Material should be written with lay person language at a _____ grade level to promote general patient understanding.

8. Copies of teaching materials should be available in other _____ when possible.

9. One of the major problems with delivering quality patient education in the ambulatory setting is the lack of _____.

10. Many times the key to patient understanding and _____ is involvement of family members.

Word List
Risk
Self-paced
Languages
Compliance
Resources
Time

Perception
Physical
Sixth to eighth
Informed

TRUE OR FALSE

Directions: Circle the best answer.

11.   T   F   A holistic model for patient education means designing a patient teaching plan that focuses on the patient's disease without concern for the patient's ability to pay for care.

12.   T   F   If a patient is in pain, it is best to get the patient teaching session completed immediately so the patient can go home and rest.

13.   T   F   Nonverbal communication is important when interacting with patients who have a language barrier.

14.   T   F   Lecture is an effective method for teaching a patient with diabetes how to give insulin injections.

15.   T   F   Providing an 83-year-old patient a videotape about diabetes is an effective teaching method.

16.   T   F   Teaching interventions should be postponed if the patient is extremely anxious or agitated.

17.   T   F   Demonstration/return demonstration is an excellent method for teaching a patient how to change a dressing.

CHAPTER **29**

Assisting with the Primary Physical Examination

MULTIPLE CHOICE

Directions: Circle the letter of the choice that best completes the statement or answers the question.

1. If you are interested in working with patients of all ages who seek help for a wide variety of disorders, employment with which medical specialist would be your best choice?
   a. family practitioner
   b. oncologist
   c. internist
   d. physical medicine physician

2. During a physical examination, the physician discovers the presence of bruits. What method would the physician use to make this discovery?
   a. manipulation
   b. palpation
   c. percussion
   d. auscultation

3. The usual sequence of the general physical examination involves moving:
   a. from the head toward the feet
   b. from the center of the body
   c. from the area with symptoms
   d. from the trunk and then outward to the limbs

4. With whom can you ethically discuss patient information that is gathered during the physical examination?
   a. your co-workers who do not work with this patient
   b. your family members who do not know this patient
   c. the physician who performed the examination
   d. family members of the patient who are involved in the patient's care

5. Which examination position requires the most careful monitoring of patients to ensure their safety from falls?
   a. dorsal recumbent
   b. knee-chest
   c. lithotomy
   d. Trendelenburg's

6. The physician performs manipulation during the physical examination to gain information about the:
   a. condition of internal organs
   b. irregularities that can be felt just beneath the skin
   c. range of motion of a joint
   d. strength of the muscles

7. Which examination position is used for obstetrical/gynecological examinations?
   a. dorsal recumbent
   b. knee-chest
   c. lithotomy
   d. Trendelenburg's

8. Which examination position is used in emergencies for patients in shock?
   a. dorsal recumbent
   b. knee-chest
   c. lithotomy
   d. Trendelenburg's

9. Which examination position is used for rectal or sigmoid examinations?
   a. dorsal recumbent
   b. knee-chest
   c. lithotomy
   d. Trendelenburg's

10. Which examination position requires the medical assistant to raise the head of the bed to a 30-degree to 45-degree angle?
    a. dorsal recumbent
    b. Fowler's
    c. lithotomy
    d. semi-Fowler's

11. The physician asks the medical assistant to position a patient on the examination table so that the patient can breathe more easily. The most appropriate position is:
    a. dorsal recumbent
    b. jackknife
    c. lithotomy
    d. semi-Fowler's
    e. Trendelenburg's

12. Which of the following pulses is palpated on either side of the trachea?
    a. apical
    b. brachial
    c. carotid
    d. radial
    e. temporal

13. Subjective information that should be included in the patient's record is:
    a. personal data
    b. physical examination findings
    c. results of tests
    d. vital signs
    e. x-ray examination reports

14. Which of the following information in the medical record is considered subjective?
    a. diagnosis
    b. examination
    c. medical history
    d. prognosis
    e. x-ray examination report

15. Which of the following information is objective data?
    a. family history
    b. past history
    c. social history
    d. patient symptoms
    e. physical examination

16. After a patient interview by the medical assistant, the medical assistant should record each of the following EXCEPT:
    a. chief symptom
    b. examination narrative
    c. family medical history
    d. medication allergies
    e. past medical history

17. "Return to clinic in 2 weeks" is:
    a. subjective
    b. objective
    c. assessment
    d. plan

18. "My throat hurts when I swallow" is:
    a. subjective
    b. objective
    c. assessment
    d. plan

19. The artery used in the measurement of blood pressure in the leg is the:
    a. brachial
    b. carotid
    c. popliteal
    d. radial
    e. temporal

20. Which of the following positions is most appropriate for a patient with severe hypotension?
    a. dorsal recumbent
    b. jackknife
    c. lithotomy
    d. semi-Fowler's
    e. Trendelenburg's

21. Which of the following positions is achieved by lying prone with the head and legs lowered and the buttocks elevated?
    a. dorsal recumbent
    b. lithotomy
    c. proctologic
    d. Sims'
    e. Trendelenburg's

22. Which of the following positions is most appropriate for a patient undergoing breast examination?
    a. knee-chest
    b. prone
    c. Sims'
    d. supine
    e. Trendelenburg's

23. After a proctoscopic examination, the patient should be helped to the upright position slowly to prevent:
    a. defecation
    b. diarrhea
    c. flatulence
    d. intestinal torsion
    e. syncope

TRUE OR FALSE

Directions: Circle the best answer.

24.   T   F   When using proper body mechanics, medical assistants should twist their body in the direction of the object to be lifted.

25.   T   F   The medical assistant should push a heavy item rather than trying to pull it.

26.   T   F   Bending both the knees and the back is the best method for picking up a heavy object.

27.   T   F   When transferring a patient from a wheelchair to the examination table, the medical assistant should always assist the patient on the weak side.

COMPLETION

Directions: Fill in the blank with the best answer.

28. A(An) _____ is composed of two or more types of tissues that form together to perform a particular function.

29. A body _____ is composed of several organs and their associated structures.

30. A(An) _____ is a medical instrument that is used to inspect the inner structures of the eye.

31. _____ _____ are used to test a patient's ability to conduct vibrations through bone.

32. A(An) _____ is used to examine the external auditory canal and tympanic membrane.

33. _____ is a method of examination that uses tapping or striking the body with fingers or a small hammer to determine alterations in sound or vibration.

34. A physician using the technique of _____ touches a patient to determine the size and consistency of a tumor.

35. Measuring the circumference of an infant's head is an example of _____.

36. For administration of a rectal suppository, the patient would be placed in the _____ position.

37. The _____ position is used for vaginal examinations.

38. A patient with severe shock may be placed in a _____ position.

39. The abbreviation _____ means the patient's eyes react normally during the physical examination.

40. The sinuses are visualized during the physical examination with passing light through the nasal passages with a technique called _____.

Word List
Lithotomy
Mensuration
Ophthalmoscope
Organ
Otoscope
Palpation
PEARL
Percussion
Sims'
System
Transillumination
Trendelenburg's
Tuning forks

CHAPTER **31**

Pharmacology Math

MULTIPLE CHOICE

Directions: Circle the letter of the choice that best completes the statement or answers the question.

1. One teaspoon is equal to _____ or _____.
   a. 5 cc, 5 ml
   b. 15 cc, 15 ml
   c. 30 cc, 30 ml
   d. 60 cc, 60 ml

2. One fluid ounce is equal to _____ or _____.
   a. 20 cc, 20 ml
   b. 15 cc, 15 ml
   c. 25 cc, 25 ml
   d. 30 cc, 30 ml

3. The formula for calculation of pediatric doses by weight is called:
   a. Fried's Law
   b. Clark's Rule
   c. Young's Rule
   d. West's Nomogram

4. The formula for calculation of pediatric doses by age in months is called:
   a. Fried's Law
   b. Clark's Rule
   c. Young's Rule
   d. West's Nomogram

5. The formula for calculation of pediatric doses by age in years is called:
   a. Fried's Law
   b. Clark's Rule
   c. Young's Rule
   d. West's Nomogram

6. Which of the following is a metric unit of volume?
   a. ounce
   b. milliliter
   c. milligram

7. Which of the following is a metric unit of weight or mass?
   a. ounce
   b. liter
   c. gram

8. Which of the following is a metric unit of length?
   a. centimeter
   b. milliliter
   c. milligram
   d. kilogram

9. Which of the following is an apothecary measure?
   a. gram
   b. grain
   c. ounce
   d. cubic centimeter

10. Which of the following is a household measure?
    a. gram
    b. grain
    c. drop
    d. cubic centimeter

11. Your patient is to receive Precef 20 mg/kg every 12 hours. The patient weighs 88 lb. What is the correct dosage?
    a. 500 mg
    b. 600 mg
    c. 800 mg
    d. 1000 mg

12. You need to give Lanoxin 0.125 mg. All you have is 0.250 mg/tablet. How much do you give?
    a. 2 tablets
    b. 5 tablets
    c. ½ tablet

13. A child who weighs 70 lb weighs how many kilograms?
    a. 140 kg
    b. 154 kg
    c. 32 kg
    d. 30 kg

14. How many milligrams equal 150 mcg ?
    a. 0.015 mg
    b. 0.15 mg
    c. 1.5 mg
    d. 15 mg

15. How many liters equal 1500 cc?
    a. 1.5 L
    b. 15 L
    c. 150 L
    d. 0.15 L

16. How many cubic centimeters equal 2.5 teaspoons?
    a. 10 cc
    b. 15 cc
    c. 5 cc
    d. 12.5 cc

17. How many milligrams equal 0.75 g?
    a. 75 mg
    b. 750 mg
    c. 7.5 mg
    d. 7500 mg

18. How many fluid ounces equal 90 ml?
    a. 20 fl oz
    b. 3.5 fl oz
    c. 3 fl oz
    d. 4 fl oz

19. How many milliliters equal 45 minims?
    a. 3 ml
    b. 30 ml
    c. 5 ml
    d. 0.3 ml

20. How many grains equal 1.2 grams?
    a. 36 grain
    b. 16.2 grain
    c. 18 grain
    d. 9 grain

21. How many tablespoons equal 16 oz?
    a. 8 T
    b. 32 T
    c. 24 T
    d. 12 T

22. How many ounces equal 150 cc?
    a. 50 oz
    b. 3.2 oz
    c. 32 oz
    d. 5 oz

SHORT ANSWER

Directions: Given the following information, calculate the amount (milliliter or tablet) of medication you should administer to the patient. Round to the closest half milligram or tablet.

These problems are each stated a little differently, but they all require the same information—dosage per kilogram of body weight or total dosage.

23. Timmy is scheduled for surgery in the morning. The physician orders 2 mg of medication per kg of body weight. The label on the bottle reads 0.5 g/5 ml. Timmy weighs 50 lb. How many milliliters do you give?

24. Juan is admitted with a diagnosis of meningitis. The physician orders 10 mg of medication per kg of body weight. The label on the bottle reads 1000 mg/ml. How many milliliters do you give if Juan weighs 108 lb?

25. Peter is to have 1 mg of a medication per kg of body weight. The label reads 10 mg/tablet. Peter weighs 88 kg. How many tablets do you give?

26. Mary Alice is being discharged today. Dr. Good has ordered a stat dose of medication 1 hour before she leaves the hospital to prevent car sickness on the long drive home. He tells you to give her 15 mg per kg of body weight. The label on the bottle reads 1.5 g/2 ml. Mary Alice weighs 120 lb. How many milliliters do you give?

27. Gary is to have 3 mg of medication per kg of body weight. The label on the bottle reads 0.3 g/ml. Gary weighs 100 lb. How many milliliters do you give?

28. Carolyn is to have 3 mg of medication per kg of body weight. Carolyn weighs 75 kg. Calculate the total milligrams of medication she should receive.

29. Inez weighs 145 lb. She is to have 2 mg of medication per kg of body weight. Calculate the total milligrams of medication she should receive.

30. The physician orders 20 mg of Garamycin. Available is 40 mg/ml. How many minims do you give?

31. The physician orders 100 mg of a medication. You have 250 mg/ml on hand. How many milliliters do you give?

32. Tim is to have 2 mg/kg of body weight of a certain medication. Tim weighs 75 kg. The medication is available in 500 mg/ml. How many milliliters do you administer?

CHAPTER **33**

Assisting with Medical Emergencies

MULTIPLE CHOICE

Directions: Circle the letter of the choice that best completes the statement or answers the question.

1. The patient faints in the reception room and falls to the floor. The medical assistant should:
   a. place a pillow under the patient's head and shoulders, keeping the feet and legs flat
   b. place a pillow under the patient's head and shoulders
   c. roll the patient onto the right side
   d. check for a pulse
   e. keep the patient's head and shoulders flat and raise the legs

2. Which of the following emergency situations should be managed first?
   a. hemorrhage
   b. shock
   c. occluded airway
   d. severe chest pain
   e. fractured bone

3. The first step in rendering first aid to a patient who appears to have stopped breathing is to:
   a. check for a pulse
   b. check for a medical alert bracelet
   c. begin chest compressions
   d. begin fluid resuscitation
   e. get the crash cart

4. On discovering an unresponsive person, the medical assistant should first assess the person's:
   a. airway
   b. blood pressure
   c. heart sounds
   d. pulse
   e. skin color

5. The initial step in giving first aid to a patient with a second-degree chemical burn is to:
   a. apply a burn ointment
   b. break the blisters
   c. cover with dry gauze
   d. flood the affected area with water
   e. give pain medication

6. Before CPR is initiated on an adult, the presence of circulation is usually determined with palpation of which pulse?
   a. brachial
   b. carotid
   c. femoral
   d. popliteal
   e. radial

7. The first treatment for a patient in insulin shock is administration of:
   a. insulin
   b. furosemide (Lasix)
   c. glucose
   d. normal saline solution
   e. lactated Ringer's solution

8. A patient is having a grand mal seizure. Which of the following is the MOST appropriate step for the medical assistant to protect the patient?
   a. administer small amounts of liquid
   b. apply wrist restraints
   c. hold the patient's head in an upright position
   d. loosen clothing around the patient's neck
   e. place a padded tongue blade in the patient's mouth

9. Before CPR is initiated on an infant, the presence of circulation is usually determined with palpation of which pulse?
   a. brachial
   b. carotid
   c. femoral
   d. popliteal
   e. radial

10. _____ is used to control hemorrhage and shock.
    a. Lanoxin
    b. Epinephrine
    c. Lidocaine
    d. Syrup of ipecac
    e. Valium

11. _____ is used for congestive heart failure.
    a. Lanoxin
    b. Epinephrine
    c. Lidocaine
    d. Syrup of ipecac
    e. Valium

12. _____ is used to induce vomiting.
    a. Lanoxin
    b. Epinephrine
    c. Lidocaine
    d. Syrup of ipecac
    e. Valium

13. _____ is used to control seizures.
    a. Lanoxin
    b. Epinephrine
    c. Lidocaine
    d. Syrup of ipecac
    e. Amytal

14. _____ is used as a topical anesthetic.
    a. Lanoxin
    b. Epinephrine
    c. Lidocaine
    d. Syrup of ipecac
    e. Valium

15. An AED is used to treat:
    a. CVA
    b. aneurysms
    c. seizures
    d. heart rhythm

16. A CVA is a:
    a. heart attack
    b. stroke
    c. seizure
    d. defibrillator

17. Syncope is:
    a. heart attack
    b. stroke
    c. seizure
    d. fainting

18. A sprain is:
    a. a fracture
    b. a ligament injury
    c. not treated
    d. a muscle injury

19. A strain is:
    a. a fracture
    b. a ligament injury
    c. not treated
    d. a muscle injury

20. An epistaxis is a:
    a. redness
    b. ligament injury
    c. nosebleed
    d. bruise

TRUE OR FALSE

Directions: Circle the best answer.

21. T F If a patient calls the physician's office with an immediate life-threatening emergency, place them on hold while you activate EMS.

22. T F Documentation in the patient's chart of an emergency phone call that has not resulted in a physician office visit is not necessary.

23. T F Symptoms of a heart attack in female patients include dizziness and syncopal episodes.

24. T F The physician must write a prescription for home oxygen use.

25. T F When clearing an obstructed airway in a conscious adult victim, administer a series of five abdominal thrusts.

26. T F A blind oral finger sweep should be used to remove a foreign airway obstruction in all age groups of choking victims.

27. T F To dislodge a foreign object from the airway of an infant, the chest thrusts are applied in the same position as those used for infant CPR.

28. T F Septic shock may be seen with severe congestive heart failure.

29. T F A patient with diabetes may go into shock with an overdose of insulin.

30. T F Excessive loss of blood can lead to cardiogenic shock.

31. T F If a patient reports an animal bite without a break in the skin, the patient can be instructed to wash the area well and observe for signs of infection.

32. T F A patient with burns must receive a tetanus shot if more than 6 years have passed since the last immunization.

33. T F A patient undergoing anticoagulant therapy should be seen immediately for any bleeding wound.

34. T F If a patient calls for an appointment after a head injury and clear drainage from the nose is reported, the patient should be seen by the physician first thing tomorrow.

35. T F A patient with abdominal pain accompanied by tarry stools should be seen immediately.

36. T F Application of a match or nail polish to the site of a tick bite is an effective method for prevention of Lyme disease.

37. T F If a patient is bleeding profusely from an arm laceration, apply direct pressure to the radial artery.

38. T F Mild frostbite may be treated by gently rubbing the affected extremity.

CHAPTER **34**

Assisting in Ophthalmology and Otolaryngology

MULTIPLE CHOICE

Directions: Circle the letter of the choice that best completes the statement or answers the question.

1. While playing tennis, Ms. Salinas is hit in the eye with a ball and has pain and swelling. Who should she call for an appointment?
   a. ophthalmologist
   b. optician
   c. optometrist
   d. any of the above

2. The average person blinks two to three times every second for the eyes to:
   a. rest briefly
   b. cleanse themselves
   c. refocus
   d. avoid eyestrain

3. The experience of seeing is initiated by the stimulation of the:
   a. lens
   b. rods and cones
   c. fovea centralis
   d. optical nerve

4. Which potentially destructive disorder of the eye is characterized by increased fluid inside the eyeball?
   a. cataract
   b. conjunctivitis
   c. glaucoma
   d. strabismus

5. Where is the tuning fork placed during the Weber test?
   a. on the mastoid process
   b. the center of the top of the head
   c. 1 inch from the opening of the ear canal
   d. 1 foot from the front of the face

6. When instilling ear drops in an adult who is lying down, in which direction should you gently pull the pinna to straighten the ear canal?
   a. up and back
   b. straight down
   c. down and away from the head
   d. straightening the canal is not necessary if the patient is lying on the side

7. Which preparation or instruction may negatively affect the accuracy of the Snellen visual acuity test?
   a. illuminating the chart with a bright light
   b. instructing the patient to keep both eyes open during testing
   c. having the patient sit during the test
   d. allowing the patient to squint

8. In which circumstances must sterile technique be used with ophthalmic procedures?
   a. only when the eye is lacerated or ulcerated
   b. during all examination and testing procedures
   c. when any instrument or application touches the eye or surrounding area during instillation of any irrigation solution or medication

9. An instrument used to measure intraocular pressure is a(an):
   a. ophthalmoscope
   b. optometer
   c. ophthalmometer
   d. tonometer

10. Inflammation of the eardrum is called:
    a. myringectomy
    b. myringoplasty
    c. myringititis
    d. myringotomy

11. During testing of a patient's visual acuity, the patient reads the 20/20 line with the right eye and misses one letter. The visual acuity should be recorded as:
    a. O.D. 19/20
    b. O.D. 20/20-1
    c. O.S. 19/20
    d. O.S. 20/20-1
    e. O.U. 19-20

12. During testing of a patient's visual acuity, the patient reads the 20/20 line with the left eye. The visual acuity should be recorded as:
    a. O.D. 19/20
    b. O.D. 20/20-1
    c. O.S. 19/20
    d. O.S. 20/20
    e. O.U. 19-20

13. During testing of a patient's visual acuity, the patient reads the 20/25 line with both eyes. The visual acuity should be recorded as:
    a. O.D. 19/20
    b. O.D. 20/20-1
    c. O.S. 19/20
    d. O.S. 20/20
    e. O.U. 20/25

14. When testing a patient's far visual acuity, the medical assistant uses which type of chart?
    a. Snellen
    b. Ishihara
    c. Rosenthal

15. When testing a patient's near visual acuity, the medical assistant uses which type of chart?
    a. Snellen
    b. Ishihara
    c. Rosenthal

16. When testing a patient for color blindness, the medical assistant uses which type of chart?
    a. Snellen
    b. Ishihara
    c. Rosenthal

17. A cloudy lens is called:
    a. glaucoma
    b. cataract
    c. ptosis
    d. stye

18. Increased intraocular pressure is called:
    a. glaucoma
    b. cataract
    c. ptosis
    d. stye

19. A drooping eyelid is:
    a. glaucoma
    b. cataract
    c. ptosis
    d. stye

20. When instilling ear drops in a child, pull the pinna:
    a. up and back
    b. down and back

COMPLETION

Directions: Fill in the blank with the best answer.

21. Extreme sensitivity to light is called _____.

22. _____ are structures that are found in the retina and make color perception possible.

23. _____ causes the auditory ossicles to become fixed, resulting in a vibration hearing deficit.

24. A _____ medication causes the pupil to constrict.

25. _____ errors occur when the eye is unable to focus light effectively on the retina.

26. Individuals over the age of 40 years have a decrease in the elasticity of the internal lens of the eye. This is called _____.

27. Nearsightedness, or _____ occurs when light rays entering the eye focus in front of the retina.

28. When light focuses behind the retina, the patient is diagnosed with _____.

29. A surgical procedure called _____ _____ can correct myopia.

30. Amblyopia is an example of the failure of the eyes to track together, known as the condition of _____.

31. A child with _____ has involuntary movement of one or both eyes. This condition is often seen with multiple congenital abnormalities.

32. The medical term for a stye is a _____.

33. _____ is a highly infectious disease typically caused by the staphylococcal bacteria and resulting in edema, purulent discharge, and inflammation of the eye.

34. Inflammation of the glands and lash follicles along the margins of the eyelids is called _____.

35. _____ _____ results in the loss of central vision and ultimately leads to blindness.

36. The middle ear contains the three ossicles: the _____, _____ and _____.

37. The _____ _____ in the inner ear are responsible for maintaining balance and equilibrium.

38. The _____ within the cochlea is lined with hair-like sensory cells that are surrounded by nerve fibers that stimulate the eighth cranial nerve and produce sound.

39. _____ is a sensorineural hearing loss that occurs with aging.

40. The medical term for swimmer's ear is _____ _____.

41. _____ _____ causes destruction of the hair cells of the cochlea with recurring attacks of vertigo, nausea, and progressive hearing loss.

Word List
Blepharitis
Cones
Conjunctivitis
Hordeolum
Hyperopia
Incus
Macular degeneration
Malleus
Ménière's disease
Miotic
Myopia
Nystagmus
Organ of corti
Otitis externa
Otosclerosis
Photophobia
Presbycusis
Presbyopia
Radial keratotomy
Refractive
Semicircular canals
Stapes
Strabismus

CHAPTER **35**

Assisting in Dermatology

MULTIPLE CHOICE

Directions: Circle the letter of the choice that best completes the statement or answers the question.

1. Why is the dermis layer sometimes referred to as the "true skin?"
   a. it is the outer layer that is visible to others
   b. it comprises the largest percentage of total skin mass
   c. it provides the body with protection from dehydration
   d. it contains the substance that gives the skin its distinctive color

2. What is one of the principal functions of the subcutaneous layer of the skin?
   a. to provide insulation for the body
   b. to produce oil to soften and protect the skin
   c. to house the sweat glands that function as temperature regulators
   d. to synthesize vitamin D

3. Which type of lesion is a sign of a partial thickness (second-degree) burn?
   a. pustule
   b. bulla
   c. ulcer
   d. wheal

4. Which statement does NOT describe a result of a full-thickness (third-degree) burn?
   a. severe pain immediately after the injury
   b. need for skin grafting
   c. danger of infection
   d. damage to all skin layers

5. Which is NOT an appropriate action to take in treatment of frostbite?
   a. using a heat source of up to 105°F
   b. taking time to monitor vital signs periodically during treatment
   c. warming the area with an external even heat source
   d. gently rubbing the affected area

6. Antipruritics are useful in treating which of the following conditions?
   a. acne
   b. herpes zoster
   c. macules
   d. nail fungus

7. Which highly contagious disorder is caused by streptococci and characterized by itchy vesicles and pustules?
   a. impetigo
   b. eczema
   c. scabies
   d. psoriasis

8. Which statement describes a major advantage of topical over systemic drugs?
   a. topical drugs are less likely to cause side effects
   b. topical drugs provide relief more quickly
   c. topical drugs are less costly for the patient
   d. topical drugs are easier to administer

9. What is a major preventive action that patients can take to avoid malignant neoplasms?
   a. use tanning beds rather than direct sun
   b. use lotions with a high SPF
   c. refrain from picking at acne lesions
   d. avoid direct contact with infected individuals

10. When obtaining a wound culture, it is important NOT to:
    a. remove too much exudates
    b. irritate the wound by inserting the swab too deeply
    c. use cotton swabs to collect the sample
    d. all of the above

11. When educating patients about the care of their skin, it is best to:
    a. avoid endorsing any particular product brands
    b. confine information to health rather than cosmetic issues
    c. refer them to outside sources, such as allergists and dietitians
    d. emphasize preventive measures that help promote healthy skin
    e. a, b, and d are correct

12. The word that means "the study of the skin" is:
    a. dermatitis
    b. dermatology
    c. dermopathy
    d. dermal

13. The meaning of the word *intradermal* pertains to:
    a. "upon the skin"
    b. "under the skin"
    c. "below the skin"
    d. "within the skin"

14. A surgical repair of the nose is called:
    a. rhinoplasty
    b. rhinorrhea
    c. rhinorrhagia
    d. rhinomycosis

15. Which of the following is NOT considered to be one of the three layers in the integumentary system?
   a. epidermis
   b. dermis
   c. hair papilla
   d. subcutaneous

16. The part of the integumentary system containing fat as a stored energy source is the:
   a. sebaceous glands
   b. epidermis
   c. dermis
   d. subcutaneous

17. A blister is called a:
   a. macule
   b. papule
   c. bulla
   d. pustule

18. A freckle is called a:
   a. macule
   b. papule
   c. bulla
   d. pustule

19. A raised lesion is called a:
   a. macule
   b. papule
   c. fissure

20. Redness of the skin is:
   a. cyanosis
   b. jaundice
   c. ecchymosis
   d. erythema
   e. pruritis

21. A bruise is also known as:
   a. cyanosis
   b. jaundice
   c. ecchymosis
   d. erythema
   e. pruritis

22. Itching is called:
   a. cyanosis
   b. jaundice
   c. ecchymosis
   d. erythema
   e. pruritis

23. Blueness of the skin is:
    a. cyanosis
    b. jaundice
    c. ecchymosis
    d. erythema
    e. pruritis

24. Yellow-colored skin is:
    a. cyanosis
    b. jaundice
    c. ecchymosis
    d. erythema
    e. pruritis

25. Which highly contagious disorder is caused by the itchmite?
    a. impetigo
    b. eczema
    c. scabies
    d. psoriasis

TRUE OR FALSE

Directions: Circle the best answer.

26.   T   F   Patients with metastasis have distant spread of a cancerous tumor.

27.   T   F   Benign tumors invade the basement membrane of surrounding tissues.

28.   T   F   A benign tumor has anaplastic changes.

29.   T   F   Grading of a tumor requires a pathological assessment of the level of cellular differentiation.

30.   T   F   The physician orders a series of diagnostic tests to determine the stage of the tumor.

31.   T   F   A patient scheduled for allergy skin tests does not need to stop taking prescription antihistamines before the procedure.

32.   T   F   Skin testing on young children is typically done on both forearms.

33.   T   F   A wheal forming at the site of a skin test indicates an allergic reaction to the serum.

34.   T   F   Patients should remain in the office for a minimum of 15 minutes after skin testing is completed for observation for adverse reactions to the procedure.

35.   T   F   Scratch allergic testing is more accurate than intradermal injections of potential allergens.

36.   T   F   The RAST test can be used to verify the presence of an allergic reaction.

37.   T   F   Chemexfoliation may cause increased levels of photophobia.

COMPLETION

Directions: Fill in the blank with the best answer.

38. The medical term for partial or complete lack of hair is _____.

39. The signs and symptoms of _____ _____ include cyanosis, numbness, tingling, and pain, especially in the extremities, as a result of intermittent attacks of ischemia.

40. When a physician removes dead or foreign material from a wound site, the procedure is called _____.

41. Small, purple, hemorrhagic patches on the skin that are frequently associated with bleeding disorders or liver disease are called _____.

42. An increase in the number of cells is called _____.

43. Cells that are in a primitive form and are diagnostic of a cancer-producing tumor are called _____.

Word List
Alopecia
Anaplastic
Debridement
Hyperplasia
Petechiae
Raynaud's phenomenon

CHAPTER **38**

Assisting in Obstetrics and Gynecology

MULTIPLE CHOICE

Directions: Circle the letter of the choice that best completes the statement or answers the question.

1. The cervix controls the opening to which organ?
   a. fallopian tube
   b. ovary
   c. uterus
   d. vagina

2. Which STD is a leading cause of female sterility?
   a. candidiasis
   b. gonorrhea
   c. chlamydia
   d. herpes
   e. b and c are correct

3. Which of the following is NOT a means of transmitting the HIV virus?
   a. breastfeeding
   b. blood transfusion
   c. sexual intercourse
   d. hugging

4. Which type of examination usually involves the taking of pelvic measurements?
   a. new patient visit
   b. diagnosis of PID
   c. initial prenatal visit
   d. consultation regarding contraception

5. Which is the most effective method of birth control?
   a. condom
   b. diaphragm
   c. IUD
   d. OCPs

6. Which method of birth control has the highest failure rate?
   a. condom
   b. diaphragm
   c. IUD
   d. birth control pills

7. Menses lasting longer than 7 days is:
   a. metrorrhagia
   b. menorrhagia
   c. amenorrhea
   d. dysmenorrhea

8. Bleeding between menses is:
   a. metrorrhagia
   b. menorrhagia
   c. amenorrhea
   d. dysmenorrhea

9. Pain or cramps with menstruation is:
   a. metrorrhagia
   b. menorrhagia
   c. amenorrhea
   d. dysmenorrhea

10. Failure to have a menstrual period is:
    a. metrorrhagia
    b. menorrhagia
    c. amenorrhea
    d. dysmenorrhea

11. Candidiasis is characterized by:
    a. itching
    b. bleeding
    c. infertility
    d. ulceration

12. Genital herpes is characterized by:
    a. itching
    b. bleeding
    c. infertility
    d. ulceration

13. Syphilis is associated with:
    a. itching
    b. bleeding
    c. infertility
    d. chancre

14. HPV is associated with:
    a. cancer
    b. bleeding
    c. infertility
    d. ulceration

15. _____ is the stage of labor when the baby is born.
    a. Stage I
    b. Stage II
    c. Stage III

16. _____ is the stage of labor when the placenta is delivered.
    a. Stage I
    b. Stage II
    c. Stage III

17. _____ is the stage of labor when the cervix dilates.
    a. Stage I
    b. Stage II
    c. Stage III

18. Which type of abortion can result in a D&C?
    a. complete
    b. spontaneous
    c. missed
    d. threatened

19. Which type of abortion is characterized by spotting without dilation of the cervix?
    a. complete
    b. spontaneous
    c. missed
    d. threatened

TRUE OR FALSE

Directions: Circle the best answer.

20.   T   F   Extensive growth of the endometrium is seen during the luteal phase of menstruation.

21.   T   F   Lupron injections may be prescribed for advanced endometriosis.

22.   T   F   Pregnancy is recommended to women with endometriosis because it frequently cures the disorder.

23.   T   F   PID is a major cause of infertility.

24.   T   F   Fibroid tumors of the uterus are considered precancerous in nature and must be excised.

25.   T   F   Fibrocystic breast disease causes firm nonmovable masses throughout the breasts that increase in tenderness in association with the menstrual cycle.

26.   T   F   Ovarian cancer can be diagnosed with a PAP smear.

27.   T   F   The leading gynecological cause of mortality in women is breast cancer.

28.   T   F   A cystocele is the protrusion of the bladder into the rectal wall.

29.   T   F   Teratogens are substances that result in severe fetal deformities.

30.   T   F   The most crucial period for fetal organ development is the third trimester.

31.   T   F   Effacement is the opening of the cervix that occurs during the birth process.

32.   T   F   Another word for pregnancy is parturition.

33.   T   F   An ectopic pregnancy is one that occurs in the inferior uterine wall.

34.   T   F   Perimenopause may last as long as 10 years.

35.   T   F   Recent research indicates HRT protects postmenopausal women from heart disease.

36.   T   F   A major advantage of using a colposcope to collect a cervical biopsy is that the suspected area can be visualized during the procedure and the tissue gathered from the most atypical area.

37.   T   F   Cryosurgery is used to treat cervical ulcers.

38.   T   F   Determination of the EDD is typically done via sonogram.

39.   T   F   An elevated AFP level may indicate the infant has a neural tube defect.

40.   T   F   Mammography uses sonograms to create an image of the breast.

COMPLETION

Directions: Fill in the blank with the best answer.

41. _____ is the initial milk that is rich in nutrients and immune properties and is expressed from the breasts immediately after the birth of an infant.

42. The medical term for a herniation of part of the spinal cord and its meninges from a congenital opening in the vertebral column is a _____.

43. _____ is the thinning of the cervix during labor and is measured from 0 to 100%.

44. _____ is the opening of the cervix during labor and is measured in centimeters.

45. When a disease or condition has no known cause, it is considered _____ in nature.

46. The medical term for the act or process of giving birth is _____.

47. A woman is considered _____ if she has had two or more pregnancies.

Word List
Colostrum
Dilation
Effacement
Idiopathic
Multiparous
Myelomeningocele
Parturition

CHAPTER **39**

Assisting in Pediatrics

MULTIPLE CHOICE

Directions: Circle the letter of the choice that best completes the statement or answers the question.

1. During which period in a child's life is weight gain the fastest in proportion to the child's total weight?
   a. first 6 months
   b. 6 months to 1 year
   c. preschool
   d. adolescence

2. Which human characteristic is NOT measured with the Denver II Development Screening Test?
   a. socialization
   b. verbal ability
   c. intelligence
   d. muscular control

3. Myringotomy may be necessary when a child has chronic:
   a. colic
   b. otitis media
   c. asthma
   d. croup

4. In which illness or condition are dehydration and subsequent electrolyte imbalance a particular concern in children?
   a. colic
   b. influenza
   c. hepatitis B
   d. diarrhea

5. Which condition, if left untreated, can lead to heart and kidney disease?
   a. tonsillitis
   b. Reye's syndrome
   c. hepatitis B
   d. chicken pox

6. At which age is the first dose of MMR vaccine recommended?
   a. 2 months
   b. 4 months
   c. 12 months
   d. 4 years

7. To which degree of accuracy should the child's head circumference be measured?
   a. $\frac{1}{8}$ inch
   b. $\frac{1}{4}$ inch
   c. $\frac{1}{2}$ inch
   d. $\frac{3}{4}$ inch

8. What method of evaluation is used to detect microcephaly?
   a. culture of infectious material
   b. developmental screening test
   c. laryngoscopy
   d. measurement of head circumference

9. Colic in infants is most often characterized by all EXCEPT:
   a. intermittent occurrence
   b. mild abdominal distress and crying
   c. disappearance by the age of 4 months
   d. allergies to cow's milk
   e. a, c, and d

10. Which common medication is not recommended for children because of its link to a sometimes fatal disease?
    a. acetaminophen
    b. aspirin
    c. ibuprofen
    d. penicillin

11. Which organization should you contact to obtain a current schedule of recommended immunizations?
    a. American Medical Association
    b. Occupational Safety and Heath Administration
    c. American Academy of Pediatrics
    d. individual vaccine manufacturers

12. A BRAT diet is used to treat:
    a. colic
    b. diarrhea
    c. constipation
    d. childhood obesity

13. The common cold is caused by:
    a. bacteria
    b. fungi
    c. virus

14. A middle ear infection is called:
    a. otitis media
    b. otitis externa
    c. otalgia
    d. meningitis

15. Swimmer's ear is called:
    a. otitis media
    b. otitis externa
    c. otalgia
    d. meningitis

16. A sore throat is commonly caused by:
    a. staph
    b. strep
    c. H. flu
    d. HBV

17. Another name for chicken pox is:
    a. rubella
    b. rubeola
    c. varicella
    d. herpes simplex

18. Tetanus is part of which immunization:
    a. HBV
    b. Hib
    c. DPT
    d. MMR

19. Routine head circumference is recommended for children until age:
    a. 6 months
    b. 12 months
    c. 3 years
    d. 10 years

20. Infants should be placed to sleep on their:
    a. left side
    b. back
    c. stomach
    d. right side

TRUE OR FALSE

Directions: Circle the best answer.

21.   T   F   Children with asthma typically have a productive cough with rales.

22.   T   F   Rescue inhalers are used for long-term prevention of bronchospasms in children with asthma.

23.   T   F   The flu vaccine is recommended for any child 3 months and older.

24.   T   F   A child diagnosed with conjunctivitis can return to school after 24 hours of antibiotic treatment.

25.   T   F   The Hib vaccine prevents meningitis.

26.   T   F   Viral meningitis is much more serious than the bacterial forms.

27.   T   F   Newborns are typically given the first dose of HBV vaccine before discharge to home.

28.   T   F   Cystic fibrosis is an inherited disorder caused by both parents being carriers.

29.   T   F   One of the most serious health problems associated with cystic fibrosis is the formation of thick mucus within the bronchioles that may lead to pulmonary obstruction.

30.   T   F   Duchenne's muscular dystrophy is an inherited disorder passed from father to son.

31.   T   F   The DTaP vaccine provides immunization against diphtheria, tetanus, and polio.

32.   T   F   The normal pediatric pulse range increases with the decreasing age of the child.

33.   T   F   The respiratory rate of an infant should be around 20 breaths per minute.

34.   T   F   The medical assistant is not responsible for reporting suspected child abuse to appropriate authorities.

CHAPTER **40**

Assisting in Orthopedic Medicine

MULTIPLE CHOICE

Directions: Circle the letter of the choice that best completes the statement or answers the question.

1. The type of bone that is composed of a diaphysis and two epiphyses serves mainly to:
   a. allow the body to stand upright
   b. store white blood cells
   c. protect internal organs
   d. encase nerve pathways

2. Which type of muscle is responsible for moving fluids through the urinary system?
   a. skeletal
   b. smooth
   c. striated
   d. voluntary

3. What is the principal reason physical activity is the preferred treatment for patients with muscular dystrophy?
   a. it strengthens the remaining muscle fibers
   b. it reverses the progression of the disease
   c. it prevents the patient from becoming overweight
   d. it replaces the protein in the muscles

4. A goniometer is used in the orthopedic examination to measure:
   a. muscular strength
   b. gait
   c. spinal curves
   d. joint range of motion

5. A patient who reports occasional acute pain in a big toe may have:
   a. osteoarthritis
   b. gouty arthritis
   c. tendonitis
   d. rheumatoid arthritis

6. Spongy porous bone tissue is called:
   a. bone marrow
   b. fossa
   c. sinus
   d. joint

7. Loss of bone mass is known as:
   a. osteolysis
   b. osteodystrophy
   c. osteoporosis
   d. osteoclasis

8. Lateral curvature of the spinal column is known as:
   a. osteoporosis
   b. lordosis
   c. scoliosis
   d. kyphosis

9. A sac of fluid near a joint is known as:
   a. tendon
   b. synovial membrane
   c. bursa
   d. ligament

10. Backward (upward) bending of the foot is known as:
    a. extension
    b. dorsiflexion
    c. pronation
    d. abduction

11. Visual examination of a joint with an endoscope is known as:
    a. bone scan
    b. arthrography
    c. arthrocentesis
    d. arthroscopy

12. A word that means pain in a joint is:
    a. arthralgia
    b. arthritis
    c. arthrocentesis
    d. arthroplasty

13. A surgical puncture of a joint to remove fluid is called:
    a. arthrodesis
    b. arthroplasty
    c. arthrocentesis
    d. arthrogram

14. An abnormal posterior thoracic spinal curvature is called:
    a. spondylitis
    b. kyphosis
    c. scoliosis
    d. lordosis

15. An anterior lumbar curvature of the spine that becomes abnormally exaggerated is known as:
    a. spondylitis
    b. kyphosis
    c. scoliosis
    d. lordosis

16. Several terms are used in anatomy and physiology to describe body movements. Which of the following is commonly described as bending?
    a. flexion
    b. extension
    c. abduction
    d. adduction

17. A type of movement that results in moving a part away from the midline of the body is:
    a. rotation
    b. extension
    c. abduction
    d. adduction

18. As soon as possible after a musculoskeletal injury, RICE therapy should be initiated. This stands for:
    a. resistance, increased extension, cold, and exercise
    b. rest, ice, compression, and elevation
    c. rest, ice, compression, and exercise
    d. resilience, ice, closure, and elevation

19. All of the following are true about fibromyalgia EXCEPT:
    a. it occurs more frequently in men than women
    b. it is associated with sleep disorders
    c. it is frequently seen in patients with lupus
    d. it causes chronic pain and fatigue

20. The typical treatment for fractures includes:
    a. NSAIDs
    b. reduction
    c. immobilization
    d. all of the above

21. Which of the following is true of Lyme disease?
    a. it is restricted to young children
    b. it is contracted through the bite of a flea
    c. it is a form of infectious arthritis
    d. it cannot be cured

22. Which of the following is NOT a risk factor for osteoporosis?
    a. a female over the age of 50 years
    b. alcohol abuse
    c. smoking
    d. obesity

23. Application of heat to a musculoskeletal injury results in:
    a. vasoconstriction, numbness, and increased metabolism
    b. increased blood flow, reduced muscle spasms, and local warmth
    c. vasodilation, local anesthesia, and increased blood viscosity
    d. muscle relaxation, decreased blood flow, and numbness

TRUE OR FALSE

Directions: Circle the best answer.

24.   T   F   A spiral fracture in a young child is suspicious of a child abuse injury.

25.   T   F   A greenstick fracture is typically seen in pediatric patients under the age of 14 years.

26.   T   F   The physician must perform a reduction for a displaced fracture.

27.   T   F   Osteomalacia in children is called rickets.

28.   T   F   One method of treating osteoporosis is rest and non–weight bearing exercise.

29.   T   F   Rheumatoid arthritis is caused by an autoimmune reaction against the synovial membrane that lines joints throughout the body.

30.   T   F   Heat application is contraindicated over scar tissue.

31.   T   F   Electric heating pads can be safely left in place up to 1 hour if the patient does not report any problems with circulation.

32.   T   F   Slight erythema is normal after the application of a moist hot pack or a paraffin bath.

33.   T   F   With therapeutic ultrasonography, the applicator should be focused directly over the affected bone.

34.   T   F   Passive exercise of an injured muscle can be accomplished with electric muscular stimulation.

35.   T   F   A TENS unit can play an integral role in the management of chronic pain.

36.   T   F   When a patient is fitted for crutches, the elbow should be bent approximately 45 degrees when holding the handgrips.

CHAPTER **41**

Assisting in Neurology and Mental Health

MULTIPLE CHOICE

Directions: Circle the letter of the choice that best completes the statement or answers the question.

1. The cranial nerves belong to which part of the nervous system?
   a. autonomic
   b. central
   c. parasympathetic
   d. peripheral

2. The point at which the neuron makes contact with the adjacent nerve cell is called the:
   a. axon
   b. dendrite
   c. nucleus
   d. synapse

3. The most common reasons that many neurological problems are not diagnosed in the early stages include all of the following EXCEPT:
   a. society has attached a stigma to neurological disorders
   b. patients may be unaware of symptoms
   c. the symptoms may occur in seemingly unrelated parts of the body
   d. fewer diagnostic procedures are available than for other body systems

4. Which condition is not usually associated with injuries caused by accidents?
   a. hemiplegia
   b. cerebral concussion
   c. quadriplegia
   d. paraplegia

5. A patient who describes seeing an aura before the onset of a severe headache often has a sign of:
   a. future CVA
   b. migraine headache
   c. epilepsy
   d. brain tumor

6. A patient calls to report symptoms that are commonly associated with the flu. The patient has not improved after 2 weeks of rest and may have:
   a. ALS
   b. CVA
   c. encephalitis
   d. MS

7. If a patient has delirium, the patient:
   a. cannot be awakened from an unconscious state
   b. has mental illness
   c. is temporarily unable to connect with the environment
   d. is in danger of permanent brain damage

8. For which neurological disorder should patients with hypertension and elevated cholesterol be monitored?
   a. CVA
   b. brain tumors
   c. migraines
   d. ALS

9. In what way does the medical assistant contribute most to the diagnosis of neurological disorders?
   a. conducting diagnostic tests
   b. careful observation of and listening to patients
   c. positioning patients for neurological examinations
   d. providing patient instruction

10. Which of the following means inflammation of the covering of the brain?
    a. meningitis
    b. poliomyelitis
    c. meningocele
    d. meningomyelitis

11. The medical term that means a condition of difficulty in swallowing is:
    a. dysphasia
    b. dysphagia
    c. bradyphagia
    d. bradyphasia

12. Which of the following words means "pertaining to the head and to the tail?"
    a. anterolateral
    b. dorsocephalad
    c. cephalocaudal
    d. anteroposterior

13. The tough outer layer of the meninges is the:
    a. pia mater
    b. arachnoid layer
    c. subdural space
    d. dura mater

14. Cognex and Aricept are used to treat:
    a. CVA
    b. epilepsy
    c. Alzheimer's disease
    d. migraine headaches

15. Which statement is NOT true of TIAs?
    a. they result from short-term ischemic episodes
    b. they may be precursors to a CVA
    c. they cause permanent neurological dysfunction
    d. they indicate the need for comprehensive diagnostic evaluation

16. Which statement is NOT true of absence or petit mal seizure?
    a. it causes a momentary loss of contact with reality
    b. it may occur without the awareness of others
    c. it must be treated aggressively
    d. it has a clonic/tonic phase

17. Parkinson's disease:
    a. affects women more than men
    b. is caused by a deficiency of the neurotransmitter dopamine
    c. is progressive and has no cure
    d. all are true
    e. b and c are true

18. Which statement is NOT true of multiple sclerosis?
    a. it is most frequently diagnosed in women living in Southern climates
    b. it causes a wide range of neurological problems
    c. it is a progressive neurological disorder without a known cure
    d. patients with MS have a repeated cycle of exacerbation of symptoms and remission

19. What diagnostic studies does the medical assistant expect the physician to order for a patient suspected of having a brain tumor?
    a. ophthalmoscopic examination
    b. CT scan
    c. bone scan
    d. a and b are correct

20. Which statement is NOT true of ALS?
    a. it is a progressive neurological disease that results in muscle atrophy
    b. death usually occurs because of respiratory failure
    c. it occurs most frequently in women in their 30s
    d. the etiology is unknown

TRUE OR FALSE

Directions: Circle the best answer.

21.　T　F　Encephalitis occurs because of a severe bacterial infection.

22.　T　F　A positive Brudzinski sign is indicative of meningitis.

23.   T   F   A concussion is a much more serious injury to the brain than a contusion.

24.   T   F   A subdural hematoma causes a rapid increase in intracranial pressure with sudden severe headaches and projectile vomiting.

25.   T   F   A patient with a spinal cord injury that caused complete transection of the cord resulting in paraplegia can still walk with assistance.

26.   T   F   Bell's palsy is a sudden paralysis of the tenth cranial nerve.

27.   T   F   Paresthesia is the abnormal feeling of burning or stinging that accompanies nerve compression.

28.   T   F   Lumbar puncture to collect CSF does not necessarily have to be conducted as a sterile procedure.

CHAPTER **42**

Assisting in Endocrinology

MULTIPLE CHOICE

Directions: Circle the letter of the choice that best completes the statement or answers the question.

1. Which of the following regulates the amount of calcium in the blood and bones?
   a. parathyroid hormone
   b. thyroxine
   c. thyroid-stimulating hormone
   d. prostaglandins

2. Cushing's disease is:
   a. a thyroid gland disorder
   b. hypofunction of the adrenal cortex
   c. a pancreatic disease
   d. hyperfunction of the adrenal cortex

3. Acromegaly is characterized by:
   a. hyperfunctioning of the pituitary gland after puberty
   b. adenomas of the pituitary gland during adulthood
   c. hyperfunctioning of the pituitary gland before puberty
   d. a and b

4. Hypopituitary dwarfism:
   a. causes enlargement of extremities
   b. is caused by failure to produce GH
   c. is caused by a tumor of the sella turcica
   d. is the result of hyperfunctioning of the pituitary gland

5. Myxedema is:
   a. adrenal gland hypofunction
   b. hirsutism and virilism
   c. advanced hypothyroidism in adulthood
   d. hot tumor areas in the thyroid gland

6. Which one of the endocrine glands produces epinephrine and norepinephrine?
   a. thyroid
   b. adrenal
   c. pituitary
   d. thymus

7. Which of the endocrine glands is divided into anterior and posterior lobes?
   a. thyroid
   b. adrenal
   c. pituitary
   d. thymus

8. Which endocrine gland requires iodine to produce its hormone?
   a. thyroid
   b. thymus
   c. gonads
   d. parathyroid

9. The islets of this endocrine gland regulate the levels of glucose in the blood. This gland is the:
   a. parathyroid gland
   b. thyroid gland
   c. pineal gland
   d. pancreatic gland

10. A disease that results in the enlargement of bones of the hands, feet, jaws, and cheeks in adults is:
    a. acroarthritis
    b. acromegaly
    c. arthralgia
    d. gigantism

11. Which endocrine gland stimulates synthesis and dispersion of melanin pigment in the skin?
    a. anterior pituitary
    b. parathyroid
    c. thyroid
    d. hypothalamus

12. Which endocrine gland regulates electrolyte and fluid homeostasis?
    a. thyroid
    b. parathyroid
    c. cortex of adrenal glands
    d. pancreatic islets

13. Which disorder is caused by an overactive thyroid?
    a. Cushing's
    b. Addison's
    c. diabetes
    d. Graves'

14. Which disorder is caused by an overactive adrenal gland?
    a. Cushing's
    b. Addison's
    c. diabetes
    d. Graves'

TRUE OR FALSE

Directions: Circle the best answer.

15.   T   F   Diabetes insipidus is related to glucose metabolism.

16.   T   F   Endemic goiters occur because of lack of iodine in the diet in specific geographical locations.

17.   T   F   Cretinism occurs when the thyroid fails to develop properly in an adolescent.

18.   T   F   Exophthalmia occurs in hypothyroidism.

19.   T   F   Polyphagia associated with diabetes mellitus means the patient is extremely thirsty.

20.   T   F   Diagnostic criteria for diabetes mellitus include an FBS greater than 126 mg/dl on more than one occasion.

21.   T   F   The normal FBS range is 80 to 120 mg/dl.

22.   T   F   The diagnostic criterion for diabetes mellitus type 1 is the absence of insulin production.

23.   T   F   Diabetes mellitus type 1 has a chronic onset and is seen in patients over the age of 30 years.

24.   T   F   Patients with diabetes mellitus type 1 must take multiple oral or injected doses of insulin throughout the day.

25.   T   F   Patient activity level does not affect the type and amount of insulin prescribed.

26.   T   F   The best method for teaching patients with diabetes how to perform glucometer testing is with a handout.

27.   T   F   Diabetes mellitus type 2 occurs much less frequently than type 1.

28.   T   F   A strong relationship exists between family history of the disease and the development of diabetes mellitus type 1.

29.   T   F   Oral hypoglycemics are used to treat diabetes mellitus type 2.

30.   T   F   Patients with diabetes mellitus type 2 have a problem with target cell response to insulin.

31.   T   F   The goal of diabetic management is to maintain blood glucose levels slightly above normal.

32.   T   F   Hyperglycemia may occur if the patient takes too much insulin and does not eat enough.

33.   T   F   Severe hypoglycemia causes ketoacidosis with resultant acetone or "fruity" breath.

34.   T   F   Diabetic retinopathy occurs because of hypoglycemic episodes that damage the blood vessels in the retina.

35.   T   F   Diabetic nephropathy is the leading cause of renal failure in the United States.

36.   T   F   Persons with diabetes are at no greater risk of CVD than are persons without diabetes.

37.   T   F   As part of diabetic foot care, patients should be instructed to never apply lotion to the feet.

CHAPTER **44**

Assisting in Cardiology

MULTIPLE CHOICE

Directions: Circle the letter of the choice that best completes the statement or answers the question.

1. Which heart chamber receives oxygenated blood from the lungs?
   a. left atrium
   b. right atrium
   c. left ventricle
   d. right ventricle

2. What is the principal sign of coronary artery disease?
   a. damaged heart valves
   b. inflammation of the blood vessels
   c. reduction of the blood supply to the myocardium
   d. irregular heartbeat

3. If a patient has tachycardia, this means that:
   a. the heart rate is faster than normal
   b. the patient has difficulty breathing when lying down
   c. the patient has dizzy spells
   d. the heartbeat is irregular

4. What takes place as a result of a myocardial infarction?
   a. the heartbeat becomes very irregular
   b. a major blood vessel bursts
   c. a portion of the heart muscle dies
   d. a major artery becomes blocked

5. A bruit noted during auscultation in the area of a blood vessel is often a sign of:
   a. an aneurysm
   b. an embolus
   c. phlebitis
   d. a thrombus

6. The _____ is the blood vessel that carries oxygen-rich blood from the lungs to the heart.
   a. pulmonary vein
   b. pulmonary artery
   c. superior vena cava
   d. inferior vena cava

7. Contraction phase of the heartbeat is called:
   a. diastole
   b. systole
   c. tachycardia
   d. pacemaker

8. The _____ is the saclike membrane surrounding the heart.
   a. endocardium
   b. bundle of His
   c. pericardium
   d. sinoatrial node

9. Sensitive tissue in the right atrium wall that initiates the heartbeat is known as the:
   a. tricuspid
   b. atrioventricular node
   c. bundle of His
   d. sinoatrial node

10. Blood vessels branching from the aorta to carry oxygen-rich blood to the heart muscle are called:
    a. venae cavae
    b. coronary arteries
    c. carotid arteries
    d. renal arteries

11. Cyanosis is characterized by which of the following?
    a. caused by hypoxia
    b. yellow coloration of the skin
    c. associated with a hemangioma
    d. a form of atherosclerosis

12. In the conduction system of the heart, which of the following is responsible for initiating a heartbeat?
    a. Purkinje fibers
    b. bundle of His
    c. atrioventricular node
    d. sinoatrial node

13. The signal from the sinoatrial (SA) node is then picked up by which of the following?
    a. atrioventricular node
    b. aorta
    c. Purkinje fibers
    d. bundle of His

14. The part of the conduction system of the heart that wraps around the outer walls of the ventricles is the:
    a. bundle branches
    b. Purkinje fibers
    c. bundle of His
    d. aorta

15. The blood vessel branching from the heart that carries deoxygenated blood to the lungs is called the:
    a. vena cava
    b. pulmonary artery
    c. carotid artery
    d. renal artery

16. The blood vessel that carries deoxygenated blood to the heart is called the:
    a. vena cava
    b. pulmonary artery
    c. carotid artery
    d. renal artery

17. Which drug is used for congestive heart failure?
    a. digoxin (Lanoxin)
    b. fluoxetine (Prozac)
    c. gemfibrozil (Lopid)
    d. triazolam (Halcion)
    e. warfarin (Coumadin)

18. Which drug is used as an anticoagulant?
    a. digoxin (Lanoxin)
    b. fluoxetine (Prozac)
    c. gemfibrozil (Lopid)
    d. triazolam (Halcion)
    e. warfarin (Coumadin)

19. What is another name for a heart attack?
    a. CVA
    b. MI
    c. MS
    d. CHF

20. Which is the most common route of administration of nitroglycerin?
    a. sublingual
    b. intradermal
    c. intramuscular
    d. intravenous
    e. subcutaneous

TRUE OR FALSE

Directions: Circle the best answer.

21.   T   F   MI symptoms in women include acute chest pain.

22.   T   F   Thrombolytic treatment to dissolve coronary artery blockage must be started within 3 hours of the onset of the episode.

23.   T   F   CABG procedures involve the insertion of a flexible catheter into a blocked coronary artery and the insertion of a stent to maintain the patency of the artery.

24.   T   F   Chronic hypertension may result in left ventricular hypertrophy.

25.   T   F   Essential hypertension is the result of an underlying pathological condition in another body system.

26.   T   F   Patients with primary hypertension may be asymptomatic until serious health problems occur.

27.   T   F   Left-sided heart failure causes pulmonary edema, dyspnea, orthopnea, and tachycardia.

28.   T   F   Patients with CHF must pay particular attention to a sudden gain in weight.

29.   T   F   Rheumatic heart disease develops because of an antigen-antibody reaction several weeks after an untreated staphylococcal infection.

30.   T   F   Patients with rheumatic heart disease may be prescribed life-long antibiotic prophylaxis for invasive medical procedures.

31.   T   F   A DVT may be a life-threatening problem because of the potential of embolus creation.

32.   T   F   Patients with DVTs are treated immediately with anticoagulant therapy. The therapy is discontinued 2 weeks after the onset of symptoms.

33.   T   F   A bruit may be palpated over the site of an abdominal aneurysm.

34.   T   F   A Doppler study uses a sonographic beam that picks up the speed of WBCs in the arteries being tested.

35.   T   F   Echocardiography is used in the diagnosis of incompetent cardiac valves.

CHAPTER **45**

Assisting in Geriatrics

MULTIPLE CHOICE

Directions: Circle the letter of the choice that best completes the statement or answers the question.

1. Which of the following diseases is NOT associated with aging?
   a. hypertension
   b. diabetes mellitus type 2
   c. arteriosclerosis
   d. diabetes mellitus type 1

2. Which of the following disorders is associated with aging?
   a. constipation
   b. diarrhea
   c. hematuria
   d. asthma

3. Which of the following disorders is associated with bone loss?
   a. osteoarthritis
   b. osteoporosis
   c. rheumatory arthritis
   d. rheumatic fever

4. Which of the following is a clouding of the lens of the eye?
   a. cataract
   b. glaucoma
   c. macular degeneration

5. Which of the following disorders is associated with joint pain in older adults?
   a. osteoarthritis
   b. osteoporosis
   c. rheumatory arthritis
   d. rheumatic fever

6. Which of the following is caused by increasing pressure inside the eye?
   a. cataract
   b. glaucoma
   c. macular degeneration

7. Hearing loss in older adults is called:
   a. presbycusis
   b. presbyopia
   c. tinnitus

8. Vaginal dryness is treated with:
   a. lubricant
   b. douching
   c. estrogen cream
   d. a and c

TRUE OR FALSE

Directions: Circle the best answer.

9. T F Aging people are resistant to change and are unable to learn new things.

10. T F All aging people have a certain amount of hearing and vision loss.

11. T F The myocardium becomes less efficient as we age.

12. T F Older patients first diagnosed with diabetes mellitus have the same symptoms as younger patients: polyuria, polydipsia, and polyphagia.

13. T F Older patients are more prone to pernicious anemia.

14. T F Aging causes a loss of subcutaneous fat, resulting in difficulty with the regulation of body temperature.

15. T F Seborrheic keratosis development is common in aging patients.

16. T F Muscular decline is unavoidable with increased age.

17. T F Stroke victims should be supported on the strong side when walking or transferring.

18. T F Risk factors for osteoporosis include smoking, Asian descent, and a large skeletal frame.

19. T F Decubitus ulcers form because of chronic ischemia to tissue.

20. T F The aging brain is the same size and weight as other brains.

21. T F Older individuals take longer to process information.

22. T F Sedentary lifestyle and social isolation increase the risk of cognitive decline.

23. T F The first stage of Alzheimer's disease affects the patient's ability to make decisions and remember simple tasks.

24. T F Alzheimer's disease is diagnosed with blood work and the use of MRI.

25.   T   F   Older patients need as much as eight times more light to read but also have a problem with glare.

26.   T   F   A direct relationship exists between hearing loss and the development of depression.

27.   T   F   If an older person has difficulty hearing, shouting in the good ear is an effective way to communicate.

28.   T   F   The effects of sleep disorders in aging persons may be confused with dementia.

29.   T   F   Older learners are easily distracted and may have short-term memory loss.

CHAPTER **46**

Principles of Electrocardiography

MULTIPLE CHOICE

Directions: Circle the letter of the choice that best completes the statement or answers the question.

1. If a patient has tachycardia, this means that:
   a. the heart rate is faster than normal
   b. the patient has difficulty breathing when lying down
   c. the patient has dizzy spells
   d. the heartbeat is irregular

2. If a patient has bradycardia, this means that:
   a. the heart rate is faster than normal
   b. the heart rate is slower than normal
   c. the patient has chest pain
   d. the heartbeat is irregular

3. If the ECG recording appears as a series of interruptions on the baseline, you should:
   a. check for nearby electric appliances
   b. ask the patient to lie still
   c. help the patient to relax and stay warm
   d. check the cable connections to the electrodes

4. In which direction should lead connectors on electrodes be pointed when attached to the patient in preparation for the ECG?
   a. toward the head
   b. toward the feet
   c. away from the body midline
   d. toward the center of the body

5. On an ECG recording, five 5-mm boxes are seen between the R waves. What is the patient's heart rate per minute?
   a. 60 bpm
   b. 65 bpm
   c. 70 bpm
   d. 75 bpm

6. On an ECG recording, seven QRS complexes are seen on a 6-second strip. What is the patient's heart rate per minute?
   a. 60 bpm
   b. 65 bpm
   c. 70 bpm
   d. 75 bpm

7. If the ECG recording appears as a series of small uniform spikes in the baseline, you should:
   a. check for nearby electric appliances
   b. ask the patient to lie still
   c. help the patient to relax and stay warm
   d. check the cable connections to the electrodes

8. If the ECG recording appears with the baseline rising and falling, you should:
   a. check for nearby electric appliances
   b. ask the patient to lie still
   c. help the patient to relax and stay warm
   d. check the cable connections to the electrodes
   e. b and c are correct

9. If the ECG recording appears as a series of irregular jagged peaks, you should:
   a. check for nearby electric appliances
   b. ask the patient to breathe through the mouth
   c. help the patient to relax and stay warm
   d. check the cable connections to the electrodes

10. A monitor that a patient wears for 24 hours is called a(an):
    a. 12-lead
    b. Holter
    c. halter
    d. echocardiogram

11. In a standard 12-lead ECG, the measurement of current that the heart muscle produces between the right arm electrode and left arm electrode is known as the:
    a. standard limb lead I
    b. standard limb lead II
    c. standard limb lead III
    d. augmented lead – AVL

12. The greatest deflection from the baseline on the electrocardiogram is the:
    a. P wave
    b. T wave
    c. ST segment
    d. QRS complex

13. Which deflection from the baseline represents the repolarization of the ventricles?
    a. P wave
    b. T wave
    c. ST segment
    d. QRS complex

14. What part of the ECG complex represents the atrial depolarization?
    a. P wave
    b. T wave
    c. ST segment
    d. QRS complex

15. In a standard 12-lead ECG, the measurement of current that the heart muscle produces between the midline to the left arm electrode is known as the:
    a. standard limb lead I
    b. standard limb lead II
    c. standard limb lead III
    d. augmented lead–AVL

TRUE OR FALSE

Directions: Circle the best answer.

16. T   F   The precordial leads, which include aVR and aVL, record the electric activity between specific points on the chest wall and within the heart.

17. T   F   The patient must be placed in the supine position for an ECG, even with symptoms of dyspnea and orthopnea.

18. T   F   Patients should hold their breath during the brief seconds necessary to record an ECG.

19. T   F   Documentation for an ECG should include whether the patient smoked a cigarette within 15 minutes of the procedure.

20. T   F   Digitalis toxicity may cause specific ECG changes.

21. T   F   One of the most specific ECG changes that occurs in patients with an MI is elevated T waves.

22. T   F   There are no eating restrictions when a patient is scheduled for a stress test.

COMPLETION

Directions: Fill in the blank with the best answer.

23. The P wave occurs during the contraction of the _____ and shows the beginning cardiac depolarization.

24. The QRS complex shows the contraction of both _____ and also reflects the completion of cardiac depolarization.

25. The T wave indicates ventricular recovery or _____ of the ventricles.

26. The _____ on an ECG machine makes the image on the ECG paper.

27. ECG paper has horizontal and vertical lines at _____ intervals.

28. Every fifth line on ECG paper, both vertically and horizontally, is darker than the other lines and creates a large square measuring _____ on each side.

29. One large 5-mm square passes the stylus every _____ seconds.

30. The normal-speed ECG paper travels past the stylus at a rate of _____ mm per second.

31. The first three leads recorded are called the standard or _____ limb leads because they each use two limb electrodes to record the heart's electric activity.

32. Lead _____ records the electric activity between the right arm and the left leg. Lead _____ records the electric activity between the right arm and the left arm.

33. Lead _____ records the electric activity between the left arm and the left leg.

34. _____ records the activity from midway between the left leg and the left arm to the right arm.

35. _____ records the activity from midway between the right arm and the left leg to the left arm.

36. _____ records the activity from midway between the right arm and the left arm to the left leg.

37. The precordial or chest leads are _____ and are designated V_1, V_2, V_3, V_4, V_5, and V_6.

38. The _____ _____ is a combination of all of the electric events occurring in the heart during a single heartbeat.

39. Initiation of the electric activity of the heart occurs in specialized tissue called the _____ _____, which is located in the superior posterior wall of the right atrium.

40. The AV node sends the electric impulse through the _____, which stimulates the right and left ventricular walls.

41. The distal-most portions of the electric system of the myocardium are the _____.

42. _____ _____ _____ refers to a regular heart rate that ranges from 60 to 80 bpm.

43. The _____ is the electric recording of the heart at rest.

44. A _____ _____ _____ is an ectopic ventricular beat that occurs without a preceding P wave.

45. There is no pulse when the patient is in _____ _____.

46. In the case of _____, the patient exhibits general malaise and muscle cramps. The condition may occur if diuretics are used without potassium supplementation.

47. _____ _____ occurs when the atria are beating at an extremely rapid rate of up to 400 bpm.

48. A cardiac _____ _____ is a diagnostic procedure performed to evaluate the patient's myocardial response to measured exercise.

Word List
I
II
III
0.2
25
1-mm
5 mm
Atria
Atrial flutter
aVF
aVL
aVR
Baseline
Bipolar
Bundle of His
Cardiac cycle
Hypokalemia
Normal sinus rhythm
Premature ventricular contraction
Purkinje fibers
Repolarization
Sinoatrial node
Stress test
Stylus
Unipolar
Ventricles
Ventricular fibrillation

CHAPTER 47

Assisting with Diagnostic Imaging

MULTIPLE CHOICE

Directions: Circle the letter of the choice that best completes the statement or answers the question.

1. _____ is fluoroscopic examination of the esophagus, stomach, and duodenum with oral administration of barium sulfate as a contrast medium.
   a. CT scan
   b. MRI
   c. Lower GI
   d. Upper GI

2. The part of the sonography machine that is in contact with the patient is called the:
   a. gantry
   b. cathode
   c. transducer
   d. table

3. The doughnut-shaped portion of a CT scanner that surrounds the patient and functions, at least in part, to gather imaging data is called the:
   a. gantry
   b. contrast medium
   c. transducer
   d. table

4. _____ is fluoroscopic examination of the colon, usually with rectal administration of barium sulfate as a contrast medium.
   a. CT scan
   b. MRI
   c. Lower GI
   d. Upper GI

5. A badge for monitoring radiation exposure to personnel is called a:
   a. gantry
   b. dosimeter
   c. transducer
   d. roentgen

6. The computerized x-ray imaging method that provides axial and three-dimensional scans is commonly called a:
   a. CT scan
   b. MRI
   c. sonogram
   d. upper GI

7. Radiographic examination of the urinary tract with intravenous injection of an iodine contrast medium is called:
   a. CT scan
   b. MRI
   c. IVU
   d. fluoroscopy

8. _____ is direct observation of the x-ray image in motion.
   a. CT scan
   b. MRI
   c. IVU
   d. Fluoroscopy

9. _____ is an imaging method that uses a magnetic field and radiofrequency pulses to create computer images of both bones and soft tissues in multiple planes.
   a. CT scan
   b. Ultrasound
   c. MRI
   d. IVU

10. _____ is an imaging method that uses radioactive materials injected or ingested into the body to provide information about the function of organs and tissues.
    a. Nuclear medicine
    b. Ultrasound
    c. MRI
    d. IVU

11. Directional terms are used in describing relative positions of body parts. Which of the following terms means "toward the head?"
    a. superior
    b. inferior
    c. anterior
    d. posterior

12. Which term is used in medical terminology to describe "front" or "in front of?"
    a. superior
    b. inferior
    c. anterior
    d. posterior

13. What word in medical terminology is used to mean "toward the feet?"
    a. superior
    b. inferior
    c. anterior
    d. posterior

14. What term is used in anatomy and physiology to mean "back" or "in back of?"
    a. superior
    b. inferior
    c. anterior
    d. posterior

15. The word used in medical terminology to mean "toward the midline of the body" is:
    a. medial
    b. lateral
    c. ventral
    d. dorsal

16. What word means "toward the side of the body" or "away from the midline?"
    a. medial
    b. lateral
    c. ventral
    d. dorsal

17. What word is used in medical terminology to mean "toward or nearest the trunk of the body?"
    a. proximal
    b. distal
    c. superficial
    d. deep

18. To indicate that something lies nearer the surface, we use the term:
    a. proximal
    b. distal
    c. superficial
    d. deep

19. The word used in anatomy and physiology to mean "farther away from the body surface" is:
    a. proximal
    b. distal
    c. superficial
    d. deep

20. What word means "farther away" or "farthest from the trunk or the point of origin of a body part?"
    a. proximal
    b. distal
    c. superficial
    d. deep

21. The body is divided into subdivisions or smaller segments to facilitate the study of the body as a whole or individual organs. What plane divides the body into two equal right and left halves?
    a. midsagittal plane
    b. frontal plane
    c. transverse plane
    d. crosswise plane

22. The plane that divides the body into anterior and posterior portions is called the:
    a. sagittal plane
    b. frontal plane
    c. midsagittal plane
    d. transverse plane

23. Which plane of the body is synonymous with a horizontal or crosswise plane?
    a. sagittal plane
    b. frontal plane
    c. midsagittal plane
    d. transverse plane

TRUE OR FALSE

Directions: Circle the best answer.

24.   T   F   Patients with cardiac pacemakers are restricted from MRI examinations.

25.   T   F   A patient is exposed to an average amount of radiation during an MRI procedure.

26.   T   F   Nuclear medicine scans provide clear detailed images of anatomic structures.

27.   T   F   Thallium is a nuclear medicine that helps visualize the condition of the myocardium during a stress test.

28.   T   F   A barium enema is conducted before a sigmoidoscopy for best visualization of the colon.

29.   T   F   All radiographic examinations requiring the use of iodine uptake should be scheduled before a lower GI series.

30.   T   F   The purpose of intensifying screens is to reduce the amount of x-ray exposure necessary for an accurate view.

31.   T   F   X-ray film boxes should be stored flat with the expiration date visible.

32.   T   F   Potential formation of cataracts is a concern for radiographers who work extensively with fluoroscopy.

33.   T   F   A parent, rather than a professional radiographer, should hold a child in position for an x-ray examination.

COMPLETION

Directions: Fill in the blank with the best answer.

34. The plane that divides the body into anterior and posterior parts is called _____.

35. The radiographic view in which the coronal plane of the body or body part is parallel to the film plane (AP or PA) is _____ projection.

36. The radiographic view in which the sagittal plane of the body or body part is parallel to the film is called _____.

37. The radiographic view in which the body or body part is rotated so that the projection is neither frontal nor lateral is called _____.

38. The frontal projection in which the patient is prone, or facing the x-ray film or image receptor, is called _____.

39. The plane that divides the body into right and left parts is called _____.

40. The plane that divides the body into superior and inferior parts is called _____.

41. The radioactive substance administered to a patient for nuclear medicine imaging procedures is called _____.

42. Another name for an x-ray examination is _____.

43. AP stands for _____.

44. _____ is a treatment procedure that uses a catheter to open or widen a blood vessel.

45. A fluoroscopic examination of a joint that uses contrast medium to visualize the soft tissue components is a(an) _____.

46. Another term for _____ is diagnostic ultrasound, which uses sound waves to produce images of soft tissue.

47. A(An) _____ is a moving grid device that prevents scatter radiation from fogging an x-ray film.

48. A(An) _____ substance is easily penetrated by x-rays and appears dark on radiographs.

49. A(An) _____ substance is not easily penetrated by x-rays and appears light on radiographs.

50. A(An) _____ is conducted through a lumbar puncture and the injection of an iodine contrast medium.

51. _____ is a therapeutic technique conducted by the radiologist that uses a catheter to block a blood vessel and prevent hemorrhage.

52. _____ ultrasound can be used to detect vascular disease, such as atherosclerosis and venous thrombosis.

53. A(An) _____ light beam helps the radiographer vary the size of the radiation field and properly align the x-ray cassette tray.

Word List
Angioplasty
Anteroposterior
Arthrogram
Bucky
Collimator
Coronal or frontal plane
Doppler
Embolization
Frontal
Lateral
Myelogram
Oblique
Posteroanterior
Radiograph
Radiolucent
Radiopaque
Sagittal
Sonography
Tracer
Transverse

CHAPTER **48**

Assisting in the Clinical Laboratory

MULTIPLE CHOICE

Directions: Circle the letter of the choice that best completes the statement or answers the question.

1. Which of the following results do you expect from a procedure considered to be a screening test?
   a. specific gravity = 1.025
   b. hematocrit = 44%
   c. occult blood = positive
   d. hemoglobin = 15 g/dl

2. The act passed by Congress to establish quality standards for all laboratory testing is referred to as:
   a. FDA
   b. CDC
   c. CLIA
   d. MSDS

3. Categories of tests performed in the clinical laboratory are assigned by the FDA on the basis of the:
   a. potential risk to public health
   b. expense to the patient
   c. ease of performance
   d. instrumentation and supplies needed

4. Laboratory tests performed in a physician's office are most likely to be categorized as:
   a. waived
   b. moderate-complexity
   c. high-complexity
   d. a and b

5. Which of the following is NOT a waived test?
   a. dipstick urinalysis
   b. fecal occult blood
   c. Gram staining
   d. spun microhematocrit

6. As you are reading an article in a professional publication, you come across a new test for serum cholesterol. You wonder whether that test might be appropriate for use in the physician's office where you work. What website should you visit to determine the CLIA categorization of the test?
   a. www.cdc.gov
   b. www.epa.gov
   c. www.osha.gov
   d. www.fda.gov

7. A blood culture and sensitivity (C&S) test is most likely performed in which division of the clinical laboratory?
   a. urinalysis
   b. chemistry
   c. hematology
   d. microbiology

8. You are preparing a chemical hygiene plan for your employer and need copies of the material safety data sheets (MSDS) for several products in use in your laboratory. The first step is to contact:
   a. the manufacturer of the product
   b. the CDC
   c. an OSHA representative
   d. a sales representative

9. In the identification system of the National Fire Protection Association, the white diamond indicates:
   a. the flammability of the chemical
   b. special hazards of the chemical
   c. the reactivity/stability of the chemical
   d. the health hazard of the chemical

10. A chemical that is extremely hazardous to one's health has a number _____ in the _____ diamond on the National Fire Protection Association label.
    a. 10, blue
    b. 4, yellow
    c. 4, blue
    d. 10, yellow

11. Which of the following is LEAST likely to prevent the spread of infection in a laboratory?
    a. using a special container for sharps
    b. washing the hands
    c. using sterile cups in urine collection
    d. cleaning with a chemical disinfectant

12. The pledge of healthcare professionals to work to achieve the highest degree of excellence in the care given to every patient is otherwise known as:
    a. chain of custody
    b. quality assurance
    c. quality control
    d. incident reporting

13. Every time you open a new container of urine dipsticks, you dip one in a special solution provided by the manufacturer and compare the results on the dipstick with a standard chart. You know that the readings typically are high. The special solution you are using is known as a(an):
    a. control
    b. standard
    c. aliquot
    d. referral specimen

14. Before determining a urine specific gravity with a refractometer, you place a drop of special solution on the instrument and adjust the instrument until the scale reads 1.000. The special solution you are using is known as a(an):
    a. control
    b. standard
    c. aliquot
    d. referral specimen

15. Your first task when you arrive at the laboratory in the morning is to check the temperature of the refrigerator/freezer. The values you expect are:
    a. refrigerator = 4°C; freezer = 0°C
    b. refrigerator = 40°C; freezer = 32°C
    c. refrigerator = 0°C; freezer = 8°C
    d. refrigerator = 10°C; freezer = 0°C

16. The most common temperature for an incubator in the microbiology laboratory is:
    a. 25°C
    b. 37°C
    c. 10°C
    d. 121°C

17. You are required to transfer 10 ml of urine from a 24-hour specimen into a special tube to be sent to a referral laboratory. You:
    a. pour the urine into the tube, estimating the amount
    b. use a graduated cylinder to measure the urine and then pour it into the tube
    c. use a serologic pipet to transfer the urine into the tube
    d. use a beaker to measure 10 ml and pour it into the tube

18. Which type of pipet must be drained completely to ensure accuracy of measurement?
    a. TD
    b. TC

19. Pipets used to prepare reagents include:
    a. serologic
    b. graduated
    c. volumetric
    d. b and c
    e. all of the above

20. Which of the following is most accurate to measure 500 ml?
    a. 500-ml volumetric flask
    b. 500-ml beaker
    c. 500-ml graduated cylinder
    d. 500-ml Erlenmeyer flask

21. You mix 2 ml of a patient's serum with 18 ml of diluent to prepare a:
    a. 2:18 dilution
    b. 1:9 dilution
    c. 1:20 dilution
    d. 1:10 dilution

22. You need to prepare a 1:10 dilution of a serum sample obtained from an infant. Because you have a small amount of sample, you use a micropipettor to measure 0.5 ml, which you then add to:
    a. 9.5 ml diluent
    b. 4.5 ml diluent
    c. 5.0 ml diluent
    d. 50 ml diluent

23. The ocular of the microscope generally magnifies the image:
    a. 2 times
    b. 5 times
    c. 10 times
    d. minimally

24. The microscope component that directs the light up through the stage is the:
    a. condenser
    b. iris diaphragm
    c. ocular
    d. magnification system

25. The microscope component that regulates the amount of light passing through the specimen is the:
    a. condenser
    b. iris diaphragm
    c. ocular
    d. magnification system

26. When the 40× objective is in place on the microscope, the total magnification of the specimen is:
    a. 40×
    b. 4×
    c. 400×
    d. 80×

27. Immersion oil can be used with which of the following objective lenses of the microscope?
    a. 40×
    b. 100×
    c. 10×
    d. both a and b

28. The high-power lens of the microscope is the:
    a. 40× objective
    b. 10× objective
    c. 100× objective
    d. 4× objective

29. The low-power lens of the microscope is the:
    a. 40× objective
    b. 10× objective
    c. 100× objective
    d. 4× objective

30. A centrifuge is used to:
    a. separate liquids from solids
    b. separate blood cells from serum or plasma
    c. separate crystals from urine
    d. all of the above

31. Balancing a centrifuge requires that:
    a. all tubes in the load have an equal amount of liquid of the same viscosity
    b. all tubes in the load are of equal size and shape
    c. all tubes in the load have a partner in that they are directly across from one another in the rotor holder
    d. all of the above

32. Preventing aerosolization in a centrifuge can be accomplished by ensuring that:
    a. the tubes have an equal amount of fluid
    b. the atmosphere has 5% carbon dioxide
    c. the tubes are tightly capped
    d. rubber cups are in the bottom of the carriers

33. An autoclave can best be compared with a(an):
    a. oven
    b. deep fryer
    c. pressure cooker
    d. washing machine

34. The word *autoclaved* appears on special tape used in an autoclave only if the temperature has reached:
    a. 121°C
    b. 254°C
    c. 100°C
    d. 212°F

35. Carbon dioxide is used in the _____ to _____.
    a. autoclave, increase the partial pressure of gases
    b. centrifuge, prevent aerosolization of liquids
    c. incubator, enhance the growth of pathogens
    d. laboratory, decontaminate surfaces

TRUE OR FALSE

Directions: Circle the best answer.

36. T   F   Laboratories that perform moderate-complexity to high-complexity testing are required to submit to unannounced inspections every 2 years.

37. T   F   When using a fire safety blanket, be sure to wrap the person securely in the blanket to smother the flames.

38. T   F   A qualitative test determines the exact amount of analyte in a patient's body fluid.

39. T   F   The most effective means of preventing infection is the use of latex gloves.

40. T   F   The military clock time of 1735 hours corresponds to 5:35 AM on the Greenwich clock.

41. T   F   The gram is the unit of mass in the metric system.

42. T   F $10^{-6} \, \mu m = 1 \, m$

43. T   F   The longer the objective of the microscope, the greater the magnification of the lens.

44. T   F   To obtain the maximum resolution in microscopy, the illumination must be decreased as the magnification is increased.

45. T   F   A centrifuge load always contains an even number of tubes.

COMPLETION

Directions: Fill in the blank with the best answer.

46. CLIA is an abbreviation for _____ _____ _____ _____.

47. The _____ fire extinguisher is one that can be used on all types of fires.

48. Mr. Rodriguez delivers a 24-hour urine specimen to the laboratory. Dr. Lim directs you to send the specimen to the referral laboratory for mercury testing. The sample that you pour into a smaller container is called a(an) _____.

49. The stepwise method used to collect, process, and test a specimen used as evidence in a legal case is termed _____.

50. An order found on a laboratory requisition indicating that the test must be done immediately is called _____

Word List
ABC
Aliquot
Chain of custody
Clinical Laboratory Improvement Amendments
Stat

CHAPTER **50**

Assisting in Phlebotomy

MULTIPLE CHOICE

Directions: Circle the letter of the choice that best completes the statement or answers the question.

1. Which of the following Vacutainer tubes is routinely used for hematology testing?
   a. lavender-topped
   b. red-topped
   c. green-topped
   d. light-blue–topped

2. No anticoagulants are found in the:
   a. lavender-topped Vacutainer tube
   b. red-topped Vacutainer tube
   c. green-topped Vacutainer tube
   d. yellow-topped Vacutainer tube

3. If a laboratory test requires serum, which Vacutainer tube is the tube of choice?
   a. lavender-topped
   b. red-topped
   c. green-topped
   d. yellow-topped

4. Blood or body fluid cultures require the use of a:
   a. lavender-topped Vacutainer tube
   b. red-topped Vacutainer tube
   c. green-topped Vacutainer tube
   d. yellow-topped Vacutainer tube

5. For collection of blood specimens during a glucose tolerance test, which type of tube is used?
   a. lavender-topped Vacutainer tube
   b. red-topped Vacutainer tube
   c. gray-topped Vacutainer tube
   d. yellow-topped Vacutainer tube

6. Mr. Johnson currently is taking heparin after heart valve-replacement surgery. He is admitted to the emergency department and needs several chemistry tests to be performed stat. Which Vacutainer tube do you most likely draw?
   a. lavender-topped
   b. yellow/gray-marbled–topped
   c. green-topped
   d. yellow-topped

7. _____ is an anticoagulant that prevents platelet clumping and preserves the appearance of blood cells for microscopic preparation.
   a. Thrombin
   b. Sodium heparin
   c. Ethylenediamine tetraacetic acid (EDTA)
   d. Sodium polyanetholsulfonate

8. The slant at the open end of a needle used for venipuncture is termed the:
   a. lumen
   b. bevel
   c. shaft
   d. bore

9. The needle size most commonly used for adult venipuncture is:
   a. 18 gauge
   b. 10 gauge
   c. 12 gauge
   d. 21 gauge

10. The needle size most commonly used by the blood bank for donations is:
    a. 16 gauge
    b. 10 gauge
    c. 35 gauge
    d. 21 gauge

11. The needle size most commonly used on infants or elderly patients is:
    a. 16 gauge
    b. 23 gauge
    c. 35 gauge
    d. 21 gauge

12. Plasma could be retrieved from a:
    a. red-topped Vacutainer tube
    b. lavender-topped Vacutainer tube
    c. gray-topped Vacutainer tube
    d. b and c only
    e. a, b, and c

13. A short-draw, or QNS sample, is less of a problem with a:
    a. red-topped Vacutainer tube
    b. light blue–topped Vacutainer tube
    c. gray-topped Vacutainer tube
    d. lavender-topped Vacutainer tube

14. A tourniquet is used during the phlebotomy procedure to:
    a. collapse the artery
    b. prevent venous flow out of the site
    c. cause the vein to bulge
    d. both b and c
    e. all of the above

15. A tourniquet should remain tied on a patient's arm no longer than:
    a. 3 minutes
    b. 2 minutes
    c. 5 minutes
    d. 1 minute
    e. necessary

16. Without a clot activator, whole blood typically clots in:
    a. 1 to 2 minutes
    b. 60 to 90 minutes
    c. 30 to 60 minutes
    d. 5 to 10 minutes

17. Thixotropic gel, found in the SST red and gray marbled–topped Vacutainer tube:
    a. has the same density as red blood cells
    b. is more dense than red blood cells and less dense than serum
    c. is more dense than red blood cells and less dense than white blood cells
    d. is less dense than red blood cells but more dense than serum

18. The _____ is the portion of the venipuncture needle that fits into the syringe or Vacutainer adapter.
    a. shaft
    b. bevel
    c. hub
    d. retractable sheath

19. The laboratory requisition indicates that you are to collect a venous blood specimen for hematology testing, serum chemistry testing, and coagulation studies. What is the proper order of collection for these tubes?
    a. red, light-blue, lavender
    b. yellow, red, light-blue
    c. light-blue, red, lavender
    d. two lavender, red

20. You are required to collect a venous sample for a typical hematology test, the complete blood count. You collect a:
    a. red-topped and a lavender-topped
    b. yellow-topped, red-topped, light-blue–topped, green-topped, and a lavender-topped
    c. lavender-topped
    d. red-topped

21. A syringe is preferred over a Vacutainer collection when:
    a. the patient's veins are fragile
    b. the sample must be drawn from the hand veins
    c. many tests have been ordered and multiple tubes must be drawn
    d. a and b
    e. a, b, and c

22. Leaving a tourniquet tied on a patient's arm for longer than the recommended time results in:
    a. syncope
    b. hemoconcentration
    c. hematoma formation
    d. bifurcation

23. Before a routine venipuncture or capillary puncture, the site is typically cleaned with:
    a. isopropyl alcohol
    b. ethyl alcohol
    c. povidone-iodine solution
    d. soap and water

24. Before collection of a blood culture, the venipuncture site is typically cleaned with:
    a. isopropyl alcohol
    b. ethyl alcohol
    c. povidone-iodine solution
    d. soap and water

25. With a routine venipuncture, the angle in which the needle enters the arm should be:
    a. 80 to 90 degrees
    b. 180 degrees
    c. 15 to 30 degrees
    d. 0 to 5 degrees

26. During a routine venipuncture, when should the phlebotomist request that the patient "make a fist"?
    a. after applying the tourniquet and before inserting the needle
    b. after the last tube has been drawn
    c. after the procedure is complete and the gauze has been applied so that bleeding stops
    d. only if a tourniquet is not used

27. During a routine venipuncture, when should the phlebotomist request that the patient "release the fist"?
    a. when the procedure is complete, after the tourniquet is removed
    b. when the last tube has filled, before the tourniquet is removed
    c. when blood enters the first tube being drawn
    d. when the procedure is complete and the bleeding has stopped

28. During a routine venipuncture, when is the correct time to remove the tourniquet?
    a. immediately after the needle punctures the vein
    b. as the last tube to be drawn begins to fill
    c. after the last tube has been drawn and the needle has been removed from the vein
    d. after the vein has been located, before the venipuncture actually begins

29. The vein(s) that can be used for routine venipuncture is(are):
    a. median cephalic
    b. median basilic
    c. supplementary cephalic
    d. a and b
    e. a, b, or c

30. A winged-infusion set is also known as a:
    a. hemoguard tube
    b. Velcro tourniquet
    c. butterfly needle
    d. luer adapter

31. A needlestick is more likely to happen if:
    a. an attempt is made to recap a needle
    b. a needle of inappropriate gauge is used
    c. a Vacutainer set is used to obtain a specimen
    d. needles are immediately retracted into a safety device after use
    e. all of the above

32. Mrs. Rogers was experiencing a successful venipuncture when petechiae arose on her forearm.
    This was the result of:
    a. allergy to the antiseptic used to cleanse the area
    b. the needle puncturing completely through the vein
    c. the tourniquet being applied too tightly
    d. a rare genetic disorder
    e. all of the above

33. A hematoma can be caused by:
    a. excessive probing to locate a vein
    b. failure to insert the needle far enough into the vein
    c. the needle penetrating all the way through a vein
    d. all of the above

34. Blood obtained via capillary puncture can be collected:
    a. in microtainer tubes
    b. in capillary tubes
    c. in microhematocrit tubes
    d. onto filter paper
    e. all of the above

35. The device used for dermal puncture is a:
    a. Unopette
    b. lancet
    c. butterfly
    d. Vacutainer

TRUE OR FALSE

Directions: Circle the best answer.

36.   T   F   The red/gray-marbled–topped Vacutainer tube contains silica particles to enhance clotting and a thixotropic gel to assist in the separation of serum and blood cells.

37.   T   F   Concerning venipuncture needles, the smaller the gauge, the larger the lumen of the needle.

38.   T   F   The smaller the gauge of the venipuncture needle, the less likely that hemolysis of blood cells will occur.

39.   T   F   The NCCLS has recommended the drawing of a red-topped "waste" tube before drawing a light-blue–topped Vacutainer tube because thromboplastin released from cells during the venipuncture can interfere with coagulation testing.

40.   T   F   Once the top of a Vacutainer tube has been punctured, it cannot be reused, even if the needle that punctured it was sterile.

41.   T   F   When drawing a venous blood sample from the hand, a tourniquet should never be used.

42.   T   F   Verbal consent from a patient is necessary before a venipuncture.

43.   T   F   Capillary blood is a mixture of arterial blood and venous blood.

44.   T   F   During insertion of the needle into the vein during a routine venipuncture, the bevel of the needle should be facing down.

45.   T   F   While one is obtaining capillary blood, it is important to squeeze and "milk" the finger to obtain an adequate amount of blood.

COMPLETION

Directions: Fill in the blank with the best answer.

46. The largest of the Vacutainer tubes typically used for phlebotomy fills to a volume of 10 ml. Approximately _____ tubes are needed to fill a pint (473 ml).

47. The mnemonic that is useful for remembering the order of drawing blood is

_____.

48. _____ is the liquid portion of the blood that contains clotting agents.

49. The typical site for a capillary puncture on an adult is the _____ finger.

50. The typical site for a capillary puncture on an infant is the medial or lateral side of the

_____.

Word List
Heel
Plasma
Ring or fourth
Stop Red Light Green Light Ready Go
47

CHAPTER **51**

Assisting in the Analysis of Blood

MULTIPLE CHOICE

Directions: Circle the letter of the choice that best completes the statement or answers the question.

1. Erythrocytes have a typical _____ shape from _____.
   a. concave, the presence of oxygen gas
   b. oval, their short life span
   c. convex, adequate hemoglobin concentration
   d. concave, the lack of a nucleus

2. Granular leukocytes:
   a. have granules in the nucleus of the cell
   b. function primarily in the plasma
   c. act as phagocytes
   d. all of the above

3. Antibodies:
   a. are produced by plasma cells
   b. are protein molecules
   c. can neutralize viruses and toxins directly
   d. all of the above

4. Dr. Lim orders an H&H, ESR, and reticulocyte count for Mr. Robertson, a healthy adult male. What should the phlebotomist do?
   a. draw three lavender-topped Vacutainer tubes
   b. perform a fingerstick for the hematocrit and draw a lavender-topped Vacutainer for the remaining tests
   c. draw one red-topped Vacutainer tube
   d. draw one lavender-topped Vacutainer tube

5. A hemolyzed specimen has the least detrimental effect on:
   a. the erythrocyte count
   b. the hematocrit
   c. the white blood cell differential
   d. the ESR

6. The reference value for the red blood cell count in a healthy adult male is:
   a. 0.45 to 0.60 million/mm^3
   b. 4.5 to 6.0 million/ml
   c. 4.5 to 6.0/ml
   d. 4.5 to 6.0 million/mm^3

7. Platelets:
   a. can be seen as large nucleated purple cells in a Wright-stained preparation
   b. are elevated in the disorder thrombocytopenia
   c. are fragments of a larger cell called a poikilocyte
   d. none of the above

8. In performance of a microhematocrit:
   a. whole coagulated blood must be used
   b. the capillary tube must be completely filled and sealed on one end
   c. the open end of the capillary tube should be placed against the rubber gasket of the centrifuge
   d. the capillary tubes should be centrifuged in a labeled, sealed Vacutainer tube

9. The buffy coat:
   a. is a layer of thrombocytes between the plasma and cells in a centrifuged microhematocrit tube
   b. can be seen in a centrifuged microhematocrit tube but not in a centrifuged Vacutainer tube
   c. is white in color
   d. is removed for Wright staining during the differential portion of the CBC

10. A decreased hematocrit value could be the result of:
    a. polycythemia vera
    b. excessive squeezing of the finger during collection
    c. anemia
    d. a and b
    e. b and c

11. The copper sulfate method for hemoglobin determination is:
    a. a qualitative test
    b. based on the specific gravity of hemoglobin
    c. commonly used to screen blood donors
    d. all of the above

12. While Mr. Chakrabarti's hematocrit is spinning in the centrifuge, you perform an automated hemoglobin test on a sample of his blood and record the value as 15 g/dl. You do a quick mental calculation and expect that the hematocrit value will be approximately:
    a. 5%
    b. 45 g/dl
    c. 5 g/dl
    d. 45%

13. With a manual blood cell count, which counting squares are used to determine the number of red blood cells?
    a. the center squares
    b. the corner squares
    c. all squares
    d. all squares but the center squares

14. Materials necessary for a manual blood cell count include all of the following EXCEPT a:
    a. Unopette diluting device
    b. hemacytometer
    c. microscope
    d. Coulter counter

15. Which component of the complete blood count is not necessary in calculation of the red cell indices?
    a. differential
    b. hemoglobin
    c. hematocrit
    d. erythrocyte count

16. A properly prepared wedge smear:
    a. has blood covering one half to three quarters of the slide
    b. is dried quickly with forceful blowing
    c. has a blunt edge
    d. should be dried with the "heel" end up before staining

17. The Wright staining procedure:
    a. involves several steps
    b. fixes the blood smear to the slide with a buffer
    c. stains the cells with a single dye, such as methylene blue
    d. gives leukocytes a green metallic sheen

18. When stained with the Wright stain, the cytoplasm of segmented neutrophils appears _____ and cytoplasmic inclusions appear _____.
    a. light pink, pink
    b. light pink, orange
    c. light pink, blue-black
    d. blue-gray, bubbly

19. With microscopic examination of a Wright-stained blood smear, a large cell with a cerebriform nucleus and a blue-gray cytoplasm that has a ground-glass appearance is most likely a:
    a. band neutrophil
    b. monocyte
    c. basophil
    d. thrombocyte

20. Which of the following is an abnormal value for a differential?
    a. 50% to 65% segmented neutrophils
    b. 0 to 7% band neutrophils
    c. 25% to 40% lymphocytes
    d. 50% to 70% basophils

21. A white blood cell differential typically involves the enumeration of:
    a. 500 cells
    b. 10 cells
    c. 100 cells
    d. 1000 cells

22. A differential reveals hypochromic, anisocytic erythrocytes that exhibit poikilocytosis. The cells appear:
    a. abnormally pale and varied in size and shape
    b. normally stained but abnormally large, lacking the typical concave shape
    c. abnormally pale, varied in size, but normal in shape
    d. darkly stained and varied in size and shape

23. The ESR test results:
    a. are diagnostic for rheumatoid arthritis
    b. vary greatly between genders and as a person ages
    c. are obtained with a complex, automated test
    d. are reported in percentage/hour

24. Several tests have been developed to determine ESR values, including the Wintrobe, Westergren, Landau-Adams, and ESR-10 tests. Regardless of the test used:
    a. the amount of blood that fills the tube remains the same
    b. the duration of the test remains the same
    c. the size of the tube used remains the same
    d. the value reported (mm/hour) remains the same

25. The protime is:
    a. also known as prothrombin time
    b. performed to evaluate warfarin or Coumadin therapy
    c. performed on a specimen collected in a light-blue–topped Vacutainer tube
    d. all of the above

26. A prozone reaction, resulting in a false-negative result, occurs in:
    a. coagulation testing
    b. certain serological tests
    c. manual red blood cell counting
    d. the ESR

27. Solid surfaces used in solid-phase immunoassay include:
    a. plastic cartridges
    b. horse erythrocytes
    c. bacteria, such as *Helicobacter pylori*
    d. all of the above

28. Which of the following immunoassay detects abnormal antigen in a patient specimen?
    a. bladder tumor–associated antigen test
    b. *Helicobacter pylori* test
    c. infectious mononucleosis test
    d. all of the above

29. Heterophile antibodies:
    a. are produced by persons afflicted with bladder cancer
    b. agglutinate sheep red blood cells
    c. are nonspecific antibodies produced in response to infection with Epstein-Barr virus
    d. cause B lymphocytes to transform

30. A person with type O blood:
    a. has O antigens on the surface of the red blood cells
    b. has anti-A and anti-B antibodies in circulation
    c. has no circulating ABO antibodies
    d. has agglutination of both the anti-A and the anti-B antisera in the blood typing test

31. A blood typing test is performed on an obstetrics patient. The following results are obtained:
    anti-A antiserum (blue) = no agglutination
    anti-B antiserum (yellow) = agglutination
    anti-D antiserum (clear) = agglutination

    Which of the following is correct?
    a. The patient has A-negative blood type.
    b. The patient has antibody to the Rh factor.
    c. The patient is a candidate for Rho(D)immune globulin.
    d. The patient has B-positive blood type.

32. When is administration of Rho(D)immune globulin absolutely necessary?
    a. if an Rh-negative mother gives birth to an Rh-positive stillborn
    b. if an Rh-positive mother gives birth to an Rh-negative baby
    c. if both mother and baby are Rh-negative
    d. if an Rh-negative man fathers an Rh-negative baby

33. Which of the following is not detected in liver panel testing?
    a. GGT
    b. ALT
    c. ALP
    d. CBC

34. Electrolytes detected in an electrolyte panel test include:
    a. T_3
    b. Na^+
    c. O_2
    d. Fe^{+++}

35. Troponin is a component of a(an):
    a. liver panel
    b. renal panel
    c. cardiac panel
    d. electrolyte panel

36. Hormones detected in a thyroid panel include:
    a. thyroxine
    b. triiodothyronine
    c. thyroid-stimulating hormone
    d. all of the above

37. HDL:
    a. transports cholesterol
    b. is referred to as the "bad" cholesterol
    c. if elevated, can result in a greater risk for heart disease
    d. all of the above

38. Hemoglobin A1C is measured to monitor:
    a. anemia
    b. transfusion reactions
    c. diabetes
    d. hemolytic disease of the newborn

TRUE OR FALSE

Directions: Circle the best answer.

39.   T   F   One can easily distinguish a T lymphocyte from a B lymphocyte in a peripheral blood smear stained with Wright stain.

40.   T   F   The most important red cell index for classification of anemias as macrocytic or microcytic is the mean corpuscular volume.

41.   T   F   Blood type O is considered to be the universal donor because no anti-A or anti-B antibodies are found in the plasma.

42.   T   F   Hemoglobin A1C determination is more useful than blood glucose measurement in the management of diabetes because it provides information on the average blood sugar over a 60-day to 90-day time period.

43.   T   F   Fasting is necessary before cholesterol testing because HDL and LDL cholesterol are greatly affected by food consumption.

44.   T   F   A certified medical assistant, under CLIA guidelines, never performs drug or alcohol testing.

45.   T   F   Metabolites from abused drugs are retained for a longer period of time in the blood than in the urine, making blood the body fluid of choice for drug testing.

COMPLETION

Directions: Fill in the blank with the best answer.

46. _____ cells are the most numerous type of agranular lymphocyte and function to stimulate the activity of other T lymphocytes.

47. The smallest of the formed elements in the peripheral blood is a cell fragment that assists with clotting and is known as a _____.

48. A counting chamber known as a _____ is used to enumerate blood cells in a diluted specimen.

49. The amount or strength of antibody present at a given time in a person's serum is called the _____.

50. A _____ is performed by the immunohematology department to determine blood compatibility before a transfusion.

Word List
Helper T
Hemacytometer
Platelet or thrombocyte
Titer
Type and cross match

CHAPTER **52**

Assisting in Microbiology

MULTIPLE CHOICE

Directions: Circle the letter of the choice that best completes the statement or answers the question.

1. Which is NOT considered to be a microorganism?
   a. bacteria
   b. fungi
   c. helminth
   d. rickettsia

2. Both bacteria and fungi can be:
   a. multicellular
   b. eukaryotes
   c. prokaryotes
   d. unicellular

3. In reporting the causal organism of an infection on a laboratory requisition, it is important to give both genus and species because:
   a. there may be many species within a given genus
   b. different species may cause different diseases
   c. different species may need treatment with different antibiotics
   d. all of the above

4. In the scientific name *Escherichia coli*, coli:
   a. is the species
   b. is the genus
   c. refers to the habitat of the organism
   d. both a and c
   e. both b and c

5. Normal microbiota are:
   a. never infectious
   b. found only on the skin
   c. resistant to all antibiotics
   d. involved in homeostasis

6. An infection acquired in the hospital is called:
   a. nostral
   b. nystagmus
   c. nosocomial
   d. nonpathological

7. Collection of a throat culture requires a:
   a. sterile CCMS container
   b. BACTEC bottle
   c. Culturette transport system
   d. yellow-topped Vacutainer tube

8. Collection of a gonorrhea culture requires a:
   a. sterile CCMS container
   b. BACTEC bottle
   c. JEMBEC transport system
   d. yellow-topped Vacutainer tube

9. Collection of a urine culture requires a:
   a. sterile CCMS container
   b. BACTEC bottle
   c. JEMBEC transport system
   d. Culturette transport system

10. Collection of a blood culture requires a:
    a. sterile CCMS container
    b. Culturette
    c. JEMBEC transport system
    d. yellow-topped Vacutainer tube

11. Enteric transport media are needed for a:
    a. rectal swab
    b. throat culture
    c. blood culture
    d. urine culture

12. Diagnosis of a helminth infection requires a:
    a. stool for culture on differential media
    b. stool for O&P examination
    c. skin biopsy for fluorescent testing
    d. blood for tissue culture

13. Stuart's and Amie's media are examples of a:
    a. differential medium
    b. selective medium
    c. viral culture medium
    d. transport medium

14. Cultures for which two organisms should not be refrigerated after collection?
   a. *Escherichia coli* and *Neisseria gonorrhoeae*
   b. *Streptococcus pyogenes* and *N. gonorrhoeae*
   c. *S. pyogenes* and *Staphylococcus aureus*
   d. *S. pyogenes* and *N. gonorrhoeae*

15. Most pathogenic organisms remain viable at temperatures of:
   a. 37°C
   b. 0°C
   c. 25°C
   d. all of the above

16. An anaerobic organism is most likely isolated from a(an):
   a. abscess
   b. sputum
   c. skin scraping
   d. throat

17. An organism that is flexible as far as its oxygen requirements are concerned is called a(an):
   a. aerobe
   b. anaerobe
   c. facultative aerobe
   d. facultative anaerobe

18. Tightly coiled, spiral-shaped bacteria are called:
   a. spirilla
   b. sarcinae
   c. spirochetes
   d. streptobacilli

19. Tiny gram-negative organisms transmitted by blood-sucking insects are:
   a. rickettsia
   b. chlamydia
   c. herpes simplex
   d. ascaris

20. An organism that is unlikely to be transmitted by airborne droplets is:
   a. *Streptococcus pneumoniae*
   b. *Legionella pneumophila*
   c. *Neisseria meningitidis*
   d. *Treponema pallidum*

21. An organism that is unlikely to be transmitted by sexual contact is:
   a. *Neisseria gonorrhoeae*
   b. *Treponema pallidum*
   c. *Chlamydia trachomatis*
   d. *Clostridium botulinum*

22. An organism that is unlikely to be transmitted by food or drink consumption is:
    a. *Staphylococcus aureus*
    b. *Clostridium tetani*
    c. *Escherichia coli*
    d. *Salmonella enteritidis*

23. You observe a bacterial smear and note that the arrangement of the organisms resembles a pearl necklace. This arrangement is termed:
    a. staphylococci
    b. streptococci
    c. sarcinae
    d. streptobacilli

24. You observe a bacterial smear and note that the arrangement of the organisms resembles the stitching on jeans. This arrangement is termed:
    a. staphylococci
    b. streptococci
    c. sarcinae
    d. streptobacilli

25. A urine culture has been planted on three types of media, A, B, and C. On the all-purpose medium (A), there are more than 100 colonies; yet on medium B, there are no colonies. Medium B is most likely a(an):
    a. differential medium
    b. enriched medium
    c. selective medium
    d. transport medium

26. A urine culture has been planted on three types of media: A, B, and C. On the all-purpose medium (A), there are more than 100 white colonies. No colonies appear on medium B. On medium C, the colonies have a yellow halo on the pink-colored medium. Medium C is most likely a(an):
    a. differential medium
    b. enriched medium
    c. selective medium
    d. transport medium

27. Which color is common to both the Gram stain and the Acid-Fast stain?
    a. pink
    b. purple
    c. blue
    d. green

28. The Gram reaction a bacterium exhibits is the result of its:
    a. cell membrane phospholipids
    b. cell wall peptidoglycan
    c. gelatinous capsule
    d. wax-like cell wall lipids

29. The ideal means for sterilizing a wire inoculating loop between uses is:
    a. immersion in bleach
    b. incineration
    c. autoclaving
    d. wiping with isopropyl alcohol

30. Microscopically, a gram-positive bacillus appears as:
    a. purple spheres
    b. purple rods
    c. pink (red) spheres
    d. pink (red) rods

31. Microscopically, a sputum specimen containing AFB reveals:
    a. pink rods
    b. blue rods
    c. purple rods
    d. green rods

32. The component of the Gram stain that is responsible for the pink color of *Escherichia coli* is the:
    a. primary stain
    b. mordant
    c. decolorizer
    d. counterstain

33. The component of the Gram stain that is responsible for the purple color of *Staphylococcus aureus* is the:
    a. primary stain
    b. mordant
    c. decolorizer
    d. counterstain

34. Beta hemolysis:
    a. is best detected on sheep blood medium
    b. is caused by hemolysis of blood cells
    c. refers to a clear zone around bacterial colonies growing on sheep blood medium
    d. all of the above

35. Which part of the Gram stain is the most critical?
    a. application of crystal violet
    b. application of safranin
    c. decolorization
    d. length of time the Gram iodine remains on the slide

36. A bacterial smear is:
    a. a heavy growth of bacteria on an agar medium
    b. a suspension of bacteria allowed to air dry on a slide in preparation for staining
    c. a test done to identify the causal agent of a disease
    d. a negative political campaign in the microbial world

37. The microbiology laboratory report for Mrs. Walter's urine culture lists eight antibiotics, five of which are followed by the letter "S." This means that these antibiotics:
    a. should be avoided when treating the infection
    b. should be considered when treating the infection
    c. are likely to cause sensitivity or allergy in the patient
    d. should be retested with a more sensitive method

38. The rapid detection test that assists in the diagnosis of stomach ulcers detects:
    a. *Clostridium perfringens*
    b. *Escherichia coli*
    c. *Helicobacter pylori*
    d. *Streptococcus pyogenes*

39. A urinary tract infection can be diagnosed if an organism isolated from a CCMS specimen is found in pure culture and is present in a quantity greater than _____ per milliliter of urine.
    a. 10
    b. 100
    c. 10,000
    d. 100,000

40. A cellulose tape test for pinworms requires:
    a. a thin specimen of stool to be spread on cellulose tape to immobilize the worms
    b. a length of cellulose tape to be touched against the anal folds to collect worms
    c. temporarily taping the anus closed to trap the worms
    d. a microscope to view the eggs that have adhered to a length of cellulose tape

TRUE OR FALSE

Directions: Circle the best answer.

41.   T   F   Bacterial endospores allow a microorganism to survive harsh environments.

42.   T   F   Negative rapid strep test results must be confirmed with a throat culture because the rapid strep test is highly specific but not highly sensitive.

43.   T   F   *Candida albicans* is a typical resident bacterium of the vagina that commonly causes superinfection after treatment with antibiotics.

44.   T   F   If a CCMS specimen is collected properly, no microorganisms are ever present in normal urine.

45.   T   F   Any microorganisms isolated from a urine specimen collected from a urinary catheter are considered to be pathogenic.

COMPLETION

Directions: Fill in the blank with the best answer.

46. In observation of a skin scraping for the presence of fungal filaments, the scraping is typically placed in a drop of potassium hydroxide on a slide covered with a coverslip and observed with a microscope. This type of preparation is called a(an) _____.

47. Organisms that require special growth factors to reproduce on artificial media are called

_____.

48. Protozoa are often identified with observation of _____, the microscopic capsule-like sacs that enclose them in the larval stage.

49. A blood-sucking insect such as a mosquito is known as a(an) _____.

50. The metric unit of measurement used to report the size of bacteria and viruses is the

_____.

Word List
Arthropod
Cysts
Fastidious
Nanometer
Wet mount

CHAPTER **53**

Surgical Supplies and Instruments

MATCHING

Directions: Match each term with the correct definition below.

a. Bayonet forceps
b. Towel forceps (towel clamp)
c. Littauer stitch or suture scissors
d. Needle holders

e. Splinter forceps
f. Nasal specula
g. Probe tip is blunt

_____ 1. Blade has beak or hook to slide under sutures.

_____ 2. Jaws are shorter and look stronger than hemostat jaws.

_____ 3. Design and construction vary. Fine tip for foreign object retrieval.

_____ 4. Have very sharp hooks.

_____ 5. Valves can be spread to facilitate viewing.

_____ 6. Bandage scissors.

_____ 7. Manufactured in different lengths. Smooth-tipped. Used to insert packing into or remove objects from nose and ear.

MULTIPLE CHOICE

Directions: Circle the letter of the choice that best completes the statement or answers the question.

8. Surgical instruments are generally classified according to use. Which is NOT a classification of instrument?
   a. cutting
   b. grasping
   c. restabilizing
   d. probing and dilating

9. Which antiseptic(s) are the most effective for a surgical hand scrub or patient skin preparation for surgery?
   a. hydrogen peroxide
   b. Hibiclens
   c. isopropyl alcohol
   d. providine-iodine
   e. b and d

10. Which of these anesthetic agents are injected into subcutaneous tissue, resulting in temporary cessation of feeling at the site of the injection?
    a. Nesacaine
    b. ethyl chloride
    c. Fluori-Methane
    d. Sensorcaine
    e. a and d

11. Choose the smallest diameter of a suture strand.
    a. 0
    b. 5-0
    c. 5
    d. 1-0

TRUE OR FALSE

Directions: Circle the best answer.

12. T   F   Always lock each instrument before immersion in the chemical decontaminate to permit cleansing of the entire surface area.

13. T   F   Nylon suture is nonabsorbent and strong and has a high degree of elasticity.

14. T   F   Hydrogen peroxide is the preferred antiseptic for skin preparation before surgery.

15. T   F   After instruments have been immersed in a chemical sterilizing agent, they should be rinsed with clean bottled water.

16. T   F   The physician may spray a topical anesthetic agent, such as Fluori-Methane, on a surgical site before injecting local anesthesia.

17. T   F   Sterile technique does not have to be followed in preparation of a site for surgery.

18. T   F   Fluori-Methane causes local anesthesia by temporarily freezing tissues in the area.

19. T   F   Local anesthesia can last as long as 5 hours.

20. T   F   Epinephrine may be included in a local anesthetic because of its vasodilating effect.

21. T   F   Epinephrine is always included with local anesthetics for surgical procedures involving the digits.

22. T   F   One method of controlling epistaxis is to apply silver nitrate sticks to the bleeder site.

23. T F   Surgical sponges used to absorb blood and drainage during a surgical procedure do not have to be sterile.

24. T F   Suture scissors have a beak or hook tip that can slide under the suture for removal.

25. T F   Bandage scissors have a pointy sharp probe tip that is inserted under the bandage for removal.

26. T F   A trocar is used to dilate or open a body orifice.

27. T F   A probe is used to search for foreign objects in a wound.

28. T F   Stainless steel and chrome-plated instruments should be placed in the same basin for disinfection.

29. T F   Contaminated instruments should be placed in a container of disinfectant solution, with heavier instruments on the bottom and lighter instruments on the top.

30. T F   An effective method for disinfecting instruments that are contaminated with dried blood and secretions is to soak the closed instruments in a mild detergent.

31. T F   Detergent used for cleansing of surgical instruments should have a low pH to prevent damaging the instruments.

32. T F   Use of an ultrasonic washer is an effective and safe method for cleaning instruments with sharp edges.

33. T F   If instruments must be cleaned by hand, the medical assistant should always wear disposable latex gloves to prevent injury or exposure to contaminants.

COMPLETION

Directions: Fill in the blank with the best answer.

34. A _____ is a metal probe that is inserted into or passed through a catheter, needle, or tube to clear the equipment of secretions or to help pass it into a body orifice.

35. _____ refers to a body cavity or canal that is in its normal open position, such as the trachea remaining open during surgery.

36. _____ is a procedure that scrapes a body cavity or internal organ (such as the uterus) with a surgical instrument.

37. A localized collection of pus that causes tissue destruction is called a(an) _____.

38. A complication of surgery or certain disease conditions is the formation of a(an) _____, which is an abnormal, tube-like connection between internal organs (such as between the rectum and the vagina) or from an internal organ to the body surface.

39. Opening or widening the circumference of a body orifice (such as the cervix) with a surgical instrument is called _____.

40. The medical term for cutting tissue with a surgical instrument is _____.

41. A(An) _____ drain may be placed in a wound at the end of a surgical procedure to drain excess fluid from the site.

42. Nasal packing material used for the treatment of epistaxis should be coated with _____ to prevent trauma to the site during removal.

43. _____ resemble gears that have three or more positions and are located just below the ring handle of an instrument so that the instrument can be locked into a particular position.

44. The ridged teeth on the inner surface of the tip of some instruments are called _____. They help prevent tissue from slipping out of the jaws of the instrument.

45. _____ were originally designed to stop bleeding or to clamp cut vessels during a surgical procedure.

46. _____ forceps are small (4 inches) and are used to clamp small vessels or tissues.

47. _____ _____ forceps come in different lengths and are used to grasp tissue, muscles, or skin surrounding a wound.

48. Sterile _____ forceps are used to arrange items on a sterile tray.

49. _____ are used to hold tissue away from the surgical incision to better expose the surgical site.

50. A(An) _____ is a fiberoptic instrument that is used to visualize the anus and rectum.

51. A(An) _____ surgical needle comes packaged with the suture material attached to the needle.

Word List
Abscess
Allis tissue
Curettage
Dilation
Dissect
Fistula
Hemostats
Mosquito
Patency
Penrose
Ratchets
Retractors
Serrations
Sigmoidoscope
Stylus
Swaged
Transfer
Vaseline or petroleum jelly

CHAPTER **54**

Surgical Asepsis and Assisting with Surgical Procedures

MATCHING

Directions: Match each term with the correct definition below.

a. Permeable
b. Contamination
c. Asepsis
d. Disease
e. Chronic
f. Infection
g. Antiseptic
h. Edema
i. Spores
j. Pathogens
k. Germicides
l. Pyemia
m. Acute
n. Sterilization
o. Disinfection
p. Microorganisms
q. Sanitization

_____1. Invasion of body tissues by microorganisms that then proliferate and damage tissues.

_____2. Living organisms that can only be seen with a light microscope.

_____3. Disease-causing microorganisms.

_____4. Allows a substance to pass or soak through.

_____5. Presence of pus-forming organisms in the blood.

_____6. Reducing the number of microorganisms to a relatively safe level.

_____7. Thick-walled dormant form of bacteria, very resistant to disinfection measures.

_____8. Complete destruction of all forms of microbial life.

_____9. Chemical agents that kill pathogens.

_____10. Having a rapid onset and severe symptoms.

_____11. Substance that kills microorganisms.

_____12. Being free from infection or infectious materials.

_____13. Persisting for a prolonged period of time.

_____14. Becoming unsterile by contact with any nonsterile material.

_____15. Pathological process having a descriptive set of signs and symptoms.

_____16. Destruction of pathogens by physical or chemical means.

_____17. Swelling between layers of tissue.

TRUE OR FALSE

Directions: Circle the best answer.

18.   T   F   Air currents carry bacteria, so body motions and talking over a sterile field should be kept to a minimum.

19.   T   F   Infection can cause death in some circumstances.

20.   T   F   A sterile field can get wet.

21.   T   F   Sterile team members should always face each other.

22.   T   F   Always keep the sterile field in your view.

23.   T   F   Never turn your back on a sterile field or wander away from it.

24.   T   F   When autoclaving, place a gauze sponge around the tips of sharp instruments to prevent them from piercing the wrapping material.

25.   T   F   Nonsterile persons should never reach over a sterile field.

26.   T   F   All hinged instruments are wrapped in the open position to allow full steam penetration of the joint.

27.   T   F   When using sterilizing bags, insert the grasping end of the instruments last.

28.   T   F   Techniques for medical asepsis create a sterile environment.

29.   T   F   Venipuncture should be conducted with sterile technique.

30.   T   F   The recommended temperature for sterilization in an autoclave is a minimum of 230°F.

31.   T   F   Unwrapped items in an autoclave require more time to sterilize than wrapped items.

32.   T   F   Wet steam in an autoclave can be caused with placement of cold instruments in a hot chamber.

33.   T   F   Storing an autoclave pack that has a small tear in the wrapper for up to 2 weeks is acceptable.

34.   T   F   After autoclaving, a change in the color of the dye of the autoclave tape indicates that the pack is sterile.

35.   T   F   A wet instrument pack is automatically considered contaminated.

36.   T   F   Plastic-wrapped autoclave packs are considered sterile up to 6 months.

37.   T   F   Chemical sterilization requires immersion of the items in the chemical mixture for a minimum of 24 hours.

38.   T   F   Patient and practitioner eyes must be protected during laser surgical procedures.

39.   T   F   The medical assistant should wear clean gloves when decontaminating the postsurgical room.

40.   T   F   Erythema or edema at the surgical site without the presence of fever does not have to be reported to the physician.

41.   T   F   A large gaping wound that must heal from the bottom of the wound outward heals by first intention.

42.   T   F   Suppuration can cause problems with wound healing.

43.   T   F   A bandage must be applied with sterile technique.

COMPLETION

Directions: Fill in the blank with the best answer.

44. _____ _____ is the destruction of microbes after they leave the body.

45. _____ is the complete destruction of all forms of microbial life.

46. _____ are disease-causing microorganisms.

47. Sterilization _____ _____ placed in the center of a large pack are the best indicators of proper sterilization in an autoclave.

48. _____ uses a high-frequency current to cut through tissue and seal blood vessels.

49. Very low temperatures are used in _____ to destroy tissue by freezing it on contact.

50. A(An) _____ wound is infected with pathogens.

51. The _____ phase of wound healing is when fibrin is deposited at the site and clotting begins.

52. The _____ phase of wound healing is when collagen closes the gap between tissues and scar tissue forms.

53. A(An) _____ is a sterile covering that is placed directly over the wound.

Word List
Cryosurgery
Dressing
Electrocautery
Final or remodeling
Indicator strips
Lag
Medical asepsis
Pathogens
Septic
Sterilization

Surgery Review

Directions: Circle the letter of the choice that best completes the statement or answers the question.

1. What is the term for tumorous growths that include stems and might be found growing in the intestines?
   a. abscesses
   b. cysts
   c. lesions
   d. polyps

2. Betadine is used as an antiseptic for all of the following procedures EXCEPT:
   a. rinsing surgical instruments after use
   b. preparing patient skin for surgery
   c. applying as topical ointment
   d. scrubbing hands in preparation for surgery

3. Which of the following is used as a protective coating for ulcers and abrasions on the surface of the skin?
   a. iodoform gauze strips
   b. tincture of benzoin
   c. Vaseline
   d. ethyl chloride

4. What is the principal use of hemostat forceps?
   a. holding suture needles
   b. pulling tissue away from incisions
   c. grasping other instruments
   d. clamping and holding tissue

5. Which characteristic is NOT descriptive of bandage scissors as compared to other surgical scissors?
   a. thinner blades
   b. blunter
   c. more angular
   d. asymmetrical

6. Which type of retractor is the medical assistant most often required to hold in place to keep tissue away from incisions made during minor office surgeries?
   a. Army-Navy handheld
   b. Crile malleable
   c. Weitlander
   d. Senn

7. Which instrument is commonly used to improve the surgeon's access to body cavities?
   a. curette
   b. probe
   c. speculum
   d. trocar

8. Which of the following instruments would NOT normally be used in a pediatric office?
   a. skin hook
   b. sigmoidoscope
   c. transfer forceps
   d. Mayo scissors

9. What type of needle would you order for the superficial skin repairs commonly performed in the family practice offices?
   a. straight, cutting edge, eyeless
   b. straight, cutting edge, with eyelet
   c. curved, tapered, eyeless
   d. curved, cutting edge, eyeless

10. Hydrogen peroxide in solution form is useful for all of the following EXCEPT:
    a. cleaning skin abrasions
    b. irrigating wounds
    c. assisting with debridement
    d. serving as a strong antiseptic

11. Which of the following actions is LEAST likely to contaminate a sterile field or instrument?
    a. excessive talking over the field
    b. loose hair of a sterile team member
    c. nonsterile person entering the room
    d. brushing instrument against edge of sterile tray

12. Before the beginning of a surgical procedure, a nonsterile person reaches over the sterile tray you have just set up. You should:
    a. ask him to leave the area immediately
    b. start from the beginning and prepare a new tray
    c. advise the physician and ask for directions
    d. prepare a new tray only if the field was actually touched

13. A responsibility of the specially trained medical assistant during laser surgery is the suctioning of the plume in order to avoid:
    a. obstruction of the physician's view
    b. potential infection at the surgical site
    c. destruction of health tissue
    d. fire hazard with equipment

14. The principal purpose of endoscopic procedures is to make it possible for the surgeon to:
    a. operate on extremely small structures using a microscope
    b. directly view internal organs through a tube
    c. perform surgery on the urinary system
    d. use laser technology

15. Which of the following should NOT be done when properly setting up a sterile tray?
    a. position it just below waist level for easy monitoring
    b. ensure that the tray is completely dry before it is draped
    c. consider the outer 1-inch margin to be contaminated
    d. wear sterile gloves when arranging surgical instruments on the tray

16. When you are putting on sterile gloves before assisting with a surgical procedure, it is critical that you:
    a. touch only the inside surfaces of both gloves
    b. hold your hands close to your body
    c. do not touch the gloves' outer surfaces with your bare hands
    d. unfold the cuffs before pulling them on

17. If you are the only assistant working with a physician as he performs a minor surgical procedure, which statement most completely describes at which points you must perform surgical hand scrubs?
    a. after gathering all equipment and supplies and before setting up the sterile field
    b. before beginning to assist with the procedure on the patient
    c. before positioning the patient and arranging the sterile packs
    d. before preparing the surgical site on the patient

18. What is usually the most important consideration when positioning a patient for surgery that involves the use of a local anesthetic?
    a. convenience of the medical team
    b. comfort of the patient
    c. placement of the equipment
    d. preference of the physician

19. When performing a skin prep prior to surgery, a standard recommendation for the medical assistant is to:
    a. remove all resident bacteria from the patient's skin
    b. use medical asepsis throughout the procedure
    c. shave the area before the skin prep
    d. scrub the area for at least 5 minutes

20. All of these rules must be followed when preparing a sterile surgical tray EXCEPT:
    a. after set up it must be continually monitored
    b. keep hands in view below the waist
    c. the outer 1 inch of the tray drape is considered nonsterile
    d. a duplicate set of sterilized instruments should be available

21. Which of the following would NOT be appropriate for giving a patient information about postsurgical self-care at home?
    a. call her the day following surgery with instructions
    b. give her written materials to take home
    c. ask her to call if she has any questions
    d. give very clear oral instructions before she leaves the office

22. Which type of bandage is NOT recommended for general use in securing dressings?
    a. plain gauze roller
    b. plain elastic cloth
    c. adhesive
    d. elastic cloth with adhesive backing

23. Which of the following is NOT an appropriate responsibility for the medical assistant in the performance of office surgery?
    a. prepare needed medications for use during the surgery
    b. give postoperative care and instructions to patients
    c. advise the patient about nonsurgical treatment alternatives
    d. ensure that there is a signed patient consent form on file

24. Which of the following instruments is MOST appropriate for use when setting up a sterile tray?
    a. curette
    b. insufflator
    c. retractor
    d. transfer forceps
    e. tenaculum

25. An instrument used to scrape cerumen from the ear is:
    a. a speculum
    b. a catheter
    c. a snare
    d. a curette
    e. an extractor

26. Which of the following instruments is MOST appropriate for use during a gynecological exam?
    a. curette
    b. insufflator
    c. retractor
    d. speculum
    e. tenaculum

Clinical Review

Directions: Circle the letter of the choice that best completes the statement or answers the question.

1. The section of the medical history whose purpose is to help uncover existing or potential health problems is called the:
   a. database
   b. past history
   c. social history
   d. systems review

2. What does it mean when medical assistants display empathy when dealing with patients?
   a. they feel sorry for patients who have serious health problems
   b. they are able to hear what the patient says without judging the content
   c. they can detach themselves emotionally from the problems of their patients
   d. they truly like and care about each of their patients

3. While you are taking the medical history of a new patient, he mentions having occasional headaches that are quite painful. What is the best way for you to proceed with the interview?
   a. express concern and note this information in writing
   b. ask him a direct question about the pain
   c. reassure him that it is probably nothing serious
   d. ask him an open-ended question about the headache

4. Which statement best describes what it means to have good rapport with patients?
   a. you use language that they understand
   b. they respect you as a professional
   c. you have smooth, pleasant relationships with them
   d. you are friendly and reassuring

5. Which of the following abilities possessed by the medical assistant will most influence the overall quality of the medical history?
   a. sympathetic
   b. note taking
   c. demonstrating care and concern
   d. asking questions

6. If a patient displays nervous tapping and fidgeting during the medical history interview, it is best to:
   a. politely let him know that the behavior is disruptive
   b. say nothing, but note it in the history
   c. ask questions to explore reasons for the nervousness displayed
   d. ignore it and proceed with the interview

7. What action do viruses take when they enter the body's cells?
   a. multiply and form colonies
   b. produce poisonous secretions
   c. incorporate into the cell's reproductive material
   d. create resistant spores

8. Which is the only time it is considered appropriate procedure to recap a needle?
   a. a biohazard sharps container is not close by
   b. the procedures performed do not involve venipuncture
   c. you know the patient is free of infectious disease
   d. after withdrawing medication from a vial

9. Which activity must be recorded on a documented schedule in order to meet OSHA standards?
   a. cleaning of work areas
   b. purchase of syringes and needles
   c. use of controlled medications
   d. laundering of uniforms

10. What information is provided by the culture tube indicator used to test the effectiveness of a sterilization process?
    a. maximum temperature reached during the sterilization process
    b. presence of microorganisms in the items that were sterilized
    c. highest pressure reached during the sterilization process
    d. the presence of spores in the autoclave

11. Rapidly boiling water is an effective means of:
    a. disinfection
    b. sanitization
    c. sterilization
    d. all of the above

12. If a person is a carrier of an infectious disease, this means that he:
    a. has passed the acute stage of the disease
    b. is asymptomatic but can transmit the infection to another person
    c. has passed the incubation stage of the disease
    d. is known to have transmitted the disease to others

13. Which type of contact is a form of direct transmission?
    a. contaminated food
    b. urine from reservoir host
    c. dirty instruments
    d. disease-carrying insects

14. If a bedridden patient is experiencing chills and shivering, what effect would you expect this to have on his body temperature?
    a. increase
    b. decrease
    c. remain the same
    d. it would depend on his age

15. How do rectal and axillary temperatures compare with oral temperatures?
    a. both are lower
    b. both are higher
    c. axillary higher, rectal lower
    d. rectal higher, axillary lower

16. What is considered the least invasive and most accurate method of taking a patient temperature?
    a. oral
    b. aural
    c. rectal
    d. axillary

17. Which of the following should be noted when palpating the radial pulse?
    a. the color of the skin
    b. the condition of the local artery
    c. the temperature of the extremity
    d. the rhythm of the heartbeat
    e. b and d are true

18. What would be considered a normal pulse for an average-sized 37-year-old patient in good health?
    a. 50-60
    b. 60-70
    c. 50-70
    d. 60-80

19. A person suffering from pneumonia may experience difficulty in breathing. This condition is called:
    a. apnea
    b. bradypnea
    c. dyspnea
    d. orthopnea

20. Which of the following factors would most likely cause a decrease in blood pressure?
    a. hemorrhage
    b. increase in blood volume
    c. obesity
    d. cholesterol deposits in the arteries

21. If a patient is diagnosed with secondary hypertension, this means that:
    a. her condition has worsened from essential hypertension
    b. she has the most serious form of hypertension
    c. she has the most common form of hypertension
    d. the hypertension is associated with another disease

22. Which sequence proceeds from the most simple to the most complex body unit?
    a. tissue, cell, organ, system
    b. system, organ, tissue, cell
    c. cell, tissue, organ, system
    d. cell, organ, tissue, system

23. All of the following are types of tissue cells EXCEPT:
    a. connective
    b. muscle
    c. nervous
    d. skeletal

24. Identify the body system and organ that are incorrectly matched.
    a. integumentary: hair
    b. endocrine: sebaceous glands
    c. respiratory: pharynx
    d. lymphatic: thymus

25. If a patient describes symptoms that indicate possible abnormalities of the kidneys, to which specialist would he be referred?
    a. endocrinologist
    b. podiatrist
    c. nephrologist
    d. proctologist

26. Which instrument would you hand the physician when he is preparing to determine the condition of the tympanic membrane?
    a. ophthalmoscope
    b. otoscope
    c. speculum
    d. tuning fork

27. During a physical examination, the physician discovers the presence of bruits. What method would she be using to make this discovery?
    a. manipulation
    b. palpation
    c. percussion
    d. auscultation

28. If the physician wishes to determine the amount of air present in an organ, which method of examination would he use?
    a. auscultation
    b. mensuration
    c. palpation
    d. percussion

29. Draping the patient to expose the area to be examined helps:
    a. preserve patient privacy and increase the efficiency of the exam
    b. decreasing the dignity and comfort of the patient
    c. ensuring that the physician has complete visibility of the area
    d. demonstrating the competency of the medical assistant

30. The usual sequence of the general physical examination involves moving:
    a. from the head toward the feet
    b. from the center of the body
    c. from the area where there is a complaint
    d. from the trunk and then outward to the limbs

31. If a speculum is to be used during a vaginal examination, which patient position should be used?
    a. prone
    b. Sims'
    c. dorsal recumbent
    d. lithotomy

32. Which of the following is NOT a responsibility of the medical assistant in conducting the physical examination?
    a. preparing and draping the patient
    b. preparing the examination room
    c. setting out the equipment to be used
    d. informing the patient of any findings and diagnoses

33. Which layer of the heart performs the work of contracting and forcing blood into the vessels?
    a. endocardium
    b. epicardium
    c. myocardium
    d. pericardium

34. What is the principal sign of myocardial ischemia?
    a. damaged heart valves
    b. inflammation of the blood vessels
    c. reduction of the blood supply to the heart muscle
    d. irregular heart beat

35. What takes place as a result of a myocardial infarction?
    a. the heartbeat becomes very irregular
    b. a major blood vessel bursts
    c. a portion of the heart muscle dies
    d. a major artery becomes blocked

36. A correct statement about the arteries is that they:
    a. transport only oxygenated blood
    b. have thinner walls than the veins
    c. have a series of interior valves
    d. carry blood away from the heart

37. A bruit noted during auscultation in the area of a blood vessel is often a sign of:
    a. an aneurysm
    b. an embolus
    c. phlebitis
    d. a thrombus

38. If the ECG recording appears as a series of irregularly-sized jagged peaks, you should:
    a. check for nearby electrical appliances
    b. use disposable stick-on electrodes
    c. help the patient to relax and stay warm
    d. check the cable connections to the electrodes

39. On an ECG recording, there are five 5-mm boxes between the R waves. What is the patient's heart rate per minute?
    a. 60 beats
    b. 65 beats
    c. 70 beats
    d. 75 beats

40. Which structure is classified as part of the upper respiratory tract?
    a. bronchi
    b. larynx
    c. lung
    d. trachea

41. Which statement is the best description of the process of ventilation?
    a. Downward movement of the diaphragm to allow air to enter the lungs.
    b. Exchange of oxygenated air and waste gases.
    c. Transport of oxygen from the outside environment into the alveoli.
    d. Signal from the brain that initiates the breathing cycle.

42. Crackling sounds heard upon auscultation of the chest are known as:
    a. dyspnea
    b. phlegm
    c. pulmonary consolidation
    d. rales

43. Dust particles containing bacteria that are reactivated in moist environments are a means of transmitting:
    a. emphysema
    b. pneumoconiosis
    c. tuberculosis
    d. hay fever

44. In order to obtain a useful evaluation of pulmonary function in the asthma patient, you must administer the test when the patient:
    a. has suffered a spasm in the bronchial tubes within the previous hour
    b. is experiencing a bronchial spasm
    c. has already been evaluated with chest radiographs
    d. has taken medication to expand the bronchi

45. In order to obtain a reliable throat culture for testing, it is essential to:
    a. swab only the back of the throat and the tonsils
    b. obtain at least two samples
    c. ensure that the patient does not gag
    d. include material from the back of the tongue

46. Which respiratory action is initiated by a signal from the medulla oblongata?
    a. expiration
    b. inspiration
    c. ventilation
    d. exhalation

47. Which diagnostic test of the respiratory system requires written patient consent?
    a. bronchoscopy
    b. mantoux
    c. spirometry
    d. chest x-ray

48. The structure of the eye that produces tears is called the:
    a. aqueous humor
    b. conjunctiva
    c. lacrimal gland
    d. opaque sclera

49. When irrigating a patient's eye to relieve inflammation, which of the following is not an appropriate practice?
    a. warming solution to 98.6 degrees
    b. using sterile technique
    c. directing solution toward inner contour of eye
    d. turning patient's head toward the unaffected eye

50. How would you record the results of a Snellen test in which the patient read the 60 line at 20 feet with the right eye?
    a. 60/20 OD
    b. 60/20 OS
    c. 20/60 OD
    d. 20/60 OS

51. Which of the following is an appropriate reason for irrigating the eye?
    a. removing a foreign body
    b. testing for pressure inside the eyeball
    c. dilating the pupils
    d. treating an infection

52. In which section of the digestive tract are bile and pancreatic enzymes added to the bolus to aid in its breakdown into useable elements?
    a. colon
    b. duodenum
    c. jejunum
    d. stomach

53. If a patient reporting abdominal pain points to the area in which the stomach is located, what would you note to indicate location on his chart?
    a. LLQ
    b. LUQ
    c. RLQ
    d. RUQ

54. Which disorder has vague symptoms that patients tend to ignore, resulting in diagnosis being delayed until the disease has reached an advanced stage?
    a. gastric ulcers
    b. gastric cancer
    c. ulcerative colitis
    d. duodenal ulcers

55. The only characteristic that the five types of hepatitis have in common is:
    a. organ that is most affected
    b. severity of the symptoms
    c. availability of a vaccine
    d. route of transmission

56. In order to confirm a diagnosis of gallstones, all of the following tests may be ordered EXCEPT:
    a. cholecystogram
    b. cholangiogram
    c. serum bilirubin
    d. endoscopy

57. When positioning a patient for a proctologic exam, it is critical that the:
    a. drape wraps securely around the patient's legs
    b. patient feels comfortable
    c. body is flexed at the hip joint
    d. legs are placed lower than the head

58. The cervix controls the opening to which organ?
    a. fallopian tube
    b. ovary
    c. uterus
    d. vagina

59. What action takes place during the follicular phase of the menstrual cycle?
    a. release of the ovum from the ovary
    b. sloughing of the endometrium from the uterus
    c. production of human chorionic gonadotropin (hCG)
    d. contraction of the uterus

60. At which time during pregnancy is the formation of all the baby's cells completed?
    a. conception
    b. first trimester
    c. second trimester
    d. third trimester

61. Which type of exam usually involves the taking of pelvic measurements?
    a. new patient visit
    b. diagnosis of PID
    c. initial prenatal visit
    d. consultation regarding contraception

62. By which age have most children lost their "baby fat?"
    a. two
    b. three
    c. five
    d. eight

63. Which condition, if left untreated, can lead to heart and kidney disease?
    a. tonsillitis
    b. Reye's syndrome
    c. hepatitis B
    d. chickenpox

64. As you are preparing a 3-year-old child to be examined by the physician, you note severe bruises on his chest and abdomen. What is the first action that you should take?
    a. contact the local child abuse authorities
    b. notify the pediatrician immediately
    c. ask the parent for an explanation
    d. ask the child what happened

65. What method of evaluation is used to detect microcephaly?
    a. culture of infectious material
    b. developmental screening test
    c. laryngoscopy
    d. measurement of head circumference

66. The purpose of Varivax vaccine is to provide protection against which of the following diseases?
    a. chickenpox
    b. influenza
    c. measles
    d. polio

67. Which condition is not usually associated with injuries caused by accidents?
    a. hemiplegia
    b. cerebral concussion
    c. quadriplegia
    d. paraplegia

68. Carpel tunnel syndrome is most likely to appear in:
    a. office workers
    b. motorcycle riders
    c. people with hypertension
    d. people over age fifty

69. Which action is appropriate when assisting a person suffering from an epileptic seizure?
    a. place item that cannot be swallowed in mouth to prevent biting tongue
    b. call for an ambulance or transport victim to hospital
    c. restrain violent movements that may cause self-injury
    d. turn victim onto side with cushion under head

70. What is one of the principal functions of the subcutaneous layer of the skin?
    a. provide insulation for the body
    b. produce oil to soften and protect the skin
    c. house the sweat glands that function as temperature regulators
    d. synthesize Vitamin D

71. Which type of lesion is a sign of a partial-thickness burn?
    a. pustule
    b. vesicle
    c. ulcer
    d. wheal

72. Which condition requires the patient to clean, wash, and/or spray all items with which he has had contact?
    a. eczema
    b. psoriasis
    c. pediculosis
    d. tinea corporis

73. When communicating with patients in the dermatology office, it is best to:
    a. express optimism about the outcome of their treatment
    b. give requested advice about their condition and treatment
    c. share stories about patients with similar problems whose conditions were cured
    d. be supportive and complement them on small improvements

74. When obtaining a wound culture, it is important NOT to:
    a. remove too much exudates
    b. irritate the wound by inserting the swab too deeply
    c. use cotton swabs to collect the sample
    d. all of the above

75. The medical term for a crack in the skin, such as is caused by certain fungi, is:
    a. fissure
    b. ulcer
    c. scale
    d. wheal

76. The purpose of synovial fluid is to:
    a. increase strength
    b. produce red blood cells
    c. lubricate
    d. store minerals

77. The protective cushions that are located throughout the musculoskeletal system are called:
    a. bursea
    b. synovial sacs
    c. articular cartilage
    d. fibrous capsules

78. Which disease or condition can result in the nonsurgical fusion of bone ends within a previously moveable joint?
    a. herniated disk
    b. kyphosis
    c. lordosis
    d. rheumatoid arthritis

79. Which of the following symptoms reported by a patient is most common for a bone fracture?
    a. discoloration
    b. lack of movement
    c. pain
    d. swelling

80. A goniometer is used in the orthopedic exam to measure:
    a. muscular strength
    b. gait
    c. spinal curves
    d. joint range of motion

81. What value is used in measuring normalcy of muscle strength?
    a. a designated degree of strength for the patient's age, size, and gender
    b. the length of time a given position can be held
    c. the equality of strength of each side of the body
    d. the proportional strength of different sections of the body

82. A patient who reports occasional, acute pain in a big toe may be suffering from:
    a. osteoarthritis
    b. gouty arthritis
    c. tendonitis
    d. rheumatoid arthritis

83. Which of the following tasks would NOT be done by the medical assistant without special training?
    a. maximizing patient comfort
    b. assisting patients with ambulation
    c. applying casts
    d. ensuring patient safety

84. In which order does urine move through the organs of the urinary tract from the formation of urine to the outside environment?
    a. ureters – kidneys – urinary bladder – urethra
    b. urinary bladder – kidneys – ureters – urethra
    c. kidneys – ureters – urinary bladder – urethra
    d. urethra – kidneys – ureters – urinary bladder

85. One important function of the nephron unit is to:
    a. reabsorb fluid needed by the body
    b. allow urine to flow into the urethra
    c. assist in the regulations of blood pressure
    d. produce calcium using Vitamin D

86. Hydronephrosis is commonly caused by:
    a. renal calculi
    b. pyelonephritis
    c. polycystic kidneys
    d. glomerulonephritis

87. If a patient reports that he experiences pain when urinating, what is the proper term for noting this symptom on his chart?
    a. anuria
    b. dysuria
    c. pyuria
    d. urea

88. If a middle-aged patient is diagnosed with benign prostate hypertrophy, this means that he:
    a. has difficulty enjoying sexual relations
    b. will experience decreased fertility
    c. is likely to develop cancer of the prostate
    d. has a condition that is common for men in his age group

89. When explaining laboratory procedures to male patients that involve the urinary or reproductive systems, it is best to:
    a. explain clearly, never assuming that the patient knows what to do
    b. avoid embarrassment by being as brief as possible
    c. provide detailed written, rather than oral, instructions
    d. have the physician or male medical assistant speak with the patient

90. A woman in her mid-fifties who does not exercise and has a low-calcium diet is most at risk for:
    a. arthritis
    b. osteoporosis
    c. loss of muscle tissue
    d. hot flashes

91. In the United States, which body system exhibits the most health problems that could be prevented by the practice of better personal habits over the life span?
    a. respiratory
    b. integumentary
    c. cardiovascular
    d. gastrointestinal

92. Which of the following can cause conditions such as sleep disorders and an altered mental state in the elderly?
    a. menopause
    b. medications
    c. depression
    d. normal body changes

93. Which statement most accurately describes the changes in sleep patterns common to most elderly people?
    a. REM sleep time decreases
    b. Non-REM sleep time decreases
    c. Increasing insomnia is a natural part of aging
    d. Amount of sleep needed increases significantly

94. If a patient has prepared a living will, this means that he has:
    a. made provisions for the payment of future medical care
    b. ensured that his wishes for medical care are followed in case of incapacitation
    c. requested complete information about future medical treatments
    d. determined who will take care of his affairs after his death

95. All of the following are common changes that occur with age and should be considered when working with older patients EXCEPT:
    a. inability to learn new things
    b. decreased depth perception
    c. inability to comfortably deal with glare
    d. decreased response to temperature changes

96. An elderly patient is brought to the office by his son with whom he lives. When explaining his new arthritis medication, you should:
    a. discuss the treatment with the son
    b. speak directly with the patient
    c. use very simple language in your explanations
    d. give the son information that he can take and explain to his father

97. Which statement is TRUE concerning the use of lead aprons when performing x-rays?
    a. Their use depends on the length of the procedure.
    b. They are unnecessary if the patient is not pregnant.
    c. They are necessary only if you suspect the x-ray tube has a leak.
    d. They should be worn by both patients and personnel.

98. Which task related to the taking of x-rays is NOT a duty within the scope of practice of the medical assistant in many states?
    a. giving pre- and post-x-ray patient instructions
    b. operating x-ray equipment
    c. managing films and reports
    d. positioning patients

99. Under which patient condition is the application of heat appropriate as a treatment modality?
    a. presence of malignancy
    b. acute inflammation
    c. badly strained muscle
    d. pregnancy

100. With which form of treatment is it easiest to cause serious burns and therefore, must be used with great caution?
    a. hot compresses
    b. heating pads
    c. ultraviolet radiation
    d. hot soak

CHAPTER **55**

Career Development and Life Skills

MULTIPLE CHOICE

Directions: Circle the letter of the choice that best completes the statement or answers the question.

1. The best way to earn a favorable evaluation on your externship is to:
    a. demonstrate integrity and practice high ethical standards
    b. be friendly with your supervisor and other senior staff members
    c. impress the physician with your knowledge and skills
    d. demonstrate your willingness by performing tasks that have not been assigned to you before yours are completed

2. Which statement is TRUE regarding the status of students during the externship, as compared with the status of regular employees?
    a. they should not waste the supervisor's time asking a lot of questions
    b. they cannot be sued for medical malpractice
    c. attendance expectations are generally less strict for them
    d. they are expected to perform under the same professional standards

3. Which of the following is the MOST appropriate expectation for you to have of your externship experience?
    a. if you do good work, you will be offered employment
    b. you will feel prepared to perform any duty assigned to you on the first day
    c. you will have many opportunities to practice the skills in which you are competent
    d. you are inexperienced and will be given the lower-level office tasks

4. When is the best time to gather information and explore your personal preferences about where you would like to work?
    a. while reviewing help-wanted ads that describe employer requirements
    b. during employment interviews with potential employers
    c. before you begin to search for a position
    d. after interviewing with several employers

5. The MOST effective way to conduct a search for employment is to:
    a. approach potential employers only when you feel completely confident about your skills
    b. devote time and attention to it as if it were a job
    c. ask the placement office at your school to set up interviews for you
    d. only apply for positions that seem perfectly suited to your preferences

6. If you prepare a chronological list of events, this means that they are organized:
   a. in the order of time in which they occurred
   b. in strict alphabetic order
   c. in their order of importance
   d. in the order of easiest to most difficult

7. What is the principal difference between the personal inventory and the resume?
   a. the resume never includes information about extracurricular activities
   b. the resume contains actual dates of past employment
   c. the personal inventory does not require regular updating
   d. the personal inventory contains more complete and detailed information

8. It is usually appropriate to include all of the following items in your resume EXCEPT:
   a. your salary history and current requirements
   b. your professional employment objective
   c. employment history that is not in the medical field
   d. education that was not related to medical assistant training

9. If you are interested in a position advertised in the newspaper that includes a mailing address but does not have a telephone number listed, it is a good idea to:
   a. show your initiative by looking up the telephone number and calling the office
   b. send your resume along with a cover letter in which you express your interest in the position
   c. not send a resume because this office does not appear serious about filling the position
   d. send only a letter of inquiry and a resume when it is requested

10. What is the best action to take if an employer asks if you are married?
    a. advise the interviewer that it is illegal to ask this question
    b. ignore the question by pretending you did not hear it
    c. politely ask the interviewer if you can respond to questions that relate directly to the job
    d. you are required to answer it truthfully

11. What is the best attitude to display when applying for your first position as a medical assistant?
    a. willing to take any position offered
    b. eager to get the position
    c. prepared and self-confident
    d. modest and aware of your inexperience

12. Which of the following can be assessed with a resume?
    a. your dependability
    b. your loyalty to the employer
    c. your ability to work as a team member
    d. the extent of your clinical and administrative experience

13. When applying for a position for which you are qualified, which of the following actions would MOST likely increase your chances of being hired?
    a. writing a polite note thanking the employer for the interview
    b. making frequent telephone calls to express your interest in the position
    c. getting to know the office staff at the site where you wish to work
    d. not inquiring about salary or work hours at the interview

14. Under what circumstances is it appropriate to include extracurricular activities on your resume?
   a. when they are related to the job requirements of the medical assistant
   b. when they demonstrate your ability to organize your time
   c. when you have won awards for achievement in those areas
   d. all of the above

15. When developing career objectives, the medical assistant should ask:
   a. Where am I today?
   b. Where will I be in five years?
   c. What additional skills do I need to get where I want to go?
   d. all of the above

16. The best job search method listed is:
   a. employment agencies
   b. networking
   c. mailing resumes
   d. newspaper ads

17. The cover letter:
   a. is always optional
   b. should only be sent when an interview has been arranged
   c. should always be sent along with a resume
   d. should be approximately two pages

18. Which of the following is NOT an action word?
   a. increased
   b. streamlined
   c. taught
   d. from

19. Which of the following interview questions should NOT be asked in an interview?
   a. Tell me about yourself.
   b. Who do you most admire?
   c. Who takes care of your children while you work?
   d. Why would you be successful in this position?

20. Which of the following is a reason why a person might NOT be hired after an interview?
   a. poor personal appearance
   b. overbearing personality
   c. making excuses for poor performance
   d. all of the above

TRUE OR FALSE

Directions: Circle the best answer.

21.   T   F   The demands of the medical profession make it an often stressful environment.

22.   T   F   Good self-esteem is a result of knowing strengths are overcoming weaknesses.

23.   T   F   Students may lose future income tax refunds if they do not repay their student loans.

24.   T   F   A 2-week notice should be given before leaving a job.

25.   T   F   Loan companies rarely grant a student a deferment.

26.   T   F   Salary expectations should be listed on the resume.

27.   T   F   It is a good idea to include a photograph with a resume.

28.   T   F   The purpose of the cover letter is to get the employer to look at the resume, and the purpose of the resume is to get the job.

29.   T   F   The four phases of a job interview include the preparation, the actual interview, the follow-up, and the negotiation.

30.   T   F   It is acceptable for a new employee to arrive late to work as long as it is no more than twice a month.

COMPLETION

Directions: Fill in the blank with the best answer.

31. A return offer made by one who has rejected an offer or job is called a(an) _____ offer.

32. A(An) _____ is a postponement, especially of a student loan.

33. The exchange of information or services among individuals, groups, or institutions is known as _____.

34. The medical assistant must exercise _____ and not respond in kind to patients who are disagreeable.

35. A person with good _____ is motivated, able to express love, and capable of handling criticism.

36. The _____ period is a time for the new medical assistant to become oriented to the facility.

37. There should be no _____ on a resume.

38. Performance _____ rarely have perfect ratings.

39. _____ skills are those that can be taken from one job to another.

40. _____ comments help the medical assistant to perform better and take on more responsibility.

41. Remember to be completely _____ when completing a job application and resume.

42. Follow-up calls should be limited to no more than _____ per week.

43. Never speak _____ about former employers.

44. There are _____ ways of introducing oneself to an employer without bluntly asking for a job.

45. When conducting the job search, the medical assistant may wish to write a brief _____ of the ideal medical assisting job.

46. Medical assistants must evaluate their own _____ and weaknesses.

47. _____ skills are the abilities that the medical assistant needs to perform the job.

48. It is helpful to list goals in a(an) _____ place at home.

49. It is helpful to conduct _____ interviews for practice.

50. Consequences or something produced by a cause are called _____.

51. Having a clear, decisive relevance to the matter at hand is being _____.

52. _____ is reading and marking corrections.

53. The failure to pay financial debts, especially student loans, is called _____.

54. To correct by removing errors is to _____.

55. Something that is marked by compact, precise expression is _____.

56. Performing well on _____ may be one of the best ways to secure a job.

57. _____ each resume to get better results during the job search.

58. Recent trends indicate that a good rule of thumb is to allow one page for every _____ years of experience.

59. Pay particular attention to all _____ of appearance when preparing for the job interview.

60. Some medical assistants make _____ early on a new job, such as complaining or gossiping.

Word List
Networking
Negatively
Default
Appraisals
Prominent
6
Counteroffer

Honest
Pertinent
Transferable
Mock
Aspects
Deferment
Two
Proofreading
Self-esteem
Synopsis
Succinct
Self-control
Subtle
Rectify
Errors
Job
Target
Constructive
Ramifications
Mistakes
Probationary
Strengths
Externships

Medical Terminology Review

Directions: Indicate the response that best defines these medical terms.

1. Gastrotomy is:
   a. gastric resection
   b. intestinal incision
   c. tumor of the stomach
   d. incision of the stomach

2. Osteitis is:
   a. incision of the bone
   b. removal of bone
   c. inflammation of a joint
   d. inflammation of a bone

3. Cystoscopy is:
   a. study of cells
   b. visual examination of cells
   c. removal of the urinary bladder
   d. visualization of the urinary bladder

4. Hepatoma is:
   a. incision of the kidney
   b. tumor of the liver
   c. a blood mass
   d. inflammation of the liver

5. All the following are endocrine glands EXCEPT:
   a. thyroid gland
   b. adrenal gland
   c. mammary gland
   d. pituitary gland

6. Iatrogenic:
   a. produced by treatment
   b. produced by the mind
   c. cancer producing
   d. pertaining to producing a tumor

7. Electroencephalogram is:
   a. a record of the electricity in the brain
   b. record of electricity in the heart
   c. x-ray of the head
   d. x-ray of the chest

8. Cancerous tumor:
   a. hematoma
   b. neurotomy
   c. carcinoma
   d. carcinogenic

9. Microscopic examination of living tissue:
   a. incision
   b. pathology
   c. biopsy
   d. autopsy

10. Removal of a gland:
    a. gastrectomy
    b. gastric
    c. adenectomy
    d. nephrectomy

11. Decrease in numbers of red blood cells:
    a. erythrocytosis
    b. pancytopenia
    c. thrombocytosis
    d. erythrocytopenia

12. Pain in a joint:
    a. ostealgia
    b. arthritis
    c. arthroalgia
    d. arthralgia

13. A platelet is:
    a. hematoma
    b. leukocyte
    c. erythrocyte
    d. thrombocyte

14. Abnormal condition of the mind:
    a. psychosis
    b. meningitis
    c. encephalopathy
    d. psychogenic

15. The process by which food is burned to release energy:
    a. anabolism
    b. phagocytosis
    c. catabolism
    d. protein synthesis

16. Glycosuria is:
    a. high amount of glucose in the blood
    b. sugar in the liver
    c. excretion of glucose in the urine
    d. urea in the kidney

17. The space in the chest between the lungs is called the:
    a. peritoneum
    b. esophagus
    c. mediastinum
    d. pleural cavity

18. The voice box is the:
    a. pharynx
    b. larynx
    c. esophagus
    d. cricoid process

19. Cranial means pertaining to:
    a. the brain
    b. the skull
    c. the scalp
    d. under the head

20. Adipose means pertaining to:
    a. cartilage
    b. bone
    c. nervous tissue
    d. fat

21. Viscera are:
    a. cells in the blood
    b. internal organs
    c. cavities of the body
    d. tissues compose of cartilage

22. Distal means:
    a. pertaining to the surface
    b. pertaining to the middle
    c. near the beginning of the structure
    d. far from the beginning of the structure

23. Chondr/o means:
    a. below
    b. bone
    c. flesh
    d. cartilage

24. Muscular wall separating the abdominal and thoracic cavities:
    a. pleura
    b. mediastinum
    c. diaphragm
    d. peritoneum

25. Prolapse:
    a. -poiesis
    b. -ptosis
    c. -plasty
    d. -plasm

26. Death:
    a. neur/o
    b. nephr/o
    c. nucle/o
    d. necr/o

27. Small artery is a(an):
    a. capillary
    b. arteriole
    c. venule
    d. lymph vessel

28. A blood cell that produces antibodies:
    a. erythrocyte
    b. platelet
    c. lymphocyte
    d. basophil

29. Opposite of -malacia is:
    a. -plasia
    b. -emia
    c. -sclerosis
    d. -megaly

30. Instrument to record:
    a. -scope
    b. -graphy
    c. -scopy
    d. -graph

31. Pertaining to the opposite side:
   a. bilateral
   b. contralateral
   c. unilateral
   d. sagittal

32. Metamorphosis:
   a. paralysis of limbs
   b. spread of a cancerous growth
   c. precancerous
   d. change in shape or form

33. Hypertrophy:
   a. shrinking in development
   b. poor development
   c. increase in cell size
   d. increase in cell numbers

34. Antigens:
   a. streptococci
   b. antitoxins
   c. foreign substances that trigger an immune response
   d. antibiotics

35. Dia-:
   a. flow
   b. down, lack of
   c. complete, through
   d. against

36. Brady-:
   a. fast
   b. short
   c. slow
   d. irregular

37. Tachycardia:
   a. bad, painful swallowing
   b. near the windpipe
   c. rapid breathing
   d. rapid heart rate

38. The first part of the large intestine:
   a. ileum
   b. jejunum
   c. duodenum
   d. cecum

39. Muscular wave-like movement to transport food through digestive system:
    a. mastication
    b. regurgitation
    c. emulsification
    d. peristalsis

40. Celiac means pertaining to the:
    a. abdomen
    b. stomach
    c. small intestine
    d. spleen

41. Stomat/o means:
    a. roof of the mouth
    b. mouth
    c. stomach
    d. tongue

42. Membrane that connects parts of the small intestine:
    a. anastomosis
    b. ileum
    c. mesentery
    d. pylorus

43. Difficult, painful swallowing:
    a. borborygmus
    b. nausea
    c. eructation
    d. dysphagia

44. Spitting up blood from the respiratory tract and lungs:
    a. hematemesis
    b. menorrhagia
    c. hemoptysis
    d. hemolysis

45. Suture:
    a. -rrhapy
    b. -rrhagia
    c. -rrhaphy
    d. -stasis

46. Difficult digestion:
    a. deglutition
    b. dysphagia
    c. aphagia
    d. dyspepsia

47. Flow, discharge:
    a. -ectasis
    b. -lysis
    c. -rrhea
    d. -emesis

48. Anastomosis:
    a. ileostomy
    b. cholecystojejunostomy
    c. colonotomy
    d. gingivectomy

49. The ovum is also known as the:
    a. female gonad
    b. female gamete
    c. embryo
    d. none of the above

50. Respiratory disorder in the neonate:
    a. pyloric stenosis
    b. hydrocele
    c. kernicterus
    d. hyaline membrane disease

51. Finger-like ends of the uterine tubes are called:
    a. ligaments
    b. papillae
    c. fimbriae
    d. labia

52. Removal of a uterine tube and ovary:
    a. hysterectomy
    b. salpingectomy
    c. salpingo-oophorectomy
    d. hysterotomy

53. The male gamete:
    a. contains 46 chromosomes
    b. spermatozoa
    c. testicle
    d. scrotum

54. The hair-like tail region of the sperm cell is called:
    a. cilia
    b. sperm head
    c. flagellum
    d. fimbriae

55. Inflammation of the glans penis:
    a. orchitis
    b. hydrocele
    c. balanitis
    d. epididymitis

56. Nerves that carry impulses toward the brain and spinal cord:
    a. afferent
    b. efferent
    c. motor
    d. a and c

57. Chemical released at ends of nerve cells:
    a. cerebrospinal fluid
    b. acetylcholine
    c. lymph
    d. norepinephrine

58. Part of the nerve cell that first receives the nerve impulse:
    a. axon
    b. cell body
    c. neurilemma
    d. dendrite

59. Space between nerve cells is called the:
    a. subdural space
    b. ventricle
    c. synapse
    d. stimulus

60. Paralysis of four extremities:
    a. quadriparesis
    b. quadriplegia
    c. paraparesis
    d. paraplegia

61. A blood vessel that carries oxygen-poor blood from the heart to the lungs:
    a. pulmonary vein
    b. pulmonary artery
    c. superior vena cava
    d. inferior vena cava

62. Contraction phase of the heartbeat:
    a. diastole
    b. systole
    c. tachycardia
    d. pacemaker

63. Saclike membrane surrounding the heart:
    a. Endocardium
    b. Bundle of His
    c. Pericardium
    d. Sinoatrial node

64. Sensitive tissue in the right atrium wall that initiates the heartbeat:
    a. tricuspid
    b. atrioventricular node
    c. bundle of His
    d. sinoatrial node

65. Blood vessels branching from the aorta to carry oxygen rich blood to the heart muscle:
    a. venae cavae
    b. coronary arteries
    c. carotid arteries
    d. renal arteries

66. Cyanosis:
    a. caused by hypoxia
    b. yellow coloration of the skin
    c. associated with a hemangioma
    d. a form of atherosclerosis

67. Tubes that bifurcate from the windpipe:
    a. alveoli
    b. bronchioles
    c. adenoids
    d. bronchi

68. Nasopharyngeal lymphatic tissue:
    a. soft palate
    b. adenoids
    c. paranasal sinuses
    d. epiglottis

69. Removal of the voice box:
    a. laryngectomy
    b. tracheotomy
    c. esophagectomy
    d. pharyngectomy

70. Hypercapnia is related to one of the following:
    a. level of carbon dioxide in the lungs
    b. level of nitrogen in the blood
    c. level of carbon dioxide in the blood
    d. level of nitrogen in the lungs

71. Pass of a tube through the mouth into the trachea:
    a. endotracheal intubation
    b. tracheostomy
    c. thoracentesis
    d. laryngoscopy

72. PPD:
    a. pulmonary function test
    b. type of lung x-ray
    c. tuberculin test
    d. drug used to treat pneumonia

73. Protein threads that form the basis of a clot:
    a. fibrinogen
    b. globulin
    c. hemoglobin
    d. fibrin

74. Pigment produced from the breakdown of hemoglobin:
    a. serum
    b. albumin
    c. globulin
    d. bilirubin

75. Immature cell
    a. band cell
    b. hemocytoblast
    c. megakaryocyte
    d. all of the above

76. Excessive bleeding caused by congenital lack of factor VIII:
    a. idiopathic thrombocytopenic purpura
    b. granulocytosis
    c. polycythemia vera
    d. hemophilia

77. Lymph contains all of the following *except*:
    a. erythrocytes
    b. water
    c. protein
    d. leukocytes

78. Humoral immunity:
    a. involves B-cells
    b. involves plasma cells
    c. antibody production
    d. all of the above

79. T-cells:
    a. are important in cell-mediated immunity
    b. are lymphocytes and secrete interferon
    c. act as helper or suppressor cells
    d. all of the above

80. Organ in the mediastinum that produces T cell lymphocytes:
    a. spleen
    b. bone marrow
    c. thymus
    d. heart

81. Spongy, porous bone tissue:
    a. yellow bone marrow
    b. haversian canals
    c. sinus
    d. cancellous

82. Poor formation of bone:
    a. osteolysis
    b. osteodystrophy
    c. myelopoiesis
    d. osteoclasis

83. Lateral curvature of the spinal column:
    a. osteoporosis
    b. lordosis
    c. scoliosis
    d. kyphosis

84. Sac of fluid near a joint:
    a. tendon
    b. synovial membrane
    c. bursa
    d. ligament

85. Backward (upward) bending of the foot:
    a. extension
    b. dorsiflexion
    c. pronation
    d. abduction

86. Visual examination of a joint with an endoscope:
    a. bone scan
    b. arthrography
    c. arthrocentesis
    d. arthroscopy

87. Xer/o means:
    a. dry
    b. scaly
    c. yellow
    d. white

88. Moles that can develop into malignant melanoma:
    a. basal cell carcinomas
    b. squamous cell carcinomas
    c. verrucae
    d. dysplastic nevi

89. Yellowish region in the retina; contains the fovea centralis:
    a. optic disk
    b. posterior chamber
    c. macula lutea
    d. choroid

90. Adjustment of the lens by the ciliary body:
    a. accommodation
    b. refraction
    c. photophobia
    d. amblyopia

91. Ciliary body:
    a. phak/o
    b. cycl/o
    c. irid/o
    d. dacry/o

92. Myopia:
    a. nearsightedness
    b. farsightedness
    c. astigmatism
    d. strabismus

93. Ossicle:
    a. incus
    b. pinna
    c. malleus
    d. a and c

94. Myring/o:
    a. cerumen
    b. tympanic membrane
    c. stapes
    d. cochlea

95. Regulates the amount of calcium in the blood and bones:
    a. parathyroid hormone
    b. thyroxine
    c. thyroid-stimulating hormone
    d. prostaglandins

96. Cushing's disease is:
    a. a thyroid gland disorder
    b. hypofunction of the adrenal cortex
    c. a pancreatic disease
    d. hyperfunction of the adrenal cortex

97. Type I diabetes mellitus occurs because of:
    a. malfunction of the anterior pituitary
    b. failure of the beta cells of the pancreas to produce insulin
    c. increased resistance to insulin at the target cells
    d. obesity

98. Acromegaly is characterized by:
    a. Hyperfunctioning of the pituitary gland after puberty
    b. Adenomas of the pituitary gland during adulthood
    c. Hyperfunctioning of the pituitary gland before puberty
    d. a and b

99. Achondroplastic dwarf:
    a. enlargement of extremities
    b. caused by genetic defect in cartilage formation that affects the growth of bone
    c. caused by tumor of the sella turcica
    d. hyperfunctioning of the pituitary gland

100. Myxedema is:
    a. adrenal gland hypofunction
    b. hirsutism and virilism
    c. advanced hypothyroidism in adulthood
    d. hot tumor areas in the thyroid gland

Computer Terminology Review

Directions: Using the Word List below, complete the following sentences.

1. Pressing and releasing the button on a mouse once is a _____.

2. A graphical representation of a program, file, or disk is an _____.

3. A storage site for data is a _____.

4. The ability to store information is the _____.

5. A program like Windows that manages the operation of the computer is _____ software.

6. Moving an object to another location is called _____.

7. Rows that contain various buttons for routinely performed tasks is a _____.

8. A button with an open square _____ and enlarges the window.

9. A graphical representation of a directory that can store documents is a _____.

10. A program or file that is built into a program that can assist the user is called _____.

11. _____-clicking an icon can start a program.

12. A shaded sliding box that is used to move through a document is called the _____bar.

13. _____-clicking once can access a menu.

14. Windows _____shows the hierarchy of all of the folders and sub-folders on a computer.

15. A list of commands is a _____.

16. A _____ box pops up and requires the user to enter additional information.

17. The _____ allows the user to move between running programs to open documents.

18. The window in which you are working is the _____ window.

19. _____ software is designed to perform a specialized function or specific tasks.

20. Starting a computer is called _____.

21. Temporary storage for a deleted file is the _____ bin.

22. A button that decreases the size of a window is called _____.

23. Documents or programs stored on a computer are called _____.

24. The graphical representation of a computer's local system is called _____ _____.

25. The box on a screen that contains a running program is a _____.

WORD LIST
Active
Application
Booting
Click
Dialog
Disk
Double
Dragging
Explorer
File
Folder
Help
Icon
Maximizes
Memory
Menu
Minimize
My Computer
Operating
Recycle
Right
Scroll
Taskbar
Toolbar
Window

Answer Key for Student Study Guide Exercises

CHAPTER 1

Part I.
A.
1. G
2. C
3. F
4. A
5. D
6. B
7. E

B.
1. critical thinking
2. professional behaviors
3. learning style(s)
4. empathy
5. processing
6. perceiving

Part II.

Stage 1	Stage 4
Stage 2	Stage 3

Part III.
1.
a. determine your purpose
b. identify your main concern
c. be organized
d. stop procrastinating
e. remember you

2.
a. make your work meaningful
b. plan work deadlines
c. ask for help
d. prioritize
e. reward yourself

Part IV.
1. T
2. F
3. F
4. T
5. T
6. T
7. T

Part V.
Students will record their own ideas, pair up with a partner, and then share their ideas with the class.

Part VI.
Have students write a short plan for their academic success. Have them sign it so that they will feel committed to applying the new strategies.

Part VII.
1. Determine your individual learning style and how it applies to your ability to learn new material.
2. Make sure you read directions carefully and, if possible, begin with the easiest or shortest questions to build your confidence. Be aware of the amount of time allotted for the examination and pace yourself accordingly.

Chapter 1 Quiz
1. Dependability, respectful patient care, empathy, initiative, and positive teamwork
2. Empathy
3. Reflection
4. Private
5. F
6. T
7. List two of the following: determine your purpose, identify your main concerns, be organized, stop procrastinating, remember you
8. Mind maps: spider, fishbone, cycle, and chain of events

CHAPTER 2

Part I.
1. caduceus
2. Moses
3. Hippocrates
4. Galen
5. Vesalius
6. Harvey
7. Leeuwenhoek
8. Hunter
9. Jenner
10. Semmelweis
11. Pasteur
12. Lister
13. Long
14. Curie
15. Nightingale
16. Barton
17. Sanger

18. Ross
19. Sabin
20. Ho
21. Koop

WORD FIND

Part II.

1. World Health Organizations
2. Department of Health and Human Services
3. United States Army Medical Research Institute of Infectious Diseases
4. Center for Disease Control and Prevention
5. National Institutes of Health
6. Clinical Laboratory Improvement Act
7. Occupational Safety and Health Administration

Part III.

1. sole proprietorship
2. partnership
3. corporation
4. chiropractor
5. osteopathic
6. dentist
7. optometrist
8. podiatrist
9. Medical technologists
10. Physician assistants
11. Nurse anesthetists
12. Physical therapists

Chapter 2 Quiz

1. B
2. Medical laboratory technician
3. B
4. True
5. paramedic
6. respiratory therapists
7. T
8. dentists
9. b
10. C

CHAPTER 3

Part I.

1. Versatile: Embracing a variety of subjects, fields, or skills; having a wide-range of abilities
2. Cross-training: Training in more than one area, so that a multitude of duties may be performed by one person, or so that substitutions of personnel may be made when necessary or in emergencies,
3. Phlebotomy: The invasive procedure used to obtain a blood specimen for testing, experimentation, or diagnosis of disease.
4. CEUs: Credits for courses, classes, or seminars related to an individual's profession, designed to promote education and to keep the professional up-to-date on current procedures and trends in their field: often required for licensing.

Part II.

Over the years as the practice of medicine has become more organized and complicated, some physicians hired nurses to help in their office practices. As more years past, physicians realized a need for an assistant with both administrative and clinical training. So many physicians began training nurses or other office individuals to help with all of the office duties. Community colleges and junior colleges began offering training programs to meet this need for a more versatile office employee. Today, medical assisting is one of the most respected allied health fields in the industry.

Part III.

A
1. Administrative
2. Clinical

B
Answers may include the following: filing, patient registration, mail processing, coding

C
Answers may include the following: assisting with physical exams, laboratory tests, and diagnostic tests. Students will share their preferences

regarding the area in which they most enjoy working.

Part IV.

A

1. Classroom training
2. Externships/internships
3. Continuing education

B

1. Courtesy
2. Capacity for teamwork
3. Positive attitude
4. Enthusiasm
5. Initiative
6. Dedication

C

1. To keep current with rapid changes within the profession
2. To earn CEUs

Part V.

Students will write a dress code.

Part VI.

1. Certified medical assistant
2. AAMA
3. CAAHEP and ABHES
4. RMA

Chapter 3 Quiz

1. d
2. True
3. True
4. False
5. False
6. True
7. CMA
8. False

CHAPTER 4

Part I.

1. morale
2. commensurate
3. Procrastination
4. insubordination
5. competence
6. detrimental
7. Professionalism

Part II.

1. loyalty
2. dependability

3. courtesy
4. initiative
5. flexibility
6. credibility
7. confidentiality
8. attitude

Part III.

1. Personal problems
2. Rumors
3. Personal phone calls
4. Office politics
5. Procrastination

Students will examine their own weaknesses regarding deterrents to professionalism.

Part IV.

Students will rate themselves.

Part V.

Answers may include the following:

1. Write down the exact doses of medications, repeat the verbal orders back to Dr. Ross
2. Approach coworkers with courtesy and professionalism.
3. Neatness is important to patient care; records need to be neat for legal reasons.
4. She needs to be professional, yet she may want to let her coworkers know that she is going through a difficult time. She should not bring personal problems to work.
5. Offer verbal instructions and ask the patient to repeat them. Use pictures to convey the instructions.

Chapter 4 Quiz

1. b
2. False
3. b
4. True
5. Rumor
6. Teamwork
7. True
8. c

CHAPTER 5

Part I.

1. ambiguous
2. battery
3. caustic
4. vehemently

5. litigious
6. volatile
7. stereotype
8. feedback

Part II.
1. Closed
2. Closed
3. Open
4. Closed
5. Closed
6. Closed
7. Closed
8. Closed
9. Open
10. Closed

Part III.
1. Projection
2. Denial
3. Regression
4. Repression
5. Verbal aggression
6. Compensation
7. Rationalization
8. Apathy
9. Displacement
10. Physical avoidance
11. Sarcasm

Part IV.
1. Physical impairment
2. Language
3. Prejudice
4. Stereotyping
5. Perception

Part V.
Answers may include the following:
1. Physical needs must be met first; oxygenation is a basic need.
2. Healthcare workers cannot help others if they become injured themselves.
3. Hunger is a basic level need in Maslow's hierarchy of needs.

Chapter 5 Quiz
1. None
2. c
3. True
4. True
5. Open
6. Sarcasm

7. True
8. B

CHAPTER 6

Part I.
1. D
2. G
3. F
4. E
5. C
6. A
7. B

Part II.
1. (B) Beneficence
2. (N) Nonmaleficence
3. (V) Veracity
4. (F) Fidelity

Part III.
A
a. Gathering relevant information
b. Identifying the type of ethical problem
c. Determining the ethics approach to use
d. Explore the practical alternatives
e. Complete the action

B
1. False
2. True
3. True

Part IV.
Discuss these ethical dilemmas with the class.

Part V.
Discuss this scenario with the class.

Chapter 6 Quiz
1. Answers may include the following: fidelity, veracity, justice, beneficence, nonmaleficence
2. Etiquette
3. b
4. True
5. True
6. True
7. A physician accepts payment from another physician solely for the referral of a patient; both physicians are guilty of an unethical practice called fee splitting.
8. The substitution of another surgeon without the patient's consent is called ghost surgery.

CHAPTER 7

Part I.

1. Arbitration
2. Assault
3. Bailiff
4. Code of Federal Regulations (CFR)
5. Fine
6. Battery
7. Judicial
8. Law
9. Felony
10. Libel
11. Subpoena
12. Verdict
13. Prudent
14. Municipal
15. Misdemeanor

WORD FIND

Part II.

1. a. Misdemeanors
   b. Felonies
   c. Treason

2. a. Tort law
   b. Contract law
   c. Administration law

3. a. Manifestation of assent
   b. The contract must involve legal subject matter
   c. Both parties must have the legal capacity to enter into a contract
   d. Must be some type of consideration which is an exchange of something of value

4. Abandonment

5. a. Professional care is being discontinued
   b. The physician will provide copies of the patients records to another physician upon request
   c. The patient should seek the attention of another physician as soon as possible

6. certified mail, return receipt requested

Part III.

1. deposition
2. duces tecum
3. reasonable doubt
4. preponderance of the evidence
5. damages
6. expert witnesses

Answers may include the following:

1. Direct cause is missing; no injury
2. Discuss this scenario with the class. No legal duty exists. Ask the class if there is an ethical duty, however.
3. Dereliction of Duty
4. Punitive damages are awarded by the courts as punishment for gross negligence.

Part IV.

1. • within the state
   • requirements
   • suspension or revocation

2. a. conviction of a crime
   b. unprofessional conduct
   c. personal or professional incapacity

Chapter 7 Quiz

1. b
2. HIPAA
3. d
4. True
5. True
6. statute of limitations
7. True
8. emancipated minor
9. d
10. d

CHAPTER 8

Part I.

1. Applications
2. Artificial intelligence
3. ASC II
4. Back-up

5. Byte
6. Cache
7. Cookies
8. Cursor
9. Database
10. Disk
11. eCommerce
12. email
13. Font
14. Format
15. gigabyte
16. Hard copy
17. Hub
18. HTML
19. Icon
20. Input
21. Java
22. Megabyte
23. Megahertz
24. Modem
25. Multimedia
26. Output
27. Router
28. Scanner
29. URL
30. Virtual Reality
31. Zip drive

Part II.
A. 1. ROM (read only memory)
   2. RAM (random access memory)

B. Discuss and demonstrate various ways to perform these ten tasks.

Part III.
A. 1. Input
    2. Input
    3. Output
    4. Input
    5. Storage
    6. Storage
    7. Storage
    8. Input
    9. Storage
    10. Input

B. 1. Performs repetitive tasks
   2. Reduces errors
   3. Speeds up production
   4. Recalls information on command
   5. Saves time
   6. Reduces paperwork

7. Allows for more creative and productive use of the worker's time.

Part IV.
A. Answers may include the following:
   1) input—keyboard, scanner, mouse,
   2) processing—CPU,
   3) storage—CD-ROM, Zip drive, floppy disks,
   4) output—printers, modems

B. Discuss results of student investigations in class.
C. Discuss results of student investigations in class.

D. 1. Work surface
   2. Storage
   3. Monitors
   4. Adjustable chairs
   5. Keyboard
   6. Mouse
   7. Lighting

Chapter 8 Quiz
1. megahertz
2. true
3. It is fast and gives good copy
4. monitors, printers, CPU, keyboard
5. local-area network
6. Programs that are designed to perform certain tasks
7. 1 million bytes
8. True
9. storage
10. True

CHAPTER 9

Part I.
1. B
2. D
3. H
4. G
5. F
6. I
7. E
8. A
9. M
10. P
11. N
12. O
13. K
14. C
15. L
16. J

Part II.
Student to complete three telephone message forms.

Part III.
A. 3, 2, 5

B. 1. Allow caller to hang up first
   2. Thank caller for calling
   3. Close conversation with a form of good-bye
   4. Replace cradle gently
C. 1. Hang up and drive
   2. Turn off cell phone during meetings
   3. Respect personal space
   4. Keep it charged

Part IV.
Answering the phone call takes priority.

Chapter 9 Quiz
  1. clarity
  2. 11:00 am
  3. true
  4. automatic call routing
  5. answering service
  6. chest pain, fainting, shortness of breath, seizures, head injuries
  7. inflection
  8. monotone
  9. True
 10. lower your voice, avoid getting angry, offer friendly assurance that the issue is important and will be investigated

CHAPTER 10

Part I.
  1. Disruption
  2. Established patients
  3. Expediency
  4. Integral
  5. Interaction
  6. Intermittent
  7. Interval
  8. Matrix
  9. No show
 10. Prerequisite
 11. Proficiency
 12. Socioeconomic
 13. Triage

Part II.
A. Students will complete two reminder cards.
B. Discuss any questions students may have regarding scheduling.

C. Discuss any questions students may have regarding scheduling.

Part III.
A. 1. patient need
   2. physician preference and habits
   3. available facilities

B. 1. The size should conform to the desk space available.
   2. It should be large enough to accommodate the practice.
   3. It should open flat for easy writing and reference.
   4. It should allow space for writing when, who, and why.

Part IV.
Scheduled Appointments: Studies have shown that practitioners are able to see more patients with less pressure when their appointments are scheduled.

Open Office Hours: The facility is open at given hours of the day or evening, and the patients are "scheduled" by the physician by mentioning to the patient to return "in a couple of weeks". At intermittent times the patients come in, knowing in advance they will be seen in the order of their arrival.

Flexible Office Hours: Many health care providers are now turning to extended-day and flexible office hours. Scheduling evening and weekend hours may increase the size of the practice, due to the convenience that is offered to the patients.

Wave Scheduling: Assumes that the actual time needed for all of the patients seen will average out over the course of the day. Instead of scheduling patients at each twenty minute interval, wave scheduling places three patients in the office at the same time, and they are seen in the order of their arrival. Thus, one person's late arrival will not disrupt the entire schedule.

Modified Wave Scheduling: There are several ways to modify the wave schedule. One method is to have two patients scheduled to come in at 10:00 am, and a third at 10:30 am. This hourly cycle is repeated throughout the day. Another application would have patients scheduled to arrive at given intervals during the first half of the hour, and none scheduled to arrive during the second half of the hour. Physicians can modify wave scheduling to best suit the clinic's needs.

Double Booking: Booking two patients to come in at the same time, both of whom are to be seen by the physician, is poor practice. Of course, if each is expected to only take five minutes, there is no harm in telling both to come at the same time and reserving a 15-minute period for the two. This is simply one method of wave scheduling. However, if each patient requires 15 minutes, two will require 30 minutes. This must be reflected in the scheduling. It is not considered double booking if a patient comes to the office to receive a treatment by someone other than the physician, such as a physical therapy modality or an allergy injection.

Grouping Procedures: Scheduling based on the grouping or categorizing of procedures. For instance, obstetricians often schedule pregnant patients on different days than the regular gynecology patients.

Advance Booking: Appointments made months in advance. Patients are given appointment cards; each card should mention that patients must give 24-hours notice if they are unable to keep the time reserved for them.

Chapter 10 Quiz

1. no-show
2. established
3. triage
4. size and space needed and number of physicians that will be making appointments
5. True
6. open office hours
7. extended-day and weekend hours
8. wave
9. end
10. recorded or documented

CHAPTER 11

Part I.

1. Amenity: Something conducive to comfort, convenience, or enjoyment
2. Intercom: A two-way communication system with a microphone and loudspeaker at each station for localized use
3. Progress notes: Notes used in the patient chart to track the progress and condition of the patient

4. Demographic: The statistical characteristics of human populations (as in age or income) used especially to identify markets

Part II.

1. Fervent
2. Flagged
3. Harmonious
4. Immigrant
5. Perception
6. Phonetic
7. Sequentially

Part III.

A. Discuss results of student investigations in class.
B. Examine the days scheduled appointments. She needs to consult the appointment book.
C. Pull charts for the next day's schedule

Part IV.

A. Discuss students' thoughts and concerns as a class.
B. Create a transparency master using p. 74 as a template; have students design a registration form as a class.
C. Answers may include the following: turning off equipment, locking up cash, preparing exam rooms for the next day, emptying trash, and arming the security system.
D. Lead the class in a discussion on asking for payment.
E. Have students role play and practice interviewing Mr. Shapiro.

Chapter 11 Quiz

1. replenish supplies, pull patient charts
2. phonetic
3. False
4. It may interfere with lab work.
5. demographic
6. Prearrange to interrupt the doctor via intercom or schedule the patient at the end of the day.
7. lock files and safe, turn off lights, set alarm, leave lab specimens in the appropriate place
8. Your balance is _____, will you be writing a check or would you like to charge it to a credit card?
9. what to remove and how to put on the gown
10. ventilation, lighting, comfortable seating

CHAPTER 12

Part I.

1. Watermark: A marking in paper resulting from differences in thickness usually produced by pressure of a projecting design in the mold or on a processing roll and visible when the paper is held up to the light.
2. Portfolio: A set of pictures, drawings, documents, or photographs either bound in book form or loose in a folder.
3. Ream: A quantity of paper being 20 pounds or variously 480, 500, or 516 sheets.
4. Archived: To file or collect records or documents in or as if in an archive.
5. Flush: Directly abutting or immediately adjacent, as set even with an edge of a type page or column; having no indention.

Part II.

A A. Letterhead
    B. Date
    C. Inside address
    D. Salutation
    E. Paragraph 1
    F. Paragraph 2
    G. Complimentary closing
    H. Signature
    I. Typed signature
    J. Reference initials
    K. Enclosures
    L. Copies

B. JIM SMITH MD
   301 WEST HUGHES ST.
   CHICAGO, IL 54321

   MS. CINDY JOHNSON
   SUITE 409
   1467 E. GREEN ST.
   BAYFIELD, GA 12345

   MS. JOSE KELLEY
   321 MEMORIAL LANE
   WEST COLUMBIA, FL 98765

Part III.

A. Answers may include the following: pc, printer, word processor, typewriter
B. Answers may include the following: pens, letterhead, stationary, continuation pages, envelopes, printer
C. $8\frac{1}{2} \times 11$

D. 1. 10 envelope (business envelope)—Fold 1/3 up from the bottom and make a crease; fold top down to within 3/8″ of bottom crease.
   2. $6\frac{3}{4}$ envelope—bring bottom edge to within 3/8″ of top edge and crease. Then fold from the right edge and make a fold a little less than 1/3 the width of the sheet and crease, fold left edge and bring to 3/8″ of previous crease.
   3. Window envelope—fold letter by bringing bottom 2/3 of letter up and crease; then fold top back to the crease. The address should be facing forward.

E. 1. Heading
   2. Opening
   3. Body
   4. Closing

F. 1. Name of the addressee
   2. Page number
   3. Date

Part IV.

A. Registered Mail—a piece of mail that helps trace delivery. The mail is accounted for from time of mailing until the time of delivery and is transported separately from other mail under a special lock.
Certified Mail—used for documents that would not be difficult to replace. A record is kept of delivery.
B. Students will compose a letter.
C. Students will compose a memo.
D. Students will design a fax cover sheet.

Chapter 12 Quiz

1. bond
2. collect on delivery
3. Domestic
4. A portfolio is a set of samples or examples bound in a folder or notebook.
5. ream
6. watermark
7. annotating
8. continuation

CHAPTER 13

Part I.

1. Alphanumeric
2. Audit
3. Augment
4. Caption

5. Chronologic time
6. Dictation
7. Direct filing system
8. Indirect filing system
9. Microfilm
10. Objective
11. Shingling
12. Subjective
13. Tickler
14. Transcription

Part II.

A. 1. Second shelf, second from the right
   2. First shelf, first from the left
   3. Second shelf, fourth from the left
   4. Second shelf, fourth from the right

B. 1. Before Michael Smith
   2. After Michael Smith
   3. After Ann Davis
   4. After Joe Brown

Part III.

A. Year the patient was seen, name, drug allergies, record number, the number of folders for patient

B. ***Vertical drawer file cabinet***
   Advantages and disadvantages: locks, easy to move, top heavy, hard to access, only one drawer can be opened at one time, a drawer left open may cause trauma

   Wall lateral, open shelves, or shelf file
   Advantages and disadvantages: easy access, holds more materials, faster retrieval, lack of security, less protection from fire and water damage

   Rotary circular files or compressible or rolling shelves
   Advantages and disadvantages: saves space, expensive, limited access to other files, less privacy

   Revolving or rotating file system
   Advantages and disadvantages: can be locked, expensive, not all records are available at the same time

Part IV.

A. 1. Disk—a device with a magnetic surface capable of storing computer input
   2. Microfilm—rolled film bearing photographic record or reduced scale of printed or graphic matter
   3. Microfiche—a flat sheet bearing a photographic record on a reduced scale of the printed or graphic matter.

B. Outguides help the medical assistant or other staff to locate and track missing files.

Chapter 13 Quiz

1. active, inactive, closed
2. name of person who has the record, date
3. lack of security
4. False
5. True
6. The facility owns the record. The patient owns the information.
7. dictation
8. False
9. Problem-oriented medical record
10. transcription

CHAPTER 14

Part I.

A. 1. account balance
   2. credit
   3. debit
   4. accounts receivable ledger
   5. debit cards
   6. disbursements
   7. fee profile
   8. fiscal agent
   9. guarantor
   10. payables
   11. fee schedule
   12. Pegboard system
   13. posting
   14. premium
   15. professional courtesy
   16. receipts, receivables
   17. third party payor
   18. transaction

B. 1. Usual: Physician's usual fee for a service
   2. Customary: Range of usual fees charged for the same service by physicians with similar training and experience for the geographic and socioeconomic area.
   3. Reasonable: Usually applies to a service or procedure that is exceptionally difficult or complicated, requiring extraordinary time or effort on the part of the physician.

C. 1. B
   2. D
   3. C
   4. A

D. 1. deduct amount from checking account
   2. add amount to patient's account balance

E. 1. Day sheet
   2. Patient ledger
   3. Encounter form

Part II.

A. 1. $250
   2. $60
   3. $55
   4. Treadmill stress test; 93015
   5. Insulin

Part III.

A. 1. 99212; $48; 90788-$30; Dx code 463
   2. 99245; $250; 93000; $55; 786.50-diagnosis
   3. 99203; $60; 90782; $18; 782.1-diagnosis

B. Discuss with class.
C. Discuss with class.

Part IV.

A. 1. skip
   2. bill or letter
   3. 40 to 60

B. 1. send no more statements
   2. mark the ledger
   3. refer the patient to the agency
   4. report any payments made to the office
   5. call the agency with any new information
   6. don't call the agency frequently

C. 1. Regulation Z of the Truth in Lending Act: Insures disclosure of interest rates
   2. Small Claims Court: Amounts vary from state to state; no lawyer needed; inexpensive way to collect delinquent accounts

D. Use role plays and class discussions to examine students concerns and thoughts about collections.

Chapter 14 Quiz

1. Truth in Lending
2. a person who has no forwarding address or other means of communication
3. no attorney fees
4. True
5. accounts receivable
6. write-it once system
7. credit
8. guarantor
9. encounter form or superbill
10. Usual customary and reasonable

CHAPTER 15

Part I.

1. lozenge
2. section mark
3. bullet
4. triangle
5. beginning, end
6. female
7. male
8. 4th
9. 5th
10. brackets
11. parentheses
12. colons
13. braces

Part II.

Diagnosis	ICD-9 Code
1. Polycystic kidney	753.12
2. Amenorrhea	626.0
3. Measles	055.9
4. Hematuria	599.7
5. Catatonic schizophrenia, chronic	295.22
6. Cancer of the duodenum (neoplasm)	152.0
7. Nodular tuberculosis (lung)	011.1
8. High blood pressure	401.9
9. Left-sided congestive heart failure	428.1
10. Croup	464.4
11. Ear wax	380.4
12. Exophthalmos R/T thyroid	376.2
13. Gout	274.9
14. Active rickets	268.0
15. Cat scratch fever	078.3
16. Benign prostatiac hypertrophy (enlarge prostate)	600.0
17. Encephalitis from West Nile virus	062.9

Diagnosis	ICD-9 Code
18. Thrush	112.0
19. Parkinson's disease	332.0
20. Senile cataract	366.10
21. Huntington's chorea	333.4
22. Mitral valve prolapse	424.0
23. Transient ischemic attack	435.9
24. Asthma	493.90
25. Cushing's syndrome	255.0

Diagnosis	V Code
1. Ear piercing	V50.3
2. Gynecologic exam	V72.3
3. Annual physical	V70.0
4. Venereal disease exposure	V01.6
5. History of mental illness	V11.9

Situation	E-Code
1. Bathtub drowning	E910.4
2. Rattlesnake bite	E905.0
3. Sunstroke	E900.0
4. Pedestrian hit by a train	E801.2
5. Parachute failure	E843.7

Part III.

A. 1. 5 appendices; 17 chapters
2. Volume I
3. Alphabetical

B. 1. 401.9, 274.9
2. 464.4, 112.0
3. 600.0, 599.7
4. 4228.1, 274.9

Part IV.

A. ICD-9 is a great spelling tool.

B. 1. T
2. F
3. F
4. T
5. T

Chapter 15 Quiz

1. True
2. True
3. physicals or other types of preventative services
4. emergencies, accidents
5. unspecified (not otherwise specified)
6. preexisting
7. comorbidity
8. complication
9. ancillary diagnostic services
10. principal diagnosis

CHAPTER 16

Part I.

A. 1966, procedures, services
B. Evaluation and Management
C. CPT-4
D. October
E. Bundled
F. Unbundled
G. Upcoding
H. Downcoding

Part II.

Procedure	CPT Code
1. Liver biopsy, needle	47000
2. Cholecystectomy	47562
3. Newborn circumcision	54150
4. Gastric motility study	91020
5. Right heart catheterization	93501
6. Intradermal allergy testing	95015
7. Removal of foreign body from nose	30300
8. X-ray examination of ankle, three views	73610
9. CAT scan of arm with contrast	73201
10. Partial thromboplastin time	85730

Find the Appropriate Modifier	Modifier
1. Bilateral	-50 Omit these answers
2. Two surgeons	-62
3. Repeat procedure same surgeon	-76
4. Multiple procedures	-51

Part III.

A. 1. new
2. revision
3. add-on
4. modifier
5. guidelines, referenced
6. Assistant
7. Surgical

B. 1. E&M
2. Anesthesia
3. Surgery
4. Radiology
5. Pathology and lab

Part IV.

A. Type of service, place of service, patient status
B. Problem focused, expanded problem focused, detailed, comprehensive
C. Straightforward, low-complexity, moderate complexity, high complexity
D. 1. V70.0; 99205
   2. 281.9; 99212
   3. 180.9, 308.5; 99214, 88141

Chapter 16 Quiz

1. True
2. 11
3. straightforward, low, moderate, high
4. problem-focused, expanded, detailed, comprehensive
5. 21
6. Current Procedural Terminology
7. bundled
8. modifier
9. morbidity
10. mortality

CHAPTER 17

Part I.

Advantages of paper claims:
- Documentation explaining unusual circumstances can be readily attached.
- Start-up cost is minimal
- Forms are readily available
- Accepted by most third-party payers

Disadvantages of paper claims:
- Completing forms is labor intensive
- Costs of mailing, follow-up, and resubmission can become excessive
- Greater chance for rejection
- Cash flow is delayed due to slower reimbursements
- Require a lot of storage space

Advantages of electronic claims:
- Cost savings due to shortened preparation time
- Cost savings in postage
- Reduced claim rejection
- Quicker payment turnaround time
- Generation of claim status reports

Disadvantages of electronic claims:
- Computer hardware/software glitches and/or power outages that delay preparation and/or transmission
- Issue of creating electronic attachment(s)
- Initial start-up is expensive

Part II.

A and B. Discuss and complete the forms as a class.

Part III.

1. 3 visits
2. $30
3. $75
4. $15
5. $32
6. $22

Part IV.

Answer any questions students may have about completing the HCFA form using their own insurance information. The instructor may want to complete this exercise as well so that the students will have an example.

Chapter 17 Quiz

1. False
2. optical character
3. clean
4. 11
5. 21
6. CMS 1500
7. assignment of benefits
8. beneficiary
9. carrier
10. provider identification

CHAPTER 18

Part I.

1. Allowed charge: The maximum amount of money that many third-party payors will pay for a specific procedure or service. Often based on the UCR fee.
2. Authorization: A term used by managed care for an approved referral.
3. Benefits: The amount payable by the insurance company for a monetary loss to an individual insured by that company, under each coverage.
4. Birthday rule: When an individual is covered under two insurance policies, the insurance plan of the policyholder whose birthday comes first in the calendar year (month and day—not year) becomes primary.
5. Coordination of benefits: The mechanism used in group health insurance to designate the order in which multiple carriers are to pay benefits to prevent duplicate payments.
6. Copayment: A copayment (or coinsurance) is a policy provision frequently found in medical insurance, whereby the policyholder and the insurance company share the cost of covered losses in a specified ratio (i.e., 80/20—80 percent by the insurer and 20 percent by the insured).
7. Deductible: A specific amount of money a patient must pay out-of-pocket up front before the insurance carrier begins paying. Often this amount is anywhere from $100 to $1000. This deductible amount must be met on a yearly or per incident basis.
8. Government plan: An insurance or health care plan that is sponsored and/or subsidized by the state or federal government, such as Medicaid and Medicare.

9. Group policy: Insurance written under a policy that covers a number of people under a single master contract issued to their employer or to an association with which they are affiliated.
10. Health insurance: Protection in return for periodic premiums, which provides reimbursement of monetary losses due to illness or injury. Included under this heading are various types of insurance such as accident insurance, disability income insurance, medical expense insurance, and accidental death and dismemberment insurance. Also known as accident and health insurance or disability income insurance.
11. HMO: An organization that provides a wide range of comprehensive health care services for a specified group at a fixed periodic payment. HMOs can be sponsored by the government, medical schools, hospitals, employers, labor unions, consumer groups, insurance companies, and hospital-medical plans.
12. Indemnity plan: Traditional health insurance plan that pays for all or a share of the cost of covered services, regardless of which doctor, hospital, or other licensed health care provider is used. Policyholders of indemnity plans and their dependents choose when and where to get health care services.
13. Individual policy: An insurance policy designed specifically for the use of one person (and his or her dependents) not associated with the amenities of a group policy, namely higher premiums. Often referred to as "personal insurance."
14. Managed care: An umbrella term for all health care plans that provide health care in return for preset monthly payments and coordinated care through a defined network of primary care physicians and hospitals.
15. Medical savings account: A tax-deferred bank or savings account combined with a low-premium/high-deductible insurance policy, designed for individuals or families who choose to fund their own health care expenses and medical insurance.
16. Medically indigent: An individual who can afford to pay for his or her normal daily living expenses but cannot afford adequate health care.
17. Medically necessary: A decision-making process used by third-party payors to decide

whether a patient's symptoms and diagnosis justify specific medical services or procedures. (Also known as medical necessity.)

18. Participating provider: A physician or other health care provider who enters into a contract with a specific insurance company or program, and by doing so, agrees to abide by certain rules and regulations set forth by that particular third-party payor.

19. Policyholder: The individual in whose name an insurance policy is written and who pays the premium. The "holder" of the policy.

20. Primary diagnosis: The condition or chief complaint for which a patient is treated in outpatient (physician's office or clinic) medical care.

21. Principal diagnosis: A condition established after study that is chiefly responsible for the admission of a patient to the hospital. Used in coding inpatient hospital insurance claims.

22. Premium: The periodic (monthly, quarterly, or annual) payment of a specific sum of money to an insurance company for which the insurer, in return, agrees to provide certain benefits.

23. RBRVS: Resource-based relative value system. A fee schedule designed to provide national uniform payment of Medicare benefits after being adjusted to reflect the differences in practice costs across geographic areas.

24. Rider: A special provision or group of provisions that may be added to a policy to expand or limit the benefits otherwise payable. It may increase or decrease benefits, waive a condition or coverage, or in any other way amend the original contract.

25. Self-insured plans: Insurance plans funded by organizations having a big enough employee base that they can afford to fund their own insurance program.

26. Service benefit plan: Plans that provide their benefits in the form of certain surgical and medical services rendered rather than cash. A service benefit plan is not restricted to a fee schedule.

27. Workers' compensation: Insurance against liability imposed on certain employers to pay benefits and furnish care to employees injured, and to pay benefits to dependents of employees killed in the course of or arising out of their employment.

28. Utilization review: A review of individual cases by a committee to make sure that services are medically necessary and to study how providers use medical care resources.

Part II.
A. 1. Group policies
2. Individual policies
3. Government plans
4. Self-insured plans
5. Medical savings account

B. 1. Hospitalization
2. Surgical
3. Basic medical
4. Major medical
5. Disability (income loss)
6. Dental
7. Vision care

Part III.
A. 1. Health care costs are usually contained
2. There are established fee schedules
3. Authorized services are usually paid
4. Most preventive medical treatment is covered
5. Patient out-of-pocket expenses tend to be smaller than traditional insurance

B. 1. Access to specialized care and referrals can be limited
2. Physician choices in treatment of patients can be limited
3. Amount of paperwork may be increased
4. Treatment may be delayed due to preauthorization requirements
5. Reimbursement is historically less than traditional insurance

Part IV.
1. Medicare is for older adults or patients on disability or social security. Medicaid is a government insurance for providing medical care for the medically indigent.
2. CHAMPUS: covers military dependents; CHAMPVA: covers veterans; TRICARE: managed care for military personnel and dependents
3. Medicare Part A: hospitalization coverage; Medicare Part B: covers doctors' bills (Part B is optional and a premium is charged)
4. An HMO (Health Maintenance Organization) is more limited than the more flexible PPO (Preferred Provider Organization) option.
5. Worker's compensation provides treatment, rehabilitation, and income protection for work-related injuries.

Chapter 18 Quiz
1. True
2. Medical savings
3. catastrophic
4. Relative-based relative value
5. True
6. Champus or Tricare
7. deductible
8. co-pay
9. co-insurance
10. group

CHAPTER 19

Part I.
1. B
2. O
3. J
4. A
5. G
6. L
7. H
8. I
9. F
10. K
11. E
12. D
13. N
14. M
15. C

Part II.
A. 1. Bank draft – A check drawn by a bank against funds deposited to its account in another bank
   2. Cashier's check – Bank's own check drawn on itself and signed by a bank official
   3. Certified check – Depositor's own check, on the face of which the bank has placed the word "certified" or "accepted" with the date and a bank official's signature
   4. Limited check – Limiting the amount written on the check or the time during which it can be presented for payment
   5. Money order – Used for paying bills by mail when an individual does not have a checking account
   6. Traveler's check – Designed for persons traveling where personal checks may not be accepted, or for use when it is inadvisable to carry large sums of money
   7. Voucher check – A detachable voucher form that is used to itemize or specify the purpose for which the check is drawn

B. The transactions in the box below should be recorded on the patient ledger in the proper columns.

Patient's balance = $20

C. 1. Blank: payee signs only his or her name
   2. Restrictive: specifies purpose of endorsement
   3. Special: includes words specifying the person to whom the endorser makes the check payable
   4. Qualified: disclaiming or destroying any future liability of endorser

D. 1. As checks from patients and other sources arrive, they should be recorded on the ledger and immediately stamped with the restrictive endorsement "for Deposit Only."
   2. Some insurance checks or drafts require a personal signature endorsement.

E. 1. There is the possibility of a stop-payment order.
   2. The check may be lost, misplaced, or stolen.

Date	Professional service	Charge	Payment	Adjustment	Balance
	Previous Balance				$267.00
6-1-xx	Office visit	76.00			$343.00
6-1-xx	Paid co-pay ck 2365		10.00		$333.00
6-13-xx	Insurance		55.00		$278.00
6-13-xx	Insurance adjustment			11.00	$267.00
6-14-xx	Returned check #2365	10.00			$277.00
6-14-xx	Fee: returned check	10.00			$287.00

3. Delay may cause the check to be returned because of insufficient funds.
4. The check may have a restricted time for cashing.
5. It is a courtesy to the payer.

Part III.
A. 94-72/1224
B. 678800470
C. 1837, 1838, and 1839
D. checks provided
E. checks provided
F. checks provided; total in bank after writing checks is $4696.96
G. form provided
H. itemized on p. 125
I. Chronological "tickler file"

Part IV.
1. See form on Student Study Guide, p. 126
2. See form on Student Study Guide, p. 126
3. No; the balance is $4616.96 in reconciliation
4. A HMO (Health Maintenance Organization) is more limited than the more flexible PPO (Preferred Provider Organization) option.
5. Provides treatment, rehabilitation, and income protection for work-related injuries.

Chapter 19 Quiz
1. False
2. first
3. voucher
4. Lost or missing checks
5. fraud
6. holder
7. drawer
8. payee
9. disbursements
10. mail

CHAPTER 20

Part I.
1. cohesive
2. embezzlement
3. incentives
4. morale
5. insubordination
6. reprimands

Part II.
A. Answers may include the following:
- Preparing and updating policy and procedure manuals
- Developing job descriptions
- Recruiting new employees
- Orientation and training
- Performance and salary reviews
- Dismissal of employees
- Planning staff meetings
- Maintaining staff harmony
- Establishing work flow guidelines
- Improving office efficiency
- Supervising the purchase and care of equipment
- Educating patients
- Eliminating time-wasting tasks for the physician
- Practice marketing
- Customer service

B. Discuss this advertisement with the class.

C. 1. Mutual accountability
2. Common purpose and goals
3. Fairly small size
4. Common approach
5. Complementary skills

Part III.
1. After call to order
2. New business
3. Old business
4. Shortens meetings, keeps the group on track, avoids omission of topics, and informs group of planned topics

Part IV.
A. Discuss results of student response and tally the results.

B. 1. Medical assistants and nurses are supervised by MDs and follow orders of the MD
2. Secretary, maintenance, and lab
3. Clinical supervision needed by MD
4. No

C. 1. Charismatic
2. Transactional
3. Transformational

Chapter 20 Quiz
1. charismatic, transactional, transformational
2. democratic, autocratic, laissez-faire
3. False
4. peer
5. True
6. agenda
7. embezzlement

8. insubordination
9. reprimand
10. chain of command

CHAPTER 21

Part I.
1. Objectives
2. Outreach
3. Marketing
4. Prosthetics
5. Tangible
6. Target market

Part II.
A. Product, placement, price, promotion
B. Assessment, research, plan the concept, execution, evaluation.
C. Answers may include the following: sponsoring Little League sports teams or bowling leagues, participating in charity events as a staff, United Way payroll deductions, blood drives, participating in health fairs.
D. There is a difference between advertising and public relations. Advertising could be defined as "creating or changing attitudes, beliefs and perceptions by influencing people with purchased broadcast time, print space, or other forms of written/visual media." Broadcast time could be in the form of TV commercials, radio, or audio-visual aids. Print could be a newspaper, magazine, or trade journal, while written/visual media may be a flier, brochure, or billboard. Public relations are influential as well, using news broadcasts, radio reports, and magazine or newspaper articles to reach people. Most public relations efforts are free, but it is often difficult to get others interested enough in the activities the medical office is planning to warrant coverage.
E. There are several phrases that could be considered the "deadly sins" of customer service. These phrases should never be used when relating to patients and visitors:

- "I don't know"
- "I don't care"
- "I can't be bothered"
- "Ask someone else"
- "It's not my job"
- "It's not my fault"
- "I know that"
- "I'm right, you're wrong"

F. There are four basic steps involved in building a website for the medical practice. These steps include the following:

- Define the objectives of the website
- Design the pages
- Locate a web server where the pages can be uploaded
- Upload the page to the web server

Part III.
Discuss results of student research in class.

Part IV.
Answers may include the following: other doctors (such as consultants), pharmaceutical company representatives, equipment vendors, and fellow employees.

Chapter 21 Quiz
1. product, placement, price, and promotion
2. newspaper columns, free websites, health fairs
3. a word or graphic that links to another website
4. evaluation
5. True
6. The process of promoting a product or service
7. assessment
8. web address
9. target market
10. internet service provider

CHAPTER 22

Part I.
1. B
2. F
3. K
4. A
5. G
6. C
7. J
8. H
9. I
10. E
11. D

Part II.
A. AHIMA
B. HIPAA
C. JCAHO

Part III.

Form provided. Discuss student responses as a class.

Part IV.

Create a transparency master using p. 140 as a template; work with students to reword the confidentiality statement so that it would be appropriate for a medical practice setting.

Chapter 22 Quiz

1. encrypted
2. total quality management
3. Joint Commission on Accreditation of Healthcare Organizations
4. National Center for Health Statistics
5. an unexpected outcome involving death or serious injury relating to healthcare
6. Health Insurance Portability and Accountability Act
7. AHIMA
8. that it can be trusted and that it is accurately reported
9. to determine if claims should be paid
10. authentication

CHAPTER 23

Part I.

1. Assets: The entire property of a person, association, corporation, or estate applicable or subject to the payment of debts.
2. Accounts payable: Debts incurred and not yet paid.
3. Accounts receivable: Amounts owed to the physician.
4. Accounts receivable trial balance: A method of determining that the journal and the ledger are in balance.
5. Accrual basis of accounting: Method of accounting where income is recorded when earned, and expenses are recorded when incurred.
6. Balance sheet: A financial statement for a specific date that shows the total assets, liabilities, and capital of the business.
7. Bookkeeping: The recording of business and accounting transactions.
8. Cash basis of accounting: Method of accounting where income is recorded when received, and expenses are recorded when paid.
9. Cash flow statement: A financial summary for a specific period that shows the beginning balance on hand, the receipts and disbursements during the period, and the balance on hand at the end of the period.
10. Disbursements Journal: A summary of accounts paid out.
11. Equities: The money value of a property or of an interest in a property in excess of claims or liens against it.
12. Fiscal year: An accounting period of twelve months.
13. In balance: The total ending balances of patient ledgers equal total of accounts receivable control.
14. Invoice: A paper describing a purchase and the amount due.
15. Liabilities: Something that is owed; a debt.
16. Packing slip: An itemized list of objects in a package.
17. Petty cash fund: A fund maintained to pay small unpredictable cash expenditures.
18. Statement: A request for payment.
19. Statement of income and expense: A summary of all income and expenses for a given period.
20. Trial balance: A method of checking the accuracy of accounts.

Part II.

A. Accounting is a system of recording, classifying, and summarizing financial transactions. Bookkeeping is mainly the recording part of the accounting process.

B. 1. First, use good penmanship so that the records are clearly legible, even years later. Use the same pen style and ink consistently.
    2. Keep columns of figures straight and write well-formed figures
    3. Carry decimal points correctly.

C. Single-entry, double-entry, pegboard

D. 1. Errors are not easily detected.
    2. There are no built-in controls.
    3. Periodic analyses are inadequate for financial planning.

Part III.

A. Answers may include the following: Auto expense, dues and meetings, equipment, insurance, medical supplies, office expenses, printing, postage, and stationery, rent and maintenance, salaries, taxes and licenses, travel and entertainment, utilities, miscellaneous, and personal withdrawals.

B. Purchase order forms provided. Discuss results of student research and completion of forms in class.

Part IV.

A. Petty cash request form provided. Discuss completion of form in class.

B. Write a check for cash, cash the check at the bank, and then replenish forms and document.

C. Checks provided. Discuss completion of checks in class. The final balance is $2679.97

D. 1. Social Security number application form
2. Wage and tax statement
3. Transmittal of income and tax statement
4. Employee withholding allowance

Chapter 23 Quiz

1. invoice
2. packing
3. four
4. a withholding certificate
5. Federal Unemployment Tax Act
6. the recording part of bookkeeping
7. cash and accrual
8. amounts paid out
9. petty cash
10. single entry, double-entry, pegboard

CHAPTER 24

Part I.

1. Anaphylaxis: Exaggerated hypersensitivity reaction which, in severe cases, leads to vascular collapse, bronchospasm, and shock.

2. Antibody: Immunoglobulin produced by the immune system in response to bacteria, viruses, or other antigenic substances.

3. Antigen: Foreign substance that causes the production of a specific antibody.

4. Antiseptic: Pertaining to substances that inhibit the growth of microorganisms such as alcohol and betadine.

5. Autoimmune: Disturbance in the immune system in which the body reacts against its own tissue. Examples of autoimmune disorders include multiple sclerosis, rheumatoid arthritis, and systemic lupus erythematosus.

6. Contaminated: Soiled with pathogens or infectious material; nonsterile.

7. Germicides: Agents that destroy pathogenic organisms.

8. Pathogenic: Pertaining to disease-causing microorganisms.

9. Permeable: To pass or soak through

10. Relapse: The recurrence of the symptoms of a disease after apparent recovery.

11. Remission: The partial or complete disappearance of the clinical and subjective characteristics of a chronic or malignant disease.

12. Vector: An animal, usually an insect or tick, that transmits the causative organisms of disease.

Part II.

Infectious Agent

E   A
D   B
     C

Part III.

A. 1. Blood vessel dilation at the site of invasion causing heat and inflammation
2. Blood vessel walls become more permeable causing edema and pain.
3. Chemostaxis, or the release of chemical agents, causes the attraction of WBCs to the site.
4. Finally phagocytosis results in the engulfing and destruction of microorganisms and damaged cells.

B. 1. Destroyed pathogens, cells, and WBCs collect in the area and form a thick, white substance called pus.
2. If the pathogenic invasion is too great for localized control, the infection may collect in the body's lymph nodes, where more WBCs are present to help fight the battle. This causes swollen glands or *lymphadenopathy.*
3. A systemic infection, also called blood poisoning; septicemia could ultimately affect the entire body. Without appropriate medical intervention, death can occur.

C. 1. Acute infection – rapid onset of symptoms but last a relatively short time.
2. Chronic infection – persist for long period of time, sometimes for life.
3. Latent infection – persistent infection in which the symptoms cycle through periods of relapse and remission.
4. Slow infection – progress over very long periods of time.

Part IV.

A. 1. virus
   2. bacteria
   3. protozoa
   4. fungi
   5. rickettsia

C. 1. Cocci (spherical)
   2. Bacilli (rod)
   3. Sprilla (spiral)

D. 1. Gloves
   2. Gowns
   3. Goggles

B.

Organism	Transmission	Symptoms	Specimens	Tests
HIV	Contact with an infected person's blood and/or blood contaminated body fluids, semen, CSF, synovial and amniotic fluids	Weight loss, chronic fevers, lymphadenopathy, recurrent infections, oral lesions	Blood	HIV serologic tests; ELISA test; positive Western blot
AIDS	Contact with an infected person's blood and/or blood contaminated body fluids, semen, CSF, synovial and amniotic fluids	Kaposi's sarcoma, pneumocystitis carinii pneumonia, candidiasis	Blood	HIV serologic tests, ELISA test, positive Western blot
HAV	Fecal-oral route Contact with carrier, contaminated food or water	Mild fever, malaise, nausea, headache, jaundice	Blood	IgM, IgG
HBV	Blood, body fluids, contaminated instruments	Dark urine, light stools, liver tenderness	Blood	HbsAg, anti-HBc, Anti-HBs
HDV	Requires the presence of HBV	Jaundice, cirrhosis	Blood	Anti-HDV
HCV	Blood transfusions, hemodialysis, IV drug users	Jaundice, chronic liver disease, cirrhosis, hepatocellular carcinoma	Blood	Transaminase levels, anti-HCV
HSV	Direct contact	Causes cold sores and genital herpes, painful papules and vesicles	Swab of vesicles	Culture and cytology
Varicella-zoster virus (VZV)	Direct contact	Vesicles, pustules, fever, general malaise, painful area along nerve pathway with herpes zoster	Swab of vesicles	Culture and cytology, clinical diagnosis

4. Masks
5. Lab coats
6. Face shields

E. 1. Urticaria
2. Dermatitis
3. Conjunctivitis
4. Rhinitis
5. Asthma
6. Anaphylaxis

Part V.
1. PPE
2. Training
3. Medical surveillance
4. Hep B immunization
5. Record keeping of workplace injuries
6. Labeling harzardous materials
7. Engineering controls

Part VI.
1. *Disinfection* is the process of killing pathogenic organisms or of rendering them inactive. It is not always effective against spores, the tubercle bacilli, and certain viruses.
2. *Medical asepsis* is defined as the removal or destruction of disease causing organisms *after they leave the body.*
3. *Asepsis* means freedom from infection or infectious material. Surgical asepsis is defined as the destruction of organisms *before they enter the body.*
4. Proper *hand washing* depends on two factors: running water and friction.
5. *Sanitization* is the cleansing process that decreases the number of microorganisms to a safe level as dictated in public health guidelines.
6. *Sterilization,* or the destruction of all microorganisms, is essential when conducting surgical asepsis.

Part VII. Discuss results of student research on hand washing in class.

Chapter 24 Quiz
1. remission
2. a
3. blood, CSF, vaginal secretion, saliva, etc
4. Centers for Disease Control and Prevention
5. F
6. itching, rash, wheezing, etc
7. T

8. sterilized
9. Occupational Safety and Health Administration
10. runny nose

CHAPTER 25

Part I.
1. Database
2. Past medical history
3. Family history
4. Social history
5. Review of systems

Part II. Discuss student responses.

Part III.
The three processes of active listening are:

Restatement – simply paraphrasing or repeating the patient's statement with phrases such as "You are saying…"

Reflection – repeating the main idea of the conversation while also identifying the feelings of the sender

Clarification – seeks to summarize or simplify the sender's thoughts and feelings as well as to resolve any confusion in the message

The receiver of a message attaches meaning to a message based on the linear communication model whereby communication is described as an interactive process involving the sender of the message, the receiver, and the crucial component of feedback to confirm the reception of the message.

Part IV. Discuss results of student observations. Four important rules to remember in preparing the appropriate environment for patient interaction include:
1. Insure privacy
2. Avoid interruption
3. Provide comfort
4. Take notes

Part V.
1. Open-ended
2. Closed-ended
3. Closed-ended
4. Open-ended
5. Closed-ended
6. Closed-ended

7. Open-ended
8. Closed-ended
9. Closed-ended
10. Closed-ended

Part VI. Ask students to share their examples with the class.

Part VII.
1. The environment should be safe and attractive.
2. Do not keep children and their caregivers waiting any longer than necessary since they become anxious and/or distracted quickly.
3. Do not offer a choice unless the child can truly make one. If part of the treatment requires that the child receive an injection, asking her if she'd like her shot now will get an automatic "No". However, giving her a choice of stickers after the injection is appropriate.
4. Praising the child during the examination helps decrease anxiety and increase self-esteem. When possible, direct questions toward the child so he or she feels part of the process.
5. Involving the child in the exam by permitting her to manipulate the equipment may help relieve anxiety. If possible, use your imagination and make a game of the assessment or the procedure.
6. A typical defense mechanism seen in sick or anxious children is regression. The child may refuse to leave her mother's lap or want to hold a favorite toy during the procedure as a comfort measure. Look for signs of anxiety such as thumb sucking or rocking during the assessment.
7. Listen to parents' concerns and respond truthfully to questions.

Part VIII.
1. Symptom
2. Symptom
3. Symptom
4. Sign
5. Sign
6. Symptom
7. Sign
8. Symptom
9. Sign
10. Symptom

Part IX.
1. Right pt, right chart
2. Black
3. Date/Time/Signature
4. Onset/Duration/Quality/Aggravating Factors
5. 1-10
6. Single-line through error and write "error" above the line with the date, initials, and then write correction
7. Late entry – record date and time of note and document with late entry for date and time, then include necessary information
8. Care of patient and legal documentation

Part X.
A. 1. Database
   2. Problem List
   3. Plan
   4. Progress Notes

B. Subjective
   Objective
   Assessment
   Plan
   Evaluation

C. Source-oriented medical record

D. 1. H&P
   2. Progress Notes
   3. Lab Results
   4. Consults

E. Computerized medical record

Part XI.
1.
S: chest pain of 4 on a 1-10 scale and sweating for 2 hours, left arm pain
O: T-99, P-68, R-24, irregular pulse

2.
S: sore throat of 7 on a 1-10 scale, fever for 2 days, exposed to strep last week
O: T-102.4, P-108, R-20, erythematous popular rash across chest

3.
S: headache with pain of 8 on a 1-10 scale, nausea for 3 days, dizziness, eyes hurt
O: T-97.6, P-110, R-20, pale, damp skin

4.
S: low back pain of 5 on 1-10 scale, c/o blood in urine
O: T-98.7, P-98, R-20, ecchymosis across flank

Chapter 25 Quiz

1. T
2. T
3. T
4. T
5. Chief
6. Rapport
7. Database
8. Social
9. Family
10. T

CHAPTER 26

Part I.

1. emotional, social, psychological, economic, physical, spiritual

Part II.

1. Provide knowledge and skills to promote health.
2. Include family and significant others
3. Encourage patient ownership
4. Promote safe and appropriate use of medication and treatments
5. Encourage adaptation to healthy behaviors
6. Provide information on accessing community resources

Part III.

1. Perception
2. Need for information
3. Age and developmental level
4. Mental and emotional state
5. Culture and diversity
6. Learning style
7. Physical disability

Part IV.

1. Address patient by last name
2. Be courteous; use formal communication
3. Use gestures, tone
4. Use pictures or handouts
5. Monitor body language
6. Use simple words
7. Demonstrate all procedures
8. Use an interpreter when available

Part V.

Flexible, what, when

Part VI.

1. Learning style
2. Age/developmental level

3. Defense mechanisms
4. Language
5. Motivation
6. Physical limitations
7. Emotional/mental state
8. Cultural and ethnic background
9. Pain
10. Time limitations

Part VII.

1. Written materials written in lay language on 6 to 8th grade level
2. Information is well-organized
3. Material is accurate
4. Professional format and appealing
5. Obtain copies in other languages when possible

Part VIII.

1. Reinforce physician instructions and information
2. Encourage patient to take an active role in their health
3. Use each patient interaction as an opportunity to contact health teaching
4. Keep information relevant to patient needs
5. Establish and maintain patient rapport
6. Communicate clearly
7. Be sensitive to patient factors
8. Modify the teaching plan as needed to best meet needs of patient

Part IX. Printed, internet, resources, return, family

Part X. Have students present a patient education program on a selected topic; have them use the teaching plan checklist as a peer evaluation tool.

Chapter 26 Quiz

1. Consider all aspects of a patient's life.
2. medication and healthy lifestyles
3. True
4. videos, brochures, handouts
5. True
6. family
7. True
8. language and physical conditions (eyesight, hearing)
9. assessment
10. Have them restate, repeat, or demonstrate what they have learned.

CHAPTER 27

Part I.

A. 1. Low iron
   2. Low fiber, high fats
   3. Low fiber, low water
   4. High carbohydrates
   5. High fat
   6. High fat, high sodium
   7. Low calcium

B. 1. roughage
   2. Carbohydrates
   3. Fat
   4. antioxidants
   5. Proteins
   6. fat, water
   7. Electrolytes

Part II.

A. 1. 35 and 16
   2. 41 and 104
   3. 0.68
   4. Answers will vary.

B. 1. maintenance of body temperature
   2. Acts as solvent and medium for biochemical reactions
   3. Acts as the vehicle for transport of substances
   4. Acts as lubricant for joints and mucous membranes

Part III.

A.
A. Fats, oils, and sweets
B. Milk, yogurt, and cheese group
C. Vegetable group
D. Meat, poultry, fish, dry beans, eggs, and nuts group
E. Fruit group
F. Bread, cereal, rice, and pasta group

B.
1. $1\frac{1}{4}$ cup
2. 110
3. Less than 1 gram
4. Carbohydrate, sodium

Part IV.

Discuss results of student research in class.

Chapter 27 Quiz

1. complete and incomplete
2. HDL and LDL
3. decreases unhealthy cholesterol
4. bulimia and anorexia
5. olive and canola
6. calorie
7. carbohydrates
8. roughage
9. saturated and unsaturated
10. C and E

CHAPTER 28

Part I.

1. Apnea: Absence or cessation of breathing
2. Arrhythmia: Irregular heart rhythm
3. Bradycardia: A slow heartbeat; a pulse below 60 beats per minute
4. Bradypnea: Respirations that are regular in rhythm but slower than normal in rate
5. Dyspnea: Difficult or painful breathing
6. Febrile: Pertaining to an elevated body temperature
7. Hyperlipidemia: Excess of fats or lipids in the blood plasma
8. Hypertension: High blood pressure (systolic pressure consistently above 140 mm Hg and diastolic pressure above 90 mm Hg)
9. Hyperventilation: Abnormally prolonged and deep breathing usually associated with acute anxiety or emotional tension
10. Hypotension Blood pressure that is below normal (systolic pressure below 90 mm Hg and diastolic pressure below 50 mm Hg)
11. Orthopnea: Individual must sit or stand to breathe comfortably
12. Rales: Abnormal or crackling breath sounds during inspiration
13. Rhonchi: Abnormal rumbling sounds on expiration that indicate airway obstruction by thick secretions or spasms
14. Syncope: Fainting; a brief lapse in consciousness
15. Tachycardia: Rapid but regular heart rate exceeding 100 beats per minute
16. Tachypnea: Respirations that are rapid and shallow; hyperventilation
17. Vertigo: Dizziness

Part II.

1. Temperature
2. Pulse
3. Respiratory rate
4. Blood pressure

Part III.

1. Height
2. Weight
3. Fat composition
4. Head and chest circumference

Part IV.

1. T
2. T
3. T
4. F

Part V. See Table 28-1 in text.

Part VI.

A. 1. Continuous
    2. Intermittent
    3. Remittent
    4. Rectal
    5. Axillary
    6. Rectal
    7. Digital, blue, rectal
    8. Tympanic, bilateral otitis externa, cerrumen
    9. Axillary
    10. Rectal, Sims

B. 1. 100.4
   2. 99.5
   3. 98.6
   4. 100.9, 3 weeks, 1 week

C. 1. 37
    2. 98.6
    3. 36.4
    4. 100.4
    5. 37.4
    6. 96.8
    7. 40
    8. 107.6
    9. 38.3
    10. 105.8
    11. 38.9
    12. 109.4

Part VII.

1. Temporal
2. Carotid
3. Apical
4. Brachial
5. Radial
6. Femoral
7. Popliteal
8. Dorsalis pedis

Part VIII.

1. inspiration and expiration
2. rate, rhythm, and depth
3. 2, 16

Part IX.

1. arteries
2. pulse pressure
3. systolic, diastolic

Phase I	Phase V	Document B/P
110	80	110/80
204	114	204/114
116	72	116/72
98	56	98/56
142	88	142/88

Part X.

1. T 98.7 (O) P 60 (A) R 22 B/P 152/98 Lying 114/75 Standing
2. T 96.8 (T) P 86 (R) R 18 B/P 132/76 L 128/80 R
3. T 101.2 (R) P 100 R 20 B/P 126/70
4. T 97.5 (AX) P 78 (C) R 20 B/P 120/PAP

Chapter 28 Quiz

1. systolic pressure
2. 18
3. palpated
4. 64.4 kg
5. 160.6#
6. T
7. T
8. F
9. temporal
10. T

CHAPTER 29

Part I.
1. transillumination
2. uremia
3. sclera
4. murmur
5. nodule
6. bruit

Part II.
A. 1. epithelial
   2. connective
   3. muscle
   4. nervous

B. 1. Tissue: Similar cells working together
   2. Organ: Two or more tissues working together
   3. System: Two or more organs working together

C. Refer to Table 29-1 in the textbook.

Part III.
A. 1. Room preparation
   2. Patient preparation
   3. Assisting the doctor

Part IV.
1. Tongue depressor
2. Reflex hammer
3. Tuning fork
4. Stethoscope
5. Tape measure
6. Nasal speculum
7. Opthalmascope
8. Otoscope

Part V.
1. Looking
2. Touching
3. Tapping
4. Listening
5. Measuring
6. Moving

Part VI.
1. Fowlers
2. Supine
3. Dorsal recumbent
4. Lithotomy
5. Sims
6. Prone

7. Left lateral
8. Knee chest

Part VII.
1. High-pitched sounds
2. Low-pitched sounds

Chapter 29 Quiz
1. Urinary
2. ear
3. d
4. nervous
5. musculoskeletal system
6. GI
7. lymphatic and hematic
8. Sims (left)
9. F
10. T

CHAPTER 30

Part I.
1. E
2. C
3. B
4. A
5. F
6. D

Part II.
A. 1. Food and Drug Administration
   2. Drug Enforcement Agency
   3. Federal Trade Commission

B. 1. FTC
   2. FDA
   3. DEA
   4. DEA
   5. FDA
   6. DEA

C. 1. Written in ink or typed
   2. Prescribed date
   3. Full name and address of the patient
   4. Name, address, and DEA number of the physician
   5. Amount prescribed written out (ten rather than 10), usually for small quantities of the drug
   6. Manually signed by the physician although the medical assistant can prepare the prescription for the physician signature.

Part III.

Schedule	Guidelines	Drug Examples
I	No accepted medical use High potential for abuse Possession of these drugs is illegal	Heroin, LSD, marijuana, Quaalude, mescaline, peyote, amphetamine variations
II	Accepted for medical use but with severe restrictions High potential for abuse May cause severe psychological or physical dependence	Opium, morphine, methadone, cocaine, amphetamine, cannabis, barbiturates, Ritalin, Percodan, Dilaudid, Demerol, codeine
III	Accepted for medical use Potential for abuse less than I or II May cause moderate to low physical dependence or high psychological dependence Includes combination drugs that contain limited amounts of narcotics or stimulants	Paregoric, Tylenol with codeine, Benzphetamine, suppositories with barbiturates, anabolic steroids including testosterone
IV	Accepted for medical use Low potential for abuse May cause limited physical or psychological dependence in comparison to schedule III drugs Includes minor tranquilizers and hypnotics	Equanil, Librium, Valium, Dalmane, Dalmane, Chloral Hydrate, Darvon, Talwin, Xanax, Halcion, Restoril, Tranxene, Ativan
V	Accepted for medical use Low potential for abuse May cause limited physical or psychological dependence in comparison to schedule IV drugs Includes drug mixtures containing limited amounts of narcotics	Cough medicines containing codeine, Donnagel, Lomotil

Part IV.
1. T
2. F
3. T
4. T
5. T

Matching
1. B
2. D
3. A
4. E
5. C

Part V.
1. Absorption
2. Distribution
3. Metabolism
4. Excretion

Part VI. Discuss findings of small group discussions.

Part VII. Answers may include the following:
Analgesic
Action: Lessens the sensory function of the brain
Example: Aspirin; acetaminophen

Anesthetic
Action: Produces insensibility to pain or the sensation of pain
Example: Bupivacaine (Marcaine)

Antibiotic
Action: Kills or inhibits the growth of microorganisms
Example: Cefaclor (Ceclor)

Antidepressant
Action: Treats depression
Example: Fluoxetine (Prozac)

Antihistamine
Action: Counteracts the effects of histamine by blocking action in tissues
Example: Brompheniramine maleate (Dimetane)

Antihypertensive
Action: Blocks nerve impulses that cause arteries to constrict; slows heart rate, decreasing its contractibility; restricts the hormone aldosterone in the blood
Example: Atenolol (Tenormin)

Antiinflamatory
Action: Acts as anti-inflammatory or antirheumatic
Example: Nonsteroidal (NSAIDs): Ibuprofen (Advil, Motrin)

Antineoplastic
Action: Inhibits the development of and destroys cancerous cells
Example: Interferon alfa-2a (Roferon-A)

Antiussive (cough suppressant)
Action: Inhibits the cough center
Example: Narcotic: Codeine sulfate; nonnarcotic: Dextromethorphan

Part VIII. Discuss student responses.

Chapter 30 Quiz

1. Answers may include the following: the rate at which body tissues absorb a drug; where a drug is distributed or localized in the tissues; the route by which a drug is excreted; and toxicity.
2. cathartic (laxative)
3. T
4. F
5. T
6. T

7. a. Chemical
   b. Generic
   c. Brand

8. Physician's Desk Reference

CHAPTER 31

Part I. Discuss results of student research in class.

Part II.
A. 1. centi
   2. deci
   3. milli
   4. micro
   5. deka
   6. hecto
   7. kilo

B.
   1. 1500
   2. 0.05
   3. 3000
   4. 2
   5. 2500
   6. 500
   7. 0.5
   8. 750
   9. 1000
  10. 1

Part III.
A. 2—II
   3—III
   4—IV
   6—VI
   7—VII
   8—VIII
   9—IX
   15—XV
   20—XX
   30—XXX
   40—XL
   50—L
   60—LX
   70—LXX
   80—LXXX

Abbreviations and symbols
1. oz, ℥
2. tsp
3. mg
4. gr
5. pt
6. ʒ
7. tbsp

Conversions
1. 20
2. 10
3. 6
4. 30 mL/oz

Part IV.

Pounds to Kilograms

1. 68
2. 35
3. 10
4. 95
5. 29
6. 90
7. 51
8. 74
9. 6
10. 2

Inches to Centimeters

1. 155 cm
2. 85
3. 242.5
4. 60, 150
5. 74″, 185 cm

Part V.

Decimals to Percentages

1. 75
2. 33
3. 25
4. 100%
5. 50

Part VI.

1. x = 9
2. x = 3
3. x = 40
4. x = 4
5. x = 25

Part VII.

1. 2 (Keflex 500 mg/Label reads 250 mg capsule)
2. 2 (Lasix 40/Label reads 20 mg tablet)
3. 3 (Zoloft 75 mg/Label reads 25 mg tablet)
4. 3 (Claritin 30 mg/Label reads 10 mg tablet)
5. 4 (Prilosec 40 mg/Label reads 10 mg capsule)
6. 1.5 (Celebrex 150/Label reads 100 mg tablet)
7. ¹/₄ (Vioxx 12.5/Label reads 50 mg)
8. ¹/₂ (Lanoxin .125/Label reads .25 tablet)
9. 4 (Coumadin 20 mg/Label reads 5 mg tablet)
10. .5 (Augmentin 250/Label reads 500 mg per 5 ml)
11. 8 (Prednisone 40 mg/Label reads 5 mg tablet)
12. 2 (Prozac 20 mg/Label reads 10 mg capsule)
13. ¹/₂ (Synthroid/Label reads 88 mg per tablet)
14. 3 (Zocor 60 mg/Label reads 20 mg tablet)
15. 2 (Glucophage 1 g/Label reads 500 mg tablet)
16. 2 (Zestril 2.5 mg/Label reads 5 mg tablet)
17. 4 (Norvasc 10 mg/Label reads 2.5 mg tablet)
18. 3 (Cipro 750 mg/Label reads 250 mg tablet)
19. 4 (Zyrtec syrup mg/Label reads 5 mg/5 ml)
20. 2 (Zovirax 200 mg/Label reads 400 mg tablet)

Part VIII.

Fried's Law

1. Penicillin 12000 U
2. Benadryl 20 mg
3. Tylenol 80 mg
4. Sudafed 4 mg

Clark's Rule

1. Penicillin 14667 U
2. Benadryl 4 mg
3. Tylenol 180 mg
4. Sudafed 15 mg

West's Nomogram

1. Penicillin 29412 U
2. Benadryl 9 mg
3. Tylenol 176 mg
4. Sudafed 25 mg

Part IX.

1. 19 KG, 19 mg
2. 8 mg
3. 9 mg
4. 330 mg
5. 106 mg
6. 0.5 mL
7. 0.5 mL
8. 148 mg
9. 2.5 mL
10. 0.5 mL

Part X. Discuss results of student research in class.

Chapter 31 Quiz

1. 8
2. 5
3. 30
4. b
5. b
6. cc
7. IV
8. 3
9. F
10. 2.2

CHAPTER 32

Part I.
1. A
2. M
3. K
4. O
5. Q
6. C
7. I
8. N
9. J
10. P
11. L
12. D
13. B
14. H
15. G
16. E
17. F

Part II.
1. Drug
2. Route
3. Time
4. Dose
5. Patient
6. Technique
7. Documentation

Solid Oral Forms
1. Made to cut or split
2. Compressed powder
3. Decreased acidity
4. Gelatin coated particles
5. Oblong tablet
6. Dissolves at different times

Liquid Oral Forms
1. Sugar and water
2. Volatile oil in water
3. Contains alcohol
4. Insoluble drug in liquid
5. Oil mixture
6. Minerals in water
7. Alcohol and plant extract
8. Sweetened

Mucous Membrane Forms
1. Cheek
2. Tongue
3. Upper respiratory and lungs

Topical Forms
1. Medication applied to the skin
2. Also applied to the skin, but have a higher portion of oil than do lotions
3. Semi-solid medication in oil base
4. Absorbed slowly through the skin

Parenteral Forms
1. Glass container with a stopper
2. Glass container that must be broken to obtain medication
3. Use for more than one dose
4. Ready to inject
5. Tubex or other holder/plunger required

Vial or Ampule?
A. vial
B. vial
C. ampule

1. V
2. A
3. A
4. V
5. V
6. A
7. V
8. A
9. A
10. A

Routes of Parenteral Administration
1. IM
2. SQ
3. ID
4. IV

True or False
1. T
2. T
3. T
4. T
5. T
6. F
7. T
8. T
9. F
10. F

Create a transparency master using p. 221 as a template; have students label the syringes as indicated.

Part III.

Anterior: A, B, C (from top to bottom of figure)
Posterior: A, D (from top to bottom of figure)
Pediatric Sites: vastus lateralis
Student to draw arrow; always pull the pinna down

Part IV.

Discuss student responses.

Extra for Experts

Sample Prescription
Discuss individual sections of the written
prescription with the class.
Superscription – Patient's name, address, and date
Inscription – Name of the drug, dosage form, and
strength
Subscription – Directions for the pharmacist–size
of each dose, amount to dispense, and drug form
Sig – Directions for patient – Instructions on how
to take medication
Refills – Number of refills allowed
Directions for taking Tylenol #3: Take one or two
by month every 4-6 hours as needed for pain.

Spell out the following abbreviations.

1. every 4 hours
2. 3 times per day
3. 4 times per day
4. twice per day
5. every 3 hours
6. at bedtime
7. before meals
8. after meals
9. as needed
10. by mouth
11. nothing by mouth
12. per rectum
13. intravenously
14. subcutaneously
15. intramuscularly
16. sublingual
17. everyday
18. every other day
19. every morning
20. every evening

Chapter 32 Quiz

1. T
2. 1
3. F
4. D
5. A

6. cc
7. bevel
8. subcutaneous
9. T
10. F

CHAPTER 33

Part I.

A. 1. Blue color of the mucous membranes and
    body extremities caused by lack of oxygen
   2. Difficult or painful breathing
   3. A hemorrhagic skin discoloration
      commonly called bruising
   4. A substance that causes vomiting
   5. Rapid, random, ineffective contractions of
      the heart
   6. Blood in the urine
   7. Space in the center of the chest under the
      sternum
   8. The muscular lining of the heart
   9. Pertaining to the death of cells or tissue
   10. Visual sensitivity to light
   11. Excessive thirst
   12. Excreting large amounts of urine
   13. Temporary neurological symptoms because
       of a gradual or partial occlusion of a cerebral
       blood vessel

B. 1. First aid
   2. Automated external defibrillator
   3. Cardiopulmonary resuscitation
   4. Cerebrovascular accident
   5. Transient ischemic attack
   6. Myocardial infarction
   7. Myocardial infarction

C. 1. Sweating (*diaphoresis*)
   2. Nausea or indigestion
   3. Shortness of breath (SOB)
   4. Cold and clammy skin
   5. Feeling weak (*general malaise*)

D. 1. Anaphylactic
   2. Insulin
   3. Psychogenic
   4. Hypovolemic
   5. Cardiogenic
   6. Neurogenic
   7. Septic

E. RICE
   1. Rest
   2. Ice

3. Compression
4. Elevation

F. Answers may include the following: symptoms related to shock; severe, constant pain or waves of pain; bloody or tarry stools; pregnancy or a missed menstrual period; continuous vomiting or severe constipation; chest pain, SOB, or continuous cough

Part II.
1. Heat stroke
2. Muscle cramps
3. Heat exhaustion

Part III.

Emergency Situation	Triage Questions	Home Care Advice
Syncope	Was the patient injured? Does the patient have a history of heart disease, seizures, or diabetes?	Does not necessarily indicate a serious disease. If injured from a fall, the patient may need to be treated. Patient should get up very slowly to prevent recurrence, take it easy, and drink plenty of fluids. If patient is to be seen, someone should accompany him or her to the clinician's practice.
Animal bites	What kind of animal? (pet or wild)? How severe is the injury? Where are the bites? When did the bite occur?	Health department or police should be notified. Every effort must be made to locate the animal and monitor its health. If the skin is not broken then wash well and observe for signs of infection
Insect bites and stings	Does the patient have a history of anaphylactic reaction to insect stings? Is the patient having difficulty breathing, have a widespread rash, or having trouble swallowing?	If there is a history of anaphylaxis and the patient has an EpiPen system, it should be administered immediately and EMS notified. Activate EMS if having systemic symptoms. An antihistamine (Benadryl) relileves local pruritis.
Asthma	Does the patient show signs of cyanosis? Has the patient used the prescribed inhalers?	If the asthmatic is unable to speak in sentences, color is poor, and struggling to breathe even after inhaler use they should be seen immediately or EMS activated.
Burns	Where are the burns located and what caused them? Are there signs of shock. i.e., moist clammy skin, altered consciousness, rapid breathing and pulse? Are there signs of infection (foul odor, cloudy drainage) in a burn more than 2 days old?	Activate EMS for burns on the face, hands, feet, and perineum or those caused by electricity, a chemical, or associated with inhalation. Activate EMS if there are signs of shock. Patient must receive tetanus shot if it has been more than 10 years since last one. Schedule an urgent appointment if signs of infection are reported

Emergency Situation	Triage Questions	Home Care Advice
Wounds	Is the bleeding steady or pulsating? How and when did the injury occur? Does the patient have any bleeding disorders or on anticoagulant drugs? Is the wound open and deep?	Pulsating bleeding usually indicates arterial damage; activate EMS. If from a powerful force other injuries may exist. Patient taking anticoagulants, with diabetes or anemia; schedule an urgent appointment. Gaping, deep wound requires sutures.
Head injury	Did the patient pass out or have a seizure? Is the patient confused, vomiting, or is there clear drainage from nose or ears?	If the answer is "yes" to any of these symptoms. EMS should be activated.

Chapter 33 Quiz

1. automatic external defibrillator
2. grand mal
3. chest pain, nausea, diophoresis, arm pain
4. faint
5. hemorrhage, allergies, infection, heart attacks
6. T
7. T
8. Steri-strips, sutures, dressings, butterflies
9. 911 or EMS
10. Triage

CHAPTER 34

Part I.

1. b
2. g
3. f
4. a
5. l
6. n
7. m
8. i
9. j
10. k
11. h
12. d
13. e
14. c

Part II.

1. Ishihara
2. Snellen
3. Rosenbaum

Part III.

A
A. Outer canthus
B. Sclera and conjunctiva
C. Pupil

B
A. Helix of pinna
B. Tragus
C. External auditory canal
D. Lobule

Part IV.

A.
1. Stye
2. Chalazion

Part V.

A. OD 20/20   OS 20/15   OU 20/20
B. OD 20/20   OS 20/30   OU 20/20

You can have the patient point in the direction that the E faces.

Part VI. Discuss results of student research in class.

Part VII.

A. 1. Weber
   2. Rinne

B. Students will assess their near acuity.

Part VIII.
1. 380.12
2. 381.01
3. 380.15
4. 381.10
5. 380.4

Part IX.
A. 1. Hyperopia
   2. Myopia
   3. Presbyopia or astigmatism

B. 1. Keratitis
   2. Conjunctivitis
   3. Lephritis
   4. Hordeolum

C. 1. Corneal abrasions
   2. Cataract
   3. Glaucoma
   4. Macula degeneration

D. 1. Nares and turbinates
   2. a. Nasal speculum
      b. Pen light

E. Answers may include the following: otitis media would refer to an inner ear infection; otitis externa would refer to an outer ear infection (or swimmer's ear).

F. Hyperopia is farsightedness and myopia is nearsightedness

Chapter 34 Quiz
1. myopia
2. right eye
3. Ishihara
4. left eye
5. a. open-angle glaucoma
   b. closed-angle glaucoma
6. farsightedness
7. true
8. a. hyperopia
   b. myopia
   c. presbyopia
9. pertaining to the ear
10. Rinne

CHAPTER 35

Part I.
1. Bilirubin: Orange-colored pigment in bile, which when it accumulates leads to jaundice

2. Cryosurgery: Technique of exposing tissue to extreme cold to produce a well-defined area of cell destruction
3. Debridement: Removal of foreign material and dead, damaged tissue from a wound
4. Ecchymosis: Bluish-black skin discoloration produced by hemorrhagic areas
5. Electrodesiccation: Destructive drying of cells and tissue by means of short high-frequency electrical sparks
6. Exacerbation: An increase in the seriousness of a disease marked by greater intensity in the signs and symptoms
7. Hyperplasia: An increase in the number of cells
8. Jaundice: Yellow discoloration of the skin and mucous membranes
9. Keratin: Very hard, tough protein found in hair, nails, and epidermal tissue
10. Leukoderma: White patches on the skin
11. Opaque: Not translucent or transparent
12. Remission: Partial or complete disappearance of the signs and symptoms of a disease

Part II.
1. Sebum
2. Dermis
3. Flora
4. Impetigo
5. Acne
6. Eczema

Part III.
A. Epidermis
B. Dermis
C. Subcutaneous tissue

Part IV.
1. Athlete's foot
2. Jock itch
3. Ringworm
4. Onychomycosis
5. Itch mite
6. Lice
7. Wart
8. Cellulitis

Part V.
A. Answers will vary.
B. Answers will vary.

Part VI.
1. Retin-A, benzoyl
2. tetracycline
3. isotretinoin (Accutane)

4. Elimite, Kwell
5. Herpes zoster
6. Lotrimin, Nizoral, Mycostatin
7. Zovirax
8. Allergies

Part VII.
A. Discuss student responses.

B. 1. Scratch test
   2. Intradermal
   3. Patch test
   4. RAST—Radioallergosorbent

C. 1. Asymmetry: one half of the mole does not match the other half
   2. Border: edges of the mole are blurred or irregular
   3. Color: color of the mole is not the same throughout
   4. Diameter: larger than 6 mm, about the size of a pencil eraser

Part VIII.
1. 052.9
2. 053.9
3. 052.9
4. 054.9
5. 053.9
6. 054.10
7. 054.4
8. 053.71
9. 054.3
10. 054.6

Part IX.
A. 1. Macule: skin lesion that is flat and less than 1 cm in diameter
   2. Papule: small solid raised skin lesion less than 1 cm in diameter
   3. Plaque: flat, often raised patch on the skin
   4. Fissure: crack-like lesion of the skin
   5. Pustule: small round elevation of the skin containing fluid that is usually purulent
   6. Vesicle: small, thin-walled, raised skin lesion containing clear fluid
   7. Bulla: thin-walled blister containing clear serous fluid greater than 1 cm in diameter
   8. Cyst: closed sac in or under the skin containing fluid or semi-solid material
   9. Ulcer: circumscribed craterlike lesion, may be shallow or deep
   10. Wheal: individual lesion of urticaria, such as a pimple

B. 1. Impetigo
   2. Acne
   3. Furuncles and carbuncles
   4. Cellulitis
C. 1. Seborrheic dermatitis
   2. Contact dermatitis
   3. Eczema
   4. Psoriasis
   5. Systemic lupus erythematosus
   6. Scleroderma.

Seven Warning Signs of Cancer
1. Change in bowel or bladder habits
2. A sore that will not heal
3. Unusual bleeding or discharge
4. Thickening or lump in breast or elsewhere
5. Indigestion or difficulty swallowing
6. Obvious change in a wart or mole
7. Nagging cough or hoarseness

Appearance Modification
1. Chemical Peel
2. Dermabrasion
3. Laser Resurfacing

Chapter 35 Quiz
1. Shingles
2. Human papilloma virus
3. fungal
4. itching
5. jock itch, ringworm, athletes' foot
6. Scabies and lice
7. ecchymosis
8. superficial, partial thickness, and full thickness
9. Systemic lupus erythematosus
10. second-degree

CHAPTER 36

Part I.
1. Anastomosis
2. Fecalith
3. Fissures
4. Flatus
5. Hepatomegaly
6. Ileocecal valve
7. Ileostomy
8. Melena
9. Polyps

Part II.
1. Obturator
2. Peristalsis
3. Lithotripsy

Part III.

A. 1. common bile duct
   2. small
   3. villi

B. The large intestine is made up of the cecum (extending from it is the vermiform appendix), ascending colon, transverse colon, descending colon, sigmoid colon, rectum, and anal canal.

C
1. Peritoneum: membrane that covers the abdominal wall and organs of the abdominal cavity.
2. Mesentery: a peritoneal fold that attaches the jejunum and ileum to the posterior abdominal wall.
3. Omentum: a fold of fatty peritoneal tissue that contains multiple lymph nodes and hangs from the stomach like an apron covering the anterior transverse colon and the small intestine
4. Adhesions: bands of scar tissue that bind together two anatomical surfaces that are normally separate.

D. Left side of figure: liver
   Right side of figure (from top to bottom): diaphragm, spleen, stomach

Part IV.

1. Gastroenterologists
2. Hiatal hernia, GERD, ulcers
3. Food poisoning, dumping syndrome, irritable bowel syndrome, appendicitis, Crohn's, colitis, celiac, hernia, hemorrhoids, diverticular disease
4. Hepatitis, and gallstones

Part V. See Table 36-1

Part VI. Discuss results of student research in class.

Part VII.

Clo-test *(H. pylori),* H&H, hemoccult, endocsopy, upper GI, barium swallow. See Table 36-4.

Part VIII.

A. See Table 36-5
   1. 562.02
   2. 562.01
   3. 562.12
   4. 562.01
   5. 562.10

Part IX.

A. 1. B
   2. A
   3. C

B. 1. RUQ
   2. RLQ
   3. LUQ
   4. RUQ
   5. LUQ

C. *H. pylori*
D. True
E. Knee chest: Safety concerns always have to be addressed while a patient is in this position. Privacy is also an issue.
F Sims' position

Chapter 36 Quiz

1. R. hypochondriac
2. R. iliac/lingual
3. pyloric stenosis
4. pouches in the intestines
5. Vitamin C and red meats
6. A
7. T
8. *H. pylori* and excess acid
9. gallstones
10. Salmonella

CHAPTER 37

Part I.

1. Albuminuria: Abnormal presence of albumin in the urine
2. Azotemia: Retention in the blood of excessive amounts of nitrogenous wastes
3. Casts: Fibrous or protein material molded to the shape of the part in which it has accumulated and thrown off into the urine in kidney disease.
4. Copulation: Sexual intercourse
5. Erythropoietin: Substance released from the kidney and liver that promotes red blood cell formation
6. Urgency: Sudden, compelling desire to urinate and the inability to control its release
7. Urology: the study of the urinary tract in both male and female patients

Part II.

1. Urethritis
2. Cystitis
3. Pyelonephritis
4. Glomerulonephritis

Part III.

A. inguinal canal
B. Vas deferens

C. Epididymis

D. testes

Part IV.

1. To relieve urinary retention
2. To obtain a sterile urine sample
3. To measure the amount of residual urine in the bladder
4. To obtain a urine sample when it cannot be obtained by any other method
5. To empty the bladder before and/or during surgery or before specific diagnostic procedures.

Part V.

Date, Time. In and Out cath for UA. 460 cc clear/dark orange urine. Pt. tolerated procedure without difficulty.

_____ signature

Part VI.

A. Discuss results of student research in class.

B.

Part VII.

A. Refer to Table 37-1 in textbook.

B. 1. Creatinine – Nitrogenous wastes from muscles metabolism excreted in urine

2. BUN (Blood urea nitrogen) Blood test to detect renal disease

3. UA (Urinalysis): A common laboratory examination used to diagnose and evaluate diseases in mulitple body systems

Part VIII.

1. 600.9
2. 600.0
3. 600.3
4. 601.0
5. 601.1

Disease (Causative Organism)	Signs and Symptoms	Treatment
Chlamydia (Chlamydia trachomatis)	May be asymptomatic; dysuria; itching and white discharge from penis	Azithromycin (Zithromax) or Doxycycline (Vibramycin)
Genital herpes simplex virus (HSV-2)	Painful genital vesicles and ulcers; erythema and pruritus; tingling or shooting pain 1 to 2 days before outbreak; cycle through episodes. Viral shedding may occur during asymptomatic periods.	Antiviral therapy during episodes shorten duration of lesions; Acyclovir (Zovirax), Famciclovir (Famvir), or Valacyclovir (Valtrex)
Genital warts (human papillomavirus, HPV)	Most prevalent STD; period of communicability is unknown; genital pinhead lesions may or may not be visible; warts tend to recur	Goal of treatment is to remove symptomatic warts; cryotherapy for lesions; Podoflox solution or Imiquimod cream to lesions
Gonorrhea (N. gonorrhoeae) bacteria	Dysuria; whitish discharge from penis that may become yellow-green; testicular pain	Cefixime (Suprax), Azithromycin, Doxycycline
Syphilis (T. pallidum): Spirochete bacteria	Six stages that can affect multiple body systems; 10- to 90-day incubation; initial sign is a painless lesion, or chancre, at the exposure site (penis); serous discharge from chancre; lymphadenopathy. If not diagnosed and treated, will advance to further stages.	Penicillin G (Wycillin); if allergic to penicillin, Doxycycline or Tetracycline

Part IX.

A

1. Epididymis: Long, coiled tube where the sperm are stored until maturation. Peristaltic waves in the epididymis help the sperm move into the *vas deferens*.
2. Balanitis: Inflammation of the glans penis and of the mucous membrane beneath it.
3. Impotence: Inability to achieve and maintain an erection sufficient for intercourse.
4. Infertility: The inability to produce offspring
5. Prostatitis: Inflammation of the prostate
6. BPH: Benign prostatic hyperplasia
7. Cryptorchidism: The failure of one or both testes to descend into the scotum.
8. Hydrocele: A build up of fluid in the scrotum
9. Enuresis: Inability to control urination
10. Renal calculi: Small stones created when salts in the urine collect in the kidney or when fluid intake is low creating a highly concentrated filtrate.

B. Inguinal: Males are at risk for developing a hernia in this area because the testes descend through this canal after birth. The muscle wall is weakest in the inguinal area.

Chapter 37 Quiz

1. blood pressure
2. red blood cells
3. undescended testes
4. Kidney, ureters, bladder
5. Answers will vary.
6. F
7. The inability to control urination
8. a. Peritoneal
   b. Hemodialysis
9. intravenous pyelogram
10. Renal cortex

CHAPTER 38

Part I.

1. Rectocele: A protrusion of the rectum into the posterior wall of the vagina
2. Uterine prolapse: The uterus loses its supportive structure and drops into the vagina. This may involve the descent of the cervix into the vagina or be both the uterus and the cervix protruding from the vaginal opening

3. Cystocele: A protrusion of the bladder into the anterior wall of the vagina.
4. PID – pelvic inflammatory disease: Any acute or chronic infection of the reproductive system ascending from the vagina, cervix, uterus, fallopian tubes, and ovaries
5. Endometriosis: Abnormal condition characterized by ectopic growth and function of endometrial tissue
6. Dilation and curettage: The widening of the cervix and scraping of the endometrial wall of the uterus
7. Abruptio placenta: The placenta detaches from the uterine wall prior to the birth of the fetus
8. Placenta previa: The placenta implants in the lower uterine segment
9. Hysterectomy: The surgical removal of the uterus.

Part II.

1. Multiparous
2. Colostrum
3. Stereotactic
4. Metrorrhagia
5. Menorrhagia
6. Amenorrhea
7. Oligomenorrhea

Part III.

A. follicular (Proliferative), luteal (Secretory), menstrual phase

B.
A. Labia majora
B. Mons pubis
C. Clitoris
D. urethral orifice
E. Labia minora
F. Vagina
G. Anus

Part IV.

A. Abdominal pain (new or more severe)
   Chest pain (new or more severe)
   Headache (new or more severe)
   Eye problems (new or more severe)
   Severe leg pain

B. 1. Chlamydia
   2. Gonorrhea
   3. Syphilis

C. Trichomoniasis

D. 1. Genital herpes
   2. Genital warts

E. 1. Fibroid
   2. Ovarian
   3. Fibrocystic breast disease

F. 1. Cervical
   2. Endometrial
   3. Ovarian
   4. Breast

G. Stage I. Dilation, effacement
   Stage II. Birth of the fetus
   Stage III. Placenta and amniotic membranes

Part V.
1. Spontaneous
2. Complete
3. Incomplete
4. Missed
5. Threatened

Part VI. A.

Type	Failure Rate	Contraindications	Side Effects
Condom (Barrier method)	2-10%	Allergic reactions to latex and other materials used in manufacturing condoms.	Possible allergic response to spermicide
Diaphragm or cervical cap (Barrier method)	2-19%	Latex, rubber, or spermicidal allergy; uterine prolapse; severe cystocele or rectocele.	Increased risk for UTI (diaphragm); increased risk abnormal Pap (cap)
Intrauterine device (IUD)	2-6%	Cervicitis, vaginitis, endometriosis, pelvic infection, Hx of STD or ectopic pregnancy	Increased risk of PID; spotting in 10-15% of users.
Depo Provera (DMPA)	0.5%	Intention of becoming pregnant within 1 year; breast cancer; liver disease	Return of fertility may be delayed 10-18 months; headache, weight gain, depression possible.
Norplant	0.5%	Thrombolytic or liver disease; vaginal bleeding; breast or genital tract cancer	Irregular bleeding frequent; headaches, weight gain, depression possible
Oral contraceptives (OCPs)	1%	Thromblytic, liver, or coronary artery disease; breast, liver, reproductive tract cancer; smoker over 35; diabetes; sickle cell disease	Nausea, breakthrough bleeding, breast tenderness, fluid retention; hypertension, elevated lipid levels

B. Discuss results of student research in class.

Part VII.
1. Ultrasonography: High-frequency sound waves used to produce images of soft tissues and fluid within the body
2. Chronic villus sampling: Cellular screening performed between 8 and 12 weeks of gestation for early detection of genetic or chromosomal disorders
3. Amniocentesis: Needle aspiration of amniotic fluid at 14 to 16 weeks' gestation to determine genetic and chromosomal abnormalities or inherited metabolic disorders
4. Alpha-fetoprotein (AFP): Maternal blood sample analyzed for the early diagnosis of neural tube defect or fetal congenital anomalies
5. Mammography: An x-ray image of the breast tissue performed to identify abnormal masses
6. Colposcopy: Visual examination of the vagina and the cervical surfaces through the use of a colposcope. The colposcope is a macroscope with a light source and a magnifying lens making it possible
7. Cryosurgery: A procedure done to treat chronic cervicitis and cervical erosion problems through the use of freezing temperatures

Part VIII.
1. 626.0
2. 626.6
3. 626.1
4. 626.2
5. 626.7

Part IX.
A. Lithotomy
B. Vaginal speculum
C. Gloves and lubricant

Chapter 38 Quiz
1. candidiasis
2. excessive menstrual blood loss
3. having given birth to more than 1 child
4. Pelvic Inflammatory Disease
5. a. gonorrhea or Chlamydia
   b. has been known to develop after pelvic surgery or abortion
6. T
7. absence of menstruation (for at least 6 months)
8. a. palpation or breast self examination
   b. mammogram
9. cervical cancer
10. 8

CHAPTER 39

Part I.
1. F
2. C
3. H
4. A
5. E
6. B
7. D
8. G

Part II.
1. *Colic* is a spasm of the GI tract usually seen in the newborn period or in early infancy, and is characterized by abdominal distress, usually in the late afternoon and evening. The cause is unknown, but it is thought that improper feeding techniques, overeating, swallowing excessive air while eating, and an allergy to cow's milk are all possible causes.

2. *Diarrhea* is the presence of loose, watery stools that can be caused by a variety of different microorganisms, including bacteria, viruses, and parasites. However, children can sometimes have diarrhea without having an infection, such as when diarrhea is caused by food allergies or as a result of taking medicines such as antibiotics.

3. *Infectious rhinitis,* also known as the common cold, is characterized by nasal congestion, low-grade fever, and general malaise. Most colds are self-limiting and run their course in about a week. In infants and young children, the primary concern is nasal congestion and loss of appetite.

4. *Asthma* is a chronic breathing disorder and is the most common chronic health problem among children. Asthma is the result of two specific reactions—bronchospasm and inflammation that produce a wheezing respiration.

5. *Bronchiolitis* is a viral infection of the small bronchi and bronchioles that usually affects children under 3 years of age. The infection varies in severity and is seen in children with a family history of asthma and those children exposed to cigarette smoke.

6. *Influenza* is an acute, highly contagious viral infection of the respiratory tract. Its highest incidence is in schoolchildren, but it is most severe in infants and toddlers. It is transmitted by direct contact with moist secretions. Children tend to have high fevers with influenza and are susceptible to pulmonary complications.

7. *Diphtheria* is an acute, contagious bacterial infection characterized by the production of a systemic toxin and a false membrane lining of the mucous membrane of the throat.

8. *Tetanus* is an acute, potentially fatal infection of the central nervous system as a result of a penetrating contaminated wound.

9. *Meningitis* is an inflammation of the membranes that cover the brain and spinal cord. The cause of this inflammation is infection with either bacterial or viruses. The cause of the inflammation may be either bacterial or viral.

10. *Hepatitis B virus* is a serious and potentially chronic infection of the liver. The virus can be transmitted across the placenta to a fetus or to the infant during the birth process if the mother is infected.

11. *Reye's syndrome* has been linked to the use of aspirin during a viral illness. It is an acute and sometimes fatal illness that is characterized by fatty invasion of the inner organs, especially the liver, and swelling of the brain.

12. *Cystic fibrosis* is an autosomal recessive genetic disorder (both parents are carriers) that causes exocrine glands to produce abnormally thick secretions. The lungs and pancreas are primarily affected causing the build up of mucus in the lungs and blockage of the pancreatic ducts, which prevents the excretion of pancreatic digestive enzymes and results in malabsorption problems in the child.

13. *Muscular dystrophy* is an X-linked genetic disease (passed from mothers to sons) that causes progressive muscle degeneration. The disease usually develops before age 5 with muscular weakness, frequent falls, waddling gait, possible swallowing problems, and difficulty climbing stairs.

14. *Rubella,* or *German measles,* is a contagious viral disease characterized by fever, symptoms of a mild upper respiratory tract infection, lymph node enlargement, arthralgia, and a diffuse, fine, red, maculopapular rash.

15. *Poliovirus* is the causative organism of poliomyelitis. There are three serologically distinct types of this very small RNA virus. Asymptomatic, mild, and paralytic forms of the disease occur.

Part III.

1. 6 months
2. 2
3. 18

Part IV.

A.

1. walk; is more autonomous; is toilet trained; sits at the table and eats with the family; can make simple sentences and understands the word "no"; vocabulary consists of up to 900 words; imitates by using verbal gestures that he or she has seen used

2. the child becomes increasingly independent; initiates activities; has mastered many gross motor skills; is perfecting fine motor development; uses full simple and even complex sentences but remains quite literal; mastering nonverbal communication skills; vocabulary includes more than 2000 words; during this period, children need to develop social skills, such as sharing and taking part in peer-group activities.

3. fine motor skills and can paint, draw, and play an instrument: enjoys team activities; expands reading and writing skills; intellectual skills are developing; refining social skills; sense of self-achievement and self-worth is developing; learning and testing the rules for socializing outside the immediate family as an independent individual.

4. attempting to establish an adult identity; experimenting with adult roles and behavior patterns. Traditional values learned in childhood may be questioned; peer relationships take on new importance; developing the emotional maturity and motivation to make beneficial decisions; looks to family for encouragement and guidance in making decisions that will help develop self-confidence, to become patient and less impulsive and self-centered.

B.

Complaint	Triage Questions
Pain	Onset, frequency, duration of pain. On a scale of 1-10, how severe is the pain? Where is the exact location? Was there any accident involved (include details)? Has the pain gotten worse over time? Has the pain interfered with sleep? Is there associated fever, vomiting, diarrhea, or rash?
Gastro-intestinal	Onset, duration, frequency of symptoms. Has the child been vomiting longer than 24 hours without improvement? Is the child receiving clear liquids only? Is the child dehydrated (dry mouth, no urination in 8-10 hours, listless)? If diarrhea, were there more than 5-6 watery stools in 12 hours? Does the child have other symptoms (vomiting, fever over 103°, rapid breathing)?

Complaint	Triage Questions
Respiratory	Onset, duration, frequency of symptoms. Describe the child's breathing. Has child been diagnosed with breathing disorder? Is prescribed treatment being used? Are there any other symptoms (severe headache, stiff neck, fever, cough)? If coughing, what does it sound like? Are there signs of a sore throat or earache?

Part V.

Divide 20 by 2.2

20 lbs divided by 2.2 = 9.09 kg

Part VI. Discuss results of student research in class.

Part VII.

1. Standing, kicking, running, balance
2. Word comprehension, follow simple commands, use of subjects, counting
3. Reaching, grasping, piling blocks, drawing
4. Playing games, using fork and spoon, dressing, brushing teeth

Part VIII.

A. Answers may include the following:
1. Position healthy full-term infants on their back or side to sleep.
2. Stairs should be carpeted and protected with nonaccordian gates.
3. Install and maintain smoke detectors on each floor and near sleeping areas.
4. Develop and practice a plan of escape in the event of a fire
5. Put a self-latching lock on basement stairs.
6. Store dangerous products out of reach in cabinets with locks.
7. Post the numbers of the Poison Control Center and the child's physician on all phones.
8. Teach children to call 911.
9. Regularly inspect toys for sharp or removable parts.
10. Use an approved car seat that is appropriate for the child's age.

B. All threats to a child's physical and/or mental welfare must be reported

Part IX.

1. Bananas, rice, applesauce, and tea
2. Immunization against measles, mumps, and rubella
3. Immunization against diphtheria, pertussis, and tetanus
4. Scoliosis

Chapter 39 Quiz

1. Asthma
2. Croup
3. Varicella
4. meningitis
5. Mumps, measles, and rubella
6. pediatrics
7. 7 to 7.5 pounds
8. 2
9. colic
10. viral

CHAPTER 40

Part I.

1. Kyphosis: An excessive backward curvature of the thoracic spine
2. Lordosis: Abnormal or excessive curves toward the front of the body in the thoracic or lumbar region
3. Luxation: Dislocation of a bone from its normal anatomical location
4. Subluxation: Incomplete dislocation
5. Thoracic: Referring to the chest
6. Tendon: Fibrous band of tissue that attaches muscle to bone
7. Ligament: Slightly elastic band of tissue binding joints together and connecting various bones and cartilages

Part II.

1. Crepitation: A crackling sound made when joints move.
2. Epiphysis: both ends of long bones that allow for the growing of the bone prior to adulthood.
3. Corticosteroids: natural or synthetic hormones associated with the adrenal cortex used to treat inflammatory conditions
4. Goniometer: an instrument used to measure angles of a joint
5. Ligament: slightly elastic band of tissue binding joints together and connecting various bones and cartilages

Part III.

A.

A. Head of humerus

B. Humerus

C. Radius

D. Ulna

E. Carpals

F. Metacarpals and phalanges

G. Greater trochanter

H. Head of femur

I. Lesser trochanter

J. Femur

K. Patella

L. Fibula

M. Tibia

N. Tarsals

O. Metatarsals

P. Phalanges

B.

A. origin

B. tendons

C. muscle

D. tendon

E. insertion

C.

Voluntary

Smooth

Cardiac

D.

1. T

2. F

3. T

4. T

5. T

Part IV.

Arm

1. Rotate

2. Extend

3. Supinate/pronate

4. Adduct

Hip/Leg

1. Abduct

2. Flex

3. Hyperextend

4. Extend

Head

1. Flex/extend

2. Rotate

Foot

1. Dorsiflex

2. Plantar flex

3. Eversion

4. Inversion

B. Gout: Syndrome caused by inflammatory response to uric acid production resulting in crystal formation in joints.
Osteoarthritis: Degenerative joint disease that is not associated with inflammation.
Rheumatoid arthritis: Systemic autoimmune disease causing chronic inflammation of connective tissues, primarily in the joints.

Part V. The photos show Herberden nodes, ulnar deviation, swan-neck deformity, and Boutonniere deformity. These deformities are seen with rheumatoid arthritis.
How long have you had the pain and tenderness?
Rate the pain on a scale of 1-10, with 1 being little pain and 10 being unbearable pain.
When did the abnormal functions of the hand first appear?
Has anyone in your family had arthritis?
What anti-inflammatory drugs are you taking?
How long have you taken these medications?

Part VI. Discuss results of student research in class.

Part VII.

A. For scoliosis assessment, have the patient lean forward and allow arms to dangle. From the rear view, assess the height of the patient's scapula.

B. ESR (Erythrocyte sedimentation rate): the speed of settling of red blood cells in a vertical glass. Increased rate indicates inflammation.

Part VIII.

1. 724.3

2. 724.02

3. 724.2

4. 724.1

5. 724.70

Part IX.

1. D

2. F

3. A

4. J

5. N
6. B
7. I
8. H
9. C
10. G
11. M
12. L
13. K
14. E

Chapter 40 Quiz

1. Tibia
2. twelve
3. open
4. Systemic lupus erythematosus
5. Rheumatoid
6. diaphysis
7. arthritis
8. tendon
9. ligament
10. extend

CHAPTER 41

Part I.

1. Anoxia: Absence of oxygen in the tissues
2. Ataxia: Failure or irregularity of muscle actions and coordination
3. Atrophy: Decrease in the size of a normally developed organ
4. Coma: An unconscious state from which the patient cannot be aroused
5. Diplopia: Double vision
6. Gait: The way a person walks

Part II.

1. Idiopathic: Unknown cause.
2. Ipsilateral: Pertaining to the same side of the body.
3. Contralateral: Pertaining to the opposite side of the body.

Part III.

A. 1. Parietal
   2. Occipital
   3. Cerebellum
   4. Frontal lobe
   5. Temporal lobe
   6. Pons
   7. Medulla oblongata

B.
1. CSF (cerebrospinal fluid) is a clear fluid that circulates continuously through the ventricles and around the brain and spinal cord and carries nutrients and removes wastes.
2. Controls balance, equilibrium, posture, and muscle coordination.
3. Controls reflexes such as moving the eyes; serves as a sensory relay station for input coming into the brain from the body.
4. Has vital role in vision, hearing, respirations, heart rate, blood pressure, and waking and sleeping.
5. Control of the autonomic nervous system that is responsible for maintaining homeostasis where higher learning and most thinking take place.
6. Spinal nerves carry information to and from your brain through the spinal cord and relay information to and from the sense organs and muscles of the face and neck.
7. Extend from the CNS to control activities of the face and head.
8. Autonomic nerves control homeostasis, or keep the body running smoothly, much like a thermostat controls the temperature in a room.

C

CN I:	Olfactory
CN II:	Optic
CN III:	Oculomotor
CN IV:	Trochlear
CN V:	Trigeminal
CN VI:	Abducent
CN VII:	Facial
CN VIII:	Acoustic
CN IX:	Glossopharyngeal
CN X:	Vagus
CN XI:	Spinal accessory
CN XII:	Hypoglossal

Part IV.

A. An embolus is foreign material blocking a blood vessel, frequently a blood clot that has broken away from some other part of the body. A thrombus is a blood clot adhered to a vessel.
B. T
C. Stroke
D. T
E. aura
F. petit mal

G. Parkinson's, mask, rigidity, viral, dopamine
H. Multiple sclerosis
I. Amyotrophic lateral sclerosis
J. Bell's palsy
K. median, wrist

Part V.
1. post-traumatic stress syndrome
2. attention deficit disorder
3. learning disability
4. Answers may include the following: hopelessness, sadness, anger, irritability, sleeping too much or too little, constipation, irregular menses, loss of interest in sex, social withdrawal, and low self-esteem.

Part VI. Discuss results of student research in class.

Part VII.
1. Magnetic Resonance Imaging creates a hologram to show the location of tumors, plaques, or bleeding within the brain using magnetic fields.
2. Computed Tomography uses computer processing to generate an x-ray image showing the various tissue densities in transverse sections (slices) of various body tissues.
3. Electroencephalography (EEG) is the recording of changes in the electrical impulses in various areas of the brain by means of electrodes placed on the scalp, on the brain surface, or within the brain itself.
4. Lumbar puncture (spinal tap) is done to collect several ml of CSF to be cultured, analyzed for glucose and protein, and examined through the microscope for the presence of bacteria and blood cells.

Part VIII.
A. 1. 73221
   2. 70450
   3. 95819
   4. 62270

B. 1. 342.10
   2. 342.01
   3. 342.90
   4. 342.12
   5. 342.02

Part IX.
1. CVA: Cerebral vascular accident or stroke that occurs when a vessel in the brain ruptures or totally occludes as a result of cerebrovascular disease.

2. ALS: Amyotrophic lateral sclerosis is a progressive, destructive neurologic disease that results in muscle atrophy.
3. MS: Multiple sclerosis results from progressive inflammation and deterioration of the myelin sheaths, leaving the nerve fibers exposed and leading to a variety of neurological symptoms.
4. PTSD: Post-traumatic stress disorder may follow the person who was a part of or witnessed some terrifying, horrendous, or violent physical or emotional event.
5. ADD: Attention deficit disorder is a condition that has such symptoms as short attention span, easy distractibility, lack of self control, impulsive behavior, and hyperactivity.
6. TIA: Transient ischemic attacks are also called mini-strokes that occur when the blood supply to a particular part of the brain is inadequate for a short period of time, usually seconds to minutes.

Chapter 41 Quiz
1. 20%
2. cerebrum
3. cerebellum
4. smell
5. parasympathetic
6. Cerebrovascular accident
7. Transient Ischemic Attack
8. Parkinson's
9. Multiple sclerosis
10. Bell's palsy

CHAPTER 42

Part I.
1. C
2. A
3. B

Part II.
1. Polydipsia
2. ACTH
3. Insulin
4. Ketosis
5. TSH
6. Polyphagia
7. ADH
8. Polyuria

Part III.

1. oxytocin, antidiuretic hormones

2. a. Thyroid stimulating hormone (TSH)
   b. Adrenocorticotropic hormone (ACTH)
   c. Prolactin (PRL)
   d. Growth hormone (GH)
   e. Follicle stimulating hormone (FSH)
   f. Luteinizing hormone (LH)

3. a. Gigantism
   b. Acromegaly
   c. Dwarfism

Part IV.

A.

Location	Disease	Common Signs/Symptoms
Adrenal cortex	Addison's	Weakness, decreased endurance, bronzing of skin, anorexia, dehydration, weight loss, decreased tolerance to cold, anxiety, depression; labs: low serum levels of sodium and glucose; increased potassium levels
	Cushings	Obese trunk, but normal extremities; thin skin, slow to heal, Moonlike face
	Pheochromocytoma	Headache, palpitation, sweating, nervousness, hyperglycemia, nausea, vomiting, syncope.

Location	Disease	Signs/Symptoms
Pancreas	Diabetes mellitus	glucosuria, polyuria, polydipsia, polyphagia, rapid weight loss, drowsiness and fatigue, itching of the skin, visual disturbances, and skin infections.
	Hyperinsulinism	Hypoglycemia, hunger, shakiness, and diaphoresis

Location	Disease	Signs/Symptoms
Pituitary gland (anterior lobe)	Acromegaly	Gradual, marked enlargement of bones of face, jaw and extremities. Tongue may also enlarge.
	Gigantism	Long bones grow excessively; person may reach 8 ft tall
	Dwarfism	Extreme short stature; associated with differing levels of mental retardation

Location	Disease	Signs/Symptoms
Pituitary gland (posterior gland)	Diabetes insipidus	Extreme polyuria and polydipsia

Location	Disease	Signs/Symptoms
Thyroid diseases	Hyperthyroidism	Nervousness, tremor, constant hunger, weight loss, fatigue, intolerance to heat, palpitations, diarrhea, may have exopthalmos
	Hypothyroidism	Weight gain, mental and physical lethargy, dry skin, constipation, arthritis, intolerance to cold, slowing of metabolic process.

B. Type 1 diabetes usually develops before the age of 30 and is characterized by a complete absence of insulin production. Patients need daily insulin injections to survive. Type 2 diabetes develops gradually because of an insufficient amount of insulin or resistance at the target cell site or both.

C. Insulin shock occurs if an adult patient's blood glucose level is below 45 to 60 mg/dl. In the case of a diabetic coma, the diabetic is unable to use glucose for energy because insulin is either absent or insufficient or there is resistance to insulin at the target cell site and glucose levels build in the blood causing loss of consciousness.

D.
1. Polyuria: excessive urine production.
2. Polydipsia: excessive thirst.
3. Polyphagia: increased appetite.

E. 2-4, strokes, coronary artery disease, cigarette smoking
F. new blindness
G. Kidney

Part V.
A. Students to document correctly. Discuss diabetic foot care.

Part VI.

Synthroid	Hypothyroidism
Hydrocortisone	Adrenal insufficiency
DDAVP	Treat diabetes insipidus
Diabeta	Oral hypoglycemic, diabetes mellitus, Type 2: Stimulates pancreatic islet beta cell insulin release
Glucophage	Oral Hypoglycemic, diabetes mellitus, Type 2: decreases hepatic glucose production and intestinal absorption
Glynase	Oral Hypoglycemic, diabetes mellitus, Type 2: Stimulates pancreatic islet beta cell insulin release
Micronase	Oral hypoglycemic, diabetes mellitus, Type 2: Stimulates pancreatic islet beta cell insulin release
Glucovance	Oral hypoglycemic, diabetes mellitus, Type 2: combination drug
Avandia	Oral hypoglycemic, diabetes mellitus, Type 2: Increases insulin sensitivity
Actos	Oral hypoglycemic, diabetes mellitus, Type 2: Increases insulin sensitivity

Part VII.
A.
1. TSH: Indicates how hard the pituitary gland is having to work in order to stimulate or suppress the thyroid gland.
2. Sodium: Detects hyponatremia and hypernatremia. These are low and high electrolyte levels.
3. Potassium: Detects hypokalemia and hyperkalemia. These are low and high electrolyte levels.
4. Fasting blood sugar: Blood sugar drawn after a period of not eating. Shows blood sugar at lowest level.
5. Glucose tolerance test: The patient drinks a high-glucose fluid and the blood sugar is checked at several intervals. Shows the body's ability to use large doses of insulin within 2-3 hours.
6. Glycohemoglobin: Measures the average blood sugar over a period of months.

Part VIII.
1. Hypoglycemia, Insulin shock, juvenile (uncontrolled) 250.83
2. Ketoacidosis, NIDDM (Uncontrolled) 250.12
3. Hyperosmolar nonketotoic coma, insulin dependent (uncontrolled) 250.23
4. Controlled juvenile diabetes 250.01
5. Uncontrolled Non-Insulin Diabetes 250.02
6. Diabetes type 2: 250.00
7. Controlled Adult Onset Diabetes 250.00
8. Uncontrolled IDDM 250.03
9. Diabetic Cataract, Controlled, Juvenile onset 250.51 and 366.41
10. Diabetic Renal Failure, NIDDM (Uncontrolled) 250.42 and 583.81

Part IX.
1. T
2. F
3. increase
4. thyroid
5. T

Part X. Students to follow a diabetic diet for 24 hours. Discuss results of student research in class.

Chapter 42 Quiz
1. oxytocin
   antidiuretic hormone
2. gigantism, acromegaly
3. Grave's
4. increases
5. insulin dependent, noninsulin dependent

6. T
7. High
8. b
9. what the glucose levels have been for the past 2-3 months.
10. T

CHAPTER 43

Part I.

A.

Apnea	Absence of breathing
Atelectasis	Collapsed lung
Dyspnea	Difficulty breathing
Empyema	Accumulation of pus in the pleural space
Hempotysis	Expectoration of blood
Hemothorax	Accumulation of blood and fluid in the pleural cavity
Hypercapnia	Greater than normal amounts of carbon dioxide in the blood
Hyperpnea	Deep, rapid, labored respiration that may occur because of exercise or pain and fever.
Hypoxemia	Low level of oxygen in the blood
Orthopnea	Person must sit or stand to breathe comfortably
Pleurisy	Inflammation of the parietal pleura causing dyspnea and stabbing pain; friction rub may be auscultated
Pneumothorax	Collection of air or gas in the pleural space causing the lung to collapse
Pyothorax	Collection of pus in the pleural cavity from infection
Rhinoplasty	Plastic surgery to repair or alter the structure of the nose
Rhinorrhea	Excessive watery drainage from the nose
Tachypnea	Abnormally rapid rate of breathing
Thoracotomy	Surgical opening into the thoracic cavity

Part II.

1. Lung
2. Mantoux
3. Oximetry
4. Endoscopic

Part III.

A.

1. Anterior axillary
2. Mid-axillary
3. Posterior axillary

B.

1. Respiratory center
2. Pharynx
3. Esophagus
4. Mediastinum
5. Right lung
6. Diaphragm
7. Sinuses
8. Nasal cavity
9. Tongue
10. Epiglottis
11. Larynx
12. Trachea
13. Bronchial tube
14. Bronchioles and alveoli
15. Bronchus
16. Left lung

C.

1. Right upper lobe
2. Right middle lobe
3. Right lower lobe
4. Left upper lobe
5. Left lower lobe

Part IV.

True or False

1. T
2. T

Matching

1. B
2. C
3. A

Part V.

A. Students to practice documentation.

Part VI.

A.

Drug	Usage
Oxygen	Treat shortness of breath or when pulse oximeter shows saturation less than 90-92%
INH	Treat those with positive TB test but without secondary infection. Must take for 6-12 months.
Allegra	Antihistamine, used to treat allergies
Rifampin	To treat active TB; given with INH, pyrazomamide, streptomycin
Zyrtec	Antihistamine, used to treat allergies
Prednisone	Used with various respiratory problems to treat tissue inflammation
Ventolin	Rescue inhaler for asthma
Azmacort	Inhaler to treat tissue inflammation

B.
1. Nasal cannula
2. Simple face mask
3. Non-rebreathing face mask

Part VII.
A. Clubbing of nails. It is usually a result of longterm hypoxia.

B.
1. Complete blood count: Includes a differential count to determine whether the asthma attack is allergy related
2. Chest radiographs: Show changes in the lungs from the mucous obstructions
3. Spirometric evaluation: Measures the degree of airflow obstruction

Part VIII.
1. 492.8
2. 491.0
3. 491.8
4. 493.90
5. 493.10
6. 490
7. 493.0
8. 494.1

Part IX.
1. T

2. a. Skin test
   b. Chest x-ray
   c. Sputum culture

3. Lower

4. a. Nose
   b. Pharynx
   c. Larynx

Chapter 43 Quiz
1. asthma, emphysema, and chronic bronchitis
2. no breathing
3. pharyngitis
4. lungs
5. colds, sinusitis
6. T
7. hoarseness
8. B
9. runny nose
10. trachea

CHAPTER 44

Part I.
A. 1. Murmur
   2. Intermittent
   3. Lupus

Part II.
1. peri
2. epi
3. myo
4. endo

Part III.
A. Aorta
B. Pulmonary arteries
C. Pulmonary vein
D. Left atria
E. Aortic valve
F. Mitral valve
G. Left ventricle
H. Superior vena cava
I. Pulmonic valve
J. Right atria
K. Tricuspid valve
L. Inferior vena cava

Part IV.

A. Coronary artery disease

B.
1. Abdominal or mid-back pain
2. Jaw pain
3. Indigestion
4. Extreme fatigue
5. Aching in both arms

C.
1. Current chest pain that is crushing, pressing, or radiating to the arms, upper back, or jaw
2. Sweating, difficulty breathing, nausea, indigestion, or dizziness
3. A history of coronary artery disease, myocardial infarction, or angina
4. A change in the pattern of the angina
5. Chest pain that occurs when resting or with minimal exertion

D.
Stroke, AMI, CHF, renal failure, angina

E.
Death of cardiac muscle following clot formation inside the coronary arteries

F.

Type	Definition	Cause
Cardiogenic	Low cardiac output due to inability of heart to pump	Acute MI, arrhythmias, pulmonary embolism, and CHF
Hypovolemic	Excessive loss of blood or body fluids	GI bleeding; internal or external hemorrhage; excessive loss of plasma or body fluids; burns
Neurogenic	Peripheral vascular dilation due to neurologic injury or disorder	Spinal cord injury, emotional stress, drug reaction
Anaphylactic	Systemic hypersensitivity to an allergen causing respiratory distress and vascular collapse	Drug, vaccine, shellfish, nuts, insect venom, or chemical
Septic (septicemia)	Systemic vasodilation due to the release of bacterial endotoxins	Systemic infection or bacteremia

Part V. Students will practice documentation.

Part VI.
1. atenolol, metoprolol, propranolol (beta blockers end in "lol")
2. benazepril, catopril, enalapril (generic names end in "pril")
3. atorvastatin, lovastatin, simvastatin (cholesterol meds end in "statin")
4. warfarin
5. digoxin
6. hydrochlorothiazide, furosemide, triamterene and HCTZ

Part VII.
1. EEG or EKG: Electrocardiograph: used to provide information on electrical impulses of the heart that provide heart rhythm.
2. CPK and LDH: Cardiac enzymes: shows heart muscle damage
3. ESR: Erythrocyte sedimentation rate show inflammatory processes.

Part VIII.
1. 391.2
2. 391.1
3. 391.0
4. 391.0
5. 391.1

Part IX.
1. atria, ventricles
2. SA
3. Congestive heart failure
4. Left-sided
5. Right, right
6. T

Chapter 44 Quiz
1. Lasix, HCTZ, Dyazide
2. Heart attack

3. a
4. Mitral value prolapse
5. Insufficient (weak and floppy), stenosis (stiff)
6. Cor pulmonale
7. left
8. b
9. digxoin
10. Septic, anaphylactic, cardiogenic, neurogenic, hypovolemic

CHAPTER 45

Part I.

1. Disease is normal and unavoidable.
2. Older workers are less productive than younger one.
3. Most older people end up in long-term care facilities.
4. Most aging people have no interest in, or capacity for, sexual relations.
5. Aging people are resistant to change and cannot learn new things

Part II.

Body System	Age-Related Changes	Health Promotion
Cardiovascular	Arteriosclerosis and atherosclerotic plaque build up reduces blood flow to major organs; hypertension. #1 killer of women and men in their 60s	Exercise regularly; control weight; diet rich in fruits, vegetables, and whole grains; monitor cholesterol and blood glucose levels
Central nervous system	Brain shrinks by 10% between 30 and 90; takes longer to learn new material; attention span and language remains same. Depression, vascular disease, and drug reactions may be cause	Aerobic exercise to increase blood flow to CNS and maintaining mental activities
Endocrine	Women over age 50 have sharp decline in estrogen and men more gradual decline in testosterone	Possible hormone repleacement therapy
Gastrointestinal	Decline in gastric juices and enzymes by age 60; decreased peristalsis w/increased constipation; some nutrients not absorbed as well	High-fiber diet to prevent constipation and diverticulitis; exercise and folic acid reduce risk of colon cancer
Musculoskeletal	Muscle mass decreases; tendency to gain weight; gradual loss of bone density; deterioration of joint cartilage	Strength training to increase muscle mass; stretching to remain limber; exercise; vitamin D and calcium supplements
Pulmonary	At age 55 the lungs become less elastic and the chest wall gradually stiffens making oxygenation more difficult	Quit smoking and do regular aerobic exercise
Sensory organs	Hearing intact through mid-50s but declines by 25% by age 80; oral problems common; skin thins and loses elasticity with age; presbyopia after 40; cataracts common after 60	Avoid exposure to loud noise and use hearing aids; maintain good dental hygiene; avoid sun damage to skin; annual eye examinations and diets rich in dark green leafy vegetables to avoid cataracts and macular degeneration

Body System	Age-Related Changes	Health Promotion
Urinary	Kidneys become less efficient; bladder muscles weaken; 1/3 of seniors experience incontinence; prostate enlargement common	Pelvic exercises, drugs, or surgery for incontinence; annual PSA monitoring for males
Sexuality	Impotence not a symptom of normal aging; men over age 50 may have some altered function. Menopause causes vaginal narrowing and dryness causing painful intercourse	Men should maintain cardiovascular health with exercise, weight control, no smoking. Women use vaginal lubricants or estrogen cream

Part III.

1. Recommend a home humidifier to obtain artificial humidification.
2. Advise elderly patients to bathe less frequently using warm water, NOT hot water.
3. Recommend that patients use a mild soap or cleansing cream such as Aveenobar, Basis, or Dove soap.
4. Remind the patient to wear protective clothing in cold weather.
5. Suggest establishing a regimen of moisturizers for treatment of dry skin.
6. Creams and moisturizers should be applied *after* getting out of the bathtub or shower to decrease the possibility of falls.

Part IV.

1. Use assistive devices such as adaptive silverware, tub seat or shower chair, electric razor, and reaching devices.
2. Assist with gripping devices as needed (wait for the patient to place his or her hand around a cup or help them with it before letting go).
3. Need more time to complete tasks but prefer to do so independently so *slow down.*
4. Stroke victims should be supported on the weak side when walking or transferring from chair to examination table.
5. Physician may recommend physical therapy for range of motion exercises.
6. Encourage activity; lack of activity causes decreased ability to function.

Part V.

1. Perform regular hearing and vision testing so that patients are aware of possible dangers.
2. Family and patient should be educated on the side effects of medications, especially those that may make the patient dizzy or sleepy.

3. Limit the use of alcohol.
4. If needed, use assistive devices consistently for support.
5. Wear low-heeled, rubber-soled shoes with good support.
6. Avoid going outside in icy weather.
7. Encourage regular weight-bearing exercise for bone strength.
8. Assess the home for possible dangers; keep emergency numbers handy.

Part VI.

1. Hypertension, diabetes, heart disease since they decrease blood flow to the brain.
2. Environmental exposure to lead.
3. High stress levels.
4. Sedentary lifestyle and lack of social interaction.
5. Environmental exposure to lead.
6. Low education level.
7. Smoking and substance abuse.

Part VII.

1. First Stage: Occurs 2 to 4 years leading up to diagnosis; memory loss affects job performance; confusion and disorientation common; mood or personality changes; has difficulty making decisions, paying bills, gets lost easily, withdraws from others, loses things.
2. Second Stage: Two to 10 years after diagnosis; increased memory loss and confusion; shorter attention span; restless; makes constant repetitive statements; exhibits problems with reading, writing, and numbers; may be irritable or suspicious; exhibits motor problems; has difficulty recognizing close friends and family members.
3. Terminal Stage: One to 3 years; does not recognize family; weight loss; unable to care for self; incontinent of bladder and bowel; requires complete care.

Part VIII. Use expanded speech, gestures, demonstrations, or written instructions in block print. If the message must be repeated, paraphrase or find other words to say the same thing.

Part IX. Kyphosis is pictured. People with osteoporosis can develop a hunchback appearance. Calcium supplements and estrogen replacement for females during menopause is recommended. The deformity is commonly called a dowager's hump.

Chapter 45 Quiz

1. a. Dry skin
   b. Seborrheic keratosis
2. male balding
3. b
4. Presbycusis is associated with normal aging and causes a decreased ability to hear high frequencies and to discriminate sounds.
5. Glaucoma results from a blockage to the outflow of aqueous humor, which causes an increase in intraocular pressure and damage to the optic nerve
6. Cloudy or opaque areas in the eye lens
7. Falls
8. Do Not Resuscitate
9. Viagra
10. Periodic limb movement disease

CHAPTER 46

Part I.

1. D
2. E
3. A
4. B
5. L
6. M
7. N
8. G
9. H
10. I
11. C
12. J
13. K
14. F

Part II.

1. 28742 atria
2. 8368742537 (ventricles)
3. 8378446 (vertigo)
4. 243872283 (bifurcate)

Part III. (1) The electrical conduction system of the heart originates the cardiac impulse in the sinoatrial (SA) node and the wave passes to the atrioventricular (AV) node. The AV node sends the impulse to the bundle of His, to the bundle branches, continuing to the muscle fibers known as the Purkinje fibers. The Purkinje fibers totally encase both ventricles causing the ventricles to contract.

Structures of the Heart

1. Aorta
2. Pulmonary artery
3. Pulmonary vein
4. Mitral valve
5. Purkinje fibers
6. Right and left bundles
7. Left ventricle
8. Inferior vena cava
9. Right ventricle
10. Tricuspid valve
11. AV node
12. SA node
13. Superior vena cava

Precordial Leads

1. A. V1, B. V2, C. V3, D. V6, E. V4, F. V5
2. Students will draw in correct lead placement. Refer to Figure 46-5 in textbook.
3. Normal sinus rhythm
4. Sinus bradycardia
5. Sinus tachycardia
6. Ventricular tachycardia
7. Ventricular fibrillation
8. Asystole
9. Defibrillation is used to correct v-tach and v-fib. Both are deadly dysrhythmias.

Part IV.

1. P
2. QRS
3. PR
4. Repolarization
5. 5
6. 0.04
7. 0.2
8. right, left
9. II
10. Left
11. AVR
12. AVL

13. AVF
14. 10
15. wandering
16. Somatic tremor
17. Baseline interruption
18. AC
19. Stress
20. Holter

Part V.
A. dots and dashes
B. VR VL VF
C. V1, V2, V3, V4, V5, and V6

Part VI.
1. 93010
2. 93005
3. 93230
4. 93227

Part VII.
1. b
2. Chest
3. a
4. 1 mm every second
5. augmented
6. a. LL
   b. RA
   c. RL
7. a. AVR
   b. AVL
   c. AVF
8. a. V1
   b. V2
   c. V3
   d. V4
   e. V5
   f. V6
9. Atrial depolarization
10. Premature ventricular contractions

Chapter 46 Quiz
1. depolarization
2. QRS
3. ST
4. 1
5. bipolar
6. SA
7. tachycardia
8. bradycardia
9. arrhythmia or dysrhythmia
10. False

CHAPTER 47

Part I.
1. Radiography
2. radiopaque
3. Fluoroscopy
4. CT
5. Nuclear

Anatomical Position Matching
1. G
2. K
3. L
4. A
5. F
6. H
7. B
8. I
9. D
10. E
11. C
12. J
13. N
14. M

Part II.
1. 674 (MRI)
2. 7666472749 (sonography)
3. 5283725 (lateral)
4. 6254Q83 (oblique)
5. 29425 (axial)

Part III.
1. Superior
2. Proximal
3. Posterior (dorsal)
4. Anterior (ventral)
5. Inferior
6. Sagittal plane
7. Frontal plane
8. Lateral

Part IV.
1. T
2. F
3. T
4. lead
5. roentgen
6. rad
7. rem
8. T

Part V.
A. Posterioanterior (PA)
B. Anterioposterior (AP)
C. Right lateral

Part VI.
1. 71260
2. 71020
3. 71550
4. 71010

Part VII.
1. prone
2. recumbent
3. dorsal recumbent
4. lateral recumbent
5. ventral recumbent
6. supine
7. upright

Chapter 47 Quiz
1. fluoroscopy
2. angiography
3. facing
4. lateral
5. transverse
6. radiograph
7. CT
8. mammogram
9. MRI
10. contrast media

CHAPTER 48

Part I.
1. Hemolyzed
2. Pipet
3. Analyte
4. Specimen
5. Carcinogenic
6. Resolution
7. Aliquot
8. Caustic
9. Diluent
10. Anticoagulant
11. Stat
12. Teratogenic
13. Exudates
14. Hematoma
15. Cerebrospinal fluid
16. Preservatives
17. Referral laboratory

Part II.
1. ASCP
2. AMT
3. AAMA
4. ABHES

Part III.
1. Precise meter always reads 10% too high; accurate meter is correct within 5 to 9%
2. a. 1350
   b. 0150

3. A. Eyepieces
   B. Revolving nosepiece
   C. Arm
   D. Objectives
   E. Stage
   F. Iris diaphragm lever
   G. Condenser
   H. Mechanical stage
   I. Light source
   J. Fine adjustment
   K. Coarse adjustment
   L. Base

Part IV.
1.
A. When you enter and before leaving this area
B. Before and after every patient procedure
C. After contact with body fluid even if gloves were worn
D. Before and after eating
E. Before and after using the restroom

2.
A. Physical
B. Chemical
C. Biological

3. Qualitative – positive or negative showing the quality is either present or not
   Quantitive – a numerical value that precedes the quantity that is present

4.
A. Urinalysis
B. Hematology
C. Blood chemistry
D. Microbiology

5. A. B
   B. A
   C. D
   D. C
   E. D

F. B
G. C
H. B

6. Materials Safety Data Sheet
7. U.S. Department of Labor's Occupational Safety and Health Administration sets safety standards for laboratories
8. Clinical Laboratory Improvement Amendments: waived test and moderate-and high-complexity tests
9. Physician's name, account number, and phone number
   Patient's full name, surname first
   Patient's address
   Patient's insurance information
   Patient's age, date of birth, and gender
   Source of specimen
   Date and time of collection
   Specific tests requested
   Medications the patient is taking
   Possible diagnosis
   Indication of whether test is stat

Part V.
1. a. F 98.6*   C 37*
   b. F 59*-86*   C 15*-30*
   c. F 32*   C 0*
   d. F35*-46*   C 2*-8*

2. Left cylinder 20 mL
   Right cylinder 80 mL
   a. 9 mL
   b. 18 mL
   c. 19 mL
   d. 45 mL
   e. balancing—tubes of equal size and volume are directly across from each other

Part VI. Dysuria, urinalysis

Part VII.
1. T
2. 400
3. F
4. arm, base

Chapter 48 Quiz
1. aliquot
2. hemolyzed
3. Material safety data sheets
4. when you leave or enter the lab, before and after eating, before and after going

to the restroom, after each contact with blood or body fluids, after removing gloves
5. to ensure accuracy and eliminate errors
6. waived
7. CLIA
8. quantitative
9. qualitative
10. OSHA

CHAPTER 49
Part I.
1. Myoglobinuria
2. Phenylalanine
3. Ischemia
4. Enzymatic reaction
5. Polymorphonuclear
6. Glycosuria
7. Mononuclear
8. Refractile
9. Renal threshold
10. Filtrate

Part II.
1. PH
2. Foam
3. odor
4. Casts

Part III.
A.
1. Spleen
2. Renal artery
3. Renal vein
4. Left kidney
5. Inferior vena cava
6. Abdominal aorta
7. Common iliac vein
8. Common iliac artery
9. Urethra
10. Urinary bladder
11. Right ureter
12. Right kidney
13. 10th rib
14. Liver
15. Adrenal glands

B.
1. renal artery
2. renal vein
3. renal pelvis

4. ureter
5. renal cortex
6. medulla
7. renal capsule
8. calyx
9. renal pyramid
10. arteries and veins

Part IV.

A.
1. Random specimen
2. First morning specimen
3. Two hour postprandial urine
4. Twenty-four hour urine specimen
5. Second-voided specimen
6. Catheterized specimen
7. Suprapubic specimen
8. Clean catch, midstream urine specimen

B.
1. Physical
2. Chemical
3. Microscopic

C. The urinometer is a sealed glass float with a calibrated paper scale in its stem.
D. The refractometer measures the refraction of light through solids in a liquid.
E. Clinitest tablets test based on glucosuria and is used to detect other sugars present in urine. Acetest tablets test for the presence of ketones in urine.
F. To measure the protein in the urine
G. Detects the presence of hCG in urine which is based upon reactions that occur between antibodies and antigens.
H. Detects human chorionic gonadotropin, a hormone produced by the placenta.

Part V.

1. A. RBC
   B. WBC

2. A. Bacteria
   B. Flagellates
   C. Yeasts

Part VI.

1. 81002
2. 81003
3. 81000
4. 81001

Part VII. Students are to draw urine crystals. Calcium oxalate is shaped like kites. Triple phosphates are shaped like envelopes.

Chapter 49 Quiz

1. 12
2. Clean catch mid-stream
3. 20
4. Void, discard, record time, save urine for 24 hours, keep on ice, void at same time the next a.m., save, and transport on ice
5. clear, straw, yellow, amber
6. kidneys
7. nephron
8. 1200
9. date, time, name, type of collection
10. specific gravity

CHAPTER 50

Part I.

1. Bifurcation
2. Hematocrit
3. Serum
4. Plasma
5. Hemoconcentration
6. Syncope
7. Hemolysis
8. Thixotropic gel
9. Antiseptic

Phone-etics Game

1. EDTA
2. serum
3. stat
4. latex

Part III.

1. a. Evacuated tube
   b. Stopper
   c. Barrel adapter or needle holder
   d. double-pointed needle or multisample needle
   e. Bevel
   f. Flange
   g. sheathed needle
   h. Hub
   i. Shaft
   j. Point

2. a. Cephalic vein
   b. Median cephalic vein
   c. Supplementary cephalic vein

d. Basilic vein
e. Median basilic vein
f. Median antebrachial vein

Part IV.

A.
1. Unlabeled or mislabeled specimen
2. Quantity not sufficient (QNS)
3. Defective tube
4. Incorrect tube used for test ordered
5. Hemolysis
6. Anticoagulated
7. Improper storage and handling

B.
1. Blood culture
2. Red
3. Light
4. Green
5. Lavender
6. Red/gray
7. gray

Part V.

A.
1. Clean gloves
2. Cotton balls
3. Lancet holder
4. Sealing clay
5. Lancet stages
6. Slides
7. Gauze
8. Capillary tubes
9. Needle unit for microsample collection
10. Adapter
11. Butterfly adapter
12. Capillary collection tubes
13. Alcohol preps
14. Alcohol

B.
1. Elderly patients
2. Pediatric patients (especially under the age of 2)
3. Frequent glucose monitoring
4. Patients with burns or scars in venipuncture sites
5. Obese patients
6. Patients receiving IV therapy
7. Patients who have had mastectomy

C. Capillary
D. microtainer
E. planter
F. True

G. 70% isopropyl alcohol
H. povidone (Betadine)

Chapter 50 Quiz

1. Red
2. coagulation
3. EDTA
4. green
5. cephalic
6. phlebotomy
7. superficial
8. the point of forking or separating into two branches
9. without delay
10. the liquid portion of blood after it is clotted

CHAPTER 51

Part I.

1. A
2. I
3. B
4. D
5. G
6. H
7. E
8. F
9. K
10. C
11. J

Part II.

1. CBC
2. Hct
3. hgb
4. RBC
5. ESR

Part III.

A. 1. RBCs
2. platelets
3. basophil
4. neutrophil
5. eosinophil
6. lymphocyte
7. monocyte

B. Students will practice this exercise with an actual blood smear.

Part IV.

A. plasma, erythrocytes, leukocytes, thrombocytes
B. Hemoglobin, 120

C. Neutrophils, eosinophils, basophils
D. Lymphocytes, monocytes
E. Thrombocytes
F. Calcium, thromboplastin, prothrombin, fibrin
G. Prothrombin time

H. 1. 3
   2. negative
   3. 3
   4. A
   5. positive
   6. 67
   7. AB
   8. 167

I. 1. Blood glucose
   2. Cholesterol
   3. Hemoglobin A1C

Part V. Many RBCs, 2 WBCs (1 seg, 1 lymphocyte)

Part VI.
1. 85014
2. 85013
3. 85015
4. 85008

Chapter 51 Quiz
1. thrombocytes
2. to count cells
3. glucose, cholesterol, HA1C
4. toxicology
5. layers of white cells or platelets that are found between the plasma and the packed RBCs after centrifuging whole blood
6. hematology
7. CBC
8. plasma
9. leukocytes
10. erythrocytes

CHAPTER 52
Part I.
1. Nosocomial
2. Pathogen
3. Pure culture
4. Organelle
5. Nanometer
6. Microorganism
7. Eukaryote
8. Fastidious
9. Cyst
10. Specimen
11. Prokaryote

12. Broad-spectrum antimicrobial agent
13. In vitro
14. Asepsis
15. Macromolecules
16. Tissue culture
17. Antimicrobial
18. Molecule
19. Wet mount
20. Viable
21. Transport medium

Part II.
1. ova
2. broth
3. agar

Part III.
A.
1. Bacilli (rods)
2. Cocci (spheres)
3. Curved rods
4. Small bacteria

B.
1. Amoebas
2. Flagellates
3. Ciliates
4. Sporozoa

C.
1. Nematodes
2. Helminthes
3. Arthropods

D.
1. Yeasts
2. Molds

Part IV.
A. aerobes, anaerobes
B. Mycology
C. Protozoa
D. Gram stain is used in the microbiology laboratory and acid stain is used in the identification of mycobacteria.

E.
1. All purpose: Used to support the growth of a wide variety of bacteria; will not support growth of fastidious bacteria
2. Selective: Supports the growth of one type of organism while inhibiting the growth of others
3. Differential: Contains chemicals or dyes that alter the appearance of certain bacterial types

4. Enriched: Contains complex organic materials that certain fastidious species must have in order to multiply

F. Refer to Table 52-1 in textbook.

Part V.

What are the ways that I can prevent extraneous microorganisms from contaminating this sample? What can I do to prevent myself from becoming infected while I collect this sample?

Students are to draw a properly streaked plate in the circle provided.

Part VI.
1. 87045
2. 87040
3. 87070
4. 87070
5. 87046

Chapter 52 Quiz
1. blood agar
2. E. coli
3. KOH (potassium hydroxide)
4. shapes, structure, gram staining ability, acid fast
5. pinworms
6. cocci
7. bacilli
8. alcohol
9. Epstein Barr virus
10. pathogen

CHAPTER 53

Part I.
1. curettage
2. dilatation
3. fascia
4. fistula
5. lumen
6. cannula
7. obturator
8. abcess
9. patency
10. polyps
11. stylus
12. dissect

Part II.
A.
1. Operating table
2. Clock with a second hand sweep
3. Operating light
4. Sitting stools
5. Mayo stand

B.
1. Sterile water
2. Saline solution (0.9%)
3. Betadine
4. Hibiclens

C.
1. Fluori-methane 15%
2. Ethyl chloride
3. Caine (lidocaine)

D.
1. Epinephrine
2. Silver nitrate

E.
1. Cutting
2. Grasping
3. Retracting
4. Probing and dilating

Part III.
1. A. 23 blade
   B. 22 blade
   C. 21 blade
   D. 20 blade
   E. 15 blade
   F. 12 blade
   G. 11 blade
   H. 10 blade
   I. 17 blade
   J. 9 blade

2. Blade handle
3. Sharp/sharp straight operating scissors, sharp/blunt straight operating scissors, blunt/blunt straight operating scissors
4. Tissue/thumb forceps
5. Straight and curved hemostats
6. Suture removing scissors
7. Towel clamp
8. Needle holder
9. Splinter forcep
10. Sponge forceps
11. Bandage scissors

Part IV.
A. 1. True
   2. False
   3. False
   4. True

B. 1. C
   2. D
   3. E
   4. B
   5. F
   6. G
   7. A

C. Discuss results of student research in class.

Chapter 53 Quiz

1. scissors
2. retractors
3. forcep
4. clamp
5. 0.9%
6. caine
7. curettage
8. obturator
9. antiseptics or skin preps
10. packing

CHAPTER 54

Part I.

1. F
2. P
3. J
4. A
5. L
6. Q
7. I
8. N
9. K
10. M
11. G
12. C
13. E
14. B
15. D
16. O
17. H

Part II. Students are to rate themselves on their knowledge of the procedures listed.

Part III. Informed, what, why, risks and benefits, sign, discussion, consents, refuses, family member, document, sedative, never

Part IV.

A.
1. Redness around the operative site
2. Bleeding from the wound
3. Fever
4. Swelling
5. Increasing or severe pain

B.
1. True
2. True
3. False
4. True
5. True
6. True
7. True
8. True
9. False
10. True

Chapter 54 Quiz

1. grounding pad
2. True
3. flexible
4. freezing
5. Informed
6. gas, steam, chemical, and dry heat
7. autoclave
8. change colors when exposed to steam to show article has been autoclaved
9. date, name of contents, initials
10. 28 or 6

CHAPTER 55

Part I.

1. D
2. B
3. H
4. P
5. N
6. G
7. O
8. K
9. I
10. F
11. J
12. E
13. M
14. A
15. C
16. L

Part II.

A.

1. Networking
2. Contacting employers directly
3. Newspaper ads
4. Employment agencies
5. Joining professional societies
6. Volunteering
7. Mailing resumes
8. Cold calling
9. Performing well on externships

Discuss strategies for completing the job application.

Discuss preparation of the draft resume.

Part III. Discuss student evaluations of the sample cover letter.

Part IV. Discuss student career goals.

Chapter 55 Quiz

1. resume
2. False
3. networking, direct contact
4. True
5. preparation, interview follow-up, and negotiation
6. newspapers, agencies, callings, sending resumes
7. to get attention and provide introductory information
8. Where am I today? Where will I be in ten years? What skills will I need to get there?
9. someone neat, dependable, good clinical and verbal skills
10. job skills, self-management skills, and transferable skills

Answer Key for Critical Thinking Exercises

Unit 1

1-1 Students will create a plan for academic improvement.

1-2 Have students identify how they process and perceive information.

1-3 Students will describe times when learning was enjoyable.

1-4 Have students identify their own effective time management strategies.

1-5 Students will identify a problem and practice brainstorming for solutions and/or using the pros-and-cons method for creating solutions.

1-6 Discuss various barriers to learning and have students implement four new study skills during the upcoming week.

1-7 Students are asked to try four new test-taking strategies.

2-1 Have students share their opinion about who they think influenced medicine the most.

2-2 After students read about the pioneers of medicine, ask them whom they would have like to have worked with.

2-3 Have students do a poster presentation on someone that influenced modern medicine, but who is not listed in their textbook. Discuss how medical assistants might influence medicine.

2-4 Ask students to investigate local hospitals and find out about medical staff privileges.

2-5 Ask students to compare MDs, DOs, and chiropractors.

3-1 Discuss with the class how they might explore administrative and clinical roles in a variety of practice settings. Have the students research medical specialties, focusing on at least two areas that could serve as potential career paths

3-2 Single parents may need to investigate insurance benefits, retirement, and family sick leave very carefully before choosing a position.

3-3 Students should pay close attention, follow instructions, ask pertinent questions, and be courteous. Sandra may wish to join or form a study group or ask the instructor for additional assistance.

3-4 Problems with externships should be reported to the instructor immediately. Students may be asked to assist with filing and other routine tasks as assigned by the office manager. Sandra can learn some on-the-job tips from her co-workers.

3-5 Medical assisting organizations allow student membership at a reduced rate. Students may attend local, state, and national meetings.

3-6 Certification can often mean more opportunities for advancements and higher salaries. It is important for graduates to network and attend educational programs. Ask the students to find out which certification exams are offered in your area.

4-1 Students should display honesty, integrity, courtesy, initiative, and dependability.

4-2 Karen can demonstrate loyalty by doing the best job possible and taking the initiative to learn new skills as opportunities present.

4-3 Students should be willing to learn new skills under the appropriate supervision. Preparation for the next day includes pulling charts, restocking supplies, and cleaning work area.

4-4 Karen should try her best to focus on her work responsibilities. She can make telephone calls to check on her grandmother during scheduled break times.

4-5 Explain office policies to the visitor and offer to meet off-site for lunch once a week. She can make telephone calls to check on her grandmother during scheduled break times.

4-6 Setting priorities may involve making a list of important activities. For example, a key goal for the new medical assistant could be to always be on time (or early) for work.

5-1 Touch conveys compassion. Laughter can relieve stress if used at the appropriate moment.

5-2 Have Mrs. Cloyd repeat the directions back to you. Make eye contact with the patient.

5-3 Allow Sarah to discuss her fears. Explore her feelings about the impact of this decision.

5-4 They have opposing wishes. They need to avoid using defense mechanisms.

5-5 Assess for defense mechanisms. Smile and focus on communicating care and compassion. Try not to appear stressed or rushed.

5-6 Yes, help Sarah learn more about the stages of grief. Allow her to discuss these feelings.

5-7 Have the students identify community resources that are available for the terminally ill and their family.

5-8 It is best to have a will if they are dependents and heirs, even for small estates.

5-9 Physical needs must be met before high level functioning can be achieved. Sarah must take care of herself so that she will be able to care for her mother.

5-10 Encourage an open discussion about the funeral and business affairs.

6-1 Ethical and morale opinions are based in cultural and religious beliefs. Although it is a completely acceptable practice to depend on groups and committees to guide ethical decisions, the responsibility for making these decisions ultimately rests with the individual.

6-2 Some couples prefer to remain anonymous. Some may fear becoming emotionally involved with the birth mother. Some adoptive parents prefer to participate in the birth experience.

6-3 How will the family react if there is a genetic defect? Ask the class to share their opinions about prenatal genetic testing.

6-4 Monica needs to openly discuss her wishes will her family. A donor card may be helpful. It is imperative that she make her wishes known to family.

6-5 Monica is not able to divulge any information. Ask the class how they would handle this situation.

7-1   Yes, if Dr. Patrick saw the patient, there is a contractual agreement.

7-2   No, always, encourage patients to follow instructions.

7-3   No, tell them that the doctor is unable to accepting them as a new patient. Offer them a list of area physicians.

7-4   Many Supreme Court decisions have had an impact on the medical profession. For example, Roe versus Wade helped legalize first trimester abortion.

7-5   Sometimes giving unsolicited information can harm a case.

7-6   She should disclose this information to the practice attorney. She is ethically and legally obligated to tell the truth.

7-7   Obviously, the prosecution failed to prove to the jury that he was guilty of the crime.

7-8   Punitive damages are awarded in cases of gross negligence. Some states are considering placing a cap on monetary awards.

7-9   The medical assistant should offer to refer these questions to the physician.

7-10   Report the concerns to the office manager and expect total confidentiality.

7-11   She should include all staff members that use needle safety devices.

7-12   Offer the instruction immediately and annually. Document each set of instruction.

7-13   Lynda does not have to offer a reason for the declination.

Unit 2

8-1   Peer training might work. The benefits of closing the office for one day to educate the other employees about the system may be well worth losing a day of patient visits.

8-2   Pirating software is illegal and unethical. There is no recourse if software fails and information is lost or hardware damaged.

8-3   The speed of the printer, price of toner and ink, and warranty information should be considered.

8-4   One price is thirty cent per CD-R disk and the other is thirty-three cents each. It depends on how many CD-Rs you expect to use during the coming year.

8-5   Digital photos of the staff can be added to the practice web site. Patient photos can be placed on the chart for name recognition. Wounds can be photographed at various stages of healing. Always obtain a patient's written permission before taking a photograph.

8-6   Limit personal Internet use to authorized breaks. Most practices do not allow for computer games or downloading from the Internet.

9-1   She will have to speak more slowly. If Ashlynn does receive personal calls at work, she should politely remind the caller that her office has policies regarding telephone use and that it is important that she keep the business lines free for incoming calls.

9-2   Notify the involved employees at once that their conversation was overhead. If this behavior continues and you feel that there are confidentiality issues, discuss the situation with the office manager.

9-3 Discuss these concerns with the office manager. However, the office manager or physician will have the final say.

9-4 Ask students to respond to this scenario.

9-5 She should remain calm, ask to place the caller on hold, and then transfer them to the manager.

9-6 Automated systems should always have a way to bypass the menu and ring directly to a telephone attendant. Help an older patient determine which department that they call most often, and write down those extensions as menu options they should dial.

10-1 Ask the doctor if there is anything that Ramona can do to help her get back on schedule.

10-2 She can arrange for an on-site demo.

10-3 Have the class discuss this innovative scheduling plan.

10-4 Remain calm and courteous. Repeat the offer to reschedule the patient.

10-5 Point out to the patient that he is often late, and offer a time slot that would work better for his schedule. If he continues to be late, schedule him in the last slot of the day, and ask him to arrive 10 minutes earlier than actually scheduled.

11-1 She may decide to included artwork, plants, and warm, comfortable seating.

11-2 Provide a designated children's area with safe toys and activities.

11-3 Georgina could make a chart of the necessary duties; this way duties will rotate and everyone shares the responsibility.

11-4 Some practices use photographs of patients on their file folder. Some medical assistants try name association. If all else fails, just apologize and say, "I'm sorry, I can't seem to remember your name."

11-5 Have blank charts pre-prepared. Some practices mail out information forms in advance and ask the patient to complete it before they arrive.

11-6 Schedule her for the first appointment in the morning. Georgina could say something like, "I'm sorry, I would love to sit and talk, but I must finish some work now."

12-1 Sort the mail into payments, urgent, routine, and junk mail. Process payments and urgent mail first.

12-2 He can place reorder reminders in boxes of supplies.

12-3 He should point out the error in a respectful manner to avoid embarrassing the manager.

12-4 With the doctor's permission, use a signature stamp or sign and co-sign the letter.

12-5 Privacy is a concern with e-mail. An e-mail can be forwarded without your knowledge. An important memo may need to be sent by e-mail with a written memo to follow.

12-6 He might call the patient and let her know that the check was received and the patient may opt to come in and write a new check before it is deposited. He should notify the manager.

12-7 See if he can get more information to include advantages and disadvantages of the system. He could also do a cost comparison.

12-8 Compare UPS, FedEx, regular mail, and private couriers. Research the reliability, dependability, and integrity of a private courier before switching.

13-1 Explain office policy regarding the release of medical records. Never release records to a third party without the patient's signed consent or consent from their legal guardian.

13-2   Explain than unauthorized access is prevented by passwords and firewalls.

13-3   SOAP is a format that is used in the progress notes of the POMR system.

13-4   Don't be judgmental. Explain that everyone is asked the same questions for safety reasons. If he refuses to answer, let the physician know.

13-5   Draw one single line through the error, write the corrected abbreviation above it, date and initial the change.

13-6   Search the Internet or consult a law book at the local library to find a copy of a Power of Attorney. Never call the attorney without your employer's permission.

13-7   Use a cassette recorder and a keyboard. Take a medical terminology refresher course at a local trade school or on-line. Use reference books, such as drug guides, medical dictionaries, and coding books to increase your knowledge of terminology.

13-8   Alphabetical filing is straightforward and easy to set up and use, requiring only a file cabinet or shelf, folders, and some divider guides. However, alphabetical filing can become time consuming as the number of patient files increases. Another drawback is that the correct spelling of the name must be known. Numeric filing requires the use of an alphabetical cross-reference to find a given file. Numeric filing does offer the advantages of unlimited expansion without periodic shifting of folders, additional confidentiality, and time-savings in that retrieving and refiling of records can occur quickly.

13-9   The tickler file is a useful reminder for recurring events such as payments, meetings, and the anticipated return of x-ray reports and laboratory reports.

Unit 3

14-1   She could design a brochure or instruction sheet that explains basic insurance concepts.

14-2   Myra could ask this patient to come into the manager's office to discuss these complaints.

14-3   Ask the class to discuss this scenario.

14-4   Myra could make a pocket card for him to take to the hospital to track visits. She could also request copies of his hospital dictations.

14-5   She could ask to look at the EOB and call the insurance company.

14-6   Myra should excuse herself, check with the office manager, and then collect the card as instructed. She could suggest that the patient call the credit card company.

14-7   Immediately reprint the itemized bill for the patient.

14-8   Offer to have Dr. Wallace get in touch with Dr. Franklin's office as soon as Dr. Wallace returns from the meeting.

14-9   Ask the collection company for their policy. Notify the physician if you feel that the company is violating the Fair Credit Collection Act.

15-1   She could visit the NCHS web site or refer to the Federal Register.

15-2   Kay should make sure that the practice owns the updated coding books and software.

15-3   Kay has a legal and ethical responsibility to code the diagnosis as documented in the patient's medical record.

15-4   Code the symptom or chief complaint.

16-1   Both codes are found in an index and confirmed in another section.

16-2   E&M codes also take in to consideration the medical decision making component.

16-3   Practice coding this scenario with the class.

17-1   She can watch the entire claims process and learn firsthand from someone who files claims electronically.

17-2   Have students role play the assignment of benefits scenario.

17-3   Refer to the section of your textbook titled Common Problem Areas on page 321.

17-4   A delay in claims payment results in decreased cash flow.

17-5   The claim may be able to be resubmitted with added documentation. Discuss this claim with the physician.

18-1 $1000 minus $250 equals $750. Twenty percent of 750 is $150.

18-2   Beverly could keep current by reading AMA publications and attending continuing education programs.

18-3   Beverly could explain the situation when the patient first presents an insurance card or when the patient calls for an appointment.

18-4   Usually calling the insurance company for pre-certification results in maximum payment for procedures, tests, and surgeries. This saves the patient money.

18-5   Look at the EOB. Determine if the deductible was met. Check the patient's card to see if they have Part A and B. Part B is optional and covers the doctor's bill.

19-1   Contact various banks or visit their web site for information on e-banking and M-banking.

19-2   Laura could explain the difference between checking, savings, and money market accounts.

19-3   She should check the disbursements journal, call the bank, or check on-line to see if the check has cleared. If it cannot be traced, she should consider stopping payment.

19-4   Laura should not accept this check, stating that it is against office policy to accept a check written for more than the amount due and returning cash for the difference between the amount of the check and the amount owed.

19-5   Consider office policy. If it meets with the approval of your office manager, call and verify the amount of the check with the bank.

Unit 4

20-1   Treat employees with courtesy and respect. An assessment of employee perceptions will be useful in planning to build on practice strengths and improve weak areas.

20-2   Leadership, a caring attitude, and being approachable are some of the qualities of a good manager. Ask the class to discuss traits of a poor manager.

20-3   Talking with employees about their personal and professional goals is a good strategy for discovering employees' motivations for working.

20-4   Katherine could praise Jewel's good points before pointing out her weaknesses.

20-5   Discuss these social scenarios in class.

20-6   Katherine may want to wait until after she interviews Carol to decide whether or not to hire this applicant. Telephone communication skills are important in the medical office.

20-7   This comment could be the result of an isolated experience or personality clash. Ask the applicant how she perceived her previous job.

20-8   Assign a competent staff member to serve as a mentor for the new employee.

20-9   Katherine should remain calm. Have the class role play this scenario.

20-10   Monitor the situation very closely. Go over medication policies with the entire staff. Confront the employee if you feel it is warranted.

21-1   She could ask one of her professors for assistance. Staff may have good marketing ideas. They may decide to make a brochure, web site, or place a newspaper ad.

21-2   The Area Planning Commission, Chamber of Commerce, and telephone directory may be of assistance. Be sure to collect demographic information about the population and the names of major employers in the area.

21-3   She can make calls to area clinics or ask the insurance companies for usual and customary rates.

21-4   The American Red Cross, newspapers, the local hospital and library may be useful. Monica's clinic could host a health fair or BP screening at a local business.

21-5   Discuss these ideas with the class. Have students compile a list of resources and community organizations that are available in your area.

21-6   The "Frequently Asked Questions" section of the web site may ultimately save the staff time by decreasing telephone inquires.

22-1   Organizations offer professional recognition, networking, and opportunities to earn CEUs.

22-2   This information is used for coding, DRGs, and analysis of statistical trends. The doctor could be misdiagnosing patients.

22-3   Physicians must authenticate charts by initials entries.

22-4   The hospital employee could conduct patient education, plan a health fair, or make brochures.

22-5   Individuals who are not involved with a patient's care should not have access to their records.

22-6   Explain how trends are examined and patient safety is impacted by quality assurance. Adherence to QA policy should be mandated.

23-1   Brenda should show this employee the financial impact of her mistakes. Make sure a calculator is readily available. If a verbal warning goes unheeded, issue a written warning.

23-2   Check the disbursement records. Call the bank and consider stopping payment.

23-3   Employees should never use petty cash for anything other than office incidental expenses.

23-4   The peg board system is often considered the easiest to use.

23-5   The mistake could be in an individual account. Notify the account and physician if it is a significant error.

23-6   Brenda should look up the itemized purchase order. If she has not ordered the item, she should return the merchandise.

23-7   Discuss the results of this investigation with the class.

23-8   Yes, but she may end up owing taxes at the end of the year.

23-9   Brenda might suggest leasing the needed equipment. Assess the cost of repairs versus purchasing. Leasing may be a short-term solution.

Unit 5

24-1   The medical assistant should practice universal precautions, use good hand-washing, and disinfect all surfaces that the patient touched.

24-2   Inflammation exhibits redness, pain, and edema.

24-3   We use universal blood and body fluid precautions on all patients.

24-4   Ask students to make posters showing their mind maps.

24-5   Immediately wash the area, provide first aid, report the incident to the office manager, and follow the exposure policy.

24-6   Ask students to outline the important concepts of sanitization and disinfection.

25-1   Ask students to share their list of the five "things" they value most with the class.

25-2   Have students write a short essay about their personal biases.

25-3   Mr. Gonzales is exhibiting denial. Consider showing him his past B/P readings and educating him about the risks of hypertension.

25-4   Subjective: sore throat, pain on a scale of 5 on a 1-10 scale
Objective: Temperature, rash on chest

26-1   Ask students to share their assessment of Mr. Ignatio's learning needs.

26-2   Ideas that would be most useful might include demonstrations and pictures.

26-3   Have students document this scenario.

27-1   High fiber foods include raw fruits, bran, vegetables, and greens. Fiber clears LDL and inhibits synthesis of cholesterol in the liver.

27-2   Marcia can recommend that the patient decrease consumption of red meats and saturated fats. Increase consumption of fatty fish, olive and canola oil.

27-3   She could give him a copy of a BMI nomogram.

27-4   Have students develop a meal plan for a 1200-calorie diabetic diet.

27-5   Discuss the Heart Healthy Diet that is described in Table 27-7.

27-6   She may have bulimia. Marcia should encourage her to seek counseling.

27-7   Discuss the benefits of walking 30 minutes each day.

28-1   The child should be seen today.

28-2   37.2 degrees C   38.9 degrees C
        129.6 degrees F   138.6 degrees F

28-3   Tympanic
        Oral
        Tympanic
        Oral
        Tympanic

28-4   Try radial and consider confirming with apical.

28-5   Try to watch some part of the sweater that is rising and failing.

28-6   Discuss diet, smoking, exercise, and medications.

28-7   Ask students to practice documenting the series of vital signs.

28-8   191.4 pounds
        67.27 kilograms

28-9   Discuss this scenario with the class.

29-1   Felicia needs to update his insurance information, go over changes in the medical history, take vital signs, and obtain labwork and ECG.

29-2   Sims
        Lithotomy
        Prone
        Fowler's
        Supine
        Trendlenburg

29-3   Discuss this scenario with the class.

29-4   Ask students to write a teaching plan for this patient.

Unit 6

30-1   The orientation should include the DEA regulations for controlled substances.

30-2   The disposal should be witnessed and documented. Many medical assistants put wasted tablets in the biohazard box.

30-3   Lipitor 20 mg
        Sig: 1 qd @ hs
        Disp: 28
        Refill: 2

30-4   Cardizen is a calcium channel blocker that slows heart rate and decreases blood pressure by relaxing smooth muscle. It can cause swelling of the hands and feet. Her weight and renal function may alter the distribution and excretion of the drug.

31-1   0.45 L equals 450 milliliters.

31-2   Administer 2.9 or 3 cc of Acetaminophen. Have someone double check the calculation.

32-1   Dorothy should always consider the "seven rights" of drug administration.

32-2   Ask students to discuss the guidelines for successful medication administration to children as well as those for administration to geriatric patients.

32-3   Document the date, time, and drug dosage given in the office as well as the Rx information.

32-4   PPD .1ml ID R. forearm, date, time, and instructions given.

32-5   Have students describe a vastus lateralis injection for an infant and practice documenting the injection in this scenario.

Unit 7

33-1   Is he alert? Is there active bleeding? Thoroughly document the information gathered as well as any actions taken.

33-2   Ask students to role-play the on-site emergency.

33-3   Discuss this scenario with the class.

33-4   Mr. Antonio needs to be evaluated for a TIA in the local ER as soon as possible.

33-5   Keep the mother on the line and contact poison control. EMS should be activated. Tell her *not* to give Ipecac to the drowsy child.

34-1   Ask students to discuss Hyperopia, Myopia, Presbyopia, and Astigmatism.

34-2   Author to supply.

34-3   Irrigate OD with NS until clear.

34-4   Humorsol 0.25% 1 gtt OD.

34-5   Ask students to properly document this procedure as well as the results.

35-1   Reinforce good handwashing techniques. Disinfect all surfaces that the patient touched. Use universal blood and body fluid precautions.

35-2   Wash clothes and bedding in hot water. If the daughter's coat touches others in the coat-rack, all of the coats should be dry-cleaned.

35-3   Do not pop blisters. Apply a sterile dressing. Ask him to come to the office so that Dr. Lee may examine him.

35-4   Ask students to compare and contrast the patch, intradermal, and RAST tests.

36-1   Ask students to write a plan for a GI in-service training session.

36-2   Ask students to role-play these four scenarios.

36-3   Have students design a brochure about IBS.

36-4   Use universal precautions to avoid exposure to hepatitis B, C, D, and E in the medical office.

36-5   Ask about the onset, duration, and related symptoms.

36-6   Students may use Table 36-5 as a reference for designing a handout.

37-1   Ask students to discuss their ideas and opinions.

37-2   Have students discuss the prep and procedure for a cystogram and IVP.

37-3   The female patient should wipe from the front to the back after toileting. She should also avoid bubble baths.

37-4 Divide the class into two groups. Ask students to do some research on these two procedures and then make posters about their findings on hemodialysis and peritoneal dialysis.

37-5 Ask the class to compare and contrast BHP and prostate cancer.

37-6 Review and discuss Table 37-2 with the class.

38-1 Encourage students to create their own contraceptive reference sheet.

38-2 Discuss the physiology, symptoms, causes, treatments, and fertility issues related to endometriosis.

38-3 This patients needs teaching about all STDs and the importance of safe sex and HIV prevention. HPV is often associated with cervical cancer.

38-4 Soy products, Vitamins E and B6, calcium, and exercise are useful nonpharmaceutical treatments during menopause.

39-1 Ask about gross motor, language, fine motor, and personal skills. Offer to schedule a routine check-up with the doctor or refer the call to the doctor.

39-2 Ask if the child is alert. Does he have a fever? Can the child tolerate fluids? This child should be seen today.

39-3 Does the child have a fever? What is the child's disposition? The child should be seen as soon as possible.

39-4 Avoid aspirin for pediatric fevers. Find out if she can tolerate fluids.

39-5 DPT, Hib, and IPV are given at 4 months. Some children experience fever, irritability, drowsiness, and malaise.

39-6 Ask students to create a safety checklist for a pediatric office.

40-1 Encourage students to share their ideas about this scenario with the class.

40-2 The mechanism of injury will aid in a complete assessment and appropriate diagnosis.

40-3 Elevate the extremity. Apply ice and assess distal pulses.

40-4 Immobilization of the patient's shoulder and arm is a priority. Kaiwan should apply an ice pack.

40-5 Ask the doctor if he can examine the patient in a chair.

40-6 A goniometer is used to measure ROM while a patient is in a relaxed position.

40-7 Ask students to role-play this scenario.

40-8 Remove the wax and assess the skin for burns. In the future, Kaiwan should test the temperature of the paraffin bath by using a meat or candy thermometer in the hot wax.

40-9 The cast needs to dry. Also, the patient's circulation must be assessed after the cast hardens.

40-10 Demonstrations and written handouts will work well.

41-1 Ask students to develop a teaching plan. A model or chart of the brain and spinal cord might be helpful.

41-2 Have students practice by role-playing this scenario.

41-3 Ask students to share their ideas bout how they might approach Mr. Jackson.

41-4 Ask someone to call 911. Explain to the patient that you are sending help. Stay on the line. This could be a cerebrovascular accident (CVA).

41-5   Ask students to design a brochure about the risks of G-force injuries on amusement rides. Such a brochure should include the fact that roller coasters are a great cause for concern. Some coasters subject riders to G-forces greater than astronauts are subjected to during space shuttle liftoff.

41-6   Ask students to develop a brochure or handout on hand injury information. Rather than permitting the patient to take one of the brochures before the physician approves it, Mai could offer to mail one to the patient after the brochure is approved.

41-7   Ask students to role-play this scenario.

41-8   Mai should notify the doctor and ask him to speak with the mother about her concerns.

42-1   Pituitary, thyroid, parathyroid, adrenals, pancreas, ovaries, and testes are common causes of endocrine dysfunction.

42-2   Hyper and Hypopituitarism can result if there is a problem with the anterior pituitary. Examples of two such health problems could be gigantisms and dwarfisms.

42-3   Hyperthyroidism causes a high metabolism, fast heart rate, weight loss, and the sensation of being hot. Hypothyroidism causes a slow metabolism, a slow heart rate, weight gain, and the sensation of being cold.

42-4   Discuss the life-style changes that the diabetic patient must make. Miguel should inform Carlos that many drug companies offer glucose machines to the needy.

42-5   Work with students to develop teaching plans for hypoglycemia and hypergylcemia.

42-6   Ask students to make posters describing diabetic foot care.

43-1   When documenting this information, Michael should use terms such as dyspnea, hemoptysis, othopnea, rhinorrhea, tachypnea, cyanosis, effusion and atelectasis.

43-2   A chest X-ray and sputum cultures will be ordered. INH and rifampin are anti-TB drugs. All residents will need PPDs.

43-3   Ask students to develop a FAQ list about asthma and emphysema. Have students identify community resources.

43-4   Michael could have Cinda observe him as he administers the spirometer test. Michael should explain that successful spirometry requires the application of a consistent technique for preparing the patient, explaining and performing the procedure, and determining the results.

43-5   Discuss the procedure for collecting a sputum specimen.

44-1   Anna should offer to call 911. If the patient refuses, Anna needs to document that in the chart and encourage the patient to come to the office immediately.

44-2   Discuss telephone screening for chest pain with the class.

44-3   Anna can help patients by teaching them how to take their own blood pressure, providing brochures that reinforce the necessity of monitoring BP, and helping them to understand that this condition cannot be cured but can be controlled. Ask students to locate education materials about hypertension and make a list of places, such as drug stores, that offer BP checks.

44-4   Anna could explain that salt and sodium cause fluid retention which places an increased workload on the heart. She could emphasize that daily weights are an important indicator of fluid volume and retention.

44-5   Anna should encourage this patient to walk around at work, wear support hose, and avoid smoking if taking birth control pills.

45-1   Ask students to share their ideas and opinions with the class.

45-2   Bill could suggest that this patient use milder soap, bathe less often, and use moisturizers.

45-3   Ask the class to review both boxes on this page and then apply this information to the critical thinking application.

45-4   Bill could let this patient's family know that during this stage of Alzheimer's disease, patients may be irritable, have trouble recognizing family and friends, and may experience more confusion.

45-5   Ask students to prepare a poster about age-related sensorimotor changes and some helpful interventions for each.

45-6   Ask students to develop a plan for this in-service.

Unit 8

46-1   Marcus should review the instruction manual or procedure. He could observe co-workers performing the procedure and then practice until he feels comfortable with this machine.

46-2   Ask the class to role-play this scenario.

46-3   Marcus should go ahead and place the chest leads. However, he might want to get someone to double check his lead placement.

46-4   Marcus should notify the doctor and/or call 911. He should also prepare to administer oxygen and emergency medications as ordered.

46-5   Pull the charts and prepare the ECG mounting cards with all of the appropriate information. (Author to review response.)

46-6   He could use the older electrodes or borrow a box from another medical office.

46-7   Marcus should explain to this patient that a stress test is performed under close supervision with constant cardiac monitoring.

46-8   Marcus should ask Mrs. Jamison if she wore the monitor while in the shower.

47-1   Inquire about the patient's symptoms of hypoglycemia and her last home monitor results. Move the procedure to the earliest, so the patient can eat as soon as possible. Notify the radiographer that the procedure has been rescheduled.

47-2   Sara should notify the doctor so that a pregnancy test can be ordered for Ingrid.

47-3   Increase fluid intake during the prep. The prep consists of laxatives, enemas, and suppositories. Dr. Roberts will decide which prep to give.

47-4   Ask the class to respond to this legal and ethical situation.

48-1   These results are quantitative and the units are missing from the notations.

48-2   Cultures are done in microbiology.

48-3   She should consult with OSHA, CLIA, and NCCLS in developing suggestions for expanding on-site laboratory testing.

48-4   Ask students to discuss standardization as well as high, low, and normal controls.

48-5   TD pipettes will deliver the specified amount by drawing up to the calibration mark. Allow fluid to drain vertically and unassisted.

49-1   Cultures are done on urines in sterile containers.

49-2   Refrigerate specimens after 30 minutes. CCMS urines are used for cultures.

49-3   Amber urine is more concentrated. Cloudiness may mean infection or abnormal cells.

49-4   Yes, she should proceed with the chemical analysis of each specimen in exactly the same manner. Mrs. Carpenter may be dehydrated. Ms. Winfrey may have a UTI. Mr. Parks may be diabetic.

49-5   The doctor might find white blood cells.

50-1   Supplies to perform venipuncture include evacuated blood tubes, needles, tourniquets, alcohol, cotton balls, band-aids, lancets, and butterflies. The room should be equipped with needleboxes, gloves, emergency supplies, eye wash, and a hand-washing sink.

50-2   Discuss this situation with the class. Melissa will need a butterfly and a small blue-top tube to draw from the hand.

50-3   Report all exposures to the office manager. The manager will follow the exposure control plan. Use universal precautions, gloves, and other engineering controls to prevent accidental needlesticks.

50-4   Ask the class to role-play using this scenario.

50-5   Leah should withdraw the needle and then apply pressure. She should also administer first aid for syncope.

50-6   Ask the mom if she would like to hold Garrett in her lap. Leah will need a lancet, alcohol, capillary tubes, cotton ball, and band-aid to perform the capillary puncture.

51-1   Red tops are for CBCs. It can show WBCs, RBCs, platelets, Hgb, and Hct.

51-2   Hct plus or minus 3, then divide by three. Yes, the Hgb could be on the low side of normal.

51-3   O positive shows agglutination with anti-D, but not with anti A and B.

51-4   This test shows the average blood sugar over the past two months.

51-5   BUN and creatinine are part of a renal profile.

51-6   Anemia is characterized by a low Hbg and low Hct.

52-1   Discuss the procedure for collecting wound cultures, universal precautions, and hand-washing.

52-2   *E. coli* is a gram negative flagellated bacilli.

52-3   It would appear as a gram positive cluster of spheres.

52-4   Fungal specimens must be treated with KOH. Normal skin flora is not pathogenic.

52-5   Differential media will be used an incubated at 37 degrees C.

52-6   The drug that is least toxic and most economical will be prescribed in most cases.

52-7   The number of colonies observed in each 24 hours period will be documented.

52-8   Strict handwashing is encouraged. Aaron and his mother should avoid touching the area.

Units 9 and 10

53-1   The medical assistant should check to make sure there are sutures, tape, sponges, iodoform packing, syringes, needles, lidocaine, Vaseline gauze, and disposable scalpel blades are on hand for upcoming surgeries.

53-2   Nasal speculum and bayonet forceps can be added to a standard suture tray.

53-3   Have the students read the section on care and handling of instruments. Ask them to write a sample policy.

54-1   She should read the section on sanitization of instruments and autoclave safety.

54-2   The integrity of the sterile package could be compromised. Melissa should address her concerns with the office manager.

54-3   They should be totally reprocessed and dated. Because these packages of sterilized instruments are not marked with dates, Melissa has no way of knowing how long ago the instruments were autoclaved.

54-4   Author to supply response.

54-5   Gloves with visible blood go in a biohazard waste container.

54-6   Notify the doctor that the patient thinks she is having a "cyst removed" from her breast. The consent could be incorrect, or the patient may not understand the procedure.

54-7   Melissa needs to remove the glove immediately. She should inspect her skin and provide first aid. Any injury should be reported immediately. The scalpel is no longer sterile.

54-8   Evidence of good circulation should be documented. The patient could have permanent damage if the bandage occludes circulation. This situation could lead to a liability case.

55-1   An employee with a good attitude shows initiative, dependability, and a willingness to learn. Ask the class to describe an employee or potential employee with a bad attitude.

55-2   Have students list and describe their strengths. Ask them to give examples of each of these strengths.

55-3   Ask students to share their goals with regard to the first position they would like to hold as a medical assistant.

55-4   Allow students to share their brainstorming ideas about networking.

55-5   Ask students to bring in "help wanted" ads from the local paper. Divide the class into groups and have them discuss prospective positions.

55-6   Maybe Lisa should not remove the mention of her volunteer experience since volunteer work shows interest in the community.

55-7   Unusual fonts may not transmit well. Lisa could resave a file with the font standardized, and then e-mail it.

55-8   Those questions are not appropriate. Discuss this scenario with the class.

55-9   Report this incident to the office manager immediately.

55-10   She may need to compare benefits, work environment, and opportunities for advancement.

Transparency Masters

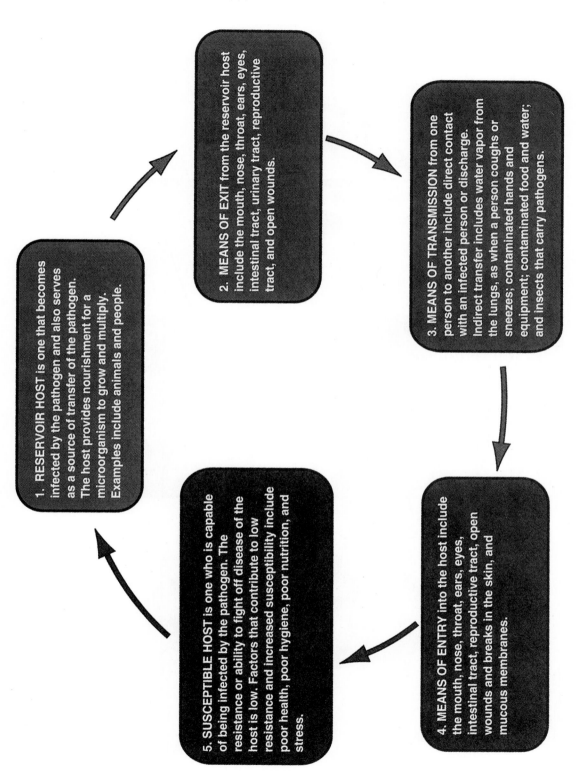

1. RESERVOIR HOST is one that becomes infected by the pathogen and also serves as a source of transfer of the pathogen. The host provides nourishment for a microorganism to grow and multiply. Examples include animals and people.

2. MEANS OF EXIT from the reservoir host include the mouth, nose, throat, ears, eyes, intestinal tract, urinary tract, reproductive tract, and open wounds.

3. MEANS OF TRANSMISSION from one person to another include direct contact with an infected person or discharge. Indirect transfer includes water vapor from the lungs, as when a person coughs or sneezes; contaminated hands and equipment; contaminated food and water; and insects that carry pathogens.

4. MEANS OF ENTRY into the host include the mouth, nose, throat, ears, eyes, intestinal tract, reproductive tract, open wounds and breaks in the skin, and mucous membranes.

5. SUSCEPTIBLE HOST is one who is capable of being infected by the pathogen. The resistance or ability to fight off disease of the host is low. Factors that contribute to low resistance and increased susceptibility include poor health, poor hygiene, poor nutrition, and stress.

TM 2
Balance of body temperature

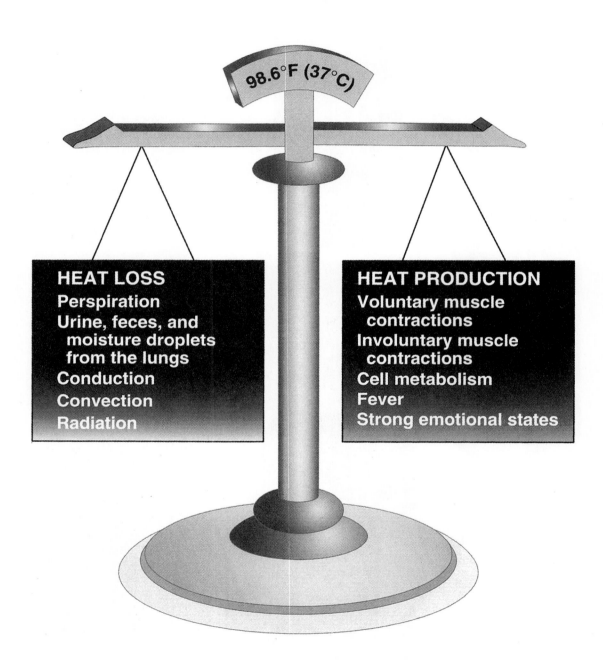

98.6°F (37°C)

HEAT LOSS
Perspiration
Urine, feces, and
moisture droplets
from the lungs
Conduction
Convection
Radiation

HEAT PRODUCTION
Voluntary muscle
contractions
Involuntary muscle
contractions
Cell metabolism
Fever
Strong emotional states

TM 3

Terms to describe body temperature

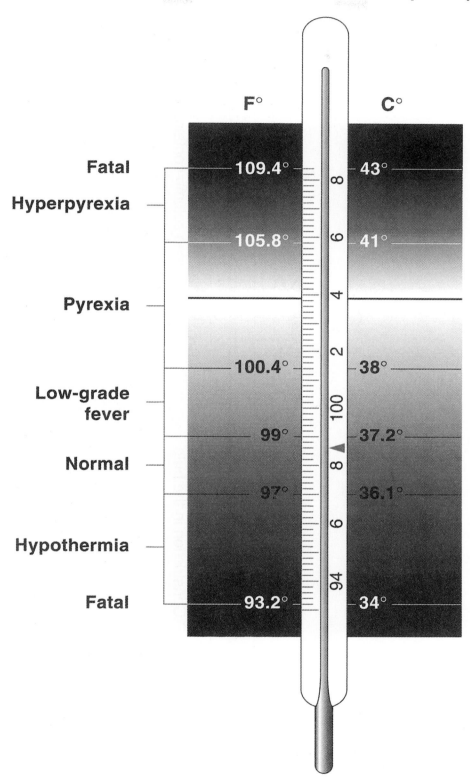

	F°	C°
Fatal	109.4°	43°
Hyperpyrexia		
	105.8°	41°
Pyrexia		
	100.4°	38°
Low-grade fever		
	99°	37.2°
Normal		
	97°	36.1°
Hypothermia		
Fatal	93.2°	34°

TM 4
Parts of a mercury glass thermometer

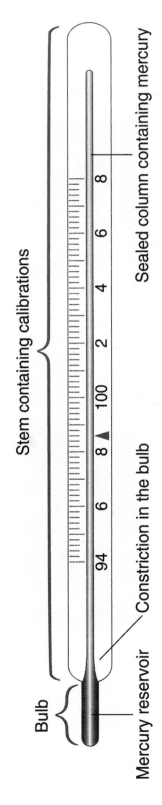

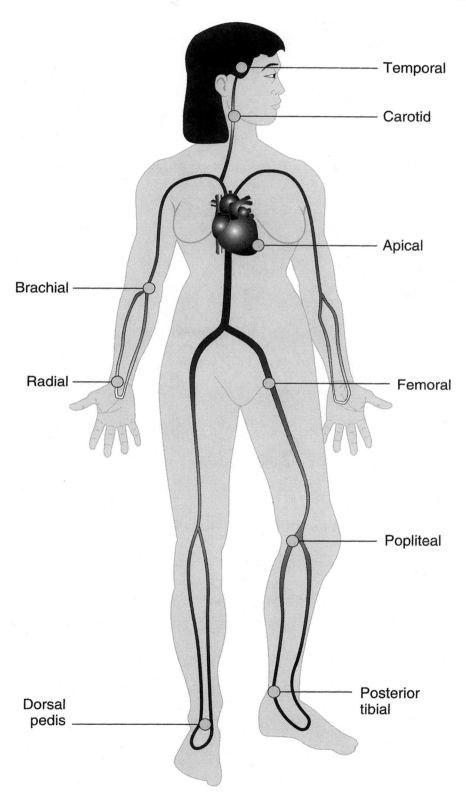

Temporal

Carotid

Apical

Brachial

Radial

Femoral

Popliteal

Posterior
tibial

Dorsal
pedis

TM 6
Location of the apical pulse

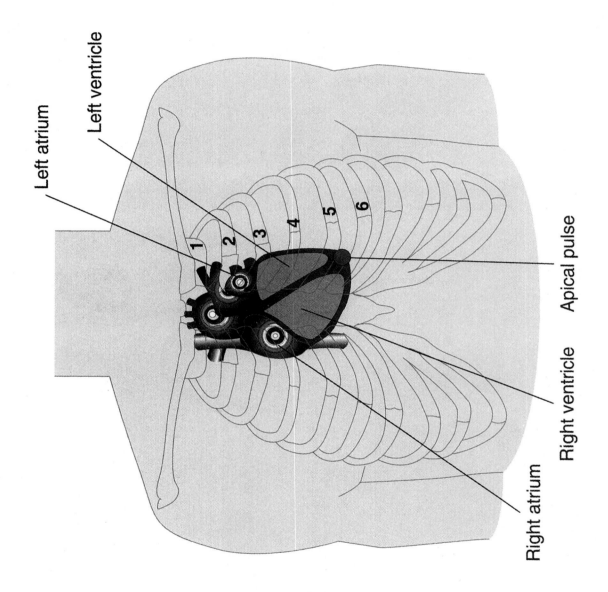

Left atrium

Left ventricle

Apical pulse

Right ventricle

Right atrium

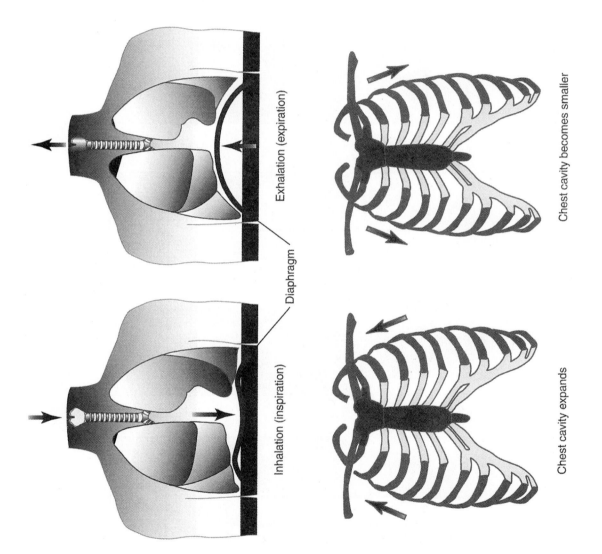

Exhalation (expiration)

Chest cavity becomes smaller

Diaphragm

Inhalation (inspiration)

Chest cavity expands

TM 8
Sounds of Kortkoff

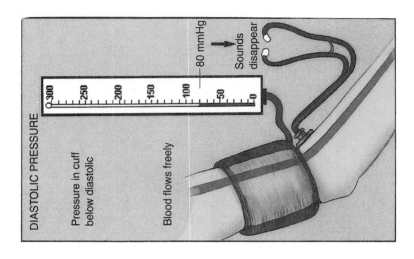

DIASTOLIC PRESSURE

Pressure in cuff below diastolic

Blood flows freely

80 mmHg → Sounds disappear

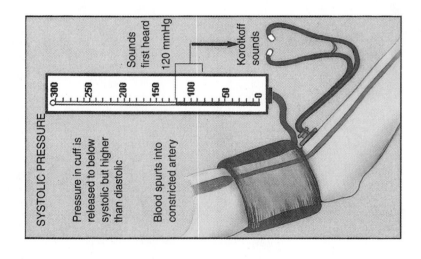

SYSTOLIC PRESSURE

Pressure in cuff is released to below systolic but higher than diastolic

Blood spurts into constricted artery

Sounds first heard
120 mmHg → Korotkoff sounds

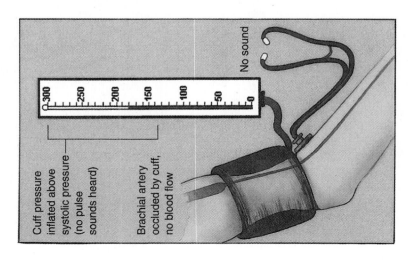

Cuff pressure inflated above systolic pressure (no pulse sounds heard)

Brachial artery occluded by cuff, no blood flow

No sound

TM 9
Autoclave cycle

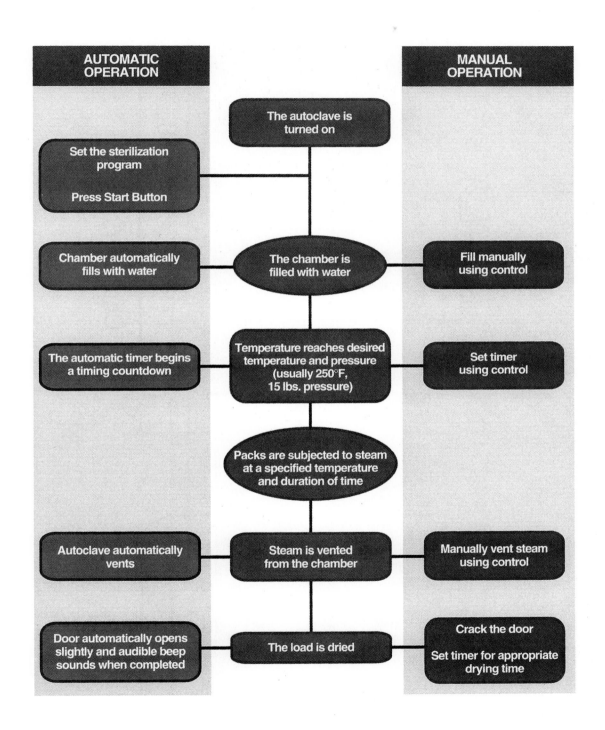

AUTOMATIC OPERATION

MANUAL OPERATION

The autoclave is turned on

Set the sterilization program

Press Start Button

The chamber is filled with water

Chamber automatically fills with water

Fill manually using control

Temperature reaches desired temperature and pressure (usually 250°F, 15 lbs. pressure)

The automatic timer begins a timing countdown

Set timer using control

Packs are subjected to steam at a specified temperature and duration of time

Steam is vented from the chamber

Autoclave automatically vents

Manually vent steam using control

The load is dried

Door automatically opens slightly and audible beep sounds when completed

Crack the door

Set timer for appropriate drying time

TM 10

Arrangement of packs in the autoclave

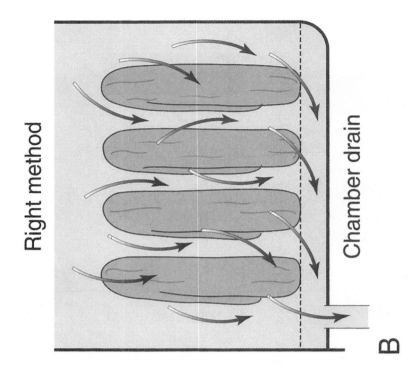

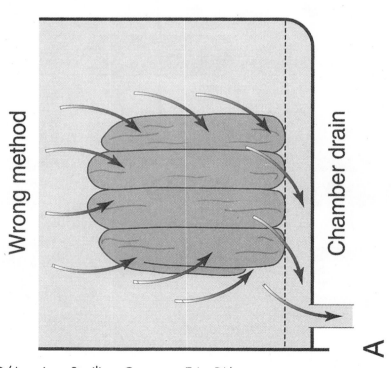

(Courtesy of AMSCO/American Sterilizer Company, Erie, PA)

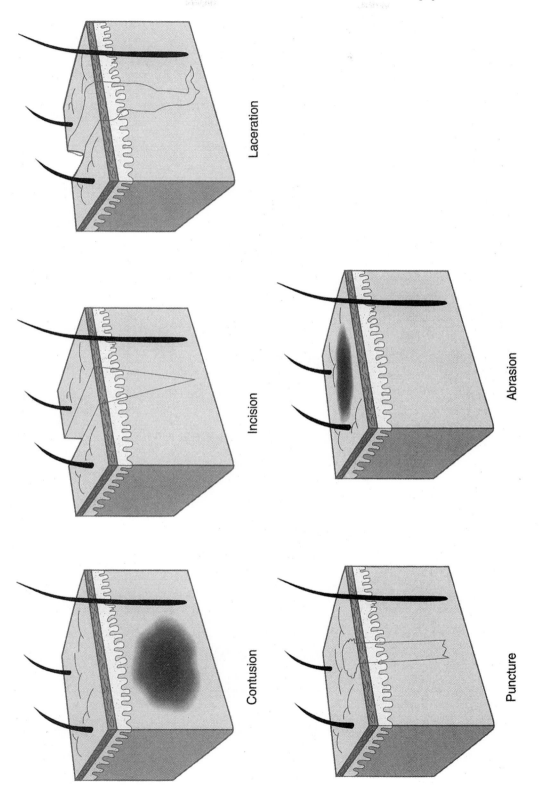

TM 12

An example of a prescription

Larry Douglas, M.D.
11 West Union Street
City, State
740-641-8993

① PATIENT_____Holly Roberts_____AGE___24___

ADDRESS_____72 Hill St., City, St._____DATE__7/12/2002__ ②

③ ℞

④ (Inscription)⎰ Amoxil   250 mg

⑤ (Subscription)⎰ Disp: #40

⑥ (Signature)⎰ Sig: $\frac{\cdot}{1}$ po   tid X 10 days

☐ Dispense as Written

☒ Label

☒ Generic Equivalent OK

⑧ Refill ⟨None,⟩ 1, 2, 3, 4, 5   Larry Douglas   M.D.

DEA #_____ ⑦

TM 13
Parts of a needle and syringe

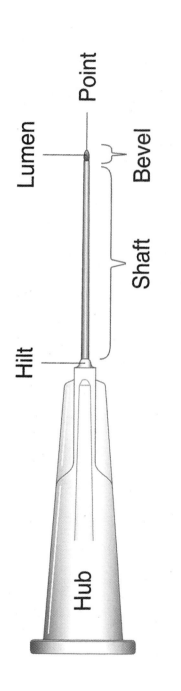

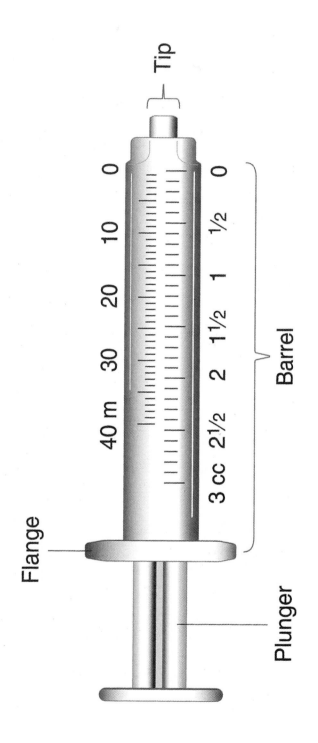

Point

Lumen

Bevel

Shaft

Hilt

Hub

Tip

0

10

20

30

40 m

½

1

1½

2

2½

3 cc

Barrel

Flange

Plunger

TM 14

Type of syringes

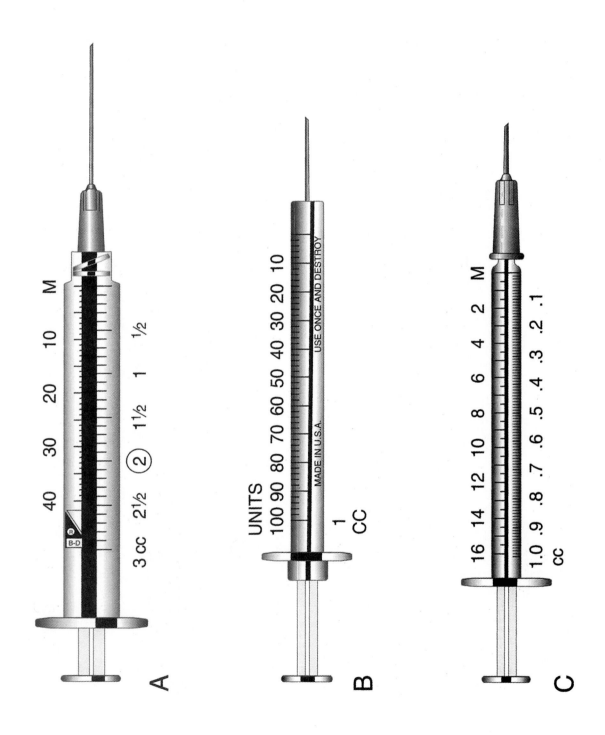

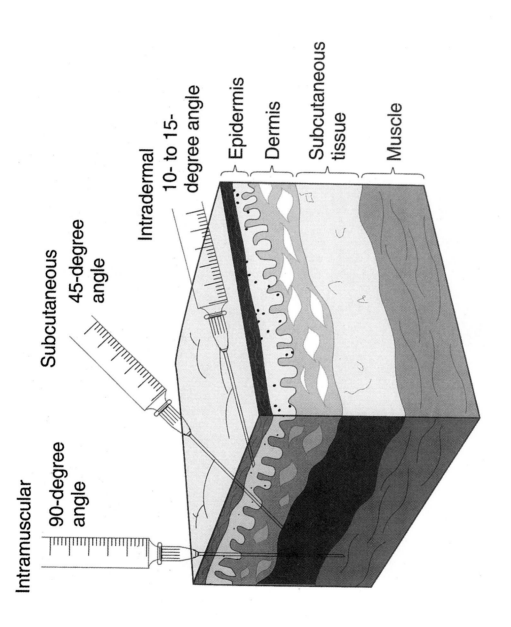

TM 16
Sites for subcutaneous injections

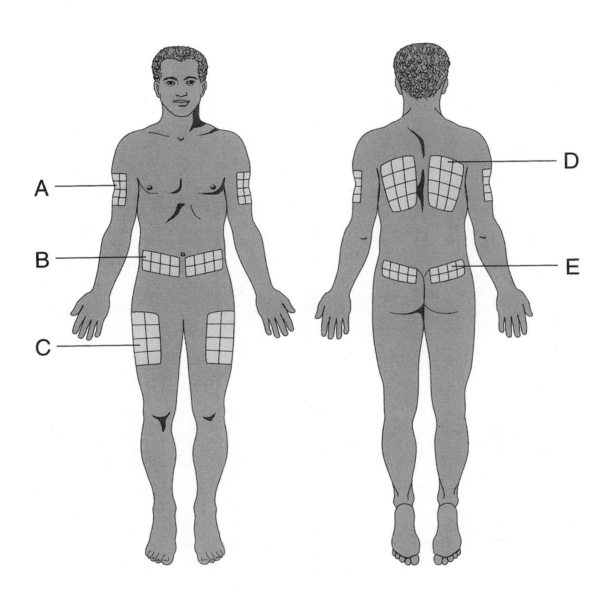

A

B

C

D

E

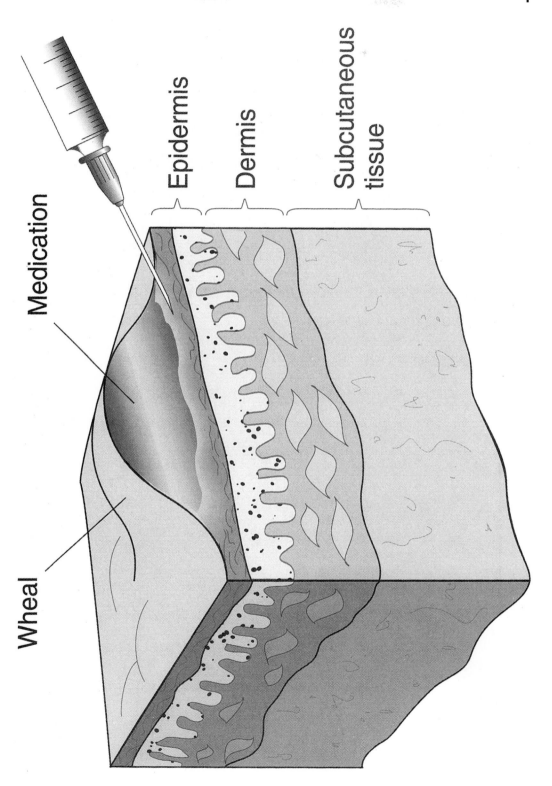

TM 17
Intradermal injection

Epidermis

Dermis

Subcutaneous tissue

Medication

Wheal

TM 18
Skin prick testing

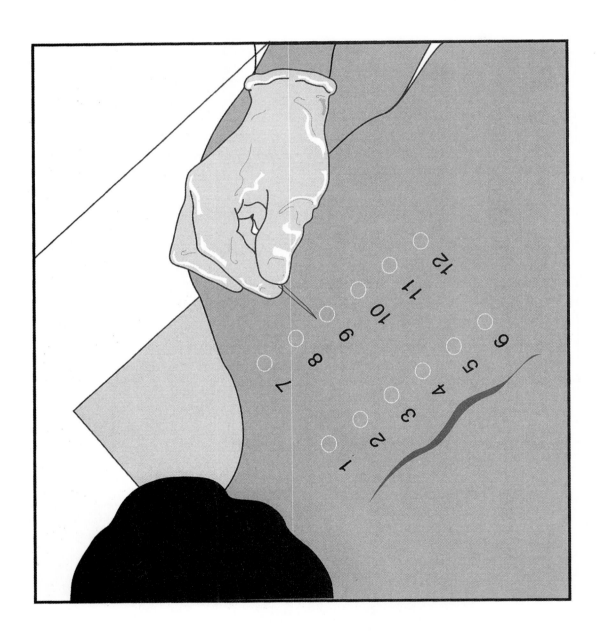

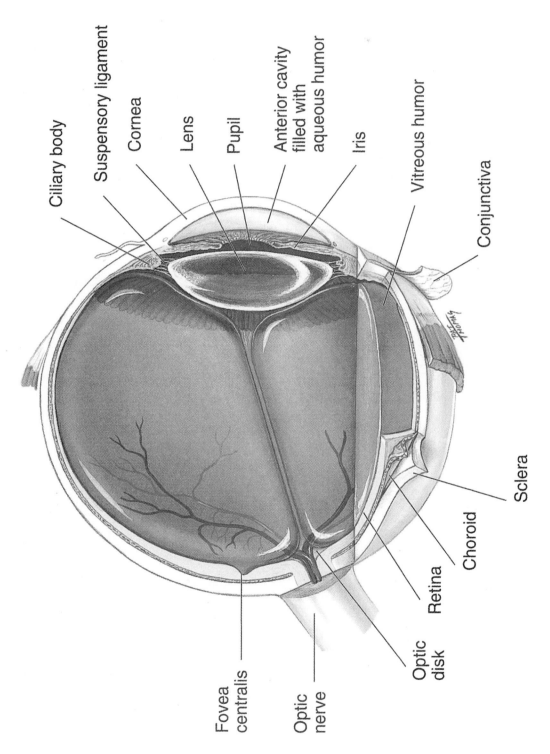

Ciliary body

Suspensory ligament

Cornea

Lens

Pupil

Anterior cavity filled with aqueous humor

Iris

Vitreous humor

Conjunctiva

Sclera

Choroid

Retina

Optic disk

Optic nerve

Fovea centralis

(From Applegate EJ: *The Anatomy and Physiology Learning System*, Philadelphia, WB Saunders, 1995.)

TM 20
Refraction

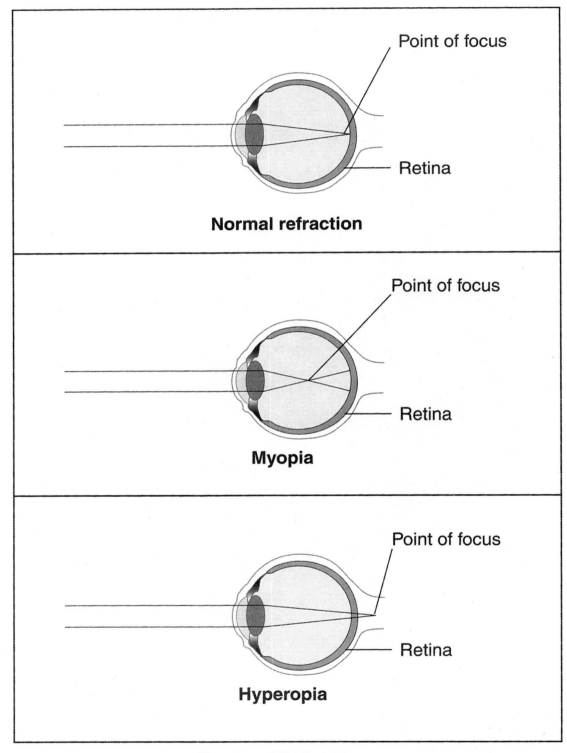

Normal refraction

Myopia

Hyperopia

Errors of Refraction

TM 21
Snellen eye chart

Based on a visual angle of one minute.

NO. 2867-1240

$\frac{20}{200}$	**E**	200 FT. 61 M — **1**
$\frac{20}{100}$	**F P**	100 FT. 30.5 M — **2**
$\frac{20}{70}$	**T O Z**	70 FT. 21.3M — **3**
$\frac{20}{50}$	**L P E D**	50 FT. 15.2 M — **4**
$\frac{20}{40}$	**P E C F D**	40 FT. 12.2 M — **5**
$\frac{20}{30}$	**E D F C Z P**	30 FT. 9.14 M — **6**
$\frac{20}{25}$	**F E L O P Z D**	25 FT. 7.62M — **7**
$\frac{20}{20}$	**D E F P O T E C**	20 FT. 6.10 M — **8**
$\frac{20}{15}$	**L E F O D P C T**	15 FT. 4.57M — **9**
$\frac{20}{13}$	**F D P L T C E O**	13 FT. 3.96M — **10**
$\frac{20}{10}$	**P E Z O L C F T D**	10 FT. 3.05M — **11**

TM 22
Structure of the ear

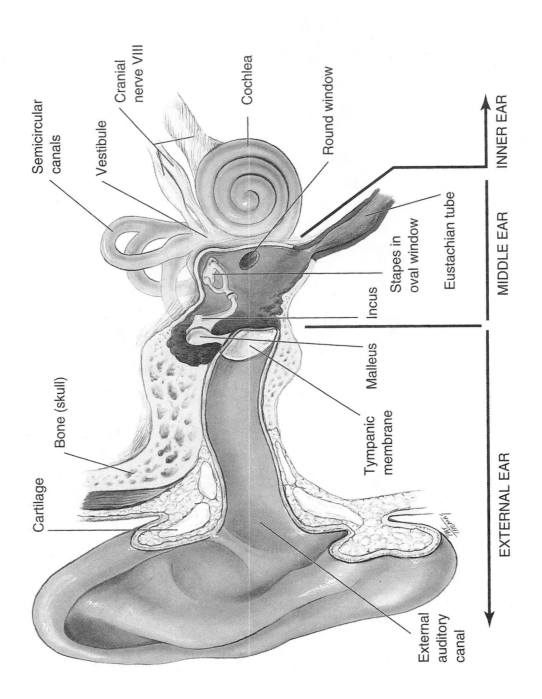

Semicircular canals

Vestibule

Cranial nerve VIII

Cochlea

Round window

INNER EAR

Eustachian tube

MIDDLE EAR

Stapes in oval window

Incus

Malleus

Tympanic membrane

Bone (skull)

Cartilage

EXTERNAL EAR

External auditory canal

(From Jarvis C: *Physical Examination and Health Assessment*, Philadelphia, WB Saunders, 1980

TM 23
Effects of the local application of heat and cold

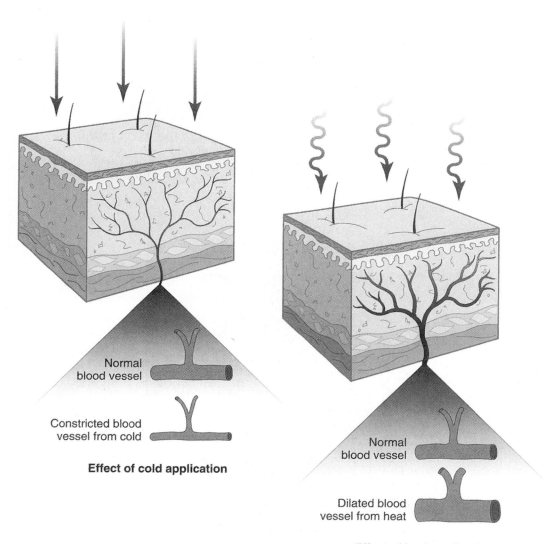

Normal
blood vessel

Constricted blood
vessel from cold

Effect of cold application

Normal
blood vessel

Dilated blood
vessel from heat

Effect of heat application

(From Wood LA, Rambo, BJ: Nursing Skills for Allied Health Services, Vol. 2, Philadelphia, WB Saunders, 1980)

TM 24
Types of casts

Short arm cast

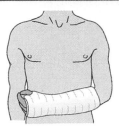

Extends from below the elbow to the fingers.

Long arm cast

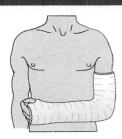

Extends from the axilla to the fingers, usually with a bend in the elbow.

Short leg cast

Begins just below the knee and extends to the toes; a walking heel is usually attached to a lower extremity cast so that the patient is able to ambulate.

Long leg cast

Extends from the midthigh to the toes.

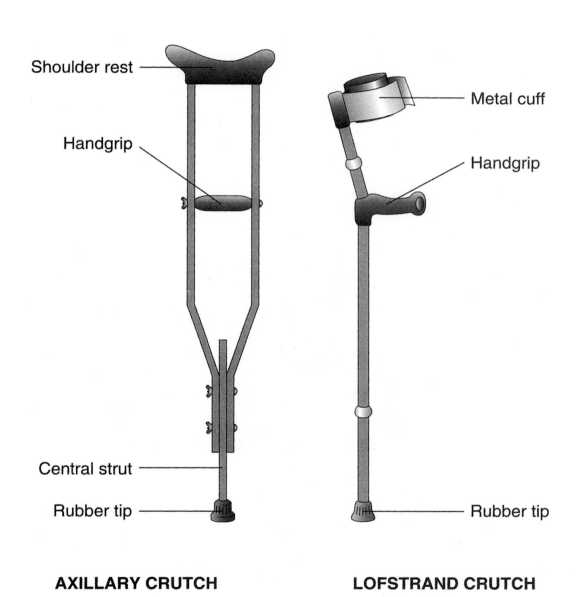

Shoulder rest

Handgrip

Central strut

Rubber tip

Metal cuff

Handgrip

Rubber tip

AXILLARY CRUTCH

LOFSTRAND CRUTCH

TM 26
The Bimanual pelvice examination

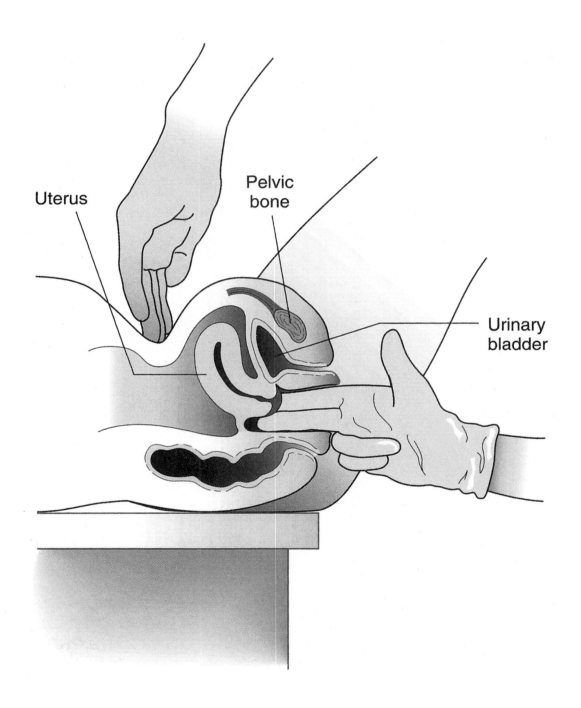

Uterus

Pelvic bone

Urinary bladder

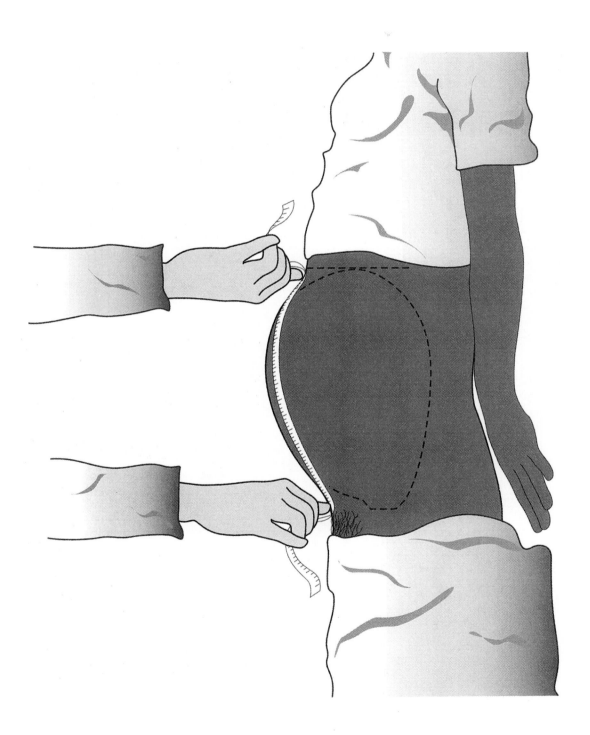

TM 28

Growth chart for length and weight of girls, birth to 36 months

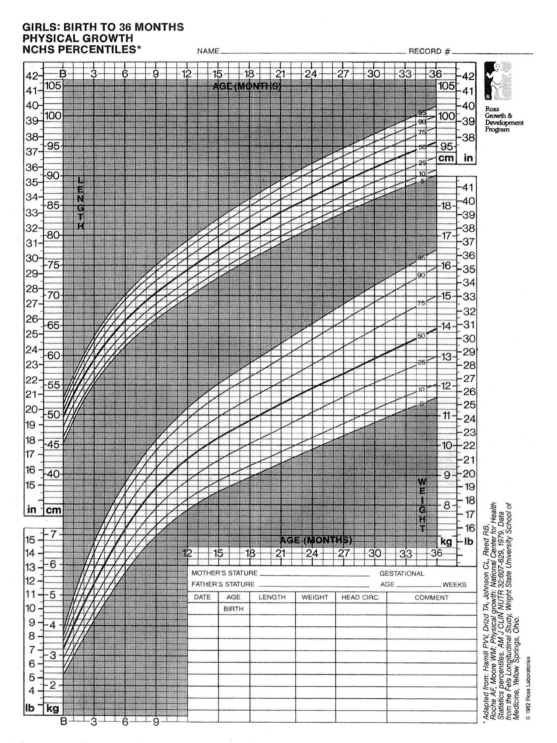

**GIRLS: BIRTH TO 36 MONTHS
PHYSICAL GROWTH
NCHS PERCENTILES***

NAME _____ RECORD # _____

Ross Growth & Development Program

MOTHER'S STATURE _____ GESTATIONAL
FATHER'S STATURE _____ AGE _____ WEEKS

DATE	AGE	LENGTH	WEIGHT	HEAD CIRC.	COMMENT
	BIRTH				

*Adapted from: Hamill PVV, Drizd TA, Johnson CL, Reed RB, Roche AF, Moore WM: Physical growth: National Center for Health Statistics percentiles. AM J CLIN NUTR 32:607-629, 1979. Data from the Fels Longitudinal Study, Wright State University School of Medicine, Yellow Springs, Ohio.

© 1982 Ross Laboratories

(Adapted from Hamill PVV et al: *National Center for Health Statistics percentiles, Am J Clin Nutr* 32:607-629, 1979. Data from the National Center for Health Statistics (NCHS), Hyattsville, MD)

TM 29
Growth chart for head circumference of girls, birth to 36 months

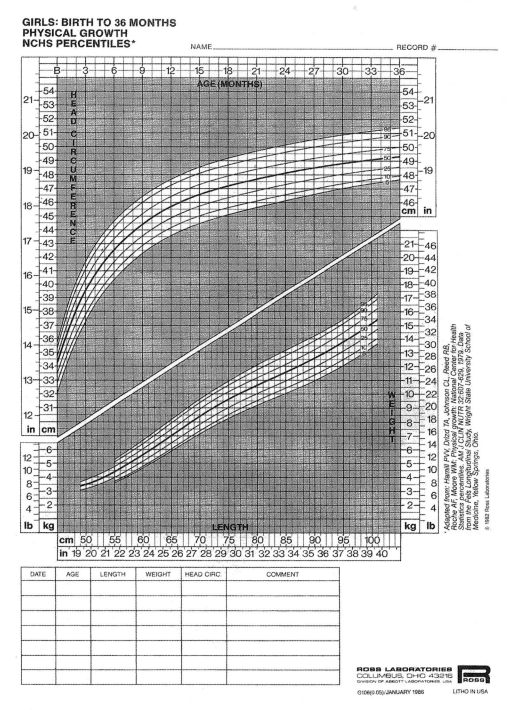

GIRLS: BIRTH TO 36 MONTHS
PHYSICAL GROWTH
NCHS PERCENTILES*

NAME_____ RECORD #_____

* Adapted from: Hamill PVV, Drizd TA, Johnson CL, Reed RB, Roche AF, Moore WM: Physical growth: National Center for Health Statistics percentiles. AM J CLIN NUTR 32:607-629, 1979. Data from the Fels Longitudinal Study, Wright State University School of Medicine, Yellow Springs, Ohio.

© 1982 Ross Laboratories

DATE	AGE	LENGTH	WEIGHT	HEAD CIRC.	COMMENT

ROSS LABORATORIES
COLUMBUS, OHIO 43216
DIVISION OF ABBOTT LABORATORIES, USA

G106(0.05)/JANUARY 1986   LITHO IN USA

(Adapted from Hamill PVV et al: *National Center for Health Statistics percentiles, Am J Clin Nutr* 32:607-629, 1979. Data from the National Center for Health Statistics (NCHS), Hyattsville, MD)

TM 30
Diagram of the heart

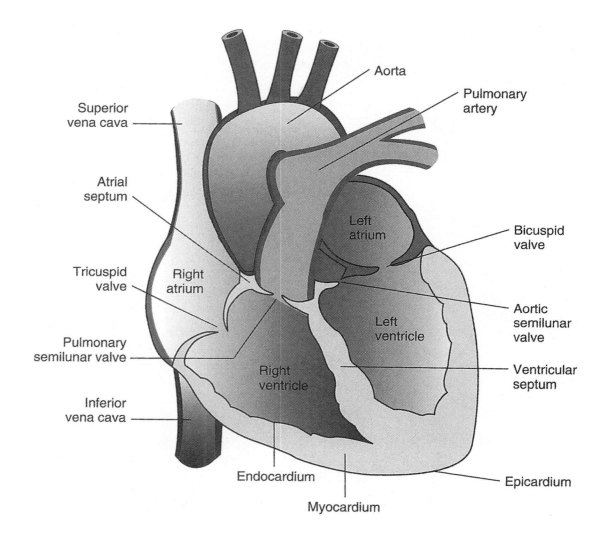

Superior
vena cava

Atrial
septum

Tricuspid
valve

Right
atrium

Pulmonary
semilunar valve

Inferior
vena cava

Endocardium

Myocardium

Right
ventricle

Aorta

Pulmonary
artery

Left
atrium

Bicuspid
valve

Aortic
semilunar
valve

Left
ventricle

Ventricular
septum

Epicardium

TM 31

Conduction system of the heart

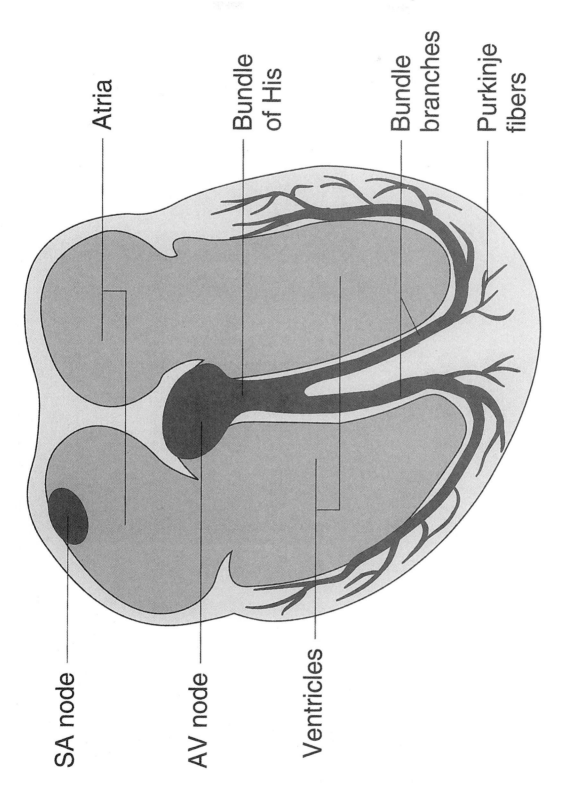

Atria

Bundle of His

Bundle branches

Purkinje fibers

SA node

AV node

Ventricles

TM 32
ECG cycle

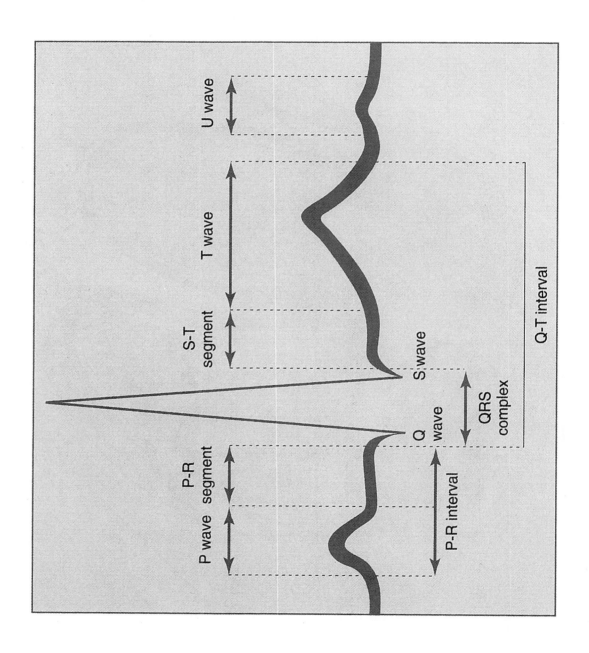

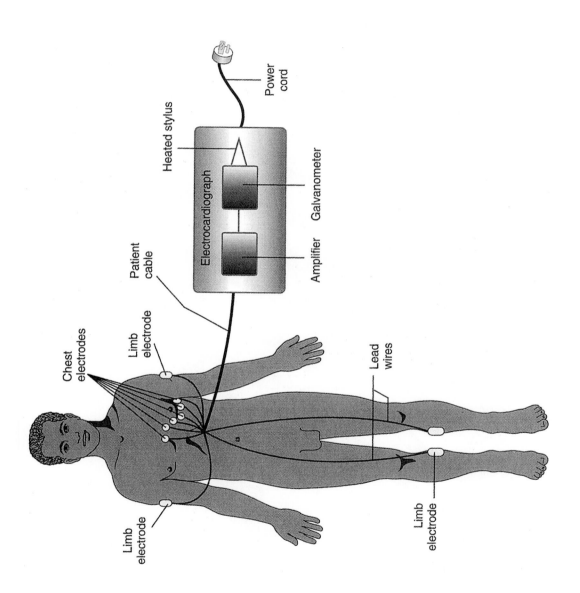

Power cord

Heated stylus

Galvanometer

Electrocardiograph

Amplifier

Patient cable

Chest electrodes

Limb electrode

Lead wires

Limb electrode

Limb electrode

TM 34
Chest leads

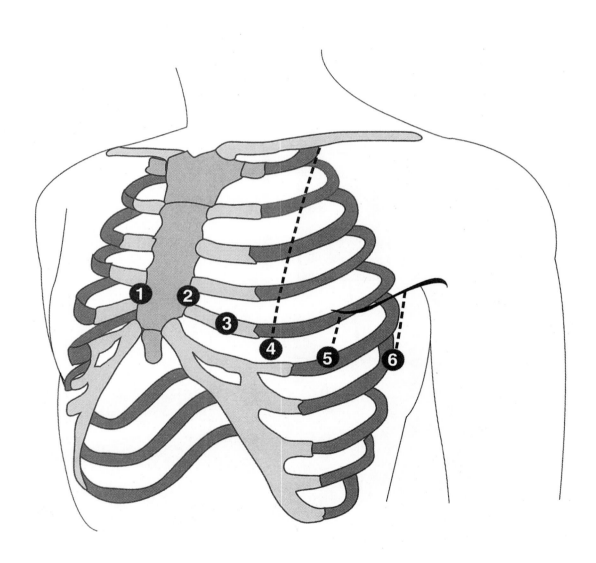

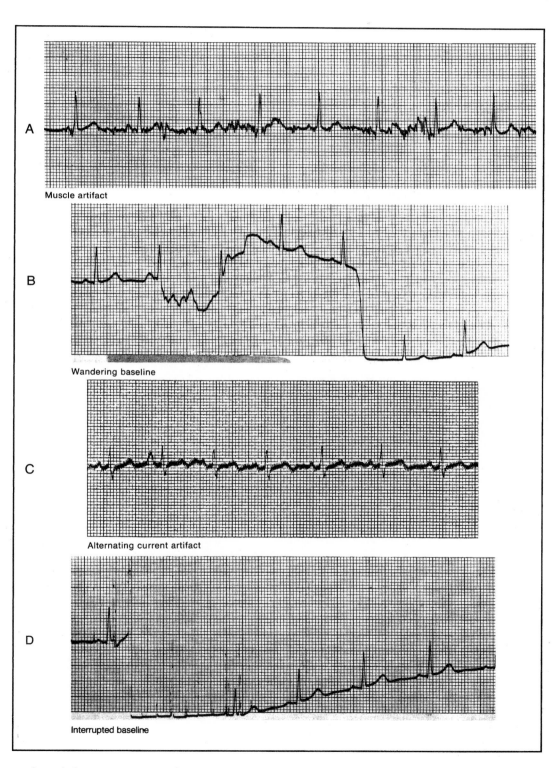

A — Muscle artifact

B — Wandering baseline

C — Alternating current artifact

D — Interrupted baseline

(Courtesy of Burdick Corporation, Milton, WI)

TM 36
Structures making up urinary system

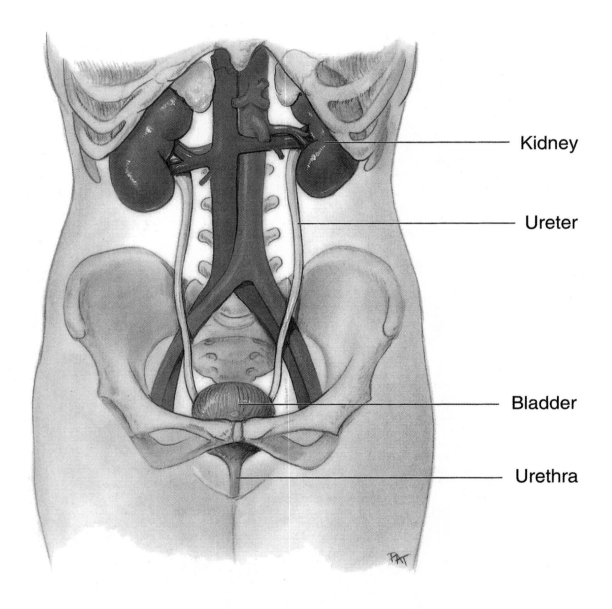

Kidney

Ureter

Bladder

Urethra

(From Applegate EJ: *The Anatomy and Physiology Learning System*, Philadelphia, WB Saunders, 1995.)

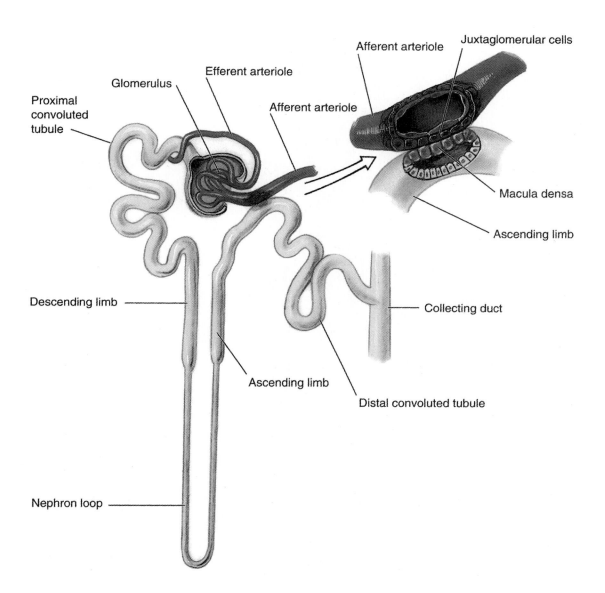

Proximal convoluted tubule

Glomerulus

Efferent arteriole

Afferent arteriole

Afferent arteriole

Juxtaglomerular cells

Macula densa

Ascending limb

Descending limb

Ascending limb

Collecting duct

Distal convoluted tubule

Nephron loop

(From Applegate EJ: *The Anatomy and Physiology Learning System*, Philadelphia, WB Saunders, 1995.)

TM 38
Antecubital veins

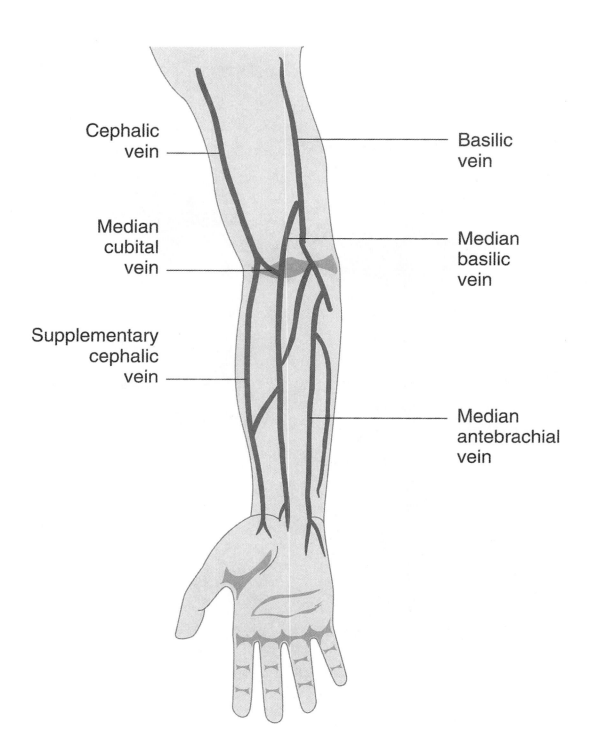

Cephalic vein

Median cubital vein

Supplementary cephalic vein

Basilic vein

Median basilic vein

Median antebrachial vein

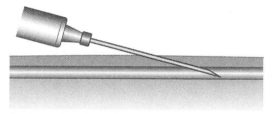

A   Correct insertion of the needle into the vein.

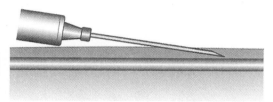

B   Improper angle of insertion (<15°), causing the needle to enter above the vein.

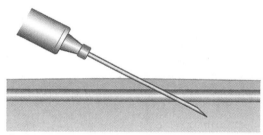

C   Improper angle of insertion (>15°), causing the needle to go through the vein.

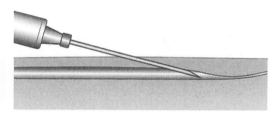

D   Collapsed vein (most likely to occur in persons with small veins).

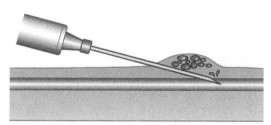

E   The beveled opening is partially within and partially outside of the vein, causing a hematoma.

TM 40
Hematocrit test results

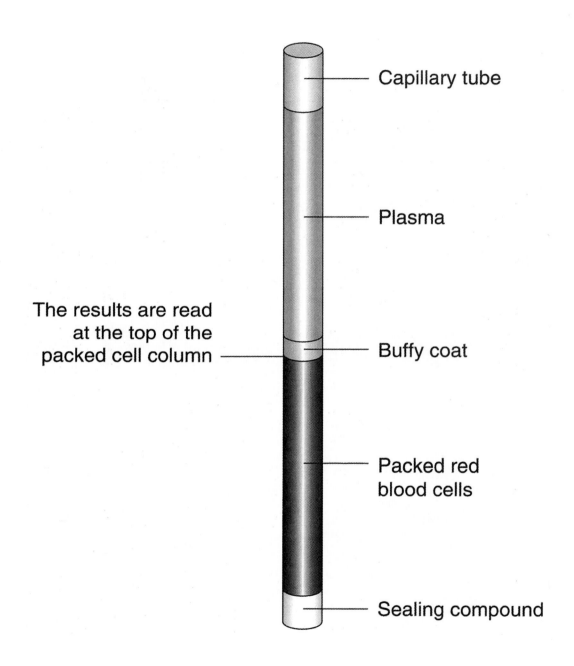

Capillary tube

Plasma

The results are read
at the top of the
packed cell column

Buffy coat

Packed red
blood cells

Sealing compound

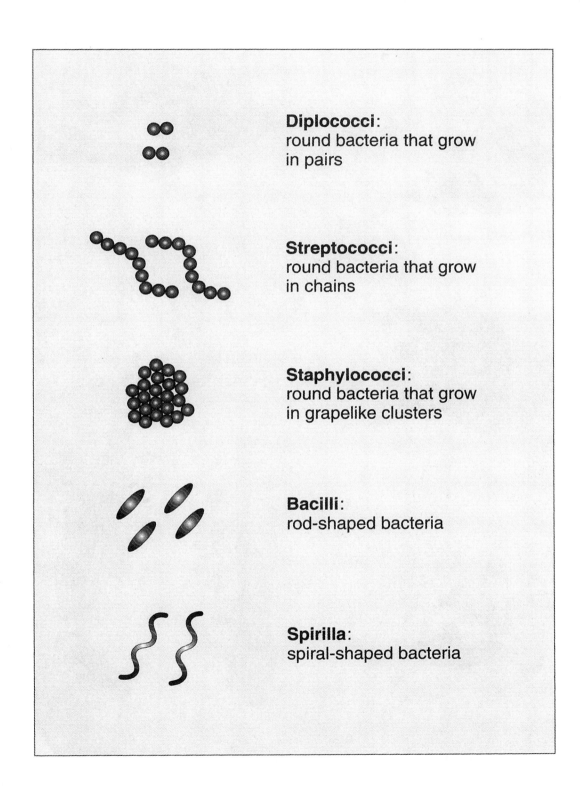

Diplococci:
round bacteria that grow
in pairs

Streptococci:
round bacteria that grow
in chains

Staphylococci:
round bacteria that grow
in grapelike clusters

Bacilli:
rod-shaped bacteria

Spirilla:
spiral-shaped bacteria

TM 42
Location of pressure points

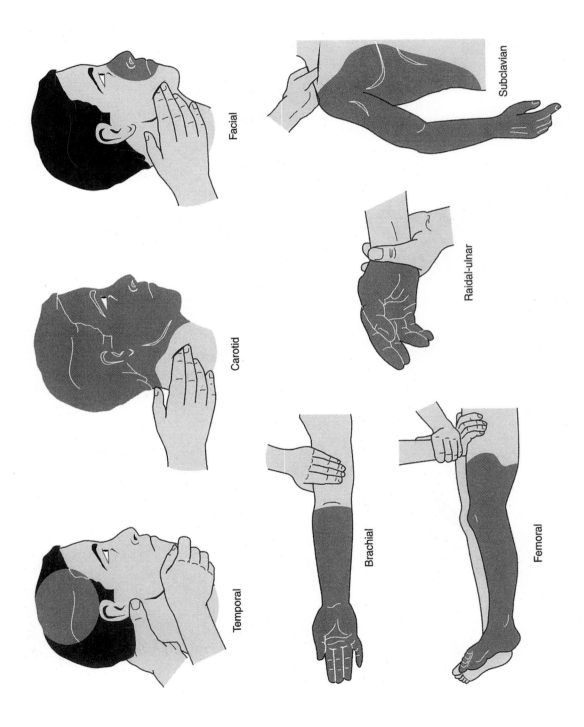

Facial

Subclavian

Carotid

Raidal-ulnar

Temporal

Brachial

Femoral

(From Miller BF, Keane CB: Encyclopedia and Dictionary of Medicine, Nursing, and Allied Health, ed 6, Philadelphia, WB Saunders, 1997)

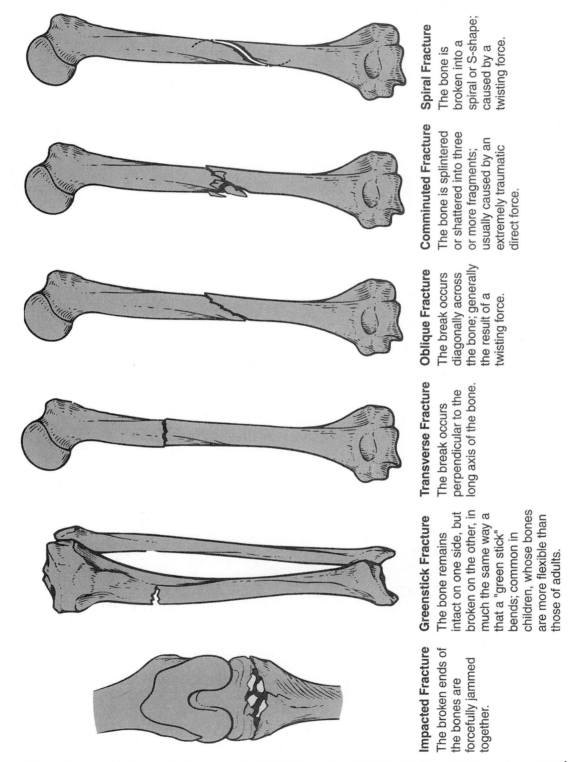

Spiral Fracture The bone is broken into a spiral or S-shape; caused by a twisting force.

Comminuted Fracture The bone is splintered or shattered into three or more fragments; usually caused by an extremely traumatic direct force.

Oblique Fracture The break occurs diagonally across the bone; generally the result of a twisting force.

Transverse Fracture The break occurs perpendicular to the long axis of the bone.

Greenstick Fracture The bone remains intact on one side, but broken on the other, in much the same way a that a "green stick" bends; common in children, whose bones are more flexible than those of adults.

Impacted Fracture The broken ends of the bones are forcefully jammed together.

(Adapted from Copass M, Soper R, Eisenberg M: EMT Manual, ed 2 Philadelphia, WB Saunders, 1991)

TM 44
Types of burns

Burn type	APPEARANCE	SENSATION	COURSE
SUPERFICIAL BURN	Mild to severe erythema; skin blanches with pressure	Painful; Hyperesthetic; Tingling; Pain eased by cooling	Discomfort lasts about 48 hours; Desquamation peeling in 3–7 days
PARTIAL-THICKNESS BURN	Large thick-walled blisters covering extensive area (vesiculation); Edema; mottled red base; broken epidermis; wet, shiny, weeping surface	Painful; Sensitive to cold air	Superficial partial-thickness burn heals in 14–21 days; Deep partial-thickness burn requires 21–28 days for healing; Healing rate varies with burn depth and presence or absence of infection
FULL-THICKNESS BURN	Variable, e.g., deep red, black, white, brown; Dry surface; Edema; Fat exposed; Tissue disrupted	Little pain; Insensate	Full-thickness dead skin suppurates and liquefies after 2–3 weeks; Spontaneous healing impossible; Requires removal of eschar and subsequent split or full-thickness skin grafting; Hypertrophic scarring and wound contractures likely to develop without preventive measures

EPIDERMIS
Sweat duct
Capillary
Sebaceous gland
Nerve endings
DERMIS
Hair follicle
Sweat gland
Fat
Blood vessels
SUBCUTANEOUS TISSUE

(From Polaski, AL, Tatro SE: Luckmann's Core Principles and Practice of Medical-Surgical Nursing, Philadelphia, WB Saunders, 1996)

TM 45
Telephone message form

MESSAGE FROM										

For Dr.	Name of Caller	Rel. to pt.	Patient	Pt. Age	Pt. Temp.	Message Date	Message Time	Urgent
							PM	☐YES ☐NO

Message: | Allergies

Respond to Phone #	Best Time To Call	Pharmacy Name/#	Patient's Chart Attached	Patient's Chart #	Initials
	AM PM		☐YES ☐NO		

DOCTOR–STAFF RESPONSE

Doctor's/Staff Orders/Follow-up Action

	Call Back	Chart Mes.	Follow-up Date	Follow-up Completed–Date/Time	Response By:
	☐YES ☐NO	☐YES ☐NO		PM	

(From Potter BA: *Instructor's Manual and Curriculum Guide for Medical Office Administration: A worktext,* Philadelphia, Saunders, 2003)

TM 46

Appointment book page

			DAY / DATE				
			8	00			
				15			
				30			
				45			
			9	00			
				15			
				30			
				45			
			10	00			
				15			
				30			
				45			
			11	00			
				15			
				30			
				45			
			12	00			
				15			
				30			
				45			
			1	00			
				15			
				30			
				45			
			2	00			
				15			
				30			
				45			
			3	00			
				15			
				30			
				45			
			4	00			
				15			
				30			
				45			
			5	00			
				15			
				30			
				45			

TM 47
Patient registration form

REGISTRATION
(PLEASE PRINT)

Home Phone:_____   Today's Date:_____

PATIENT INFORMATION

Name_____ Soc. Sec.#_____
_____ Last Name _____ First Name _____ Initial

Address _____

City_____ State_____ Zip_____

Single____ Married____ Widowed____ Separated____ Divorced____ Sex M____ F____ Age____ Birthdate_____

Patient Employed by_____ Occupation_____

Business Address_____ Business Phone_____

By whom were you referred? _____

In case of emergency who should be notified?_____ Phone_____
_____ Name _____ Relation to Patient

PRIMARY INSURANCE

Person Responsible for Account _____
_____ Last Name _____ First Name _____ Initial

Relation to Patient_____ Birthdate_____ Soc. Sec.#_____

Address (if different from patient's) _____ Phone_____

City_____ State_____ Zip_____

Person Responsible Employed by_____ Occupation_____

Business Address_____ Business Phone_____

Insurance Company _____

Contract #_____ Group #_____ Subscriber #_____

Name of other dependents covered under this plan _____

ADDITIONAL INSURANCE

Is patient covered by additional insurance? ____Yes ____No

Subscriber Name_____ Relation to Patient_____ Birthdate_____

Address (if different from patient's) _____ Phone_____

City_____ State_____ Zip_____

Subscriber Employed by_____ Business Phone_____

Insurance Company_____ Soc. Sec.#_____

Contract #_____ Group #_____ Subscriber #_____

Name of other dependents covered under this plan _____

ASSIGNMENT AND RELEASE

I, the undersigned, certify that I (or my dependent) have insurance coverage with _____
_____ Name of Insurance Company(ies)
and assign directly to Dr._____ insurance benefits, if any, otherwise payable to me for services rendered. I understand that I am financially responsible for all charges whether or not paid by insurance. I hereby authorize the doctor to release all information necessary to secure the payment of benefits. I authorize the use of this signature on all insurance submissions.

_____   _____   _____
Responsible Party Signature   Relationship   Date

ORDER # 58-8425 • © 1996 BIBBERO SYSTEMS, INC. • PETALUMA, CALIFORNIA • TO REORDER CALL TOLL FREE: (800) 242-2376 OR FAX: (800) 242-9330

TM 48
Encounter form

LIC. # 999999
S.S. # 111-22-3333
UPIN # A12365

JANE A. SMITH, M.D.
Reproductive Endocrinology
123 FIRST AVENUE
ANYTOWN, N.Y. 22222

TELEPHONE: (212) 555-4444
FAX: (212) 555-4545

PATIENT'S LAST NAME	FIRST		INITIAL	BIRTHDATE	SEX	TODAY'S DATE
				/ /	☑ FEMALE	/ /

ADDRESS	CITY	STATE	ZIP	RELATION TO SUBSCRIBER	REFERRING PHYSICIAN

SUBSCRIBER OR POLICYHOLDER | INSURANCE CARRIER

ADDRESS	CITY	STATE	ZIP	INS. ID	COVERAGE CODE	GROUP

OTHER HEALTH COVERAGE?
☐ NO ☐ YES
IDENTIFY

DISABILITY RELATED TO: ☐ IND.
☐ ACCIDENT ☐ PREGNANCY
☐ OTHER

DATE SYMPTOMS APPEARED,
INCEPTION OF PREGNANCY, OR
ACCIDENT OCCURRED: / /

ASSIGNMENT & RELEASE: I hereby assign my insurance benefits to be paid directly to the undersigned physician. I am financially responsible for non-covered services. I also authorize the physician to release any information required to process this claim.
SIGNED: (Patient, or Parent, if Minor)   DATE: / /

(Left margin: PATIENT INFORMATION)

✔ DESCRIPTION	CODE	FEE	✔ DESCRIPTION	CODE	FEE	✔ DESCRIPTION	CODE	FEE
OFFICE VISIT			**OFFICE PROCEDURES**			**LABORATORY - IN OFFICE**		
New Patient			Sperm Wash	58323		Pregnancy Test	85160	
Consultation	99204		Cauterization of Cervix	57510		Urinalysis	81002	
Comprehensive	99205		Cervical Biopsy	57500		Stool Occult Blood	82270	
OFFICE VISIT			Endocervical Curettage	57505		Lyme Titer	86317	
Established Patient			Endometrial Biopsy	58100		Estradiol	82670	
Limited	99211		Office Endometrial Curettage	58102		Chemistry	80019	
Intermediate	99212		Post Coital Test	89300		CBC, pit., Diff.	85024	
Extended	99213		Artificial Insemination	58310		T3 Uptake	84479	
Comprehensive	99214		Pelvic Sonogram	76856		T4	84435	
Comprehensive	99215		Vulvar Biopsy	56600		TSH	84443	
SURGERY			Bilateral Mammogram	76091		ESR	85650	
D & C	58120		Unilateral Mammogram	76090		Pregnancy Test	84702	
Pregnancy Termination	59840		Breast Ultrasound	76645		FSH	83000	
Laparoscopy	56305		Abdominal Ultrasound	76700		Prolactin	84146	
Hysteroscopy	56351		Polypectomy	57500				
Laporotomy	49000							
Myomectomy	58140							
Hysterectomy	58150							

DIAGNOSIS: **ICD-9**

☐ Abortion, Incomplete 634.71	☐ Diabetes Mellitus 250.0	☐ Hyperthyroidism 242.9
☐ Abortion, Spontaneous 634.90	☐ Dysmenorrhea 625.3	☐ Hypothyroidism 244.9
☐ Alopecia 704.09	☐ Dyspareunia 625.0	☐ Infertility 628.9
☐ Amenorrhea 626.0	☐ Dysuria 788.1	☐ Luteal Phase Insufficiency .628.8
☐ Anemia 285.9	☐ Ectopic Pregnancy 633.9	☐ Menometrorrhagia 626.2
☐ Anovulation 628.0	☐ Edema 782.3	☐ Menopausal Syndrome ...627.2
☐ Atrophic Vaginitis 627.3	☐ Endometrial Hyperplasia .621.3	☐ Menorrhagia 626.2
☐ Breast Cyst 610.1	☐ Endometriosis 617.0	☐ Monilial Vaginitis 112.1
☐ Breast Mass 611.72	☐ Fatigue 780.7	☐ Obesity 278.0
☐ Breast Pain 611.71	☐ Fibrocystic Breast Disease .610.1	☐ Osteoarthritis 715.9
☐ Cervical Polyp 622.7	☐ Galactorrhea 676.6	☐ Osteopenia 733.9
☐ Cervicitis 616.0	☐ Headache 784.0	☐ Osteoporosis 733.0
☐ Condyloma 091.3	☐ Hemorrhoids 455.6	☐ Ovarian Cyst 620.2
☐ Cyclic Adrenal Hyperplasia .255.2	☐ Herpes 054.1	☐ Ovarian Insufficiency ...256.3
☐ Cystocele 618.0	☐ Hypercholesterolemia ...272.0	☐ Pelvic Pain 625.9
☐ Cystitis 595.9	☐ Hyperprolactinemia 253.1	☐ Polycystic Ovary Syndrome 256.4
	☐ Hypertension 401.9	☐ Postmenopausal Bleeding .627.1

☐ Pregnancy V22.2
☐ Pregnancy Termination ...V72.4
☐ Premature Ovarian Failure .256.3
☐ Premenopausal Menorrhagia .627.0
☐ Prolactinoma 253
☐ Prolapsed Uterus 618.1
☐ Rectocele 569.1
☐ Thyroiditis 245.2
☐ Trichomonas 131.0
☐ Urinary Tract Infection ...599.0
☐ Uterine Fibroids 218.9
☐ Vasomotor Instability 780.2
☐ Vaginitis 616.1
☐ Vulvitis 616.1

DIAGNOSIS: (IF NOT CHECKED ABOVE)

ADDITIONAL INFORMATION:

DOCTOR'S SIGNATURE

SERVICES PERFORMED AT: ☐ OFFICE   ☐ University Hospital   ☐ Day Surgery / University Hosp.
345 Second Avenue   678 Third Avenue
Anytown, N.Y. 23333   Anytown, N.Y. 23444

REFERRING PHYSICIAN:

ACCEPT ASSIGNMENT? ☐ YES ☐ NO

TOTAL TODAY'S FEE

PREVIOUS BALANCE

INSTRUCTIONS TO PATIENT FOR FILING INSURANCE CLAIMS:

1. COMPLETE UPPER PORTION OF THIS FORM; SIGN AND DATE.
2. MAIL THIS FORM DIRECTLY TO YOUR INSURANCE COMPANY. YOU MAY ATTACH YOUR OWN INSURANCE COMPANY'S FORM IF YOU WISH, ALTHOUGH IT IS NOT NECESSARY.
PLEASE REMEMBER THAT PAYMENT IS YOUR OBLIGATION, REGARDLESS OF INSURANCE OR OTHER THIRD PARTY INVOLVEMENT.

AMT. REC'D. TODAY

NEW BALANCE

INSUR-A-BILL ® BIBBERO SYSTEMS, INC. • PETALUMA, CA • © 5/95 (SB M-N)   (REV. 9/96)

RECORDS RELEASE AUTHORIZATION

TO _____
Doctor or Hospital

_____
Address

I HEREBY AUTHORIZE AND REQUEST YOU TO RELEASE TO:

ALL RECORDS IN YOUR POSSESION CONCERNING _____

_____ ILLNESS AND/OR

TREATMENT DURING THE PERIOD FROM _____ TO _____.

NAME _____ TEL. _____

ADDRESS _____

SIGNATURE _____ DATE _____
(If relative, state relationship)

WITNESS _____ DATE _____

25-8104 © 1973 BIBBERO SYSTEMS, INC., PETALUMA,, CA.

TM 50
Day sheet

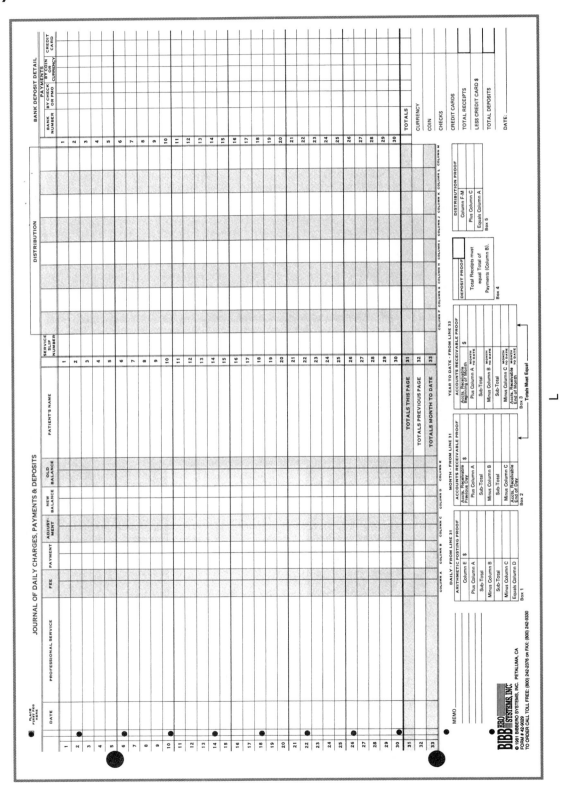

TM 51
Patient ledger card

STATEMENT

LEONARD S. TAYLOR, M.D.
2100 WEST PARK AVENUE
CHAMPAIGN, ILLINOIS 61820

TELEPHONE 351-5400

DATE	FAMILY MEMBER	PROFESSIONAL SERVICE	CHARGE	CREDITS		BALANCE
				PAYMENTS	ADJ.	
				BALANCE FORWARD ▷		

Form 1625

PAY LAST AMOUNT IN THIS COLUMN △

OC - OFFICE CALL	INS - INSURANCE	PE - PHYSICAL EXAMINATION
HC - HOUSE CALL	OB - OBSTETRICAL CARE	EKG - ELECTROCARDIOGRAM
HOSP - HOSPITAL CARE	PAP - PAPANICOLAOU TEST	XR - X-RAY
L - LABORATORY	OS - OFFICE SURGERY	M - MEDICATION
I - INJECTION	HS - HOSPITAL SURGERY	NC - NO CHARGE

(Courtesy Colwell Systems, Inc., Champaign, IL)

TM 52
CMS 1500 form

(Modified from Fordney M: *Insurance Handbook for the Medical Office*, ed 8, Philadelphia, Saunders, 2004)

TM 53
Managed care referral form

MANAGED CARE PLAN
TREATMENT AUTHORIZATION REQUEST

TO BE COMPLETED BY PRIMARY CARE PHYSICIAN
OR OUTSIDE PROVIDER

Health Net ☐	Met Life ☐
Pacificare ☐	Travelers ☐
Secure Horizons ☐	Pru Care ☐

Member No. _____

Patient Name: _____ Date: _____

M _____ F _____ Birthdate_____ Home telephone number_____

Address _____

Primary Care Physician _____ Provider ID#_____

Referring Physician _____ Provider ID#_____

Referred to _____ Address_____

_____ Office telephone no. _____

Diagnosis Code _____ Diagnosis _____

Diagnosis Code _____ Diagnosis _____

Treatment Plan: _____

Authorization requested for procedures/tests/visits:

Procedure Code_____ Description _____

Procedure Code _____ Description _____

Facility to be used: _____ Estimated length of stay _____

Office ☐   Outpatient ☐   Inpatient ☐   Other ☐

List of potential consultants (i.e., anesthetists, assistants, or medical/surgical):

_____

Physician's signature   _____

TO BE COMPLETED BY PRIMARY CARE PHYSICIAN

PCP Recommendations:_____ PCP Initials _____

Date eligibility checked_____ Effective date _____

TO BE COMPLETED BY UTILIZATION MANAGEMENT

Authorized _____ Not authorized _____

Deferred _____ Modified _____

Authorization Request#_____

Comments: _____

TM 54
Check

1837

DATE _____
TO _____
FOR _____

BALANCE BROUGHT FORWARD		
DEPOSITS		
BALANCE		
AMT THIS CK		
BALANCE CARRIED FORWARD		

BLACKBURN PRIMARY CARE ASSOCIATES, PC
1990 Turquiose Drive
Blackburn, WI 54937
608-459-8857

1837
94-72/1224

DATE _____

PAY TO THE ORDER OF _____ $ _____

_____ DOLLARS

DERBYSHIRE SAVINGS Member FDIC
P.O. BOX 8923
Blackburn, WI 54937

FOR _____

⑈055003⑈ 446782011⑈ 678800470

1838

DATE _____
TO _____
FOR _____

BALANCE BROUGHT FORWARD		
DEPOSITS		
BALANCE		
AMT THIS CK		
BALANCE CARRIED FORWARD		

BLACKBURN PRIMARY CARE ASSOCIATES, PC
1990 Turquiose Drive
Blackburn, WI 54937
608-459-8857

1838
94-72/1224

DATE _____

PAY TO THE ORDER OF _____ $ _____

_____ DOLLARS

DERBYSHIRE SAVINGS Member FDIC
P.O. BOX 8923
Blackburn, WI 54937

FOR _____

⑈055003⑈ 446782011⑈ 678800470

1839

DATE _____
TO _____
FOR _____

BALANCE BROUGHT FORWARD		
DEPOSITS		
BALANCE		
AMT THIS CK		
BALANCE CARRIED FORWARD		

BLACKBURN PRIMARY CARE ASSOCIATES, PC
1990 Turquiose Drive
Blackburn, WI 54937
608-459-8857

1839
94-72/1224

DATE _____

PAY TO THE ORDER OF _____ $ _____

_____ DOLLARS

DERBYSHIRE SAVINGS Member FDIC
P.O. BOX 8923
Blackburn, WI 54937

FOR _____

⑈055003⑈ 446782011⑈ 678800470

(From Hunt SA: *Fundamentals of Medical Assisting,* Philadelphia, Saunders, 2002)

CHECKING ACCOUNT DEPOSIT TICKET

Horizons Healthcare Center
123 Main Ave.
Farmington, ND 58000

Date

State Bank of Farmington
500 Main Ave.
Farmington, ND

41-764
4536

USE OTHER SIDE FOR
ADDITIONAL LISTINGS

BE SURE EACH ITEM IS PROPERLY
ENDORSED

FOR USE IN LEARNING ACTIVITIES ONLY

CASH		
C H E C K S		
TOTAL FROM OTHER SIDE		
TOTAL		
LESS CASH RECEIVED		
NET DEPOSIT		

1: 45367647 " : 7868765765 08 " 330112

CHECKS AND OTHER ITEMS ARE RECEIVED FOR DEPOSIT SUBJECT TO THE TERMS OF THIS BANK'S COLLECTION AGREEMENT

DEPOSIT TICKET
FOR CLEAR COPY, PRESS FIRMLY WITH BALL POINT PEN.

State Bank of Farmington
500 Main Ave.
Farmington, ND 58000

DATE _____

CHECKS AND OTHER ITEMS ARE RECEIVED FOR DEPOSIT SUBJECT TO THE PROVISIONS OF THE UNIFORM COMMERCIAL CODE OR ANY APPLICABLE COLLECTION AGREEMENT

	DOLLARS	CENTS
CURRENCY		
COIN		
LIST EACH CHECK		
1.		
2.		
3.		
4.		
5.		
6.		
7.		
8.		
9.		
10.		
11.		
12.		
13.		
14.		
15.		
16.		
17.		
18.		
19.		
20.		
PLEASE ENTER TOTAL.		
TOTAL DEPOSIT		

PLEASE BE SURE ALL ITEMS
ARE PROPERLY ENDORSED

DEPOSITS MAY NOT BE AVAILABLE
FOR IMMEDIATE WITHDRAWAL

TOTAL ITEMS

50-17
223 0107

1: 45890277 " : 6334792445 08 " 6221

(From Potter BA: *Medical Office Administration: A worktext,* Philadelphia, Saunders, 2003)

TM 56
Pegboard system

RECORD OF CHECKS DRAWN BY _____

MONTH OF _____

BALANCE FORWARD

BALANCE

DEPOSITS — DATE | AMOUNT

NET SALARY

OTHER

SWT

FWT

F.I.C.A.

S.D.I.

GROSS

DESCRIPTION–NON PAYROLL CHECKS

NET AMOUNT OF CHECK

CHECK NO.

DATE

CHECK ISSUED TO

MEMO

FIRST CHECK

State Bank of Farmington
500 Main Avenue
Farmington, ND 58000

98-95
1251

№ 7388

DOLLARS

Horizons Healthcare Center
123 Main Avenue
Farmington, ND 58000

PAY

TO THE ORDER OF

PLEASE DETACH BEFORE CASHING

DATE | REF. | AMOUNT | DATE | REF. | AMOUNT

TOTAL AMOUNT

DATE | CHECK NO. | AMOUNT

GROSS SALARY | F.I.C.A. | FED'L. W/H | STATE W/H | OTHER | NET SALARY

S.D.I.

THIS IS A STATEMENT OF PAYMENT OR EARNINGS & DEDUCTIONS

NAME OR S.S.N.

PERIOD FROM _____ TO _____

Horizons Healthcare Center

TO REORDER CALL TOLL FREE 800-BIBBERO (IN CA)
OR 800–358-8240 (REST OF U.S.A.)
BIBBERO SYSTEMS, INC.
PETALUMA, CA

44-10501 © 1972

LAST CK

TOTAL THIS PAGE

TOTAL PREVIOUS PAGE

TOTAL TO DATE

(From Potter BA: *Medical Office Administration: A worktext*, Philadelphia, Saunders, 2003)

Andrus/Clini-Rec®
General Health History Questionnaire
Male or Female

C
O
N
F
I
D
E
N
T
I
A
L

INSTRUCTIONS TO MY PATIENT

One of the most important parts of the medical record your doctor keeps for you is a health history concerning your past and present health problems, and any personal information which might affect the state of your health.

Your answers will be treated confidentially, as are all parts of your visit. Please return this questionnaire to your doctor or to the doctor's nurse or assistant after you complete it.

Take all the time you need to complete this questionnaire. Answer each question as best you can by filling in the information asked for or by putting an "X" in the appropriate space. Choose the answer to each question which in your mind comes closest to applying to you.

If there is any question you have difficulty answering, just circle the question. You can discuss it with the doctor when you return the questionnaire.

If you have completed this questionnaire at home, be sure to bring it with you so that you and the doctor can go over your answers during your appointment within a confidential setting.

If this is a RE-EXAMINATION and you have previously filled out one of these "Patient Administered Comprehensive Health History Questionnaires", fill in PART A - Present Health History, sections I & II. *You do not* have to redo sections III & IV, or PART B - Past History.

Any changes which have occurred since you last filled out the questionnaire should be noted.

Created and Developed by
"Medical Economics" Professional Systems

BIBBERO SYSTEMS, INC.
1300 N. McDOWELL BLVD.
PETALUMA, CA 94954
DISTRIBUTOR

TM 58
Health history form (cont'd)

ANDRUS/CLINI-REC HEALTH HISTORY QUESTIONNAIRE

Chart No. _____

Identification Information

Today's Date _____

Name _____ Date of Birth _____

Occupation _____ Marital Status _____

PART A – PRESENT HEALTH HISTORY

I. CURRENT MEDICAL PROBLEMS
Please list the medical problems for which you came to see the doctor. About when did they begin?

Problems   Date Began

_____   _____

_____   _____

_____   _____

What concerns you most about these problems?

_____

_____

If you are being treated for any other illness or medical problems by another physician, please describe the problems and write the name of the physician or medical facility treating you.

Illness or Medical Problem   Physician or Medical Facility   City

_____   _____   _____

_____   _____   _____

II. MEDICATIONS
Please list all medications you are now taking, including those you buy without a doctor's prescription (such as aspirin, cold tablets or vitamin supplements).

_____ _____ _____ _____

_____ _____ _____ _____

III. ALLERGIES AND SENSITIVITIES
List anything that you are allergic to such as certain foods, medications, dust, chemicals or soaps, household items, pollens, bee stings, etc., and indicate how each affects you.

Allergic To: Effect   Allergic To: Effect

_____ _____ _____ _____

_____ _____ _____ _____

IV. GENERAL HEALTH, ATTITUDE AND HABITS

How is your overall health now?....................	Health now:	Poor _____ Fair _____ Good _____ Excellent _____
How has it been most of your life?.................	Health has been:	Poor _____ Fair _____ Good _____ Excellent _____

In the past year:

Has your appetite changed?....................	Appetite:	Decreased _____ Increased _____ Stayed same _____
Has your weight changed?.....................	Weight:	Lost _____ lbs. Gained _____ lbs. No change _____
Are you thirsty much of the time?...............	Thirsty:	No _____ Yes _____
Has your overall 'pep' changed?.................	Pep:	Decreased _____ Increased _____ Stayed same _____
Do you usually have trouble sleeping?.............	Trouble sleeping:	No _____ Yes _____
How much do you exercise?.....................	Exercise:	Little or none _____ Less than I need _____ All I need _____
Do you smoke?...............................	Smokes:	No _____ Yes _____ If yes, how many years? _____
How many each day?..........................		_____ Cigarettes _____ Cigars _____ Pipesfull
Have you ever smoked?........................	Smoked	No _____ Yes _____ If yes, how many years? _____
How many each day?..........................		_____ Cigarettes _____ Cigars _____ Pipesfull
Do you drink alcoholic beverages?...............	Alcohol:	No ____ Yes ____ I drink ____ Beers ____ Glasses of wine _____ Drinks of hard liquor - per day
Have you ever had a problem with alcohol?.........	Prior problem:	No _____ Yes _____
How much coffee or tea do you usually drink?.......	Coffee/Tea:	_____ cups of coffee or tea a day.
Do you regularly wear seatbelts?.................	Seatbelts:	No _____ Yes _____

DO YOU:	Rarely/ Never	Occasionally	Frequently	DO YOU:	Rarely/ Never	Occasionally	Frequently
Feel nervous?	_____	_____	_____	Ever feel like committing suicide?	_____	_____	_____
Feel depressed?	_____	_____	_____	Feel bored with your life?	_____	_____	_____
Find it hard to make decisions?	_____	_____	_____	Use marijuana?	_____	_____	_____
Lose your temper?	_____	_____	_____	Use "hard drugs"?	_____	_____	_____
Worry a lot?	_____	_____	_____	Do you want to talk to the			
Tire easily?	_____	_____	_____	doctor about a personal matter? No _____ Yes _____			
Have trouble relaxing?	_____	_____	_____				
Have any sexual problems?	_____	_____	_____				

C
O
N
F
I
D
E
N
T
I
A
L

PART A – PRESENT HEALTH HISTORY (continued)

IV. GENERAL HEALTH, ATTITUDE AND HABITS (continued)

Have you recently had any changes in your: If yes, please explain:

Marital status?	No_____ Yes_____	_____
Job or work?	No_____ Yes_____	_____
Residence?	No_____ Yes_____	_____
Financial status?	No_____ Yes_____	_____
Are you having any legal problems or trouble with the law?	No_____ Yes_____	_____

PART B – PAST HISTORY

C O N F I D E N T I A L

I. FAMILY HEALTH

Please give the following information about your immediate family:

Relationship	Age, if Living	Age At Death	State of Health Or Cause of Death
Father	_____	_____	_____
Mother	_____	_____	_____
Brothers and Sisters	_____	_____	_____
	_____	_____	_____
	_____	_____	_____
Spouse	_____	_____	_____
Children	_____	_____	_____
	_____	_____	_____
	_____	_____	_____

Have any **blood relatives** had any of the following illnesses? If so, indicate relationship (mother, brother, etc.)

Illness	Family Members
Asthma.	_____
Diabetes.	_____
Cancer.	_____
Blood Disease	_____
Glaucoma.	_____
Epilepsy	_____
Rheumatoid Arthritis	_____
Tuberculosis	_____
Gout.	_____
High Blood Pressure	_____
Heart Disease	_____
Mental Problems.	_____
Suicide.	_____
Stroke	_____
Alcoholism	_____
Rheumatic Fever.	_____

II. HOSPITALIZATIONS, SURGERIES, INJURIES

Please list all times you have been hospitalized, operated on, or seriously injured.

Year	Operation, Illness, Injury	Hospital and City
_____	_____	_____
_____	_____	_____
_____	_____	_____

III. ILLNESS AND MEDICAL PROBLEMS

Please mark with an (X) any of the following illnesses and medical problems you have or have had and indicate the year when each started. If you are not certain when an illness started, write down an approximate year.

Illness	(x)	(Year)	Illness	(x)	(Year)
Eye or eye lid infection	____	_____	Hernia	____	_____
Glaucoma	____	_____	Hemorrhoids	____	_____
Other eye problems	____	_____	Kidney or bladder disease	____	_____
Ear trouble	____	_____	Prostate problem (male only)	____	_____
Deafness or decreased hearing	____	_____	Mental problems	____	_____
Thyroid trouble	____	_____	Headaches	____	_____
Strep throat	____	_____	Head injury	____	_____
Bronchitis	____	_____	Stroke	____	_____
Emphysema	____	_____	Convulsions, seizures	____	_____
Pneumonia	____	_____	Arthritis	____	_____
Allergies, asthma or hay fever	____	_____	Gout	____	_____
Tuberculosis	____	_____	Cancer or tumor	____	_____
Other lung problems	____	_____	Bleeding tendency	____	_____
High blood pressure	____	_____	Diabetes	____	_____
Heart attack	____	_____	Measles/Rubeola	____	_____
High cholesterol	____	_____	German measles/Rubella	____	_____
Arteriosclerosis (Hardening of arteries)	____	_____	Polio	____	_____
Heart murmur	____	_____	Mumps	____	_____
Other heart condition	____	_____	Scarlet fever	____	_____
Stomach/duodenal ulcer	____	_____	Chicken pox	____	_____
Diverticulosis	____	_____	Mononucleosis	____	_____
Colitis	____	_____	Eczema	____	_____
Other bowel problems	____	_____	Psoriasis	____	_____
Hepatitis	____	_____	Venereal disease	____	_____
Liver trouble	____	_____	Genital herpes	____	_____
Gallbladder trouble	____	_____	HIV test	____	_____
			AIDS	____	_____

TM 60
Health history form (cont'd)

PART C – BODY SYSTEMS REVIEW

Please answer all of the following questions.

Circle any questions you find difficult to answer.

<u>MEN</u>: Please answer questions 1 through 12, then skip to question 18.

<u>WOMEN</u>: Please start on question 6.

MEN ONLY

1. Have you had or do you have prostate trouble? . . . . No _____
2. Do you have any sexual problems or a problem with impotency? . . . . No _____
3. Have you ever had sores or lesions on your penis? . . . . No _____
4. Have you ever had any discharge from your penis? . . . . No _____
5. Do you ever have pain, lumps or swelling in your testicles? . . . . No _____

Check here if you wish to discuss any special problems with the doctor . . . .

MEN & WOMEN　　　　　　　　　　　　　　　　　　　　　　Rarely/ Never

6. Is it sometimes hard to start your urine flow? . . . . _____
7. Is urination ever painful? . . . . _____
8. Do you have to urinate more than 5 times a day? . . . . _____
9. Do you get up at night to urinate? . . . . _____
10. Has your urine ever been bloody or dark colored? . . . . _____
11. Do you ever lose urine when you strain, laugh, cough or sneeze? . . . . _____
12. Do you ever lose urine during sleep? . . . . _____

WOMEN ONLY　　　　　　　　　　　　　　　　　　　　　　　Rarely/ Never
Do you:
13.　a. Have any menstrual problems? . . . . _____
　　b. Feel rather tense just before your period? . . . . _____
　　c. Have heavy menstrual bleeding? . . . . _____
　　d. Have painful menstrual periods? . . . . _____
　　e. Have any bleeding between periods? . . . . _____
　　f. Have any unusual vaginal discharge or itching? . . . . _____
　　g. Ever have tender breasts? . . . . _____
　　h. Have any discharge from your nipples? . . . . _____
　　i. Have any hot flashes? . . . . _____
14. How many times, if any, have you been pregnant? . . . .
15. How many children born alive? . . . .
16. Are you taking birth control pills? . . . . No _____
17. Do you examine your breasts for lumps? . . . . No _____
17a. What was the date of your last menstrual period? . . . .

Check here if you wish to discuss any special problem with the doctor . . . .

MEN & WOMEN　　　　　　　　　　　　　　　　　　　　　　Rarely/ Never
18. In the past year have you had any:
　　a. Severe shoulder pain? . . . . _____
　　b. Severe back pain? . . . . _____
　　c. Muscle or joint stiffness or pain due to sports, exercise or injury? . . . . _____
　　d. Pain or swelling in any joints not due to sports, exercise or injury? . . . . _____

19. Do you have dry skin or brittle fingernails? . . . . No _____
20. Do you bruise easily? . . . . No _____
21. Do you have any moles that have changed in color or in size? . . . . No _____
22. Do you have any other skin problems? . . . . No _____

23. In the last 3 months have you had:
　　a. A fever that lasted more than one day? . . . . No _____
　　b. Sores or cuts that were hard to heal? . . . . No _____
　　c. Any cold sores (fever blisters)? . . . . No _____
　　d. Any lumps in your neck, armpits or groin? . . . . No _____
　　e. Do you ever have chills or sweat at night? . . . . No _____
24. Have you traveled out of the country in the last 2 years? . . . . No _____

25. Write in the dates for the shots you have had: . . . .

26. Have you had a tuberculin (TB) skin test? . . . . No _____
　　If so, was it negative or positive? . . . . Neg _____
27. Have you had an HIV test for AIDS? . . . . Neg _____

PLEASE TURN THIS PAGE

REMOVE THIS PAGE AFTER COMPLETING QUESTIONNAIRE

28. Do you wear eyeglasses? . . . . No_____
29. Do you wear contact lenses? . . . . No_____
30. Has your vision changed in the last year? . . . . No_____

Rarely/Never

31. How often do you have:
   a. Double vision? . . . . _____
   b. Blurry vision? . . . . _____
   c. Watery or itchy eyes? . . . . _____
32. Do you ever see colored rings around lights? . . . . _____
33. Do others tell you you have a hearing problem? . . . . _____
34. Do you have trouble keeping your balance? . . . . _____
35. Do you have any discharge from your ears? . . . . _____
36. Do you ever feel dizzy or have motion sickness? . . . . _____
37. Do you have any problems with your hearing? . . . . No_____
38. Do you ever have ringing in your ears? . . . . No_____

Rarely/Never

39. How often do you have:
   a. Head colds? . . . . _____
   b. Chest colds? . . . . _____
   c. Runny nose? . . . . _____
   d. Stuffed up nose? . . . . _____
   e. Sore/hoarse throat? . . . . _____
   f. Bad coughing spells? . . . . _____
   g. Sneezing spells? . . . . _____
   h. Trouble breathing? . . . . _____
   i. Nose bleeds? . . . . _____
   j. Cough blood? . . . . _____
40. Have you ever worked or spent time:
   a. On a farm? . . . . No_____
   b. In a mine? . . . . No_____
   c. In a laundry or mill? . . . . No_____
   d. In very dusty places? . . . . No_____
   e. With or near toxic chemicals? . . . . No_____
   f. With or near radioactive materials? . . . . No_____
   g. With or near asbestos? . . . . No_____

Rarely/Never

41. Do you get out of breath easily when you are active (like climbing stairs)? . . . . _____
42. Do you ever feel light-headed or dizzy? . . . . _____
43. Have you ever fainted or passed out? . . . . _____
44. Do you sometimes feel your heart is racing or beating too fast? . . . . _____
45. When you exercise do you ever get pains in your chest or shoulders? . . . . _____
46. Do you have any leg cramps or pain in your thighs or legs when walking? . . . . _____
47. Do you ever have to sit up at night to breathe easier? . . . . _____
48. Do you use two pillows at night to help breathe easier? . . . . _____
49. Would you say you are a restless sleeper? . . . . _____
50. Are you bothered by leg cramps at night? . . . . _____
51. Do you sometimes have swollen ankles or feet? . . . . _____

Rarely/Never

52. How often, if ever:
   a. Are you nauseated (sick to your stomach)? . . . . _____
   b. Do you have stomach pains? . . . . _____
   c. Do you burp a lot after eating? . . . . _____
   d. Do you have heartburn? . . . . _____
   e. Do you have trouble swallowing your food? . . . . _____
   f. Have you vomited blood? . . . . _____
   g. Are you constipated? . . . . _____
   h. Do you have diarrhea (watery stools)? . . . . _____
   i. Are your bowel movements painful? . . . . _____
   j. Are your bowel movements bloody? . . . . _____
   k. Are your bowel movements dark or black? . . . . _____
53. Have you ever had a sigmoidoscopy? . . . . No_____

PLEASE TURN TO BACK PAGE AND COMPLETE QUESTIONS ON NUTRITION.

TM 62
Health history form (cont'd)

BODY SYSTEMS REVIEW

VISION / HEARING

Yes_____		Wears eyeglasses
Yes_____		Wears contacts
Yes_____		Vision changes in last year

Occasionally	Frequently	
_____	_____	Double vision
_____	_____	Blurred vision
_____	_____	Watery/itchy eyes
_____	_____	Sees halos
_____	_____	Hearing problem
_____	_____	Loses balance
_____	_____	Discharge from ears
_____	_____	Dizzy / motion sickness

Yes_____	Hearing Problems	
Yes_____	Ringing in ears	

NOSE / THROAT / RESPIRATORY

Occasionally	Frequently	
_____	_____	Head colds
_____	_____	Chest colds
_____	_____	Runny nose
_____	_____	Head congestion
_____	_____	Sore / hoarse throat
_____	_____	Coughing spells
_____	_____	Sneezing spells
_____	_____	Trouble breathing
_____	_____	Nose bleeds
_____	_____	Cough blood

Yes_____	Worked on a farm
Yes_____	Worked in a mine
Yes_____	Worked in a laundry/mill
Yes_____	Worked in high dust concentrations
Yes_____	Exposed to toxic chemicals
Yes_____	Exposed to radioactive materials
Yes_____	Exposed to asbestos

CARDIOVASCULAR

Occasionally	Frequently	
_____	_____	Out of breath quickly when exercising
_____	_____	Dizziness
_____	_____	Fainted
_____	_____	Rapid heartbeat
_____	_____	Chest/shoulder pains in exercise
_____	_____	Pain in thighs or legs when walking
_____	_____	Sits up at night to breathe easier
_____	_____	Breathing problems during sleep
_____	_____	Restless sleeper
_____	_____	Leg cramps at night
_____	_____	Swollen ankles/feet

DIGESTIVE

Occasionally	Frequently	
_____	_____	Nauseated
_____	_____	Stomach pains
_____	_____	Burps after eating
_____	_____	Heartburn
_____	_____	Trouble swallowing food
_____	_____	Vomited blood
_____	_____	Constipated
_____	_____	Diarrhea
_____	_____	Painful bowel movements
_____	_____	Bloody bowel movements
_____	_____	Dark bowel movements
Yes_____ Date_____		Date of last sigmoidoscopy?

C O N F I D E N T I A L

MALE GENITAL

Prostate trouble	Yes _____
Sexual problems or Impotency	Yes _____
Sores or lesions on penis	Yes _____
Discharge from penis	Yes _____
Pain or swelling in testicles	Yes _____
Special problem	[____]

URINARY

	Occasionally	Frequently
Hard to start urine flow	_____	_____
Painful urination	_____	_____
Frequency while awake	_____	_____
Frequency while asleep	_____	_____
Urine dark color, or bloody	_____	_____
Lose urine: strain, laugh, cough, sneeze	_____	_____
Lose urine: sleep	_____	_____

FEMALE GENITAL

	Occasionally	Frequently
Menstrual problem	_____	_____
Premenstrual tension	_____	_____
Heavy menstrual bleeding	_____	_____
Painful menstruation	_____	_____
Bleeds between periods	_____	_____
Vaginal discharge, itching	_____	_____
Tender breasts	_____	_____
Discharge from nipples	_____	_____
Hot flashes	_____	_____
Pregnancies	. . . _____	
Children born alive	. . . _____	
Taking birth control pills	Yes _____	
Monthly breast examination	Yes _____	
Last menstrual period	Date _____	
Special problem	[____]	

MUSCULOSKELETAL

	Occasionally	Frequently
Shoulder pain	_____	_____
Severe back pain	_____	_____
Muscle/joint problems due to exercise	_____	_____
Joint problems not due to exercise	_____	_____

SKIN

Dry skin/brittle fingernails	Yes _____
Bruise easily	Yes _____
Mole change	Yes _____
Other skin problems	Yes _____

GENERAL

In last 3 months:

Fever over 24 hours	Yes _____
Sores/cuts hard to heal	Yes _____
Herpes simplex	Yes _____
Lumps in neck/armpits/groin	Yes _____
Has chills/sweats at night	Yes _____

Yes, Traveled in: _____

No shots in last 5 years			
	Measles _____	Smallpox _____	
	Mumps _____	Tetanus _____	
	Polio _____	Typhoid _____	

Date of last TB skin test	Yes _____	Date _____
Positive TB test	Pos _____	
HIV test	Pos _____	Date _____

C O N F I D E N T I A L

STOCK NO. 19-711-4 5/83

Page 3

NUTRITION AND DIET

1. How many meals do you eat each day? . . . . _____ Meals each day

2. Do you usually eat breakfast? . . . . ☐ No ☐ Yes Breakfast

3. Do you diet frequently and/or are you now dieting? . . . . ☐ No ☐ Yes Diets

4. Do you consider yourself . . . . ☐ Underweight ☐ Overweight ☐ Just right? Weight

5. Do you snack? . . . . ☐ More than once a day ☐ Usually daily ☐ Rarely? Snacks

6. Do you add salt to your food at the table? . . . . . . ☐ Almost always ☐ Sometimes ☐ Rarely Salts food

7. Check the frequency you eat the following types of foods:

	More than once daily	Daily	3 times weekly	Once weekly	Twice monthly	Less or never
a. Whole grain or enriched bread or cereal						
b. Milk, cheese, or other dairy products						
c. Eggs						
d. Meat, Poultry, Fish						
e. Beans, Peas, or other legumes						
f. Citrus						
g. Dark green or deep yellow vegetables						

List any food supplements or vitamins you take regularly: _____

Additional Patient Comments: _____

_____

_____

_____

_____

_____

_____

Thanks for completing this questionnaire. Please review for skipped questions, sign your name on the space to the right and return it to the physician or assistant. If you wish to add any information, please write it in the spaces provided above.

Patient's Signature _____

Physician's Notes: _____

_____

_____

_____

_____

_____

C O N F I D E N T I A L

To order, call or write:
Bibbero Systems, Inc.
1300 N. McDowell Blvd., Petaluma, CA 94954-1180
Toll Free: 800-BIBBERO (800 242-2376)
Or Fax: 800-242-9330
STOCK NO. 19-711-4   5/83

TM 64
Physical exam form

Andrus/Clini-Rec®
BIBBERO SYSTEMS, INC.

COMPREHENSIVE
PHYSICAL EXAMINATION
MALE OR FEMALE
NEW OR ESTABLISHED PATIENT
CPT # 99201 - 99215

(For Office Use Only)

TODAY'S DATE _____

NAME _____ AGE _____ YRS. OLD   DATE OF BIRTH _____

Key: [O] Neg. Findings [+] Positive Findings [X] Omitted [✔] See Notes/CIRCLE WORDS OF IMPORTANCE & EXPLAIN

C O N F I D E N T I A L

1	GEN. APPEARANCE	[ ]	Apparent Age/Nutrition/Development/Mental & Emotional Status/Gait/Posture/Distress/Speech –
2	HEAD / SCALP	[ ]	Size/Shape/Tender over Sinuses/Hair/Alopecia/Eruption/Masses/Bruit –
3	EYES	[ ]	Conjunct/Sclerae/Cornea/Pupils/EOM's/Arcus/Ptosis/Fundi/Tension/Eyelids/Pallor/Light/Bruit –
4	EARS	[ ]	Ext. Canal/TM's/Perforation/Discharge/Tophi/Hearing Problem/Weber/Rinne –
5	NOSE / SINUSES	[ ]	Septum/Obstruction/Turbinates/Discharge –
6	MOUTH / THROAT	[ ]	Odor/Lips/Tongue/Tonsils/Teeth/Dentures/Gums/Pharynx –
7	NECK	[ ]	Adenopathy/Thyroid/Carotids/Trachea/Veins/Masses/Spine/Motion/Bruit –
8	BACK	[ ]	Kyphosis/Scoliosis/Lordosis/Mobility/CVA/Bone/Tenderness –
9	THORAX	[ ]	Symmetry/Movement/Contour/Tender –
10	BREASTS	[ ]	Size/Size-Consistency/Nipples/Areolar/Palpable Mass/Discharge/Tenderness/Nodes/Scars –
11	HEART	[ ]	Rate/Rhythm/Apical Impulse/Thrills/Quality of Sound/Intensity/Splitting/Extra Sounds/Murmurs –
12	CHEST / LUNGS	[ ]	Excursion/Dullness or Hyperresonance to Percussion/Quality of Breath Sounds/Rales/Wheezing/Rhonchi/Diaphragm/Rubs/Bruit –
13	ABDOMEN	[ ]	Bowel Sounds/Appearance/Liver/Spleen/Masses/Hernias/Murmurs/Contour/Tenderness/Bruit/Inguinal Nodes –
14	GROIN	[ ]	Hernia/Inguinal Nodes/Femoral Pulses –
15	MALE GENITALIA	[ ]	Penis/Testes/Scrotum Epididymis/Varicocele/Scars/Discharge –
16	FEMALE GENITALIA	[ ]	Vulva/Vagina/Cervix/Uterus/Adnexa/Rectocele/Cystocele/Bartholin Gland/Urethra/Discharge – PAP Smear (if done ✔) ☐
17	EXTREMITIES	[ ]	Deformity/Clubbing/Cyanosis/Edema/Nails/Peripheral Pulses/Calf Tenderness/Joints for Swelling/ROM –
18	SKIN	[ ]	Color/Birthmarks/Scars/Texture/Rash/Eczema/Ulcers –
19	NEUROLOGICAL	[ ]	DTR's/Babinski/Cranial Nerves/Motor Abnormalities/Tremor/Paralysis/Sensory Exam – (touch, pin prick, vibration)/Coordination/Romberg –
20	MUSCULAR SYSTEM	[ ]	Strength/Wasting/Development –
21	RECTAL EXAM	[ ]	Sphincter Tone/Hemorrhoids/Fissures/Masses/Prostate/Stool Guaiac (if done ✔) ☐ Pos ☐ Neg –

Impression: ☐ Check If Normal Physical Examination
Summary: _____

_____

_____Signature _____ Date _____

ORDER # **19-744-1** • © 1982 BIBBERO SYSTEMS, INC. • PETALUMA, CA.TO REORDER CALL TOLL FREE: (800) BIBBERO (800-242-2376) OR FAX (800) 242-9330   MFG IN U.S.A.   (REV. 4/96)

TM 65
Physical exam form (cont'd)

COMPREHENSIVE
PHYSICAL EXAMINATION
(continued)

(For Office Use Only)

CONFIDENTIAL

Body Area Number	REMARKS:	PHYSICIAN'S NOTES:

HEIGHT _____	**VISION**			**AUDIOMETRIC TESTING**			**BLOOD PRESSURE**

VISION

Without Glasses

Far   R 20/   L 20/

Near   R 20/   L 20/

With Glasses

R 20/   L 20/

R 20/   L 20/

Tonometry   R _____ L _____

Colorvision _____

Peripheral Fields R ____ L____

HEIGHT _____

WEIGHT _____

BUILD _____

PULSE _____

RESP. _____

TEMP. _____

AUDIOMETRIC TESTING

	250	500	1000
R	_____	_____	_____
L	_____	_____	_____

	2000	4000	8000
R	_____	_____	_____
L	_____	_____	_____

Gross Hearing _____

BLOOD PRESSURE

Sitting

R   /   L   /

Standing

R   /   L   /

Lying

R   /   L   /

Diagnostic Tests:	**Results:**

The space below is provided for additional information when these data are being forwarded to a hospital, insurance company, a referral physician, etc.

Significant Comments/Recommendations:

Physician's Name _____

Address _____

Telephone (_____) _____

TM 66
Progress notes form

PATIENT'S NAME _____ ☐ FEMALE ☐ MALE   Date of Birth:_____ / ___ / _____

DATE	PATIENT VISITS AND FINDINGS

ALLERGIC TO _____

ORDER #25-7133 • © 1999 BIBBERO SYSTEMS, INC. • PETALUMA, CA   TO REORDER CALL 800-BIBBERO (800-242-2376) OR FAX (800) 242-9330 MFG IN USA   PAGE_____ of_____

Petty Cash Log

Date	Description	Amount	Balance

(From Potter BA: *Medical Office Administration: A worktext,* Philadelphia, Saunders, 2003)

TM 68
Release of medical records form

AUTHORIZATION FOR RELEASE OF INFORMATION

SECTION A: Must be completed for all authorizations.

I hereby authorize the use/disclosure of my health information as described below. I understand that this authorization is voluntary. I understand that any and all records, whether written, oral or in electronic format are confidential and cannot be disclosed without my prior written authorization except as otherwise provided by law. I understand that a photocopy or fax of this authorization is as valid as the original.

Patient Name: _____

Date of Birth: _____

Person(s)/organizations authorized to use/disclose information (from): _____

Person(s)/organizations authorized to receive the information: _____

Information that may be used/disclosed:
(Include dates where appropriate, e.g., medications dispensed in December 2002 or EKG Report performed in June 2000)

❑ Record of Visits (all) _____
❑ Record of Visit(s) (Specific) _____
❑ Discharge Summary _____
❑ History/Physical _____
❑ Consultation Report(s) _____
❑ Operative Report(s) _____
❑ Problem List _____
❑ Progress Notes _____
❑ Immunization Record(s) _____
❑ Medication Record(s) _____

❑ Laboratory Report(s) _____
❑ X-Ray, MRI, CT _____
❑ Echo, Stress Tests, Holters _____
❑ EKG Report _____
❑ Mental Health/Alcohol/Drug Abuse Treatment ____
❑ AIDS or HIV Information _____
❑ Hepatitis Information _____
❑ Entire Medical Record _____
❑ Statement of Charges/Payments _____
❑ Other _____

SECTION B: Must be completed only if a health provider or a health plan has requested the authorization.

1. The health plan or health care provider must complete the following:

   a. The information will be used/disclosed for the following purposes:

   ❑ Continued Patient Care
   ❑ Disability Determination
   ❑ Personal Use

   ❑ Attorney/Legal
   ❑ Insurance Claim
   ❑ Other _____

   b. Will the health care provider or health plan requesting the authorization receive financial or in-kind compensation in exchange for using or disclosing the health information described above?   Yes _____   No _____

2. I understand that my health care and payment for my health care will not be affected if I do not sign this form.

3. I understand that I may inspect and copy any information to be used or disclosed.

SECTION C: Must be completed for all authorizations.

1. I understand that I may revoke this authorization at any time by notifying the Health Information Management Department in writing. I understand that the revocation will not apply to information that has already been released in response to this authorization. This authorization expires _____
(Insert applicable date or event that triggers expiration)

2. I understand that, if my protected health information is disclosed to someone who is not required to comply with the federal privacy protection regulations, then such information may be re-disclosed and would no longer be protected.

_____
Signature of Patient or Representative

_____
Today's Date

_____
Printed Name of Patient's Representative (if applicable)

_____
Relationship to Patient

#25-8401 • 12/02 • BIBBERO SYSTEMS, INC • PETALUMA, CA

TO REORDER FORMS: (800) BIBBERO (800 242-2376) OR FAX: (800) 242-9330

TM 69

Revocation of authorization to release medical records form

REVOCATION OF AUTHORIZATION TO RELEASE MEDICAL RECORDS

_____ , who resides at _____
Name   Street Address

_____ , hereby revokes authorization to the physician, hospital, clinic,
City/State/Zip

lab, radiology center or other healthcare provider listed below:

_____
Name

_____
Street Address

_____
City/State/Zip

to disclose information from the medical records of:

_____
Name

_____
Street Address

_____
City/State/Zip

My revocation extends to the data or documents I have initialed below:

_____ Records of visits (all visits)

_____ Record of visit for a specific date or dates, including or limited to _____

_____ Copies of records or reports provided to the above named (i.e. hospital, lab, etc.)

_____ Statements of charges or payments

_____ Mental health, alcohol and/or drug abuse treatment _____

_____ HIV information

_____ Hepatitis information

_____ Other (specific) _____

This revocation is given freely with the understanding that:

1. Disclosures made in good faith may have already occurred based upon my previously issued authorization and that this revocation cannot apply retroactively to such disclosures. I also understand that the disclosure of health information may be required by law in some instances, such as for the reporting of communicable diseases.
2. The facility, it's employees, officers, and physicians are hereby released from any legal responsibility or liability for disclosure of the information I authorized previously.

_____   _____   _____
Patient's Printed Name   Social Security # (for identification purposes only)   Date

_____   _____
Patient's Signature (or Guardian, if for a minor)   Revocation Date (if other than 60 days from date above)

_____   _____
Witness   Date

#25-8402 • 12/02 • BIBBERO SYSTEMS, INC • PETALUMA, CA   TO REORDER FORMS: (800) BIBBERO (800 242-2376) OR FAX: (800) 242-9330 MFG IN U.S

TM 70
Non-disclosure agreement form

EMPLOYEE/SERVICE PROVIDER NON-DISCLOSURE AGREEMENT

Office Name: _____   Date: _____

Address: _____   Phone: _____

Employee/Service Provider Name: _____

☐ Employee ☐ Service Provider Employed By:

_____
Name

_____
Street Address

_____
City/State/Zip

I have been asked by_____ to reaffirm my commitment made at the time of my employment/assignment to protect the confidentiality of health information. I understand that _____ reminds its employees, volunteers, and service providers of their confidentiality obligations on a periodic basis to help ensure compliance, due to the significance of this issue. By my signature below, I acknowledge that I agree to uphold, as a condition of my employment or as provider of service to_____, the confidentiality of protected health information.

_____ has a legal and ethical responsibility to safeguard the privacy of all patients and protect the confidentiality of their health information. In the course of my employment/assignment at _____, I may have access to or come into possession of confidential patient information, even though I may not be directly involved in providing patient services.

I understand that such information must be maintained in the strictest of confidence. As a condition of my employment/assignment, I hereby agree, unless directed by my supervisor, that I will not at any time during or after my employment/assignment with _____ disclose any patient information to any person whatsoever or permit any person whatsoever to examine or make copies of any patient reports or other documents prepared by me, or to which I have free access, or that may come into my possession, or under my control, or use patient information, other than as necessary in the course of my employment/assignment.

I understand that violation of this agreement could result in disciplinary action, up to and including termination and/or legal action.

Employee's/Service Provider's Name (Printed): _____ Date: _____

Employee's/Service Provider's Signature: _____ SS # _____

Witness Name (Printed): _____

Witness Signature: _____

HIPAA Privacy Training Completed: _____No _____Yes (Date: _____)

Patient Sign-In

Date: _____

Please sign-in and notify us if:
you are a new patient, you insurance, telephone number or address have changed.

NO.		Please Print Name	Appt. Time	Time Seen	Appointment with	Note if first visit, new phone, address or insurance change
1	1					
2	2					
3	3					
4	4					
5	5					
6	6					
7	7					
8	8					
9	9					
10	10					
11	11					
12	12					
13	13					
14	14					
15	15					
16	16					
17	17					
18	18					
19	19					
20	20					
21	21					
22	22					
23	23					

ITEM 051-1667/14037

TM 72
Protected health information disclosure form

PROTECTED HEALTH INFORMATION (PHI) DISCLOSURE RECORD

Patient Name: _____ DOB: _____/_____/_____
Month   Day   Year

Authorized Methods of Communication (✔ Check all that apply)			
❏ *Residence Telephone*	❏ *Work Telephone*	❏ *Written Correspondence*	❏ *Other (Specify)*
Number: ( )	Number: ( )	❏ Mail/Delivery Service	
❏ Leave call back number only; do not leave message	❏ Leave call back number only; do not leave message	❏ Fax: ( )	
❏ Okay to leave detailed message with person	❏ Okay to leave detailed message with operator	❏ E-Mail @ Residence:	
❏ Okay to leave detailed message on answering machine	❏ Okay to leave detailed message on personal voice mail	❏ E-Mail @ Work:	

Patient Signature: _____ Date: _____

		Record of Disclosures			
Date Of Disclosure	Disclosed to: Name & Address or Contact Number	Description of PHI Disclosed and Purpose of Disclosure (If a copy of the authorization or request is attached, check ❏ below.)	Type of Disclosure *Enter T, P, or O	Person Disclosing	Method of Disclosure **Enter M, P, F, E, or OT
		❏			
		❏			
		❏			
		❏			
		❏			
		❏			
		❏			
		❏			
		❏			
		❏			

*T = Treatment, P = Payment, O = Health Care Operations Activities
**M = Mail, P = Telephone, F = Fax, E = E-Mail, OT = Other (and specify mode of delivery)

Procedure _____

Task:

Condition: Equipment and Supplies:

Standards: Complete the procedure and all critical steps in _____ minutes with a minimum

score of _____ % within three attempts.

Scoring: Divide points earned by total possible points. Failure to perform a critical step that is indicated
with an asterisk (*), will result in an unsatisfactory overall score.

Time began _____ **Time ended** _____

Steps	Possible Points	First Attempt	Second Attempt	Third Attempt
1.	_____	_____	_____	_____
2.	_____	_____	_____	_____
3.	_____	_____	_____	_____
4.	_____	_____	_____	_____
5.	_____	_____	_____	_____
6.	_____	_____	_____	_____
7.	_____	_____	_____	_____
8.	_____	_____	_____	_____
9.	_____	_____	_____	_____
10.	_____	_____	_____	_____
11.	_____	_____	_____	_____
12.	_____	_____	_____	_____
13.	_____	_____	_____	_____
14.	_____	_____	_____	_____
15.	_____	_____	_____	_____

Documentation in the Medical Record

_____

_____

_____

_____

Comments:

Total Points Earned _____ Divided by _____ Total Possible Points = _____ % Score

Instructor's Signature _____

Outline of PowerPoint Slides

CHAPTER 1: Becoming a Successful Student

Student Success
- To become a successful medical assistant, you must first become a successful student.
- Discover the way you learn best.
- Use multiple strategies to assist you in your journey toward success.

Keys to Success
- Consider your history as a student. What helped you be successful? What needs improvement?

Learning Style
- You have developed a method for perceiving and processing information.
- This method is called your learning style.

Perceiving Information
- To learn new material, two things must happen: first, your perception of information helps you examine the material and recognize it as real.

Processing Information
- The next step is processing the information, internalizing it, and making it your own. With various learning styles, you can combine different methods of perceiving and processing information.

Perceiving
- Concrete perceivers learn through direct experience by doing, acting, sensing, or feeling.
- Abstract perceivers take in information through analysis, observation, and reflection.

Active Processors
- Active processors make sense of the new material by jumping in and doing things immediately.

Reflective Processors
- Reflective processors, however, think about the information before they internalize it, preferring to observe and consider.

Stage 1
- Stage 1 learners, with a concrete/reflective style, want to know the purpose of the information and have a personal connection to the content. They consider many different points of view, observe others, and plan before taking action.

Stage 2
- Stage 2 learners, with an abstract/reflective style, learn for the sheer pleasure of learning.
- They arrange new material in a logical and clear manner.
- Although they plan studying and create ways of thinking, they do not always consider the practical application of the material.

Stage 3
- Stage 3 learners, with an abstract/active style, want to experiment and test the knowledge they learn.

Stage 4
- Stage 4 concrete/active learners are concerned about how they can use what they learn to make a difference in their lives.

CHAPTER 2: The Healthcare Industry

The History of Medicine
- Aesculapius, son of Apollo, was revered as the god of medicine. Early Greeks worshiped his healing powers and built temples in his honor.

- The staff of Aesculapius depicts a serpent encircling it, and signifies the art of healing. It has been adopted by the AMA as the symbol of medicine.

The Caduceus

- The mythological staff of Apollo, the caduceus, encircled by two serpents, is the insignia of the United States Army Medical Corps—not a symbol of the medical profession.

Medicine in Ancient Times

- In the Egyptian, Babylonian, and Assyrian societies, physicians used the little knowledge they had to treat illness and injury.
- Moses, around 1205 BC, presented rules of health and so is considered the first public health officer.
- Hippocrates
  - Born in 450 BC
  - Best remembered for the Hippocratic Oath
  - Hippocratic Oath has been administered to physicians for more than 2000 years
- Galen
  - A Greek physician known as the Prince of Physicians
  - Considered the Father of Experimental Physiology and the first experimental neurologist

Distribution of Knowledge

- Before the invention of the printing press, very little exchange of scientific knowledge and ideas occurred.
- In the 17th century, European academies or societies were formed and participants met to discuss subjects of mutual interest.

British Influence

- One of the earliest of the academies was the Royal Society of London, formed in 1662.
- The passage of the Medical Act of 1858 was one of the most important events in British medicine.

Vesalius

- Andreas Vesalius (1514–1564), a Belgian anatomist, is known as the Father of Modern Anatomy.
- His work broke with traditional beliefs in Galen's theories.

Harvey and Leeuwenhoek

- In 1628, William Harvey (1578–1657) announced his discovery that the heart acts as a muscular pump, forcing and propelling the blood throughout the body.

- Anton Van Leeuwenhoek (1632–1723) used a simple biconvex lens to magnify microscopic organisms and structures never seen before.

Malpighi and Hunter

- In 1661, Marcello Malpighi described the pulmonary and capillary network connecting the smallest arteries with the smallest veins.
- The English scientist, John Hunter (1728–1793), is known as the Founder of Scientific Surgery.

Jenner and Semmelweis

- Edward Jenner (1749–1823), a student of John Hunter, is considered one of the immortals of preventive medicine for his discovery of the smallpox vaccine.
- Ignaz Philipp Semmelweis (1818–1865), known as the Savior of Mothers, directed his students to wash and disinfect their hands before delivering infants.

Pasteur and Lister

- Pasteur (1822–1895) was a chemist whose studies in bacteriology made him one of the most famous men in medical history.
- Joseph Lister (1827–1912) revolutionized surgery by using Pasteur's discoveries. He understood the similarity between the infections in postsurgical wounds and the processes of putrefaction.

Koch and Long

- Robert Koch (1843–1910) is a familiar name to all bacteriologists, because of his famous Koch's Postulates, criteria that must be satisfied for an organism to be accepted as the causative agent of a disease.
- Crawford Williamson Long (1815–1878) was the first to use ether as an anesthetic agent.

Roentgen and the Curies

- Roentgen discovered the x-ray in 1895 while experimenting with electrical currents passed through sealed glass tubes.
- Marie and Pierre Curie discovered radium in 1898; they were awarded the 1902 Nobel Prize in Physics for their work on radioactivity.

Johns Hopkins

- In the United States, medical education was greatly influenced by the Johns Hopkins University Medical School in Baltimore in partnership with Johns Hopkins Hospital, with teaching and research by members of the medical faculty.

Women in Medicine

- Florence Nightingale (1820–1910), founder of modern nursing, is fondly called "the lady with the lamp."

- Clara Barton (1821–1912) organized a Red Cross Committee in Washington, forming the American Red Cross.
- Elizabeth Blackwell (1821–1910) was the first woman in the United States to receive the Doctor of Medicine degree.

Sanger and Kübler-Ross

- Margaret Sanger (1883–1966), a nurse in New York, became the American leader of the birth control movement.
- Dr. Elisabeth Kübler-Ross, a Swiss-born psychiatrist, was shocked at the treatment of terminally ill patients at her hospital in New York. Her best-seller, *On Death and Dying,* helps professionals and laypersons to understand the stages of grief.

Salk, Sabin, and Barnard

- Jonas Edward Salk and Albert Sabin almost eradicated polio, once the killer and crippler of thousands in the United States. Developed in 1952, the polio vaccine was later distributed nationally.
- Christian Barnard, a South African surgeon, performed the first human heart transplant in 1967.

World Health Organization

- The World Health Organization, founded in 1948, is a specialized agency of the United Nations. It promotes cooperation between nations in controlling and eliminating diseases.

Department of Health and Human Services

- DHHS includes more than 300 programs in medical and social science research, immunization, financial assistance for low-income families, child support enforcement, improvement of infant and maternal health, child and elder abuse prevention, as well as programs for elderly Americans.

USAMRIID

- The United States Army Medical Research Institute of Infectious Diseases protects military service members and conducts key research programs in national defense and infectious diseases.
- The USAMRIID is equipped to study Biosafety Level IV viruses and pathogens.

Centers for Disease Control and Prevention

- Headquartered in Atlanta, GA
- Leading U.S. federal agency concerned with the health and safety of people throughout the world

- A clearinghouse for information and statistics associated with healthcare

National Institutes of Health

- The NIH uncovers new knowledge leading to better health for everyone. As a part of the public health service, it supports and conducts biomedical research into the causes and prevention of diseases and provides biomedical information to the healthcare professions.

Types of Healthcare Facilities

- Hospitals
- Ambulatory care
- Diagnostic laboratories
  - POLs, or "privately owned laboratories"
- Home health agencies

Medical Practices

- Sole proprietorship
- Partnerships
- Group practice
- Corporations

Healthcare Professionals

- Doctors of medicine
- Doctors of osteopathy
- Doctors of chiropractic
- Dentists
- Optometrists
- Doctors of podiatric medicine
- Other doctorates

Licensed or Certified Professionals

- Physician assistants
- Nurse practitioners
- Nurse anesthetists
- Registered nurses
- Licensed practical/vocational nurses
- Medical technologists
- Medical laboratory technicians
- Physical therapists
- Respiratory therapists
- Occupational therapists
- Diagnostic medical and cardiac sonographer
- Radiology technicians
- Paramedics and emergency medical technicians
- Registered dieticians

CHAPTER 3: The Medical Assisting Profession

Medical Assisting
- According to the United States Department of Labor's Occupational Outlook Handbook, medical assisting will be one of the ten fastest growing occupations through the year 2008.

The History of Medical Assisting
- The first medical assistant was probably a neighbor of a physician who helped when an extra pair of hands was needed.
- As the practice of medicine became more complicated, some physicians hired registered nurses to help in their offices.

Need for Trained Assistants
- As record keeping, data reporting, and business details became more important, physicians needed assistants with both administrative and clinical training.

Training and Certification
- Community and junior colleges first offered training programs in the late 1940s. Local and state medical assistant organizations began around 1950, with certifying examinations soon after.

The Medical Assistant's Scope of Practice
- Medical assistants work under the direct supervision of a physician and perform tasks delegated by the doctor or supervisor.
- Medical assistants perform administrative and clinical duties.

Classroom Training
- Many community colleges, junior colleges, and private career institutions offer formal training in medical assisting.
- After receiving a certificate or diploma, students may complete additional requirements to obtain an associate degree.

Length of Training
- Courses in community colleges usually last 1 to 2 years, with enrollment 2 or 3 times per year. In private career institutions, training usually takes 7 to 10 months, with enrollment as often as monthly.

Externships/Internships
- Most medical assisting training programs require an externship or internship before graduation.
- This on-the-job training allows the student to use classroom skills with actual patients and staff members.

Continuing Education
- Continuing education classes enhance the knowledge of the professional medical assistant.
- Continuing education units (CEUs) may be required to maintain certification.

Good Health and Grooming
- Good health requires adequate sleep, balanced meals, and enough exercise to keep fit.
- Good grooming requires attention to the details of personal appearance.

Dress for Success
- Suitable Dress
  - Uniforms or scrubs should be laundered daily.
  - Spotless and comfortable, shoes should be appropriate for a uniform. White shoes must be kept white by daily cleansing.

Professional Organizations
- American Association of Medical Assistants and Certified Medical Assistants
- American Medical Technologists and Registered Medical Assistants

American Association of Medical Assistants
- Certified Medical Assistants

AAMA
- The AAMA, formally organized in 1956 as a federation of several state associations, has 43 state societies and more than 350 local chapters.

AAMA National Certification
- The organization, with national headquarters in Chicago, Illinois, established a national certification program for medical assistants.

Accreditation
- The AAMA has established the accreditation of medical assisting training programs in community colleges and private career institutes and has set the minimal standards for entry-level medical assistants.

CMA Examination
- Since 1963, the AAMA has administered the CMA examination for the CMA credential or Certified Medical Assistant title. Examinations are given in January and June of each year at more than 280 centers.
- Certification is available to graduates of programs accredited by the CAAHEP or by ABHES.
- Recertification is required every 5 years through CEUs or reexamination.

American Medical Technologists
- Registered medical assistants

RMA Program

- In the early 1970s, the American Medical Technologists (AMT) began offering a certifying examination leading to the Registered Medical Assistant program within the AMT organization in 1976.

RMA Examination

- The RMA examination can be scheduled nearly every day of the year, other than Sundays and holidays, at Prometric Testing Centers, with more than 300 locations throughout the United States.

RMA Eligibility

- Applicants for the RMA examination must be graduates of a medical assisting course accredited by ABHES or by CAAHEP.

CMA vs. RMA

- Both certifying examinations are national credentials. The CMA credential is offered by the American Association of Medical Assistants, and the RMA credential is offered by the American Medical Technologists.
- Both of these examinations are voluntary.
- Most employers today require at least one certification.

CHAPTER 4: Professional Behavior in the Workplace

Professionalism

- Characteristics of professionalism include loyalty, dependability, courtesy, initiative, flexibility, credibility, confidentiality, and a good attitude.

Confidentiality

- Confidentiality is vitally important.
- Patients depend on medical personnel to keep their health information confidential and private.

Breach of Confidentiality

- Breach of patient confidentiality may lead to immediate termination. It can likewise result in litigation between the patient and the physician.

Professional Behavior

- Professionalism includes conforming to the technical and ethical standards of a profession, exhibiting courtesy, being conscientious, and conducting oneself in a business-like manner.
- Professionalism is vitally important in the medical profession.

Patient Care

- Because most patients are not at their best when visiting the physician's office, the attitude of the staff is important in patients' feeling at ease.

Empathy

- Medical assistants need patience when working with those who are ill.
- A smile or a reassuring pat on the back will be encouraging.

Office Politics

- Office politics can be negative or positive. Use of others for self-promotion or taking credit for a team effort is negative.

Constructive Office Politics

- Strategically planning for advancement by outstanding performance, dependability, and teamwork shows proper use of office politics.

Sensitivity to Others

- Knowing when to speak and when to listen will help the medical assistant.

Teamwork

- Teamwork makes any job easier to complete.

Helping Coworkers

- The medical assistant who helps those overwhelmed with duties may find co-workers who will help when the situation is reversed.

Trading Duties

- If two assistants have duties they dislike, trading the duties may satisfy both.

Insubordination

- Insubordination, being disobedient, is grounds for immediate dismissal.

Following Orders

- The medical assistant should carry out an order unless it is unlawful or unethical.

Conflict Resolution

- If the medical assistant believes that a duty should have been performed by someone else or if it should not have been performed, the supervisor should be consulted.

Consultation with Supervisor

- Discuss the issue and attempt to reach an agreement about the appropriateness of performing the task in the future.

Order of Importance

- Performing tasks in the order of importance can help the medical assistant to accomplish more.

Evaluating Tasks

- Ranking jobs can be used for work, home, and extracurricular activities. Tasks can be divided into those that must, should, or could be done each day.

Setting Priorities

- Within each category, number the tasks in the order in which they should be completed.

Goal Monitoring

- Goals should be written and reviewed often to check progress.

Subdivision of Goals

- Taking small steps toward goals will help assure that they are eventually reached. Set goals in each area of life and divide them into manageable parts.

Evaluation of Goals

- Goals should not be unreasonable or unattainable, but should provide the opportunity for small successes on the way to the ultimate goal.

CHAPTER 5: Interpersonal Skills and Human Behavior

First Impressions

- The opinions formed in the early moments of meeting someone remain in our thoughts long after the first words are spoken.

Providing Service

- Patients should be offered the best customer service available.

Welcoming the Patient

- When the patient approaches, even though you are wearing a name badge, introduce yourself and smile with your face, your voice, and your eyes.
- Genuinely welcome the patient.

Positive Impressions

- Once an impression is formed in the patient's mind, it is very difficult to change, so make the first impressions positive.

Verbal Communication

- Verbal communication depends on words and sounds.
- The voice lifts at the end of a question and it drops at the end of a statement.

Speech Skills

- Speak clearly, and enunciate words properly.
- Always speak at a clearly audible level, but at times it will be necessary to increase or decrease the volume of speech.
- Maintain eye contact.

Nonverbal Communication

- Some messages are conveyed without words.
- Body language, gestures, and mannerisms may or may not match the words a person speaks.

Appearance and Communication

- Appearance is an integral part of nonverbal communication.
- How can appearance influence communication?

Spacing Guidelines

- Public space is usually accepted as a distance of 12 to 25 feet, and social space as 4 to 12 feet.
- Personal space ranges from 1.5 to 4 feet, and intimate contact includes physical touching to about 1.5 feet.

Touch

- Touch is a powerful communicator: it can be comforting or promote a sexual harassment suit.
- Do not, however, be afraid to touch the patient appropriately.
- Appropriate touching would include a pat on the back or a squeeze of the hand.

Posture

- Posture can signal depression, excitement, anger, or an appeal for help.
- When the physician sits at the front of the chair and leans forward, he or she appears caring and interested.

Positioning

- Sitting behind a desk lends an air of authority.
- Standing or sitting across a room may convey a negative message of denying involvement or reluctance to talk.

The Communication Process

- The sender is the person who sends a message through a variety of different channels (spoken words, written messages, and body language).

Sender and Receiver

- The sender encodes the message, choosing a specific way of expression with words and other channels.
- The receiver decodes the message according to understanding what is communicated.

Feedback

- Feedback can be verbal expressions or body language, such as a simple nod of understanding.

Listening

- People need to know that they are being heard.
- The first rule of listening is to look at the speaker and pay attention.

Open-ended Questioning
- An open-ended question, requiring more than a "yes" or "no" answer, forces the patient to provide more detail and expand on thoughts.

Defense Mechanisms
- Verbal aggression
- Sarcasm
- Rationalization
- Compensation
- Regression
- Repression
- Apathy
- Displacement
- Denial
- Physical avoidance
- Projection

Conflict
- Conflict is the struggle resulting from incompatible or opposing needs, drives, wishes, or external or internal demands.

Assertion versus Aggression
- Conflict is not always negative.
- Assertion is stating or declaring positively, often forcefully or aggressively.
- Too much aggression can seem pushy, so it should be controlled and used appropriately.

Barriers to Communication
- Physical impairment
- Language
- Prejudice
- Stereotyping
- Perception

Maslow's Hierarchy of Needs
- Basic human needs involve our physical well-being: food, rest, sleep, water, air, and sex.
- The second level includes issues related to safety in our homes and our environments.
- The third level involves our needs for love, a sense of belonging, and interaction with others.
- The fourth level relates to our self-esteem.
- The last level is self-actualization, in which we maximize our potential.

A Good Night's Sleep
- The two main phases of sleep are NREM (non–rapid eye movement) and REM (rapid eye movement).
  - During NREM sleep, the eyes are fairly still, and the body relaxes and slows.
  - After the body moves through the four stages of NREM, it enters REM sleep, during which the brain is highly active, and the eyes move rapidly, and dreaming occurs.

Healthful Nutrition
- A balanced diet ensures that our organs and systems function at optimal levels.
- Exercise regularly and take walks to provide cardiovascular benefits.
- Don't skip meals in an effort to lose weight, but choose smaller portions and eat a variety of healthy foods.
- Avoid unhealthy snacks and sodas, and drink at least 8-10 glasses of water every day.

Healthy Self-Esteem
- Self-esteem is having confidence and satisfaction in oneself. To have good self-esteem, an individual must be self-aware. That means taking an honest look at your strengths and your weaknesses.

CHAPTER 6: Medicine and Ethics

Ethics
- Ethics: thoughts, judgments, and actions on issues that have implications of moral right and wrong.

Etiquette
- Etiquette deals with courtesy, customs, and manners.
- Ethics should not be confused with etiquette.

Rights
- Rights: claims made by a person or group on society, a group, or an individual.

Ethical Distress
- Ethical distress is a problem to which there is an obvious solution, but a barrier hinders the action that should be taken.

Ethical Dilemma
- An ethical dilemma is a situation with two or more solutions, but in choosing one, something of value is lost.

Dilemma of Justice
- A dilemma of justice involves allocation of benefits and their fair distribution.

Locus of Authority
- Two or more authority figures, each with an idea of how to handle a situation, are the center of locus-of-authority issues.

The Ethical Decision-making Process
- Making an ethical decision is easier with a logical approach and a five-step process.

Five-step Process
The steps include:
- gathering relevant information.
- identifying the type of ethical problem.
- determining the ethics approach to use.
- exploring the practical alternatives
- completing the action.

Using the Five Steps
- Gather relevant information.
- Identify the type of problem.
- Determine the ethical approach to use.
- Explore alternatives.
- Make the decision and complete the action.

AMA Code of Ethics
- The AMA's Code of Ethics has four components:
  - principles of medical ethics
  - the fundamental elements of the patient-physician relationship
  - current opinions of the CEJA with annotations
  - reports of the CEJA

CEJA Opinions
- Although healthcare professionals do not have to abide by the opinions of the Council on Ethical and Judicial Affairs (CEJA), many professionals practice in accordance with these opinions.

Ethical Duty
- A duty is an obligation that a person has or is perceived to have.
- Nonmaleficence refers to refraining from harming the self or another person.
- Beneficence refers to bringing about good.
- Fidelity is the concept of keeping promises.
- Veracity refers to the duty to tell the truth.
- Justice, in relation to medical ethics, deals with the fair distribution of benefits and burdens among individuals or groups with legitimate claims on those benefits.

Ethical Problems
- Ethical distress: problem faced when a certain course of action is indicated, but some hindrance or barrier prevents that action.
- The professional knows the right thing to do, but for whatever reason, cannot do it.
- Ethical dilemma: situation in which two or more choices are acceptable and correct, but doing one precludes doing another. Something of value may be lost if a second choice is eliminated.
- The proverbial "rock and a hard place," whereby a choice must be made that has a greater effect than may be seen on the surface.
- Dilemma of justice: this problem focuses on the fair distribution of benefits. Dilemmas of justice include those found with organ donations and distribution of scarce or expensive medications.
- In locus-of-authority issues, two or more authority figures have their own ideas about how a situation should be handled, but only one authority will prevail. If one physician believes a patient should have surgery and another does not, how does the patient decide?

The Ethical Medical Assistant
- An ethical medical assistant will not participate in known substandard or unlawful practices, especially those that might be harmful to patients.

Keeping Informed
- The medical assistant has an ethical obligation to be aware of current developments that affect the practice of medicine and care of the patients.

Continuing Education
- Membership in a professional organization provides continuing education to maintain knowledge and skills.

Confidentiality
- Confidentiality is of major importance.
- It is unethical to reveal patient confidences to anyone including family, spouse, best friends, and other medical assistants.
- Breach of patient confidentiality is sufficient reason for immediate termination.

HIV
- Some individuals might be concerned about reporting to various agencies, but unique identifiers maintain the confidentiality of those tested for HIV.
- With these identifiers, patients have much less fear of discrimination due to HIV.

Genetic Testing
- Many ethical concerns surround the advent of genetic testing, such as how the information will be used and who will have access to it.
- Discrimination could be possible with the knowledge of a person's genetic blueprint.

CHAPTER 7: Medicine and Law

Law
- Law: a binding custom or practice of a community; a rule of conduct or action prescribed or formally recognized as binding or enforceable by a controlling authority.
- Law: the system by which society gives order to our lives.

Statutes and Regulations
- Legal issues are interwoven in many aspects of medical practice, and the wording of statutes and regulations is often long and complicated.

Lawsuits
- Medical assistants, as well as all staff members and physicians, must take steps, in today's litigious society, to protect themselves from lawsuits.

Jurisprudence
- Jurisprudence: the science and philosophy of law
  - Juris: law, right, equity or justice
  - Prudentia: skill or good judgment

U.S. Constitution
- The United States Constitution, the supreme law of the land, takes precedence over federal statutes, court opinions, and state constitutions.

Acts, Statutes, and Ordinances
- A law enacted by Congress is called an act.
- Statutes are enacted by state legislative bodies.
- Local governments create and enact ordinances.

Precedents
- Much of our law is based on previous judicial and jury decisions, which are called precedents. Often judges and juries follow precedents when making a decision.

Criminal and Civil Law
- The two basic categories of jurisprudence are criminal law and civil law.

Criminal Law
- Criminal law governs violations punishable as offenses against the state or government. Such offenses involve the welfare and safety of the public rather than of one individual.
- Misdemeanors
- Felonies
- Treason

Misdemeanors
- A minor crime, called a misdemeanor, is punishable by fine or imprisonment of 1 year or less in a city or county jail rather than in a penitentiary.

Felonies
- A felony is a major crime, such as murder, rape, or burglary, and is punishable by imprisonment for more than 1 year.

Treason
- Treason is the attempt to overthrow the government. High treason is a serious threat to the stability or continuity of the government, such as an attempt to kill the president.

Civil Law
- Civil law is concerned with acts that involve relationships of individuals with other individuals, organizations, or government agencies and include the following.
  - Tort law
  - Contract law
  - Administrative law

Tort Law
- Tort law provides a remedy for harm from the wrongful acts of others, as in medical professional liability or medical malpractice.

The Four Ds of Tort
- Four elements must be established in every tort action.
  - Duty
  - Dereliction of duty
  - Direct cause
  - Damages

Duty
- First, the plaintiff must establish that the defendant was under a legal duty to act in a particular fashion.

Dereliction of Duty
- Second, the plaintiff must demonstrate that the defendant breached this duty.

Direct Cause
- Third, the plaintiff must prove that the breach of the legal duty proximately caused some injury or damage.

Damages
- Fourth, the plaintiff must prove damages, the injury or loss suffered.

Contract Law
- A contract is an agreement creating an obligation.
- A contract does not have to be formalized in writing.
- Oral contracts also are valid in many states.

Elements of a Contract
- First, there must be manifestation of assent or a "meeting of the minds," proven by an "offer"

and the "acceptance" of that offer, with agreement on the intent of the contract.

- Second, the contract must involve legal subject matter. An illegal obligation, like a gambling contract, is not enforceable.
- Third, both parties must have the legal capacity to enter into a contract (adults of sound mind, or an emancipated minor).
- Last, there must be consideration, an exchange of something of value (for example, money for the physician's time).

Offers

- The physician invites an offer by establishing availability.
- The patient accepts the invitation and makes an offer by arriving for or requesting treatment.

Acceptance of Offer

- The physician accepts the offer by accepting the patient and undertaking treatment.
- The physician may explicitly accept the patient's offer or implicitly accept the offer by exercising their independent medical judgment on behalf of the patient.

Liability

- The patient's responsibility in this agreement includes the liability for payment for services and a willingness to follow the advice of the physician.

Administrative Law

- Administrative law involves regulations set forth by governmental agencies.
  - The laws that allow the Internal Revenue Service to collect taxes and pursue restitution are administrative laws.
  - Other agencies involved with administrative law include the Social Security Administration, OSHA, Immigration & Naturalization Service, and the Centers for Medicare & Medicaid Services (formerly HCFA).

Professional Negligence

- Professional negligence in medicine may be:
  - malfeasance, the performance of an act that is wholly wrongful and unlawful
  - misfeasance, the improper performance of a lawful act
  - nonfeasance, the failure to perform an act that should have been performed

Prudent Care and Conduct

- In medicine, negligence is defined as the performance of an act that a reasonable and prudent physician *would not* do or the failure to do an act that a reasonable and prudent physician *would do*.
- The standard of prudent care and conduct is not defined by law, but is determined by a judge or jury, usually with the help of expert witnesses.

Contributory Negligence

- Contributory negligence exists when the patient contributes to his or her own condition. It can lessen the damages that can be collected or even prevent them from being collected.

Types of Damages

- Nominal damages
- Punitive damages
- Compensatory damages
- General damages
- Special damages

Standards of Care

- The courts hold that a physician must
  - use reasonable care, attention, and diligence in the performance of professional services
  - follow his or her best judgment in treating patients
  - possess and exercise the best skill and care that are commonly possessed and exercised by other reputable physicians in the same type practice in the same or a similar locality

Implied Consent

- A physician must have consent to treat a patient: this consent is usually implied by the patient's appearance at the office for treatment.
- This implied consent is sufficient for common or simple procedures that involve little risk.

Informed Consent

- Informed consent involves the patient's understanding of the condition and a full explanation of the plan for treatment.
- The physician must provide the patient or the patient's legal representative with enough information to decide whether to undergo the treatment or seek an alternative.
- The patient either refuses to consent to the proposed therapy or consents and signs a consent form.

Minors

- Consent is not required for minors when
  - consent may be assumed, as in a life-threatening situation
  - a treatment is required by law, such as a vaccination or radiograph for school entry or safety

- a court order has been issued, as when parents withhold consent for a necessary treatment for religious reasons

Emancipated Minor
- Emancipation varies from state to state. An emancipated minor is a person younger than the age of majority (usually 18 to 21 years) who is
  - married
  - in the armed forces
  - living separate and apart from parents or a legal guardian
  - self-supporting

Statutes of Limitations
- A statute of limitations defines a period after which a lawsuit cannot be filed. It varies from state to state, and differs for various types of litigation.

Depositions
- A deposition is testimony taken from a party or witness to the litigation (the deponent) and is not limited to the parties named in the lawsuit.
- A witness may be summoned by subpoena for the deposition. The deposition is usually taken under oath in an attorney's office in the presence of a court reporter. The person giving the deposition is called the deponent.
- The transcribed deposition is sent to the deponent for review, and the deponent may request corrections in the document.

Legal Disclosures
- Certain infectious diseases
- Births and deaths (in some states, detailed information about stillbirths is required)
- Results of violence, such as gunshot wounds, knife injuries, or poisonings
- Death from accidental, suggestive, or unexplained causes
- In some states, occupational diseases and injuries.

Discussion of Laws
- Patient Self-Determination Act
- Patient Bill of Rights
- Controlled Substances Act of 1970
- Uniform Anatomical Gift Act
- Health Insurance Portability and Accountability Act of 1996 (HIPAA)
- Occupational Safety and Health Act and the Bloodborne Pathogens Standard of 1992
- Clinical Laboratory Improvement Act (CLIA)

Licensure
- Examination
- Reciprocity
- Endorsement

Registration and Reregistration
- Periodic reregistration is necessary annually or biennially.
- A physician can be concurrently registered in more than one state.
- The issuing body notifies the physician when reregistration is due.

Requirements for Renewal
- Continuing education units (CEUs) are granted for attending approved seminars, lectures, scientific meetings, and formal courses in accredited colleges and universities.
- A total of 50 hours a year is the average requirement for license renewal.
- The medical assistant may assist the physician to arrange for completing the required units for license renewal.

Revocation or Suspension
- Conviction of a crime
- Unprofessional conduct
- Personal or professional incapacity

CHAPTER 8: Computers in the Medical Office

Computers in Medicine
- The development of software, the decrease in cost of computer hardware, and the time saving that the computer brings to the office make it well worth the investment.

Computer Literacy
- Computers are now standard equipment in healthcare facilities. Medical assistants must have a good understanding of the way computers work and their capabilities.

Advantages of Computer Use
- Computers assist workers in medical offices by
  - performing repetitive tasks
  - reducing errors
  - speeding production
  - recalling information on command
  - saving time
  - reducing paperwork
  - allowing more creative and productive use of the worker's time

Input
- Input: any information that enters the computer, from commands that are entered from the keyboard to data entered from another computer or input device, like a scanner, a mouse, or a keyboard.

Processing
- Processing: act of manipulating the data in the computer to carry out a certain task.

Output
- Output: anything that exits the computer such as binary numbers, characters, pictures, printed pages, or the image on the monitor.
- Output devices include monitors, speakers, and printers.

Storage
- Retaining data or applications is called storage.
- Data can be stored on disks, CDs, or on separate drives, such as a zip drive.

Hardware
- The physical pieces that can be touched and seen are called hardware.
- Most personal computers have a microprocessor, monitor, keyboard, mouse, and printer.

Microprocessor
- The microprocessor contains the logic circuitry, which carries out the instructions of a computer's programs.
- Microprocessors, sometimes called "central processing units," are differentiated by three basic elements:
  - Bandwidth
  - Clock speed
  - Instruction set

Hardware Devices
- Monitor
- Keyboard
- Mouse
- Printer

Inside the Computer
- Motherboard
- Disk drives
- CD-ROM
- Expansion boards
- Software
- Modems

Peripheral Devices
- Speakers and microphone
- Scanner
- Digital camera
- Zip drive

System Software
- System software is the operating system of the computer, allowing it to run and carry out its functions.

Applications Software
- Applications software, the programs that carry out the work, include Microsoft Office, MediSoft, and Medical Manager.

Applications Programs
- Application programs perform word processing, billing, accounting, appointment setting, insurance form preparation, payroll, and database management.

File Formats
- JPEG stands for *joint photographic experts group* and is often used for photographs.
- GIF stands for *graphics interchange format,* which supports color and is often used for scanned images and illustrations other than photographs.
- DOC: a file that includes the extension *.doc* is created by a word processor or word-processing software, and stands for *document.*
- TXT: a text file usually has the extension *.txt* after its name. Characters in a text file are represented by their ASCII codes.
- RTF stands for *rich text format.* This type of file combines ASCII codes with special commands that distinguish variations, such as a certain font.
- BMP: bit-mapped graphics are indicated by the extension *.bmp.* These are compiled by a graphics image set in rows or columns of dots.

Computer Networking
- A LAN is a *local-area network,* or a computer network spanning a relatively small area. Most LANs are contained in a single building or group of buildings, but LANs can be connected to other LANs at a distance.

Networks
- MAN stands for *metropolitan-area network,* spanning an area that does not exceed a metropolitan area or city, and connects several LANs.
- WAN: a *wide-area network,* spans a relatively large geographic area and typically consists of two or more LANs or MANs. These networks can be connected through public networks, such as a telephone system, or through leased lines or satellites. The largest WAN is the Internet.
- A HAN is a *home-area network,* which connects computers in a user's home.

- A CAN is a *campus-area network,* often used on college campuses and sometimes on military bases.

Servers

- File servers store files, and database servers process database queries.
- Some servers are *dedicated* servers, meaning they perform tasks only as a server, although a server also may operate as a normal computer.

The Internet

- The Internet is a global network connecting millions of computers.
- Each computer connected to the Internet is called a host and is independent of all the others.
- Internet Service Providers (ISPs) are companies that provide access to the Internet.

Domains

- .com
  - for commercial businesses
- .org
  - for organizations, usually nonprofit
- .edu
  - for educational institutions
- .gov
  - for governmental agencies
- .net
  - for network organizations

Browsers

- The most commonly used browsers are Netscape Navigator and Microsoft Internet Explorer.
- These browsers display graphics as well as text and can present multimedia information, the quality of which is dependent on the computer system and the Internet connection speed.

Computer Security

- Encryption is the translation of data into a code not readily understood by most users.
- Firewalls prevent individuals from accessing private networks.
- Passwords

Viruses

- Viruses are programs or pieces of code, usually loaded onto a computer without the owner's knowledge, that can act like a physical virus.
- Anti-virus software is an important part of any computer system.

Computers and Ergonomics

- Repetitive strain injury (RSI)
- Eyestrain

CHAPTER 9: Telephone Technique

Incoming Calls

- Calls to the physician's office come from a wide variety of sources.
- Patients, both new and established, may call to set appointments.

Business Calls

- Insurance companies may seek information about a claim. Hospitals, nursing facilities, or other healthcare units may report the progress of a patient. Laboratory results may come in for a patient who is very ill.

Miscellaneous Calls

- Routine sales calls and telemarketing calls come to the office, in addition to personal calls to the physician and staff members.

Telephone Voice

- A pleasing telephone voice is friendly and uplifting.

Pitch Variation

- The pitch of the voice should be varied.
- Avoid speaking in a monotone.

Courtesy

- Always be courteous and use tact, and talk directly into the handset so that the caller can clearly hear what is being said.

Handset

- The telephone handset should be held in the center, with the mouthpiece about 1 inch in front of the lips.

Mouthpiece Position

- Do not hold the mouthpiece beneath the chin, because your voice may not be heard clearly.

Receiver Position

- To avoid sore muscles and neck problems, do not lean the head downward to hold the phone between the ear and the shoulder.

Customer Service

- Be courteous to patients and other callers.

Staff Attitude

- Customer service is important because many patients have choices of healthcare providers. Attitude of staff members may play a large part in this decision.

Making a Practice Grow

- Good patient care ensures that patients will refer other patients to the physician, and this is one of the best ways to see a practice grow.

The Physician
- The physician's time is centered around the patients, but it would be physically impossible for the physician to speak with all those who wish to talk.

Screening Calls
- The medical assistant must make decisions as to which calls should be put through to the doctor.

Take a Message
- Attempt to determine the caller's needs and how those needs can be resolved.

If the Doctor is Busy
- The patient on the telephone should understand that the patient being examined must have the doctor's full attention.

Seven Parts of a Message
- Seven distinct items are needed for a phone message.
  - The name of the person to whom the call should be directed
  - The name of the person calling
  - The caller's telephone number
  - The reason for the call
  - The action to be taken
  - The date and time of the call
  - The initials of the person taking the call

Angry Callers
- Never return anger when a caller is angry.
- Remain calm and speak in tones slightly quieter than those of the caller to prompt the caller to lower his or her tone.
- Offer to help and ask questions to gain control of the conversation, moving it toward a solution.
- Do not argue with angry callers.

Complaints
- Handle a caller with a complaint as you would an angry caller. Remain calm and offer help.
- Take a serious interest in what the caller has to say: his or her concerns are important to the staff and the physician.
- Determine exactly what the caller wants or expects to resolve the problem.
- Always follow up on complaints and be sure that they were resolved as much as possible.

Emergencies
- When an emergency call comes to the medical office,
  - obtain a phone number where the caller can be reached, and
  - ask about the chief symptoms and when they started. Has the patient had similar symptoms in the past, and what happened then.
  - Determine if the patient is alone, has transportation, or needs an ambulance. In severe emergencies, do not hang up the phone until the ambulance or police arrive.

Emergency Phone Numbers
- The telephone book contains several sections of useful information, such as area codes, emergency service information, long-distance calling information, time zones, government listings, and community service numbers.
- Tear these pages out; place them in clear sheet protectors and in a binder for easy reference.

CHAPTER 10: Scheduling Appointments

Scheduling Appointments
- The medical assistant must consider the patients' needs, the physician's preferences, and the available facilities.

Patient and Physician Preferences
- Schedule the patient at his or her most convenient time to avoid no-shows. The physician will outline preferences; that should be of high priority.

Flexible Scheduling
- Most physicians are flexible and will make adjustments according to the needs of the office.
- The facilities in the office are perhaps the most inflexible: if a certain room or piece of equipment is being used by one patient, it usually cannot be used by another.

The Appointment Book
- If there are multiple physicians, the book should be arranged so that each doctor is readily identified.

Book Choice
- Books that open flat are much easier to handle.
- The book should provide enough space to write all of the patient information needed in the various time slots, such as the name, phone number, and reason for the visit.

Computerized Scheduling
- Computerized scheduling programs provide ease in operation and in making changes.

- The computer can quickly find the first available time.

Scheduling Appointments
- Most programs can prepare reports and notify patients by e-mail of an impending appointment.
- Web-based self-scheduling programs allow patients to see the physician's available appointments and book their own dates and times.

Self-scheduling
- Self-scheduling would vastly reduce calls to the office.
- Patients could make an appointment 24/7.

Types of Schedules
- Open office hours allow patients to come when it is convenient and wait in turn to see the doctor.
- Scheduling specific appointments is the most popular method of seeing patients.

Flexible Scheduling
- Flexible office hours include evenings and weekends.
- Many offices have some flexible scheduling because most families now consist of two working parents.

Wave Schedules
- Wave scheduling brings two to three patients to the office at the same time, and they are seen in the order of their arrival.
- This scheduling can be modified to suit the needs of the facility.
- Other scheduling methods include double-booking and grouping of like procedures.

Delays
- When the office is running 15 minutes late, briefly explain the delay to the waiting patients, and offer to reschedule their appointments.
- Keep the patients informed of wait times until the schedule resumes.

Patient Choice
- Giving the patient a choice in appointment times is a part of good service.

Appointment Book as Evidence
- The appointment schedule might be called into a court of law, so the handwriting in the book must be completely legible.
- The person testifying in court should be able to read all entries.
- Scribbled, messy handwriting implies incompetence; the courtroom is not the place for this impression.

Meeting Appointment Times
- Patients who generally arrive late might be told to arrive 15 minutes before their scheduled time.
- Some offices book these patients as the last appointment of the day; if they do not arrive promptly, they do not see the physician.
- The office can work with the patient to choose the best times.

Missed Appointments
- Although some patients accidentally forget the appointment with the physician, others are habitually careless.
- Emergencies often arise and some patients cannot get away from their own offices or other obligations to visit the doctor.
- The patient may not keep an appointment to avoid dealing with health issues.

CHAPTER 11: Patient Reception and Processing

Mission Statement
- The office mission statement explains why the office exists. Some physicians develop the mission statement themselves, outlining their vision and reasons for entering medical practice.

Statement Development
- Some doctors allow the office staff to assist in statement development. Employees should promote its ideas to all patients and visitors.

Waiting Room Features
- Office amenities include such things as a VCR, television, computer, telephone, and a desk where patients can sit and balance a checkbook or review work.
- These features make the time productive instead of wasteful.

Preparation for Patients
- Some offices prepare for patient arrivals the evening before, and some in the morning.
- Patient charts should be reviewed, checking for completed lab tests, posting of results, and to assure that ample progress notes exist for this visit.

Room Checks
- Rooms should be checked and inventoried for supplies and for a clean, neat appearance.

Greeting Patients
- People like hearing their own names; a better relationship is built between the staff and patients when the names are used often.
- Patients feel that the office staff cares enough about them to acknowledge them.

Preparing the Patient
- The medical assistant should escort the patient to the exam room and other areas of the office. Tell the patient when to disrobe and exactly what should be removed.

Assisting the Patient
- Take care that the patients' purse or wallet is in a secure place. Be sure that doors do not open and expose the disrobed patients. Instruct them as to when they may leave, or whether they should wait after seeing the physician.
- Ask often if the patient has any questions.

Patient Charts
- Some medical offices place patient charts in a door file to alert the physician that the patient is ready.
- The chart may be placed horizontally or vertically, one meaning that the patient is ready for the doctor, and the other meaning that the doctor is finished with the patient.
- Other offices place the charts in door files in a certain order. For example, if exam rooms 1, 2, and 3 are available, patients are seen in that order.

Talkative Patients
- Talkative patients are sometimes lonely and enjoy social interaction.
- Be as courteous as possible with talkative patients, explaining that another patient is waiting or the physician needs assistance.
- When this is said with a smile, most patients understand.

Closing the Office
- Develop a checklist of closing duties to help recall what to do before leaving for the day.
- Post a list of closing duties near the exit.

Summary
- Personal touches will help the patient to feel at home and comfortable in the office.
- An attractive reception area with various office amenities will provide a warm atmosphere.
- Using the patient's name frequently will convey a sense of caring.

CHAPTER 12: Written Communications and Mail Processing

Office Equipment
- The medical assistant is responsible for making certain that equipment is in good working order.
- Mail warranties when new equipment is purchased, and follow the correct maintenance procedures to keep machines working at an optimal level.
- Order supplies before running out, and compare prices to find the best price.

Stationery
- Four basic sizes of letterhead stationery include
  - Standard or letter-size stationery, which is most commonly used for business purposes, is $8\frac{1}{2} \times 11$ inches.
  - Monarch or executive stationery is $8\frac{1}{4} \times 10\frac{1}{2}$ inches and is used for informal business correspondence.
  - Baronial stationery is $5\frac{1}{2} \times 8\frac{1}{2}$ inches.
  - Legal stationery is $8\frac{1}{2} \times 14$ inches.

Parts of Speech
- The medical assistant should be familiar with the various parts of speech and how to use them correctly in a sentence.
- Nouns name something, such as a person, place, or thing; pronouns are substitutes for nouns.
- Verbs are action words, and express movement, a condition, or a state of being.
- Adjectives usually describe nouns, whereas adverbs usually describe verbs.
- Prepositions are connecting words, as are conjunctions.
- Interjections show strong feelings and are often followed by an exclamation point.

Communication Tools
- A personal tool collection will assist the medical assistant with written communications.
- An up-to-date dictionary, a medical dictionary, a composition handbook, an English language reference manual, and a thesaurus will be valuable additions to the tool library.

Answering Correspondence
- Read the piece carefully.
- Use a highlighter to mark questions that must be answered, or write notes in pencil.
- A draft of the reply should be written first and then rewritten in its final form.

Saving Samples

- Develop a portfolio that includes sample letters and other types of communications.
- Once a letter is written, it can be saved on the computer or on a disk, or printed and placed in a binder for easy viewing.
- Note on each example the file name as it is saved on the computer, so that the document can be easily found again when needed.

Letter Styles

- Block is an efficient, but less attractive letter style, wherein all lines begin flush with the left margin of the paper.
- Modified block is similar, but some lines begin at the center of the page instead of the left margin.
- Modified block with indented paragraphs is identical to block style, with the exception of the indention of the paragraphs.
- Simplified letter style contains lines that begin flush at the left margin, but other items are omitted, such as the salutation and complimentary closing.

Parts of the Business Letter

- The four standard parts of a business letter are the heading, the opening, the body, and the closing.
- The heading includes the letterhead and date line, whereas the opening includes the inside address and any attention or salutation line.
- The body is the message of the document, and the closing is the signature, complimentary closing, reference initials, and special notations.

Postal Rates

- Save money by consulting the post office about better rates and using zip codes. Consult a local post office when mailing in bulk for the best rates.

CHAPTER 13: Medical Records Management

Equipment and Supplies

- Several types of equipment and supplies are necessary to manage patient records.
- Open shelving allows maximal use of color-coded charts, which make finding misfiles quick and easy.

- Many file folder and forms styles are available.
- Physician and staff members' preferences are important, as are cost and availability.
- Be conservative when ordering supplies and purchasing equipment.

Filing

- Five basic steps are involved in filing documents.
  - The papers are conditioned, which is the preparatory stage for filing.
  - Releasing the documents means that they are ready to be filed and some type of mark is placed on the document to indicate this.
  - Indexing dictates where the document should be filed, and coding is placing some type of mark on the paper relative to that decision.
  - Sorting is placing the files in filing sequence.
  - The last step is the actual filing and storing of the document.

Filing Systems

- In alphabetic filing, documents are filed in alphabetic order.
- Numeric filing systems use a number code to give order to the files.
- An alphanumeric system is a combination of the two.

Color Coding

- Color coding helps to keep patient charts in order and to swiftly locate misfiled charts.
  - The medical assistant can tell at a glance when a chart is out of place.
  - Color coding also makes retrieval and refiling quick and easy.

Accuracy of Records

- Accurate medical records assure proper care. The record also allows continuity of care between providers, so that no lapse in treatment occurs.
- The record proves in court that certain treatments and procedures were performed, so it can be excellent legal support if it is well maintained and accurate.
- Medical records also aid researchers with statistical information.

Ownership of Records

- The physician owns the physical medical record, whereas the patient owns the information.

Problem-oriented Record

- The problem-oriented medical record categorizes each problem that a patient has and elaborates on the findings and treatment plan.

Detailed progress notes are kept for every individual problem.

- This method addresses each of the patient's concerns separately, whereas a traditional record addresses all problems and concerns at once.
- The problem-oriented medical record helps to address all individual problems.

Subjective Data

- Subjective information is provided by the patient, whereas objective information is provided by the physician.
- Subjective information includes the patient address, social security number, insurance information, and the patient's explanation of the medical condition.

Objective Data

- Objective information is obtained through the questions the physician asks and the observations made during the examination.

Chart Corrections

- When making corrections to a patient chart, draw a single line through the incorrect information, and then initial and date it.
- Some offices require a notation of "Corr." or "correction" on the chart as well. Never try to alter the medical record or cover up an error in charting.

CHAPTER 14: Professional Fees, Billing, and Collecting

Medical Fees

- Medical services are valuable to the patient and the physician sets fees based on three factors.

Fee Determination

- The physician offers the patient his *time,* and makes the most accurate *judgments* possible about the patient's medical condition.
- The *services* provided to the patient also figure into the fees set for various procedures.
- Many third-party payers use the usual, customary, and reasonable method of determining fees.
- The usual fee is what the physician normally charges for a given service.
- The customary fee is the range of fees charged by physicians with similar experience in the same geographic area.
- Services or procedures that are exceptionally complicated or require extra time deserve a fee that may be higher than usual.

Fee Estimates

- Providing estimates for medical care helps patients to plan and avoids the possibility of later misquoting the fee.
- The office staff should keep a copy of the estimate in the patient's chart.

Professional Courtesy

- Some physicians choose to extend professional courtesy to other physicians, medical professionals, and medical staff employees.
- The physician either discounts or eliminates the charges for all or part of the services provided.
- This decision is made by the physician.

Payment for Services

- Payment for medical services is usually received at the time of service.
- When extension of credit is offered, internal billing is necessary.

External Billing

- Some offices contract with external billing services.
- Often patients have insurance or a managed care policy that pays at least part of the bill. When patients fail to meet their obligations, outside collection services may be used.

Itemized Bills

- The first statement should always be itemized to provide the patient and the guarantor with a record of each procedure and each charge. Insurance companies require itemized bills.

Financial Problems

- Rarely do patients not wish to meet their obligations by paying bills, but some are not able to pay for medical services. If they do not have health insurance, obtaining medical care is difficult.
- The patient's financial problems may be temporary or may be a long-standing situation.
- Only a few patients are actually unwilling to pay, so work with the patient to develop a payment plan that can be met.

Skips

- Immediate action should be taken when the office classifies a patient as a "skip." Call all possible telephone numbers the patient has given.
- Do not reveal that the patient owes money. If you leave a message, do not indicate that the call is from a physician's office.
- The employer may be called if the patient has not given specific instructions not to call the place of business.
- Never communicate with a third party more than once unless invited to call back.

- A certified letter may be sent with a request for address corrections; the new address is often obtainable.
- Unless the "skip" is found quickly, the account is generally turned over to a collection agency.

Collections

- For collection calls, call within accepted hours, 8 AM to 9 PM.
- Be sure to identify correctly the person speaking, and always be respectful and courteous.
- Keep the conversation business-like and professional.
- Keep a positive attitude, and convey to the patient that the call is to help devise a way to meet the obligations to the physician.
- Never threaten the patient, and make every effort to get a commitment as to when payment can be expected.
- Most important, follow up on collection calls to assure that patients send the payment as promised.

CHAPTER 15: Basics of Diagnostic Coding

ICD Codes

- Why use ICD codes?
- In addition to the logistical layout of a standard system used in billing, some reasoning behind using ICD-9-CM codes includes:
  - Enhance data storage and retrieval
  - Maximize reimbursement by accurate coding
  - Shorten claims-processing time
  - Measure compliance with clinical guidelines

Volume I

- Volume I contains five appendices and 17 chapters. This is referred to as the Tabular List.

Disease Classification

- This volume classifies diseases and injuries according to etiology and organ system:
  - Anatomic system type of condition
  - Related groups of codes
  - Three-digit codes (category codes)
  - Fourth digit (subcategory codes)
  - Fifth digit (subclassification codes)

Chapter Subdivisions

- Each of the 17 chapters in Volume I is subdivided as follows:
  - Section: Group of three-digit code numbers describing a general disease category.
  - Category: A three-digit code representing a specific disease within the section.
  - Subcategory: A further breakdown of the category, assigning a fourth digit.
  - Sub-classification: Five-digit code giving the highest level of definition.

Volume II

- Volume II contains an Alphabetical Index of disease and injury.
- This volume contains more information than contained in the Tabular List and is divided into three sections:
  - Index of diseases
  - Poison and external causes of adverse affects of drugs and other chemical substances
  - Alphabetical index of external cause of injury and poisoning

Symbols

- ☐ The "lozenge" symbol precedes a disease code to indicate that the content of a four-digit category has been moved or modified.
- § The "section mark" symbol is used only in the Tabular List of Diseases; it precedes a code denoting a footnote on the page.
- ● The "bullet" symbol indicates a new entry.
- ▲ The "triangle" indicates a revision in the tabular list and a code change in the alphabetical index.
- ►◄ These symbols mark both the beginning and ending of new or revised text.
- ♀ Female diagnosis only.
- ♂ Male diagnosis only.
- √4th Code requires a fourth digit.
- √5th Code requires a fifth digit.

Abbreviations

NEC Not elsewhere classifiable. The category number for the term including NEC is used only when the coder lacks the information necessary to code the term to a more specific category.

NOS Not otherwise specified or "unspecified."

Punctuation

[ ] Brackets enclose synonyms, alternative wordings, or explanatory phrases.

( ) Parentheses enclose supplementary words that may be present in the statement of a disease or procedure without affecting its code number.

: Colons appear in the Tabular List after an incomplete term that needs a modifier to make it assignable to a category.

{ } Braces enclose a series of terms, each of which is modified by the statement to the right of the brace.

Other Features

Bold: used for all codes and titles in the Tabular List.

Italicized: used for exclusion notes and to identify a diagnosis that cannot be used as primary.

Assigning ICD-9-CM Codes

- The following steps are always necessary to assign the appropriate ICD-9-CM code.

Steps in Code Assignment

- Identify the key terms in the diagnostic statement.
- The definitive diagnosis should be coded first.

Preexisting Conditions

- Check documentation regarding preexisting conditions.
- Be sure this condition is currently being treated.

Unverified Conditions

Ethical Responsibility

- If a patient requests that a different (incorrect) diagnosis be used, because the insurance company will not reimburse, you must code the diagnosis correctly.

No Diagnosis

- If no definitive diagnosis is made, code the symptoms.

CHAPTER 16: Basics of Procedural Coding

CPT

- Why use CPT?
- Medicare and most commercial insurance companies use CPT to identify and classify claims for payment.
- CPT is not recognized in some settings or under special guidelines of an insurance company.

Uses of CPT

- Physician practices use CPT to
  - Submit claims
  - Track utilization
  - Measure physician productivity

Format of CPT

- Levels I and II
  - Level I (one) are national codes developed by AMA and contained in current CPT Manual. They are five-digit codes and two-digit modifiers.
  - Level II (two), known as HCPCS, are national codes developed by CMS to describe medical services and supplies not covered in CPT. They consist of alpha characters (between A and V) and four digits. Modifiers are either alphanumeric or two letters (between AA and VP).
- Level III
  - Level III (three) are local codes. Unlike Levels I and II, these codes are not common to all carriers. They are assigned by local Medicare carriers to describe new procedures not yet in Levels I and II. These codes start with a letter (W–Z) followed by four digits. When the HIPAA standards for electronic transactions are implemented, Level III (three) codes will no longer be recognized.

Symbols

Understanding symbol meaning is crucial to accurate coding.

- ● New procedure
- ▲ Code revision
- + CPT add-on codes
- Ø Exempt from the use of modifier –51
- ►◄ Revised guidelines, cross-references and explanations
- → With a circle around it, refers to *CPT Assistant*
- * Surgical procedure only

Classifications of Sections

- **Section** is a general grouping of codes like Surgery, Medicine, Laboratory, or Radiology. It is the largest grouping.
- **Subsection** better defines the section.
- **Subheading** further defines the subsection.
- **Category** includes the specific procedures to find the correct code.

CPT Updates

- Know your CPT code book: because of yearly changes, you must read the *introduction, guidelines,* and *notes.*

Services Provided

- Review all services and procedures performed, and include all medications administered and trays and equipment used on that day.

Consult Index

- Find the procedures and/or services in the index in the back of the CPT book. This will direct you to a code (not a page number), which may be listed as a procedure, body system, service, or abbreviation (this will usually refer you to the full spelling).

Read Carefully
- Read the description in the code and any related descriptions after a semicolon to find the most accurate code.

To Code a Service
- If the service is an Evaluation and Management code, identify
  - A new or established patient
  - Is this a consultation?
  - Where the service was performed
  - Review the documentation to determine the level of service
  - Is there is a reason to use a modifier?
  - Assign the five-digit CPT code

Modifiers
- Modifiers explain circumstances that alter a service.
- Sometimes more than one modifier is needed, so the first modifier used is –99 or 09999.

Understanding Evaluation and Management
- Type of service
  - Services covered in the E&M section are Physician visits in all locations for "well" and "sick" visits, Patient transport, Case management services, Preventive medicine services, and prolonged services.
- Place of service
- For payment purposes, the place of service must match the type of service. Some examples of places of service include
  - Office (11)
  - Patient's home (12)
  - Inpatient hospital (21)
  - Outpatient hospital (22)
- Patient status
  - Many of the CPT codes are classified by whether a patient is new or established.
    - A new patient is new to the practice or has not been seen by the specialty in group practice for more than 3 years.
    - An established patient has a continuing relationship with the practice and is unlikely to depart from the baseline health.

Levels of E&M Services
- Problem focused: A problem-focused history concentrates on the chief complaint; it looks at symptoms, severity, and duration. It usually does not include a ROS or family and social history.

- Expanded problem focused: The physician also includes a review of systems that relate to the chief complaint. Usually a family and social history is not included.
- Detailed: The physician documents a more extensive history, ROS, and will document pertinent family and social histories.
- Comprehensive: The physician documents responses to all of the components listed. This is usually done on an initial visit with patients who have a significant history of illness.

Medical Decision Making
- Straightforward: one diagnosis/management option, one test ordered or reviewed, and full recovery expected.
- Low complexity: limited (two) diagnosis/management options, limited (two) tests ordered or reviewed, and low risk of complications.
- Moderate complexity: multiple (three) diagnoses/management options, moderate (three) data ordered or reviewed, and moderate risk of complications and/or death if they are not treated.
- High complexity: extensive (four or more) diagnoses/management options, extensive (four or more) data ordered or reviewed and the high risk of complications to the patient if these conditions are not treated.

Examination of Body Areas and Organ Systems
- Body areas: Head including face and neck; chest, including breasts and axillas; abdomen; genitourinary; back, including spine; and extremities.
- Organ systems: Constitutional; eyes, ears, nose, throat, and mouth; cardiovascular; respiratory; gastrointestinal; genitourinary; musculoskeletal; skin; neurologic; psychiatric; and hematological/lymphatic.

Types of Examination
- Problem-focused: Limited to the single body area or single system mentioned in the chief complaint.
- Expanded problem-focused: In addition to the limited body area or system, related body areas/organ systems are examined.
- Detailed: An extended examination of related body areas/organ systems.
- Comprehensive: A "complete" multisystem examination.

CHAPTER 17: The Health Insurance Claim Form

Insurance Claims
- For a better understanding of the medical insurance claims process, the medical assistant should familiarize himself or herself with the language and terms used.

Paper and Electronic Claims
- Insurance claims can be submitted in paper and electronic forms, with advantages and disadvantages for both. Electronic claims normally have fewer errors and are paid faster.

Clean Claims
- Clean claims can be processed and paid quickly.
- Dirty claims contain errors and/or omissions that often result in rejection, thus greatly slowing reimbursement.

Claim Cycle
- The insurance claim cycle begins when the patient first makes an appointment.
- An established list of guidelines for HCFA-1500 form completion includes obtaining a signed authorization to release information.

HCFA-1500
- HCFA-1500 claim form completion requirements vary from payor to payor.

Payor Requirements
- Familiarization with each major payor's unique requirements will maximize reimbursement.

OCR Scanning
- Optical character recognition (OCR) scanning is the electronic transfer of information from claim forms to data banks that simplify and speed the claims process.

Guidelines for Claims
- Specific guidelines should be followed precisely to facilitate OCR scanning.

Claim Rejections
- Claim rejection and delay cost time and money.
- Proven methods of preventing claim rejections should be established and adhered to.

Tracking Claims
- Track claims once they are submitted.
- Create and use an insurance claim register, or log, to track claims.
- Establish a routine for claims follow-up.

CHAPTER 18: Third-Party Reimbursement

Coordination of Benefits (COB)
- The policyholder's own insurance plan is primary.
- If the policyholder is laid off or retired and is not a Medicare recipient, the policyholder's plan pays second.

Primary Coverage
- Primary coverage for dependents of the policyholder is determined by the birthday rule.
  - The insurance plan of the policyholder whose birthday comes first in the calendar year (month and day, not year) provides primary coverage for each dependent.

Length of Coverage
  - If neither situation applies, the plan that has been in existence longer is the primary payer.

Divorce and Separation
- The primary plan for dependents of legally separated or divorced parents is more complicated.

Custodial Parent
- The birthday rule is in effect if the custodial parent of the dependent has not remarried. If the custodial parent has remarried, that parent's plan is primary.

Responsible Party
- If the court has decreed one parent the responsible party, that parent's policy is primary (not always the parent with legal custody of the child).

COB Law
- If one of the plans originated in a state without the COB law, the plan that originated in a state with COB law will determine the order of benefits.

Purpose of Insurance
- The medical assistant should understand the purpose of health insurance to facilitate his or her knowledge and to educate patients. The trend for "preventive medicine" can be appreciated.

Diverse Policies
- Insurance policies are available in a variety of forms.

Types of Policies
- Various types of insurance policies are available in each policy category.

- It is important to understand and appreciate that many people in this country cannot afford and do not receive quality health care.

Policy Combinations

- Insurance packages can be tailored to each individual or group, with limitless combinations of benefits (e.g., surgical, basic medical, and major medical).

Payment Methods

- Benefits are determined and paid in indemnity schedules, service benefit plans, determination of the UCR fee, or relative value studies.
- The medical assistant should understand the ramifications of all.

Healthcare Cost

- The cost of quality health care has skyrocketed.
- Healthcare reform methods seek to contain these costs.

Healthcare Cost Reform

- Individual state laws have improved.
- Keep current by reading pertinent magazines and periodicals and pay close attention to news broadcasts.

Managed Care

- Managed care describes a variety of health plans developed to provide services at lower costs.
- The various types of managed care (e.g., HMO, IPS, PPO) function differently. Managed care has positive and negative effects on modern medicine.

Managed Care Options

- The maze of managed care options creates confusion: there are three HMO plans alone.

Other Options

- In PPOs, physicians sign a contract to allow PPO members a discount for healthcare services.
- The medical assistant should research the most common options in the area of practice and concentrate on them.

Third-party Payors

- Other major third-party payors are Blue Cross/ Blue Shield, Medicaid, Medicare, CHAMPVA/ TRICARE, and Workers' Compensation.

Medicare and Medicaid

- Medicare is the largest third-party insurer, providing quality healthcare for the elderly and select other groups.
- Medicaid is another government-sponsored healthcare plan.

Workers' Compensation

- Workers' Compensation covers employees who are injured or who become ill because of accidents or adverse conditions in the workplace.
- Disability programs reimburse for monetary losses because of an inability to work, not covered under Workers' Compensation.

Verifying Benefits

- Problems can be prevented for the patient and the medical office if the medical assistant verifies insurance benefits before services are rendered.

Patients and Coverage

- Gather as much information as possible about the patient's insurance coverage.
- Discuss with all new patients the established policy of the medical office regarding the insurance claims process and the collection of fees not covered by their policy.

Payment for Services

- Fees for medical procedures and services differ from office to office.
- Until the advent of managed care, most physicians operated on a *fee-for-service* basis.

Influences on Charges

- In recent years, government and managed care organizations have greatly influenced what healthcare providers can charge.
- Many third-party payors base reimbursements on what is referred to as the *allowable charge*.
- Other fee-schedule types include the Relative Value Scale (RVS) and the Resource-Based Relative Value Scale (RBRVS).

CHAPTER 19: Banking Services and Procedures

Electronic Banking

- The Internet has changed conventional banking as we know it.
- E-banking advantages and disadvantages should be thoroughly researched before opening an online account.

Negotiable Instrument

- For an instrument (e.g., check) to be "negotiable," it must meet certain criteria:
  - Be written and signed by a maker,
  - Contain a promise or order to pay a sum of money,

– Be payable on demand or at a fixed future date, and

– Be payable to order or bearer.

Checks

- Advantages of using checks include
  - safety and convenience,
  - quick calculation, and
  - a permanent record for taxes.

Bank Accounts

- Checking accounts, savings accounts, and money market savings accounts are slightly different, and each has special uses.

Voiding a Check

- If a mistake is made on a check, mark it VOID, and write a new check. Some banks accept minor errors if the maker initials the error. Erasures and whiteout are not allowed.

Endorsements

- The four kinds of endorsements are:
  - Blank endorsement, in which the payee signs his or her name on the back of the check
  - Restrictive endorsement, which specifies the bank and the account into which funds are to be deposited
  - Special endorsement, which names a person as payee on the back of the check
  - Qualified endorsement, which disclaims future liability. This type of endorsement is used when the person who accepts the check has no personal claim in the transaction.

Returned Checks

- When a deposited check is returned, the maker should be asked to remedy the situation by either immediately depositing funds in the account to cover the check, or using cash or a money order.

Reconciling a Statement

- The procedure for reconciling a bank statement is simple and straightforward.

CHAPTER 20: Medical Practice Management

Importance of Management

- The office manager runs the business aspects of the office so the physician can focus on good patient care.
- A high degree of trust is placed in the office manager.

Management Skills

- A good office manager is fair and flexible.
- Good communications skills and attention to details are necessary.
- Caring about the employees is essential.
- Remaining calm in a crisis, using of good judgment, and organizing tasks are important.

Leaders

- Charismatic leaders inspire allegiance and dedication while encouraging individuals to overcome obstacles.
- The transactional leader is structured and organized, hardworking, and a planner.
- The transformational leader is effective during times of transition and at building relationships.

Power

- Power can be both positive and negative, but should not be manipulative or coercive.
- Expert power is based on a high degree of knowledge.
- Legitimate power is that of position or status, whereas referent power is granted from subordinates to those who lead by example.

Motivation

- Employees are motivated by money, praise, insecurity, honor, prestige, needs, love, fear, and satisfaction.
- The effective manager discovers what motivates employees.
- Intrinsic motivation comes from within the employee, whereas, extrinsic motivation has an outside source.

Preventing Burnout

- Asking for help can prevent burnout: managers often do not delegate as much as they should.
- Exercise, rest, and understanding one's limitations help prevent burnout.
- Focused goals help the manager work toward the most critical tasks.

Personnel Records

- Resumes and applications should be accurate and complete.
- Gaps in employment dates should be explained, and the office manager should verify any references.
- Information should be legible and consistent.

Choosing among Applicants

- After interviewing a prospective candidate, the office manager should verify the resume and application, and check several references.

- Compare the candidates and choose the top two or three for a second interview.

Choosing Staff
- Involve other staff members in choosing new employees for the office.

Mentors
- Mentors offer information regarding policies and procedures.
- The new employee can approach the mentor with questions.

Staff Meetings
- Staff meetings may relay information, solve a problem, or brainstorm ideas.
- Some meetings are work sessions; others may discuss new policies or changes in procedures.

CHAPTER 21: Medical Practice Marketing and Customer Service

Preparation
- Before implementing marketing strategies, first evaluate what is currently being done.

Developing a Plan
- Decide the objectives of the marketing plan and how they will be measured.
- Develop a specific plan and timeline for each phase.

Target Market
- A target market is a very specific group that the medical facility wishes to serve.
- Where the individuals live, their lifestyle, and their personalities are all ways to classify them as a specific target market.

Identifying a Target Market
- To identify a target market, ask "Who is our patient?", "What does our patient want?", and "Why?"
- Answers to these questions will help design a marketing plan.

Suggestions
- Patients and employees often see the facility from different points of view; their suggestions can enhance the atmosphere and services.

Marketing Plan
- A marketing plan addresses the "four p's"
  - product
  - placement
  - price
  - promotion

The Four P's
- The product of a medical office includes the services and any retail items.
- Placement includes the location of the office and its convenience (and placement of retail items).
- Price represents the charges for goods and services.
- Promotion entails the ways in which the services are promoted.

Plan Development
- First assess past efforts and the results.
- Then develop the plan; such a plan should include very specific steps.
- Execute the plan.

Evaluation
- After the plan is executed, evaluate its effectiveness and determine whether the goals were met.
- The evaluation is important in planning future marketing strategies.

Public Relations
- Involvement in the community is an excellent way to promote the medical profession and to remain in the public eye, resulting in new patients. The public sees medical professionals as caring and compassionate; volunteer activities reinforce this attitude.

Advertising
- Advertising can create or change attitudes, beliefs, and perceptions through purchased broadcast time, printed material, or other forms of communication.

Public Relations
- Public relations rely more on news broadcasts or reports, magazine or newspaper articles, and radio reports.

Promotional Opportunities
- The new medical practice can place an announcement in the newspaper.
- Some physicians hold an open house and invite the public.
- A website may be listed on business cards and stationery.
- Community service and volunteer activities that mention the practice will also spread the word.

Patient Relations
- Identifying with the patient and expressing understanding of the patient's concerns are effective customer service tools.

Customer Service
- Tell the patient that a problem can be resolved.
- Four magic words in customer service are, "Let me help you."

Customers
- External customers are patients.
- Staff members and employees are internal customers who derive a sense of satisfaction in working for the medical office.
- The internal customers are just as important as the external customers.

CHAPTER 22: Health Information Management

Health Information
- Physicians and employees of medical facilities use health information to assure continuity of care from provider to provider, to assist manufacturers in determining side effects of drugs, to provide statistical information regarding diagnoses, and to help the medical facility plan for future needs and capital equipment.

Characteristics of Good Data
- Validity: The accuracy of the information.
- Reliability: The information can be counted on to be accurate, and medical decisions can be made based on it.
- Completeness: The information is available in its entirety.
- Timely information: The provider can make decisions based on the latest data about a patient or a treatment.

More Characteristics
- Relevance: The health information is useful.
- Accessibility: The information is easily available to the provider.
- Security: The effort to keep unauthorized people from accessing health information.
- Legality: The correctness of the information and its authentication by the healthcare provider.

Quality Assurance
- Four concerns of quality assurance include the overuse, underuse, misuse, and variations in use of healthcare services.
  - Overuse: Excessive and cause cost increases, as in using the emergency room for nonemergencies

  - Underuse: Patients do not take advantage of many services, especially if they are at-risk patients

Misuse and Variations
  - Misuse: Reflects errors, such as lab errors or misdiagnoses
  - Variations: In various parts of the country, individuals use services in different ways, influencing the quality of care

HIPPAA
- The Health Insurance Portability and Accountability Act supports patient privacy issues. The act gives information about who accesses their records. They must give specific authorization for the use and dissemination of the information contained in the medical record.

Health Statistics
- The National Center for Health Statistics is a part of the Centers for Disease Control.
- Health statistics allow providers to give better treatment.

Disease Outbreaks
- If an area has an outbreak of a disease, the physician may be better prepared to cope with patients, treating them faster and promoting a full recovery.

Health Data and Vital Statistics
- The NCHS compiles information about HIV infections, teen pregnancies, and other vital health data for medical professionals.
- Statistics kept by the NCHS include alcohol and drug use information, births, deaths, communicable diseases, infant health and mortality, and life expectancy.

Quality Management
- Total quality management is based on the leadership of top management, and supported by the involvement of all employees and departments.

Accreditation
- The Joint Commission on Accreditation of Healthcare Organizations is a nonprofit organization that offers voluntary accreditation services. More than 17,000 healthcare facilities in the United States are accredited by JCAHO.

Standards and Quality Assurance
- Without strong health care standards, quality cannot exist.
- The focus of quality assurance has shifted from just meeting the minimal standards to providing optimal quality.

Standards of Excellence

- People expect quality healthcare. Those organizations who seek accreditation or focus on quality will exceed standards, not just meet them.

CHAPTER 23: Management of Practice Finances

Financial Records

- Business records show how much was earned, how much was collected, how much is owed, and the distribution of expenses.

Accounts Payable and Receivable

- Accounts payable: The amount of money owed by a business, but not yet paid.
- Accounts receivable: The amount owed to the business, but not yet paid.

Bookkeeping Systems

- The three most common bookkeeping systems include the single-entry system, double-entry system, and pegboard system.

Single-entry Method

- The single-entry method is the oldest and uses a general journal, a cash payment journal, and an accounts receivable ledger.
- Payroll records and petty cash records also may be included.

Double-entry System

- The double-entry system requires an entry on each side of the accounting equation.
- The sides must always balance.
- Double-entry is more difficult to use than the single-entry system.

Pegboard System

- The pegboard system may be expensive at first, but allows the performance of several accounting functions at one time.
- It is often called the *write-it-once* system.

Trial Balance

- A trial balance reflects discrepancies between the journal and the ledger. It does not reveal errors in the individual accounts, but will show errors in the overall balances.

Employment Records

- The Internal Revenue Service requires that several employment records be kept for four years:
  - Social Security number of the employee
  - Number of withholding allowances claimed
  - Amount of gross salary
  - All deductions for Social Security and Medicare taxes; federal, state, and city or other subdivision withholding taxes; state disability insurance; and state unemployment tax

Deductions

- Several deductions are required by law, based on the total earnings of the employee; the number of withholding allowances claimed; the marital status of the employee; and the length of the pay period.

Reports

- Five common reports are used for accounting:
  - The statement of income and expense
  - The cash flow statement
  - The trial balance
  - The accounts receivable trial balance
  - The balance sheet

Withholding

- The Employee's Withholding Allowance Certificate, or form W-4, specifies the number of withholding allowances the employee claims.
- The more allowances claimed, the less taken from the employee's paycheck.

Deductions

- The Federal Insurance Contributions Act requires that money be deducted from wages for Medicare and social security programs: 1.45% for the Medicare contribution and 6.2% for social security.
- Both the employer and employee contribute these amounts.

Budget

- The physician's office sets a budget each fiscal year to prepare for all of the expenses involved in running the office.

Budget Planning

- Without a well-planned budget, the physician cannot control expenses. The expenditures from the past year should be evaluated, paying particular attention to the expenses that exceeded expected amounts.

CHAPTER 24: Infection Control

Infectious Disease

- Pathogenic microorganisms include viruses, bacteria, protozoa, fungi, and rickettsia.

Chain of Infection

- The chain of infection causes the spread of infectious disease.
- It consists of the infectious agent and the host, continues with the means or portal of exit from the host, the mode of transmission, the means or portal of entry into a new host, and the presence of a susceptible host.
- To stop the spread of infection, at least one of these links must be broken.

The Inflammatory Response

- The inflammatory response is the body's reaction to a foreign substance or antigen.
- The release of inflammation mediators, through three separate actions, results in an increase of white blood cells (WBCs) at the site of the injury.

Site of Injury

- Blood vessels dilate, causing an increase in the local blood flow, resulting in redness or inflammation and heat.
- Blood vessel walls become more permeable, which helps in releasing WBCs to the site.

WBC Protection

- The WBCs form a fibrous capsule around the injury, protecting surrounding cells from damage or the source of infection.

Plasma and Edema

- Blood plasma also filters out of the more permeable vessel walls, resulting in edema, which puts pressure on the nerves and causes pain.

Chemotaxis

- Finally, chemotaxis, the release of chemical agents, attracts WBCs.
- WBCs engage in phagocytosis, or the engulfing and destruction of microorganisms and damaged cells.

Pus Formation

- Destroyed pathogens, cells, and WBCs collect and form a thick, white substance called pus.

Immunity

- The body's immune system operates on two different levels:
  - Humoral immunity creates specific antibodies to combat antigens.
  - Cell-mediated immunity attacks the source of the infection at the cellular level.

Disease Types

- Acute diseases have a rapid onset and short duration.
- Chronic diseases last over a long period, perhaps a lifetime.

- Latent diseases cycle through relapse and remission phases.

Antibiotics

- Bacterial infections can be treated with antibiotics, but viral infections, because they involve viral takeover of cellular DNA or RNA material, cannot.

Infectious Body Fluids

- OSHA has designated certain body fluids including cerebrospinal fluid (CSF), synovial, pleural, pericardial, peritoneal, mucous, and amniotic fluids as potentially infectious with bloodborne pathogens, as may be blood, vaginal and seminal secretions, saliva, and human tissue.

Protective Equipment

- Protective equipment must be used if you will be involved in any of these activities:
  - Touching a patient's blood and body fluids, mucous membranes, or broken skin
  - Handling items and surfaces contaminated with blood and body fluids
  - Performing venipuncture, finger punctures, injections, and other vascular-access procedures
  - Assisting with any surgical procedure. If a glove is torn or an injury occurs, the glove is removed and replaced with a new glove. The instrument is removed from the sterile field.
  - Handling, processing, and disposing of all specimens of blood and body fluids
  - Cleaning and decontaminating spills of blood or other body fluids

Exposure Control Plan

- The Exposure Control Plan must contain specifics on controls for bloodborne pathogens including PPE, training, hepatitis B immunization, record keeping, and the labeling and disposal of all biohazard waste.

Follow-up

- Postexposure follow-up involves immediate cleansing of the site, examination of the source individual and worker's blood, administration of prophylactic medications, health counseling, and confidential treatment of all medical records.

Guidelines

- The OSHA Compliance Guidelines stipulate the management and implementation of barrier protection devices, environment protection, housekeeping controls, and administration of hepatitis B immunization.

Asepsis

- Medical asepsis: Removal or destruction of pathogens
- Surgical asepsis: Destruction of all microorganisms
- Medical aseptic techniques: Create an environment as free of pathogens as possible
- Surgical aseptic, or sterile technique: Used when the patient's skin or mucous membranes are disrupted
- Sanitization: The cleaning of contaminated articles or surfaces to reduce the numbers of microorganisms
- Disinfection: The process of killing pathogenic organisms
- Sterilization: The destruction of all microorganisms

Infection Control Techniques

- The medical assistant teaches patients about infection control and the potential danger of blood and body fluids, including demonstrating aseptic techniques, the management of infectious materials at home, and the importance of frequent and consistent hand washing.

Infection Control

- The medical assistant applies infection control procedures to prevent cross-contamination and the development of nosocomial infections.

CHAPTER 25: Patient Assessment

Holistic Care

- Holistic care includes assessing the patient's health status with physical, cognitive, psychosocial, and behavioral data.

The Medical History

- The medical history consists of the patient's database, past medical history, family and social histories, and the review of systems.

Preparing The Appropriate Environment

- Ensure privacy.
- Refuse interruptions.
- Prepare comfortable surroundings.
- Take judicious notes.

Open-Ended Questions

- "What brings you to the doctor?"
- "How have you been getting along?"
- "You mentioned having dizzy spells. Tell me more about that."

Closed Questions

- "Do you have a headache?"
- "What is your birth date?"
- "Have you ever broken a bone?"

Health History of a Child

- The environment should be safe and attractive.
- Do not keep children and their caregivers waiting any longer than necessary.
- Do not offer a choice unless the child can truly make one. While giving a child a choice of stickers after receiving an injection is appropriate, asking her if she'd like her shot now is not.

Child's Examination

- Praising the child helps decrease anxiety. When possible, direct questions toward the child so he or she feels part of the process.
- Involve the child by permitting her to manipulate the equipment.
- Use your imagination to make a game of the assessment or the procedure.
- A typical defense mechanism seen in sick or anxious children is regression. The child may refuse to leave her mother's lap or want to hold a favorite toy during the procedure. Look for signs of anxiety such as thumb sucking or rocking.

Helping Relationship

- Develop a professional helping relationship with patients.
- The helping relationship recognizes the impact of patient anxieties on interactions and responses to treatment.

Linear Communication

- The Linear Communication Model illustrates an interactive process between the sender and receiver of the message; feedback is a crucial part of the process.

Active Listening

- Active-listening techniques include restatement, reflection, and clarification.
- The medical assistant can listen to and appropriately respond to the patient's main point.

Nonverbal Messages

- Approximately 90% of patient interactions occur through nonverbal language.
- Successful patient interaction has congruent verbal and nonverbal messages.

Listening Strategies

- Listen to the main points.
- Attend to both verbal and nonverbal messages.
- Be patient and nonjudgmental.
- Don't interrupt.

- Never intimidate your patient.
- Use active-listening techniques: restatement, reflection, and clarification.

Communication Styles

- Certain communication styles can be misleading or restrict the patient's response.
- Avoid providing reassurance, giving advice, using medical terminology, asking leading questions, and talking too much.
- These interfere with gathering complete data and are an obstacle to developing rapport.

Communication Skills

- Patients use defense mechanisms to protect themselves in emotionally challenging situations.
- Consistently apply nonjudgmental therapeutic communication skills to maintain professional relationships.

Interview Styles

- Therapeutic communication techniques vary with the patient.
- Be aware of how to interact most effectively with young children, adolescents, adults, and their families.
- Age-specific interview styles assure clear communication.

Patient Interview

- The patient interview is divided into the introduction, the body, and the summary or closing.
- Use professional interview techniques such as empathetic patient care, sensitivity to patient diversity, active-listening skills, appropriate non-verbal communication, attention to the interview environment, avoidance of communication barriers, and use open and closed questions and/or statements.

Documentation

- Accurate and complete documentation is a necessary skill.
- Describe the patient's chief complaint, all pertinent signs and symptoms, and demonstrate the correct use of medical terminology and appropriate abbreviations.
- Correct any error in the medical record according to legally approved methods.

Medical Record Systems

- Medical record systems include the POMR method, which uses SOAPE charting to define the patient's health problems.
- The most frequently used is the SOMR, which organizes patient data into specific sections. The CMR organizes computer records for patient data.

Initial Interview

- The perfect time to initiate patient education is during the initial patient interview.

Risk Management

- Risk-management practices focus on reducing the chances of professional liability claims.
- Accurate and complete documentation on the patient's chart is crucial.
- Maintaining strict confidentiality of patient information and factual, nonjudgmental, legible recording of patient data are essential.

CHAPTER 26: Patient Education

Holistic Patient Education

- The holistic model suggests patient education should consider all aspects of patient life including physical, psychological, emotional, social, economic, and spiritual needs.

Guidelines for Patient Education

- Provide knowledge and skills that promote recovery and health
- Include family in education interventions
- Encourage patient ownership of the education process
- Promote safe use of medications and treatments
- Encourage healthy behaviors
- Provide information on community resources.

Patient Factors that Affect Learning

- Perception of disease versus the actual state of disease
- Need for information
- Age and developmental level
- Mental and emotional state
- The influence of multicultural and diversity factors
- Individual learning style
- Impact of physical disabilities.

Language Barriers

- For patients with language barriers, address the patient formally and courteously.
- Use nonverbal language to promote understanding.
- Integrate pictures or models.
- Observe the patient for understanding or confusion.
- Use simple lay language.
- Demonstrate procedures.
- Teach in small manageable steps.

- Provide written instructions.
- Use an interpreter when one is available.

Barriers

- Potential barriers include patient learning style; physical limitations; age and developmental level; emotional or mental state; use of defense mechanisms; cultural or ethnic factors; language; pain; motivation; and limited time.

Materials and Methods

- Effective methods include printed materials, videos, and approved Internet sites to gather information.
- Refer patients to community resources and experts.
- Use demonstration/return demonstration of medical skills and patient journals of events; be sure to involve family members in the education process.

Teaching Plan

- Assess learning needs
- Determine teaching priorities
- Use appropriate teaching materials and methods
- Gather feedback repeatedly to assure understanding and eliminate learning barriers
- Summarize the material at the end of each session
- Plan for the next meeting
- Evaluate the effectiveness of the session
- Completely and accurately document the details of the teaching intervention.

Reinforce Physician Instructions

- Reinforce physician instructions and information by encouraging patients to take an active role in their health
- Use "teaching moments" effectively by keeping information relevant to the patient; communicating clearly; being aware of learning factors; and being flexible with the teaching plan.

Patient Education

- Appropriate patient education reflects the patient Bill of Rights emphasis on confidentiality and informed consent.

Risk Management Practices

- Risk management practices include accurate and complete documentation of sessions and sensitivity to the diverse needs of the patient.

CHAPTER 27: Nutrition and Health Promotion

Nutrients

- Nutrients consist of carbohydrates, fats, proteins, vitamins, minerals, and water.
- They provide energy, protection, and insulation; build and repair tissues; and regulate metabolic processes.

Carbohydrates and Fiber

- Carbohydrates provide a ready source of energy.
- Dietary fiber maintains regularity and helps to prevent cancer and heart disease.

Carbohydrates

- Carbohydrates (CHO) are composed of carbon, hydrogen, and oxygen and are primarily plant products.
- They are divided into three groups: simple sugars, complex carbohydrates (starch), and dietary fiber.

Fats and Proteins

- Dietary fat provides essential fatty acids and is needed for the absorption of fat-soluble vitamins. Adipose tissue helps protect the organs of the body, insulates, and is a concentrated form of stored energy.
- Protein builds and repairs tissue and assists with metabolic functions.

Fat

- Fat is used to back up carbohydrates as a concentrated form of fuel that produces 9 kcal/g of energy.
- Dietary fats, or lipids, provide essential fatty acids for the absorption of fat-soluble vitamins.

Fatty Acids

- Fatty acids can be either saturated or unsaturated. A saturated fatty acid contains all the hydrogen possible and therefore is denser, heavier, and solid at room temperature.

Saturated Fats

- Examples of saturated fats are dairy products, eggs, lard, meat, and hydrogenated fats such as margarine.
- Fats in soft-type margarines are partially hydrogenated and usually soft at room temperatures.
- Most saturated fats come from animal sources.

Unsaturated and Monounsaturated Fats

- Unsaturated fatty acids can take on more hydrogen and therefore are less heavy and less dense.

- Fatty acids with one unfilled hydrogen bond are called monounsaturated. Olives and olive oil, peanuts and peanut oil, canola oil, pecans, and avocados contain monounsaturated fats.

Polyunsaturated Fats

- Polyunsaturated fats, such as safflower, corn, cottonseed, and soy oils have two or more unfilled hydrogen bonds, are found in plants, and are usually liquid at room temperature.

Cholesterol

- Cholesterol is synthesized only in animal tissue so is not found in plant foods.
- The primary food sources of cholesterol are egg yolks and organ meats, although all animal sources of food contain cholesterol.

HDLs

- The good fats, or high-density lipoproteins (HDLs), carry free cholesterol from body tissues to the liver for metabolism and excretion.

LDLs

- The bad fats, or low-density lipoprotein (LDLs) and very low-density lipoprotein (VLDLs), carry fat and cholesterol to the cells.
- LDLs and VLDLs form atherosclerotic plaques on arterial walls that frequently result in heart disease, hypertension, and strokes. Serum LDL levels can be improved through diet.

Antioxidants

- Our bodies protect us against toxins created by oxidation through use of antioxidant vitamins C and E and beta-carotene, but their amounts are not always sufficient.
- Antioxidants prevent cholesterol from oxidizing.

Water

- The body is approximately 80% water and can survive longer without food than it can without water.
- Water is part of almost every vital body process.

Functions of Water

- Plays a key role in the maintenance of body temperature
- Acts as a solvent and the medium for most biochemical reactions
- Acts as the vehicle for transport of substances such as nutrients, hormones, antibodies, and metabolic waste
- Acts as a lubricant for joints and mucous membranes

Functions of Protein

- Builds and repairs body tissue
- Aids in the body's defense mechanisms against disease
- Regulates body secretions and fluids
- Provides energy

Vitamins and Minerals

- Vitamins, essential for metabolic functions, are classified as either fat or water soluble. They regulate the synthesis of body tissues, aid in the metabolism of nutrients, and play a vital role in disease prevention.
- Minerals help maintain electrolytes and acid–base balance as well as regulate muscular action and nervous activities.

The Food Guide Pyramid

- The Food Guide Pyramid, developed by the government as a visual dietary guideline, is divided into six sections.
- It illustrates how the proportions of each basic food group contribute to a balanced diet.

Assessment

- The assessment of nutritional status includes an evaluation of current health and lifestyle habits as well as body fat measurements.
- Body fat can be measured as a waist-to-hip ratio, using calipers to measure fat folds, or calculating the body mass index (BMI).

Diets

- Diets can be modified to include changes in consistency and taste, monitoring caloric levels, altering amounts and types of specific nutrients, and managing the fiber content of foods.
- Diets such as the Diabetic Diet and the Heart-Healthy Diet can have significant impact on patient wellness.

Labeling Guidelines

- All food manufacturers must follow certain guidelines in labeling packages.
- Labels provide facts on the nutritional value of foods.

Eating Disorders

- Anorexia nervosa, characterized by self-induced starvation, typically affects adolescents. Those with anorexia are extremely sensitive to failure and criticism.
- They use not-eating as a way of controlling their feelings; they fear becoming grossly overweight if they allow themselves to eat.

Bulimia

- Bulimia is characterized by cycles of binging and purging.
- The person's self-worth is related to being thin.
- Some form of stress upsets the individual, who then turns to food for consolation.

Health Promotion

- Health promotion considers general wellness, adequate nutrition, environmental health and safety, health education needs, and disease prevention.
- Components include exercise, stress management, regular physical examinations, and health screening.

Treatment Compliance

- The medical assistant must understand the implications of nutrition and specific diets to be capable of answering patient questions and thereby promote compliance with treatment.

Health Problems Related to Poor Nutrition

- Anemia: Low iron or folate intake
- Cancer: High-fat, low-fiber diet
- Constipation: low-fiber, inadequate fluids; high-fat diet; sedentary lifestyle
- Diabetes: High-calorie, high-fat diet; obesity

Other Diet-Related Problems

- Hypercholesterolemia: High-fat, low-fiber diet
- Hypertension: High-calorie, high-fat diet; obesity
- Osteoporosis: Low-calcium intake; inadequate vitamin D or lack of sun exposure

CHAPTER 28: Vital Signs

Vital Signs

- The measurement of vital signs is an important aspect of every visit to the medical office.
- These signs, the human body's indicators of internal homeostasis, represent the patient's general state of health.

Variations

- Accuracy is essential. Variations may indicate the presence or disappearance of a disease process and, therefore, a change in treatment.

Cardinal Signs

- The vital signs are the patient's temperature, pulse, respiration, and blood pressure. These four signs are abbreviated TPR and BP, referred to as cardinal signs.

Other Measurements

- Anthropometric measurements include height, weight, and other body measurements, such as fat composition and head and chest circumference.

Vital Signs Measurements

- The vital signs are influenced by many factors, both physical and emotional.
- Most patients are apprehensive during an office visit, which may alter the vital signs.
- The medical assistant must help the patient relax before taking any readings.

Normal Ranges for Vital Signs

Temperature

- Body temperature is the balance between the heat lost and the heat produced by the body, measured in degrees.
- The increase in body temperature is thought to be the body's defensive reaction, to inhibit the growth of some bacteria and viruses.

Fever

- Continuous fever rises and falls only slightly during the 24-hour period. It remains above the patient's average normal range and is called continuous because that is exactly what the pattern shows.
- Intermittent fever comes and goes, or it spikes and then returns to average range.
- Remittent fever has great fluctuation but never returns to the average range. It is a constant fever with fluctuating levels and thus is remittent.

Temperatures Considered Febrile

- Rectal or aural (ear) temperatures over 100.4° F (38° C)
- Oral temperatures over 99.5° F (37.5° C)
- Axillary temperatures over 98.6° F (37° C)
- Fever of unknown origin (FUO) is a fever over 100.9° F (38.3° C) for 3 weeks in adults and 1 week in children without a known diagnosis.

Temperature Readings

- A clinical thermometer measures body temperature and is calibrated in either the Fahrenheit or the Celsius scale.
- The Fahrenheit (F) scale has been used most frequently in the United States to measure body temperature, but hospitals and many ambulatory care settings often use the Celsius scale.

Conversion Formulas

- Formulas for conversion from one system to the other
  - $C = (F - 32) \times 5/9$
  - $F = \dfrac{9 \times C}{5} + 32$

Rectal and Oral Readings

- Rectal temperatures, when taken accurately, are approximately 1° F or 0.6° C higher than oral readings.
- Axillary temperatures are approximately 1° F or 0.6° C lower than accurate oral readings.

Types of Thermometers

- Digital
- Tympanic
- Disposable
- Axillary
- Rectal

Pulse

- Pulse reflects the palpable beat of the arteries as they expand with the beat of the heart.
- An artery close to the body surface can be pushed against a bone to feel the pulse.

Pulse Sites

- The most common sites are at the following arteries: temporal, carotid, apical, brachial, radial, femoral, popliteal, and dorsalis pedis.

Characteristics of Pulse

- When you take a pulse, note four important characteristics: (1) rate, (2) rhythm, (3) volume of the pulse, and (4) condition of the arterial wall.
- Record the number of beats in 1 minute, and assess the rate, rhythm, volume, and elasticity.

Three-Point Scale for Measuring Pulse Volume

- 3 +, full, bounding
- 2 +, normal pulse
- 1 +, weak, thready

Respiration

- One complete inspiration and expiration is called a respiration.

Respiratory Rate

- Note three important characteristics:
  - Rate
  - Rhythm
  - Depth

Counting Respirations

- Patients self-consciously alter their breathing rates when they are being watched.
- Therefore, count the respirations while appearing to count the pulse.

- Keep your eyes alternately on the patient's chest and your watch while you are counting the pulse rate, and then, without removing your fingers from the pulse site, determine the respiration rate.

Respiration Rate

- Count the respirations for 30 seconds, and multiply the number by 2.
- Note and record any variation or irregularity in the rate.

Blood Pressure

- Blood pressure reflects the pressure of the blood against the walls of the arteries.
- Blood pressure is read in millimeters of mercury, abbreviated mm Hg.

Recording BP

- Blood pressure is recorded as a fraction, with the systolic reading the numerator (top), and the diastolic reading the denominator (bottom) (for example, 130/80).

Factors Affecting Blood Pressure

- Volume: Amount of blood in the arteries.
- Peripheral resistance of blood vessels: Relationship of the lumen or diameter of the vessel and the amount of blood flowing through it.
- Vessel elasticity: Vessel's capability to expand and contract to supply the body with a steady flow of blood.
- The condition of the heart muscle, or myocardium, is of primary importance to the volume of blood flowing through the body.

Hypertension

- 50 million Americans have hypertension that requires treatment.
- Prevalence increases with age; it occurs more frequently in African Americans.
- Risk factors include cigarette smoking, diabetes mellitus, hyperlipidemia, male gender, postmenopausal women, obesity, stress, and family history.
- Treatments include medications and lifestyle changes such as weight loss, limiting alcohol intake, stopping smoking, aerobic exercise, and a diet low in fat and sodium and high in fiber.
- Schedule regular follow-up visits every 3 to 6 months depending on the severity of the hypertension.

Hypotension

- Hypotension: Abnormally low blood pressure, caused by shock, both emotional and traumatic;

hemorrhage; central nervous system disorders; and chronic wasting diseases.

- Persistent readings of 90/60 mm Hg or below are usually considered hypotensive.

Measuring BP

- The sphygmomanometer must be used with a stethoscope.
- Use the inflatable cuff to obliterate (cause to disappear) circulation through an artery.
- Place the stethoscope over the artery just below the cuff, and then slowly deflate the cuff to allow the blood to flow again.
- As blood flow resumes, cardiac cycle sounds are heard through the stethoscope, and gauge readings are taken when the first (systolic) and the last (diastolic) sounds are heard.

Anthropometric Measurement

- Height
- Weight
- BMI

Conversion Formulas

- To convert kilograms to pounds:
  - 1 kilogram = 2.5 pounds.
  - Multiply the number of kilograms by 2.5.
  - Example: If a patient weighs 68 kilograms, multiply 68 by 2.2 = 149.6 pounds.

Conversion Equations

- To convert pounds to kilograms:
  - 1 pound = 0.45 kilogram.
  - Multiply the number of pounds by 0.45 or divide the number of pounds by 2.2 kg.
  - Example: If a patient weighs 120 pounds, multiply 120 by 0.45 = 54 kilograms or divide 120 by 2.2 = 54.5 kilograms.

Patient Education

- Patient education regarding vital signs includes confirming the ability of the patient to monitor vital signs at home as needed.
- Be sure to provide assistance in working home-based equipment.
- Confirm patient understanding of the need to comply with physician recommendations.

Duties of the MA

- Legal and ethical implications for the medical assistant include following physician guidelines with patient disclosure, accurate monitoring and recording of vital signs, and consistently being alert to inaccurate readings or potential carelessness.

Obtaining Vital Signs

- Correctly measure and describe all facets of each vital sign.
- Accurately and clearly document this information.
- Take advantage of all opportunities to answer questions and help the patient understand the significance of healthy vital signs.
- Maintain patient privacy throughout all procedures.
- Include family or caregivers in patient care as indicated.
- Use community resources to promote holistic patient care.
- Be sensitive to cultural and ethnic factors that may affect patient compliance.

CHAPTER 29: Assisting with the Primary Physical Examination

Organs

- An organ is composed of two or more types of tissue bound together into a more complex structure with a common purpose or function.
- It may have one or many functions and may be considered a unit in one or several systems.

Systems

- A body system is composed of several organs and their associated structures, which work together to perform a specific function.
- Of 11 systems in the human body, each system has specific units, and each performs specific functions.

Vocabulary

- Bruit: Abnormal sound or murmur heard on auscultation of an organ, vessel, or gland.
- Emphysema: Pathologic accumulation of air in the tissues or organs; in the lungs, the bronchioles become plugged with mucus and lose elasticity.
- Manipulation: Moving or exercising a body part by an externally applied force.
- Murmur: Abnormal sound heard when auscultating the heart that may or may not be pathologic.
- Nodule: Small lump, lesion, or swelling felt when palpating the skin.
- Sclera: White part of the eye that forms the orb.
- Transillumination: Inspection of a cavity or organ by passing light through its walls.

- Trauma: Physical injury or wound caused by an external force or violence.
- Uremia: Toxic renal condition characterized by an excess of urea, creatinine, and other nitrogenous end products in the blood.

Instruments

- Instruments typically are used during the physical examination to see, feel, and listen to parts of the body.
- All equipment must be in good working order, properly disinfected, and readily available.

Nasal Speculum

- Nasal speculum: Stainless-steel instrument used to inspect the lining of the nose, nasal membranes, and internal septum.
- Spreads apart to dilate the nostrils.

Ophthalmoscope

- Ophthalmoscope: Instrument used to inspect the inner structures of the eye.
- The stainless-steel handle contains batteries, onto which a head is attached, equipped with a light and magnifying lenses and an opening through which the eye is viewed.

Otoscope

- Otoscope: Instrument used to examine the external auditory canal and tympanic membrane.
- The stainless steel handle containing batteries, onto which a head is fastened.
- The head contains a light focused through a magnifying lens and disposable ear speculum.
- Examination rooms are usually equipped with wall-mounted electrical units for the ophthalmoscope, otoscope, disposable speculums, and sphygmomanometer.

Instruments

- Tongue depressor: Flat, wooden blade used to hold down the tongue when examining the throat.
- Reflex hammer: Sometimes referred to as a percussion hammer, this has a hard rubber head used to test neurological reflexes of the knee and elbow by striking the tendons.

Tuning Fork

- The tuning fork is used to check a patient's auditory acuity and to test bone vibration.
- Consists of a handle and two prongs that produce a humming sound when the physician strikes the prongs.

Stethoscope

- Stethoscope: Listening device used to auscultate certain areas of the body, particularly the heart and lungs.
- Two earpieces are connected to flexible rubber or vinyl tubing. At the distal end of the tubing is a diaphragm or bell (many have both) that enables the physician to hear internal body sounds.

Gloves

- Gloves: Disposable latex gloves protect the physician and the patient from microorganisms.
- Under Standard Precautions, gloves are to be worn whenever there is a possibility of contact with all body fluids, broken skin or wounds, or contaminated items.

Tape Measure

- Tape measure: Flexible ribbon ruler usually printed in inches and feet on one side and in centimeters and meters on the opposite side.
- Used to assess infant length and head circumference, patient wound size, etc.

Methods of Examination

- Inspection uses observation to detect significant physical features or objective data. Focus on the patient's general appearance (the general state of health, including posture, mannerisms, grooming) to more detailed observations, including body contour, gait, symmetry, visible injuries and deformities, tremors, rashes, and color changes.

Palpation

- Palpation uses the sense of touch to determine the body's condition or that of an underlying organ. Palpation may include touching the skin or the more firm feeling of the abdomen for underlying masses, and involves a wide range of perceptions: temperature, vibrations, consistency, form, size, rigidity, elasticity, moisture, texture, position, and contour.

Percussion

- Percussion involves tapping or striking the body, usually with the fingers or a small hammer, to elicit sounds or vibratory sensations, to determine the position, size, and density of an underlying organ or cavity. The effect of percussion is both heard and felt by the examiner and helps to determine the amount of air or solid matter in an underlying organ or cavity.

Auscultation

- Auscultation uses a stethoscope to listen to sounds arising from the body, distinguishing between a normal and an abnormal sound.
- Particularly useful in evaluating sounds originating in the lungs, heart, and abdomen such as murmurs, bruits, and bowel sounds.

Measurements

- Mensuration is the process of measuring.
- Measurements are recorded of the patient's height and weight, the length and diameter of an extremity, the extent of flexion or extension of an extremity, the uterus during pregnancy, the size and depth of a wound, or the pressure of a grip.

Manipulation

- Manipulation is the forceful, passive movement of a joint to determine its range of extension or flexion.

Supine

- Supine (horizontal recumbent) is used to describe the patient who is lying flat with face upward.

Dorsal Recumbent

- Dorsal recumbent position places the patient lying face upward, with the weight distributed primarily to the surface of the back, by flexing the knees so that the feet are flat on the table.
- This position relieves muscle tension in the abdomen.

Lithotomy

- Lithotomy: The patient is placed on the back, with the knees sharply flexed, the arms placed at the sides or folded over the chest, and the buttocks to the edge of the table, with the feet supported in table stirrups.

Fowler's

- Fowler's: The patient sits on the examination table with the head elevated 90 degrees or simply sits at the edge of the table.
- This position is useful for examinations and treatments of the head, neck, and chest or for patients who find it difficult to breathe lying down.

Semi-Fowler's

- Semi-Fowler's position is a modification of Fowler's position. Instead of the head at a full 90-degree angle, the head is lowered to a 45-degree angle.

Prone

- Prone: the patient is lying face down on the table, on the ventral surface of the body.

- This is the opposite of the supine position and another of the recumbent positions.

Sims'

- Sims' position is sometimes called the lateral position. The patient is placed on the left side, the left arm and shoulder are drawn back behind the body, so that the body's weight is predominantly on the chest. The right arm is flexed upward for support. The left leg is slightly flexed, and the buttocks are pulled to the edge of the table.

Knee-Chest

- Knee-Chest: The patient rests on the knees and the chest with the head turned to one side. The arms can be placed under the head for support and comfort or bent and at the sides of the table near the head. The thighs are perpendicular to the table and are slightly separated. The buttocks extend up into the air, and the back should be straight.

Trendelenburg

- Trendelenburg: The patient is supine on a table that has been raised at the lower end about 45 degrees.
- This position places the patient's head lower than the legs.

CHAPTER 30: Principles of Pharmacology

Drug Classifications

- Drugs are generally classified according to their actions on the body or according to the body system they affect.
- May have multiple actions and therefore multiple classifications.

Adrenergic

- Action: Constricts blood vessels, narrows the lumen of a vessel
- Examples: Epinephrine, phenylephrine (Neo-Synephrine)
- Primary use: Stop superficial bleeding, increase and sustain blood pressure, and relieve nasal congestion

Analgesic

- Action: Lessens the sensory function of the brain
- Examples: Nonnarcotic, aspirin; acetaminophen (Tylenol); ibuprofen (Advil, Motrin); narcotic,

meperidine (Demerol); hydrocodone (Vicodin); propoxyphene (Darvon)
- Primary use: Pain relief

Anesthetic
- Action: Produces insensibility to pain or the sensation of pain
- Examples: Bupivacaine (Marcaine); lidocaine (Xylocaine)
- Primary use: Local or general anesthesia

Antianxiety
- Action: Produces insensibility to pain or the sensation of pain
- Examples: Bupivacaine (Marcaine); lidocaine (Xylocaine)
- Primary use: Local or general anesthesia

Antibiotic
- Action: Kills or inhibits the growth of microorganisms
- Examples: Cefaclor (Ceclor); tetracycline (Acromycin); amoxicillin (Augmentin)
- Primary use: Treatment of bacterial invasions and infections

Anticholinergic
- Action: Parasympathetic blocking agent, reduces spasm in smooth muscle
- Examples: Scopolamine; atropine sulfate
- Primary use: Dry secretions

Anticoagulant
- Action: Delays or blocks the clotting of blood
- Examples: Heparin; warfarin sodium (Coumadin)
- Primary use: Treatment of blood clots

Antidepressant
- Action: Treats depression
- Examples: Fluoxetine (Prozac); imipramine pamoate (Tofranil); amitriptyline (Elavil)
- Primary use: Mood elevator

Antiemetic
- Action: Acts on hypothalamus center in the brain
- Examples: Prochlorperazine (Compazine); trimethobenzamide (Tigan); metoclopramide (Reglan)
- Primary use: Prevent and relieve nausea and vomiting

Antiepileptic (Anticonvulsant)
- Action: Reduces excessive stimulation of the brain
- Examples: Phenytoin (Dilantin); phenobarbital; carbamazepine (Tegretol)
- Primary use: Epilepsy and other convulsive disorders

Antifungal
- Action: Slows or retards the multiplication of fungi
- Examples: Miconazole (Monistat); nystatin (Mycostatin); amphotericin B
- Primary use: Treat systemic or local fungal infections

Antihistamine
- Action: Counteracts the effects of histamine; may inhibit gastric secretions
- Examples: Brompheniramine maleate (Dimetane); chlorpheniramine (Chlor-Trimeton); diphenhydramine (Benadryl); promethazine (Phenergan); cimetidine (Tagamet); ranitidine (Zantac)
- Primary use: Relief of allergies; prevention of gastric ulcers

Antihypertensive
- Action: Blocks nerve impulses that constrict arteries; or slows heart rate decreasing contractility; or restricts the hormone aldosterone in the blood
- Examples: Atenolol (Tenormin); doxazosin mesylate (Cardura); metoprolol (Lopressor); methyldopa (Aldomet)
- Primary use: Reduce and control blood pressure

Antiinflammatory
- Action: Antiinflammatory or antirheumatic
- Examples: Nonsteroidal (NSAIDs): ibuprofen (Advil, Motrin); naproxen (Naprosyn). Steroidal: dexamethasone (Decadron); prednisone (Cortisone)
- Primary use: Treatment of arthritic and other inflammatory disorders

Antineoplastic
- Action: Inhibits the development of and destroys cancerous cells
- Examples: Interferon alfa-2a (Roferon-A); hydroxyurea (Hydrea); cyclophosphamide (Cytoxan); fluorouracil (Adrucil)
- Primary use: Cancer chemotherapy

Antispasmodic
- Action: Relieves or prevents spasms from musculoskeletal injury or inflammation
- Examples: Methocarbamol (Robaxin); carisoprodol (Soma)
- Primary use: Sport injuries

Antitussive (Cough Suppressant)
- Action: Inhibits the cough center
- Examples: Narcotic: codeine sulfate; nonnarcotic: dextromethorphan (Romilar, Robitussin DM)

- Primary use: Temporarily suppresses a nonproductive cough; reduces the thickness of secretions

Bronchodilator

- Action: Relaxes the smooth muscle of the bronchi
- Examples: Aminophylline (Aminophyllin); theophylline (Theo-Dur); epinephrine (Adrenalin, Sus-Phrine); albuterol (Ventolin, Proventil); isoproterenol (Isuprel)
- Primary use: Treat asthma, bronchospasm; promotes bronchodilation

Cathartic (Laxative)

- Action: Increases peristaltic activity of the large intestine
- Examples: Magnesium hydroxide (milk of magnesia); bisacodyl (Dulcolax); casanthranol (Peri-Colace); psyllium hydrophilic muciloid (Metamucil)
- Primary use: Increases and hasten bowel evacuation (defecation)

Contraceptive

- Action: Inhibits conception
- Examples: Medroxyprogesterone acetate (Depo-Provera); norgestrel (Ovrett); ethinyl estradiol and ethynodiol diacetate (Demulen 1/35)
- Primary use: Family planning

Decongestant

- Action: Relieves local congestion in the tissues
- Examples: Ephedrine or phenylephrine (Neo-Synephrine); pseudoephedrine (Sudafed); oxymetazoline (Afrin)
- Primary use: Relief of nasal and sinus congestion due to common cold, hay fever, or upper respiratory tract disorders

Diuretic

- Action: Inhibits the reabsorption of sodium and chloride in the kidneys
- Examples: Hydrochlorothiazide (Dyazide, Esidrix, HydroDiuril); furosemide (Lasix); triamterene (Dyrenium)
- Primary use: Increases urinary output, decreases blood pressure

Expectorant

- Action: Increases secretions and mucus from the bronchial tubes
- Examples: Diphenhydramine (Benylin); guaifenesin guaiacolate (Fenesin, Robitussin)
- Primary use: Upper respiratory tract congestion

Hemostatic

- Action: Controls bleeding, a blood coagulant

- Examples: Phytonadione, vitamin K (Konakion); absorbable hemostatics, such as Gelfoam and Surgicel, are applied directly to a wound.
- Primary use: Control of acute or chronic blood-clotting disorder; formation of absorbable, artificial clot

Hypnotic (Sedative)

- Action: Induces sleep and lessens the activity of the brain
- Examples: Secobarbital (Seconal); flurazepam (Dalmane); tamazepam (Restoril)
- Primary use: Insomnia; lower doses sedate

Hormone Replacement

- Action: Replaces or compensates hormone deficiency
- Examples: Insulin (Humulin); levothyroxine sodium (Synthroid); estrogen (Premarin)
- Primary use: Maintenance of adequate hormone levels

Miotic

- Action: Causes the pupil of the eye to contract
- Examples: Carbachol (Isopto Carbachol); isoflurophate (Floropryl); pilocarpine (Isopto Carpine)
- Primary use: Counteract pupil dilation

Mydriatic (Anticholinergic)

- Action: Dilates the pupil of the eye
- Examples: Atropine sulfate (Isopto Atropine)
- Primary use: Ophthalmologic examinations

Narcotic

- Action: Depress the central nervous system and cause insensibility or stupor
- Examples: Natural narcotics: opium group (codeine phosphate, morphine sulfate): synthetic narcotics: meperidine (Demerol), methadone (Dolophine), and propoxyphene HCl (Darvon)
- Primary use: Pain relief

Sympathetic Blocking Agent

- Action: Blocks certain functions of the adrenergic nervous system
- Examples: Propranolol (Inderal); metaprolol (Lopressor); phentolamine (Regitine); prazosin (Minipress)
- Primary use: Treating cardiovascular conditions

Six Parts of a Prescription

- Superscription: Patient's name and address, the date, and the symbol Rx (for the Latin *recipe,* meaning "take").
- Inscription: Main part of the prescription; name of the drug, dosage form, and strength.

- Subscription: Directions for the pharmacist; size of each dose, amount to be dispensed, and the form of the drug such as tablets or capsules.
- Signature: Directions for the patient; usually preceded by the symbol Sig: (for the Latin *signa,* meaning "mark"). The physician indicates the instructions to tell the patient how, when, and in what quantities to use the medication.
- Refill information: May be regulated by federal law if drug is a controlled substance; must write number of times refill allowed.
- Physician signature: Must include manual signature of physician and DEA number when indicated.
- Absorption: How a drug is absorbed into the body's circulating fluids, which depend on the route by which it is administered
- Distribution: How a drug is transported from the site of administration
- Metabolism: How the drug is inactivated, including the time it takes for a drug to be detoxified and broken down into byproducts
- Excretion: The route by which a drug is excreted, or eliminated, from the body and the amount of time such a process requires

Drug Regulation
- Several federal agencies regulate drugs in the United States.
- FDA: regulates the development and sale of all prescription drugs and OTCs
- DEA: enforces laws designed to control drug abuse and also educates the public on drug-abuse prevention
- FTC regulates OTC advertisement.

DEA
- DEA regulations for the management of controlled substances include specific recordkeeping guidelines; physician registration; and the inventory, storage, and disposal of controlled substances.

Controlled Substances
- Prescriptions written for controlled substances must comply with both state and federal regulations.
- The prescription must include details on the patient; information on the physician including the DEA number; the amount of drug written out; and manually signed by the physician.

Scheduled Drugs
- Orders for Schedule II drugs cannot be phoned in except in an absolute emergency and cannot

be refilled; Schedule III, IV, and V drugs may be prescribed by phone and refilled up to 5 times in a 6-month period.
- In some states Schedule V drugs can be dispensed by the pharmacist without a physician prescription.

Drug Names
- A single drug may have as many as three names: chemical, generic, and trade.
- The chemical name is the drug's formula; the generic or official name is assigned to the drug and may reflect the chemical name.
- The trade or brand name is the name given the compound by the developing pharmaceutical company and is protected by copyright for 17 years.

Drug References
- Using drug reference materials is crucial to the safe administration of medications. Most drug reference books supply the action, indication, contraindications, precautions, adverse reactions, dosage, administration guidelines, and method of packaging.
- The most frequently consulted drug reference guide is the PDR, but package inserts also can be used.

Clinical Drug Uses
- The clinical uses of drugs include therapeutic or curative; palliative; prophylactic; diagnostic; and replacement drugs that provide substances that normally occur in the body.

Over-the-counter Drugs
- OTC drugs may interfere or interact with prescription drugs.
- Safety measures include reading directions, taking only the recommended dose, discarding when expired, informing the physician of OTC use, and being aware of OTC contraindications.

Pharmacokinetics
- Pharmacokinetics includes absorption, dependent on the routes of administration (oral, parenteral, mucous membrane, or topical); distribution through the bloodstream; metabolism in the liver; and excretion primarily through the kidneys.

Drug Action
- Multiple factors affect drug action including weight, age, gender, diurnal rhythms, pathological factors, immune responses, psychological factors, tolerance, accumulation, idiosyncrasy, and drug-to-drug interactions.

Medication Management
- The legal responsibilities include compliance with DEA regulations regarding controlled substances as well as maintaining complete and accurate documentation on all medications administered and prescribed for each patient.

CHAPTER 31: Pharmacology Math

Drug Management
- The medical assistant must be absolutely certain that the medication prepared and administered to the patient is exactly what the physician ordered.
- Although many times drugs are delivered by the pharmacy in unit dose packs, the dosage ordered may differ from the dose on hand.

Calculations
- In this case, the medical assistant must be prepared to calculate the correct dose accurately.

Dosages
- There is no margin of error in drug calculations: even a minor mistake may result in serious complications.
- The medical assistant must take meticulous care in calculating all drug dosages.

Steps of Calculations
- If the dosage ordered by the physician is different from the dosage on hand, the medical assistant must complete three basic steps.

Step 1
- Based on the type of system printed on the label, determine if the physician order is in the same mathematical system of measurement.
- If the systems vary (the order is in teaspoons but the label states the medication is prepared in ml), then accurately convert the order to match the system on the label.

Step 2
- Perform the calculation in equation form, using the appropriate formula.

Step 3
- Check your answer for accuracy, and ask someone you trust to confirm your calculations.

Complete All Three Steps
- All three of these steps must be completed before the medication is dispensed and administered.

Confirmation
- Confirm your calculations with the physician if you have any doubt of their accuracy.

Dose Calculation
- Read the label of the drug on hand accurately to determine if the physician order and the packaged drug use the same system of measurement.

Label Terms
- It is important to understand some of the basic terms used on drug labels.

Understanding Labels
- Drug label terms must be understood to implement pharmacology math formulas.

Strength
- Strength: Stated as a percentage of drug in the solution (2% epinephrine), as a solid weight (grams, milligrams, pounds, grains), or as a millequivalent or unit.

Dosage
- Dosage: The size or amount of the drug in the package. This could be in milliliters, teaspoons, or the number of tablets. For example, the label may read "Imitrex, 6 mg/0.5 ml," or 6 mg of the drug in each 0.5 ml.

Solute
- Solute: The pure drug that is dissolved in a liquid to form a solution.

Solvent
- Solvent or Diluent: The liquid, usually sterile water, that dissolves the solute.

Systems of Measurement
- Three different systems of measurement are the metric system, the apothecary system, and the household system.

Metric System
- The metric system of weights and measures is now used throughout the world as the primary system for weight (mass), capacity (volume), and length (area).
- Units in the metric system are converted by moving the decimal point in multiples of 10.

Conversions to Smaller Units
- To go from larger to smaller units of measurement, as in converting grams to milligrams, the answer will be a larger number, so move the decimal point to the right.
- Therefore, 0.35 g = 350 mg.

Conversions to Larger Units

- If converting smaller units of measurement to larger ones, the answer will be a smaller number, so move the decimal point to the left.
- For example, 150 ml = 0.15 L.

Equivalents

- The following equivalents can be used to make conversions in the metric system.

1 kg = 1000 g	1 kl = 1000 liters
1 g = 1000 mg	1 L = 1000 ml

Apothecary System

- With the apothecary system, the basic unit of weight for a solid medication is the grain (gr), and the basic unit of volume for a liquid medication is the minim.
- As in the metric system, these two units are related: the grain is based on the weight of a single grain of wheat, and the minim is the volume of water that weighs 1 grain.

Household Measurements

- The household system is used in most American households. Although this system of measurement is important for the patient at home who has no knowledge of the metric or apothecary systems, it is not completely accurate. The household system should never be used in the medical setting.

Fried's Law

- This calculation is for children younger than 1 year and is based on the age of the child in months compared with a child $12\frac{1}{2}$ years old.

$$\text{Pediatric dose} = \frac{\text{Child's age in months}}{150 \text{ months}} \times \text{Adult dose}$$

Young's Rule

- Young's rule is for children older than 1 year.

$$\text{Pediatric dose} = \frac{\text{Child's age in years}}{\text{Child's age in years} + 12} \times \text{Adult dose}$$

Clark's Rule

- This rule is based on the weight of the child.
- This system is much more accurate, because children of any age can vary greatly in size and body weight.

$$\text{Pediatric dose} = \frac{\text{Child's weight in pounds}}{150 \text{ pounds}} \times \text{Adult dose}$$

West's Nomogram

- West's nomogram calculates the body surface area of infants and young children.

Reconstitution

- Reconstituting powdered injectables requires adding an amount of solvent (as recommended on the drug label) to a vial of powdered or crystal medication.
- Once the solute and solvent are mixed in the vial, a solution of medication is formed with a strength based on equivalents printed on the drug label.

Read the Label

- Once the medication is mixed, carefully read the label to determine how much of the drug must be withdrawn to equal the physician's order.

Conversion Formula

- Use the standard conversion formula to determine the accurate dose for administration.

Responsibility

- The medical assistant who prepares, dispenses, and administers medications is ethically and legally responsible for his or her own actions.

State Laws

- Be aware of state laws that monitor medication administration by allied health workers.

CHAPTER 32: Administering Medications

Safety Precautions

- Safety precautions in the management of medication administration should be consistently applied.

Safe Administration

- Understand the physician order, look up the drug if it is unknown, and use the three label checks and the seven rights every time a drug order is completed.

Assessment Factors

- Patient assessment factors include evaluation of the patient's physical condition, holistic factors such as the patient's history, an accurate list of drug allergies, the patient's ability to understand the drug regimen and to afford the treatment, and special patient factors based on age, weight, and condition.

Precautions

- Use precautions with pregnant and lactating women; drugs can pass through the placenta into the developing fetus as well as into the breast milk.

Children's Medications
- Pediatric administration is usually based on the weight of the child. Special precautions must be used because of alterations in the absorption, distribution, metabolism, and excretion of drugs in the child's body.

Successful Approach
- Children also require a special approach for successful drug administration.

The Elderly
- Geriatric patients are more sensitive to the effects of medications because of altered metabolic rates, loss of subcutaneous fat, and accompanying chronic diseases.

Drug Interactions
- Aging patients are more likely to take more than one medication, so drug interactions are a potential problem.

Aging Patients
- A holistic approach to medication management in aging patients includes nutritional assessment, investigation of the costs, and adapted patient-education methods.

Packaging
- Oral medications include both solid and liquid preparations; mucous membrane medications are absorbed either rectally, vaginally, orally, nasally, or through the skin topically.
- Each form has specific guidelines for administration, but all require the consistent use of the three label checks and the seven rights.

Solid Oral Dosage Forms
- The basic forms are tablets, capsules, and lozenges (troches).
- Tablets are compressed powders or granules that, when wet, break apart in the stomach, or in the mouth if they are not swallowed quickly.

Tablets
- Tablets may be sugar coated to taste better, or enteric-coated, such as Ecotrin, to protect the stomach mucosa.
- Buffered tablets prevent stomach irritation by combining the drug with a buffering agent that decreases the amount of acidity in the compound. Buffered or enteric-coated tablets should never be crushed or dissolved.

Scored Tablets
- Only those tablets that are scored can be cut in half. This is accomplished with a pill cutter.

Caplets and Capsules
- Some tablets are coated with a volatile liquid that dissolves in the mouth, such as an antacid tablet. Caplets are oblong, like capsules.
- Capsules are gelatin coated and dissolve in the stomach, or they may be coated to protect them from the acid action of the stomach.

Sustained Release
- Timed- or sustained-release (SR) capsules or spansules dissolve at different rates, over a period of time. These drugs should never be crushed or dissolved.

Liquid Oral Dosage Forms
- Liquid forms differ mainly in the type of substance used to dissolve the drug: water, oils, or alcohol.
- Solutions are drug substances contained in a homogeneous mixture with a liquid.

Syrups
- Syrups: Solutions of sugar and water, usually containing flavoring and medicinal substances. Cough syrups are the most common.

Aqueous Solutions
- Aromatic waters: Aqueous solutions contain volatile oils such as oil of spearmint, peppermint, or clove.

Liquors
- Liquors contain a nonvolatile material, such as alcohol, as the solute.

Suspensions
- Suspensions are insoluble drug substances contained in a liquid.

Emulsions
- Emulsions: Mixtures of oil and water that improve the taste of otherwise distasteful products such as cod liver oil.

Mineral Suspensions
- Gels and magmas: Minerals suspended in water. Minerals settle, so products containing minerals must be shaken before use (Milk of magnesia).

Parenteral Administration
- Parenteral medications are manufactured in either ampules or single- or multi-dose vials. The drug characteristics and individual patient factors determine the correct gauge and length of needle needed.

Syringes
- The appropriate syringe is determined by the type of medication and the amount of drug. Specialty syringe units, such as the Nova Pen and the EpiPen, are designed for quick

administration of certain medications in public or in an emergency.

Guidelines

- OSHA guidelines include using syringe units with retractable needle covers and wearing disposable nonsterile gloves and protective gear when coming into contact with blood or body fluids.
- Never recap a contaminated needle, and immediately discard it into a sharps container.
- Dispose of contaminated non-sharp materials in biohazard containers.
- Disinfect contaminated work areas.
- Wash hands before and after procedures.

Routes of Administration

- Parenteral routes of administration include intradermal (ID), subcutaneous (SC), and a variety of intramuscular (IM) sites. The type of medication, the physician's order, and the unique characteristics of patients determine the route and site of administration.

Patient Education

- Patient education is absolutely crucial to the correct administration of medication at home. The patient should understand the purpose of the drug; the time, frequency, and amount of the dose; any special storage requirements; and the typical side effects.

Drug Treatment

- The more the patient knows and understands about how to take the medication and why it is prescribed, the greater the chances that the drug treatment will be successful.

MA Knowledge

- The medical assistant must be extremely knowledgeable when preparing and administering medications in the physician's office.

Clarify Questions

- If there are any questions about the order, ask for clarification before proceeding.

Legal Responsibilities

- Legal responsibilities include the prevention of error by carefully following safe practice procedures in pouring and administering drugs.

State Laws

- The medical assistant must comply with individual state laws governing medications and their administration.

Charting

- Precise charting of medication administration and the management of prescriptions cannot be overemphasized.

CHAPTER 33: Assisting With Medical Emergencies

Emergency Management

- Be familiar with the policies and procedures on the management of emergencies and maintain certification in cardiopulmonary resuscitation (CPR).
- Perform only the procedures in which you are trained.
- Always notify the physician or activate EMS if the physician is unavailable.
- Make sure the facility is accident-proof to prevent patient injuries.
- Participate in planning for emergency situations
- Post emergency telephone numbers.

Supplies

- Have a central location, either a crash cart or emergency bag, for all emergency supplies, equipment, and medication.
- Emergency supplies must be consistently inventoried and maintained.

Calm Approach

- Managing emergencies requires a calm, efficient approach to the situation.

Assessment

- Assess the nature of the emergency and determine whether EMS should be activated or if the patient requires an immediate or urgent appointment.

Record Information

- Gather as many details as possible; refer to the physician when in doubt.

Telephone Triage

- Telephone triage is one of the most important responsibilities of the medical assistant. Use emergency action principles to determine the level of patient emergency.

Triage

- Determine whether the situation is life-threatening.
- Obtain contact information about the patient and all pertinent information regarding the injury and patient signs and symptoms.

Documentation

- Share this information with the doctor, and document all details on the patient chart.

Syncope

- Was the patient injured?
- Does the patient have a history of heart disease, seizures, or diabetes?

Home Care Advice

- Syncope does not necessarily indicate a serious disease. If injured from a fall, the patient may need to be treated.
- Patient should get up very slowly, take it easy, and drink plenty of fluids.
- If patient is to be seen, someone should accompany him or her to the clinician's practice.

Animal Bites

- What kind of animal (pet or wild)?
- How severe is the injury?
- Where are the bites?
- When did the bite occur?

Home Care Advice for Bites

- Notify the health department or police.
- Locate the animal, and monitor its health.
- If the skin is not broken, wash it well and watch for signs of infection.

Insect Bites and Stings

- Does the patient have a history of anaphylactic reaction to insect stings?
- Does the patient have difficulty breathing, have a widespread rash, or have trouble swallowing?

Home Care Advice for Stings

- If there is a history of anaphylaxis and the patient has an EpiPen system, use it immediately, then notify EMS.
- Activate EMS if having systemic symptoms.
- An antihistamine (Benadryl) relieves local pruritis.

Asthma

- Does the patient show signs of cyanosis?
- Has the patient used the prescribed inhalers?

Home Care Advice for Asthma

- If the patient is unable to speak in sentences, has poor color, and struggles to breathe even after inhaler use, the patient should be seen immediately or EMS activated.

Burns

- Where are the burns, and what caused them?
- Are there signs of shock (i.e., moist clammy skin, altered consciousness, rapid breathing and pulse)?
- Are there signs of infection (foul odor, cloudy drainage) in a burn after more than 2 days?

Home Care Advice for Burns

- Activate EMS for burns on the face, hands, feet, and perineum or those caused by electricity, a chemical, or associated with inhalation.
- Activate EMS if there are signs of shock.
- Patient must receive a tetanus shot if more than 10 years has passed since she or he last had one.
- Schedule an urgent appointment if signs of infection are reported.

Wounds

- Is the bleeding steady or pulsating?
- How and when did the injury occur?
- Does the patient have any bleeding disorders or take anticoagulant drugs?
- Is the wound open and deep?

Home Care Advice for Wounds

- Pulsating bleeding usually indicates arterial damage; activate EMS.
- If from a powerful force other injuries may exist.
- If the patient takes anticoagulants or has diabetes or anemia, schedule an urgent appointment.
- Gaping, deep wound requires sutures.

Head Injury

- Did the patient faint or have a seizure?
- Is the patient confused, vomiting, or is there clear drainage from nose or ears?

Home Care Advice for Head Injury

- If the answer is "yes" to any of these symptoms, activate EMS.

Standard Precautions

- Always follow Standard Precautions when caring for a patient with a medical emergency.

Documentation

- Documentation of emergency treatment should include information on the patient; vital signs; allergies, current medications and pertinent health history; chief complaint; sequence of events including any changes in the patient's condition since the incident; and physician orders and procedures performed.

Life-Threatening Emergencies

- Life-threatening emergencies require immediate assessment, referral to the physician, and if the physician is not present, activation of EMS. While waiting for assistance, determine the presence of breathing and circulation.

Immediate Treatment
- Administer rescue breaths or CPR if indicated.
- Depending on the patient's signs and symptoms, monitor the patient for signs of a heart attack; administer the Heimlich maneuver if there is an obstructed airway; evaluate for signs of a CVA; and assess for shock.

Assessment
- Common ambulatory care emergencies require an assessment either by phone or onsite of the patient's current condition and need for physician evaluation.
- Calmly gather pertinent information from the patient and follow through with the facility's policy and physician orders on emergency management.

Patient Education
- Patients should know how to contact emergency personnel; families with young children should have poison control numbers posted.
- Educating patients on care for minor emergencies at home is an important part of telephone triage.
- Encouraging patients to participate in community safety workshops and becoming CPR certified may avoid emergencies and save lives.

Good Samaritan Laws
- They may vary from state to state but are designed to protect individuals from liability if they provide assistance at the site of an emergency.
- The law does not require a medically trained person to act, but if emergency care is given in a reasonable and responsible manner, the healthcare worker is protected from being sued for negligence.
- This protection does not extend into the workplace.

Chapter 34: Assisting in Ophthalmology and Otolaryngology

Specialties
- The ophthalmologist is a medical physician specializing in the diagnosis and treatment of the eye.
- The optometrist examines and treats visual defects.
- An optician fills prescriptions for corrective lenses.

The Eye
- The anatomy of the eye begins with the outer covering, the conjunctiva, and the three layers of tissue: sclera, choroid, and retina.
- The inner layer is where light rays are converted into nervous energy for interpretation by the brain.

Vision
- Vision begins with the passage of light through the cornea where it is refracted and then passes through the aqueous humor and pupil into the lens.

Conversion of Light
- The ciliary muscle adjusts the curvature of the lens to refract the light rays so they pass into the retina, triggering the photoreceptor cells of the rods and cones.
- Light energy is then converted into an electrical impulse, which is sent through the optic nerve to the brain where interpretation occurs.

Refractive Errors
- Refractive errors include hyperopia, myopia, presbyopia, and astigmatism.
- All are due to a problem with bending light so it can be accurately focused on the retina.
- They are usually caused by defects in the shape of the eyeball and can be corrected with glasses, contact lenses, or surgery.

Disorders
- Eye disorders can range from problems with eye movement, as in strabismus and nystagmus, to infections of the eye, including hordeolums, chalazions, keratitis, conjunctivitis, and blepharitis.
- Disorders of the eyeball include corneal abrasions, cataracts, glaucoma, and macular degeneration.

Diagnosis
- Diagnostic procedures for the eye begin with examination of the eye with an ophthalmoscope. Next the eyelids are examined for abnormalities, and the pupils are assessed for PERRLA.

Advanced Techniques
- More advanced techniques include the use of a slit-lamp to view the fine details of the eye and the exophthalmometer to measure the pressure in the central renal artery.

Assessment
- Distance visual acuity is typically assessed using a Snellen chart.

- Near visual acuity is tested with a near-vision acuity chart.
- The Ishihara test assesses color vision defects.

Irrigations
- Eye irrigations relieve inflammation, remove drainage, dilute chemicals, or wash away foreign bodies.
- Sterile technique and equipment must be used to avoid contamination.

Medication
- Medication may be instilled into the eye for treatment of an infection, to soothe an eye irritation, to anesthetize the eye, or to dilate the pupils before examination or treatment.

The External Ear
- The external ear consists of the auricle or pinna and the external auditory canal, which transmits sound waves to the tympanic membrane.

The Middle Ear
- The middle ear is an air-filled cavity that contains the ossicles. The sound vibration passes through the tympanic membrane, causing the ossicles to vibrate. This bone-conducted vibration passes through the oval window into the inner ear.

The Inner Ear
- The organ of Corti in the cochlea of the inner ear converts the sound waves into nervous energy that is sent to the brain for interpretation. The semicircular canals in the inner ear maintain equilibrium.

Conductive Hearing Loss
- A conductive hearing loss originates in the external or middle ear and prevents the sound vibrations from passing through the external auditory canal, limits the vibrations of the tympanic membrane, or interferes with the passage of bone-conducted sound in the middle ear.

Sensorineural Loss
- A sensorineural hearing loss results from damage to the organ of Corti or the auditory nerve and prevents the sound vibration from becoming nervous stimuli that can be interpreted by the brain as sound.

Otitis Externa
- Two common types of otitis are seen in patients in an otologic practice.
- The first affects the external ear canal and is called otitis externa, or swimmer's ear.

Otitis Media
- Otitis media is an inflammation of the normally air-filled middle ear, resulting in a collection of fluid behind the tympanic membrane.
- Otitis media can be either serous or suppurative. Impacted cerumen that has pushed tightly up against the eardrum is a frequent cause of conductive hearing loss.

Ménière's Disease
- Ménière's disease is a chronic, progressive condition that affects the labyrinth and causes recurring attacks of vertigo, tinnitus, a sensation of pressure in the affected ear, and advancing hearing loss.

Ear Examination
- The ear examination begins with an otoscopic examination and can include various tuning fork tests and more advanced audiometric testing.

Irrigation and Medication
- An ear irrigation removes excessive or impacted cerumen; removes a foreign body; or treats the inflamed ear with an antiseptic solution.
- Medication instilled into the ear generally softens impacted cerumen, relieves pain, or fights an infectious pathogen.

Examination of Nose and Throat
- Examination of the nose and throat begins with the nasal cavity and then the throat and the nasopharynx. Throat cultures may be done to determine the presence of a streptococcal infection.

Vision and Hearing Impairment
- Patients with vision or hearing impairments face serious challenges and require individualized attention to meet their health education needs.
- Teaching adaptations may be required for these patients.

Vision Loss
- Those with vision losses may need large-print forms and handouts, increased levels of lighting, or oral instructions rather than written ones.

Hearing Deficits
- Individuals with hearing deficits may benefit from printed instructions, demonstrations of how to manage treatments, or even sign language interpretation.
- Family members should be included in the patient's treatment plan, and referrals to appropriate community or professional resources may be very beneficial.

CHAPTER 35: Assisting in Dermatology

The Skin
- The skin
  - Acts as a barrier to protect vital internal organs against infection and injury
  - Helps dissipate heat and regulate body temperature
  - Synthesizes vitamin D when exposed to ultraviolet light
  - Responds to such sensations as heat, cold, pain, and pressure

Three Layers
- The skin is made up of three layers.
  - Epidermis, the thin uppermost layer
  - Dermis, the thicker layer beneath, often referred to as the true skin (about 90% of the skin mass)
  - Subcutaneous layer, composed primarily of fatty or adipose tissue

Diagnosis
- The diagnosis of skin lesions is based on
  - Color, level of elevation, and texture of the lesion
  - Presence of pruritus, excoriation, pain, or drainage
  - Whether the lesion is a primary or secondary growth

Infections
- Integumentary system infections include
  - Bacterial infections such as impetigo, acne vulgaris, furuncles, carbuncles, and cellulites
  - Fungal infections including a variety of tinea growths
  - Viral infections that cause warts, herpes simplex, and herpes zoster outbreaks;
  - Scabies or pediculosis infestations

Other Disorders
- Inflammatory and vascular integumentary system disorders include
  - Seborrheic dermatitis inflammations
  - Contact dermatitis
  - Eczema
  - Psoriasis
  - Two autoimmune disorders, systemic lupus erythematosus and scleroderma

Thermal Injuries
- Burns are classified as superficial (first-degree), partial-thickness (second-degree), or full-thickness (third-degree), depending on the depth of the wound.
- The most important concern in burn treatment is the prevention of infection.
- Cold injuries are usually less severe than burns, but prolonged exposure can result in infection, gangrene, amputation, and in severe situations, death.
- Frostbite can either be superficial or deep.

Cancer
- Benign masses are encapsulated; although they may grow, they remain within a confining shell.
- Malignant tumors invade and take over surrounding tissues.
- Local invasion of surrounding tissue occurs when malignant cells break through the basement membrane that separates epithelial cells from connective tissue and invade blood and lymph vessels, which can then carry the malignant cells throughout the body.

Grading
- Grading and staging describe the extent of malignant involvement so the physician can plan appropriate treatment.
- Grading is the histologic, or cellular, classification of the tumor. The more poorly differentiated the cells from the tumor, the less they look like normal cells, and the poorer the prognosis.

Staging
- Staging involves using physical examination and diagnostic tests (such as bone or liver scans) to determine the degree of tumor spread.
- The size and depth of the primary tumor, the level of lymph node involvement, and the presence of metastatic spread determines if the patient has a carcinoma in situ, a tumor that is localized to the organ of origin, a direct spread beyond the primary organ, lymph node metastasis, or a confirmed secondary tumor growth at a distant metastasis.

Warning Signs of Cancer
- The warning signs of cancer
  - Change in bowel or bladder habits
  - A sore that does not heal
  - Unusual bleeding or discharge
  - A thickening or a lump in the breast or elsewhere
  - Indigestion or difficulty in swallowing
  - An obvious change in a wart or mole
  - A nagging cough or hoarseness

Early Detection

- Any of these warning signs should be reported to the physician immediately.
- Early detection and self-examination are crucial to cancer survival.

Cancerous Lesions of the Skin

- The three cancerous lesions of the skin are basal cell, squamous cell, and malignant melanoma.
- Basal cell carcinoma is very slow growing and is the most frequently seen form of skin cancer.

Squamous Cell Carcinoma

- Squamous cell carcinoma grows rapidly and is more serious because it has a tendency to metastasize. The many forms of melanoma are all pigmented lesions (usually brown, tan, blue, red, black, or white) that are asymmetric with irregular borders and are usually larger than 6 mm.

Treatment

- Treatment depends on the type of lesion, the level of invasion, and location. The physician may surgically remove the tumor or destroy it with cryosurgery, electrodesiccation, or chemotherapeutic agents.

ABCD for Melanoma

- The ABCD rule for early detection of a malignant melanoma:
  - Asymmetry
  - Irregular border
  - Change in color
  - An increase in diameter
- If a mole displays any of these characteristics, a dermatologist should check it immediately.

Procedures

- Dermatologic procedures include:
  - Allergy skin testing that can be done with scratch, intradermal, or patch tests
  - Drawing blood for a RAST test
  - Treating allergies with immunotherapy
  - Performing a wound culture
  - Assisting with appearance-modification procedures including chemical peels dermabrasion, and laser resurfacing

CHAPTER 36: Assisting in Gastroenterology

The Gastrointestinal System

- The gastrointestinal system prepares, digests, absorbs, and excretes nutrients and waste materials.

- The gastrointestinal system begins at the mouth and ends at the anal canal.

Digestion

- The digestive process starts in the mouth with mastication and enzyme action.
- The bolus of food is swallowed and passed from the esophagus into the stomach where digestion continues with hydrochloric acid and further enzyme action.
- It ends in the duodenum with pancreatic juices and emulsification of fat by bile, excreted by the liver and stored in the gallbladder.

Absorption

- Absorption of nutrients takes place in the ileum and jejunum, with absorption of fluids in the large intestine.
- Waste materials are excreted through the anus.

Four Quadrants

- The abdominal cavity can be divided into four sections or quadrants, the right and left upper quadrants and right and left lower quadrants.

Anatomic Markers

- Another, more specific method of dividing the abdominal cavity is with nine regions:
  - Right hypochondriac, epigastric, and left hypochondriac
  - Right lumbar, umbilical, and left lumbar
  - Right inguinal, hypogastric, and left inguinal
- These anatomic markers can clearly identify the location of the gastrointestinal problem.

Symptoms

- Patients with gastrointestinal disorders may complain of:
  - Nausea with pallor, diaphoresis, and tachycardia
  - Vomiting because of pain, stress, gastrointestinal (GI) upset, or an inner ear or intracranial pressure disturbance
  - Diarrhea due to an infection, allergy, or malabsorption problem
  - Constipation because of a low-fiber diet or inadequate fluids, side effect of medication, or a bowel obstruction or tumor
  - Abdominal pain that varies in intensity and quality

Recording of Symptoms

- Identify the location of the patient's discomfort by using either abdominal quadrants or regions, and note the onset, duration, and frequency of all symptoms.

GI Cancer

- GI tumors can include:
  - Oral tumors, seen as either a white mass or an ulcer
  - Esophageal, causing dysphagia
  - Gastric, causing anorexia and weight loss, but difficult to diagnose in the early stages
  - Liver, usually secondary to metastasis from another cancerous site with hepatomegaly and portal hypertension
  - Pancreatic cancer, usually advanced when diagnosed;
  - Colorectal cancer, with changes in bowel function and anemia

Other Disorders

- Esophageal and gastric disorders include:
  - Hiatal hernias, in which part of the stomach pushes through the hiatal sphincter of the diaphragm, causing GERD
  - Peptic ulcers which are associated with *H. pylori* infections that are treated with a combination of antibiotics and proton pump inhibitors
  - Pyloric stenosis, seen most frequently in first-born male infants, causing projectile vomiting; it must be corrected by surgery
- These disorders are usually diagnosed symptomatically and with the use of a barium swallow or upper GI series of radiographs.
- Medical treatment includes the use of Propulsid, Nexium, Pepcid, Tagamet, or Zantac. Surgery may be indicated for repair of a hiatal hernia or gastric ulcers if perforation occurs.

Intestinal Disorders

- Intestinal disorders include a variety of food poisonings, all of which cause mild to severe gastroenteritis, with antiemetics and antidiarrheal medications used to control symptoms.

Dumping Syndrome

- Dumping syndrome may occur as a postsurgical complication to weight-loss surgery and results in widespread gastrointestinal complaints.

IBS

- Irritable bowel syndrome (IBS) is a recurrent functional bowel disorder causing alternating bouts of diarrhea, flatulence, and constipation.
- IBS is treated pharmaceutically with bulk-forming agents, antidiarrheals, antispasmodics, and anticholinergics.

Appendicitis

- Acute appendicitis, diagnosed by a positive McBurney's sign, is treated surgically.

Crohn's Disease

- Regional enteritis or Crohn's disease causes localized areas of ulceration in the intestinal tract and is treated medically to decrease inflammation, manage symptoms, and maintain nutritional status.

Ulcerative Colitis

- Ulcerative colitis causes inflammatory ulcers from the anus proximally through the colon. It is treated like Crohn's disease, but surgical removal of the colon is curative.

Celiac Disease

- Malabsorption disorder: Celiac disease is due to a genetic defect in the ability to metabolize gluten.

Diverticular Disease

- Diverticular disease, due to small herniations of the muscular lining of the colon, is managed with dietary changes and surgery with advanced diverticulitis.

Hernias and Varicose Veins

- If the abdominal muscles are weakened, hernias can develop; these are surgically repaired.
- Hemorrhoids, varicose veins of the anus, are treated with stool softeners, high-fiber diets, or surgical repair.

Liver Disorders

- Disorders of the liver include hepatitis, either from viral infection or chemical reaction, including alcohol abuse and a complication of drug metabolism; mild inflammation temporarily impairs function, but severe inflammation may lead to necrosis and serious complications including jaundice, cirrhosis, and portal hypertension.

Cholelithiasis or Cholecystitis

- The gallbladder stores bile excreted by the liver to aid in fat metabolism. Cholelithiasis or cholecystitis may require surgical removal of the gallbladder to relieve patient symptoms.

Hepatitis

- Hepatitis can be caused by exposure to chemicals or drug side effects. Viral hepatitis, an infection of the liver, causes an acute inflammatory process.
- Several forms of this virus: A, B, C, D, E, and G, exist.
- Hepatic cells can regenerate, so dependent on the degree of liver involvement, the patient may

recover completely or develop widespread necrosis, cirrhosis, and liver failure.

Examination
- The medical assistant's role:
  - Providing patient support and education
  - Gathering and recording complaints
  - Instilling rectal medications
  - Assisting with the examination and diagnostic procedures

Diagnostic Tests
- Diagnostic procedures:
  - Laboratory studies such as liver panels, urinary tests for bilirubin and amylase
  - Stool tests for occult blood, intestinal parasites, and fat excretion
- Radiologic and endoscopic tests:
  - Barium swallow
  - Upper GI series
  - Barium enema
  - Oral cholecystogram
  - Sigmoidoscopy
  - Colonoscopy

Proctoscopy
- The role of the medical assistant in the proctologic examination:
  - Patient support and preparation
  - Positioning and draping the patient
  - Monitoring vital signs before and during the procedure
  - Assisting the physician with the procedure

CHAPTER 37: Assisting in Urology and Male Reproduction

Urinary System
- The urinary system is made up of two kidneys located bilaterally in the retroperitoneum, two ureters, the urinary bladder, and the urethra. The urinary system removes waste products from the body.

Other Functions
- The urinary system
  - Maintains homeostasis by regulating water, electrolytes, and acid-base levels
  - Activates vitamin D, which encourages calcium ion absorption
  - Secretes the hormone erythropoietin, which helps control the rate of red blood cell formation
  - Maintains blood pressure by the secretion of the enzyme renin

Urine Production
- Three processes are involved in urine formation: filtration, reabsorption, and excretion. The outer layer of the kidney, the cortex, contains the functional nephron unit, where waste materials are filtered and substances reabsorbed.

Urine
- Waste material reaches the calyx in the form of urine, which is emptied out of the kidneys through bilateral ureters to urinary bladder. When the bladder is full, sphincters open, and urine flows into the urethra.

Mucous Membrane Lining
- The urinary tract has a continuous mucosal lining, which gives organisms that enter the urethra a direct pathway through the system.

Symptoms
- A wide range of symptoms occur in patients with disorders of the renal system; the most common involve changes in the frequency of urination, as well as dysuria (difficult or painful urination), urgency, retention, and incontinence.

Tests
- Abnormal functions of the urinary tract can be determined with urinalysis, blood urea nitrogen (BUN) levels, and with analysis of creatinine clearance.

Procedures
- Diagnostic procedures for the urologic system include:
  - Kidney-ureter-bladder radiograph (KUB), a flat plate of the abdomen that shows the size, shape, location, and malformations of the kidneys and bladder
  - Renal scanning, which is a nuclear scans to determine size, shape, and function of the kidney or to diagnose obstruction or hypertension
  - Cystography or voiding cystography is a radiograph with contrast dye to study the bladder
  - Intravenous pyelogram takes radiographs after a dye is injected to show passage through the urinary system and diagnose tumors, calculi, or obstructions
  - Renal arteriogram injects dye into the renal artery to visualize blood flow through the kidneys
  - Renal computed tomography (CT) provides transverse views of the kidneys to detect tumors, abscesses, or hydronephrosis

- Renal ultrasound can detect functional defects in the kidneys or polycystic disease
- Cystoscopy provides an endoscopic view of the urethra and bladder
- Retrograde pyelogram visualizes the bladder, ureters, and kidneys after injection of a dye

Infections

- Most urinary tract infections (UTIs) are ascending, starting with pathogens in the perineal area and infecting the continuous mucosa up through the urethra, bladder, ureters, to the kidneys.
- Infection and inflammation of the urethra is urethritis, and that of the bladder is cystitis. The resident bacterium of the colon, *Escherichia coli*, is the usual causative agent.

Pyelonephritis

- Pyelonephritis, an inflammation of the renal pelvis and kidney and the most common type of renal disease, is caused by bacteria.
- Conditions such as urinary retention or obstruction promote urinary stasis and the growth of bacteria.

Glomerulonephritis

- Acute glomerulonephritis, degenerative inflammation of the glomeruli, usually develops in children and adolescents about 2 weeks after a streptococcal infection such as strep throat or scarlet fever.
- Chronic glomerulonephritis causes progressive, irreversible renal damage; it may result in renal failure, and is caused by an antigen-antibody reaction within the glomerular capsule that ultimately destroys the nephron unit.

Renal Calculi

- Renal calculi are created when salts in the urine collect in the kidney or when fluid intake is low, creating a highly concentrated filtrate. They are common and tend to recur if the cause of formation is not treated.
- Small stones usually do not cause any difficulty until they grow large enough to lodge in the ureters or renal pelvis. Blockage can result in hydronephrosis, a backup of urine causing dilation of the calyses and increased pressure on the nephron units.

Polycystic Disease

- Polycystic kidney disease is a slowly progressive and irreversible autonomic dominant genetic disorder causing the formation of multiple grape-like cysts in the kidney.

- As the cysts enlarge, they compress the surrounding tissue, causing necrosis, uremia, and renal failure.

Bladder Cancer

- Bladder cancer is characterized by one or more tumors that can reappear. The tumors are invasive and can metastasize through the blood or surrounding pelvic lymph nodes.

Adenocarcinoma

- Adenocarcinoma of the kidney, a primary tumor that is initially asymptomatic, frequently has metastasized before being diagnosed.
- Wilms' tumor is cancer of the kidney in children due to an inherited genetic defect.

Renal Failure

- Acute renal failure has a sudden, severe onset caused by exposure to toxic chemicals, severe or prolonged circulatory or cardiogenic shock from serious burns or heart disease, or from an acute bilateral kidney infection or inflammation.
- Chronic renal failure, a slowly progressive process, is caused by the gradual destruction of the ability of the kidneys to filter waste materials. Dialysis, or cleansing of the blood, is used to treat acute renal failure until the problem is reversed or, for those patients in end-stage renal disease, until a transplant can be done.

Dialysis

- Hemodialysis uses an artificial kidney to filter out waste products in the blood and return the cleansed blood to the body.
- Peritoneal dialysis uses dialyzing fluid in the patient's abdomen to absorbs waste products, which are drained from the abdominal cavity by gravity into a container. It can be done by the patient at home.

Pediatric Disorders

- Enuresis, the inability to control urination, may be caused by physical or psychological disorders.
- Urine reflux disorder, the backward flow of urine into the ureters when voiding, is usually caused by an infection.

Cryptorchidism

- Cryptorchidism, the failure of one or both testes to descend into the scrotum, can be corrected with an orchidopexy surgical procedure.

Hydrocele

- A hydrocele, a buildup of fluid in the scrotum, may be congenital or acquired because of injury.

Male Reproductive System

- The male reproductive system is made up of a pair of testes contained in the scrotum. The testes contain the seminiferous tubules, where spermatozoa are produced. The sperm cells are tadpole-like structures, less than 0.1 mm long, that are carried to the epididymis for maturation.

Epididymis

- The epididymis, a long coiled tube, rests on the top and lateral side of each testis. Peristaltic waves in the epididymis help the sperm move into the vas deferens, where the sperm is stored until ejaculation.

Prostate

- The prostate gland surrounds the urethra at the base of the bladder. It secretes a thin fluid with an alkaline pH that neutralizes the acidic sperm-containing fluid and vaginal secretions to provide an optimal pH for fertilization.

Penis

- The organ of male copulation is the penis, which has a slightly enlarged end, called the glans penis.

Hormones

- Male sex hormones are called androgens. Testosterone stimulates the testes to enlarge, increases body hair growth, thickens skin and bone, increases muscle growth, and matures sperm cells.

Prostate Infection

- Inflammation of the prostate usually develops with infection. Symptoms are dysuria, tenderness of the prostate region, and secretion of pus from the tip of the penis.

Prostatic Hypertrophy

- The swelling of the prostate gland, benign prostatic hypertrophy, partially blocks the flow of urine, creating a medium for bacterial infection that can lead to cystitis. The diagnosis is made from patient complaints and a digital rectal examination (the physician can feel the enlarged gland). Treatment includes the use of α-adrenergic blockers or surgical removal of the prostrate gland through a transurethral resection.

Prostate Cancer

- Cancer of the prostate is common in men older than 50 and is the second highest cause of male cancer deaths. The patient may have urinary obstruction, increased bouts of urinary infection, and frequent nocturia. A digital rectal examination identifies a firm or irregular area in the prostate. The prostate specific antigen (PSA) blood test is positive.

Infections

- Male genital pathology includes epididymitis usually due to a urinary tract infection, prostatitis, or a sexually transmitted disease (STD). Patients have severe low abdominal and testicular pain and swelling and tenderness of the scrotum.
- The inflammation of the glans penis and of the mucous membrane beneath it, balanitis, occurs most often in uncircumcised patients with narrow foreskins that do not retract easily and in diabetics.
- Antibiotics are used for infections, cleansing for buildup of smegma, and avoidance of chemicals that cause reactions can help avoid the problem.

Tumors of Testes

- Testicular tumors usually occur in young men and are generally malignant. The patient complains of a hard, painless, mass affecting one testicle.
- Treatment of the tumors is usually a combination of orchiectomy, radiation therapy, and sometimes chemotherapy.

Impotence and Infertility

- Impotence is the inability to achieve and maintain an erection sufficient for intercourse. It has many causes, both psychologic and physiologic. This condition can be treated medically with Viagra.
- Male infertility may be caused by cryptorchidism, stricture, and varicoceles; low sperm count and motility; obstruction of the vas deferens, and hormonal imbalances.

STDs

- There is no cure for viral STDs such as HIV or herpes, and bacterial causes of infection are increasingly resistant to antibiotic therapy. STDs are frequently asymptomatic and can cause serious health problems, even death.
- Bacterial STDs include gonorrhea and chlamydia, infections that tend to coexist. Symptoms are associated with acute urethritis and epididymitis.

Other STDs

- Chlamydia is resistant to penicillin, so antibiotics other than penicillin should be used.
- Syphilis begins with a chancre on the male genitalia within a few days to a few weeks after exposure. It is diagnosed with the VDRL or RPR.

CHAPTER 38: Assisting in Obstetrics and Gynecology

External Genitalia
- The female reproductive system is made up of the external genitalia: the vulva, labia majora, and labia minora.

Internal Organs
- The internal organs include:
  - The vagina with rugae formation in the walls so it can expand when the baby is born
  - The bottom of the uterus, the cervix, which must dilate and efface for vaginal birth
  - The uterus with the internal lining, the endometrium, and middle lining, the myometriun
  - The fallopian tubes that extend from the fundus of the uterus and carry the fertilized egg back to the uterus
  - The ovaries that mature and excrete an egg or ovum

Menstrual Cycle
- The average menstrual cycle lasts 28 days. In the follicular phase, hormones mature a graafian follicle so that an ovum can be released while the endometrial wall is thickening.
- The ovum passes into the fallopian tube, which moves it toward the uterus. In the luteal phase, extensive growth of the endometrium continues; if conception does not occur, the menstrual cycle begins with the breakdown of the endometrium and menstrual flow.

Contraception
- Barrier contraceptive methods include the use of condoms, a diaphragm, or cervical cap. Both the diaphragm and cap use spermicidal agents as well. All barrier methods are relatively inexpensive and reversible but must be used each time there is intercourse. Hormonal contraceptives include DepoProvera injections every 12 weeks, Norplant implants that provide contraception for 5 years, or oral contraceptives that must be taken daily as prescribed.

Disorders
- Menstrual disorders include amenorrhea or the absence of menstruation for a minimum of 6 months. With oligomenorrhea, the woman has not experienced a period for from 35 days to 6 months. Abnormal menstrual bleeding includes menorrhagia, excessive menstrual blood loss, such as a menses lasting longer than 7 days. Metrorrhaghia is spotting or bleeding between menstrual cycles.

Endometriosis
- In endometriosis, functional endometrial tissue is found outside the uterus. Ectopic endometrial tissue responds to hormone changes, so it proliferates, degenerates, and bleeds as does the endometrium of the uterus throughout the menstrual cycle. This causes inflammation that recurs with each cycle, ultimately leading to adhesions and obstructions. The primary symptom of endometriosis is dysmenorrhea and frequently dyspareunia.

Infections
- Gynecological infections include a yeast infection called candidiasis; cervicitis (an inflammation of the cervix from a pathogen); pelvic inflammatory disease (PID), any acute or chronic infection of the reproductive system ascending from the vagina (vaginitis), cervix (cervicitis), uterus (endometritis), fallopian tubes (salpingitis), and ovaries (oophoritis).

Benign Tumors
- Benign tumors include uterine fibroids, composed mainly of smooth muscle and some fibrous connective tissue. Ovarian cysts are sacs of fluid or semisolid material that can occur in the follicle or the corpus luteum at any time between puberty and menopause.

PCO
- Polycystic ovary disease is a hormonal problem that causes cysts to develop over enlarged ovaries. Women with this disorder have hormonal abnormalities that cause anovulation and multiple symptoms.

Fibrocystic Breasts
- Multiple palpable nodules in the breasts are usually associated with pain and tenderness that fluctuate with the menstrual cycle. Over time the cysts enlarge, and the connective tissue of the breast is replaced with dense and firm fibrous tissue.

Malignant Tumors
- Cervical, endometrial, and ovarian cancers vary in their diagnostic features and symptoms. Breast cancer can be of multiple origins including ductal, lobular, or invasive carcinoma that has invaded surrounded tissue and metastasized. Treatment of all forms is dependent of the staging and grading of the tumors.

Cystocele

- A cystocele is a protrusion of the bladder into the anterior wall of the vagina. The bladder becomes angled, and urinary retention is common, with frequent cystitis.

Rectocele

- A rectocele, causing a protrusion of the rectum into the posterior wall of the vagina, or a uterine prolapse, where the cervix has dropped into the vaginal area, may progress to both the uterus and the cervix protruding from the vaginal opening. These structural abnormalities can be corrected with surgery.

Implantation

- Pregnancy occurs when the ovum and sperm meet in the fallopian tube, and a zygote is formed. The zygote implants in the uterine wall, and the placenta begins to form, which provides hormonal support for the pregnancy.

Embryo

- The fetus is surrounded by an amniotic sac and floats in amniotic fluid. The fetus' oxygen and nutrient needs are met by maternal blood that passes through the placenta to the umbilical cord and waste material pass out along the same path. The embryonic period ends at 12 weeks, when all tissues and organs have developed.

Fetus

- During the remainder of the pregnancy, the organs mature and begin to function, and the fetus grows.

Stages of Pregnancy and Labor

- Pregnancy is divided into trimesters. The first trimester is a crucial time for fetal organ development; the second brings quickening and many physiological changes in the mother; in the third, organ systems mature.
- Labor consists of three stages: dilation and effacement of the cervix; birth; and expulsion of the placenta.

Complications

- Complications of pregnancy begin with fertility problems and the potential loss of the pregnancy from different types of abortions (miscarriages).
- Placental abnormalities pose a threat to the well-being of the fetus.

Placental Problems

- In placenta previa, the placenta covers the cervical os; in abruptio placentae, the placenta breaks away from the uterine wall.
- Both cause maternal hemorrhage, threaten fetal oxygen supply, and require cesarean birth to protect the fetus and mother.

Maternal Disorders

- Maternal disorders include:
  - Pregnancy-induced glucose metabolic disorder
  - Gestational diabetes, which requires dietary changes and possible insulin therapy during the pregnancy
  - Hypertension, which may progress to toxemia, a life-threatening increase in blood pressure with edema, uremia, and possible seizure activity

Menopause

- Menopause is the permanent ending of menstruation because ovarian function stops. Perimenopause begins when hormone-related changes start to appear and lasts until the final menses. Some women have few or no symptoms; others have hot flashes, concentration problems, mood swings, irritability, migraines, vaginal dryness, urinary incontinence, dry skin, and sleep disorders.

Therapy

- The physician may prescribe low-dose oral contraceptives or hormone-replacement therapy; soy products or supplements; vitamin E; vitamin B6; restriction of caffeine and spicy foods; a low-fat diet high in calcium; and regular weight-bearing exercise.

MA Role

- Preparing the patient for the examination
- Equipping the room
- Making sure supplies are available and properly prepared
- Assisting with the examination
- Positioning and draping the patient
- Assisting with the Pap smear or any other procedure
- Providing support and understanding for the patient

Tests

- Diagnostic tests for the female reproductive system include:
  - Ultrasonography to determine the number of fetuses, age and sex of the fetus, fetal abnormalities, and position of the placenta
  - Chorionic villi sampling or amniocentesis to perform genetic testing for anomalies or inherited disorders

- α-Fetoprotein (AFP) blood tests to diagnose neural tube defects
- Mammography provides an x-ray image of the breast tissue to identify abnormal masses that would otherwise be undetected with a breast-palpation examination
- Colposcopy procedures visualize abnormal cervical tissue for evaluation or biopsy
- Cryosurgery treats cervical ulcers or cervicitis
- A variety of tests done during pregnancy

CHAPTER 39: Assisting in Pediatrics

Growth and Development

- The terms growth and development refer to the changes a child goes through as he or she matures.
- Growth refers to measurable changes such as height and weight, whereas development considers qualitative maturation in motor, mental, and language skills.

Growth

- By age 6 months, the child's birth weight has doubled; at 1 year it has tripled, and length has increased by 50%.
- By age 2, the child has reached approximately 50% of adult height.
- This same growth rate continues through the school-age period, 6 to 12 years, followed by a growth spurt that indicates impending puberty.
- In adolescence, ages 12 to 18 years, the adolescent gains almost half of his or her adult weight, and the skeleton and organs double in size.

Development

- Child development occurs rapidly during the first year of life, and by age 3, the child is showing increased autonomy.
- During the preschool stage, the child becomes increasingly independent, and by school age, the child has perfected fine motor skills and has expanded reading and writing skills.
- In the adolescent or transition stage, the individual attempts to establish an adult identity through trial and error by experimenting with adult roles and behavior patterns.

GI Disorders

- Pediatric gastrointestinal disorders include:
  - Infant colic
  - Diarrhea, caused by a variety of different microorganisms, treated medically when it continues for more than 2 days
  - Failure to thrive, caused by a physiological factor (such as malabsorption disease or cleft palate) or a nonorganic cause associated with the parent-child relationship
  - Obesity, with treatment for children who are more than 40% over their ideal weight

Respiratory Disorders

- Disorders of the respiratory system include the common cold, which may lead to secondary bacterial infections including strep throat or otitis media due to accumulation of either serous or suppurative fluid in the middle ear.

Croup

- Croup, a viral disorder, affects primarily the larynx with edema and spasm to the vocal cords, resulting in a high-pitched raspy cough.

Bronchiolitis and Asthma

- Bronchiolitis, a viral infection of the small bronchi and bronchioles, has an acute onset of wheezing and dyspnea because of necrosis, inflammation, edema, increased secretions, and bronchospasm in the respiratory pathway.
- Asthma causes bronchospasms that decrease the amount of air that can pass through the airways and inflammation of the bronchioles, causing edema and secretion of mucus.

Influenza

- Influenza, an acute, highly contagious viral infection of the respiratory tract, is transmitted by direct contact with moist secretions, causes high fevers and pulmonary complications.

Conjunctivitis

- Pediatric infectious diseases include conjunctivitis, caused by bacterial or viral infection, which produces a white or yellowish pus and is highly contagious.

Tonsillitis

- Tonsillitis, typically caused by Streptococcus A, causes painful, enlarged, and inflamed tonsils with fever and malaise.

Fifth Disease

- Fifth disease, also called erythema infectiosum, is a mild infection caused by parvovirus B19 with a mild fever, general malaise, and flushed cheeks.

Chickenpox

- Chickenpox, caused by a member of the herpesvirus group, involves a slight fever and skin lesions that last for about 2 weeks and usually leaves the child with lifetime immunity.

Meningitis

- Meningitis, inflammation of the membranes that cover the brain and spinal cord, is caused by bacteria or viruses; bacterial meningitis is more dangerous.

Hepatitis B

- Hepatitis B virus infection can lead to serious and chronic infection of the liver. It can be transmitted across the placenta or during the birth process if the mother is infected.

Reye's Syndrome

- Reye's syndrome is linked with the use of aspirin during a viral illness. It is characterized by fatty invasion of the inner organs, especially the liver, and swelling of the brain.

Inherited Disorders

- Pediatric inherited disorders include cystic fibrosis, an autosomal recessive genetic disorder, that causes exocrine glands to produce abnormally thick secretions. It primarily affects the lungs and pancreas, causing buildup of mucus in the lungs and blockage of the pancreatic ducts, resulting in malabsorption problems and an emphysema-like lung condition.

Muscular Dystrophy

- Duchenne's muscular dystrophy is an X-linked genetic disease
  - Progressive muscle degeneration and subsequent replacement of muscle fibers with fat and fibrous connective tissue
  - Either cardiac or respiratory failure

Vaccinations

- All children should be vaccinated against:
  - Diphtheria
  - Tetanus
  - Pertussis
  - Hepatitis B
  - *Haemophilus influnzae b* virus that can cause some forms of meningitis
  - Polio
  - Measles
  - Mumps
  - Rubella
  - Pneumonia
  - Chickenpox

Well-child Visits

- Well-child visits are typically scheduled from age 2 weeks through 15 years to maintain the health of the child with basic system examinations, immunizations, and upgrade the medical record. Sick-child visits occur whenever needed and usually on short notice.

Responsibilities of the MA

- The medical assistant is responsible for:
  - Assisting the pediatrician with examinations
  - Upgrading patient histories
  - Performing screening tests such as vision, hearing, urinalysis, and hemoglobin checks
  - Administering immunizations
  - Measuring and weighing children
  - Providing patient and caregiver support

Injuries

- The medical assistant should be involved in parent education regarding injury prevention. Unintentional injuries are the leading cause of death and disability for children in the United States, causing more childhood deaths than all diseases combined. Primary causes include motor vehicle accidents, drowning, burns, falls, poisoning, aspiration with airway obstruction, and firearms.

CHAPTER 40: Assisting in Orthopedic Medicine

Musculoskeletal System

- The main structures include
  - Skeletal muscles that provide movement
  - Tendons that connect muscles to bones
  - Bones that provide support, protection, mineral storage
  - Ligaments that connect bone to bone

Tendons and Ligaments

- Tendons are tough bands that connect muscles to bones, whereas ligaments provide support by connecting bone to bone and preventing a joint from moving beyond its normal range of motion (ROM). Ligament injury occurs when a joint is forced beyond its ROM. Bursae prevent friction between different tissues.

Disorders

- Musculoskeletal system disorders account for more missed days at work and more doctors'

office visits than nearly any other medical problems.
- Trauma
- Bacteria, fungi, or viruses
- Autoimmune disorders

Diagnosis
- Common diagnostic procedures include inspection, palpation, and percussion, along with x-ray studies. It is necessary to rule out bone fractures in many traumatic injuries with radiographs of the injured area. Other diagnostic tools include computed tomography (CT), magnetic resonance imaging (MRI), and diagnostic ultrasound.

Assistive Devices
- The most common ambulatory assistive devices are crutches, canes, walkers, and wheelchairs. Fit them properly to the patient, and give the patient adequate instruction on how to use them.

Cold Application
- Cold should always be used immediately after an injury to help decrease pain and inflammation and to inhibit additional swelling.

Heat Application
- Heat after 48 hours promotes circulation and healing, decreases swelling, and causes soft-tissue relaxation.

Physical Therapy
- Physical therapy can restore normal ROM, muscle strength, and function of the injured part. Other goals include decreasing pain and preserving muscle mass.

ROM Assessment
- In active ROM assessment or exercise, the patient provides and controls the movement.
- In passive ROM assessment or exercise, the therapist provides and controls the movement.

CHAPTER 41: Assisting in Neurology and Mental Health

Nervous System
- There are two main parts to the human nervous system:
  - The central nervous system (CNS), which includes the brain and spinal cord.
  - The peripheral nervous system (PNS), which includes all of the nerves outside of the CNS.

Nervous System Function
- The nervous system controls the body and maintains homeostasis by receiving messages in the CNS from the PNS and then sending a response to the appropriate location in the body.

Meninges
- The CNS is well protected first by bone and then by a series of membranous coverings (meninges): the dura mater, the arachnoid mater, and the pia mater.

Brain
- The brain is made up of:
  - Cerebrum (all expressions of artistic and verbal processes and thought)
  - Cerebellum (controls balance, equilibrium, posture, and muscle coordination)
  - Brainstem (vision, hearing, respirations, heart rate, blood pressure, and waking and sleeping)

Symptoms and Problems
- Symptoms of possible serious neurologic conditions:
  - Headache
  - Nausea and vomiting
  - Change in vision
  - Change in level of consciousness

Disorders from Trauma
- The most common brain disorders resulting from trauma include concussion and contusion. More severe injuries could result in intracranial bleeding.

Repetitive Stress Disorder
- The most common work-related neurologic condition is a repetitive stress disorder, carpal tunnel syndrome.

Diagnostic Tests
- Frequently used diagnostic tests include EEG, lumbar puncture, x-ray, computed tomography (CT) scan, and magnetic resonance imaging (MRI).

Depression
- Depression, among the most commonly encountered mental health disorders, has a variety of symptoms that could easily be overlooked or attributed to some other condition.

Subtle Symptoms
- Be particularly careful to recognize quite subtle signs and symptoms that can be extremely significant.

CHAPTER 42: Assisting in Endocrinology

Endocrine Hormones

- The endocrine system is a network of ductless glands and other structures that secrete hormones directly into the bloodstream. These hormones affect specific target tissues and organs.

Hormones

- Hormones are chemical transmitters produced by the body and transported to target tissue or organs by the bloodstream.

Diabetes Insipidus and Diabetes Mellitus

- Diabetes insipidus and diabetes mellitus are two different diseases.
- Diabetes insipidus is a metabolic condition characterized by excessive excretion of urine.
- Diabetes mellitus results from a deficiency or complete lack of the hormone insulin.

Pituitary Gland Disorders

- Gigantism and acromegaly are both diseases of the pituitary gland involving GH (growth hormone).
- When this condition affects children whose epiphyses have not closed, gigantism results.
- In adults, the disorder causes excessive growth of the face and extremities, called acromegaly.

Goiter

- Iodine supplements are used to reduce the size of the thyroid enlargement called a goiter.

Diabetes

- Type 1 or immune-mediated diabetes usually develops before age 30 years and is sometimes called juvenile diabetes. Type 2 diabetes mellitus develops gradually and is called maturity or adult-onset diabetes.
- Both conditions result from deficiencies of insulin, but type 1 diabetics do not produce any insulin, whereas type 2 diabetics usually produce an insufficient amount.

Food Plan

- The diabetic patient must be aware of the possible complications of the disease and the need to develop an informed food plan.

Complications of Diabetes

- Primary complications of diabetes mellitus: Hypoglycemia, ketoacidosis, and diabetic coma.
- Secondary complications can appear many years after diagnosis: Diabetic coronary artery disease, strokes, retinopathy, nephropathy, neuropathy, and atherosclerosis.

Foot Care

- Basic foot care is important for diabetic patients because of potential problems with their circulation.

Glucose Monitoring

- A fasting blood glucose sample is taken after the individual has been without food or drink (fasting) for 12 hours. It more accurately assesses the blood glucose level than a random blood glucose level.
- A glucose tolerance test (GTT) measures the body's ability to metabolize a concentrated oral glucose load. It starts with a fasting blood glucose and measures the glucose levels for from 1 to 5 hours.

Glucose Control

- Glycosylated hemoglobin level is an accurate measure of the glucose control for the preceding 5 to 6 weeks. It may be performed without a fasting specimen.

Insulin Treatment

- A type 1 diabetic can be treated with controlled doses of insulin; a mild case of type 2 diabetes can be controlled with exercise and diet. More severe cases of type 2 diabetes need medication to control sensitivity to insulin or to add insulin to the body.

Glucose Testing

- Various types of blood testing provide management options. In the clinical setting, a fasting level or a hemoglobin A1C can measure the fasting or the level of the glucose of the RBCs of the past weeks. Hand-held glucose monitors may fit the needs of the diabetic's lifestyle.

CHAPTER 43: Assisting in Pulmonary Medicine

Respiratory System

- The respiratory system
  - Exchanges oxygen from the atmosphere for carbon dioxide waste through external and internal respiration
  - Maintains the acid-base balance within the body

Respiration and Circulation

- The respiratory and circulatory systems work together to supply body cells with oxygen and remove metabolic wastes.

Respiratory Tract

- Upper respiratory tract: transports air from the atmosphere to the lungs and includes the nose, pharynx (throat), and larynx.
- Lower respiratory tract: the trachea, the bronchial tubes, and the lungs.

Bronchioles and Capillaries

- The bronchioles deposit oxygenated air into the alveoli. Surrounding each alveolus is a network of pulmonary capillaries filled with waste air.

Gas Exchange

- The oxygenated air moves through the single-celled walls of the alveoli and through the single-celled walls of these capillaries. Carbon dioxide is forced out of the capillaries, into the alveoli, and then into the bronchioles.

Ventilation

- This exchange is referred to as ventilation.
- The movement of oxygen from the atmosphere into the alveoli is called inspiration.
- The movement of the waste gases from the alveoli back into the atmosphere is called expiration.

Documentation

- Use these terms to document patient signs and symptoms.

Infections: Upper Tract

- Upper respiratory tract infections include:
  - The common cold, caused by a virus and has no cure
  - Sinusitis, which causes edema and the collection of mucus within the cavity, creating a feeling of pressure, either nasal congestion or rhinorrhea, and classic sinus headaches
  - Allergic rhinitis, a reaction of the nasal mucosa to an environmental allergen

Infections: Lower Tract

- Lower respiratory tract infections include:
  - Pneumonia, meaning inflammation of all or part of the lungs that is caused by bacteria, viruses, irritants, or other pathogens
  - Tuberculosis, caused by the bacteria *Mycobacterium tuberculosis,* transmitted by droplets of sputum from an infected host and inhaled by a susceptible host

Airway Obstructions

- Chronic obstructive pulmonary disease (COPD) is a group of diseases with chronic airway obstruction.
- Among these diseases are chronic bronchitis, bronchiectasis, asthma, pneumoconiosis, and emphysema. The patient with COPD is unable to ventilate the lungs freely, resulting in an ineffective exchange of respiratory gases.
- Treatments include bronchodilator and corticosteroid inhalers, evaluation of peak flow values, and nebulizer treatments.

Cancer

- The most prevalent neoplasms of the respiratory system are lung cancer and carcinoma of the larynx. Lung cancer is the leading cause of cancer-related deaths for both men and women and is a common site for secondary tumors from metastasis as well as primary carcinomas.

Cancer Prognosis

- Prognosis is very poor for lung cancer because early symptoms mimic chronic conditions in long-term smokers. Carcinoma of the larynx is linked to smoking and chronic alcohol consumption. Most laryngeal tumors are discovered in their early stages and have a very good prognosis.

Diagnostic Tests

- Respiratory system diagnostic procedures
  - The Mantoux intradermal test for TB
  - Pulmonary function tests, measured with a spirometer, diagnose a pulmonary abnormality and/or determine the extent of a pulmonary disease
  - Pulse oximetry, a noninvasive method of evaluating the oxygen saturation of hemoglobin in arterial blood and the pulse rate
  - Cultures performed on expectorated sputum to identify infectious pathogens
  - Bronchoscopy, viewing the larynx, trachea, and bronchi with a flexible fiberoptic instrument through which the physician can collect biopsies or bronchial washings for cytology or culture

CHAPTER 44: Assisting in Cardiology

The Heart
- The heart is a muscular organ that pumps blood through the body, circulating a continuous supply of oxygen and nutrients to the cells, and picking up the metabolic waste products.
- The three layers of tissue are surrounded by a double-membrane sac called the pericardium; the epicardium is the first layer of the heart; the middle muscular layer of the heart is the myocardium; and the inner layer, the endocardium, forms the heart valves.

Blood Flow
- The blood begins in the right atrium, which receives deoxygenated blood from the inferior and superior vena cava
- The atrium contracts, and blood passes through the tricuspid valve into the right ventricle
- The ventricle contracts, and the blood passes from the right ventricle to the lungs via the pulmonary artery
- Oxygenation occurs in the lungs, and the blood returns to the left atrium through the pulmonary veins
- The atrium contracts, and blood passes through the mitral (bicuspid) valve into the left ventricle
- The ventricle contracts, and oxygen-rich blood is sent out to the body through the aorta (the largest artery in the body)

Cardiac Disease
- Multiple risk factors for cardiac disease include:
  - Genetic predisposition and family history
  - Hypertension
  - Diabetes
  - Elevated blood cholesterol levels
- Lifestyle factors include:
  - High-fat, high-caloric diets
  - Obesity
  - Smoking
  - Lack of exercise
  - Hypertension
  - Stress

Coronary Artery Disease
- The arteries supplying the myocardium become narrowed by atherosclerotic plaques. The process causes narrowing of the lumen of the arteries and inhibition of the normal flow of blood, thus depriving the heart of an adequate nutritious blood supply.
- Symptoms: angina pectoris followed by pressure or fullness in the chest, syncope, edema, unexplained coughing spells, and fatigue.

Ischemia
- Women may exhibit a different clinical picture from that in men. Ischemia over a prolonged period leads to necrosis of a portion of the myocardium, resulting in a myocardial infarction.

Myocardial Infarction
- Symptoms of myocardial infarction are very similar to those of angina, but myocardial infarction pain lasts longer than 30 minutes and is unrelieved by rest or nitroglycerin tablets. A myocardial infarction is diagnosed by electrocardiogram changes and elevated cardiac enzymes 6 to 12 hours after the episode.

Treatment
- Medical treatment includes the use of thrombolytic medications to dissolve the coronary artery blockage, aspirin and beta blockers, angiotensin-converting enzyme (ACE) inhibitors, anticoagulants, and anticholesterol agents. When occlusion occurs in a coronary artery supplying blood to the myocardium, percutaneous transluminal coronary angioplasty or open-heart surgery may be indicated.

Hypertension
- Primary hypertension is idiopathic and is diagnosed if the patient's blood pressure is consistently above 140/90.
- Secondary hypertension occurs because of a disease process in another body system.
- Chronic elevated blood pressure can result in left ventricular hypertrophy, angina, MI, heart failure, stroke, or nephropathy.

Risk Factors
- Risk factors for developing hypertension include:
  - Family history of hypertension or stroke
  - Hypercholesterolemia
  - Smoking
  - High sodium intake
  - Diabetes
  - Excessive alcohol intake
  - Aging
  - Prolonged stress
  - Race

Congestive Heart Failure

- Congestive heart failure occurs when the myocardium is unable to pump enough blood to meet the needs of the body. It develops over time because of weakness in the left ventricle from chronic hypertension or MI of the ventricular wall; valvular heart disease; or pulmonary complications.

Heart Failure

- Typically, heart failure initially occurs on one side of the heart followed by the other side.
- Left heart failure is usually due to essential hypertension or left ventricle disease; right heart failure can develop from lung disease.

Left Heart Failure

- Left heart failure causes a backup of blood in the lungs, resulting in pulmonary edema.
- Signs and symptoms
  - Dyspnea
  - Orthopnea
  - Nonproductive cough
  - Rales
  - Tachycardia

Right Heart Failure

- Right-sided heart failure causes a backup of blood in the right atrium, which prevents complete emptying of the vena cava, resulting in systemic edema, especially in the legs and feet.
- Both types of heart failure cause fatigue, weakness, exercise intolerance, dyspnea, and sensitivity to cold temperatures.

Rheumatic Heart Disease

- Rheumatic heart disease develops because of an unusual immune reaction that occurs approximately 2 weeks after an untreated β-hemolytic streptococcal infection.

Inflammation

- Inflammation of the heart can involve all layers of heart tissue.

Endocarditis

- Endocarditis is the most common heart complication.
- Vegetations form along the outer edges of the valve cusps, causing scarring and stenosis.

Valve Disease

- Disorders of the valves of the heart may be caused by a congenital defect or an infection, such as endocarditis or rheumatic heart disease. Two specific problems can occur with valve disease.

Valve Defects

- The valve can be stenosed, restricting the forward flow of blood, or it can be incompetent, so blood can leak backward.
- The most common valve defect is mitral valve prolapse (MVP), an incompetence because of a congenital defect or due to vegetation and scarring from endocarditis.

Arteries and Veins

- Blood vessels are divided into two systems that begin and end with the heart.
  - Arteries carry oxygenated blood away from the heart
  - Capillaries are microscopic vessels responsible for the exchange of oxygen and carbon dioxide in the tissue
  - Veins carry deoxygenated blood back to the heart

Shock

- Shock, the general collapse of the circulatory system, includes decreased cardiac output, hypotension, and hypoxemia. Initial signs are extreme thirstiness, restlessness, and irritability. The body attempts to compensate for the circulatory collapse with vasoconstriction of peripheral blood vessels, causing cool, clammy skin; pallor; tachycardia; and decreased urinary output.
- Symptoms progress to a rapid, weak, and thready pulse; tachypnea; and altered levels of consciousness. If the process is not reversed, the central nervous system becomes depressed, and acute renal failure may occur.

Varicose Veins

- Varicose veins are dilated, tortuous, superficial veins that develop because the valves do not completely close, allowing blood to flow backward, thus causing the vein to distend from the increased pressure.

Deep Vein Thrombosis

- Deep vein thrombosis involves a thrombus with inflammatory changes that has attached to the deep venous system of the lower legs to cause a partial or complete obstruction of the vessel. If a thrombus becomes dislodged and begins to circulate through the general circulation, it is then called an embolus.

Disorders

- Arteriosclerosis, the thickening and loss of elasticity of arterial walls, is associated with aging. Arteriosclerosis can occur in arteries throughout the body and cause systemic ischemia and necrosis.

- Atherosclerosis, a form of arteriosclerosis, involves the formation of an atheroma (a buildup of cholesterol, cellular debris, and platelets along the inside vessel wall).
- An aneurysm is a ballooning or dilation of the wall of a vessel caused by weakening of the vessel wall.

Diagnostic Procedures
- Cardiovascular diagnostic procedures include:
  – Doppler studies of the patency of blood vessels
  – Angiography to visualize arterial pathways
  – Echocardiography to assess the structure and movement of the parts of the heart, especially the valves
  – Cardiac catheterization to visualize the heart chambers, valves, and coronary arteries

CHAPTER 45: Assisting in Geriatrics

Aging Population
- In the 2000 census, 12.4% of the U.S. population was older than 65 years. The "oldest old" (people older than 85) are the most rapidly growing age group. It is projected that people older than 65 will represent 16% of the population in 2020 and increase to 20% by 2030.

Services for the Aging
- The aging process includes the physical and sensory changes in older people. The healthcare professional recognizes the special needs of the aged and develops effective management and communication skills for better service for the older client.

Changes with Aging
- Table 45-1 in your textbook summarizes the changes in anatomy and physiology associated with aging in all body systems. Normal age-related changes can be expected and compensated for, but these become more serious in the presence of poor health habits and chronic disease.

Aging Changes
- General changes include:
  – An increase in arteriosclerosis
  – An increase in time needed to learn new material

  – A sharp decline in estrogen for women and increased risk of osteoporosis
  – An increase in malabsorption problems and constipation
  – A decrease in muscle mass
  – A tendency to gain weight
  – A deterioration of joint cartilage
  – A decreased elasticity of lung tissue
  – Presbycusis and presbyopia
  – An enlargement of the prostate and weakened bladder muscles

Management of Changes
- Age-related changes can be managed through:
  – Regular aerobic exercise and strength training
  – Weight control
  – A diet rich in fruits, vegetables, whole grains, and low in fat
  – Avoidance of sun damage to skin
  – Pelvic muscle exercises
  – Annual physical examinations with health screening

Health Issues
- The major health issues for aging people are related to an increase in atherosclerosis and potential cardiovascular disease
  – Hypertension
  – Type 2 diabetes mellitus
  – Tendency to hyperthermia and hypothermia
  – Seborrheic keratosis
  – Arthritis
  – Osteoporosis
  – Increased risk of injury from falls
  – dementia due to metabolic, cardiovascular, or Alzheimer's disease
  – pneumonia, aspiration, and reactivation of tuberculosis
  – cataracts, glaucoma, and macular degeneration;
  – depression
  – malnutrition
  – increased urinary tract infections, incontinence, and prostate enlargement
  – menopausal changes in the vaginal mucosa
  – sleep disorders such as apnea and periodic limb movement disorder (PLMD)
  – and the impact of medications on general health

MMSE
- A commonly used screening tool for dementia is the Folstein Mini Mental Status Exam, a 5-minute screening test to evaluate basic mental function in the patient's ability to recall facts, to

write, and to calculate numbers, to determine if more in-depth testing is needed.

Depression

- To screen for depression, the physician may use the Geriatric Depression Scale short form that questions the patient about daily activities, interests, and feelings. Nutritional status can be assessed through a comprehensive patient interview that considers all potential barriers to adequate nutrition.

Nutritional Status

- The nutritional status of older patients considers oral health, gastrointestinal (GI) complaints, sensorimotor changes, diet influences, and social and mental influences.

Sleep Problems

- Complaints of sleeping difficulties increase with age. Sleeping time may be slightly longer, but the quality of sleep decreases. Older people are often light sleepers and have periods of wakefulness in bed. Other factors influencing sleep patterns are medications, caffeine, alcohol, depression, and environmental or physical changes. Common sleep problems in older adults include PLMD and sleep apnea.

Caregivers

- Aging persons prefer to remain in their homes as long as possible. Adult day care centers can provide supervision for older adults who are taken care of by family members in the evening. They also serve as respite for a caregiver.

Assisted Living

- Assisted-living facilities (retirement homes or board-and-care homes) are appropriate for older adults who need assistance with some activities of daily living, such as bathing, dressing, and walking. Skilled nursing facilities provide 24-hour medical care and supervision. In addition to medical care, residents receive physical, personal, occupational, and speech therapy.

MA Role

- Develop effective communication skills reflective of age-related sensorimotor changes. To reinforce independence, aging patients require more time, and should be scheduled for longer appointments.

Elder Care

- Adequate lighting in the waiting room with forms in large print; an examination room equipped with furniture, magazines, and treatment folders especially designed for the elderly patient; and inviting a professional in the management of the elderly patient for in-service training improves the quality of elder care.

Interviews

- Ask the patient directly what is wrong rather than discussing the patient with family members.
- Give the patient your full attention rather than continuing with multiple tasks while he or she is speaking.
- Older people may take a little longer to process information, but they are capable of understanding.
- Don't hurry through explanations or questions, but take time to review a form or give instructions.
- Use referrals and community resources for patient and family support.

Communications

- Addressing the patient with an appropriate title.
- Introduce yourself and the purpose of a procedure before touching the patient.
- Establish eye contact and get the patient's attention before beginning to speak.
- Use expanded speech, gestures, demonstrations, or written instructions in block print.
- Repeat the message as needed for understanding.
- Observe the patient's nonverbal behaviors as cues to indicate if he or she understands.
- Allow time to process information.
- Avoid distractions.
- Involve family members as needed.

Legal Issues

- Legal and ethical issues for aging patients include adequate informed consent; the use of advance directives; and staying alert for signs of possible elder abuse.

CHAPTER 46: Principles of Electrocardiography

Heartbeat Origin

- The heart beats in response to an electrical signal that originates in the sinoatrial (SA) node in the right atrium, spreads over the atria, and causes atrial contraction.

Ventricular Contraction

- This impulse continues to the atrioventricular (AV) node, through the bundle of His, and then through the right and left bundle branches, eventually causing ventricular contraction.

Electrocardiogram

- The horizontal lines on the ECG paper permit the determination of the intensity of the electrical activity or the relative strength of the heartbeat.

Paper Record

- The stronger the beat, the greater the vertical deflection on the paper. The vertical lines represent time.
- The large squares each represent 0.2 seconds. Five of them equal 1 second.

Electrode Placement

- Taking an ECG requires knowledge of where to place the electrodes accurately and how to connect the leads to obtain the most accurate recording possible.

Artifacts

- The medical assistant must recognize and correct the most common types of artifacts on the ECG recording.

Preparing a Patient

- To prepare a patient for an ECG or a stress test, explain why and how the procedure is to be done.

Reducing Anxiety

- When the patients understand the test, they are much less anxious during the procedure.

P Wave

- The P wave results from the contraction or depolarization of the atria.

QRS Complex

- The QRS complex results from the contraction or depolarization of the ventricles.

T Wave

- The T wave occurs when the ventricles relax or repolarize, getting ready for the next contraction.

Leads

- The 12-lead ECG consists of three limb leads
  - I
  - II
  - III
- Three augmented leads (aVR, aVL, and aVF)
- Six precordial or chest leads (V_1, V_2, V_3, V_4, V_5, and V_6)

Heart Function

- These leads record the electrical activity from different directions, giving the physician a picture of the function of different areas of the heart.

CHAPTER 47: Assisting with Diagnostic Imaging

Radiography and Fluoroscopy

- X-ray imaging procedures have a wide variety of applications; both techniques are used for a single study.
- Radiography produces still images, usually on photographic film.
- Fluoroscopy enables the radiologist to view the x-ray image directly and to observe motion.

Magnetic Resonance Imaging

- Magnetic resonance imaging (MRI) uses a strong magnetic field and radio wave pulses to produce images of all parts of the body, including bone, soft tissue, and blood vessels.

Nuclear Medicine and Sonography

- Nuclear medicine studies demonstrate the function of organs and tissues by mapping the radiation after radioactive tracers have been ingested or injected.
- Sonography demonstrates soft tissues by using high-frequency sound waves.

Radiography

- Preparation for chest radiography involves undressing to the waist and donning a gown.
- Upper gastrointestinal (GI) series, the patient must fast and avoid drinking water, chewing gum, and smoking for at least 8 hours before the examination.
- Lower GI series, an extensive bowel cleansing, involves a low-residue or clear liquid diet, forced fluids, cathartics, a suppository, and a low-volume enema.

Preparation

- Intravenous urography (IVU): some bowel preparation, such as a cathartic on the previous evening, and nothing by mouth (NPO) orders for a period before the examination.
- CT examination of the abdomen with an oral contrast medium: After a fast, the patient must arrive at the imaging center from 1 to 2 hours in advance to drink the oral contrast medium.

X-ray Machine

- The principal components of the x-ray machine are the tube in its barrel-shaped housing. The collimator is mounted on the tube housing.

Tube Housing

- The tube housing with its attachments is mounted on the tube support, which may be suspended from the ceiling or attached to a tube stand that runs in a track on the floor.

Table and Console

- The radiographic table and an upright cassette holder provide support for the patient and the film, and incorporate a grid device. At the control console, the operator selects the exposure settings and makes the exposure. It is located in the control booth.

Body Planes

- The sagittal plane divides the body into right and left parts.
- The coronal plane divides the body into anterior and posterior parts.
- The transverse plane divides the body into superior and inferior parts.

Projections

- For a frontal projection [anteroposterior (AP) or posteroanterior (PA)], the coronal plane is parallel to the film, and the sagittal plane is perpendicular to it. For a lateral projection, the sagittal plane is parallel to the film, and the coronal plane is perpendicular to it. Neither the sagittal plane nor the coronal plane is parallel to the film on an oblique projection.

Planes

- For a PA projection, the patient is facing the film with the coronal plane parallel to the film. Lateral projections require the coronal plane to be perpendicular to the film.

More Projections

- For an oblique projection, neither the coronal nor the sagittal plane is parallel to the film. For an axial or semiaxial projection, the x-ray beam is angled toward the patient's head or feet, along the long axis of the body.

Cassette

- The image-receptor system for radiography usually consists of a cassette with two intensifying screens that give off light when stimulated by x-ray energy, and double-emulsion film that lies between the intensifying screens.

Film Exposure

- The film is exposed on both sides, principally by the light emitted from the screens. This system greatly reduces the amount of radiation and exposure time involved in making exposures compared with direct exposure of film by x-rays.

Handling Cassettes

- Cassettes are unloaded and reloaded in the darkroom under safelight illumination only.

- Ensure that the door is locked, your hands are clean and dry, and the film is not creased, bent, or scraped in loading and unloading.
- Reload the cassette with only one fresh film and latch securely.
- Keep the loading bench clean to prevent dirt from getting into the cassette.

Film Identification

- Record the identity of the patient in the image and the date and location of the examination. Serious errors in diagnosis and treatment might occur if films are not correctly identified.
- Type identification information on a card that is inserted into a photographic printer in the darkroom. The printer stamps the information on the film after it is removed from the cassette and before it is processed.

Risks

- The health risks of radiography are extremely small: a slightly increased likelihood of developing cataracts, cancer, or leukemia.
- There is a potential for minimal decrease in lifespan and for a negative outcome when exposure occurs to the abdominal area during pregnancy.
- Exposure of the reproductive organs may cause genetic changes that can be passed on to future generations.

Safety Precautions

- Stay completely behind the lead barrier of the control booth during exposures. Occupationally exposed persons must not hold patients or cassettes during exposures.
- Any staff required to be in the x-ray room should be shielded by a lead apron, should stay as far from radiation sources as possible, and should minimize the time they are in the room.

Exposure Risks

- The risks associated with x-ray exposure during pregnancy are very small unless the exposure is in excess of 5 rad to the abdominal area. These risks include spontaneous abortion, birth defects, growth retardation, and cancer or leukemia in childhood.
- Post warning signs in the x-ray department and ask women of childbearing age whether they may be pregnant.

Medical Record

- Diagnostic images are the property of the facility in which they are made. They are a part of the legal medical record and must be accessible for a period specified by state law, usually 5 to 7 years.

Borrowing Images

- To lend or transfer images to other healthcare providers, if the patient signs a release, send the images directly to the borrowing provider if possible, and keep a record of the loan.

Examinations and Interpretations

- Only licensed practitioners are permitted to order x-ray examinations or to interpret x-ray images.

CHAPTER 48: Assisting in the Clinical Laboratory

Responsibilities

- The clinical laboratory is responsible for the analysis of blood and body fluids, providing the physician with test results needed to diagnose and manage a patient's condition.

Tests

- Most physician's offices that perform laboratory testing will do routine urinalysis, complete blood counts, pregnancy testing, and throat cultures.

Regulatory Agencies

- Agencies that regulate the laboratory include the U.S. Department of Labor, the U.S. Department of Health and Human Services, and the Environmental Protection Agency (EPA). Professional agencies that provide guidelines include the national Committee for Clinical Laboratory Standards and the College of American Pathologists.

Enforcement

- All of the agencies provide recommendations for procedures in the clinical laboratory, but not all can enforce them. The U.S. Dept of Labor and the EPA can impose stiff fines for failing to follow regulations, but the standard precautions set forth by the Centers for Disease Controls are recommended but not enforceable.

Minimizing Risks

- Risks can be minimized in all areas of the laboratory by using common sense and by having a formal safety training program and an up-to-date safety manual.

Requisition

- The laboratory requisition must identify the patient, the ordering physician, the test ordered, and the details regarding the collection (such as time and source) of the specimen.

Chain of Custody

- Chain of Custody is a method to ensure that a specimen is handled in a way that will not compromise the test results.
- All individuals who handle or test the specimen must be identified in writing and provide a signature.

Quality Control

- Quality assurance involves procedures undertaken to ensure that each patient is provided excellent care.
- Quality control, ensuring that laboratory testing is accurate and reliable, is part of a quality assurance program.

Time Designations

- Greenwich time uses the designation of AM and PM, whereas military time uses the 24-hour clock. Three-fifteen PM is equivalent to 1515.

Temperature

- The Celsius (centigrade) thermometer is used in the clinical laboratory; in everyday life, we use the Fahrenheit system. The incubator is usually set at 37° C (98° F); the autoclave sterilizes at 121° C (254° F); and refrigerator temperature is 2° to 8° C (35° to 46° F).

Measurement

- Liquid volume is measured in liters; distance is measured in meters; and mass is measured in grams. Prefixes commonly used in the clinical laboratory include milli (0.001), centi (0.01), micro (0.000001), deci (0.1), and kilo (1000).

Pipettes

- Pipettes are chosen according to the job they perform. A pipetting device such as a bulb or pump should be attached, and particular attention must be given to the emptying of the pipette. Never use the mouth in pipetting.

Dilutions

- Dilutions are prepared by mixing volumes of blood, body fluids, or reagents with volumes of water, saline, or buffer.
- Dilution refers to parts in total volume and is an expression of concentration.

Microscope

- The microscope can be divided into the illumination system (light source, condenser and iris diaphragm lever); the frame (base, adjustment knobs, arm, stage, stage control); and the magnification system (objective lenses on the revolving nosepiece, oculars).

Centrifuges

- A variety of centrifuges are available. The proper tube must be used and protected from breakage; loads must be carefully balanced; specimens must be capped to prevent aerosols; and centrifuges should remain closed while in operation.

Autoclaves

- Autoclaves provide sterilization by exposing materials to steam under pressure; reaching a temperature of 121° C.
- Specialized tape or spore strips must be used to ensure that the proper temperature has been reached.

CHAPTER 49: Assisting in the Analysis of Urine

Disorder Detection

- Routine urinalysis is performed primarily as a screening test to detect metabolic and physiologic disorders.

Urine Formation

- Urine is formed through a filtration mechanism in the kidney via the nephrons. It is stored in the bladder and voided through the urethra.

Urine Collection

- Some urine collections must be timed around meals or fasts. Routine urinalysis requires no special preparation, whereas a clean-catch midstream requires cleansing of the external genitalia. Only urine that will be cultured must be collected in a sterile container.

Examination

- The physical examination of the urine involves determination of color, turbidity, and specific gravity. Odor and foam color may be noted.

Chemical Testing

- The chemical examination of urine involves determination of levels of glucose, pH, protein, ketones, blood, bilirubin, urobilinogen, nitrite, specific gravity, and leukocyte esterase.

Formed Elements

- Formed elements in the urine sediment include casts, cells, and crystals. Artifacts are not reported.

Timed Specimens

- Timed urine specimens are collected to determine the amount of an analyte in the urine during a given time frame.

Patient Instructions

- Proper patient instruction is necessary for an acceptable clean-catch midstream urine. The external genitalia are cleaned to avoid contaminating the urine.

Complete Urinalysis

- A complete urinalysis involves the physical, chemical, and microscopic assessment. The three must correlate with each other.

Supplies

- Most testing of urine requires reagent strips or tablets. These supplies must be stored in dark, cool, moisture-free areas.

Clinitest

- The Clinitest detects reducing sugars, including glucose, in the urine. It is superior to the reagent strip test because it detects sugars other than glucose.

Protein Measurement

- The sulfosalicylic acid test is a precipitation test that evaluates the amount of protein in the urine.

Pregnancy Tests

- Pregnancy tests detect human chorionic gonadotropin, a hormone produced by the placenta.

CHAPTER 50: Assisting in Phlebotomy

Venipuncture

- Venipuncture requires a double-pointed needle, evacuated collection tubes, and an adapter, or a syringe fitted with a needle, a tourniquet, an alcohol prep pad, gauze or cotton, a sterile bandage, latex gloves, and a biohazard disposal container.

Tourniquet

- The tourniquet prevents venous flow out of the site, causing the veins to bulge. This makes veins easier to locate and puncture.

The Needle

- The venipuncture needle has a shaft with one end cut at an angle (bevel). The other end attaches to the syringe or to an adapter and is called the hub.

Needle Disposal

- The opening in the tip, the lumen, is measured in gauge numbers. Needles should be disposed of in a sharps container, and the medical assistant should not recap a needle.

Syringes

- Syringes are more commonly used for blood collection from the elderly, whose veins are more fragile; from children, whose veins are small; and from the obese, whose veins are deep. Using a syringe allows a more controlled draw.

Butterfly

- A winged infusion set (butterfly) is used on blood draws from the hand and from children. The needle has a small lumen and is more easily inserted into small veins.

Anticoagulant

- Whole blood will coagulate unless mixed with an anticoagulant. The anticoagulant must be matched with the test to avoid interference with results.

Serum and Plasma

- When clotted blood is centrifuged, the cells and liquid separate; the liquid portion is the serum.
- When anticoagulated blood is centrifuged, the liquid that remains is the plasma.

Tube Additives

- Collect evacuated tubes in a specific order to prevent carryover of tube additives.

Routine Venipuncture

- Routine venipuncture begins with greeting and identifying the patient. The medical assistant then assembles the equipment, locates the vein, draws the blood, removes and properly disposes of the needle, tends to the puncture site, labels the tubes, and delivers them to the laboratory. Observe standard precautions during the procedure.

Using Tourniquets

- Tourniquets are snugly tied around the upper arm (or wrist for a hand draw) in a fashion that permits easy release. Leaving the tourniquet on for a prolonged period results in hemoconcentration.

Withdrawing Specimens

- Needles are inserted into the vein at a 15- to 30-degree angle. This angle may have to be increased for obese patients. Probing excessively may lead to a hematoma or nerve damage.

Before the needle is removed, release the tourniquet. Immediately after removal, apply pressure to the puncture site with gauze.

Vein Choice

- The median cephalic vein is the vein of choice for phlebotomy, but blood can be drawn from the cephalic vein and the median basilic vein. Avoid the basilic vein if possible.

Capillary Puncture

- Capillary puncture is the preferred test for hematocrit or hemoglobin analysis; it is routinely performed on children younger than 2 years.
- The middle two fingers (the lateral sides) are generally used for capillary puncture; in infants, the heel is the site of choice. Avoid the center of the heel.
- Capillary puncture is performed much like venipuncture. No tourniquet is used however. The first drop of blood is routinely wiped away after the puncture because it is contaminated with tissue fluid.
- Capillary blood can be collected in microtainer devices, capillary pipettes, or on filter paper test cards.

Dermal Puncture

- Dermal puncture devices are made of sharp sterile metal. Some make a cut of a specified depth, and some have internal safety devices that retract the blade after use.

CHAPTER 51: Assisting in the Analysis of Blood

Hematology

- The hematology section of the laboratory deals with:
  - Counting red blood cells, white blood cells, and platelets
  - Differentiating white blood cells on a stained smear;
  - Measuring the percentage of red blood cells in blood (hematocrit)
  - Determining the oxygen-carrying capacity of the blood (hemoglobin)

Complete Blood Count

- The complete blood cell count (CBC) is the most frequent laboratory procedure with blood. It can provide a wealth of information concerning a patient's condition.

Blood Elements

- Whole blood is composed of formed elements suspended in a clear yellow liquid portion called plasma, which makes up about 55% of the blood by volume.
- The remaining 45% consists of the formed cellular elements: erythrocytes (red blood cells), leukocytes (white blood cells), and thrombocytes (platelets). These cellular elements all have special functions.

Thrombocytes

- Thrombocytes are cytoplasmic fragments of a large cell in the bone marrow, the megakaryocyte. They are the smallest formed elements of the blood.
- They are discoid until activated, when they become globular and form finger-like cytoplasmic extensions called pseudopodia.

Plasma

- Plasma is a highly complex liquid, is involved in the structure and function of the blood cells.
- Plasma is the carrier for the formed elements and other substances such as proteins, carbohydrates, fats, hormones, enzymes, mineral salts, gases, and waste products.

Plasma Composition

- Plasma is composed of about 90% water, 9% protein, and 1% other chemical substances. When the plasma proteins and other components are used up during clotting, the remaining liquid is called serum.

Hematocrit

- The hematocrit (Hct) is the percentage of packed red blood cells in a volume of blood. The test separates the cellular elements from the plasma by centrifugation.

Hemoglobin

- The hemoglobin (Hgb) determination measures the oxygen-carrying capacity of the blood. It can be performed as part of the CBC or as an individual test.

White Blood Cell Count

- The white blood cell count approximates the total number of leukocytes in circulating blood to aid the physician in determining if an infection is present, to diagnose of leukemia, to follow the course of a disease, and to determine if the patient is responding to treatment.

White Blood Cells

- The normal white blood cell count varies with age; it is higher in newborns and decreases throughout life. The average adult range is between 4500 and 12,000 cells/mm³. Increase in the white blood cell count is called leukocytosis.

Blood Smear

- A blood smear shows the cellular components of the blood in as natural a state as possible. The morphology of the leukocytes, erythrocytes, and platelets and their size, shape, and maturity can be evaluated. Examining a blood smear is part of a CBC.

Sedimentation Rate

- The erythrocyte sedimentation rate (ESR) measures the rate of separation of erythrocytes from plasma. The test is used as a general indication of inflammation. Increases are found in acute and chronic infections, rheumatoid arthritis, tuberculosis, hepatitis, cancer, multiple myeloma, rheumatic fever, and lupus erythematosus.

Prothrombin Time

- Coagulation testing is usually performed in the hematology laboratory. A test to determine prothrombin time with a hand-held, CLIA-waived instrument uses whole blood or citrated plasma. The "protime" (or "prothrombin time") measures how well the blood clots.

Serologic Tests

- Serologic testing provides information about past or present infections by antigenantibody reactions. Most serologic testing is done with individual testing kits. The first step is to review the package insert provided by the manufacturer.

BTA Test

- CLIA-waived tests that can be performed by a medical assistant include bladder tumor–associated antigen (BTA), Helicobacter pylori antibodies, and infectious mononucleosis antibodies. The BTA test is a rapid, single-step immunoassay that detects the presence of an antigen shed by the bladder cells. Five drops of urine are placed into the sample well of the test device, and positive or negative results are provided in 5 minutes.

Blood Antigen Systems

- There are two major blood antigen systems: the ABO (or Landsteiner) system and the Rh system. In the ABO system, there are four major blood groups: A, B, O, and AB. A person is either Rh positive or Rh negative.

Chemistry

- Increasingly, clinical chemistry testing is performed in the physician's office laboratory. Several clinical chemistry tests can be performed by the medical assistant.

Glucose

- Glucose is used as a fuel by many cells in the body; it usually is the only substance used by the brain. Maintenance of blood glucose levels within the normal range is vitally important to the homeostasis of the acid–base balance of the human body, so glucose is the most frequently tested analyte.

Cholesterol

- Cholesterol is a fat-like substance (lipid) in cell membranes. It is needed to form bile acids and steroid hormones. Cholesterol travels in the blood in distinct particles containing both lipid and proteins, called lipoproteins. The cholesterol level in the blood is determined partly by inheritance and partly by acquired factors such as diet, calorie balance, and level of physical activity.

Diabetes

- Several new laboratory tests help evaluate the blood glucose level: glycohemoglobin, fructosamine, and glycosylated protein. These tests are not substitutes for monitoring blood glucose levels, but they give different information about the diabetic's health, and add a new dimension to the evaluation of diabetes.

Automated Analyzers

- Automated blood chemisty analyzers are often used to perform blood chemistry testing. Several analytes may be detected at once. A chemistry panel, such as a renal or liver panel, will determine the levels of several related analytes.

Toxicology

- Toxicology is the study of poisonous substances and their effects on the body. The toxicology laboratory tests body fluids and tissues to monitor therapeutic drugs such as digoxin (a cardiac medication) and theophylline (an asthma medication), or to detect poisonings by herbicides, metals, animal toxins, and poisonous gases (such as carbon monoxide).
- Laboratory testing for illegal drugs or alcohol may be an employment, insurance, or governmental requirement. Serum (blood) testing is a more accurate test for current impairment

and/or time of ingestion, but urine is the specimen of choice for most routine screening.

- For routine screening, a random specimen is usually collected. Safeguards ensure that the specimen is fresh and truly from the patient. In some cases, a strict chain of custody is required. The substance being tested for or its metabolite often remains in the urine much longer than the impairment or intoxication, so urine screening is favored over serum or blood screening.

CHAPTER 52: Assisting in Microbiology

Specimen Gathering

- Specimens must be collected in sterile containers. Transport systems often contain a transport medium that keeps the organisms alive, but does not let them multiply.

Incubation

- All microbes require nutrients to stay alive. Aerobes require oxygen; anaerobes die in the presence of oxygen. Most pathogens prefer an incubation temperature of 37° C.

Viruses

- Viruses differ from bacteria in that they are not cells. Viruses are composed of a core of nucleic acid surrounded by a protein coat. They do not metabolize, and they cannot replicate on their own.

Disease-causing Organisms

- Bacteria are prokaryotic, but fungi, protozoa, and parasites are eukaryotic. Many different species cause disease.

Identification

- Identification of bacteria begins with the observation of their morphology. Cocci are spherical organisms, bacilli are rod-shaped, and spirochetes are spiral-shaped.

Bacterial Arrangement

- Staphylococci are cocci in clusters, streptococci and streptobacilli are arranged in chains, and diplococci and diplobacilli are arranged in pairs.

Gram Stain

- The most important stain in microbiology is the gram stain. The four steps involve the addition of the primary stain, crystal violet; the mordant, iodine; the decolorizer, alcohol; and the counterstain, safranin. Gram-positive bacteria stain purple, and gram-negative bacteria stain pink or red.

Growth Media

- Growth media consist of nutrients selected for certain species. Media can be liquid, or they can be made solid by the addition of agar. Solid media can be prepared as petri plates or as tube media.

Media

- Media can be all-purpose and support the growth of many species or they can be selective, permitting growth of only a certain type of microbe.
- Media can allow differentiation of species based on color changes caused by different biochemical reactions. Enriched media support the growth of fastidious bacteria.

Rapid Tests

- Rapid tests identify some component of the infectious agent and do not require culture.

Susceptibility Testing

- Antimicrobial susceptibility testing uses disks impregnated with antimicrobial agents dropped onto the surface of an agar plate inoculated with a pathogen.
- The pathogen will display susceptibility, resistance, or an intermediate reaction to the antimicrobial agent. The zone of inhibition is measured around each disk and compared with a chart provided by the manufacturer.

Patient Confidentiality

- Patient confidentiality is of utmost importance, but certain infections, such as sexually transmitted diseases and tuberculosis, must be reported to the Centers for Disease Control and Prevention and to the local board of health.

CHAPTER 53: Surgical Supplies and Instruments

Supplies

- The solutions used in minor surgery include:
  - Sterile water for mixing with medications or rinsing instruments
  - Sterile saline for injection or wound irrigations
  - Antiseptic skin cleansers such as povidone/iodine (Betadine) or chlorohexidine (Hibiclens) for site preparations

  - Local anesthetics including ethyl chloride or Fluoromethane
  - Topical applications
  - Lidocaine, chloroprocaine (Nescaine), or bupivacaine (Sensorcaine) injectables

Local Anesthetics

- Local anesthetics may come packaged with or without epinephrine. The physician may use topical silver nitrate to control local bleeding.

Instruments

- Surgical instruments are classified according to their use: cutting, grasping, retracting, probing, or dilating tools.
- The components include the type of handle, the closing mechanism, and the jaws. Instrument tips may be either straight or curved.
- Surgical instruments are expensive and must be cared for properly. Examine instruments when purchased for proper working order and possible faults with mechanisms. Keep stainless steel instruments separate from other metal types.

Cleaning

- Each instrument must be cleaned according to manufacturer guidelines, unlocked, and disinfected immediately after use. Some instruments must be washed by hand in a mild, neutral pH solution with a soft brush.
- Most instruments can be cleaned with an ultrasonic washer. This prevents possible injury with sharp instruments.

Instrument Types

- The instruments used in minor surgical procedures are dependent on the type of procedure and physician preference.

Disposable Packs

- Disposable prewrapped surgical packs are widely available.
- Be familiar with what is needed for a particular procedure and with what the operating physician prefers.

Sutures

- Sutures are absorbable for internal sutures or nonabsorbable for skin closures.
- Catgut or vicryl are absorbable materials, whereas nonabsorbable sutures can be made of silk, nylon, or staples.
- Suture materials range from smaller gauges for finer tissues below 0 (aught) to thicker gauges above 0.
- Sutures come in various lengths.

Needles

- Surgical needles are either straight or curved: the sharper the curve, the deeper the surgeon can pass the needle. Most needles are manufactured with the suture material attached. The medical assistant must ask the physician for his or her preference.

CHAPTER 54: Surgical Asepsis and Assisting with Surgical Procedures

Aseptic Technique

- Proper surgical aseptic technique helps to prevent unnecessary infections in surgical patients.
- A "break" in technique can have dire consequences for the patient. Everyone on the surgical team is responsible for preventing and correcting breaks in technique.

Sterile Fields

- Air currents carry bacteria, so body motions over a sterile field and talking should be kept to a minimum.
- Sterile team members should always face each other.
- Always keep the sterile field in your view. Never turn your back on a sterile field or wander away from it.
- Nonsterile persons should never reach over a sterile field.

Sterile Surfaces

- Everything sterile is white, and everything that is not sterile is black. There is no gray!
- Sterile surfaces must never come into contact with nonsterile surfaces.

Indicators

- Indicators can be used to prove that a package was sterilized in the steam autoclave. Other indicators can prove that the contents of the package were exposed to sufficient temperature for sufficient time to achieve sterilization.

Wrapping

- Inspect muslin wrappers before each use. Discard any wrappers with holes.
- Wrap all hinged instruments in the open position to allow full steam penetration of the joint.
- Place a gauze sponge around the tips of sharp instruments to prevent them from piercing the wrapping material.

- If a number of instruments are to be placed on a stainless steel tray for wrapping, place a double-folded towel on the tray before the instruments to protect them.
- With sterilizing bags, insert the jaws of the instruments first to ensure that the grasping end of the instrument can be reached easily when the bag is opened.

Labels

- Indicate on the wrapper what is in the package, or label it with a code. This code should correspond to a list of instruments that is stored with the pack after sterilization.
- Label the contents with the date sterilized and your initials. Use a permanent marker, never a ballpoint pen.

Infection Control

- The legal and ethical concerns of infection control affect everyone on the surgical team. All individuals involved in surgical care must be aware of all legal and ethical practices that apply to excellent patient care.

Informed Consent

- Surgery cannot be legally performed without informed consent without risking the possibility of battery. The consent clearly limits what procedure can be done.

Patient Education

- Education about surgical procedures uses information sheets or pamphlets given to the patient before surgery, conversations with the patient about the procedure, and information sheets to prevent and minimize complications.

Informed Patients

- The informed patient is more relaxed, cooperative, and much more pleasant to deal with than the uninformed, frightened patient who did not receive adequate explanations.

Office Surgery

- Certain procedures should be followed before the appointment.
  - Have the necessary consent forms ready to sign.
  - Give the patient all the necessary preoperative instructions, such as medications to use and special skin-cleansing instructions.
  - Tell the patient to bring a relative or friend to drive him or her home after the surgery.
  - Tell the patient to leave jewelry and other valuables at home.
  - Call the patient the day before the scheduled surgery to confirm any special instructions.

CHAPTER 55: Career Development and Life Skills

Job-search Skills

- Approximately 85% of individuals do not have any formal training in job-search skills, so take time to learn the best methods.

Training Advantages

- Training decreases the time spent looking for work, and increases the benefits and salary offered. The medical assistant will also be more comfortable during interviews and throughout the job-search process.

Employers' Expectations

- Employers desire an employee with a good appearance, who looks as if he or she fits in the medical profession, who is dependable, and who has the skills to do the job.

Job Skills

- Job skills are those used to actually perform a job, like venipunctures or scheduling appointments.

Skills

- Self-management skills, such as honesty and dependability, are usually a part of the medical assistant's personality.
- Transferable skills can be taken from one job to another or used on any job. Examples include the ability to communicate effectively or lead and manage individuals.

Job Searches

- Networking and contacting employers directly are the two best methods of job searching.
- Networking involves individuals who can assist in finding employment, including co-workers, other students, relatives, or friends who provide leads to potential employers.

Contacting Employers

- Contacting employers directly includes taking resumes to specific offices or setting appointments to gain knowledge about the facility, and then later using that knowledge during the job search. These two methods are more effective than most traditional means of finding a job

The Resume

- Avoid errors on a resume. Be sure that everything is spelled correctly, but do not rely on the computer spell-check program alone. Proofread and have someone else proofread your resume to catch overlooked errors.
- Salary expectations should never be stated on the resume, and a photograph should not be included. Do not include personal information such as height and weight.

Preparation

- Demographic information on other employers should be taken to interviews and kept handy when filling out job applications.
- Asking for a phone book to look up the address of a former employer demonstrates a lack of preparation and planning on the part of the potential employee.

To the Instructor

SUGGESTIONS FOR WORKING WITH SECOND-LANGUAGE STUDENTS

The following are some suggestions for working with second-language students. Many of these ideas you may already use in some variation in working with all of your students.

Structured Participation with Teams and Role Play

When planning discussions and exercises for the class, look for structured ways to have the students respond orally and in writing. The student with limited English may be shy about voluntarily asking questions and participating in discussions, but they will be willing to work as part of a small team to complete an exercise, so that each member of the team has a task. They also work well with role playing when they are familiar with who they are pretending to be or what they should say. (It is amazing how lab coats, medical assistant's pins, and bathrobes help to get them into roles. It may also add a little humor and help to reduce inhibitions. Of course, some students may resist and should not be forced to wear a costume.)

Be Open to Questions

Most teachers give lip service to being open to questions, but sometimes our attitudes indicate otherwise—our body language, lack of time in and out of class, reluctance to spend time with one student at the expense of others—the reasons are myriad. This may be especially difficult for the English-as-a-Second-Language (ESL) student. They may be shy or not understand when and how to ask questions appropriately. In some cultures, asking questions may mean exposing one's ignorance or may reflect on the teacher's ability to get the information across. Students might feel that if they ask for help, they will be considered lazy or stupid. Therefore, you may need to make a special effort to encourage students to ask questions. Having a special time for questions will help (beyond the obligatory "Are there any questions?" to which shy ESL students may not respond). You may need to check specifically with the limited English student (in a way that will not be embarrassing): "Kim, is that clear for you?" You might set aside a specific time when ESL students can come to you for questions or to express feelings and frustrations. Be ready to make the first move yourself. Checking for comprehension early on and making appropriate recommendations can prevent much anguish later.

First-Language Buddies

Encourage pairing with a native speaker who is willing to practice conversation and pronunciation with the second-language speaker and to answer questions about meanings and culture. They may even wish to study together. This can give the native speaker an opportunity to learn about another culture and become more comfortable listening to and working with someone with a different language and culture.

Pocket Notebook

Ask each student to buy a small alphabetized address or notebook in which to list words in everyday speech that they have heard in class but for which they do not know the more general meaning or that have a different general usage. For example, *blanch* can refer to skin color or to cooking vegetables; void can refer to urine or to checks; and a pillow *case* can also be called a pillow *slip*. Ask to see their notebooks periodically or have a time when they can share them with you, the class, or their buddy.

Restating

Have students restate concepts or explanations in "plain English" back to you to make sure they understand the concept and will be able to explain it later to a patient. "Can you put that into your own words?" Be suspect rather than satisfied when you hear the textbook phrases coming back at you. Have students practice telling each other acronyms to make sure they can pronounce and understand them correctly.

Special Teaching Techniques

Role Playing

Role-playing is especially important for ESL students who need to practice their English as well as their medical assisting skills because they have to respond spontaneously in realistic situations. Pairing a native English speaker as the "patient" with an ESL student as the "medical assistant" elicits a natural-sounding dialogue because the native speaker probably knows something of what the patient might say and the ESL student has the opportunity to practice English. Mixing the two speakers also has the advantage of allowing the ESL student to hear natural English and the native speaker to hear accented speech to learn how to understand it better. With luck, some cross-cultural interaction will occur at the same time. Role playing works best when students know who they are to be and what they should say. Roles can be scripted at first or worked out ahead of time with the other players. It may be good to have the roles first modeled by native English speakers. As suggested earlier, use of costumes (e.g., lab coats, bathrobes) also helps.

Categorizing

Categorizing involves assigning lists of words, phrases, situations, or actions to their correct groupings; generating the words for a given category; or discovering the categories contained within a list. The student is required to think about the meaning of the words and, at the same time, practice using and writing them. If done in a group of mixed language speakers, it also necessitates the use of good English skills to accomplish the task.

Focused Grammar Exercises

Ask questions to get a specific response, which is especially crucial in the choice of verb tenses. The student should answer in the same tense or mode in which the question is asked. Here are some examples.

"When you went into the room, what was the patient doing?" *He was sitting on the floor.*
"What is he doing?" *He is sitting on the floor.*
"What just happened?" *He fell off of the examination table.*
"What was he doing when he fell?" *He was trying to get into his wheelchair.*

If the student uses the incorrect tense (*He is trying to get into his wheelchair*), the question should be asked again:

"That's what he is doing now. What *was* he doing?"

Have the students practice temporal phrases that indicate when something happens: a few minutes ago, since June, since 2:00 p.m., for 2 hours, in 15 minutes, already, just now, last week, and so on. Try not to let an incorrect usage slip by just because you understand what the student means. In another context, it may not be so clear.

If tenses and time phrases are not used and understood correctly, it can become unclear whether a task has been done or is yet to be done. Also, a patient may not know if something has happened or is yet to happen. The importance of this aspect of language cannot be overstated. The frustration of the office manager or physician is nothing compared to the well-being of the patient.

Culture

A good way to focus students on issues and to involve them in class participations is to discuss issues and attitudes they know personally. In all questions about students' native cultures and countries, be careful to be nonjudgmental in the wording of your questions, tone of voice, and comments about responses. Constructing an "unloaded" question or topic is not easy. The purpose should be to focus on the issue, elicit information, and become aware of differences and attitudes, not to evaluate them.

When we are aware of our own attitudes and biases, it is easier to handle them appropriately. Point out to students that this skill is one that medical assistants need to use in working with patients and in taking histories with their own and other cultures. It is useful to have the native-born first-language students examine the same issues in their own culture and families. Point out that all students are moving from thinking in a social context to a scientific one. Some of our attitudes will be supported, others will not. It is important for us to know where we are beginning and why. Because an instructor cannot know or teach everything about every culture, using the students to help learn about one another's culture can serve as an information gathering and sharing experience, as well as a wonderful language exercise.

One particularly interesting discussion topic is home remedies, which reflect typical treatments and attitudes about medicine in the native country. Ask the students how their parents or grandparents treated certain maladies. This points out that we are all products of our culture, whether foreign born or not. It also shows how ideas change over time, gives newcomers insights into American culture, and provides a common ground for discussion. Another topic is cultural attitudes toward such things as asking questions, working with the opposite sex, employer expectations, loyalties, family, privacy, touching, and caring for the sick and elderly. Also interesting is body language, which can be covered by demonstrating gestures and postures and discussing how they differ. Include personal space and appropriate touching in each culture. Another topic is personal feelings and attitudes about a variety of controversial issues.

Communication

Dialogues

The instructor should supply sample phrases and dialogues. Sometimes telling a second language speaker to say something is not enough. The speaker needs to know specifically what to say and how to say it. Supply or model sample phrases or actual dialogue. Problem solving is another effective way to use dialogues. Groups work together to solve a problem, then write their own dialogues for the situation. Students can present their dialogues, generated alone, in pairs, or in a group, to the class.

General Communication

Offer examples of what to say in the following types of situations: asking for clarification and requesting help; reporting, incidents, and accidents; apologizing and warning; negotiating, such as "not now, but later"; handling conflicts and complaints; making small talk and using social language. Practicing problem-solving situations in a group of first- and second-language students is an excellent way to learn together.

Verbal and Nonverbal Communication

Talk about types of nonverbal communication in the United States and other cultures. Point out when and what types of topics Americans talk about; what we say and what we do not say; and when we talk and when we do not talk. Explain how to interrupt politely and how to excuse oneself.

Pronunciation

A good pronunciation exercise is to have students practice saying and listening to acronyms and abbreviations or similar sounding word pairs with a partner. Have the listener write down what she hears and then ask for repetition when she does not understand. Then compare lists to see if the words were pronounced and heard correctly. They can then discuss the meanings of the acronyms or words.

APPENDIX B

Instructions for Transferring Files

In order for an instructor to transfer files back and forth from school to home, the instructor must first download the free version of WINZIP onto both computers.

You can download this by clicking the link below. It will automatically begin installing WINZIP to your computer.

http://www.winzip.com/downauto.cgi?winzip81.exe

Once **WINZIP** is installed the instructor can transfer files by zipping and saving the data folder to a floppy disk.

1. Double-Click on **My Computer** icon
2. Double-Click on **Local Disk** Drive

Local Disk (C:)

3. Right-Click on CompMedOffice folder and go to Add to Zip

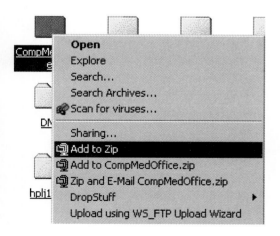

4. Next Click **I Agree**

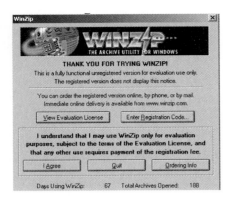

5. Next select where you want the zipped file to be sent by clicking **New.**

6. Now direct the zipped folder to the floppy disk and title the file something easy to locate such as your name and date.

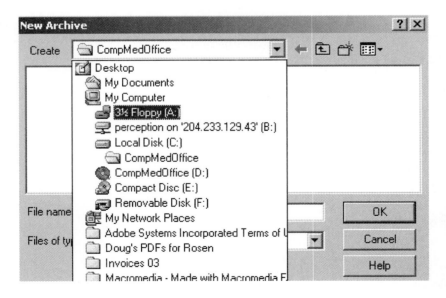

7. The file is now zipped onto a floppy disk.

8. To Unzip a file from a floppy, insert the floppy into your drive.

9. Double-click **My computer** and **3½ Floppy Drive.**

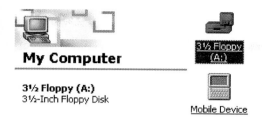

My Computer

3½ Floppy (A:)
3½-Inch Floppy Disk

3½ Floppy
(A:)

Mobile Device

10. Double-Click the zipped folder and press **I agree** and **Next.** The screen will ask what you want to do, select Unzip from an existing Zip file and press **Next.**

A screen will then ask where you want to place the unzipped files. Cllick Select different folder and place the files wherever you can locate them easily later.

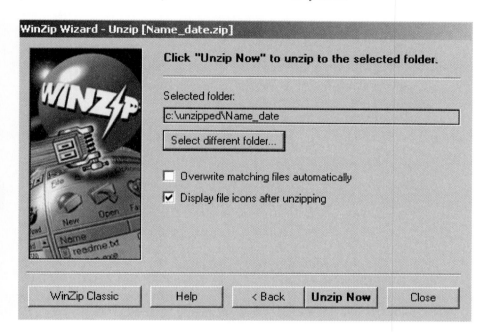

12. Open **Kinn Instructor's Curriculum Resource 2003** and click the **File** drop-down menu. Click **Open Practice** and locate the newly extracted folder. **Click on Your Name Clinic.lpf** within the folder.

This process should be repeated each time you make changes to the data files and want to transfer those changes to another computer.

Games

Introduction

Students enjoy participating in an active learning environment. The authors of this text and supplemental materials recognize that instructors often lack the time to develop and implement elaborate, fun-filled learning activities.

We have provided bingo and Jeopardy-style games. Materials needed for these activities can be downloaded, customized, and printed for classroom use. Bingo cards are available in several versions, to eliminate multiple winners. We suggest using candy, gum, or some other small treats as prizes for the winners. Also included is a blank bingo card and Jeopardy category board so that you can create and modify activities to fit your curriculum and classroom needs. These activities serve as a comprehensive and fun review for exams.

Unit 3 Card 1

U	N	I	T	3
Ancillary diagnostic services	Etiology	Fiscal intermediary	Pre-existing condition	Pre-authorization
Coding	Established patient	Site	Principal procedure	PRO
Comorbidity	Electronic billing	**Free Space**	Principal diagnosis	Participating provider
Complication	Discharge face sheet	Grouper	TEFRA	Non-participating provider
Crossover claim	DRG creep	ICD-9-CM	Uniform hospital discharge data set	New patient

Unit 3 Card 2

U N I T 3

Ancillary diagnostic services	Etiology	Fiscal intermediary	Pre-existing condition	Pre-authorization
Mandated	New patient	Site	Principal diagnosis	Established patient
Comorbidity	Electronic billing	**Free Space**	Principal procedure	Participating provider
Complication	Discharge face sheet	ICD-9-CM	TEFRA	Non-participating provider
Coding	DRG creep	Grouper	Uniform hospital discharge data set	PRO

Unit 3 Card 3

U	N	I	T	3
Ancillary diagnostic services	Mandated	Fiscal intermediary	Pre-existing condition	Comorbidity
Etiology	New patient	DRG creep	Principal diagnosis	Established patient
Pre-authorization	Electronic billing	**Free Space**	Principal procedure	Non-participating provider
Complication	Discharge face sheet	Site	ICD-9-CM	Participating provider
PRO	DRG creep	Grouper	Uniform hospital discharge data set	TEFRA

Unit 3 Card 4

U N I T 3

Participating provider	Mandated	Fiscal intermediary	Pre-existing condition	Comorbidity
Etiology	Uniform hospital discharge data set	DRG creep	Principal diagnosis	Established patient
Pre-authorization	Electronic billing	**Free Space**	Complication	Non-participating provider
ICD-9-CM	Discharge face sheet	Principal procedure	ICD-9-CM	Ancillary diagnostic services
PRO	Grouper	Site	New patient	TEFRA

Unit 4 Card 1

U	N	I	T	4

Trial balance	Daily journal	Credit column	Transaction	Superbill
Credit balance	Statement	Credit	Posting	Invoice
In balance	Discounts	**Free Space**	Debit column	Debit
Disbursements	Payables	Packing slip	Receipts	Petty cash fund
Account balance	Accrual basis of accounting	Cash basis of accounting	Bookkeeping	Credit

Unit 4 Card 2

U	N	I	T	4
Accounting equation	Daily journal	Credit column	Transaction	Superbill
Credit balance	Accounts payable	Credit	Posting	Invoice
In balance	Discounts	**Free Space**	Debit column	Receivables
Disbursements	Payables	Accounts receivable	Receipts	Petty cash fund
Account balance	Accrual basis of accounting	Cash basis of accounting	Adjustment column	Credit

Unit 4 Card 3

U	N	I	T	4
Accounting equation	Daily journal	Credit column	Transaction	Balance sheet
Accounts receivable trial balance	Accounts payable	Credit	Posting	In balance
Invoice	Discounts	**Free Space**	Debit column	Receivables
Disbursements	Debit	Accounts receivable	Receipts	Petty cash fund
Account balance	Cash basis of accounting	Accrual basis of accounting	Debit column	Credit balance

Unit 4 Card 4

U N I T 4

Accounting equation	Accounts payable	Credit balance	Transaction	Balance sheet
Accounts receivable ledger	Daily journal	Debit	Cash basis of accounting	In balance
Invoice	Account balance	**Free Space**	Credit column	Receivables
Credit	Debit column	Accounts receivable	Disbursements	Petty cash fund
Discounts	Posting	Accrual basis of accounting	Debit column	Receipts

UNIT 3

Bingo Questions

Directions: Print this file and cut the questions below into strips. Distribute copies of each of the four cards. Draw questions at random. Have students cross out the answer when the question is called.

U   A pre-existing condition that will, because of its presence with a specific principal diagnosis, cause an increase in length of stay by at least 1 day in approximately 75% of cases _Comorbidities_

U   The process of inflating diagnoses to obtain a higher payment rate _DRG creep_

U   A designated place or point _Site_

U   Federal law in 1982; contains provisions for major changes in Medicare reimbursement _TERRA_

U   A physical condition of an insured person that existed prior the insurance policy _Preexisting_

U   An entity that is composed of a substantial number of licensed doctors of medicine and osteopathy engaged in the practice of medicine or surgery in the area, or an entity that has available to it the services of a sufficient number of physicians engaged in the practice of medicine or surgery, to ensure the adequate peer review of the services provided by the various medical specialties and subspecialties _PRO Peer Review Organization_

U   Required by an authority or law _Mandated_

U   Computer software program that is used by the fiscal intermediary in all cases to assign discharges to the appropriate DRGs _Grouper_

U   A claim for benefits under both Medicare and Medicaid _Crossover_

U   A summary of the hospital stay prepared at time of patient's discharge from the hospital _Discharge Face Sheet_

U   Classifying a claim according to the cause of the disorder _Primary diagnosis_

U   A patient who has received care from the physician within the past 3 years _Established patient_

U   A physician who does not accept assignment under Medicare or the Blue Plans _Non-participating provider_

U   A procedure that was performed for definitive treatment rather than for diagnostic or exploratory purposes, or one necessary to take care of a complication; it is that procedure most related to the principal diagnosis *Principal procedure*

U   A minimum data set required to be collected for each Medicare patient on discharge *Uniform hospital discharge data set*

U   Permission by insurance carrier obtained prior to giving certain treatment to a patient *Preauthorization*

U   Services that support patient diagnoses; e.g., laboratory or x-ray *Ancillary diagnostic services*

U   A system for classifying diseases to facilitate collection of uniform and comparable health information *ICD-9-CM*

U   A patient who has not received any professional services from the physician in the past 3 years *New patient*

U   Converting verbal descriptions of diseases, injuries, and procedures into numeric and alphanumeric designations *Coding*

U   A condition that arises during the hospital stay that prolongs the length *Complication*

U   The submission of a claim via computer to computer *Electronic claim*

U   An organization that handles claims from hospitals, nursing facilities, intermediate and long-term care facilities, and home health agencies *Fiscal intermediary*

U   A physician who accepts assignment under Medicare or the Blue Plans *Participating provider*

U   That condition which, after study, is determined to be chiefly responsible for occasioning the admission of the patient to the hospital *Principal diagnosis*

N   A pre-existing condition that will, because of its presence with a specific principal diagnosis, cause an increase in length of stay by at least 1 day in approximately 75% of cases *Comorbidities*

N   The process of inflating diagnoses to obtain a higher payment rate *DRG creep*

N   A designated place or point *Site*

N   Federal law in 1982; contains provisions for major changes in Medicare reimbursement *TERRA*

N   A physical condition of an insured person that existed prior the insurance policy *Preexisting*

N   An entity that is composed of a substantial number of licensed doctors of medicine and osteopathy engaged in the practice of medicine or surgery in the area, or an entity that has available to it the services of a sufficient number of physicians engaged in the practice of medicine or surgery, to ensure the adequate peer review of the services provided by the various medical specialties and subspecialties *PRO Peer Review Oganization*

N   Required by an authority or law *Mandated*

N   Computer software program that is used by the fiscal intermediary in all cases to assign discharges to the appropriate DRGs *Grouper*

N   A claim for benefits under both Medicare and Medicaid *Crossover*

N   A summary of the hospital stay prepared at time of patient's discharge from the hospital *Discharge Face Sheet*

N   Classifying a claim according to the cause of the disorder *Primary diagnosis*

N   A patient who has received care from the physician within the past 3 years *Established patient*

N   A physician who does not accept assignment under Medicare or the Blue Plans *Non-participating provider*

N   A procedure that was performed for definitive treatment rather than for diagnostic or exploratory purposes, or one necessary to take care of a complication; it is that procedure most related to the principal diagnosis *Principal procedure*

N   A minimum data set required to be collected for each Medicare patient on discharge *Uniform hospital discharge data set*

N   Permission by insurance carrier obtained prior to giving certain treatment to a patient *Preauthorization*

N   Services that support patient diagnoses; e.g., laboratory or x-ray *Ancillary diagnostic services*

N   A system for classifying diseases to facilitate collection of uniform and comparable health information *ICD-9-CM*

N   A patient who has not received any professional services from the physician in the past 3 years *New patient*

N   Converting verbal descriptions of diseases, injuries, and procedures into numeric and alphanumeric designations *Coding*

N   A condition that arises during the hospital stay that prolongs the length *Complication*

N   The submission of a claim via computer to computer *Electronic claim*

N   An organization that handles claims from hospitals, nursing facilities, intermediate and long-term care facilities, and home health agencies *Fiscal intermediary*

N   A physician who accepts assignment under Medicare or the Blue Plans *Participating provider*

N   That condition which, after study, is determined to be chiefly responsible for occasioning the admission of the patient to the hospital *Principal diagnosis*

I   A pre-existing condition that will, because of its presence with a specific principal diagnosis, cause an increase in length of stay by at least 1 day in approximately 75% of cases *Comorbidities*

I   The process of inflating diagnoses to obtain a higher payment rate _DRG creep_

I   A designated place or point _Site_

I   Federal law in 1982; contains provisions for major changes in Medicare reimbursement _TERRA_

I   A physical condition of an insured person that existed prior the insurance policy _Preexisting_

I   An entity that is composed of a substantial number of licensed doctors of medicine and osteopathy engaged in the practice of medicine or surgery in the area, or an entity that has available to it the services of a sufficient number of physicians engaged in the practice of medicine or surgery, to ensure the adequate peer review of the services provided by the various medical specialties and subspecialties _PRO Peer Review Organization_

I   Required by an authority or law _Mandated_

I   Computer software program that is used by the fiscal intermediary in all cases to assign discharges to the appropriate DRGs _Grouper_

I   A claim for benefits under both Medicare and Medicaid _Crossover_

I   A summary of the hospital stay prepared at time of patient's discharge from the hospital _Discharge Face Sheet_

I   Classifying a claim according to the cause of the disorder _Primary diagnosis_

I   A patient who has received care from the physician within the past 3 years _Established patient_

I   A physician who does not accept assignment under Medicare or the Blue Plans _Non-participating provider_

I   A procedure that was performed for definitive treatment rather than for diagnostic or exploratory purposes, or one necessary to take care of a complication; it is that procedure most related to the principal diagnosis _Principal procedure_

I   A minimum data set required to be collected for each Medicare patient on discharge _Uniform hospital discharge data set_

I   Permission by insurance carrier obtained prior to giving certain treatment to a patient _Preauthorization_

I   Services that support patient diagnoses; e.g., laboratory or x-ray _Ancillary diagnostic services_

I   A system for classifying diseases to facilitate collection of uniform and comparable health information _ICD-9-CM_

I   A patient who has not received any professional services from the physician in the past 3 years _New patient_

I   Converting verbal descriptions of diseases, injuries, and procedures into numeric and alphanumeric designations _Coding_

I   A condition that arises during the hospital stay that prolongs the length _Complication_

I   The submission of a claim via computer to computer _Electronic claim_

I   An organization that handles claims from hospitals, nursing facilities, intermediate and long-term care facilities, and home health agencies _Fiscal intermediary_

I   A physician who accepts assignment under Medicare or the Blue Plans _Participating provider_

I   That condition which, after study, is determined to be chiefly responsible for occasioning the admission of the patient to the hospital _Principal diagnosis_

T   A pre-existing condition that will, because of its presence with a specific principal diagnosis, cause an increase in length of stay by at least 1 day in approximately 75% of cases _Comorbidities_

T   The process of inflating diagnoses to obtain a higher payment rate _DRG creep_

T   A designated place or point _Site_

T   Federal law in 1982; contains provisions for major changes in Medicare reimbursement _TERRA_

T   A physical condition of an insured person that existed prior the insurance policy _Preexisting_

T   An entity that is composed of a substantial number of licensed doctors of medicine and osteopathy engaged in the practice of medicine or surgery in the area, or an entity that has available to it the services of a sufficient number of physicians engaged in the practice of medicine or surgery, to ensure the adequate peer review of the services provided by the various medical specialties and subspecialties _PRO Peer Review Organization_

T   Required by an authority or law _Mandated_

T   Computer software program that is used by the fiscal intermediary in all cases to assign discharges to the appropriate DRGs _Grouper_

T   A claim for benefits under both Medicare and Medicaid _Crossover_

T   A summary of the hospital stay prepared at time of patient's discharge from the hospital _Discharge Face Sheet_

T   Classifying a claim according to the cause of the disorder _Primary diagnosis_

T   A patient who has received care from the physician within the past 3 years _Established patient_

T   A physician who does not accept assignment under Medicare or the Blue Plans _Non-participating provider_

T   A procedure that was performed for definitive treatment rather than for diagnostic or exploratory purposes, or one necessary to take care of a complication; it is that procedure most related to the principal diagnosis _Principal procedure_

T   A minimum data set required to be collected for each Medicare patient on discharge *Uniform hospital discharge data set*

T   Permission by insurance carrier obtained prior to giving certain treatment to a patient *Preauthorization*

T   Services that support patient diagnoses; e.g., laboratory or x-ray *Ancillary diagnostic services*

T   A system for classifying diseases to facilitate collection of uniform and comparable health information *ICD-9-CM*

T   A patient who has not received any professional services from the physician in the past 3 years *New patient*

T   Converting verbal descriptions of diseases, injuries, and procedures into numeric and alphanumeric designations *Coding*

T   A condition that arises during the hospital stay that prolongs the length *Complication*

T   The submission of a claim via computer to computer *Electronic claim*

T   An organization that handles claims from hospitals, nursing facilities, intermediate and long-term care facilities, and home health agencies *Fiscal intermediary*

T   A physician who accepts assignment under Medicare or the Blue Plans *Participating provider*

T   That condition which, after study, is determined to be chiefly responsible for occasioning the admission of the patient to the hospital *Principal diagnosis*

3   A pre-existing condition that will, because of its presence with a specific principal diagnosis, cause an increase in length of stay by at least 1 day in approximately 75% of cases *Comorbidities*

3   The process of inflating diagnoses to obtain a higher payment rate *DRG creep*

3   A designated place or point *Site*

3   Federal law in 1982; contains provisions for major changes in Medicare reimbursement *TERRA*

3   A physical condition of an insured person that existed prior the insurance policy *Preexisting*

3   An entity that is composed of a substantial number of licensed doctors of medicine and osteopathy engaged in the practice of medicine or surgery in the area, or an entity that has available to it the services of a sufficient number of physicians engaged in the practice of medicine or surgery, to ensure the adequate peer review of the services provided by the various medical specialties and subspecialties *PRO Peer Review Organization*

3   Required by an authority or law *Mandated*

3   Computer software program that is used by the fiscal intermediary in all cases to assign discharges to the appropriate DRGs *Grouper*

3   A claim for benefits under both Medicare and Medicaid _Crossover_

3   A summary of the hospital stay prepared at time of patient's discharge from the hospital _Discharge Face Sheet_

3   Classifying a claim according to the cause of the disorder _Primary diagnosis_

3   A patient who has received care from the physician within the past 3 years _Established patient_

3   A physician who does not accept assignment under Medicare or the Blue Plans _Non-participating provider_

3   A procedure that was performed for definitive treatment rather than for diagnostic or exploratory purposes, or one necessary to take care of a complication; it is that procedure most related to the principal diagnosis _Principal procedure_

3   A minimum data set required to be collected for each Medicare patient on discharge _Uniform hospital discharge data set_

3   Permission by insurance carrier obtained prior to giving certain treatment to a patient _Preauthorization_

3   Services that support patient diagnoses; e.g., laboratory or x-ray _Ancillary diagnostic services_

3   A system for classifying diseases to facilitate collection of uniform and comparable health information _ICD-9-CM_

3   A patient who has not received any professional services from the physician in the past 3 years _New patient_

3   Converting verbal descriptions of diseases, injuries, and procedures into numeric and alphanumeric designations _Coding_

3   A condition that arises during the hospital stay that prolongs the length _Complication_

3   The submission of a claim via computer to computer _Electronic claim_

3   An organization that handles claims from hospitals, nursing facilities, intermediate and long-term care facilities, and home health agencies _Fiscal intermediary_

3   A physician who accepts assignment under Medicare or the Blue Plans _Participating provider_

3   That condition which, after study, is determined to be chiefly responsible for occasioning the admission of the patient to the hospital _Principal diagnosis_

UNIT 4

Bingo Questions

Directions: Print this file and cut the questions below into strips. Distribute copies of each of the four cards. Draw questions at random. Have students cross out the answer when the question is called.

U   An account column, sometimes included to the left of the balance column, that is used for entering discounts *Adjustment column*

U   The account column on the far right that is used for recording the difference between the debit and credit columns *Balance column*

U   A financial statement for a specific date that shows total assets, liabilities, and business capital *Balance flowsheet*

U   A financial summary for a specific period that shows the beginning cash on hand, the cash income and disbursements during the period, and the amount of cash on hand at the end of the period *Cash flow statement*

U   The difference between the debit and credit totals *Balance*

U   The record of a payment received *Credit*

U   A record of all cash paid out *Cash payment journal*

U   An itemized list of objects in a package *Packing slip*

U   A fund maintained to pay small unpredictable cash expenditures *Petty cash*

U   A request for payment *Statement*

U   The act of transferring information from one record to another *Posting*

U   Cash received *Receipts*

U   A combination charge slip, statement, and insurance reporting form *Superbill*

U   The recording part of the accounting process *Bookkeeping*

U   Amounts owed to others *Payables*

U   The occurrence of a financial event or condition to be recorded _Transaction_

U   A method of checking the accuracy of accounts _Trial balance_

U   A single financial record _Account_

U   Amounts charged and not paid _Accounts payable_

U   The account column to the right of the debit column that is used for entering funds received _Credit column_

U   The book in which all transactions are first recorded; the book of original entry, or general journal _General journal_

U   Income is recorded when received, and expenses are recorded when paid _Cash basis of accounting_

U   The record of a charge or debt occurred _Debit_

U   Cash paid _Disbursement_

U   A courtesy subtraction from the patient's balance _Discount_

U   The book of original entry in accounting _Daily journal_

U   The amount of advance payment or overpayment on an account (amount of receipts exceeding amount charge) _Credit balance_

U   Total ending balances of patient ledgers equal total of accounts receivable control _In balance_

U   A paper describing a purchase and the amount due _Invoice_

U   A summary of all income and expenses for a given period _Statement of income and expenses_

U   The account column on the left that is used for entering charges _Debit column_

U   Amounts owed to the physician _Accounts receivable_

U   A summary of unpaid accounts _Accounts receivable control_

U   Assets = Liabilities + Proprietorship _Accounting equation_

U   Amounts owing from others _Receivables_

U   The combined record of all patient accounts _Accounts receivable ledger_

U   The debit or credit balance remaining in the account _Account balance_

U   A method of determining that the journal and the ledger are in balance _Accounts receivable trial balance_

U Income is recorded when earned, and expenses are recorded when incurred _Accrual basis of accounting_

U A journal summary of amounts paid out _Disbursements journal_

N An account column, sometimes included to the left of the balance column, that is used for entering discounts _Adjustment column_

N The account column on the far right that is used for recording the difference between the debit and credit columns _Balance column_

N A financial statement for a specific date that shows total assets, liabilities, and business capital _Balance flowsheet_

N A financial summary for a specific period that shows the beginning cash on hand, the cash income and disbursements during the period, and the amount of cash on hand at the end of the period _Cash flow statement_

N The difference between the debit and credit totals _Balance_

N The record of a payment received _Credit_

N A record of all cash paid out _Cash payment journal_

N An itemized list of objects in a package _Packing slip_

N A fund maintained to pay small unpredictable cash expenditures _Petty cash_

N A request for payment _Statement_

N The act of transferring information from one record to another _Posting_

N Cash received _Receipts_

N A combination charge slip, statement, and insurance reporting form _Superbill_

N The recording part of the accounting process _Bookkeeping_

N Amounts owed to others _Payables_

N The occurrence of a financial event or condition to be recorded _Transaction_

N A method of checking the accuracy of accounts _Trial balance_

N A single financial record _Account_

N Amounts charged and not paid _Accounts payable_

N The account column to the right of the debit column that is used for entering funds received _Credit column_

N   The book in which all transactions are first recorded; the book of original entry, or general journal _General journal_

N   Income is recorded when received, and expenses are recorded when paid _Cash basis of accounting_

N   The record of a charge or debt occurred _Debit_

N   Cash paid _Disbursement_

N   A courtesy subtraction from the patient's balance _Discount_

N   The book of original entry in accounting _Daily journal_

N   The amount of advance payment or overpayment on an account (amount of receipts exceeding amount charge) _Credit balance_

N   Total ending balances of patient ledgers equal total of accounts receivable control _In balance_

N   A paper describing a purchase and the amount due _Invoice_

N   A summary of all income and expenses for a given period _Statement of income and expenses_

N   The account column on the left that is used for entering charges _Debit column_

N   Amounts owed to the physician _Accounts receivable_

N   A summary of unpaid accounts _Accounts receivable control_

N   Assets = Liabilities + Proprietorship _Accounting equation_

N   Amounts owing from others _Receivables_

N   The combined record of all patient accounts _Accounts receivable ledger_

N   The debit or credit balance remaining in the account _Account balance_

N   A method of determining that the journal and the ledger are in balance _Accounts receivable trial balance_

N   Income is recorded when earned, and expenses are recorded when incurred _Accrual basis of accounting_

N   A journal summary of amounts paid out _Disbursements journal_

I   An account column, sometimes included to the left of the balance column, that is used for entering discounts _Adjustment column_

I   The account column on the far right that is used for recording the difference between the debit and credit columns _Balance column_

I   A financial statement for a specific date that shows total assets, liabilities, and business capital _Balance flowsheet_

I   A financial summary for a specific period that shows the beginning cash on hand, the cash income and disbursements during the period, and the amount of cash on hand at the end of the period _Cash flow statement_

I   The difference between the debit and credit totals _Balance_

I   The record of a payment received _Credit_

I   A record of all cash paid out _Cash payment journal_

I   An itemized list of objects in a package _Packing slip_

I   A fund maintained to pay small unpredictable cash expenditures _Petty cash_

I   A request for payment _Statement_

I   The act of transferring information from one record to another _Posting_

I   Cash received _Receipts_

I   A combination charge slip, statement, and insurance reporting form _Superbill_

I   The recording part of the accounting process _Bookkeeping_

I   Amounts owed to others _Payables_

I   The occurrence of a financial event or condition to be recorded _Transaction_

I   A method of checking the accuracy of accounts _Trial balance_

I   A single financial record _Account_

I   Amounts charged and not paid _Accounts payable_

I   The account column to the right of the debit column that is used for entering funds received _Credit column_

I   The book in which all transactions are first recorded; the book of original entry, or general journal _General journal_

I   Income is recorded when received, and expenses are recorded when paid _Cash basis of accounting_

I   The record of a charge or debt occurred _Debit_

I   Cash paid _Disbursement_

I   A courtesy subtraction from the patient's balance _Discount_

I   The book of original entry in accounting *Daily journal*

I   The amount of advance payment or overpayment on an account (amount of receipts exceeding amount charge) *Credit balance*

I   Total ending balances of patient ledgers equal total of accounts receivable control *In balance*

I   A paper describing a purchase and the amount due *Invoice*

I   A summary of all income and expenses for a given period *Statement of income and expenses*

I   The account column on the left that is used for entering charges *Debit column*

I   Amounts owed to the physician *Accounts receivable*

I   A summary of unpaid accounts *Accounts receivable control*

I   Assets = Liabilities + Proprietorship *Accounting equation*

I   Amounts owing from others *Receivables*

I   The combined record of all patient accounts *Accounts receivable ledger*

I   The debit or credit balance remaining in the account *Account balance*

I   A method of determining that the journal and the ledger are in balance *Accounts receivable trial balance*

I   Income is recorded when earned, and expenses are recorded when incurred *Accrual basis of accounting*

I   A journal summary of amounts paid out *Disbursements journal*

T   An account column, sometimes included to the left of the balance column, that is used for entering discounts *Adjustment column*

T   The account column on the far right that is used for recording the difference between the debit and credit columns *Balance column*

T   A financial statement for a specific date that shows total assets, liabilities, and business capital *Balance flowsheet*

T   A financial summary for a specific period that shows the beginning cash on hand, the cash income and disbursements during the period, and the amount of cash on hand at the end of the period *Cash flow statement*

T   The difference between the debit and credit totals *Balance*

T   The record of a payment received *Credit*

T   A record of all cash paid out *Cash payment journal*

T   An itemized list of objects in a package *Packing slip*

T   A fund maintained to pay small unpredictable cash expenditures *Petty cash*

T   A request for payment *Statement*

T   The act of transferring information from one record to another *Posting*

T   Cash received *Receipts*

T   A combination charge slip, statement, and insurance reporting form *Superbill*

T   The recording part of the accounting process *Bookkeeping*

T   Amounts owed to others *Payables*

T   The occurrence of a financial event or condition to be recorded *Transaction*

T   A method of checking the accuracy of accounts *Trial balance*

T   A single financial record *Account*

T   Amounts charged and not paid *Accounts payable*

T   The account column to the right of the debit column that is used for entering funds received *Credit column*

T   The book in which all transactions are first recorded; the book of original entry, or general journal *General journal*

T   Income is recorded when received, and expenses are recorded when paid *Cash basis of accounting*

T   The record of a charge or debt occurred *Debit*

T   Cash paid *Disbursement*

T   A courtesy subtraction from the patient's balance *Discount*

T   The book of original entry in accounting *Daily journal*

T   The amount of advance payment or overpayment on an account (amount of receipts exceeding amount charge) *Credit balance*

T   Total ending balances of patient ledgers equal total of accounts receivable control *In balance*

T   A paper describing a purchase and the amount due *Invoice*

T   A summary of all income and expenses for a given period *Statement of income and expenses*

T   The account column on the left that is used for entering charges *Debit column*

T   Amounts owed to the physician _Accounts receivable_

T   A summary of unpaid accounts _Accounts receivable control_

T   Assets = Liabilities + Proprietorship _Accounting equation_

T   Amounts owing from others _Receivables_

T   The combined record of all patient accounts _Accounts receivable ledger_

T   The debit or credit balance remaining in the account _Account balance_

T   A method of determining that the journal and the ledger are in balance _Accounts receivable trial balance_

T   Income is recorded when earned, and expenses are recorded when incurred _Accrual basis of accounting_

T   A journal summary of amounts paid out _Disbursements journal_

4   An account column, sometimes included to the left of the balance column, that is used for entering discounts _Adjustment column_

4   The account column on the far right that is used for recording the difference between the debit and credit columns _Balance column_

4   A financial statement for a specific date that shows total assets, liabilities, and business capital _Balance flowsheet_

4   A financial summary for a specific period that shows the beginning cash on hand, the cash income and disbursements during the period, and the amount of cash on hand at the end of the period _Cash flow statement_

4   The difference between the debit and credit totals _Balance_

4   The record of a payment received _Credit_

4   A record of all cash paid out _Cash payment journal_

4   An itemized list of objects in a package _Packing slip_

4   A fund maintained to pay small unpredictable cash expenditures _Petty cash_

4   A request for payment _Statement_

4   The act of transferring information from one record to another _Posting_

4   Cash received _Receipts_

4   A combination charge slip, statement, and insurance reporting form _Superbill_

4   The recording part of the accounting process _Bookkeeping_

4   Amounts owed to others _Payables_

4   The occurrence of a financial event or condition to be recorded _Transaction_

4   A method of checking the accuracy of accounts _Trial balance_

4   A single financial record _Account_

4   Amounts charged and not paid _Accounts payable_

4   The account column to the right of the debit column that is used for entering funds received _Credit column_

4   The book in which all transactions are first recorded; the book of original entry, or general journal _General journal_

4   Income is recorded when received, and expenses are recorded when paid _Cash basis of accounting_

4   The record of a charge or debt occurred _Debit_

4   Cash paid _Disbursement_

4   A courtesy subtraction from the patient's balance _Discount_

4   The book of original entry in accounting _Daily journal_

4   The amount of advance payment or overpayment on an account (amount of receipts exceeding amount charge) _Credit balance_

4   Total ending balances of patient ledgers equal total of accounts receivable control _In balance_

4   A paper describing a purchase and the amount due _Invoice_

4   A summary of all income and expenses for a given period _Statement of income and expenses_

4   The account column on the left that is used for entering charges _Debit column_

4   Amounts owed to the physician _Accounts receivable_

4   A summary of unpaid accounts _Accounts receivable control_

4   Assets = Liabilities + Proprietorship _Accounting equation_

4   Amounts owing from others _Receivables_

4   The combined record of all patient accounts _Accounts receivable ledger_

4   The debit or credit balance remaining in the account _Account balance_

4   A method of determining that the journal and the ledger are in balance *Accounts receivable trial balance*

4   Income is recorded when earned, and expenses are recorded when incurred *Accrual basis of accounting*

4   A journal summary of amounts paid out *Disbursements journal*

Unit _____ **Card** _____

B	I	N	G	O
		Free Space		

Instructions for Jeopardy Game

1. Playing this Jeopardy game is a good way to engage your students in reviewing each unit. At the end of the unit, ask each student to write one definition per category.
2. Collect the questions and assign a numeric value.
3. Divide the class into two teams.
4. Assign a scorekeeper and team leader for each team.
5. Flip a coin to decide which team goes first.
6. The first team leader chooses the first category.
7. The answer must be posed in the form of a question.
8. The team with the most points at the end of 25 questions wins.

Medical Assisting Jeopardy

Medical History	Medical Assisting Profession	Human Relations	Ethics	Law
100	100	100	100	100
200	200	200	200	200
300	300	300	300	300
400	400	400	400	400
500	500	500	500	500

Unit 1

Medical Assisting Jeopardy

Computers	Telephone Techniques	Scheduling	Mail	Filing
100	100	100	100	100
200	200	200	200	200
300	300	300	300	300
400	400	400	400	400
500	500	500	500	500

Unit 2

Medical Assisting Jeopardy

Billing	Diagnostic Coding	Procedure Coding	CMS-1500	Banking
100	100	100	100	100
200	200	200	200	200
300	300	300	300	300
400	400	400	400	400
500	500	500	500	500

Unit 3

Medical Assisting Jeopardy

Practice Manage-ment	Marketing	Customer Services	Health Info. Management	Finances
100	100	100	100	100
200	200	200	200	200
300	300	300	300	300
400	400	400	400	400
500	500	500	500	500

Unit 4

Medical Assisting Jeopardy

Infection Control	Patient Assessment	Nutrition	Vital Signs	Physical Exams
100	100	100	100	100
200	200	200	200	200
300	300	300	300	300
400	400	400	400	400
500	500	500	500	500

Unit 5

Medical Assisting Jeopardy

Drugs and Uses	Routes	Dosage Math	Sites	Technique
100	100	100	100	100
200	200	200	200	200
300	300	300	300	300
400	400	400	400	400
500	500	500	500	500

Medical Assisting Jeopardy

Medical Termino-logy	Anatomy	Physical Exam	Diagnostic Tests	Drugs and Treat-ments
100	100	100	100	100
200	200	200	200	200
300	300	300	300	300
400	400	400	400	400
500	500	500	500	500

Unit 7

Medical Assisting Jeopardy

ECG	Diagnostic Imaging	Clinical Lab/ Phlebotomy	Analysis of Blood	Micro- biology
100	100	100	100	100
200	200	200	200	200
300	300	300	300	300
400	400	400	400	400
500	500	500	500	500

Unit 8

Medical Assisting Jeopardy

Asepsis	Autoclaves	Instru-ments	Surgery	Supplies
100	100	100	100	100
200	200	200	200	200
300	300	300	300	300
400	400	400	400	400
500	500	500	500	500

Unit 9

Medical Assisting Jeopardy

		100	100	100	100
		200	200	200	200
		300	300	300	300
		400	400	400	400
		500	500	500	500

Blank

National Curriculum Competencies

AAMA ENTRY-LEVEL COMPETENCIES FOR THE MEDICAL ASSISTANT	Kinn Theory Ch/Page No.	Kinn Procedure
Administrative Competencies		
1.0 Perform Clerical Function		
1.a Schedule and Manage Appointments	Ch. 10	Procedure 10-1: Preparing and Maintaining the Appointment Book Procedure 10-2: Scheduling a New Patient
1.b Schedule Inpatient and Outpatient Admissions and Procedures	Ch. 10	Procedure 10-3: Scheduling Outpatient Admissions and Procedures Procedure 10-4: Scheduling Inpatient Admissions Procedure 10-5: Scheduling Inpatient Surgical Procedures
1.c Perform Medical Transcription	Ch.13	Procedure 13-5: Transcribing a Machine-Dictated Letter Using a Computer or Word Processor
1.d Organize Patient's Medical Record	Ch. 11 Ch. 13	Procedure 11-1: Preparing Charts for Scheduled Patients Procedure 11-2: Registering a New Patient Procedure 13-1: Initiating a Medical File for a New Patient Procedure 13-2: Preparing an Informed Consent for Treatment Form Procedure 13-3: Adding Supplementary Items to Established Patient Files
1.e File Medical Records	Ch. 13	Procedure 13-4: Preparing a Record Release Form Procedure 13-6: Filing Medical Records and Documents Using the Alphabetical System Procedure 13-7: Filing Medical Records and Documents Using the Numeric System
2.0 Perform Bookkeeping Procedures		
2.a Prepare a Bank Deposit	Ch. 19	Procedure 19-2: Preparing a Bank Deposit
2.b Reconcile a Bank Statement	Ch. 19	Procedure 19-3: Reconciling a Bank Statement
2.c Post Entries on a Daysheet	Ch. 14	Procedure 14-2: Posting Service Charges and Payments Using a Pegboard

2.d Perform Accounts Receivable Procedures	Ch. 14 Ch. 23	Procedure 14-2: Posting Service Charges and Payments Using a Pegboard
2.e Perform Accounts Payable Procedures	Ch. 19 Ch. 23	Procedure 19-1: Writing Checks in Payment of Bills
2.f Perform Billing and Collections Procedures	Ch. 14	Procedure 14-4: Preparing Monthly Billing Statements Procedure 14-5: Aging Accounts Receivables
2.g Prepare a Check	Ch. 19	Procedure 19-1: Writing Checks in Payment of Bills
2.h Establish and Maintain a Petty Cash Fund	Ch. 19	Procedure 23-1: Accounting for Petty Cash
3.0 Prepare Special Accounting Entries		
3.a Post Adjustments	Ch. 14	Procedure 14-3: Making Credit Arrangements with a Patient Procedure 14-4: Preparing Monthly Billing Statements
3.b Process a Credit Balance	Ch. 14	Procedure 14-2: Posting Service Charges and Payments Using a Pegboard
3.c Process Refunds	Ch. 14	Procedure 14-2: Posting Service Charges and Payments Using a Pegboard
3.d Post Non-sufficient Fund Checks (NSF)	Ch. 14	Procedure 14-4: Preparing Monthly Billing Statements
3.e Post Collection Agency Payments	Ch. 14	Procedure 14-5: Aging Accounts Receivables
4.0 Process Insurance Claims		
4.a Apply Managed Care Policies and Procedures	Ch. 18	Procedure 18-1: Obtaining Precertification
4.b Apply Third Party Guidelines	Ch. 17 Ch. 18	Procedure 17-1: Complete an Insurance Claim Form
4.c Obtain Managed Care Referrals and Precertifications	Ch. 18	Procedure 18-1: Obtaining Precertification Procedure 18-2: Obtaining a Managed Care Referral

AAMA ENTRY-LEVEL COMPETENCIES FOR THE MEDICAL ASSISTANT	Kinn Theory Ch/Page No.	Kinn Procedure
4.d Perform Procedural Coding	Ch. 16	Procedure 16-1: Assigning a CPT Code
4.e Perform Diagnostic Coding	Ch. 15	Procedure 15-1: ICD-9-CM Coding
4.f Complete Insurance Claim Forms	Ch. 17 Appendix B	Procedure 17-1: Complete an Insurance Claim Form
4.g Use a Physician's Fee Schedule	Ch. 18	Procedure 17-1: Complete an Insurance Claim Form
Clinical Competencies		
1.0 Fundamental Principles		
1.a Perform Hand Sterilization	Ch. 24	Procedure 24-1: Performing Medical Aseptic Hand Washing Procedure 54-3: Performing Surgical Hand Scrub
1.b Wrap Items for Autoclaving	Ch. 24 Ch. 54	Procedure 54-1: Wrapping Instruments and Supplies for Steam Sterilization in an Autoclave
1.c Perform Sterilization Techniques	Ch. 24 Ch. 54	Procedure 24-2: Sanitization of Instruments Procedure 54-2: Operating an Autoclave
1.d Dispose of Biohazardous Materials	Ch. 24 Ch. 48	Procedure 24-3: Removing Contaminated Latex Gloves Procedure 54-7: Removing Contaminated Gloves
1.e Practice Standard Precautions	Chs. 24, 48, 50, 54	Procedure 24-3: Removing Contaminated Latex Gloves Procedure 54-4: Putting on Sterile Gloves Procedure 54-5: Donning a Sterile Gown Procedure 54-6: Gloving with Sterile Gown On Procedure 54-7: Removing Contaminated Gloves
2.0 Specimen Collection		
2.a Perform Venipuncture	Ch. 50	Procedure 50-1: Collecting a Venous Blood Sample Using the Syringe Method

		Procedure 50-2: Collecting a Venous Blood Sample Using the Evacuated Tube Method
		Procedure 50-3: Performing a Butterfly Draw Using a Hand Vein
2.b Perform Capillary Puncture	Ch. 50	Procedure 50-4: Collecting a Capillary Blood Sample
2.c Obtain Throat Specimen for Microbiological Testing		Procedure 34-8: Collecting a Specimen for a Throat Culture
2.d Perform Wound Collection Procedure for Microbiological Testing	Ch. 35	Procedure 35-1: Collecting a Wound Specimen for Testing and/or Culture
2.e Instruct Patients in the Collection of a Clean-Catch, Mid-Stream Urine Specimen	Ch. 49	Procedure 49-1: Collecting a Clean-Catch Urine Specimen for Culture of Analysis
2.f Instruct Patients in the Collection of a Fecal Specimen		Procedure 52-6: Performing a Cellulose Tape Collection for Pinworms
3.0 Diagnostic Testing		
3.a Use Methods of Quality Control	Ch. 48	Procedure 49-5: Testing Urine with Chemical Reagent Strips
3.b Perform Urinalysis	Ch. 49	Procedure 49-1: Collecting a Clean-Catch Urine Specimen for Culture or Analysis
		Procedure 49-2: Assessing Urine for Color and Turbidity
		Procedure 49-3: Measuring Specific Gravity Using a Urinometer
		Procedure 49-4: Measuring Urine Specific Gravity with a Refractometer
		Procedure 49-5: Testing Urine with Chemical Reagent Strips
		Procedure 49-6: Testing Urine for Glucose with the Clinitest Method
		Procedure 49-7: Preparing Urine Specimen for Microscopic Examination
		Procedure 49-8: Performing a Pregnancy Test
		Procedure 49-9: Performing A Rapid Urine Culture Test

AAMA ENTRY-LEVEL COMPETENCIES FOR THE MEDICAL ASSISTANT	Kinn Theory Ch/Page No.	Kinn Procedure	
3.c Perform Hematology Testing	Ch. 51	Procedure 51-1:	Performing a Microhematocrit
		Procedure 51-2:	Performing a Hemoglobin Test
		Procedure 51-3:	Filling a Unopette
		Procedure 51-4:	Charging (Filling) a Hemacytometer
		Procedure 51-5:	Preparing a Smear Stained with Wright's Stain
		Procedure 51-6:	Performing a Differential Examination of a Smear Stained with Wright's Stain
		Procedure 51-7:	Performing an Erythrocyte Sedimentation Rate Using a Modified Westergren Method
		Procedure 51-9:	Determining ABO Group Using a Slide Test
		Procedure 51-10:	Determining Rh Factor Using the Slide Method
3.d Perform Chemistry Testing	Ch. 51	Procedure 49-6:	Testing Urine for Glucose With the Clinitest Method
		Procedure 51-11:	Performing a Blood Glucose Accu-Check Test
		Procedure 51-12:	Determining Cholesterol Level Using a ProAct Testing Device
3.e Perform Immunology Testing	Ch. 51	Procedure 51-8:	Mono-Test for Infectious Mononucleosis
		Procedure 51-9:	Determining ABO Group Using a Slide Test
		Procedure 51-10:	Determining Rh Factor Using the Slide Method
3.f Perform Microbiology Testing	Ch. 49	Procedure 32-4:	Giving an Intradermal Injection; Reading the Mantoux Test Results
	Ch. 52	Procedure 32-5:	Administering a Tuberculin Tine Test
		Procedure 49-7:	Preparing Urine Specimen for Microscopic Examination
		Procedure 51-5:	Preparing a Smear Stained with Wright's Stain
		Procedure 51-10:	Determining Rh Factor Using the Slide Method
		Procedure 52-1:	Preparing a Direct Smear or Culture Smear for Staining
		Procedure 52-2:	Staining a Smear With Gram's Stain
		Procedure 52-3:	Inoculating a Blood Agar Plate for Culture of Streptococcus pyogenes

3.g Screen and Follow-Up Test Results	Chs. 48, 49, 51, 52 Ch. 9	Procedure 52-6: Performing a Cellulose Tape Collection for Pinworms
3.h Perform Electrocardiograms	Ch. 46	Procedure 46-1: Obtaining a 12-Lead ECG
3.i Perform Respiratory Testing	Ch. 43	Procedure 43-1: Performing Volume Capacity Spirometric Testing
4.0 Patient Care		
4.a Perform Telephone and In-Person Screening	Ch. 9 Ch. 39	Procedure 9-1: Answering the Telephone
4.b Obtain Vital Signs	Ch. 28	Procedure 28-1: Obtaining an Oral Temperature Using a Digital Thermometer Procedure 28-2: Obtaining an Aural Temperature Using the Tympanic Thermometer Procedure 28-3: Obtaining an Auxillary Temperature Procedure 28-4: Obtaining Rectal Temperature Procedure 28-5: Obtaining an Apical Pulse Procedure 28-6: Assessing the Patient's Pulse Procedure 28-7: Determining Respirations Procedure 28-8: Determining a Patient's Blood Pressure Procedure 28-9: Measuring a Patient's Weight and Height
4.c Obtain and Record Patient History	Ch. 11 Ch. 25	Procedure 11-1: Preparing Charts for Scheduled Patients Procedure 11-2: Registering a New Patient Procedure 25-1: Obtaining a Medical History
4.d Prepare and Maintain Examination and Treatment Area	Ch. 29	Procedure 29-1: Preparing for and Assisting with the Physical Exam
4.e Prepare Patient for and Assist with Routine and Specialty Examinations	Chs. 29, 34, 36, 37, 38, 39, 40, 41, 42, 43, 44, 45, 47	Procedure 29-1: Preparing for and Assisting With the Physical Examination Procedure 34-1: Measuring Distance Visual Acuity Using the Snellen Chart Procedure 34-2: Assessing Color Acuity Using the Ishihara Test

AAMA ENTRY-LEVEL COMPETENCIES FOR THE MEDICAL ASSISTANT	Kinn Theory Ch/Page No.	Kinn Procedure
		Procedure 34-3: Irrigating a Patient's Eyes
		Procedure 34-4: Instilling Eye Medication
		Procedure 34-5: Measuring Hearing Acuity Using an Audiometer
		Procedure 34-6: Irrigating a Patient's Ear
		Procedure 34-7: Instilling Medicated Ear Drops
		Procedure 34-8: Collecting a Specimen for a Throat Culture
		Procedure 36-1: Inserting a Rectal Suppository
		Procedure 36-2: Assisting with a Colon Endoscopic Examination
		Procedure 37-1: Teaching Testicular Self-Examination
		Procedure 38-1: Assisting With Examination of the Female Patient and Pap Smear
		Procedure 38-2: Teaching the Patient Breast Self-Examination
		Procedure 38-4: Assisting with the Prenatal Examination
		Procedure 38-5: Establishing the EDD Using Nagele's Rule and Lunar Method
		Procedure 39-1: Measuring the Circumference of an Infant's Head
		Procedure 39-2: Measuring Infant Length and Weight
		Procedure 39-3: Obtaining Pediatric Vital Signs and Vision Screening
		Procedure 39-4: Applying a Urinary Collection Device
		Procedure 41-1: Assisting with Neurological Examination
		Procedure 47-1: General Procedure for X-Ray Examination
4.f Prepare Patient for and Assist with Procedures, Treatments and Minor Office Surgery	Chs. 35, 36, 37, 38, 39, 40, 41, 42, 43, 44, 45, 53, 54	Procedure 36-1: Inserting a Rectal Suppository
		Procedure 37-2: Catheterization of the Female Patient
		Procedure 37-3: Catheterization of the Male Patient
		Procedure 38-3: Preparing the Patient for Cryosurgery
		Procedure 39-4: Applying a Urinary Collection Device
		Procedure 40-1: Assisting the Patient with Cold Application
		Procedure 40-2: Assisting with Hot Moist Heat Application in the Office
		Procedure 40-3: Assisting with Therapeutic Ultrasonography

		Procedure 40-4: Assisting with Cast Application
		Procedure 40-5: Triangular Arm Sling Application
		Procedure 40-6: Assisting with Cast Removal
		Procedure 40-7: Assisting the Patient With Crutch Walking
		Procedure 41-2: Preparing the Patient for an EEG
		Procedure 41-3: Preparing the Patient for and Assisting with a Lumbar Puncture
		Procedure 43-1: Performing Volume Capacity Spirometric Testing
		Procedure 43-2: Obtaining a Sputum Sample for Culture
		Procedure 46-2: Applying a Holter Monitor
		Procedure 54-3: Performing a Surgical Hand Scrub
		Procedure 54-4: Putting on Sterile Gloves
		Procedure 54-5: Donning a Sterile Gown
		Procedure 54-6: Gloving With a Sterile Gown On
		Procedure 54-8: Skin Prep for Surgery
		Procedure 54-9: Opening a Sterile Pack and Creating a Sterile Field
		Procedure 54-10: Using Transfer Forceps
		Procedure 54-11: Pouring Solutions onto a Sterile Field(s)
		Procedure 54-12: Assisting with Minor Surgery
		Procedure 54-13: Assisting With Suturing
		Procedure 54-14: Applying/Changing a Dressing
		Procedure 54-15: Suture Removal
		Procedure 54-16: Bandaging Using Gauze and Elastic Dressing
4.g Apply Pharmacology Principles to Prepare and Administer Oral and Parenteral Medications	Chs. 30, 31, 32	Procedure 31-1: Calculating the Correct Dosage for Administration
		Procedure 31-2: Calculating the Correct Dosage for Administrating Using Two Systems of Measurement
		Procedure 31-3: Calculating the Correct Pediatric Dosage When Only an Adult Medication is Available
		Procedure 31-4: Calculating the Correct Dosage for Administration Using Body Weight
		Procedure 32-1: Dispensing and Administering Oral Medications
		Procedure 32-2: Filling a Syringe Using an Ampule
		Procedure 32-3: Filling a Syringe Using a Vial
		Procedure 32-4: Giving an Intradermal Injection
		Procedure 32-5: Administering a Tuberculin Tine Test

AAMA ENTRY-LEVEL COMPETENCIES FOR THE MEDICAL ASSISTANT	Kinn Theory Ch/Page No.	Kinn Procedure
		Procedure 32-6: Giving a Subcutaneous Injection
		Procedure 32-7: Giving an Intramuscular Injection
		Procedure 32-8: Reconstituting a Powdered Drug for Administration
		Procedure 32-9: Giving a Z-Tract Intramuscular Injection
4.h Maintain Medication and Immunization Records	Ch. 39	Procedure 30-1: Preparing a Prescription for the Physician's Signature
4.i Obtain CPR Certification and First-Aid Training	Ch. 33	Procedure 33-1: Using an Automated External Defibrillator (AED)
		Procedure 33-2: Performing Adult Rescue Breathing and One-Rescuer CPR
		Procedure 33-3: Administering Oxygen
		Procedure 33-4: Responding to an Adult With an Obstructed Airway
		Procedure 33-5: Caring for a Patient Who Has Fainted
		Procedure 33-6: Controlling Bleeding
Transdiciplinary Competencies		
1.0 Communicate		
1.a Respond to and Initiate Written Communication	Chs. 12, 40	Procedure 12-1: Composing Business Correspondence
		Procedure 12-2: Proofreading Written Correspondence
		Procedure 12-3: Preparing a FAX for Transmission
		Procedure 12-4: Opening the Daily Mail
		Procedure 12-5: Addressing Outgoing Mail Using U.S. Post Office OCR Guidelines
		Procedure 13-5: Transcribing a Machine-Dictated Letter Using a Computer or Word Processor
1.b Recognize and Respond to Verbal Communication	Chs. 5, 9, 10, 17, 18, 25, 40, 41, 42	Procedure 9-1: Answering the Telephone
		Procedure 13-5: Transcribing a Machine-Dictated Letter Using a Computer or Word Processor
		Procedure 25-1: Obtaining a Medical History

1.c Recognize and Respond to Nonverbal Communication	Chs. 5, 18, 25, 40, 41, 42	Procedure 25-1: Obtaining a Medical History
1.d Demonstrate Telephone Techniques	Ch. 9 Ch. 33	Procedure 9-1: Answering the Telephone Procedure 9-2: Taking a Telephone Message Procedure 9-3: Calling the Pharmacy With New or Refill Prescriptions
2.0 Legal Concepts		
2.a Identify and Respond to Issues of Confidentiality	Chs. 4, 6, 7, 9, 17, 18, 25, 40, 41	Procedure 25-1: Obtaining a Medical History
2.b Perform within Legal and Ethical Boundaries	Chs. 5, 6, 7, 17, 18, 19, 33, 40, 41	Procedure 17-1: Complete an Insurance Claim Form Procedure 25-1: Obtaining a Medical History Procedure 33-1: Using an Automated External Defibrillator (AED)
2.c Establish and Maintain the Medical Record	Ch. 11 Ch. 13	Procedure 11-2: Registering a New Patient Procedure 13-1: Initiating a Medical File for a New Patient Procedure 13-2: Preparing an Informed Consent for Treatment Form Procedure 13-3: Adding Supplementary Items to Established Patient Files Procedure 13-4: Preparing a Record Release Form
2.d Document Properly	Ch. 9 Ch. 13 Ch. 25 Appendix E	Procedure 9-2: Taking a Telephone Message Procedure 25-1: Obtaining a Medical History
2.e Perform Risk Management Procedures	Ch. 3, 6, 7, 24	
3.0 Patient Instruction		
3.a Explain General Office Procedures		
3.b Instruct Individuals According to Their Needs	Ch. 26	Procedure 37-1: Teaching Testicular Self Exam Procedure 38-2: Teaching the Patient Breast Self-Examination

AAMA ENTRY-LEVEL COMPETENCIES FOR THE MEDICAL ASSISTANT	Kinn Theory Ch/Page No.	Kinn Procedure
3.c Instruct and Demonstrate the Use and Care of Patient Equipment	Ch. 40	Procedure 40-7: Assisting the Patient with Crutch Walking
3.d Provide Instruction for Health Maintenance and Disease Prevention	Ch. 27	Procedure 27-1: Determining Fat-Fold Measurements Procedure 27-2: Teaching the Patient to Read Food Labels
3.e Identify Community Resources	Chs. 2, 9, 26, 27	
4.0 Operational Functions		
4.a Perform an Inventory of Supplies and Equipment	Ch. 12	
4.b Perform Routine Maintenance of Administrative and Clinical Equipment	Ch. 9	Procedure 48-1: Using the Microscope
4.c Utilize Computer Software to Maintain Systems	Ch. 8	Procedure 13-5: Transcribing a Machine-Dictated Letter Using a Computer or Word Processor

Lytec Exercises Answer Key

These student exercises can be found on the accompanying Evolve website:
http://evolve.elsevier.com/kinn/.

Lesson 1   Setting Up the Appointment Matrix and Scheduling Appointments

Name:

Date:

In this section you will perform these tasks:
• Set up your own practice by copying the Practice files.
• Set up a schedule matrix.
• Schedule appointments.
• Reschedule appointments.
• Cancel appointments.

Steps	Check Here When Completed
Open Lytec Medical 2001. On the main program menu, click File and *Open Practice*. Select *Blackburn Primary Care Associates*. To set up your own practice, right-click and select Copy from the menu. Click on the blank white space below the *Blackburn Primary Care Associates* file, right-click, and select *Paste*. This creates a copy of the lpf file. Always save your changes to this copied file. You can rename this file by selecting copied file, right-click, and select *Rename*. Shortcut: On the file menu click on *1 Copy of Blackburn Primary Care Associates.lpf* as it is listed above the word *exit*.	
On the main program menu, click *Activities*, then click *Schedule Appointments*. Shortcut: Click the 6th icon from the right on the toolbar or use *Control S* to open the Schedule Dialog box.	
The dialog box opens to the Day tab. Click today's date on the calendar to the right	

To set up the appointment Matrix for the practice, click on *Resource* button. On the resource menu, select *New Resource*.

1. Type in Dr. Howard Lawler. Set his appointments between 9 am and 5 pm in 15-minute increments. Click *OK*.

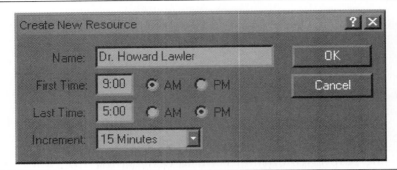

2. Type in Dr. Joanne Hughes. Set her appointments between 9 am and noon in 15-minute increments. Click *OK*.

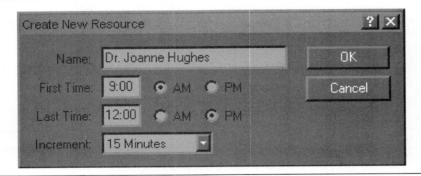

3. Type in Dr. Ralph Lopez. Set his appointments between 1 pm and 5 pm in 15-minute increments. Click *OK*.

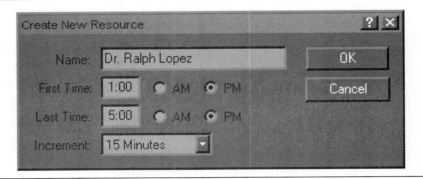

To view the appointment book, switch to the *Multiple Resource* tab.

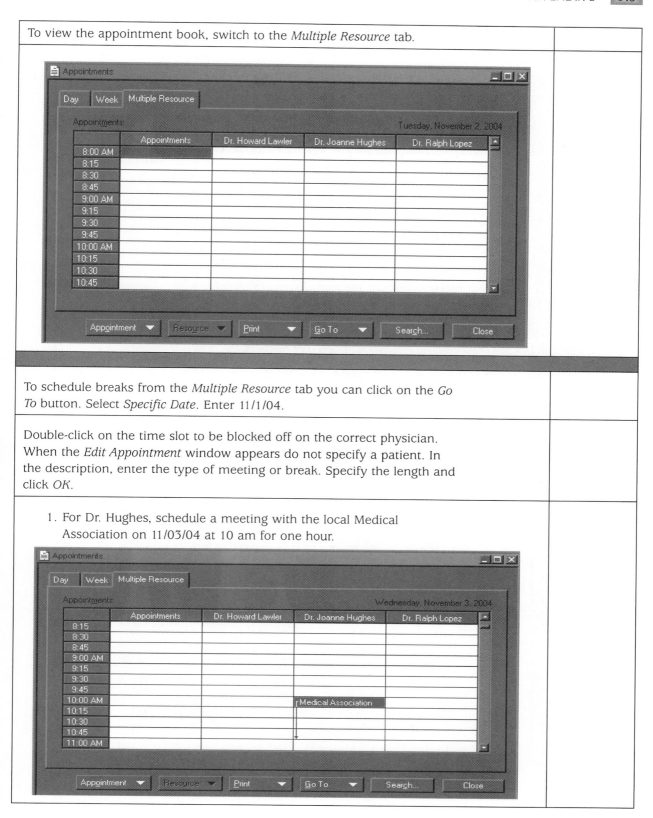

To schedule breaks from the *Multiple Resource* tab you can click on the *Go To* button. Select *Specific Date*. Enter 11/1/04.

Double-click on the time slot to be blocked off on the correct physician. When the *Edit Appointment* window appears do not specify a patient. In the description, enter the type of meeting or break. Specify the length and click *OK*.

1. For Dr. Hughes, schedule a meeting with the local Medical Association on 11/03/04 at 10 am for one hour.

2. Schedule a meeting at the hospital for Dr. Lopez on Tuesday
   11/2/04 at 3 pm for two hours.

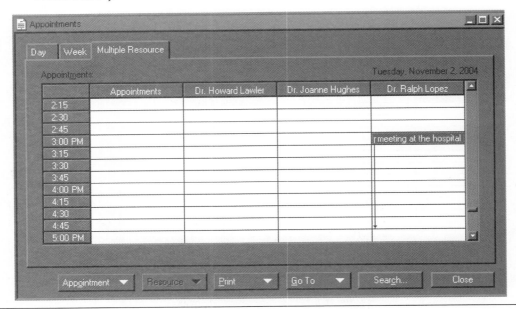

3. Enter daily lunch hours for Dr. Lawler from 12 noon until 1 pm.
   Shortcut: Use the repeated appointment function to save time. Click
   on the *Appointment* button, select *Repeating*. Click the *Add* button.
   Skip patient chart. Type in LUNCH for description. Use the
   magnifying glass to select the correct provider. Now switch to the
   When tab. Select daily. Click OK.

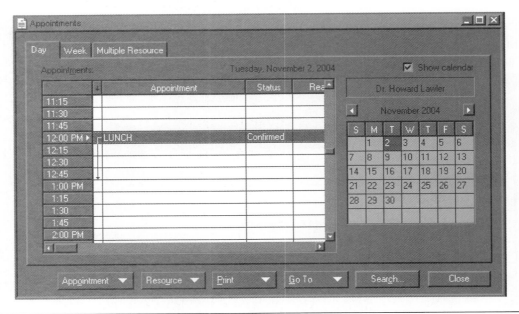

4. Switch to a different day by using the *Go To* button. Verify that Dr. Lawler's lunch break appears at the correct time each day.

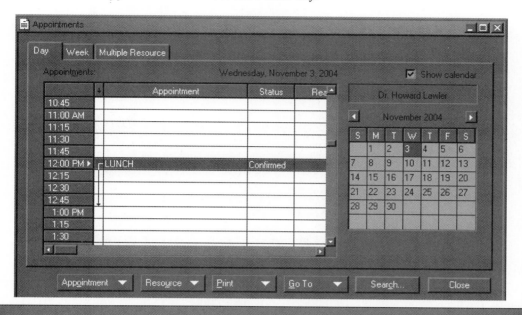

Schedule the following established patients for 11/01/04. Appointments can be entered by clicking on the appointment time in the *Multiple Resource* view. Be sure to use the magnifying glass to locate the patient name.

Shortcut: Double-clicking on the correct patient will populate all of the fields with the required patient information. Be sure to include the correct provider in the Codes section. Use the magnifying glass to pull up all reason codes. Use the *Add* button and type in the appropriate reason for the office visit. Lytec will assign a code if a description is typed in.

1. Thomas Maxwell, Sore throat, Dr. Hughes, 9 am, 15 minutes.

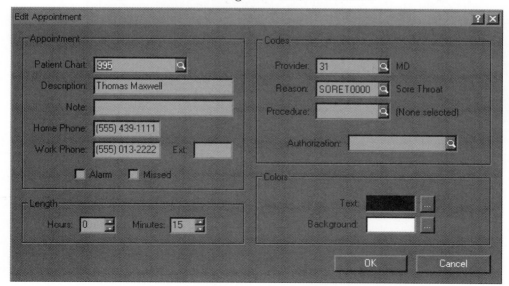

2. Lloyd Ridlon, Wound recheck, Dr. Lawler, 9 am, 15 minutes.

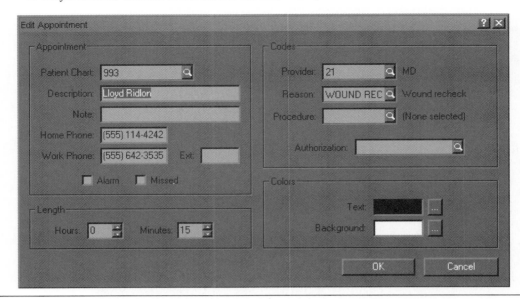

3. Daryl Saitta, Recheck hypertension, Dr. Lopez, 1 pm, 15 minutes.

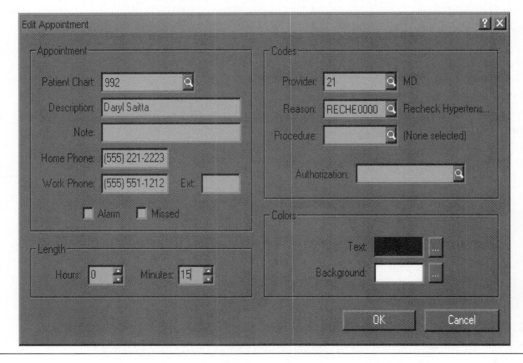

4. Maria Santos, Asthma, Dr. Hughes, 9:15 am, 30 minutes.

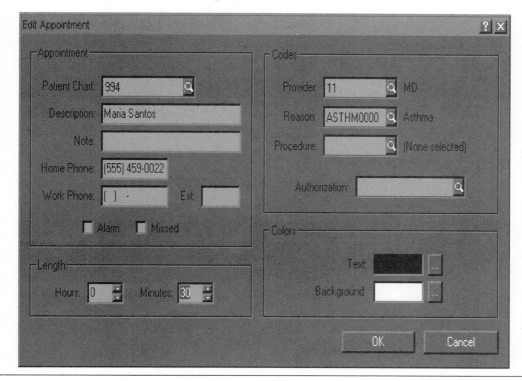

5. June St.Cyr, Chest pain, Dr. Lawler, 10 am, 30 minutes.

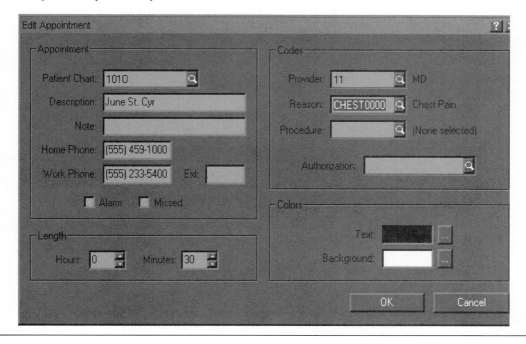

6. James Winston, Recheck heart block, Dr. Hughes, 11 am, 30 minutes.

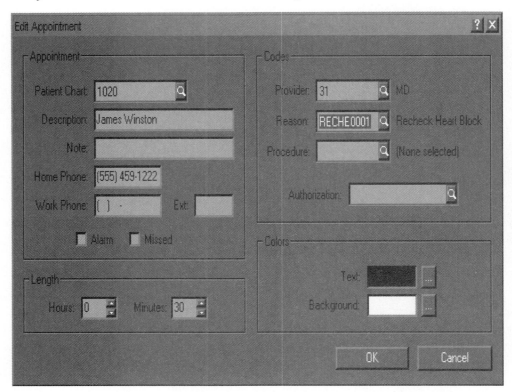

Once these tasks are complete the entire schedule should look like this.

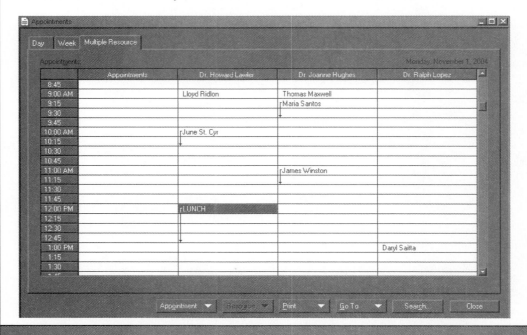

Reschedule appointments by locating the appointment, right-click, and select
Reschedule. Type in a new time or select a new date on the calendar.
Click *OK*.

1. Thomas Maxwell, Dr. Hughes, Change to 11/05/04 9 am.

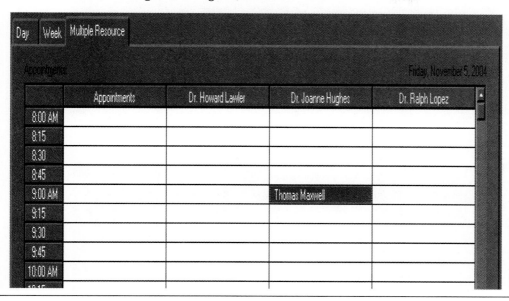

2. Lloyd Ridlon, Dr. Lawler, Change to 11 am.

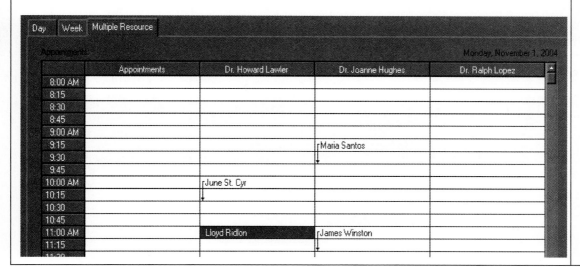

3. Daryl Saitta, Dr. Lopez, Change to 11/03/04 at 1 pm.

| Day | Week | Multiple Resource |

Appointments: Wednesday, November 3, 2004

	Appointments	Dr. Howard Lawler	Dr. Joanne Hughes	Dr. Ralph Lopez
12:00 PM		┌LUNCH		
12:15				
12:30				
12:45		↓		
1:00 PM				Daryl Saitta
1:15				

4. Maria Santos, Dr. Hughes, Change to 10:15 am.

| Day | Week | Multiple Resource |

Appointments: Monday, November 1, 2004

	Appointments	Dr. Howard Lawler	Dr. Joanne Hughes	Dr. Ralph Lopez
8:00 AM				
8:15				
8:30				
8:45				
9:00 AM				
9:15				
9:30				
9:45				
10:00 AM		┌June St. Cyr		
10:15		↓	┌Maria Santos	
10:30			↓	

5. June St. Cyr, Dr. Lawler, Change to 9 am.

| Day | Week | Multiple Resource |

Appointments: Monday, November 1, 2004

	Appointments	Dr. Howard Lawler	Dr. Joanne Hughes	Dr. Ralph Lopez
8:00 AM				
8:15				
8:30				
8:45				
9:00 AM		┌June St. Cyr		
9:15		↓		
9:30				
9:45				

6. James Winston, Dr. Hughes, Change to 9 am.

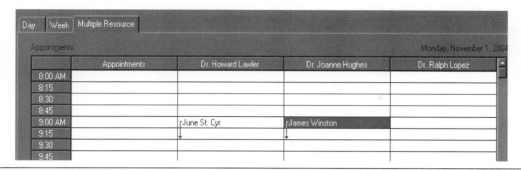

7. Change Thomas Maxwell's appointment from Dr. Hughes to Dr. Lawler on 11/05/04 by viewing the appointment in the *Multiple Resource* view. Right-click on the original appointment and *Cut*. A window will pop-up and ask if you want to delete the original appointment. Click *Yes*. Select the new time and provider, right-click, and *Paste*

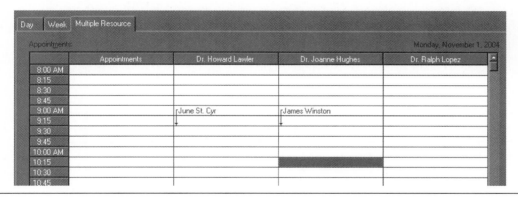

8. Use this method to cancel the appointment for Maria Santos.

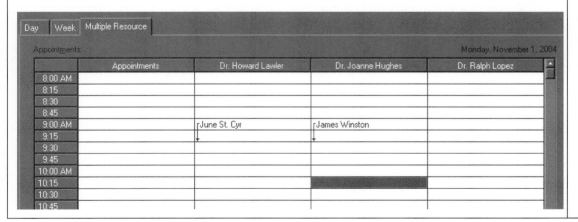

9. Reschedule Mrs. Santos for 11/02/04 for Dr. Hughes at 9 am for
   a 15 minute recheck for asthma.

	Appointments	Dr. Howard Lawler	Dr. Joanne Hughes	Dr. Ralph Lopez
8:00 AM				
8:15				
8:30				
8:45				
9:00 AM			Maria Santos	
9:15				
9:30				
9:45				

Day | Week | Multiple Resource

Appointments: Tuesday, November 2, 2004

10. Use the cut and paste method to change the time for Mrs. Santos's
    appointment to 10 am for the same doctor.

	Appointments	Dr. Howard Lawler	Dr. Joanne Hughes	Dr. Ralph Lopez
9:00 AM				
9:15				
9:30				
9:45				
10:00 AM			Maria Santos	
10:15				
10:30				
10:45				
11:00 AM				
11:15				

Day | Week | Multiple Resource

Appointments: Tuesday, November 2, 2004

Lesson 2   Recording Demographic and Insurance Information

Name:

Date:

In this section you will perform these tasks: • Register existing patients and update information. • Register new patients.	
Steps	**Check Here When Completed**
Open Lytec Medical 2001. On the main program menu, click *File* and *Open Practice*. Select *Blackburn Primary Care Associates*. If you have not done so, set up your own practice. To set up your own practice, right-click and select *Copy* from the menu. Click on the blank white space below the *Blackburn Primary Care Associates* file, right-click and select *Paste*. This creates a copy of the lpf file. Always save your changes to this copied file. You can rename this file by selecting copied file, right-click, and select *Rename*. Shortcut: On the file menu click on *1 Copy of Blackburn Primary Care Associates.lpf* as it is listed above the word *exit*.	
On the main program menu, click *Lists* and select *Patients*. The *Patients* window will open and show the first patient in the database. Click on the magnifying glass beside the patient ID number to open the *Find Patient* window. Shortcut: Click the 6th icon from the left on the toolbar or use *Control P* to open the Patients box.	

To register existing patients and update information, double-click on the correct name to view the patient information.

Type in the following changes to patient data and *Save*.

7. Thomas Maxwell, change address to 42 Delray Ave.

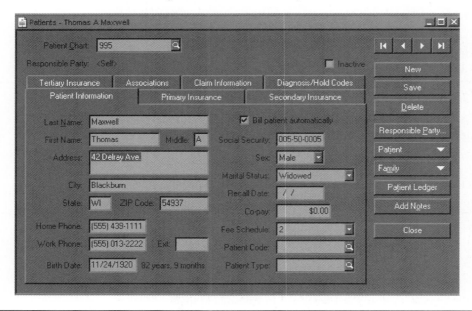

8. Lloyd Ridlon, change co-pay to $10.

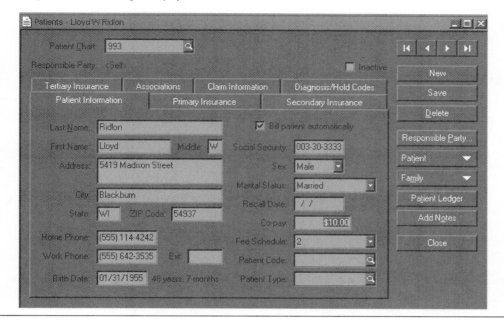

9. Daryl Saitta, change marital status to Married.

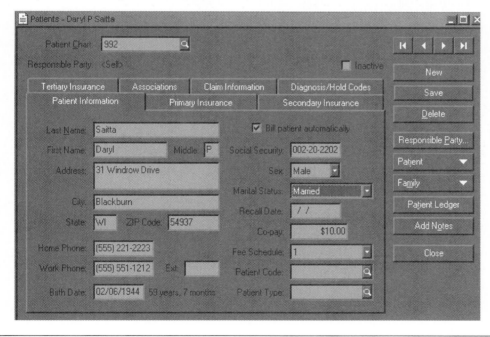

10. Maria Santos, change martial status to Divorced.

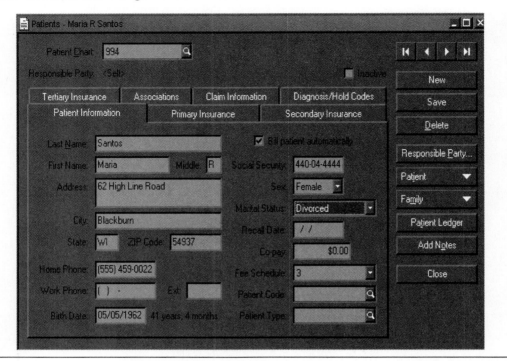

11. June St. Cyr, change work phone to 233-1212.

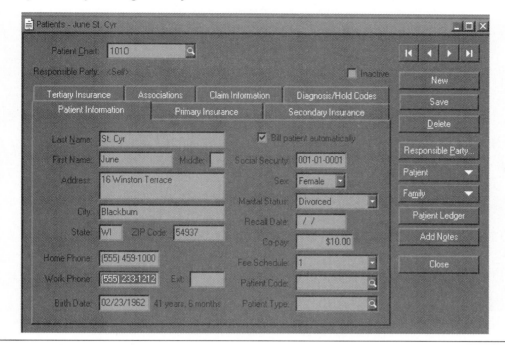

12. James Winston, change address to 32 West St.

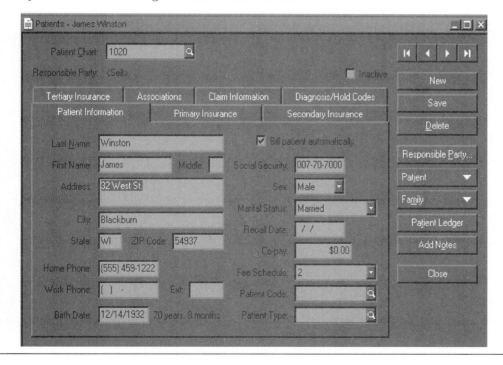

13. Mary St. Cyr, change address to 43 Magnolia Lane.

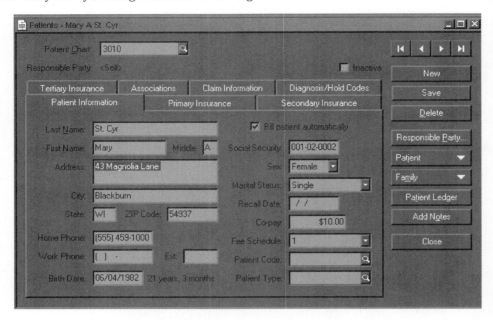

Register a new patient. In the patient window, Click *New* and type in the following information. Click *Save* when complete.

Robert H. Keese
1754 Magnolia Lane
Blackburn, WI 54937
Home phone: 555-221-4537
Work phone: 555-332-6758
SSN: 003-03-0333
Married, male, date of birth 09-10-40
Primary insurance: Standard Health Care HMO
Insured: Self through employer
Policy number: JH2269

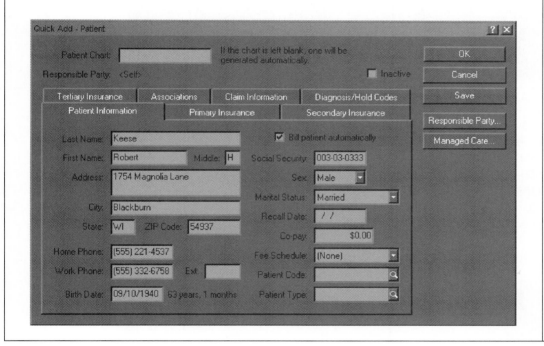

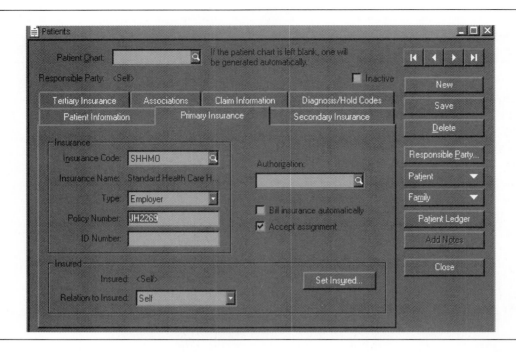

Tami Yi
543 Melbourne Avenue
Blackburn, WI 54937
Home phone: 555-221-3480
Work phone: 555-332-5648
SSN: 008-88-0888
Married, female, date of birth 06-11-37
Primary insurance: Medicare
Insured: Self
Policy number: 008-88-0888A

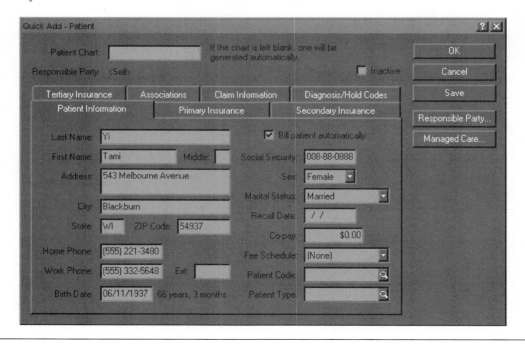

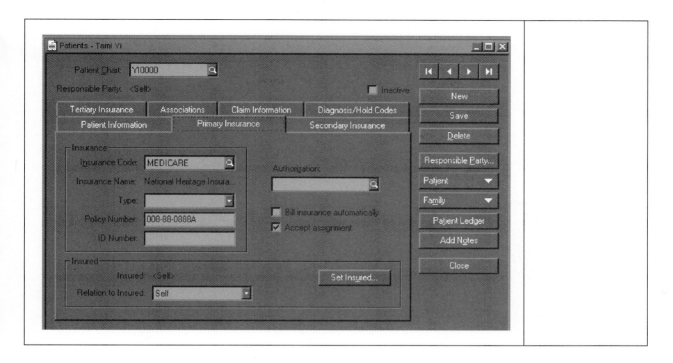

Lesson 3   Entering Patient Charges

Name:

Date:

In this section you will perform these tasks: • Enter charges from patient encounters. • Enter ICD, CPT, and POS codes for insurance processing.	
Steps	**Check Here When Completed**
Open Lytec Medical 2001. On the main program menu, click *File* and *Open Practice*. Select *Blackburn Primary Care Associates*. If you have not done so, set up your own practice. To set up your own practice, right-click and select *Copy* from the menu. Click on the blank white space below the *Blackburn Primary Care Associates* File, right-click, and select *Paste*. This creates a copy of the lpf file. Always save your changes to this copied file. You can rename this file by selecting copied file, right-click, and select *Rename*. Shortcut: On the file menu click on *1 Copy of Blackburn Primary Care Associates*. *lpf* as it is listed above the word *exit*.	
On the main program menu, click *Billing* and select *Charges and Payments*.; The *Charges and Payments* window will open. Click on the magnifying glass beside the patient chart box to open the *Find Patient* window. Shortcut: Click the 12th Icon from the left on the toolbar or use *Control B* to open the Charges and Payments box.	
Complete these steps with all charge exercises. Double-click on the correct name to view the patient information. Lytec automatically creates a new billing number for this new encounter. To view previous visit use the magnifying glass. Press *Enter* to scroll to the next field: this populates the next field.	
The provider field always defaults to the patient's primary physician. Use the magnifying glass to look up other providers. Double-click on the correct provider for this encounter.	
Tab to Created Date box and change the date of the encounter.	
Under the Co-pay field, enter $10 for Standard Health HMO. Enter $15 if the patient has Standard Health Indemnity Insurance. Use the 6th icon from the left to find insurance information for each patient.	

Click under *Billing* information to the right. Make sure the *Patient* and *Primary Insurance* boxes are checked.	
Use the Enter key to scroll to *Detail Items*. The print box should always be checked. Under *Detail Items* change date, press *Enter* to tab to the *Diagnosis and Code* area. Use the lookup feature to find the correct *Diagnosis, Procedure,* and *POS* (11 is for Doctor's Office). Press *Save* when complete.	
If the same patient has more than one charge per visit, click *New* and repeat the process for the second charge or press *Enter* in the last field of the first charge to create a new charge line.	
Type in the following charges for office visits dated 10/25/2000 and *Save*.	
14. Thomas Maxwell, Focused OV, Established patient, Dx Hyperplasia of the prostate. Saw Dr. Hughes.	
15. Thomas Maxwell, same visit, Dip urinalysis, Dx Hyperplasia of the prostate. Saw Dr. Hughes. 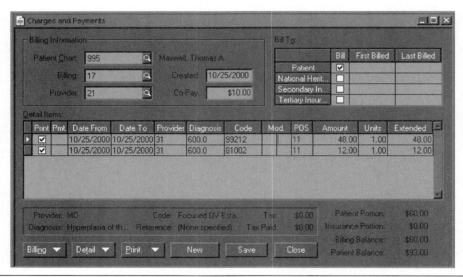	
16. Lloyd Ridlon Intermediate OV, Established patient, Dx Open Wound of the hand. Saw Dr. Lawler.	

17. Lloyd Ridlon same visit, Tetanus Shot, Dx Open Wound of the
    hand. Saw Dr. Lawler.

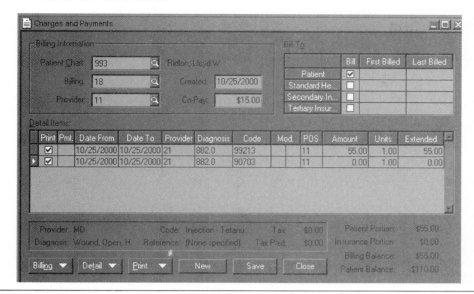

18. Daryl Saitta, Focused OV, Dx Hypertension. Saw Dr. Lopez.

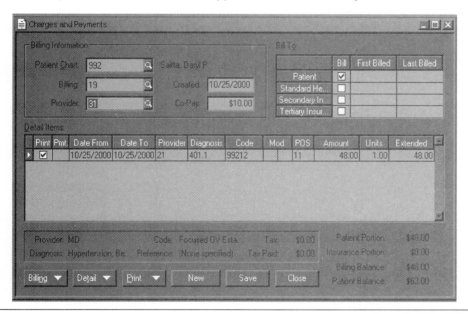

19. Maria Santos, Intermediate OV, Established patient, Dx Asthma.
    Saw Dr. Hughes.

20. Maira Santos, same visit, Spirometry, Dx Asthma. Saw Dr. Hughes.

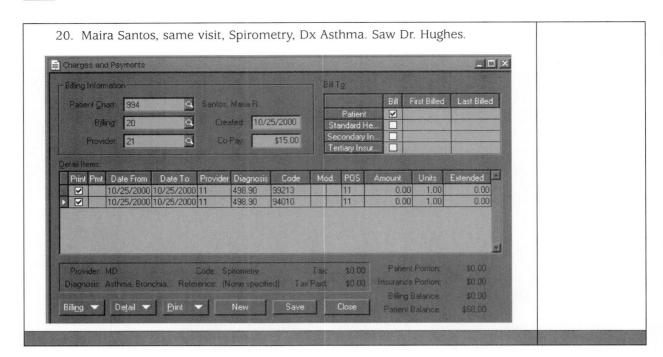

Lesson 4   Entering Payments

Name:

Date:

Steps	Check Here When Completed
In this section you will perform these tasks:	
• Enter payments from patients.	
• Enter insurance payments.	

Steps	Check Here When Completed
Open Lytec Medical 2001. On the main program menu, click *File* and *Open Practice*. Select *Blackburn Primary Care Associates*. If you have not done so, set up your own practice. To set up your own practice, right-click and select *Copy* from the menu. Click on the blank white space below the *Blackburn Primary Care Associates* file, right-click and select *Paste*. This creates a copy of the lpf file. Always save your changes to this copied file. You can rename this file by selecting copied file, right-click, and select *Rename*. Shortcut: On the file menu click on *1 Copy of Blackburn Primary Care Associates.lpf* as it is listed above the word *exit*.	
On the main program menu click *Billing* then *Apply Patient Payment*. The window will open. Click on the magnifying glass beside the patient box to open the *Find Patient window*. Shortcut: *Use Control D* to open the Apply Patient Payment box.	
Select the correct patient's name or guarantor if payment is made on behalf of the patient.	
Enter the date of the payment.	
If paid by check, enter check number under Reference.	
Enter the total of the payment under Payment Amount.	
Patient Payment: Use the lookup feature and select cash or check.	
Write off box: Select Adjustment/credit from the lookup feature.	
Select *Next* to proceed to the next screen.	
Apply payments at the billing level. Note that one payment can be applied to several bills. The payment amount at the top will automatically decrease with each posting. For example one $25 payment can be posted to both a $10 and a $15 charge.	

Post the following patient payments dated 10/25/2000.

21. Thomas Maxwell, Check #423, $25 total, Apply $10 to last change.

22. Thomas Maxwell, Apply remaining $15 to the next to the last charge. Post.

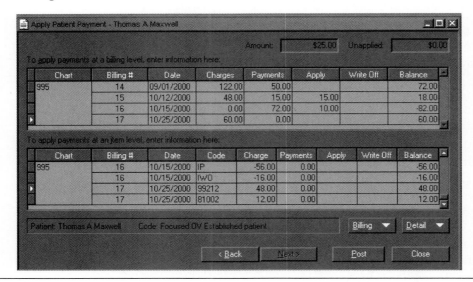

Apply Patient Payment - Thomas A Maxwell

Amount: $25.00   Unapplied: $0.00

To apply payments at a billing level, enter information here:

Chart	Billing #	Date	Charges	Payments	Apply	Write Off	Balance
995	14	09/01/2000	122.00	50.00			72.00
	15	10/12/2000	48.00	15.00	15.00		18.00
	16	10/15/2000	0.00	72.00	10.00		-82.00
	17	10/25/2000	60.00	0.00			60.00

To apply payments at an item level, enter information here:

Chart	Billing #	Date	Code	Charge	Payments	Apply	Write Off	Balance
995	16	10/15/2000	IP	-56.00	0.00			-56.00
	16	10/15/2000	IWO	-16.00	0.00			-16.00
	17	10/25/2000	99212	48.00	0.00			48.00
	17	10/25/2000	81002	12.00	0.00			12.00

Patient: Thomas A Maxwell   Code: Focused OV Established patient   Billing ▼   Detail ▼

< Back   Next >   Post   Close

23. Lloyd Ridlon, $15 Cash, Apply $15 to the last visi. Post.

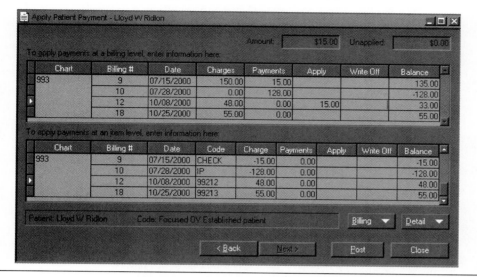

24. Daryl Saitta, Check #784, Apply $15 to last visit. Post.

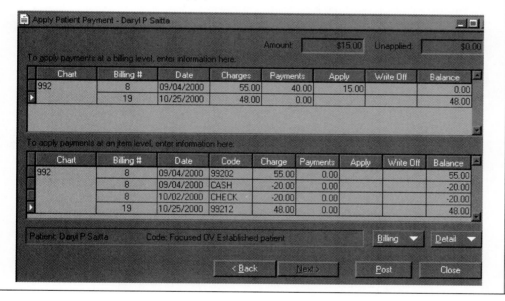

25. Maria Santos, $50, Cash, Apply $68 to balance Post.

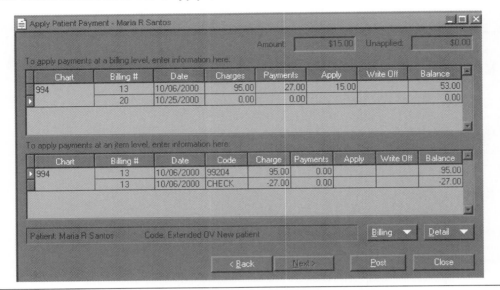

26. June St. Cyr, $15 Cash, Apply to account. Post.

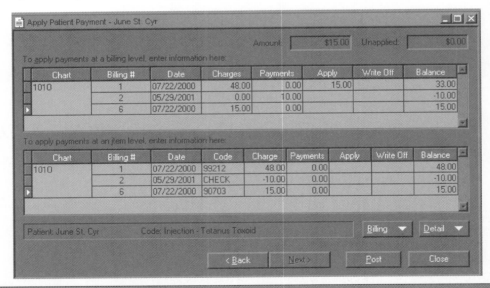

On the main program menu *Billing* then select *Charges and Payments,* and the window will open.

Shortcut: Use *Control B* to open the Charges and Payments box.	
Use the look up function to find the correct patient.	
Use the lookup function to select *Billing* information. The Detail Items will appear. Select any box on a line in the details area and press enter until a new line appears.	
On the new line enter the date of the payment and select the *Codes* area. Use the lookup function to select *Insurance Payment*. Type in amount. *Save*.	
Verify the payment by checking the patient ledger. Select *Billing* and *Patient Ledger* or *Control R*.	
Post the following insurance payments.	
1. Standard Health Insurance for Lloyd Ridln $40 check #5689.	

Patient Ledger - Lloyd W Ridlon

Please select a: ● Patient: 993   ☐ Display all family members   Sort by: Billing
○ Guarantor: Amounts: Patient/Insurance

Account activity:

Date	Chart	Billing	Provider	Code	Description	Patient	Insurance	Balance
07/15/2000	993	9			Patient co-pay	15.00	-15.00	135.00
07/28/2000	993	10	21	IP	Insurance Paym...	0.00	-128.00	7.00
07/28/2000	993	10			Not covered by i...	-128.00	128.00	7.00
10/08/2000	993	12	21	99212	Focused OV Est...	0.00	48.00	55.00
10/24/2000	993	12	21	CASH	Patient Payment ...	-15.00	0.00	40.00
10/08/2000	993	12			Patient co-pay	15.00	-15.00	40.00
10/25/2000	993	18	21	99213	Intermediate OV ...	55.00	0.00	95.00
10/25/2000	993	18	21	90703	Injection - Tetan...	0.00	0.00	95.00
10/25/2000	993	18	21	IP	Insurance Paym...	-40.00	0.00	55.00

Patient: Lloyd W Ridlon   -$113.00 $168.00 $55.00
Note: (None)
Primary: Standard Health Care   Tertiary: (None)
Secondary: (None)   Provider: MD

[Filter] [History] [Close]

2. Standard Health for Daryl Saitta for $15 check #482.

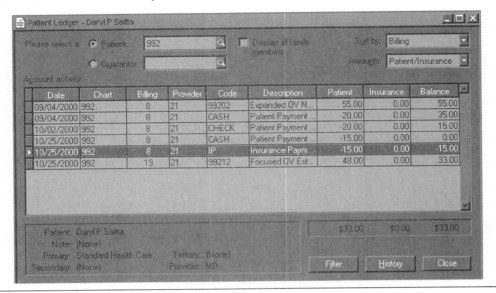

3. National Heritage Insurance for James Winston check #8753

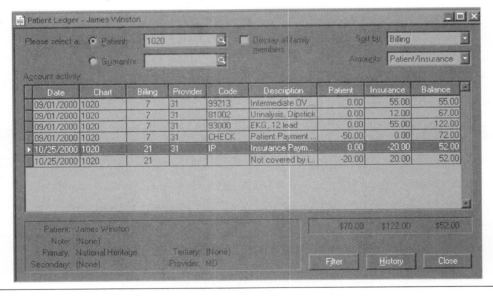

4. Standard Health Care HMO for Mary St. Cyr $15, check #657.

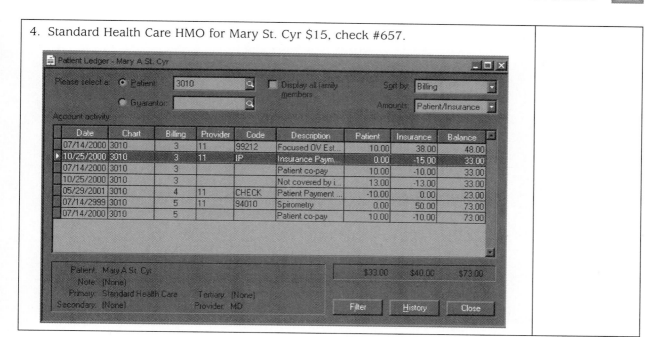

Lesson 5   Creating Receipts, Bills, and Insurance Billing

Name:

Date:

Steps	Check Here When Completed
In this section you will perform these tasks: • Print bills, receipts, and batches of statement. • Print insurance forms.	
Open Lytec Medical 2001. On the main program menu, click *File* and *Open Practice*. Select *Blackburn Primary Care Associates*. If you have not done so, set up your own practice. To set up your own practice, right-click, and select *Copy* from the menu. Click on the blank white space below the *Blackburn Primary Care Associates* file, right-click, and select paste. This creates a copy of the lpf file. Always save your changes to this copied file. You can rename this file by selecting copied file, right-click, and select *Rename*. Shortcut: On the file menu click on *1 Copy of Blackburn Primary Care Associates.lpf* as it is listed above the word *exit*.	
On the main program menu select *Billing*. Select *Charges and Payments* and the window will open. Click on the magnifying glass beside the patient chart box to open the *Find Patient* window. Shortcut: Click the 12th icon from the left on the toolbar or use *Control B* to open the Charges and Payments box.	
Continue to press *Enter* until the fields are populated. Select the appropriate billing code by using the lookup function. Make sure *Patient* and *Primary Insurance* are checked to the right in the *Bill to* section.	
Click on the Print button, select *Statement*.	
When the Select Custom Forms window opens, you may have to use the *Go Up One Level* icon to view the available forms.	
Select *Statement-Standard.lcs* and click *Open*.	
Click *Preview*. On the Preview window, click the Print icon.	

Print bills for the following patients.

27. Thomas Maxwell

Statement of Account

Blackburn Primary Care Associates

Account No.
995

Page #
1

Thomas A. Maxwell
42 Delray Ave.
Blackburn, WI 54937

Date
10/25/2000

Date	For	Description	Ref	Charges	Credits
10/25/2000	Thomas	Focused OV Established patient	17	48.00	
10/25/2000	Thomas	Urinalysis, Dipstick	17	12.00	

0 - 30 Days Current	31 - 60 Days Past Due	61 - 90 Days Past Due	91 - 120 Days Past Due	> 120 Days Past Due	Balance Due
$60.00	$0.00	$0.00	$0.00	$0.00	$60.00

Notes

28. Lloyd Ridlon

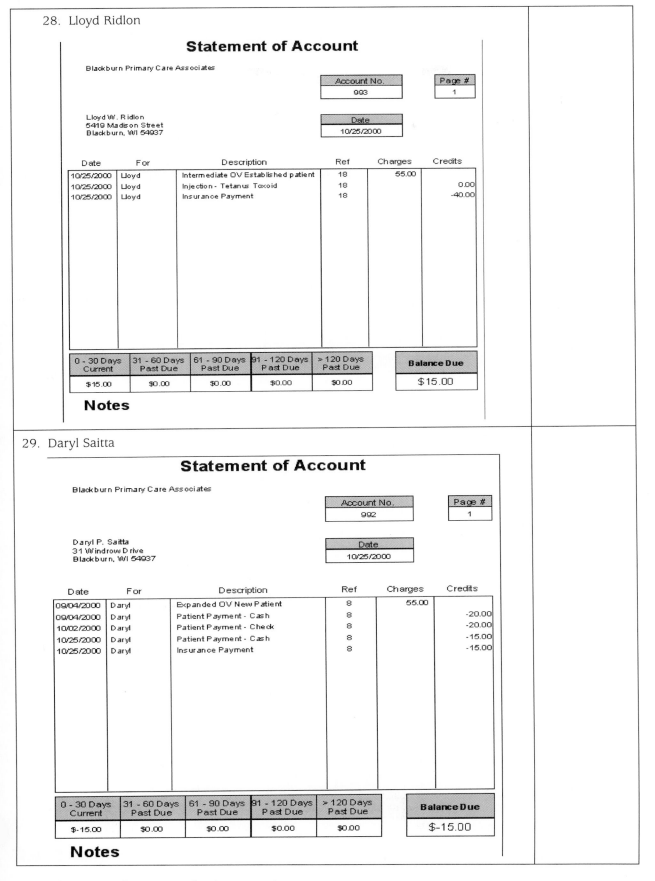

Statement of Account

Blackburn Primary Care Associates

Account No.	Page #
993	1

Lloyd W. Ridlon
5419 Madison Street
Blackburn, WI 54937

Date
10/25/2000

Date	For	Description	Ref	Charges	Credits
10/25/2000	Lloyd	Intermediate OV Established patient	18	55.00	
10/25/2000	Lloyd	Injection - Tetanus Toxoid	18		0.00
10/25/2000	Lloyd	Insurance Payment	18		-40.00

0 - 30 Days Current	31 - 60 Days Past Due	61 - 90 Days Past Due	91 - 120 Days Past Due	> 120 Days Past Due	Balance Due
$15.00	$0.00	$0.00	$0.00	$0.00	$15.00

Notes

---

29. Daryl Saitta

Statement of Account

Blackburn Primary Care Associates

Account No.	Page #
992	1

Daryl P. Saitta
31 Windrow Drive
Blackburn, WI 54937

Date
10/25/2000

Date	For	Description	Ref	Charges	Credits
09/04/2000	Daryl	Expanded OV New Patient	8	55.00	
09/04/2000	Daryl	Patient Payment - Cash	8		-20.00
10/02/2000	Daryl	Patient Payment - Check	8		-20.00
10/25/2000	Daryl	Patient Payment - Cash	8		-15.00
10/25/2000	Daryl	Insurance Payment	8		-15.00

0 - 30 Days Current	31 - 60 Days Past Due	61 - 90 Days Past Due	91 - 120 Days Past Due	> 120 Days Past Due	Balance Due
$-15.00	$0.00	$0.00	$0.00	$0.00	$-15.00

Notes

30. Maria santos

Statement of Account

Blackburn Primary Care Associates

Account No.	Page #
994	1

Maria R. Santos
62 High Line Road
Blackburn, WI 54937

Date
10/25/2000

Date	For	Description	Ref	Charges	Credits
10/06/2000	Maria	Extended OV New patient	13	95.00	
10/06/2000	Maria	Patient Payment - Check	13		-27.00

0 - 30 Days Current	31 - 60 Days Past Due	61 - 90 Days Past Due	91 - 120 Days Past Due	> 120 Days Past Due	Balance Due
$68.00	$0.00	$0.00	$0.00	$0.00	$68.00

Notes

31. June St. Cyr

Statement of Account

Blackburn Primary Care Associates

Account No.	Page #
1010	1

June St. Cyr
16 Winston Terrace
Blackburn, WI 54937

Date
10/25/2000

Date	For	Description	Ref	Charges	Credits
07/22/2000	June	Focused OV Established patient	1	48.00	
10/25/2000	June	Patient Payment - Cash	1		-15.00

0 - 30 Days Current	31 - 60 Days Past Due	61 - 90 Days Past Due	91 - 120 Days Past Due	> 120 Days Past Due	Balance Due
$33.00	$0.00	$0.00	$0.00	$0.00	$33.00

Notes

To print batches of bills, go to *Billing* and select *Print Statements* or *Control W.* Choose *Statement-Standard with Notes.lcs* on the Custom Forms Window. You may have to use the *Go Up One Level* icon to view the forms

Under the Options tab, enter the date, Standard and Dunning message, select sorting by patient name, combine family members, current month only.

Under the range tab choose the provider.

Click *Preview*. Use the arrows to view all records.

1. Print a batch of statements for Dr. Hughes.

Statement of Account

Blackburn Primary Care Associates

Account No.	Page #
993	1

Lloyd W. Ridlon
5419 Madison Street
Blackburn, WI 54937

Date
10/25/2000

Date	For	Description	Ref	Charges	Credits
10/08/2000	Lloyd	Focused OV Established patient	12	48.00	
10/24/2000	Lloyd	Patient Payment - Cash	12		-15.00
10/25/2000	Lloyd	Intermediate OV Established patient	18	55.00	
10/25/2000	Lloyd	Injection - Tetanus Toxoid	18		0.00
10/25/2000	Lloyd	Insurance Payment	18		-40.00

0 - 30 Days Current	31 - 60 Days Past Due	61 - 90 Days Past Due	91 - 120 Days Past Due	> 120 Days Past Due		Balance Due
$48.00	$0.00	$0.00	$0.00	$0.00		$48.00

Notes

Statement of Account

Blackburn Primary Care Associates

Account No.	Page #
992	1

Daryl P. Saitta
31 Windrow Drive
Blackburn, WI 54937

Date
10/25/2000

Date	For	Description	Ref	Charges	Credits
09/04/2000	Daryl	Expanded OV New Patient	8	55.00	
09/04/2000	Daryl	Patient Payment - Cash	8		-20.00
10/02/2000	Daryl	Patient Payment - Check	8		-20.00
10/25/2000	Daryl	Patient Payment - Cash	8		-15.00
10/25/2000	Daryl	Insurance Payment	8		-15.00
10/25/2000	Daryl	Focused OV Established patient	19	48.00	

0 - 30 Days Current	31 - 60 Days Past Due	61 - 90 Days Past Due	91 - 120 Days Past Due	> 120 Days Past Due	Balance Due
$33.00	$0.00	$0.00	$0.00	$0.00	$33.00

2. Print a batch of statements for Dr. Lopez.

Statement of Account

Blackburn Primary Care Associates

Account No.	Page #
995	1

Thomas A. Maxwell
42 Delray Ave.
Blackburn, WI 54937

Date
09/06/2003

Date	For	Description	Ref	Charges	Credits
10/25/2000	Thomas	Focused OV Established patient	17	48.00	
10/25/2000	Thomas	Urinalysis, Dipstick	17	12.00	

0 - 30 Days Current	31 - 60 Days Past Due	61 - 90 Days Past Due	91 - 120 Days Past Due	> 120 Days Past Due	Balance Due
$0.00	$0.00	$0.00	$0.00	$60.00	$60.00

To print an insurance claim, on the main program menu select *Billing*. Select *Charges and Payments* and the window will open. Click on the magnifying glass beside the patient chart box to open the *Find Patient* window.

Shortcut: Click the 12th icon from the left on the toolbar or use *Control B* to open the Charges and Payment box.

Continue to press *Enter* until the fields are populated. Select the appropriate billing code by using the lookup function. Make sure *Patient* and *Primary insurance* are checked to the right in the *Bill to* section.

Under the Print button, click *Primary Insurance*.

When the Select Custom Forms window opens, you may have to use the *Go Up One Level* icon to view the available forms.

Select HCFA-Standard (With Form). LCI and Click *Open*.

Click *Preview*. On the preview window, click the Print icon.

Print insurance forms for the most recent visit for the following patients.

1. Thomas Maxwell

PLEASE
DO NOT
STAPLE
IN THIS
AREA

National Heritage Insurance Co.
75 William Terry Drive
Western, WI 43502

HEALTH INSURANCE CLAIM FORM

2. PATIENT'S NAME	Maxwell, Thomas A
3. PATIENT'S BIRTH DATE	11 24 1920 SEX M [X] F [ ]
4. INSURED'S NAME	Maxwell, Thomas A
5. PATIENT'S ADDRESS	42 Delray Ave.
6. PATIENT RELATIONSHIP TO INSURED	Self [X] Spouse [ ] Child [ ] Other [ ]
7. INSURED'S ADDRESS	42 Delray Ave.
CITY	Blackburn STATE WI
8. PATIENT STATUS	Single [ ] Married [ ] Other [X]
CITY	Blackburn STATE WI
ZIP CODE	54937
TELEPHONE	(555) 439-1111
	Employed [ ] Full-Time Student [ ] Part-Time Student [ ]
ZIP CODE	54937
TELEPHONE	(555) 439-1111
11. INSURED'S POLICY GROUP OR FECA NUMBER	005-60-0005 A

MEDICARE (Medicare #) [X] MEDICAID (Medicaid #) [ ] CHAMPUS (Sponsor's SSN) [ ] CHAMPVA (VA File #) [ ] GROUP HEALTH PLAN (SSN or ID) [ ] FECA BLK LUNG (SSN) [ ] OTHER (ID) [ ]

9. OTHER INSURED'S NAME

10. IS PATIENT'S CONDITION RELATED TO:

a. EMPLOYMENT? (CURRENT OR PREVIOUS) YES [ ] NO [X]

a. INSURED'S DATE OF BIRTH 11 24 1920 SEX M [X] F [ ]

b. OTHER INSURED'S DATE OF BIRTH

b. AUTO ACCIDENT? YES [ ] NO [X] PLACE (State)

c. EMPLOYER'S NAME OR SCHOOL NAME

c. OTHER ACCIDENT? YES [ ] NO [X]

c. INSURANCE PLAN NAME OR PROGRAM: National Heritage Insurance Co.

d. IS THERE ANOTHER HEALTH BENEFIT PLAN? YES [ ] NO [X]

12. PATIENT'S OR AUTHORIZED PERSON'S SIGNATURE
SIGNED _____ DATE 09 06 2003

13. INSURED'S OR AUTHORIZED PERSON'S SIGNATURE
SIGNED _____

20. OUTSIDE LAB? YES [ ] NO [X]

21. DIAGNOSIS OR NATURE OF ILLNESS OR INJURY
1. 600.0

24. A. DATE(S) OF SERVICE From MM DD YY	To MM DD YY	B. Place of Service	C. Type of Service	D. PROCEDURES, SERVICES, OR SUPPLIES CPT/HCPCS MODIFIER	E. DIAGNOSIS CODE	F. $ CHARGES	G. DAYS OR UNITS	H. EPSDT Family Plan	I. EMG	J. COB	K. RESERVED FOR LOCAL USE
10 25 2000	10 25 2000	11			1	48 00	1				
10 25 2000	10 25 2000	11			1	12 00	1				

25. FEDERAL TAX I.D. NUMBER		26. PATIENT'S ACCOUNT NO.	27. ACCEPT ASSIGNMENT?	28. TOTAL CHARGE	29. AMOUNT PAID	30. BALANCE DUE
00-0000000 SSN [ ] EIN [X]		995	YES [X] NO [ ]	60 00	0 00	60 00

31. SIGNATURE OF PHYSICIAN OR SUPPLIER
MD
SIGNED 09 06 2003 DATE

32. NAME AND ADDRESS OF FACILITY WHERE SERVICES WERE RENDERED

33. PHYSICIAN'S, SUPPLIER'S BILLING NAME, ADDRESS, ZIP CODE & PHONE #
Blackburn Primary Care Associates
( ) -
PIN: GRP: 01-23456789

2. Llyod Ridlon

Standard Health Care Indemnity
4200 Winston Street
Western, WI 45000

HEALTH INSURANCE CLAIM FORM

PICA

1. MEDICARE	MEDICAID	CHAMPUS	CHAMPVA	GROUP HEALTH PLAN	FECA BLK LUNG	OTHER	1a. INSURED'S I.D. NUMBER (FOR PROGRAM IN ITEM 1)
(Medicare #)	(Medicaid #)	(Sponsor's SSN)	(VA File #)	[X] (SSN or ID)	(SSN)	(ID)	

2. PATIENT'S NAME (Last Name, First Name, Middle Initial)
Ridlon, Lloyd W

3. PATIENT'S BIRTH DATE MM 01 DD 31 YY 1955   SEX M [X] F

4. INSURED'S NAME (Last Name, First Name, Middle Initial)
Ridlon, Lloyd W

5. PATIENT'S ADDRESS (No., Street)
5419 Madison Street

6. PATIENT RELATIONSHIP TO INSURED
Self [X] Spouse Child Other

7. INSURED'S ADDRESS (No., Street)
5419 Madison Street

CITY Blackburn   STATE WI

8. PATIENT STATUS
Single Married [X] Other
Employed Full-Time Student Part-Time Student

CITY Blackburn   STATE WI

ZIP CODE 54937   TELEPHONE (Include Area Code) (555) 114-4242

ZIP CODE 54937   TELEPHONE (INCLUDE AREA CODE) (555) 114-4242

9. OTHER INSURED'S NAME (Last Name, First Name, Middle Initial)

10. IS PATIENT'S CONDITION RELATED TO:

11. INSURED'S POLICY GROUP OR FECA NUMBER
12345-67

a. OTHER INSURED'S POLICY OR GROUP NUMBER

a. EMPLOYMENT? (CURRENT OR PREVIOUS)
YES [X] NO

a. INSURED'S DATE OF BIRTH MM 01 DD 31 YY 1955   SEX M [X] F

b. OTHER INSURED'S DATE OF BIRTH MM DD YY   SEX M F

b. AUTO ACCIDENT? PLACE (State)
YES [X] NO

b. EMPLOYER'S NAME OR SCHOOL NAME

c. EMPLOYER'S NAME OR SCHOOL NAME

c. OTHER ACCIDENT?
YES [X] NO

c. INSURANCE PLAN NAME OR PROGRAM
Standard Health Care Indemnity

d. INSURANCE PLAN NAME OR PROGRAM NAME

10d. RESERVED FOR LOCAL USE

d. IS THERE ANOTHER HEALTH BENEFIT PLAN?
YES [X] NO   If yes, return to and complete item 9 a-d.

READ BACK OF FORM BEFORE COMPLETING & SIGNING THIS FORM

12. PATIENT'S OR AUTHORIZED PERSON'S SIGNATURE I authorize the release of any medical or other information necessary to process this claim. I also request payment of government benefits either to myself or to the party who accepts assignment below.

SIGNED _____   DATE 09 06 2003

13. INSURED'S OR AUTHORIZED PERSON'S SIGNATURE I authorize payment of medical benefits to the undersigned physician or supplier for services described below.

SIGNED _____

14. DATE OF CURRENT ILLNESS (First symptom) OR INJURY (Accident) OR PREGNANCY (LMP) MM DD YY

15. IF PATIENT HAS HAD SAME OR SIMILAR ILLNESS GIVE FIRST DATE MM DD YY

16. DATES PATIENT UNABLE TO WORK IN CURRENT OCCUPATION FROM MM DD YY TO MM DD YY

17. NAME OF REFERRING PHYSICIAN OR OTHER SOURCE

17a. I.D. NUMBER OF REFERRING PHYSICIAN

18. HOSPITALIZATION DATES RELATED TO CURRENT SERVICES FROM MM DD YY TO MM DD YY

19. RESERVED FOR LOCAL USE

20. OUTSIDE LAB? YES [X] NO $ CHARGES

21. DIAGNOSIS OR NATURE OF ILLNESS OR INJURY (RELATE ITEMS 1,2,3 OR 4 TO ITEM 24E BY LINE)
1. 882.0
2.
3.
4.

22. MEDICAID RESUBMISSION CODE   ORIGINAL REF. NO.

23. PRIOR AUTHORIZATION NUMBER

24. A DATE(S) OF SERVICE From MM DD YY	To MM DD YY	B Place of Service	C Type of Service	D PROCEDURES, SERVICES, OR SUPPLIES (Explain Unusual Circumstances) CPT/HCPCS MODIFIER	E DIAGNOSIS CODE	F $ CHARGES	G DAYS OR UNITS	H EPSDT Family Plan	I EMG	J COB	K RESERVED FOR LOCAL USE
10 25 2000	10 25 2000	11			1	55 00	1				
10 25 2000	10 25 2000	11			1	0 00	1				

25. FEDERAL TAX I.D. NUMBER SSN EIN
00-00000000 [X]

26. PATIENT'S ACCOUNT NO.
993

27. ACCEPT ASSIGNMENT? (For govt. claims, see back)
[X] YES NO

28. TOTAL CHARGE $ 55 00

29. AMOUNT PAID $ 0 00

30. BALANCE DUE $ 55 00

31. SIGNATURE OF PHYSICIAN OR SUPPLIER INCLUDING DEGREES OR CREDENTIALS (I certify that the statements on the reverse apply to this bill and are made a part thereof.)
MD
SIGNED _____ DATE 09 06 2003

32. NAME AND ADDRESS OF FACILITY WHERE SERVICES WERE RENDERED (If other than home or office)

33. PHYSICIAN'S SUPPLIER'S BILLING NAME, ADDRESS, ZIP CODE & PHONE #
Blackburn Primary Care Associates

( ) -
PIN#   GRP#

3. Daryl Saitta

PLEASE
DO NOT
STAPLE
IN THIS
AREA

Standard Health Care HMO
1500 Simmit Ave
Western, WI 43000

HEALTH INSURANCE CLAIM FORM

1. MEDICARE / MEDICAID / CHAMPUS / CHAMPVA / GROUP HEALTH PLAN / FECA BLK LUNG / OTHER
(GROUP HEALTH PLAN [X])

1a. INSURED'S I.D. NUMBER (FOR PROGRAM IN ITEM 1)

2. PATIENT'S NAME (Last Name, First Name, Middle Initial)
Saitta, Daryl P

3. PATIENT'S BIRTH DATE 02 06 1944 SEX M [X] F

4. INSURED'S NAME (Last Name, First Name, Middle Initial)
Saitta, Daryl P

5. PATIENT'S ADDRESS (No., Street)
31 Windrow Drive

6. PATIENT RELATIONSHIP TO INSURED
Self [X] Spouse Child Other

7. INSURED'S ADDRESS (No., Street)
31 Windrow Drive

CITY Blackburn **STATE** WI

8. PATIENT STATUS
Single Married [X] Other
Employed Full-Time Student Part-Time Student

CITY Blackburn **STATE** WI

ZIP CODE 54937 **TELEPHONE (Include Area Code)** (555) 221-2223

ZIP CODE 54937 **TELEPHONE (INCLUDE AREA CODE)** (555) 221-2223

9. OTHER INSURED'S NAME (Last Name, First Name, Middle Initial)

10. IS PATIENT'S CONDITION RELATED TO:

11. INSURED'S POLICY GROUP OR FECA NUMBER
000-JH2267

a. OTHER INSURED'S POLICY OR GROUP NUMBER

a. EMPLOYMENT? (CURRENT OR PREVIOUS) YES NO [X]

a. INSURED'S DATE OF BIRTH 02 06 1944 SEX M [X] F

b. OTHER INSURED'S DATE OF BIRTH SEX M F

b. AUTO ACCIDENT? YES NO [X] PLACE (State)

b. EMPLOYER'S NAME OR SCHOOL NAME

c. EMPLOYER'S NAME OR SCHOOL NAME

c. OTHER ACCIDENT? YES NO [X]

c. INSURANCE PLAN NAME OR PROGRAM
Standard Health Care HMO

d. INSURANCE PLAN NAME OR PROGRAM NAME

10d. RESERVED FOR LOCAL USE

d. IS THERE ANOTHER HEALTH BENEFIT PLAN?
YES NO [X] If yes, return to and complete item 9 a-d.

READ BACK OF FORM BEFORE COMPLETING & SIGNING THIS FORM

12. PATIENT'S OR AUTHORIZED PERSON'S SIGNATURE I authorize the release of any medical or other information necessary to process this claim. I also request payment of government benefits either to myself or to the party who accepts assignment below.

SIGNED _____ DATE 09 06 2003

13. INSURED'S OR AUTHORIZED PERSON'S SIGNATURE I authorize payment of medical benefits to the undersigned physician or supplier for services described below.

SIGNED _____

14. DATE OF CURRENT: ILLNESS (First symptom) OR INJURY (Accident) OR PREGNANCY (LMP)

15. IF PATIENT HAS HAD SAME OR SIMILAR ILLNESS GIVE FIRST DATE

16. DATES PATIENT UNABLE TO WORK IN CURRENT OCCUPATION FROM TO

17. NAME OF REFERRING PHYSICIAN OR OTHER SOURCE

17a. I.D. NUMBER OF REFERRING PHYSICIAN

18. HOSPITALIZATION DATES RELATED TO CURRENT SERVICES FROM TO

19. RESERVED FOR LOCAL USE

20. OUTSIDE LAB? YES NO [X] $ CHARGES

21. DIAGNOSIS OR NATURE OF ILLNESS OR INJURY (RELATE ITEMS 1,2,3 OR 4 TO ITEM 24E BY LINE)
1. 401.1
2.
3.
4.

22. MEDICAID RESUBMISSION CODE ORIGINAL REF. NO.

23. PRIOR AUTHORIZATION NUMBER

24. A. DATE(S) OF SERVICE From MM DD YY	To MM DD YY	B. Place of Service	C. Type of Service	D. PROCEDURES, SERVICES, OR SUPPLIES CPT/HCPCS	MODIFIER	E. DIAGNOSIS CODE	F. $ CHARGES	G. DAYS OR UNITS	H. EPSDT Family Plan	I. EMG	J. COB	K. RESERVED FOR LOCAL USE
10 25 2000	10 25 2000	11				1	48 00	1				

25. FEDERAL TAX I.D. NUMBER 00-00000000 SSN EIN [X]

26. PATIENT'S ACCOUNT NO. 992

27. ACCEPT ASSIGNMENT? (For govt. claims, see back) YES [X] NO

28. TOTAL CHARGE $ 48 00

29. AMOUNT PAID $ 0 00

30. BALANCE DUE $ 48 00

31. SIGNATURE OF PHYSICIAN OR SUPPLIER INCLUDING DEGREES OR CREDENTIALS (I certify that the statements on the reverse apply to this bill and are made a part thereof.)
MD
SIGNED _____ DATE 09 06 2003

32. NAME AND ADDRESS OF FACILITY WHERE SERVICES WERE RENDERED (If other than home or office)

33. PHYSICIAN'S SUPPLIER'S BILLING NAME, ADDRESS, ZIP CODE & PHONE #
Blackburn Primary Care Associates
( ) -
PIN# GRP# 04-578901

4. Maria Santos

Standard Health Care Indemnity
4200 Winston Street
Western, WI 45000

HEALTH INSURANCE CLAIM FORM

PICA

1. MEDICARE (Medicare #)	MEDICAID (Medicaid #)	CHAMPUS (Sponsor's SSN)	CHAMPVA (VA File #)	GROUP HEALTH PLAN (SSN or ID) [X] / FECA BLK LUNG (SSN) / OTHER (ID)

1a. INSURED'S I.D. NUMBER (FOR PROGRAM IN ITEM 1)

2. PATIENT'S NAME (Last Name, First Name, Middle Initial)
Santos, Maria R.

3. PATIENT'S BIRTH DATE MM 05 DD 05 YY 1962   SEX M [ ] F [X]

4. INSURED'S NAME (Last Name, First Name, Middle Initial)
Santos, Jose A.

5. PATIENT'S ADDRESS (No., Street)
62 High Line Road

6. PATIENT RELATIONSHIP TO INSURED
Self [ ] Spouse [X] Child [ ] Other [ ]

7. INSURED'S ADDRESS (No., Street)
62 High Line Drive

CITY
Blackburn   STATE WI

8. PATIENT STATUS
Single [ ] Married [ ] Other [X]
Employed [ ] Full-Time Student [ ] Part-Time Student [ ]

CITY
Blackburn   STATE WI

ZIP CODE
54937

TELEPHONE (Include Area Code)
(555) 459-0022

ZIP CODE
54937

TELEPHONE (INCLUDE AREA CODE)
( ) -

9. OTHER INSURED'S NAME (Last Name, First Name, Middle Initial)

10. IS PATIENT'S CONDITION RELATED TO:

11. INSURED'S POLICY GROUP OR FECA NUMBER

a. OTHER INSURED'S POLICY OR GROUP NUMBER

a. EMPLOYMENT? (CURRENT OR PREVIOUS)
YES [ ] NO [X]

a. INSURED'S DATE OF BIRTH MM DD YY   SEX M [ ] F [ ]

b. OTHER INSURED'S DATE OF BIRTH MM DD YY   SEX M [ ] F [ ]

b. AUTO ACCIDENT? PLACE (State)
YES [ ] NO [X]

b. EMPLOYER'S NAME OR SCHOOL NAME

c. EMPLOYER'S NAME OR SCHOOL NAME

c. OTHER ACCIDENT?
YES [ ] NO [X]

c. INSURANCE PLAN NAME OR PROGRAM?
Standard Health Care Indemnity

d. INSURANCE PLAN NAME OR PROGRAM NAME

10d. RESERVED FOR LOCAL USE

d. IS THERE ANOTHER HEALTH BENEFIT PLAN?
YES [ ] NO [X]   If yes, return to and complete item 9 a-d.

READ BACK OF FORM BEFORE COMPLETING & SIGNING THIS FORM

12. PATIENT'S OR AUTHORIZED PERSON'S SIGNATURE I authorize the release of any medical or other information necessary to process this claim. I also request payment of government benefits either to myself or to the party who accepts assignment below.

SIGNED _____   DATE 09 06 2003

13. INSURED'S OR AUTHORIZED PERSON'S SIGNATURE I authorize payment of medical benefits to the undersigned physician or supplier for services described below.

SIGNED _____

14. DATE OF CURRENT ILLNESS (First symptom) OR INJURY (Accident) OR PREGNANCY (LMP) MM DD YY

15. IF PATIENT HAS HAD SAME OR SIMILAR ILLNESS GIVE FIRST DATE MM DD YY

16. DATES PATIENT UNABLE TO WORK IN CURRENT OCCUPATION FROM MM DD YY TO MM DD YY

17. NAME OF REFERRING PHYSICIAN OR OTHER SOURCE

17a. I.D. NUMBER OF REFERRING PHYSICIAN

18. HOSPITALIZATION DATES RELATED TO CURRENT SERVICES FROM MM DD YY TO MM DD YY

19. RESERVED FOR LOCAL USE

20. OUTSIDE LAB? YES [ ] NO [X] $ CHARGES

21. DIAGNOSIS OR NATURE OF ILLNESS OR INJURY (RELATE ITEMS 1, 2, 3 OR 4 TO ITEM 24E BY LINE)

1. ___ . ___   3. ___ . ___
2. ___ . ___   4. ___ . ___

22. MEDICAID RESUBMISSION CODE   ORIGINAL REF. NO.

23. PRIOR AUTHORIZATION NUMBER

24. A. DATE(S) OF SERVICE From MM DD YY	To MM DD YY	B. Place of Service	C. Type of Service	D. PROCEDURES, SERVICES, OR SUPPLIES (Explain Unusual Circumstances) CPT/HCPCS	MODIFIER	E. DIAGNOSIS CODE	F. $ CHARGES	G. DAYS OR UNITS	H. EPSDT Family Plan	I. EMG	J. COB	K. RESERVED FOR LOCAL USE
10 25 2000	10 25 2000	11				1	0 00	1				
10 25 2000	10 25 2000	11				1	0 00	1				

25. FEDERAL TAX I.D. NUMBER   SSN [ ] EIN [X]
00-00000000

26. PATIENT'S ACCOUNT NO.
994

27. ACCEPT ASSIGNMENT? (For govt. claims, see back)
YES [X] NO [ ]

28. TOTAL CHARGE $ 0 00

29. AMOUNT PAID $ 0 00

30. BALANCE DUE $ 0 00

31. SIGNATURE OF PHYSICIAN OR SUPPLIER INCLUDING DEGREES OR CREDENTIALS (I certify that the statements on the reverse apply to this bill and are made a part thereof.)
MD
SIGNED _____ DATE 09 06 2003

32. NAME AND ADDRESS OF FACILITY WHERE SERVICES WERE RENDERED (If other than home or office)

33. PHYSICIAN'S & SUPPLIER'S BILLING NAME, ADDRESS, ZIP CODE & PHONE #
Blackburn Primary Care Associates
( ) -

PIN#   GRP#

5. June St. Cyr

Standard Health Care HMO
1500 Summit Ave
Westen, WI 43000

HEALTH INSURANCE CLAIM FORM

PICA	PICA

1. MEDICARE (Medicare #) | **MEDICAID** (Medicaid #) | **CHAMPUS** (Sponsor's SSN) | **CHAMPVA** (VA File #) | **GROUP HEALTH PLAN** (SSN or ID) [X] | **FECA BLK LUNG** (SSN) | **OTHER** (ID) | **1a. INSURED'S I.D. NUMBER** (FOR PROGRAM IN ITEM 1)

2. PATIENT'S NAME (Last Name, First Name, Middle Initial)
St. Cyr, June

3. PATIENT'S BIRTH DATE MM 02 DD 23 YY 1962 **SEX** M [ ] F [X]

4. INSURED'S NAME (Last Name, First Name, Middle Initial)
St. Cyr, June

5. PATIENT'S ADDRESS (No., Street)
16 Winston Terrace

6. PATIENT RELATIONSHIP TO INSURED
Self [X] Spouse [ ] Child [ ] Other [ ]

7. INSURED'S ADDRESS (No., Street)
16 Winston Terrace

CITY Blackburn **STATE** WI

8. PATIENT STATUS
Single [ ] Married [ ] Other [X]
Employed [X] Full-Time Student [ ] Part-Time Student [ ]

CITY Blackburn **STATE** WI

ZIP CODE 54937 **TELEPHONE** (Include Area Code) (555) 459-1000

ZIP CODE 54937 **TELEPHONE** (INCLUDE AREA CODE) (555) 459-1000

9. OTHER INSURED'S NAME (Last Name, First Name, Middle Initial)

10. IS PATIENT'S CONDITION RELATED TO:

11. INSURED'S POLICY GROUP OR FECA NUMBER
000-AD9876

a. OTHER INSURED'S POLICY OR GROUP NUMBER

a. EMPLOYMENT? (CURRENT OR PREVIOUS) YES [ ] NO [X]

a. INSURED'S DATE OF BIRTH MM 02 DD 23 YY 1962 **SEX** M [ ] F [X]

b. OTHER INSURED'S DATE OF BIRTH MM DD YY **SEX** M [ ] F [ ]

b. AUTO ACCIDENT? YES [ ] NO [X] **PLACE** (State)

b. EMPLOYER'S NAME OR SCHOOL NAME

c. EMPLOYER'S NAME OR SCHOOL NAME

c. OTHER ACCIDENT? YES [ ] NO [X]

c. INSURANCE PLAN NAME OR PROGRAM?
Standard Health Care HMO

d. INSURANCE PLAN NAME OR PROGRAM NAME

10d. RESERVED FOR LOCAL USE

d. IS THERE ANOTHER HEALTH BENEFIT PLAN? YES [ ] NO [X] If yes, return to and complete item 9 a-d.

READ BACK OF FORM BEFORE COMPLETING & SIGNING THIS FORM

12. PATIENT'S OR AUTHORIZED PERSON'S SIGNATURE: I authorize the release of any medical or other information necessary to process this claim. I also request payment of government benefits either to myself or to the party who accepts assignment below.

SIGNED _____ DATE 09 06 2003

13. INSURED'S OR AUTHORIZED PERSON'S SIGNATURE: I authorize payment of medical benefits to the undersigned physician or supplier for services described below.

SIGNED _____

14. DATE OF CURRENT ILLNESS (First symptom) OR INJURY (Accident) OR PREGNANCY (LMP) MM DD YY

15. IF PATIENT HAS HAD SAME OR SIMILAR ILLNESS GIVE FIRST DATE MM DD YY

16. DATES PATIENT UNABLE TO WORK IN CURRENT OCCUPATION FROM MM DD YY TO MM DD YY

17. NAME OF REFERRING PHYSICIAN OR OTHER SOURCE

17a. I.D. NUMBER OF REFERRING PHYSICIAN

18. HOSPITALIZATION DATES RELATED TO CURRENT SERVICES FROM MM DD YY TO MM DD YY

19. RESERVED FOR LOCAL USE

20. OUTSIDE LAB? YES [ ] NO [X] **$ CHARGES**

21. DIAGNOSIS OR NATURE OF ILLNESS OR INJURY (RELATE ITEMS 1, 2, 3 OR 4 TO ITEM 24E BY LINE)
1. 440.9
2. ___
3. ___
4. ___

22. MEDICAID RESUBMISSION CODE ___ ORIGINAL REF. NO.

23. PRIOR AUTHORIZATION NUMBER

24. A DATE(S) OF SERVICE From MM DD YY	To MM DD YY	B Place of Service	C Type of Service	D PROCEDURES, SERVICES, OR SUPPLIES (Explain Unusual Circumstances) CPT/HCPCS MODIFIER	E DIAGNOSIS CODE	F $ CHARGES	G DAYS OR UNITS	H EPSDT Family Plan	I EMG	J COB	K RESERVED FOR LOCAL USE
07 22 2000		11			1	48 00	1				

25. FEDERAL TAX I.D. NUMBER 00-00000000 SSN [ ] EIN [X]

26. PATIENT'S ACCOUNT NO. 1010

27. ACCEPT ASSIGNMENT? (For govt. claims, see back) YES [X] NO [ ]

28. TOTAL CHARGE $ 48 00

29. AMOUNT PAID $ 0 00

30. BALANCE DUE $ 48 00

31. SIGNATURE OF PHYSICIAN OR SUPPLIER INCLUDING DEGREES OR CREDENTIALS (I certify that the statements on the reverse apply to this bill and are made a part thereof.)
MD
SIGNED _____ DATE 09 06 2003

32. NAME AND ADDRESS OF FACILITY WHERE SERVICES WERE RENDERED (If other than home or office)

33. PHYSICIAN'S, SUPPLIER'S BILLING NAME, ADDRESS, ZIP CODE & PHONE #
Blackburn Primary Care Associates
( ) -
PIN# ___ GRP# 04-578901

Lesson 6   Electronic Claims Submission

Name:

Date:

In this section you will perform these tasks: • File an electronic claim. • Trace an electronic claim.	
Steps	**Check Here When Completed**
Open Lytec Medical 2001. On the main program menu, click *File* and *Open Practice*. Select *Blackburn Primary Care Associates*. If you have not done so, set up your own practice. To set up your own practice, right-click and select *Copy* from the menu. Click on the blank white space below the *Blackburn Primary Care Associates* file, right-click, and select Paste. This creates a copy of the lpf file. Always save your changes to this copied file. You can rename this file by selecting copied file, right-click, and select *Rename*. Shortcut: On the file menu click on *1 Copy of Blackburn Primary Care Associates.lpf* as it is listed above the word *exit*.	
On the main program menu, select *Billing*. Click on *Electronic Claims* and a submenu will appear. Shortcut: The Electronic Claims icon is the seventh from the left.	
Select *Create Insurance Claims File*. Select this option to create an insurance claims file to be sent electronically. A name will need to be assigned to the insurance claims file. Save In: Choose a folder in which to save the insurance claims file. You may want to create a special folder for electronic claims at this time. File Name: Enter a file name for the insurance claims file. Save: Click on this button to name the insurance claims file. Cancel: Click on this option to exit the dialog box.	
Once the insurance claims file has been named and saved, set the ranges for the claims to be sent.	
To send insurance claims for everything that has not been sent, leave all the ranges blank. Once an insurance claims file has been created, the date the file was created will appear in the Bill To section of the Charges and Payments window for the claims that have been sent.	

Include Claim Types: Use this section of the Dialog box to choose what claims will be included. Choose from the following:

All: Select this option to include all claim types.

Primary: Select this option to include only primary insurance claims.

Secondary: Select this option to include only secondary insurance claims.

Tertiary: Select this option to include only tertiary insurance claims.

Ranges: Enter ranges directly, or press the lookup buttons to choose ranges.

Insurance Companies: Choose a range of insurance companies for the insurance claims file.

Patients: Choose a range of patients for the insurance claims file.

Billing Numbers: Choose a range of billing numbers for the insurance claims file.

Billing Created Dates: Choose a range of billing created dates for the insurance claims file.

Patient Codes: Choose a range of patient codes for the insurance claims file.

Patient Types: Choose a range of patient types for the insurance claims file.

Providers: Choose a range of providers for the insurance claims file.

Ok: Press *OK* to create the insurance claims file.

Cancel: Press *CANCEL* to exit the Dialog box.

Once an insurance claims file has been created, transmit the file.

Practice submitting electronic claims for the most recent visits for the following patients.

6. Thomas Maxwell

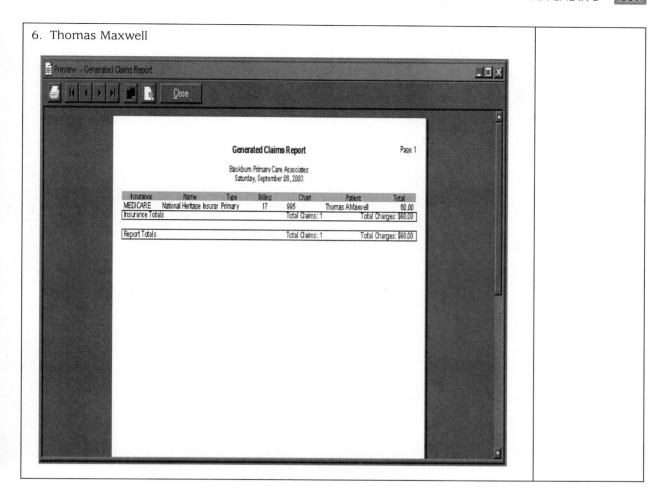

7. Lloyd Ridlon

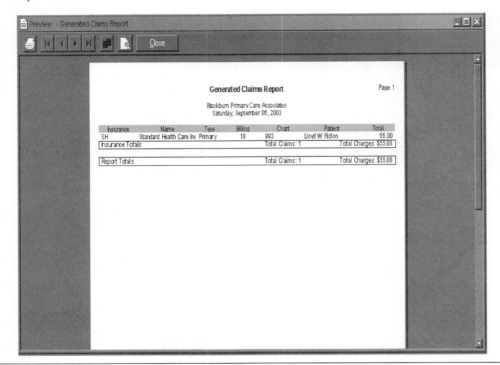

8. Daryl Saitta

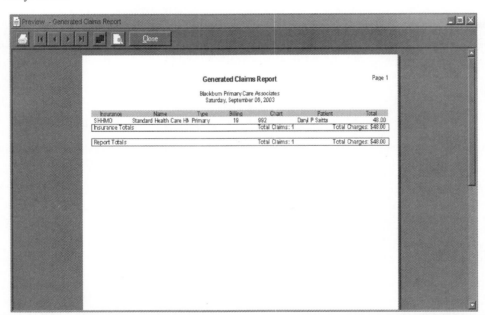

To send electronic claims, set up the electronic claims settings. This will allow the user to create an insurance claims or tracers file, transmit the file to the clearinghouse and then receive a response from the clearinghouse.

In order to transmit an insurance claims or tracers file, the electronic claims settings will need to be set up correctly. Once the Electronic Claims settings have been set up, click on this option to transmit the insurance claims or tracers file electronically.	
Locate the electronic claims or tracers file to send and press *OPEN*. The program will automatically dial the host indicated in the Electronic Claims settings and transmit the file containing the insurance claims or tracers information.	
Practice tracing claims for the following patients.	

1. Thomas Maxwell

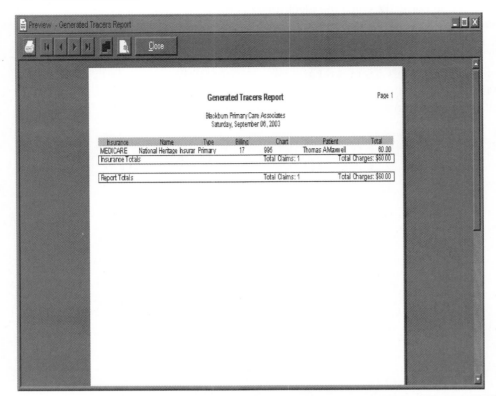

2. Lloyd Ridlon

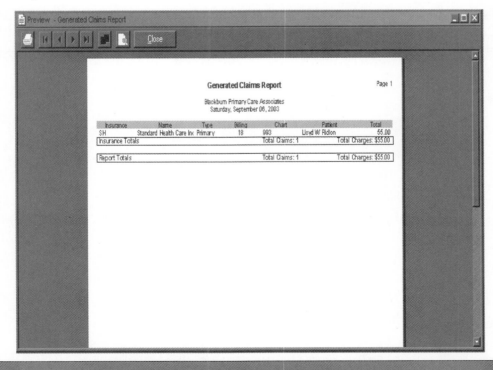

Lesson 7   Creating Reports: Day Sheets and Account Aging Reports

Name:

Date:

In this section you will perform these tasks: • Create and Print day sheets. • Create and Print account aging reports.	
Steps	**Check Here When Completed**
Open Lytec Medical 2001. On the main program menu, click *File* and *Open Practice*. Select *Blackburn Primary Care Associates*. If you have not done so, set up your own practice. To set up your own practice, right-click and select *Copy* from the menu. Click on the blank white space below the *Blackburn Primary Care Associates* file, right-click, and select *Paste*. This creates a copy of the lpf file. Always save your changes to this copied file. You can rename this file by selecting copied file, right-click, and select *Rename*. Shortcut: On the file menu click on *1 Copy of Blackburn Primary Care Associates.lpf* as it is listed above the word exit.	
On the main program menu, click on *Reports*. Select *Day Sheet* and the *Print Day Sheet* window will open.	
On the *Options* tab, click *Subtotal by Provider* and the *Close after Printing* checkboxes.	
Select Sort by *Service Date*.	
On the *Ranges* tab, enter the service date in both boxes titled Dates of Service.	
Click *Preview* and then click on the Print icon.	

Print Day Sheets for the following dates.

32. 10/12/2000

Day Sheet - Transaction Detail   Page 1

Blackburn Primary Care Associates
Saturday, September 06, 2003

Chart	Name	Billing	Date	Provider	POS	Diagnosis	Code	Amount
995	Thomas A Maxwell	15	10/12/2000	31	11		99212	48.00
		15	10/12/2000	31	11		CHECK	-15.00

Provider Totals

MD
Charges	48.00
Inventory Charges	0.00
Debit Adjustments	0.00
Refunds	0.00
Charge Backs	0.00
Patient Payments	-15.00
Insurance Payments	0.00
Credit Adjustments	0.00
Sales Tax Charges	0.00
Sales Tax Payments	0.00
Managed Care Charges	0.00
Managed Care Payments	0.00

Provider Balance	33.00

Report Totals
Charges	48.00
Inventory Charges	0.00
Debit Adjustments	0.00
Refunds	0.00
Charge Backs	0.00
Patient Payments	-15.00
Insurance Payments	0.00
Credit Adjustments	0.00
Sales Tax Charges	0.00
Sales Tax Payments	0.00
Managed Care Charges	0.00
Managed Care Payments	0.00

Report Balance	33.00

33. 07/22/2000

Day Sheet - Transaction Detail   Page 1

Blackburn Primary Care Associates
Saturday, September 06, 2003

Chart	Name	Billing	Date	Provider	POS	Diagnosis	Code	Amount
1010	June St. Cyr	1	07/22/2000	11	11	440.9	99212	48.00
		6	07/22/2000	11		882.0	90703	15.00

Provider Totals

MD
Charges	63.00
Inventory Charges	0.00
Debit Adjustments	0.00
Refunds	0.00
Charge Backs	0.00
Patient Payments	0.00
Insurance Payments	0.00
Credit Adjustments	0.00
Sales Tax Charges	0.00
Sales Tax Payments	0.00
Managed Care Charges	0.00
Managed Care Payments	0.00

Provider Balance	63.00

Report Totals
Charges	63.00
Inventory Charges	0.00
Debit Adjustments	0.00
Refunds	0.00
Charge Backs	0.00
Patient Payments	0.00
Insurance Payments	0.00
Credit Adjustments	0.00
Sales Tax Charges	0.00
Sales Tax Payments	0.00
Managed Care Charges	0.00
Managed Care Payments	0.00

Report Balance	63.00

34. 09/04/2000

Blackburn Primary Care Associates
Sunday, September 07, 2003

Chart	Name	Billing	Date	Provider	POS	Diagnosis	Code	Amount
992	Daryl P Saitta	8	09/04/2000	21	11		99202	55.00
		8	09/04/2000	21	11		CASH	-20.00

Provider Totals

MD

Charges	55.00
Inventory Charges	0.00
Debit Adjustments	0.00
Refunds	0.00
Charge Backs	0.00
Patient Payments	-20.00
Insurance Payments	0.00
Credit Adjustments	0.00
Sales Tax Charges	0.00
Sales Tax Payments	0.00
Managed Care Charges	0.00
Managed Care Payments	0.00

Provider Balance   35.00

Report Totals

Charges	55.00
Inventory Charges	0.00
Debit Adjustments	0.00
Refunds	0.00
Charge Backs	0.00
Patient Payments	-20.00
Insurance Payments	0.00
Credit Adjustments	0.00
Sales Tax Charges	0.00
Sales Tax Payments	0.00
Managed Care Charges	0.00
Managed Care Payments	0.00

Report Balance   35.00

To print batches of bills, go to *Billing* and select *Print Statements* or *Control W*. Choose Statement-Standard (with notes).lcs from the Select Custom Form window. You may have to use the *Go Up One Level* icon to view the forms.

Under the Options tab, enter the date, Standard and Dunning message, select Sort Patients by name, Combine Family Members. Select Current Month Only from Include Paid Billings.

On the *Ranges* tab, choose the provider.

Click *Preview*. Use the arrows to view all records.

3. Print a batch of statements for Dr. Hughes.

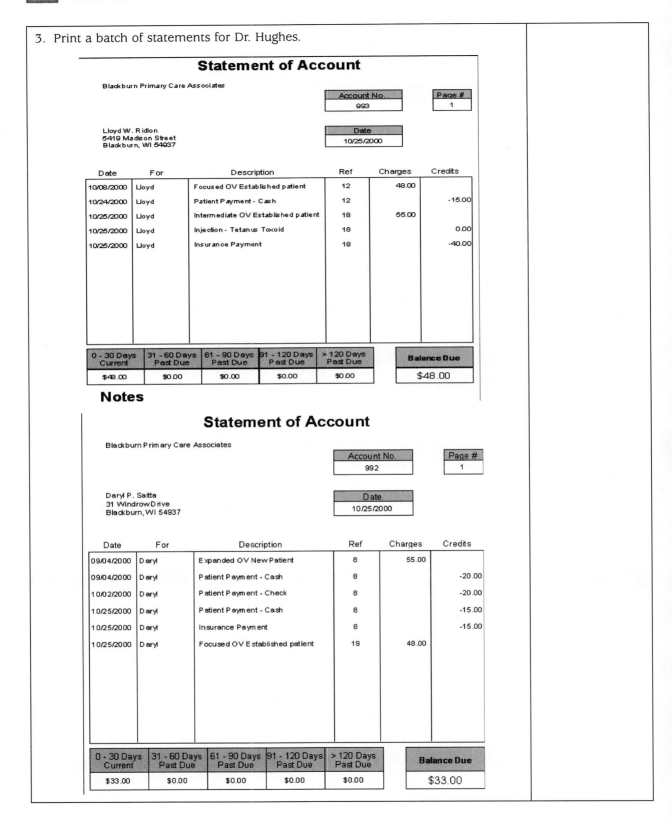

Statement of Account

Blackburn Primary Care Associates

Account No.	Page #
993	1

Lloyd W. Ridlon
5419 Madison Street
Blackburn, WI 54937

Date
10/25/2000

Date	For	Description	Ref	Charges	Credits
10/08/2000	Lloyd	Focused OV Established patient	12	48.00	
10/24/2000	Lloyd	Patient Payment - Cash	12		-15.00
10/25/2000	Lloyd	Intermediate OV Established patient	18	55.00	
10/25/2000	Lloyd	Injection - Tetanus Toxoid	18		0.00
10/25/2000	Lloyd	Insurance Payment	18		-40.00

0 - 30 Days Current	31 - 60 Days Past Due	61 - 90 Days Past Due	91 - 120 Days Past Due	> 120 Days Past Due	Balance Due
$48.00	$0.00	$0.00	$0.00	$0.00	$48.00

Notes

Statement of Account

Blackburn Primary Care Associates

Account No.	Page #
992	1

Daryl P. Saitta
31 Windrow Drive
Blackburn, WI 54937

Date
10/25/2000

Date	For	Description	Ref	Charges	Credits
09/04/2000	Daryl	Expanded OV New Patient	8	55.00	
09/04/2000	Daryl	Patient Payment - Cash	8		-20.00
10/02/2000	Daryl	Patient Payment - Check	8		-20.00
10/25/2000	Daryl	Patient Payment - Cash	8		-15.00
10/25/2000	Daryl	Insurance Payment	8		-15.00
10/25/2000	Daryl	Focused OV Established patient	19	48.00	

0 - 30 Days Current	31 - 60 Days Past Due	61 - 90 Days Past Due	91 - 120 Days Past Due	> 120 Days Past Due	Balance Due
$33.00	$0.00	$0.00	$0.00	$0.00	$33.00

4. Print a batch of statements for Dr. Lopez.

Statement of Account

Blackburn Primary Care Associates

Account No.	Page #
995	1

Thomas A. Maxwell
42 Delray Ave.
Blackburn, WI 54937

Date
09/06/2003

Date	For	Description	Ref	Charges	Credits
10/25/2000	Thomas	Focused OV Established patient	17	48.00	
10/25/2000	Thomas	Urinalysis, Dipstick	17	12.00	

0 - 30 Days Current	31 - 60 Days Past Due	61 - 90 Days Past Due	91 - 120 Days Past Due	> 120 Days Past Due	Balance Due
$0.00	$0.00	$0.00	$0.00	$60.00	$60.00

To print an insurance claim, select *Billing* from the main program menu. Select *Charges and Payments* and the window will open. Click on the magnifying glass beside the patient chart box to open the *Find Patient* window.

Shortcut: Click the 12th icon from the left on the toolbar or use *Control B* to open the Charges and Payments box.

Continue to press enter until the fields are populated. Select the appropriate billing code by using the Look Up function. Make sure *Patient* and *Primary Insurance (National Heritage)* are checked to the right in the *Bill to* section.

Under the Print button, click *Primary Insurance*.

When the Select Custom Forms window opens, you may have to use the *Go Up One Level* Icon to view the available forms.

Select HCFA-Standard (with form).lci and Click *Open*.

Click *Preview*. On the preview window, click the Print icon.

Print Insurance forms for the most recent visit for the following patients.

9. Thomas Maxwell

10. Lloyd Ridlon

PLEASE
DO NOT
STAPLE
IN THIS
AREA

Standard Health Care Indemnity
4200 Winston Street
Western, WI 45000

HEALTH INSURANCE CLAIM FORM

PICA				PICA

1. MEDICARE	MEDICAID	CHAMPUS	CHAMPVA	GROUP HEALTH PLAN	FECA BLK LUNG	OTHER	1a. INSURED'S I.D. NUMBER	(FOR PROGRAM IN ITEM 1)
(Medicare #)	(Medicaid #)	(Sponsor's SSN)	(VA File #)	(SSN or ID) X	(SSN)	(ID)		

2. PATIENT'S NAME (Last Name, First Name, Middle Initial)	3. PATIENT'S BIRTH DATE	SEX	4. INSURED'S NAME (Last Name, First Name, Middle Initial)
Ridlon, Lloyd W	01 31 1955 M X F		Ridlon, Lloyd W

5. PATIENT'S ADDRESS (No., Street)	6. PATIENT RELATIONSHIP TO INSURED	7. INSURED'S ADDRESS (No., Street)
5419 Madison Street	Self X Spouse Child Other	5419 Madison Street

CITY	STATE	8. PATIENT STATUS	CITY	STATE
Blackburn	WI	Single Married X Other	Blackburn	WI

ZIP CODE	TELEPHONE (Include Area Code)		ZIP CODE	TELEPHONE (INCLUDE AREA CODE)
54937	(555) 114-4242	Employed Full-Time Student Part-Time Student	54937	(555) 114-4242

9. OTHER INSURED'S NAME (Last Name, First Name, Middle Initial)	10. IS PATIENT'S CONDITION RELATED TO:	11. INSURED'S POLICY GROUP OR FECA NUMBER
		12345-67

a. OTHER INSURED'S POLICY OR GROUP NUMBER	a. EMPLOYMENT? (CURRENT OR PREVIOUS) YES NO X	a. INSURED'S DATE OF BIRTH	SEX
		01 31 1955 M X F	

b. OTHER INSURED'S DATE OF BIRTH SEX	b. AUTO ACCIDENT? PLACE (State)	b. EMPLOYER'S NAME OR SCHOOL NAME
MM DD YY M F	YES NO X	

c. EMPLOYER'S NAME OR SCHOOL NAME	c. OTHER ACCIDENT? YES NO X	c. INSURANCE PLAN NAME OR PROGRAM
		Standard Health Care Indemnity

d. INSURANCE PLAN NAME OR PROGRAM NAME	10d. RESERVED FOR LOCAL USE	d. IS THERE ANOTHER HEALTH BENEFIT PLAN?
		YES NO X If yes, return to and complete item 9 a-d.

READ BACK OF FORM BEFORE COMPLETING & SIGNING THIS FORM

12. PATIENT'S OR AUTHORIZED PERSON'S SIGNATURE. I authorize the release of any medical or other information necessary to process this claim. I also request payment of government benefits either to myself or to the party who accepts assignment below.

SIGNED _____ DATE 09 06 2003

13. INSURED'S OR AUTHORIZED PERSON'S SIGNATURE. I authorize payment of medical benefits to the undersigned physician or supplier for services described below.

SIGNED _____

14. DATE OF CURRENT: ILLNESS (First Symptom) OR INJURY (Accident) OR PREGNANCY (LMP)	15. IF PATIENT HAS HAD SAME OR SIMILAR ILLNESS GIVE FIRST DATE MM DD YY	16. DATES PATIENT UNABLE TO WORK IN CURRENT OCCUPATION FROM TO

17. NAME OF REFERRING PHYSICIAN OR OTHER SOURCE	17a. I.D. NUMBER OF REFERRING PHYSICIAN	18. HOSPITALIZATION DATES RELATED TO CURRENT SERVICES FROM TO

19. RESERVED FOR LOCAL USE	20. OUTSIDE LAB? YES NO X $ CHARGES

21. DIAGNOSIS OR NATURE OF ILLNESS OR INJURY (RELATE ITEMS 1, 2, 3 OR 4 TO ITEM 24E BY LINE)

1. 882.0   3. ___ ___

2. ___ ___   4. ___ ___

22. MEDICAID RESUBMISSION CODE ORIGINAL REF. NO.

23. PRIOR AUTHORIZATION NUMBER

24. A. DATES OF SERVICE						B. Place of Service	C. Type of Service	D. PROCEDURES, SERVICES, OR SUPPLIES (Explain Unusual Circumstances) CPT/HCPCS MODIFIER	E. DIAGNOSIS CODE	F. $ CHARGES		G. DAYS OR UNITS	H. EPSDT Family Plan	I. EMG	J. COB	K. RESERVED FOR LOCAL USE
From MM	DD	YY	To MM	DD	YY											
10	25	2000	10	25	2000	11			1	55	00	1				
10	25	2000	10	25	2000	11			1	0	00	1				

25. FEDERAL TAX I.D. NUMBER SSN EIN	26. PATIENT'S ACCOUNT NO.	27. ACCEPT ASSIGNMENT? (For govt. claims, see back)	28. TOTAL CHARGE	29. AMOUNT PAID	30. BALANCE DUE
00-00000000 X	993	X YES NO	$ 55 00	$ 0 00	$ 55 00

31. SIGNATURE OF PHYSICIAN OR SUPPLIER INCLUDING DEGREES OR CREDENTIALS (I certify that the statements on the reverse apply to this bill and are made a part thereof.)	32. NAME AND ADDRESS OF FACILITY WHERE SERVICES WERE RENDERED (If other than home or office)	33. PHYSICIAN'S, SUPPLIER'S BILLING NAME, ADDRESS, ZIP CODE & PHONE #
MD		Blackburn Primary Care Associates
SIGNED 09 06 2003 DATE		( ) -

11. Daryl Saitta

PLEASE
DO NOT
STAPLE
IN THIS
AREA

Standard Health Care HMO
1500 Summit Ave
Western, WI 43000

HEALTH INSURANCE CLAIM FORM

| PICA | | | | | | | | PICA |

1. MEDICARE (Medicare #) **MEDICAID** (Medicaid #) **CHAMPUS** (Sponsor's SSN) **CHAMPVA** (VA File #) **GROUP HEALTH PLAN** (SSN or ID) [X] **FECA BLK LUNG** (SSN) **OTHER** (ID)

1a. INSURED'S ID NUMBER (FOR PROGRAM IN ITEM 1)

2. PATIENT'S NAME (Last Name, First Name, Middle Initial)
Saitta, Daryl P

3. PATIENT'S BIRTH DATE
MM 02 | DD 06 | YY 1944   **SEX** M [X] F [ ]

4. INSURED'S NAME (Last Name, First Name, Middle Initial)
Saitta, Daryl P

5. PATIENT'S ADDRESS (No., Street)
31 Windrow Drive

6. PATIENT RELATIONSHIP TO INSURED
Self [X] Spouse [ ] Child [ ] Other [ ]

7. INSURED'S ADDRESS (No., Street)
31 Windrow Drive

CITY Blackburn   **STATE** WI

8. PATIENT STATUS
Single [ ] Married [X] Other [ ]

CITY Blackburn   **STATE** WI

ZIP CODE 54937   **TELEPHONE** (Include Area Code) (555) 221-2223

Employed [ ] Full-Time Student [ ] Part-Time Student [ ]

ZIP CODE 54937   **TELEPHONE** (INCLUDE AREA CODE) (555) 221-2223

9. OTHER INSURED'S NAME (Last Name, First Name, Middle Initial)

10. IS PATIENT'S CONDITION RELATED TO:

11. INSURED'S POLICY GROUP OR FECA NUMBER
000-J H2267

a. OTHER INSURED'S POLICY OR GROUP NUMBER

a. EMPLOYMENT? (CURRENT OR PREVIOUS)
YES [ ] NO [X]

a. INSURED'S DATE OF BIRTH
MM 02 | DD 06 | YY 1944   **SEX** M [X] F [ ]

b. OTHER INSURED'S DATE OF BIRTH
MM | DD | YY   **SEX** M [ ] F [ ]

b. AUTO ACCIDENT?   PLACE (State)
YES [ ] NO [X]

b. EMPLOYER'S NAME OR SCHOOL NAME

c. EMPLOYER'S NAME OR SCHOOL NAME

c. OTHER ACCIDENT?
YES [ ] NO [X]

c. INSURANCE PLAN NAME OR PROGRAM
Standard Health Care HMO

d. INSURANCE PLAN NAME OR PROGRAM NAME

10d. RESERVED FOR LOCAL USE

d. IS THERE ANOTHER HEALTH BENEFIT PLAN?
YES [ ] NO [X]   If yes, return to and complete item 9 a-d.

READ BACK OF FORM BEFORE COMPLETING & SIGNING THIS FORM

12. PATIENT'S OR AUTHORIZED PERSON'S SIGNATURE I authorize the release of any medical or other information necessary to process this claim. I also request payment of government benefits either to myself or to the party who accepts assignment below.
SIGNED _____ DATE 09 06 2003

13. INSURED'S OR AUTHORIZED PERSON'S SIGNATURE I authorize payment of medical benefits to the undersigned physician or supplier for services described below.
SIGNED _____

14. DATE OF CURRENT: ILLNESS (First symptom) OR INJURY (Accident) OR PREGNANCY (LMP)
MM | DD | YY

15. IF PATIENT HAS HAD SAME OR SIMILAR ILLNESS GIVE FIRST DATE MM | DD | YY

16. DATES PATIENT UNABLE TO WORK IN CURRENT OCCUPATION
FROM MM | DD | YY   TO MM | DD | YY

17. NAME OF REFERRING PHYSICIAN OR OTHER SOURCE

17a. I.D. NUMBER OF REFERRING PHYSICIAN

18. HOSPITALIZATION DATES RELATED TO CURRENT SERVICES
FROM MM | DD | YY   TO MM | DD | YY

19. RESERVED FOR LOCAL USE

20. OUTSIDE LAB?
YES [ ] NO [X] $ CHARGES

21. DIAGNOSIS OR NATURE OF ILLNESS OR INJURY (RELATE ITEMS 1,2,3 OR 4 TO ITEM 24E BY LINE)
1. 401.1
2. ___
3. ___
4. ___

22. MEDICAID RESUBMISSION CODE   ORIGINAL REF. NO.

23. PRIOR AUTHORIZATION NUMBER

24. A DATE(S) OF SERVICE						B Place of Service	C Type of Service	D PROCEDURES, SERVICES, OR SUPPLIES (Explain Unusual Circumstances) CPT/HCPCS	MODIFIER	E DIAGNOSIS CODE	F $ CHARGES		G DAYS OR UNITS	H EPSDT Family Plan	I EMG	J COB	K RESERVED FOR LOCAL USE
From MM	DD	YY	To MM	DD	YY												
10	25	2000	10	25	2000	11				1	48	00	1				

25. FEDERAL TAX I.D. NUMBER SSN [ ] EIN [X]
00-0000000

26. PATIENT'S ACCOUNT NO.
992

27. ACCEPT ASSIGNMENT? (For govt. claims, see back)
[X] YES [ ] NO

28. TOTAL CHARGE $ 48 00

29. AMOUNT PAID $ 0 00

30. BALANCE DUE $ 48 00

31. SIGNATURE OF PHYSICIAN OR SUPPLIER INCLUDING DEGREES OR CREDENTIALS (I certify that the statements on the reverse apply to this bill and are made a part thereof.)
MD
SIGNED _____ 09 06 2003 DATE

32. NAME AND ADDRESS OF FACILITY WHERE SERVICES WERE RENDERED (If other than home or office)

33. PHYSICIAN'S, SUPPLIER'S BILLING NAME, ADDRESS, ZIP CODE & PHONE #
Blackburn Primary Care Associates
( ) -
PIN# ___ GRP# 04-578901

12. Maria Santos

Standard Health Care Indemnity
4200 Winston Street
Western, WI 45000

HEALTH INSURANCE CLAIM FORM

PICA								PICA

1. MEDICARE ☐ (Medicare #) MEDICAID ☐ (Medicaid #) CHAMPUS ☐ (Sponsor's SSN) CHAMPVA ☐ (VA File #) GROUP HEALTH PLAN ☒ (SSN or ID) FECA BLK LUNG ☐ (SSN) OTHER ☐ (ID)

1a. INSURED'S I.D. NUMBER (FOR PROGRAM IN ITEM 1)

2. PATIENT'S NAME (Last Name, First Name, Middle Initial)
Santos, Maria R

3. PATIENT'S BIRTH DATE MM 05 DD 05 YY 1962   SEX M ☐ F ☒

4. INSURED'S NAME (Last Name, First Name, Middle Initial)
Santos, Jose A

5. PATIENT'S ADDRESS (No., Street)
62 High Line Road

6. PATIENT RELATIONSHIP TO INSURED
Self ☐ Spouse ☒ Child ☐ Other ☐

7. INSURED'S ADDRESS (No., Street)
62 High Line Drive

CITY
Blackburn   STATE WI

8. PATIENT STATUS
Single ☐ Married ☐ Other ☒
Employed ☐ Full-Time Student ☐ Part-Time Student ☐

CITY
Blackburn   STATE WI

ZIP CODE
54937

TELEPHONE (Include Area Code)
(555) 459-0022

ZIP CODE
54937

TELEPHONE (INCLUDE AREA CODE)
( ) -

9. OTHER INSURED'S NAME (Last Name, First Name, Middle Initial)

10. IS PATIENT'S CONDITION RELATED TO:

11. INSURED'S POLICY GROUP OR FECA NUMBER

a. OTHER INSURED'S POLICY OR GROUP NUMBER

a. EMPLOYMENT? (CURRENT OR PREVIOUS)
YES ☐ NO ☒

a. INSURED'S DATE OF BIRTH MM DD YY   SEX M ☐ F ☐

b. OTHER INSURED'S DATE OF BIRTH MM DD YY   SEX M ☐ F ☐

b. AUTO ACCIDENT?
YES ☐ NO ☒   PLACE (State)

b. EMPLOYER'S NAME OR SCHOOL NAME

c. EMPLOYER'S NAME OR SCHOOL NAME

c. OTHER ACCIDENT?
YES ☐ NO ☒

c. INSURANCE PLAN NAME OR PROGRAM?
Standard Health Care Indemnity

d. INSURANCE PLAN NAME OR PROGRAM NAME

10d. RESERVED FOR LOCAL USE

d. IS THERE ANOTHER HEALTH BENEFIT PLAN?
YES ☐ NO ☒   If yes, return to and complete item 9 a-d.

READ BACK OF FORM BEFORE COMPLETING & SIGNING THIS FORM
12. PATIENT'S OR AUTHORIZED PERSON'S SIGNATURE I authorize the release of any medical or other information necessary to process this claim. I also request payment of government benefits either to myself or to the party who accepts assignment below.

SIGNED   DATE 09 06 2003

13. INSURED'S OR AUTHORIZED PERSON'S SIGNATURE I authorize payment of medical benefits to the undersigned physician or supplier for services described below.

SIGNED

14. DATE OF CURRENT MM DD YY ILLNESS (First symptom) OR INJURY (Accident) OR PREGNANCY (LMP)

15. IF PATIENT HAS HAD SAME OR SIMILAR ILLNESS GIVE FIRST DATE MM DD YY

16. DATES PATIENT UNABLE TO WORK IN CURRENT OCCUPATION FROM MM DD YY TO MM DD YY

17. NAME OF REFERRING PHYSICIAN OR OTHER SOURCE

17a. I.D. NUMBER OF REFERRING PHYSICIAN

18. HOSPITALIZATION DATES RELATED TO CURRENT SERVICES FROM MM DD YY TO MM DD YY

19. RESERVED FOR LOCAL USE

20. OUTSIDE LAB? YES ☐ NO ☒ $ CHARGES

21. DIAGNOSIS OR NATURE OF ILLNESS OR INJURY (RELATE ITEMS 1,2,3 OR 4 TO ITEM 24E BY LINE)
1. ⌐ ⌐   3. ⌐ ⌐
2. ⌐ ⌐   4. ⌐ ⌐

22. MEDICAID RESUBMISSION CODE   ORIGINAL REF. NO.

23. PRIOR AUTHORIZATION NUMBER

24. A DATE(S) OF SERVICE						B Place of Service	C Type of Service	D PROCEDURES, SERVICES, OR SUPPLIES (Explain Unusual Circumstances) CPT/HCPCS	MODIFIER	E DIAGNOSIS CODE	F $ CHARGES		G DAYS OR UNITS	H EPSDT Family Plan	I EMG	J COB	K RESERVED FOR LOCAL USE
From MM 10	DD 25	YY 2000	To MM 10	DD 25	YY 2000	11				1	0	00	1				
10	25	2000	10	25	2000	11				1	0	00	1				

25. FEDERAL TAX I.D. NUMBER   SSN ☐ EIN ☒
00-00000000

26. PATIENT'S ACCOUNT NO.
994

27. ACCEPT ASSIGNMENT? (For govt. claims, see back.)
YES ☒ NO ☐

28. TOTAL CHARGE
$ 0 00

29. AMOUNT PAID
$ 0 00

30. BALANCE DUE
$ 0 00

31. SIGNATURE OF PHYSICIAN OR SUPPLIER INCLUDING DEGREES OR CREDENTIALS (I certify that the statements on the reverse apply to this bill and are made a part thereof.)
MD
SIGNED   DATE 09 06 2003

32. NAME AND ADDRESS OF FACILITY WHERE SERVICES WERE RENDERED (If other than home or office)

33. PHYSICIAN'S, SUPPLIER'S BILLING NAME, ADDRESS, ZIP CODE & PHONE #
Blackburn Primary Care Associates

( ) -
PIN#   GRP#

13. June St. Cyr

To create and print account aging reports, select *Reports* from the main program menu. Select *Aging* and then *Patient Aging*: the *Print Patient Aging* window will open.

Enter the date in the *Age From* field.

Click *Preview* and the Print icon.

Print age accounts form:

1. 11/24/2001

Patient Aging   Page 1

Blackburn Primary Care Associates
Sunday, September 07, 2003

June St. Cyr (1010)   Last payment 05/29/2001, $10.00
Responsible : Self Home : (555) 459-1000

Billing	Date	Code/CPT	Billed	Amount	Current	31-60	61-90	91-120	> 120	Total
1	10/25/2000	CASH		-15.00	-15.00					-15.00
1	07/22/2000	Patient co-pay		10.00					10.00	10.00
2	05/29/2001	CHECK		-10.00	-10.00					-10.00
Patient Total				-15.00	-25.00	0.00	0.00	0.00	10.00	-15.00

James Winston (1020)   Last payment 09/01/2000, $50.00
Responsible : Self Home : (555) 459-1222

Billing	Date	Code/CPT	Billed	Amount	Current	31-60	61-90	91-120	> 120	Total
7	09/01/2000	CHECK		-50.00	-50.00					-50.00
Patient Total				-50.00	-50.00	0.00	0.00	0.00	0.00	-50.00

Mary A St. Cyr (3010)   Last payment: 05/29/2001, $10.00
Responsible : Self Home : (555) 459-1000

Billing	Date	Code/CPT	Billed	Amount	Current	31-60	61-90	91-120	> 120	Total
3	07/14/2000	99212		48.00	10.00					10.00
3	07/14/2000	Patient co-pay		10.00					10.00	10.00
3	10/25/2000	Not covered		13.00					13.00	13.00
4	05/29/2001	CHECK		-10.00	-10.00					-10.00
5	07/14/2000	Patient co-pay		10.00					10.00	10.00
Patient Total				71.00	0.00	0.00	0.00	0.00	33.00	33.00

Daryl P Saltta (992)   Last payment 10/25/2000, $15.00
Responsible : Self Home : (555) 221-2223 Work : (555) 551-1212

Billing	Date	Code/CPT	Billed	Amount	Current	31-60	61-90	91-120	> 120	Total
8	09/04/2000	99202		55.00	10.00					10.00
8	09/04/2000	CASH		-20.00	-20.00					-20.00
8	10/02/2000	CHECK		-20.00	-20.00					-20.00
8	10/25/2000	CASH		-15.00	-15.00					-15.00
8	09/04/2000	Patient co-pay		10.00					10.00	10.00
8	10/25/2000	Not covered		20.00					20.00	20.00
19	10/25/2000	99212		48.00	10.00					10.00
19	10/25/2000	Patient co-pay		10.00					10.00	10.00
Patient Total				88.00	-35.00	0.00	0.00	0.00	40.00	5.00

Lloyd W Ridion (993)   Last payment: 10/25/2000, $40.00
Responsible : Self Home : (555) 114-4242 Work : (555) 642-3535

Billing	Date	Code/CPT	Billed	Amount	Current	31-60	61-90	91-120	> 120	Total
10	07/28/2000	Ins. ove pay		-128.00					-128.00	-128.00
18	10/25/2000	Patient co-pay		15.00					15.00	15.00
Patient Total				-113.00	0.00	0.00	0.00	0.00	-113.00	-113.00

Maria R Santos (994)   Last payment 10/06/2000, $27.00
Responsible : Self Home : (555) 459-0022

Billing	Date	Code/CPT	Billed	Amount	Current	31-60	61-90	91-120	> 120	Total
13	10/06/2000	CHECK		-27.00	-27.00					-27.00
Patient Total				-27.00	-27.00	0.00	0.00	0.00	0.00	-27.00

2. 10/12/2000

Patient Aging

Page 1

Blackburn Primary Care Associates
Sunday, September 07, 2003

June St Cyr (1010)   Last payment 05/29/2001, $10.00
Responsible : Self   Home : (555) 459-1000

Billing	Date	Code/CPT	Billed	Amount	Current	31-60	61-90	91-120	> 120	Total
1	10/25/2000	CASH		-15.00	-15.00					-15.00
1	07/22/2000	Patient co-pay		10.00		10.00				10.00
2	05/29/2001	CHECK		-10.00	-10.00					-10.00
Patient Total				-15.00	-25.00	0.00	10.00	0.00	0.00	-15.00

James Winston (1020)   Last payment 09/01/2000, $50.00
Responsible : Self   Home : (555) 459-1222

Billing	Date	Code/CPT	Billed	Amount	Current	31-60	61-90	91-120	> 120	Total
7	09/01/2000	CHECK		-50.00	-50.00					-50.00
Patient Total				-50.00	-50.00	0.00	0.00	0.00	0.00	-50.00

Mary A St Cyr (3010)   Last payment: 05/29/2001, $10.00
Responsible : Self   Home : (555) 459-1000

Billing	Date	Code/CPT	Billed	Amount	Current	31-60	61-90	91-120	> 120	Total
3	07/14/2000	99212		48.00	10.00					10.00
3	07/14/2000	Patient co-pay		10.00			10.00			10.00
3	10/25/2000	Not covered		13.00	13.00					13.00
4	05/29/2001	CHECK		-10.00	-10.00					-10.00
5	07/14/2000	Patient co-pay		10.00			10.00			10.00
Patient Total				71.00	13.00	0.00	20.00	0.00	0.00	33.00

Daryl P Saitta (992)   Last payment 10/25/2000, $15.00
Responsible : Self   Home : (555) 221-2223   Work : (555) 551-1212

Billing	Date	Code/CPT	Billed	Amount	Current	31-60	61-90	91-120	> 120	Total
8	09/04/2000	99202		55.00	10.00					10.00
8	09/04/2000	CASH		-20.00	-20.00					-20.00
8	10/02/2000	CHECK		-20.00	-20.00					-20.00
8	10/25/2000	CASH		-15.00	-15.00					-15.00
8	09/04/2000	Patient co-pay		10.00		10.00				10.00
8	10/25/2000	Not covered		20.00	20.00					20.00
19	10/25/2000	99212		48.00	10.00					10.00
19	10/25/2000	Patient co-pay		10.00	10.00					10.00
Patient Total				88.00	-5.00	10.00	0.00	0.00	0.00	5.00

Lloyd W Ridlon (993)   Last payment: 10/25/2000, $40.00
Responsible : Self   Home : (555) 114-4242   Work : (555) 642-3535

Billing	Date	Code/CPT	Billed	Amount	Current	31-60	61-90	91-120	> 120	Total
10	07/28/2000	Ins. over pay		-128.00			-128.00			-128.00
18	10/25/2000	Patient co-pay		15.00	15.00					15.00
Patient Total				-113.00	15.00	0.00	-128.00	0.00	0.00	-113.00

Maria R Santos (994)   Last payment 10/06/2000, $27.00
Responsible : Self   Home : (555) 459-0022

Billing	Date	Code/CPT	Billed	Amount	Current	31-60	61-90	91-120	> 120	Total
13	10/06/2000	CHECK		-27.00	-27.00					-27.00
Patient Total				-27.00	-27.00	0.00	0.00	0.00	0.00	-27.00